THIS IS OUR LIFE

BY THE TRAGICALLY HIP

Dear Gord,

Those melodies come back to me
Time beyond our heartbeat

GS, PL, JF & RB

THIS IS OUR LIFE

BY THE TRAGICALLY HIP

GENESIS PUBLICATIONS
SINCE 1974

10 9 8 7 6 5 4 3 2 1

ISBN: 978-1-905662-91-3

Genesis Publications Ltd
Genesis House
2 Jenner Road, Guildford
Surrey, England, GU1 3PL

www.genesis-publications.com

THERE is NO DRESS REHEARSAL, THIS IS OUR LIFE

THE TRAGICALLY HIP

AUGUST 5, 2016   MTS CENTRE   WINNIPEG, MANITOBA

CONTENTS

GORD DOWNIE

Nothing-to-do makes a searcher outta you.

"the prolific bird gets the worm"

idéal

répertoire téléphonique
adressenverzeichnis
address book
adressboekje
telefontavle
rubrica
indice
memo

G. Downie
184 Browning Ave
Toronto M4K 1W5
(416) 778·0300

Enjoy the ride!
all of this is for you...

Growing up in Amherstview, Ontario. Nothing and everything to do. We're atop the neighbourhood tobogganing spot. It looks down to the highway and the lake. Lake Ontario. There is a good swamp we look at too. Nothing-to-do makes a searcher outta you. There are endless things, places, people to search. It's a place that was hard to see past your fingertips. We had fields at the edges of us that went on, north, maybe forever.

There were cliffs to jump from into Lake Ontario. You could smoke your 12-year-old's cigarettes there. There were tireless games of shinny or foot hockey when the water froze in winter. There were places of dirt for dirt bikes. There was baseball under the lights all summer long. Basketball with chain mesh nets at the schoolyard. I'd ride my bike around. Endlessly. Throw it into high grass, hide it rather than lock it. Hang out where people might be. Oftentimes they weren't.

On my bike I might pass or run into one of my brothers or sisters. Most likely, Patrick. Pat was four years younger than me. My mom, Lorna, had not given up, not lost interest. She had lost gusto. 'Can Patrick come with you and your friends?' It wasn't really a question. It was a demand. I'm like, 'Mom. He's seven!' I'm taking Pat. I tell him to ride his bike back a bit. 'Stop asking questions.' Anyone fucks with him, or tries, gets it from me. I don't let that happen – even once. I tell him what to do – 'Inhale like this' – he doesn't.

My bedroom – a tiny place I shared with Patrick and my elder brother, Mike. Three of us in one. Mood, again, unpredictable. Perhaps it was boredom or lack of true direction, but we could tangle and we could howl with laughter. We got funny. We taught each other all of it. With what we had. With what we wanted. We moved, we read, we tucked, we hid, we stared out of grey windows, across the highway to the lake.

Next door, our sisters, Charlyn and Paula, were doing the same things differently. We were a family. Down deep we loved … us. We didn't feel inclined to worry about poor behaviour to one another. It just seemed regular. These were the days well before analysis or instruction. Lorna tried to instil instructions that were never kept. Rules that were never followed. Going that way was always challenged – and overruled. Our home was home. Who knows what that is supposed to look like? Who cares?

Gord Downie on tour in Europe, February 1993

Opposite: Downie family photos, showing Gord with his parents, Lorna and Edgar, his sisters, Charlyn and Paula, and his brothers, Mike and Patrick (top)

Pages from Gord's address book and many notebooks (bottom)

ROB BAKER

That brown Strat I got for my 13th birthday was the guitar that I played every show The Hip ever did.

My upbringing was pretty standard. I had an older brother who was incredibly athletic, so I wasn't going to define myself that way. I didn't have a hope. And I had an older sister who was a little bit of a wild child, but she had a fabulous record collection, which laid the groundwork for me. For every time she listened to one of her albums, I listened to it probably 20 times.

My folks met through figure skating. My mother was a US dance champ, born in Hollywood, California, and she came to Toronto as the visiting pro sometime in the early Fifties. My dad was putting himself through law school as a dance gigolo, so he would be a partner for hire for any girl taking their gold or silver dance test. That's how they met.

My dad, Judge Phil, was a very funny, gregarious guy. There was no physical punishment. I think he raised his voice maybe five times to me and if he raised his voice I knew it was my cue to cry because it was a very traumatic event, being so rare. There was a lot of laughing and a lot of offside joking around and it was a pretty happy household.

My dad would do this thing on Saturdays where he'd go to a local grocery store called Bennett's and he'd station himself there for two hours. And then he'd go across town to another grocery store and he'd do another two hours there. Those were his public office hours; people would come up and plead their cases in front of him, talk to him and ask him for advice. It was his way of making himself accessible as a judge, which I don't think most judges do.

As a judge in a town like Kingston, there will be people that love you and people that hate you and most of the time my dad didn't really worry about that. But there was one morning I remember when I was in grade 8 and I had to wake up early to go to a seven o'clock hockey practice. I looked out the window and saw a guy in a car parked down the street staring at our house with binoculars. When I got my cab to hockey practice, the guy was still there. And he was still there when the cab brought me back home. I woke my dad up and told him

Rob Baker with his brown Stratocaster, Alfie's (Queen's University pub), Kingston, ON, 1986 (also opposite, centre and bottom left)

Opposite: Baker family photos, including Rob with his elder brother and sister, Matthew and Vicki

Air Canada Centre, Toronto, 23 February 1999 (bottom right)

about this guy sitting at the end of the block, staring at our house. And my old man just went white.

I found out later that day that there was a credible threat to my dad's life at the time, regarding a mafia case, and that this guy at the end of the street was a police officer. My old man went to live in a hotel for a couple of weeks and us kids got shipped off to different friends and relatives and had to be taken to and from school by car. That happened a couple of times when I was growing up.

The Sinclairs moved in across the street from us when Gord was about one and a half and I was about three. We got invited over and Gordie and I played in the sandbox, and we've been playing together in some form ever since.

Gord's mom made the best hot dogs – she still does. Leona was one of the nicest people I ever met, just so sweet and she had great musical tastes. We'd go over to Gord's and his mom would have Fats Domino and Elvis and whatever was big at the time. She'd put on Otis Redding and Gordie and I would start bouncing around, ricocheting off the furniture and screaming and freaking out. Then she'd put on Henry Mancini and we'd sit down and eat our hot dogs.

As a kid, I was a little terrified of Gord's dad, Duncan. He seemed very stern and very proper compared to my parents, who were super relaxed and gregarious and social. But as time went on, I realised that Duncan was one of the sweetest guys. Leona and Duncan were my other parents, really.

My sister had a guitar that she never touched and I would listen to music and pretend I was rocking out. I pretended to play for a long time, from maybe age four or five.

But it was when I was around 11 that I really got interested in picking up an instrument. Gord's mom played piano and attempted to teach me a little bit. We had a piano in the house and I practised on that – one hand, then the other hand. I could never get them going at the same time and that's still the case.

My parents were always very encouraging about it and for my 12th birthday they got me an acoustic guitar. For Christmas that year I talked my mom into getting me an amplifier and when I got my amplifier on Christmas Day, I turned to my dad and said now I needed an electric guitar. It was all a bit of a ruse on my part.

My mother signed me up for a month of guitar lessons. I did three and said, 'That's it, I'm not going to the fourth one, I hate this.' My teacher was an old evangelical dude and it wasn't my bag at all. But my mom said that they'd paid for the fourth lesson so I had to go, and then I didn't ever have to go again. I went to my fourth lesson and there was a guy filling in, who was 16 – I would have been 12 or 13 – and he taught me how to play 'Jumpin' Jack Flash'. I said that I'd sign up for a year if this guy could be my teacher. And that's pretty much what happened. I was gone. He was called Jorgen Jensen.

I think I learned almost everything I needed to know in the first two or three lessons that I had with him, but I stuck with him for a year and a half because I enjoyed it. Then I was playing hours every day. I'm a human not meant for this life, I'm allergic to so many things – I'm allergic to grass, for God's sake – so the summers were hell for me and I just wanted to be inside all the time with my guitar.

My dad waited until my 13th birthday to buy me an electric guitar, and we went out to the music shop. There was a year-old Stratocaster hanging on the wall. I didn't know anything about Fenders and Gibsons, but this guitar looked just like the one Robbie Robertson played. That was all I needed. To get a Stratocaster as your first electric guitar was quite good. I think it was 350 bucks, which my old man thought was outrageous, but, looking back, was a pretty sweet deal.

My high school years were a grand time in my life. I was into all of it. I loved the parties and the socialising, I loved the dope, I played sports. I was a decent student until the dope got the better of that, but I was good for a while.

On Friday night there'd be a party somewhere and I'd be the guy that would show up with a big stack of records under my arm and I would take over the turntable and DJ for the evening. I had money from my job working the midnight shift at the post office, so every weekend I'd have an ounce of weed, couple hits of acid, six brand new albums, and I was loaded for beer. I was just living the dream.

Everyone smoked weed on a Friday night at a party; it wasn't a big deal. The acid scene was a little different. It was harder edged and had a more defined crowd, but it was better dollar value – more laughs for your money. By the time I finished high school, coke had crept into the scene and I'm no fan of that but it did help me stay awake to get some essays done.

Around that time my dad told me that if I ever got picked up for drunk driving or possession of weed, he would be asked to retire as a judge. I remember thinking that if I couldn't drink and I couldn't smoke then my social life was over. That lasted until the next Friday, and then I deemed that I just needed to be much more careful. I've always been very polite in any dealings with the police.

GORD SINCLAIR

We moved to our house on Churchill Crescent, right across from Robbie's mom and dad, in 1966. It was a great neighbourhood; there were lots of kids of all ages and there was always a road hockey game going on. We would go over to a friend's house first thing in the morning and we didn't have to be home until the street lights came on. Our folks never really had any idea where we were.

My mom was a school teacher and then stayed home, my dad was a dean at the university. They were both super, super musical. When my dad did his degree in veterinary medicine at the University of Guelph, he would play saxophone in a dance band on the weekends. My mom was a classically trained pianist. She came through the conservatory programme and she made me do the same. It was very draconian – you had to put balls under your hands to get the proper playing position. I was in it for a year and a half before I begged my dad to intercede.

About a week later, my dad, who's a second-generation Scottish émigré, had got me doing bagpipe lessons with the Rob Roy pipe band and never a word more was spoken about the conservatory programme. This was when I was about 12 or 13. I started learning on a little nine-note chanter and really took to it. The drone-based background with melodies in different rhythmic fields layered on top made a lot of sense to me musically. I did that until I was 16 or 17; the band used to travel around for parades and community events, and entered competitions at Highland Games, including over in Scotland. Individually, I got into this type of bagpipe music called pibroch, which was very improvisational. I guess a lot of that came out in The Hip later on, when we were jamming and whatnot. It wasn't the coolest of instruments, but it was a pretty cool foundation.

At school in grade 7, they drew lots for instruments. Everyone wanted to be the trumpet player, but I got kind of the short end of the stick and ended up playing the French horn, which, after the bagpipes, might be the most uncool instrument ever. When I got to Kingston Collegiate and Vocational Institute, I went right into the band programme. My dad still had his sax, so we got it cleaned up and I started playing that.

Gord Sinclair,
Marine Midland Arena,
Buffalo, NY,
10 February 1999

Opposite: Sinclair family photos, including Gord with his parents, Leona and Duncan, and younger brother, Colin

Being in different bands – the Rob Roy, the KC stage band and also the Fort Henry Guard, which I did as a summer job – was a great preparation for being in a rock band. At rehearsals you had to know what you were doing, because you didn't want to be the one guy laying down clams.

In my house, the academic expectations were set high. In grade 13, you took six classes. My dad told me I had to take functions, calculus, algebra, physics and chemistry and left me with one elective. I chose history. My whole peer group was kind of skewed that way from an early age. We were conditioned to work hard at school and study hard at home.

My parents were probably a little stricter than Robbie's, so I liked to goof around in his basement. We listened to records all the time, starting with his older sister's. She had the triple Woodstock record and Steppenwolf's first record, Simon & Garfunkel, stuff like that. Then, when we got old enough, we would pool our lawn-mowing money and buy records together from House of Sounds, which was a great record store in town.

One day in grade 10 or 11, Robbie conned his dad into getting him an electric guitar and announced that he was going to put a band together and I was going to be the bass player. So my mom and I went down to Tremblay's music store on Princess Street, bought a crappy old Univox bass and an amp and Robbie and I started picking out tunes and hacking our way through them. I was always very fortunate in being able to pick up pretty quickly with my ear what I was supposed to be doing. I didn't have to learn chords or anything like that. And that's kind of how it all started.

JOHNNY FAY

I figured out aged ten that I wanted to play the drums. By 14, I had decided I was going to do it for the rest of my life. I didn't know how, but I just wanted to do it and I wasn't going to let anyone talk me out of it.

The music department at KCVI was run by Ted Brown and he was a great teacher. He taught everyone in The Hip at some point. The school had gear you could sign out for a night or over a weekend, so I was always lugging stuff to and from my house.

My parents told me they'd pay for the best teachers around, but that if I wanted any equipment of my own I'd have to pay for it myself. They got me a job as a busboy working in a Greek restaurant and I learned the importance of a dollar. So many kids get drum sets, play them for two weeks and then never play them again, and so having good teachers really motivated me.

I would hightail it home as soon as I was finished at school because I just wanted to play as much as I could. I really didn't spend time doing anything else. I kept playing until my parents shut it down. Then I started playing with my mom's knitting needles because they were much quieter, but, even then, they'd tell me to stop at a certain point. I was just living, eating and breathing it.

I was diagnosed with dyslexia when I was quite young. The cool thing about dyslexia is you have things upside down and sideways, so I looked at the drum kit differently. I wanted to know what the feet were doing, because, as a drummer, if you have confidence in your feet then you're going to go places. I was also able to hear and process rhythm in a different way from other people. So I never looked at my dyslexia as a handbrake; it was actually a gift, because it made me focus on one thing and that one thing was drumming. It really helped me get to the next level.

I started studying and hyper-focusing on my favourite drummers, like Stewart Copeland (he was the reason for life, for me and other drummers, if you were growing up in the Eighties), Alan White of Yes, Steve Jordan – there were little pieces of those players that I wanted to integrate into my playing.

Johnny Fay, recording Road Apples, Kingsway *Studios, New Orleans, 1990 (right)*

Opposite: Fay family photos, including Johnny with his dad, John, and his mom, Loretta

My Italian drum teacher taught me that the bass drum is your father, the snare drum is your mother, the toms are your brothers and sisters, and the cymbals are your cousins. You don't want to invite your cousins over too much because they're too loud – keep everything nice and tight.

In 1984, when I was in grade 11, my mom had seen me look at the brochure for the Berklee College of Music in Boston. That summer she told me to pack up my things ready to go on a trip the next day. I didn't know where. We drove to Boston, parked right in front of the college building and just waltzed in through the front door. My mom said, 'My son would like to go to the summer programme here.' And the guy there said, 'You can't just show up, it doesn't work that way. Applications were done in January. I'm sorry.' My mom said, 'We drove all the way from Canada, could you at least listen to him before we go home?' So this guy – his name was Ed Saindon and he was such a nice guy – took me into a room and I played and he came out and said I was good enough to stay.

He sorted me out with a place in the dormitory and enrolled me in the classes. When he asked where my drums were, my mom said, 'Oh, they're in the car out front, we'll go get them.' But we hadn't brought any drums, so we went across the street to Daddy's Junky Music and got a set of Red Sparkle Slingerland drums. That's what I had for my time down there and it was a great little kit. I had to work some more in the Greek restaurant to pay her back.

At the time, my mom didn't know how much she was helping, but that's what great parents do – they open doors, and she was kicking doors down. She got me in there, she knew I'd be fine and I was.

It was a great, great school; there were ten drummers better than me. The other drummers might have had 90 percent talent but I had that 10 percent drive and I got that from her – she just pushed and pushed and pushed.

Summer of 1984 was the beginning of my ride. I'll never forget it. And then, once I had come back home, in October I got a call from Gord Downie to come and audition for The Hip.

Secondary School Honour Graduation Diploma
Diplôme d'études secondaires supérieures

PAUL LANGLOIS

I'm pretty lucky. I had a normal, happy childhood. Great parents. Very involved. Both teachers. And three sisters, which I think has given me, to this day, a perspective that certain people I know who didn't have sisters maybe don't have.

In high school, I was just interested in getting by – there's such social pressure in that environment, so I was probably pretty focused on navigating that. It helped a lot that my dad, Adrien 'Tic' Langlois, had been the head of phys ed at my school since 1967 and he was considered cool. So, almost from my first day of grade 9, I had older boys looking out for me.

Paul Langlois with his parents, Terry and Adrien 'Tic' Langlois (above)

Rochester Dome Arena, Rochester, NY, 8 October 1998 (right)

Opposite: Langlois family photos (top)

New York, 1990 (centre right)

Paul Langlois's live rig used for The Hip's last ten years in arenas and theatres, including three Randall amp heads, one Celestion amp and one Randall amp (bottom left) and various effects pedals, tuners and power conditioners (bottom right)

All the senior football players knew I was Tic's son. I loved high school sports and going to games – the cheerleaders, sitting with all the fans. I would say I was pretty average, not a star or anything. I was on the curling team. Gord Downie was my vice. We weren't bad. I played soccer and volleyball three out of the five high school years. I played football two out of the five years.

My mom played piano, so we always had one in the house. I think she got quite far in her grades and she encouraged us all to play. I would fiddle around just for my own amusement but I never got very far. There might have been a guitar but no one could play it, including my parents. They bought a lot of records and then my sister Michèle and I would go to the record store and come home with records, so there was a mix of our parents' music and our music. My dad listened to stuff like Johnny Cash and Elton John. So music was part of the household. It wasn't a priority, but it was highly encouraged.

When I was 13 or 14, my mom heard me singing along with my sister Monique to songs from the top 100 that year on the radio. I would have been doing it in a very shy way, but once she heard she stayed on me for years and years to learn guitar and sing because she thought I had a nice voice. I told her it wasn't my thing. So when I finally did learn guitar, which was halfway through my first year of university, she was pretty pleased. I learned the Beatles song 'And I Love Her' to give her as a present for Christmas, as I had no money. That went over well.

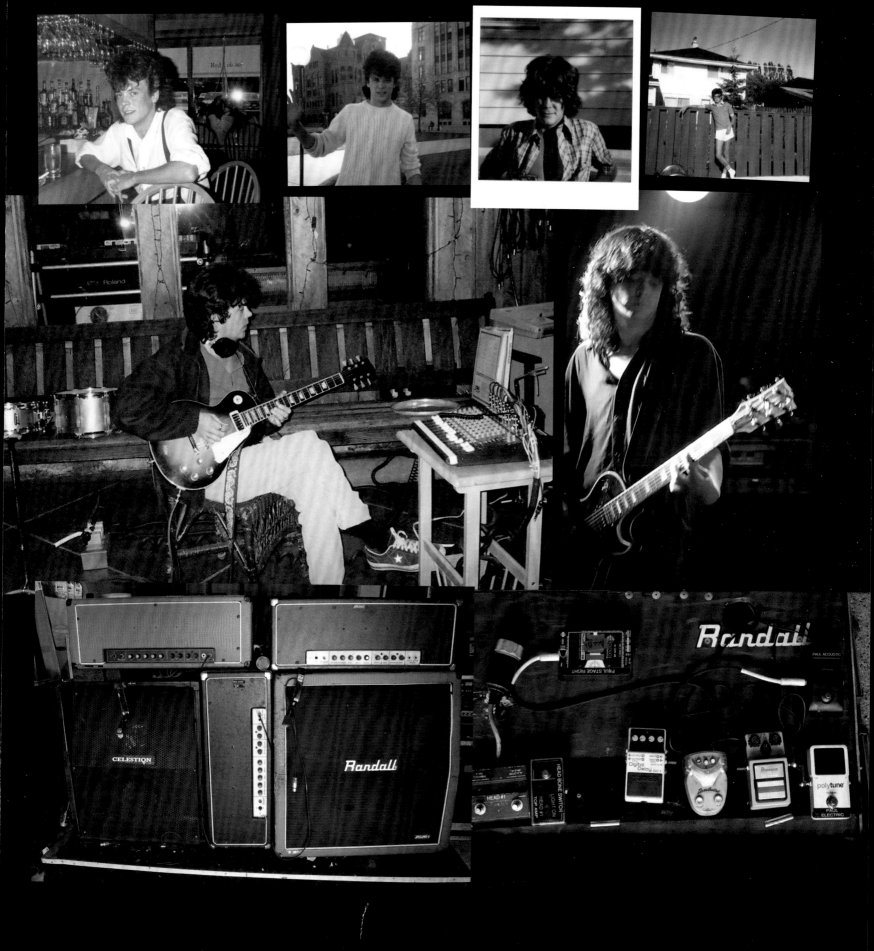

JF: KCVI is a big part of our connective tissue. Paul's dad was one of our teachers and taught us all. We all went to the same school and we're very proud of it. It was a great place to be from.

KCVI (Kingston Collegiate and Vocational Institute) yearbook photos (left to right): Rob Baker (1979), Johnny Fay (1982), Paul Langlois (1981), Gord Sinclair (1979) and Gord Downie (1981)

Opposite: Gord Downie, 1980/81 (top), Gord Downie and Paul Langlois, 1982 (bottom)

GORD S: At high school there were lots of doctors' kids and kids whose parents worked at the university in various capacities, but there were also kids whose moms and dads were doing blue-collar gigs. There are several prisons in and around Kingston, so there were lots of prison guards' kids, with different, tougher upbringings than we had.

ROB: The best thing about KCVI was how diverse the student body was. It had a reputation as being the rich kids' school – the richest kids in the city probably did go there, but I would say that a lot of the poorest kids in the city went there too, as well as the whole middle class. You were defined by where you came from economically, but I think you were defined more by what you were into.

Some kids go to a high school where everyone comes from the same economic background and they learn how to network, which is great and that'll carry you far in life, I suppose, but the skill you learn going to a public school with a diverse group of people is how to get along with people. You learn how far you can push without getting the shit kicked out of you, which is really an important lesson.

JOHNNY: Like Robbie and Gord Sinclair, I'd gone to Winston Churchill first but I knew of KCVI because my brothers had gone there. It was a really cool place. As I got into grade 9 and then grade 10, I figured out that the teachers were all about opening doors – they really wanted kids to do well.

PAUL: Robbie is two years older than me, same with Sinclair, so they were two grades ahead of Gord and me, and Johnny was two grades behind. That meant there was one year when all five of us were at KCVI at the same time. Robbie was always friendly. Everyone knew he played guitar and he was a dude but he was quite low key. My sister was in his grade, so I knew him a little bit through her. Robbie and Sinclair were in The Rodents and they were known as the cool cats – very out-there, alternative, weed-smoking, very hippie, reggae almost, mysterious. They didn't do a lot of gigs but I saw them once or twice.

Robbie was also known for bringing people back to his house to listen to a few good records. I didn't get that invite until after high school.

ROB: KCVI was definitely a clique-y place. The Jets, the Sweats, the Space Cadets, everyone had their own separate entrance and their own separate hang out areas … and you didn't cross those lines, for the most part. I did, I hung out with all of them.

The Jets were the more privileged upper-middle-class kids and they used the front door, of course. The Sweats were the ones that were mostly taking level four courses, making roach clips in metal shop and stuff like that. They'd smoke at the Earl Street entrance. And the Space Cadets were the ones that were taking acid all the time and listening to Genesis and Pink Floyd. They'd use whatever entrance they could use without getting beaten up.

I think I smoked my first joint the summer before I started grade 9. We'd smoke on weekends, then clean up our heads for the coming week. By grade 11, I was smoking weed every day – not usually before school in the morning (although sometimes), but at least every day at lunch. My first period after lunch was math and I just tanked. You can't do math when you're really high, apparently. My math mark went from a low 80s, down to a low 50s and sometimes lower. But my art mark went up and my English mark went up and my music mark was good, so it just kind of set a course for me.

GORD D: We all went to the same high school – it was like a solar eclipse. Johnny was in grade 9, and Robbie and Gord were in grade 13, and Paul and I were both in grade 11. We didn't really hang out together, obviously – probably booted Johnny out of a party or two for stealing beer.

JOHNNY: I'd seen Gord around the hallways; he sometimes wore a scarf, and he always had a book tucked under one arm and a cheerleader on his other arm. He was always nice to me but that may have been because I was friends with his little brother, Pat.

PAUL: On the very first day of grade 11, there was a new kid sitting beside me in history class, and it was Gord Downie. We hit it off pretty immediately, literally within the first couple of days. I was more established at school and had friends; he was in from Amherstview and didn't really know anyone. So I introduced him to some of my friends, invited him to do whatever I was doing and we started hanging out more and more.

We didn't have anything to do with music. It was more to do with sports and a similar style of thinking. I just thought he was cool and a nice kind of spirit to be around. We clicked right off the bat ... and it never stopped.

Gord had a pretty distinct style, even back then. He wasn't a girl chaser but there were certainly girls interested in him because of the way he dressed. And it became obvious through that first year of grade 11 that he was an athlete. Like all the kids who were good at sports, he became known. But he was also known as someone that was slightly different. He was quiet but smart and also fun and funny.

GORD S: Everyone was conscious of it when the Downies moved into town. It wasn't too long before Gord was dating the most attractive girls in school, instant cred. It was hard not to be aware of him, this tall, good-looking, athletic guy. It was a pretty big deal for a new kid to come in and crack the junior basketball team right away.

PAUL: As I got to know Gord, I saw he was much more sensitive, dynamic and emotional than I was or ever would be. I think I provided a kind of stability for him and helped him handle various people that were weirding him out. I wouldn't say I was just a listener but I was a good listener, so when he had ups and downs it was helpful for him to have me to talk to.

ROB: We had just started grade 9 and I'd just got an electric guitar and an amp. A week or two later Gord [Sinclair] had a little Traynor amp and a bass and we were on our way. Then we needed a drummer. We found a guy at school called Bill Reid and we started jamming with him. I think the first tune we played was 'Dancing Days' by Led Zeppelin.

We played a couple of times with Bill and with people that we met in band class at school, but it wasn't really working. Then we found Rick McCreary, who had become friends with Gord Sinclair because they were both big brains, and we asked him to come over one Saturday to jam. We played some songs from the first Bad Company record and 'Bastille Day' by Rush and a few other tunes that were hot at the time.

Once we'd hooked up with Rick we became The Rodents, which felt like a good name for a band. Then we became Rick and the Rodents, because you should always name your band after the drummer! Our musical tastes kind of grew and changed together; we became Clash devotees and played all those tunes, learned the Sex Pistols' album in a day.

JOHNNY: I remember a bunch of people at school being very heavily into David Bowie and circulating records when I was in grades 9 and 10, and that was a huge influence. In those days, friends would make tapes for each other. My friends turned me on to a lot of different kinds of music.

ROB: When you're a teenager, you're often trying on different identities with music and clothes. You try stuff on and see if it works for you. The Seventies was a weird time for music. If you were into rock music in the Sixties, you were into whatever was happening. But then it started to splinter into all these subgroups. I liked everything really – I loved soul music and early disco and all that, but I was a traditional rocker at heart. The Stones, AC/DC, Aerosmith, Zeppelin and Bowie – that was me.

GORD S: The Sex Pistols' first record was a big changing moment, which captured a real youthful energy. As a 16-year-old you feel like rebelling against something, but I wished I had something to rebel against. With The Clash or The Jam you're listening to English working-class protest tunes, where everyone is just pissed about something. The energy was inescapable for me and I really caught on to it. In retrospect, it was basically drum driven. Never mind fancy guitar chords and stuff like that, let's just play quarter notes and eighth notes as hard as we can. These guys hadn't gone to the Royal Conservatory of Music. They could play great but in their own way. All of a sudden there was a real licence there.

Before then, you only knew your favourite bands like The Who and Zeppelin through *Circus* and *Creem* magazines, then once every three years they would come to Maple Leaf Gardens. So they seemed totally unattainable – these were rock stars. But when punk came along, it was more attainable from a musical perspective. It's like The Clash singing 'we're a garage band'. We were a garage band, and all of a sudden we realised we could do this too. It started to consume our daily life.

Robbie had a fantastic record collection growing up, still does, so we were listening to music all the time. If we weren't down in his basement hacking away, we were up in his bedroom listening to tunes. And then we would go down and start playing the songs we were listening to and the floodgates opened.

ROB: When I was in grade 11 I played the KC talent show with Julie Thorburn (our trial lawyer three decades later when we were suing management over publishing, and now a Justice of the Superior Court of Ontario), who sang 'Wuthering Heights' by Kate Bush and I accompanied her on guitar. The next year, Gord Sinclair, Rick McCreary and I went in the talent show and played a Freddie King song, 'Hide Away', and 'Jumpin' Jack Flash' and we won. That took us to the county talent show at the Grand Theatre, which was a big deal. We had a friend, John Estabrooke, sing with us and he was a really dynamic frontman – he moved kind of like Iggy Pop. So we felt like we had something on the go. By grade 12, we were playing a lot. We played the high school dance at the end of grade 12 and then another one in grade 13.

GORD S: Playing the KCVI dance seemed like the logical extension of playing in Robbie's basement for so long. We knew the tunes and we could do it and it was an opportunity to actually play in front of people. KC had a dance once a quarter and they would always have a band come in. I'm sure it was a lot of people's first exposure to live music. Back in the day, for groups like Rush, high school dances were a good paying gig. I guess for us, in retrospect, to be the local band playing our own high school dance was a big deal for a lot of people.

ROB: Playing a high school dance is a big deal. It would have been weeks of mental preparation, thinking about your wardrobe, which shoes to wear. I would probably have restrung my guitar. We would have spent time on the set list, jigging and re-jigging. I had this schedule written out with military precision of how we were going to approach the day. It was: 3.30, pick up PA system from Renaissance Music; 4.30, set up PA system; 5.30, have dinner; 6.00, get high. The order was all laid out very clearly. And I'm sure we stuck to it because it was serious business.

We were super nervous. It was one thing to get up on stage and play two songs, and even that was terrifying, but to play a dance, you needed to get through three 45-minute sets, which was huge. We didn't have a person to do the lights. We'd made three boxes, each containing different coloured floodlights. To turn the lights on and off you had to go over while playing and kick the switch with your toe. It was ridiculous. But it really felt like the big time. We were so excited, so into it.

GORD S: We got all punked out and learned a bunch of Pistols and Clash tunes. We also played some Stones and some blues tunes. It was a punk dance but we were playing John Mayall & the Bluesbreakers. We played every tune that we could and probably repeated them. It was great.

*Rick and the Rodents
(Rob Baker, Gord Sinclair
and Rick McCreary)
in Rob's parents'
basement, early 1978*

GD: The Rodents were kind of like a punk band and very revered. Robbie walked the halls and people definitely knew who he was. It was an amazing thing.

JOHNNY: I was riding my bike with a couple of buddies one day after school around Churchill Crescent, which I later found out was where Robbie Baker lived, and I heard a band playing. It was muffled but we knew it was loud. It was those guys rehearsing for one of their gigs in the school gym.

I remember them being really cool because they played Clash tunes. Gord Sinclair was in the Fort Henry Guard so he had his hair cut pretty short and he looked like J.J. Burnel, the bass player of The Stranglers. And then there was Robbie, Andrew Grenville and Rick McCreary. I've always liked Rick's playing, he's a good drummer. They were really good. They definitely tweaked the interest of people in high school – you'd see these guys playing a gig and think that maybe you could do that too.

PAUL: I thought the school bands were cool but I never considered doing anything like that. All those guys in the bands were so cynical. They hated everything – when a band from Toronto or Ottawa or wherever came to play in the gym, the local band guys would always say that they were no good. It seemed to be a requirement to carry that little badge of cynicism with you – I guess because you were doing your own thing and trying to be the best.

School dances would be: take a bottle from your parents, put in a little bit of vodka, a little bit of whisky and a little bit of gin – a brutal mix of stuff – drink it all and head in. Or you'd smoke a couple of joints, or stand outside the beer store and ask a stranger to get you some beer. Sometimes that would be OK but other times it would go sideways and you wouldn't even make it to the gym.

It always took a long time for people to dance, which was actually good for the bands because everyone would just stand there and watch them. It's a good goal to have as a band, to get people dancing. Some things never change.

the Slinks...

ROB: When we were in grade 13, there was a competing band, The Slinks. It was like, 'Who are these young upstarts? We gotta take them down!' We had played the one dance and there was another dance coming up where this other band were also going to be playing. I remember standing outside the gym listening to them rehearsing before the dance and thinking that they sounded pretty good, which probably made me feel horrible and threatened at the time.

I would have become aware of Gord around the time of The Slinks dance and the rumour was that he was a very good front man, which would have appealed to us as we were a very good band that didn't have such a good front man.

GORD S: What our singer John Estabrooke lacked in singing, he made up for in performance energy – he did a lot of leaping about. He was a real character and a dear old friend of ours, still is. But we were always searching for a proper front man, because it's a tough gig. Mick Jagger, Roger Daltrey and Robert Plant – the rock gods with the fans blowing their hair back – they were the archetype for us. The quest for the front man was always the thing.

JOHNNY: You'd see Gord around the school hallways Monday through Friday, but at the weekend he was transformed. Gord lived for the gig. He was always planning on playing somewhere, whether it be somebody's living room or a local bar. And any time that he was going to be playing a gig, you definitely wanted to be there.

You'd go to a party at somebody's house on a Friday night and Gord and The Slinks would be unloading the gear ready to play there. One time, the basketball coach made him pick between a weekend tournament and a gig. Gord picked the music, but I think that was a hard decision for him.

PAUL: I remember being at Gord's, up in his bedroom, listening to records. He was more into music than any of my other friends were. I bought a few records and listened to them at home, but nothing like Gord. I have a vision of us walking in my neighbourhood and him telling me about this band he knew that he wanted to try singing with. And that was The Slinks, which was a group of KC guys that he was in for quite a while in high school.

That was probably a good way through his first year at school. He hadn't said anything about wanting to sing before; I just knew he listened to a lot of music. He was probably beginning to copy Bowie and Jagger and various other singers and wondering what he would sound like.

The first time I saw Gord sing was at the house of Steve Holy, The Slinks' guitar player, which is where they jammed. I can't remember what they played, but it would have been songs that were popular at the time – something by The Doors or Bowie or someone like that.

Posters hand drawn by The Slinks' bass player, Andrew Frontini, 1982

THE RETURN OF THE LEGENDS OF ROCK

The Slinks

SENSATION

SPECIAL
CES ON
QUALITY,
TOP
FORMANCE

$3.00 in advance FEB
$3.50 at the door 11th
THE POLISH HALL, 8:30
(65 Queen St)

PAUL: The first Slinks gig I saw was at a dance in gym 1. I remember being impressed that Gord had dressed up in a blazer and a shirt (which ended up being what Robbie and I wore on stage the rest of our careers). And he was dancing. He wasn't just standing there, he was really doing his thing and I was pretty floored with how good he was.

JOHNNY: Gord was extremely loyal. He would still be making music with The Slinks today, but they must have just gotten to a point where he didn't really feel that they were going to continue and he needed to do something else.

The Slinks performing at KCVI's school dance, fall 1981, featuring Gord Downie on vocals, Grant Ethier on drums, Andrew Frontini on bass, Steve Holy on guitar and Joe Pater on harmonica, guitar and keyboards

DANCE TO...

THE FILTERS

MULDOON'S
FRI. AND SAT.

ROB: It wasn't really until the summer after grade 13 that I got to know Gord Downie a bit and that was from going to a local bar, Muldoons, to see him in his next band, The Filters, which had been started by Finny McConnell, another guy from KC. Sinclair and I went down there one night and were really impressed by Gord. He could clearly sing but he was also a very dynamic front man; it was hard to take your eyes off him. I thought the tunes were a bit of a mixed bag but, all in all, it was most enjoyable for us. Sinclair and I had some conversation about needing a front man like that – we'd had that conversation a thousand times by then – but seeing Gord suddenly made that more attainable, because he lived in our town and went to our high school.

By then Sinclair was going to Queen's and I was just about to start there after taking a year off after high school, waiting for my fortune to fall into my lap (which didn't happen). He and I weren't really playing together at that time, as he was very involved with his studies at Queen's and he also had a band that I think he'd met through the Fort Henry Guard and they were playing a very different type of music than I was interested in.

GORD D: **Kingston has a bunch of bands, and everyone knows who everyone else is, especially in the music community. Plus, it's got Queen's University there, which brings in a lot of different tastes, if nothing else, and makes it a semi-fertile spawning ground for man because at least there's an open-mindedness about the city.**

Gord Downie wasn't completely sold on The Filters and he told Finny that if he was serious about this then he needed to get me to play guitar in the band. I had nothing happening, so it was perfect for me. I said that as long as I got 50 bucks a night plus expenses I'd be there. I think I played sort of a key man for Gord, so Finny needed to keep me happy to keep Gord happy. But I wasn't that hard to keep happy – free beer, $50 a night and I get to play guitar to people? Come on, I was pretty happy!

I can't really imagine why Gord wanted me in the band. I was serious about music, but I wasn't any hot shit guitar player. But I'm glad he felt that way because suddenly I was playing gigs in bars and getting paid for it and feeling like a professional musician, which is all I ever really wanted.

JOHNNY: I saw The Filters with Gord and Robbie at the Lakeview Manor where they opened up for – and blew off the stage – Platinum Blonde. It was pretty incredible. It was the only time I saw Gord perform in front of me, because soon after that I was in the band and I only ever saw his ass.

ROB: We started playing real bars. We were playing the Commodore, which was a really rough, divey, biker sort of bar on Princess Street. The place smelled of stale beer and there were fruit flies everywhere. It was known to be pretty dead, skidsville, but we sold the place out, I think, six Saturday nights. At which point the Lakeview Manor, which was the happening bar in town, came and said they'd offer us a residency if we signed a paper saying we would never play the Commodore again. So we did it. The money was good and they offered us lots of gigs over the coming year. That was really how The Filters took off and became a going concern in eastern Ontario.

GORD S: Robbie held back a year and started playing with Finny McConnell, Mauro Sepe and Gord in The Filters. I remember they played a pub, probably the Commodore, downtown. It was a proper paying bar gig, which I was impressed with at the time. The tune selection was really cool – they were doing Iggy and the Stooges and stuff like that. I remember saying to Rick at the time that if we ever put the band together again, this was the guy we needed. Gord was really authentic. When he was singing Stooges or Stones or Doors covers, he wasn't trying to sound like Iggy or Mick Jagger or Jim Morrison. He was doing his own thing and that made it all cohesive.

ROB: I liked a lot of the music The Filters were playing. Some of it I wasn't so into – The Romantics' 'What I Like About You' was a little poppy for me. It was Finny, primarily, choosing the tunes and it wasn't all my cup of tea.

I remember playing 'Vicious' by Lou Reed, and if they were going to play a Stones tune Finny wanted to do something well known like 'Get Off of My Cloud' or 'Satisfaction'.

We played a lot of gigs in town and we were also doing the eastern Ontario circuit – Gananoque, Belleville, Brockville, Trenton. Gord Downie and I were both going to Queen's by this time and suddenly we were playing gigs sometimes four or five nights a week and it was getting a little hard to keep up at university and play in this band that neither of us saw our future in.

I was trying to figure out a way forward for myself. Pete Townshend, Keith Richards, Eric Clapton, John Lennon all went to art school, so I signed up for art school, because I thought if you wanted to be in a band that was how you did it.

GORD S: I was at Queen's trying to figure out what I was going to do. I started off doing math and sciences but quickly dropped those because they were tough and my interests were elsewhere. Then I started doing history and political science courses, again still trying to figure out what I was doing. I met a guy in a political science class who was a musician and we got talking. He was putting a band together and looking for a bass player, and I was happy to be involved. We never ended up gigging but it was good to start playing again. Then when Robbie got to Queen's to do his bachelor of fine arts we started talking more and more and, sure enough, we began to jam together again. It didn't take too long for music to start becoming way more important than school. Rick was just too busy – he was in applied science, which was a tough programme, so, slowly over the four years we were at Queen's, we saw each other less and less. Robbie and I had a little more time on our hands than Rick and it felt so good to play together. Slowly, it became the thing – this is what we wanted to do.

The Filters' original 1983 line-up was Finny McConnell on guitar, Gord Downie on vocals, Mauro Sepe on drums and Kelly Campbell on bass, with the addition of Rob Baker on guitar in 1984

This page: The Filters, Lakeview Manor, Kingston, ON, 1983

Opposite: The Filters, Muldoon's, Kingston, ON, 1983

PAUL: My really good friend Mauro Sepe was a drummer in bands. Mauro, in my mind, was the best drummer in town. But one day I was at a friend's party and I heard this drumming from the basement. Someone said, 'Have you heard this kid, Johnny Fay? He's the best drummer around.' At the time, I would have been grade 11, so he would have been grade 9. I listened to him and he was maybe playing 'Tom Sawyer' or some other incredibly difficult Rush tune and my heart sank a little for Mauro, because this guy was really good.

JOHNNY: I'd heard that Rick McCreary's dad was pressing him to get a proper job. Rick had been in bands for a while, but now he felt it was important that he get through university and take a pass on music. That's how I got the gig. I'd come back from the Berklee College summer programme and I got a call from Gord Downie to come audition in Robbie's basement for a band they were starting. It was Gord, Robbie, Gord Sinclair and it had no name. Gord didn't really mention Rick, but I did do the audition on Rick's Tama Swingstars, which he'd left there.

I had confidence in myself. I told myself that the reason I was at this audition was because that's where I was supposed to be. If these guys didn't like me then somebody else would. I was going to be a drummer.

GORD D: **Johnny came over to Robbie's place and, as he likes to say, 'I got incredibly stoned and the next thing I knew, I was on the road.'**

JOHNNY: We played a song called 'I Love You, Suzanne' by Lou Reed, which we then had on the repertoire for a while. Gord Sinclair said we were going to play some obscure covers and write some original songs. There were a lot of bands that were doing nothing but covers, so I thought it was really cool that we were doing our own stuff.

Gord Downie went and talked to my parents about the band. For them it was important that I was going to be with a bunch of people that they knew and trusted to look out for me. If it had been people that my parents didn't know it might have been different. My dad just told me to get entrance to university so I had something to fall back on. But he always said, 'You gotta wake up and enjoy what you do in life. And if you're enjoying doing music, then do it.' So my mom and dad were both really supportive. This was 1984, so not a lot of parents were letting their kids go on the road.

GORD S: **Johnny sat down on Rick's kit, and right away it was like we were a band. It just felt really great with us playing off each other. And it was the first time that I'd ever been in a band with a really good singer. The vocals were always an afterthought in groups that I'd been in before.**

ROB: After just over a year The Filters had become too much work. It was Gord Downie's suggestion to form a band with Gord Sinclair at Queen's and just do it for fun, free beer and the occasional gig. The natural idea was that we'd get Sinclair, of course, and Rick McCreary, who is a killer drummer; it would basically be The Rodents with Gord Downie singing – my dream. We had a rehearsal and Rick McCreary was a no-show, so we scheduled another rehearsal, and again he was a no-show. We talked about what tunes we'd want to play but we weren't doing any playing because we didn't have a drummer. After a third no-show from Rick, we could see that he clearly wasn't going to be in the band. I think it was Gord Downie who said about a guy he knew, not very well, who was still in KC and was supposed to be a real hot shot drummer.

GORD S: When Johnny was in grade 9 and we were in grade 13, we knew of him reputationally and knew he could drum.

JOHNNY: All of our parents were really supportive. I don't think that we could have been in The Hip if it wasn't for them. Gord Sinclair's parents bought us a van. We rehearsed at Robbie's house and his dad, Judge Baker, used to lend us his cars to get to gigs. We had one of our biggest meetings at Paul's house in the basement there.

Gord Downie had a friend who I met at a high school party when I was 18. Her name was Leslie Galbraith, and she had a summer job working as a photographer's assistant for a guy in town named Joe Bronson. Joe would go off for a two-martini lunch and leave the studio unoccupied for a couple of hours. When this happened, Leslie would give us the short-notice call to come on down. She was our go-to photographer for the first year and a half or so and took a bunch of really good promo shots. She was such a good photographer that we decided we needed to bring her into the fold, so I married her.

    Gord Sinclair's looking like he just farted and we're all laughing … and if my eyes don't deceive me I think Gord Downie's got a little bit of eye-liner on, which would be about right for the time. (RB)

This page and opposite:
Early studio photos,
Kingston, ON, 1985

GORD D: When we were putting the band together, we found that *we* were the band's influences. We found that we were gravitating towards a lot of Yardbirds, early Stones, that kind of stuff. And it was solely due to the fact that that was the stuff we were listening to and we wished that other bar bands would play that stuff. So instead, we compromised and formed the band ourselves.

ROB: In the mid-Eighties it was a cover band scene, and it was the era of the tribute band – often stadium rock being delivered in pubs and small clubs. It all seemed absurd to us. We thought, if we have to play covers, why not play music suited to those cramped, sweaty venues and, for us, that harkened back to the mythical days of the early Sixties club scene in London – the Crawdaddy, the Ricky Tick, the Marquee – places where the superstar bands of the late Sixties and Seventies were just young bands learning their craft, cutting their teeth trying to put their own spin on American blues and rhythm and blues – The Beatles, The Rolling Stones, The Yardbirds, John Mayall, Them, The Pretty Things, Pink Floyd. Loud, crowded and sweaty, it was a scene, not a show, and that's the atmosphere we were going for.

GORD S: We played pretty obscure cover material – Yardbirds and Rolling Stones B-sides, songs that people wouldn't be super familiar with. That meant we were able to start slipping in our own, primarily blues-based songs without anyone noticing. Back then, some of the clubs we played didn't allow bands to do their own material.

And lo and behold, people wouldn't leave the dance floor. They dug it, and that was encouraging. People were responding to our songs, even if they didn't know that's what they were.

ROB: When one makes sourdough bread or kombucha you use a fermented starter called a mother. The mother, if nurtured and cared for, is a living culture that can last for years, even decades. Well, we used the music at the heart of the early Sixties British club scene as our mother – a culture being kept alive to help us develop a scene. There was the added advantage that the material we were working with had not been overexposed – nobody we knew was playing this music on radio or in clubs, and most of the people we knew weren't familiar with it. So, we could really take ownership of these tunes. The audience had little or no expectations of how they were supposed to sound so we could twist them, stretch them, Gord could play with and change the lyrics – it was raw material for us to use and it allowed us to find our footing and our sound, and learn how to work a room and a crowd.

1. REFORMED
2. LITTLE BY LITTLE
3.* BIG HUNK O' LOVE — SUZIE
4.* BOOM BOOM BOOM
5. MESSIN
6. IT'S MY LIFE
7. ~~JUST YOUR~~ BEDROCK
8. STUPID GIRL
9.** WITHOUT A DOUBT
10. YOU TOLD ME
11. MARY MARY
12. BREATHLESS
13. NOT FADE AWAY

Set #1
Terrapin
Oct 3/85

Grad Club – 2nd Set
1 LITTLE BY LITTLE
2 REFORMED
3 BABY BLUE BLOOD
4 SIRENS
5 HAVE MERCY
6 GOOD LOUIN
7 IT'S MY LIFE
8 COLD SHOT
9 OFF THE HOOK
10 BOOM BOOM BOOM
11 PSYCHEDELIC RAMBLINGS
12 FOR YOUR LOVE
13 HEART ATTACK LOVE
14 MARY MARY
15 HITCH HIKE
16 EVELYN
17 WOOLY BULLY
18 I'M A BELIEVER
19 ROSALYN
20 STEPPIN STONE

1. ROUTE 66
2. BIG CITY
3. BABY BLUE BLOOD
4. SIRENS
5. ~~CERTAIN GIRL~~ KING BEE ~~FOR YOUR~~
6. CERTAIN GIRL
7. CIRCUMSTANTIAL
8. I JUST WANNA FUCK
9. ~~WALKIN THE WALK~~
10. DOWN HOME GIRL
11. ROADRUNNER   Set Terr Oct
12. MISS AMANDA   WE GOT THE BEAT
13. ~~CAN YOU~~ ~~EVELYN~~
14. STRAIGHT HELL

GHOST
SURFERS | WIPE OUT | BEDROCK
WE GOT THE BEAT
(GLORIA)? / WOOLY

Night Comes Down
Ghost Surfers
Down Home Girl
King Bee
Can I Get A Witness

JOHNNY: **They gave me my musical education. Gord Sinclair gave me some Little Richard records and said we were going to try this or that song, and Robbie gave me some Stones or some blues or J.J. Cale.**

ROB: The first gig was for my fine-art end of term party in November 1984 at the Kingston Artists Association (now the Modern Fuel Gallery). We rehearsed for a couple of weeks in my parents' basement and cobbled together three sets, with two originals in each set. As we went on, that balance just shifted. Before long, half the set was original and then after two years we were playing two cover songs out of a 12-song set.

PL: The name, The Tragically Hip, is kind of tongue in cheek … 'It's so tragic, it's hip.'

GORD S: We had this gigantic repertoire of R&B, blues-based stuff, where the riffs and the beat would change but the song structure was fairly standard. Gord would learn the first verse and the chorus, and then make the rest up. That's really how he learned how to write.

We did the deep dive into The Stones and went backwards into their earlier catalogue. How did The Stones become The Stones? What were they listening to as kids? We always thought there was a lot more merit in playing 'Off the Hook' than '19th Nervous Breakdown'. And then we did the deep dive into their contemporaries – The Pretty Things and The Yardbirds, in particular.

That's what we set our sights on and so it launched us right away. It was all about the music all the time. And then it took us a long time to figure out that every night we stepped on stage was a moment of success for us. Because of the nature of our friendship, every moment that we stepped on stage was a gift.

ROB: With our first gig at the Kingston Artists Association coming up, we were tentatively called The Bedspring Symphony Orchestra, which no one thought was a good name. When Gord suggested 'The Tragically Hip', we went with it because it was better than the alternative. We thought it was funny. The upper middle-class kids who can't get the Mercedes for the weekend, who need to borrow extra money to get some coke for the party. Oh yeah, we were real punks. We really had a lot to complain about!

GORD D: It came from a Mike Nesmith video compilation tape you can buy called *Elephant Parts* – a bunch of skits. There's one skit in there that is sort of like a TV plea: 'Send some money to the Foundation for The Tragically Hip.' And that phrase has also appeared in an Elvis Costello song. It crops up every now and again, and it's just a name that we like.

Set lists and flyers for shows at the 40-capacity Terrapin Tavern, downtown Kingston, 1985

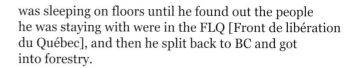

Above (l to r): Davis Manning, Gord Downie, Gord Sinclair, Rob Baker and Johnny Fay, outside Wizard of Ink tattoo studio, Kingston, ON, winter 1986

Opposite: Performing with Davis Manning at Queen's pub, Alfie's, Kingston, ON, winter 1986 (top and second row, left) and at the Horseshoe Tavern, Toronto, winter 1986 (second row, centre right and third row)

Notes on band members' profiles for the Hip fan club from one of Gord Downie's notebooks (centre right)

Contact sheet of the final band photo shoot with Davis Manning, 1986 (bottom)

ROB: One of the girls at Queen's had been cooking at logging camps around Hope, BC and a guy there had fallen in love with her and followed her back to Kingston. She wanted to unload this guy on someone and so she told us that he was a musician who played sax and guitar and asked if we'd be interested in jamming with him. I told her to send him over to our next rehearsal at Gord Sinclair's parents' house.

He showed up and played with us over the next few months and we started gigging a lot. We also got the backstory of who he was and where he came from.

Davis Manning was born in Nevada and grew up in the Vegas area (as a huge Wayne Newton fan, which was just mind-boggling to us). He was a deserter from the US Navy. He was told that if he took up a study of signals and really excelled then he would become a teacher in signals. So he really applied himself, did really well, and then they said, 'You're really good at this, you're going to Vietnam.' So he decided to split. His stepmother turned him in and he did some time in a military prison. He told us a story about how he was made to stand from sun up to sun down with his nose pressed into a chain-link fence, and every person that walked past kicked the fence. He said his whole face was abraded and blistered. Finally, he was released, but then he deserted a second time. This time, he made it to Vancouver and then ended up in Montreal, where he was sleeping on floors until he found out the people he was staying with were in the FLQ [Front de libération du Québec], and then he split back to BC and got into forestry.

GORD S: We learned an awful lot from Davis Manning. He was a real character, a bona fide hippie with all the dreams of a better world that the hippie movement involved. We got to know him socially, just sitting around and listening to him play his songs. We'd been goofing around as a band and then he hooked up with us playing the sax.

ROB: We didn't really want to be a two-guitar band at the time. We were mining something a little different, so having a sax player was awesome. Davis was about ten years older than us. We were a bunch of fresh-faced college kids and here was this old, grizzled vet. People were like, 'What's he doing with them? They must have something.'

BERNIE BREEN: Davis was special. He was a hippie, groovy man, like the cool Muppet dude with the shades and the 'tache. I loved what he brought to the band at that time. The blues are acquired and I think Davis instilled that in the guys in many ways, not just musically but in some sort of barometer of cool/crazy. And he could hit those sax solos, man.

GORD S: Davis made a lot of contributions to the group, but probably the most important was that he was a wonderful songwriter. When he wheeled into town, he already had three or four really good songs. He really pushed us to write our own material, because he knew that that was where the money was. Growing up in Kingston you see becoming a songwriter as unattainable, but he showed us that it was a real possibility.

ROB: Davis was an incredible songwriter – kind of like Jim Croce crossed with Charles Manson! He was the guy I'd always wanted to be. He'd pick up a guitar, sit down in a room full of people and have everyone spellbound for an hour just playing his songs and telling stories in between.

He was a great addition to the band, particularly at that stage when we were trying to find our way and our own voice. Davis gave us a credibility that got us in the door of places like the Terrapin Tavern, which fancied itself as a blues bar. They had live music seven nights a week, but it was a really hardcore place; Morgan Davis and all kinds of great blues acts came through there. The owner had trouble making money on the blues acts, so three or four nights a month he would have The Tragically Hip in and we would stuff the place and he'd set a new bar record every time we came. He hated us! It bummed him out that we were these young college kids and that we weren't playing straight blues. But he had to have us, and we took full advantage of that.

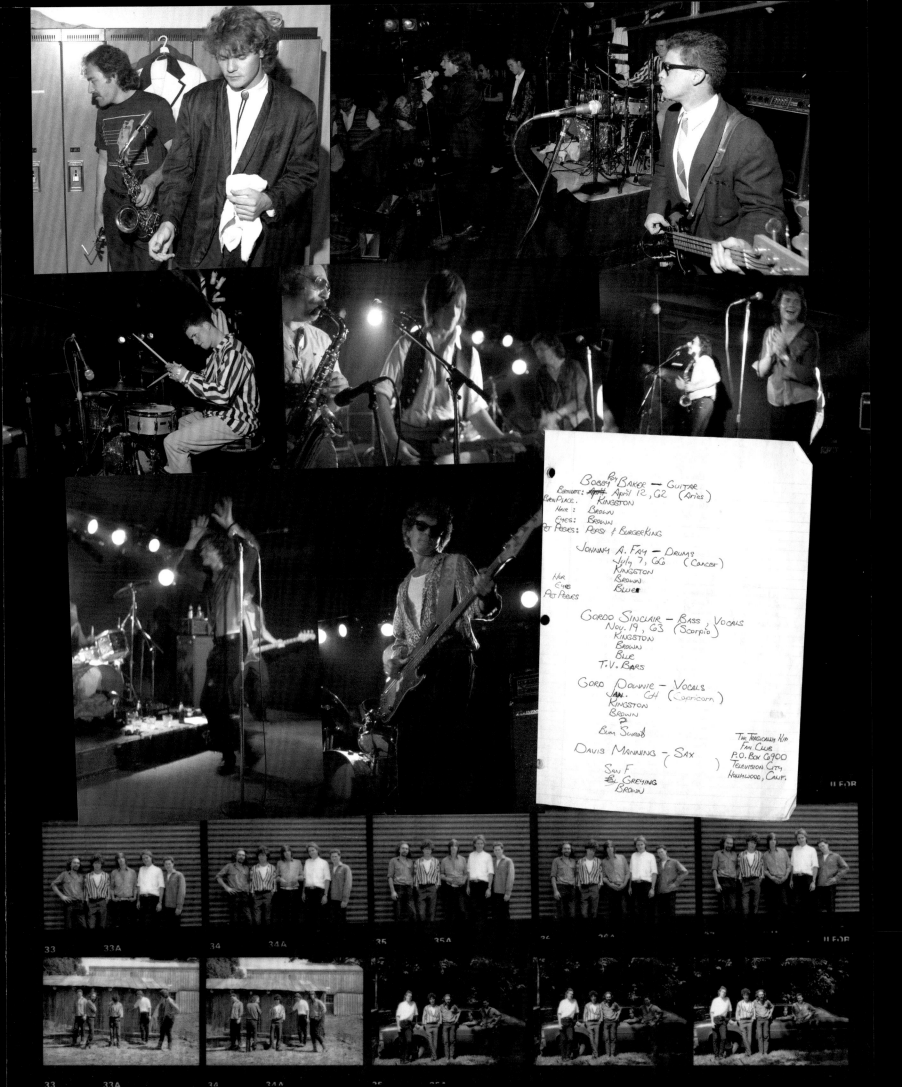

Roy
Bobby Baker — Guitar
Birthdate: April April 12, 62 (Aries)
Birthplace: Kingston
Hair: Brown
Eyes: Brown
Pet Peeves: Pepsi & BurgerKing

Johnny A. Fay — Drums
July 7, 66 (Cancer)
Kingston
Hair   Brown
Eyes   Blue
Pet Peeves

Gordo Sinclair — Bass, Vocals
Nov. 19, 63 (Scorpio)
Kingston
Brown
Blue
T.V. Bars

Gord Downie — Vocals
Jan. 64 (Capricorn)
Kingston
Brown
?
Bum Sweat

Davis Manning — Sax
San F
El Greying
Brown

The Tragically Hip
Fan Club
P.O. Box 6900
Television City
Hollywood, Calif.

TERRAPIN
TAVERN
76 PRINCESS

entertainment

JULY
29 & 30   PHIL GUY and THE CHICAGO MACHINE
Hot blues guitarist formally with Brother Buddy Guy.
31   B.B. GABOR in a rare solo appearance.

AUGUST
1 - 3   THE BEARCATS – Great Rock & Roll
5 - 6   PRAIRIE OYSTER
7   POETRY – Micheal Andre also the EZRA POUND
ART SHOW
8 - 10   BILL JOSLIN / GEORGETTE FRY
12 - 13   REGGAE
15   KAAI BENEFIT DANCE, The Tragically Hip
16   THE TRAGICALLY HIP
17   MATT "GUITAR" MURPHY
19 - 20   WILLIE P. BENNETT
21   BLUEST OF THE BLUES CONTEST, Morgan Davis
22 - 24   MORGAN DAVIS
26 - 27   GWEN SWICK BAND
28   T.B.A.
29 - 31   THE TROUBLE BOYS
SEPTEMBER
2   PRUF ROCK
3 - 4   COLIN LINDEN

JOHNNY: The Terrapin Tavern was the first Kingston bar we played. We opened for the Florida Razors, who were fronted by Tom Wilson, and he was the one that got us the gig. That was such a huge opportunity for us. Tom knew how hard it was for a young band to get a gig and he wanted to give us a break, which was very cool of him. A couple of months later, he gave us our first gig in Ottawa, at the Rainbow Bistro.

In the dressing room of the Terrapin they had beer cases for seats. I was still in high school back then and I actually did some homework down there one time. Robbie used to help me with English, Gord Sinclair was the historian. I remember doing a *Great Gatsby* paper that was due the next morning. It was after midnight and the guys were arguing about F. Scott Fitzgerald and I was taking notes.

ROB: I remember my mom and dad coming to see us at the Terrapin Tavern. As the judge in town, my dad couldn't have a drink in public – he had to be super-careful. He also knew there were lots of people in Kingston that he'd put away. But he showed up with my mom one night when we were just getting ready to take the stage. A biker friend of the band met them at the door and said, 'Judge, you have nothing to worry about here, come on in.' He led my folks up to the front, kicked some people off a table and plunked them down right in front of the stage. They had a grand time.

THE TRAGICALLY HIP

The Tragically Hip were formed on or about Christmas 1984 in Kingston. Since that time they have performed extensively in and around South Eastern Ontario, and have been received enthusiastically by audiences wherever they go. What began as a part-time pastime for a group of University friends has now become a popular attraction for everybody in the know. The Hip play music that they enjoy, which is the band's founding premise. Their blend of original and cover material is exciting and new.

The Tragically Hip is comprised of four Kingston boys: guitarist Rob Baker, drummer John Fay, bassist Gord Sinclair and vocalist Gord Downie. The addition of saxophone, both on stage and in the studio, makes the unit complete. They were, and still are, knit together by their taste in music and their devotion to live performance. Though they have developed their own style, which is reflected in the band's original material, they draw heavily on the influence of the English club scene of the early 1960's. They are not a revival band ... good music doesn't ever go away!

While they began playing the University scene, The Tragically Hip soon found that their music commanded a wider audience. Instantly, The Hip became Kingston's most popular band, playing to capacity crowds wherever they went. Now that they are finished with school, the band is anxious to take their show on the road and build the foundations for a career in music. Come and check-out The Tragically Hip ... they're it.

This page and opposite: Set lists and flyers for early gigs at Kingston venues Terrapin Tavern, Alfie's and Lakeview Manor, and Toronto venue the Horseshoe

MANOR Rock Fest Apr 27

1 CHILD OF MOON
2 BABY BLUE !
3 STRAIGHT DOWN HELL
4 THAT'S ALL RIGHT
5 HOME TOWN, BRING DOWN
6 PSYCHEDELIC
7 WISH YOU WOULD
8 EVELYN
9 NADINE
10 ALL CDN SURF CLUB
11 SHE'S A RAINBOW
12 LITTLE by LITTLE
13 HEART ATTACK LOVE
14 REFORMED
15 GROOM STILL WAITING
1000 Night Comes / It's All over Now

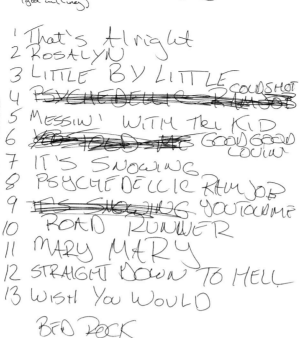

2nd Set   Manor   6 Dec
(god willing)

1 That's Alright
2 ROSALYN
3 LITTLE BY LITTLE   COLDSHOT
4 ~~PSYCHEDELIC RAMJOB~~
5 MESSIN' WITH THE KID
6 ~~IT'S TOLD STR~~ GOOD GOOD LOVIN
7 IT'S SNOWING
8 PSYCHEDELIC RAM JOB
9 ~~ITS SNOWING~~ YOUTOLDME
10 ROAD RUNNER
11 MARY MARY
12 STRAIGHT DOWN TO HELL
13 WISH YOU WOULD
BED ROCK

THE TRAGICALLY HIP

the lakeview manor
monday feb. 24

JOHNNY: My parents' house overlooked the prison and then down below the prison you could see this thing flashing away like a Las Vegas casino in the cold February night. And that was the Lakeview Manor. My mom used to pick me up from KCVI and take me down there with the drums. I knew that the exotic dancers were just about to go on, so when she asked if I needed any help getting set up I'd tell her that I'd be OK. She knew what was going on in there.

It was hard. Some nights I'd get home about three in the morning smelling like an ashtray because everyone was smoking and then I'd have to be at school at nine. But when you're that age you don't really need much sleep. It was exhilarating too, because even making 60 bucks a night I was still making more money than anyone else at school – not that that was what was driving me.

My last day of high school, I had a history exam and then I walked out, got in a car and ended up at the Horseshoe in Toronto to play what I guess was my first gig as a professional. The Horseshoe was one of the great Canadian venues of all time, so there was a lot of pressure on that gig.

THE TRAGICALLY HIP

alfie's
thurs-sat.
mar. 6-8

the Manor
Lakeview Manor Hotel

The Lakeview Manor presents

The TRAGICALLY HIP
with
BANANA REPUBLIC

UNITED WAY DAY

Sat., March 29th

Tickets - $2.50
Doors open 8 p.m.

"Give a Kid a Good Easter"

Kingston's always been a great music town with a real lack of great music venues. We never really had a Horseshoe but there were still lots of places to play. (GS)

ALFIE'S PUB

Combining spirit   with tradition

Shooters 1.5 oz	(2.32 + .23 tax) 2.55
German Helmet Kahlua, Bailey's, Peppermint Schnapps	**B52** Kahlua, Bailey's, Triple Sec
Jelly Bean Triple Sec, Tequila, Galliano, Grenadine	**Shooter McGee** Amaretto, Vodka
Golden Gael Amaretto, Galliano	**Popsicle** Bailey's, Vodka, Apricot Brandy

Cocktails 1 oz	(1.95 + .20 tax) 2.15
Bloody Mary Vodka, tomato juice	**Daiquiri** Rum, lime juice
Bloody Caesar Vodka, clamato juice	**Moscow Mule** Vodka, lime, ginger ale
Collins Liquor, lemon juice, soda	**Tequila Sunrise** Tequila, orange juice, Grenadine
	Brown Cow Tia Maria, milk

Mixed Drinks 1.5 oz	(2.32 + .23 tax) 2.55
Black Russian Vodka, Tia Maria	**Planters Punch** Dark Rum, Triple Sec, fruit juice, Grenadine
Rootbeer Tia Maria, Galliano, coke, soda	**Sinapore Sling** Gin, Cherry Brandy, soda lemon, Grenadine
Dirty Mother Tequila, Tia Maria, cream	**Harvey Wallbanger** Vodka, orange juice, Galliano
Rusty Nail Scotch, Drambuie	**Velvet Hammer** Tia Maria, Triple Sec, cream
After Eight Tia Maria, Creme de menthe, cream	

Long Drinks 2 oz	(2.77 + .28 tax) 3.05
Cheap Thrill Triple Sec, Tia Maria, orange juice, cream	**Slammer** Southern Comfort, Amaretto, fruit juice
Zombie Light Rum, Dark Rum, fruit juices	**Melon Cooler** Melon Liquer, Vodka, orange juice

House Specials 3 oz	(3.36 + .34 tax) 3.70
Millionaire Tia Maria, Bailey's, Amaretto, cream	**Cherry Bomb** Light Rum, Dark Rum, Cherry Brandy, fruit juices	**Alfie's Iced Tea** Rum, Vodka, Gin lime juice, coke

Alfie's is owned and operated by Queen's Alma Mater Society.

Framing
Travel Posters
Contemporary Art Prints
Drymounting & Laminating
Do-It-Yourself & Custom Framing
Student & Artist Discounts
546-1868
198 Princess Street at Montreal
Kingston Framewoks gallery & workshop

Sailboards
FOR SALE OR LEASE FOR A WEEKEND, WEEK, MONTH, SEASON OR TO BUY
29B Princess St. (at Clergy)
Kingston, Ontario K7L 1B5

City Sports
542-4415   542-7831

Queen's Team Orders
CRESTED SPORTSWEAR
CUSTOM CRESTING & EMBROIDERY

Pristine - 3/June/85

ROB: Davis had a darker side and he had some anger. He hated putting his fate in the hands of a bunch of 20-year-old college kids who were making it up as they went along. He thought he knew the formula and that we were getting it all wrong and it was immensely frustrating to him. There were a few instances when that frustration boiled over and finally I was tasked with letting him go.

GORD S: When Davis left we were at a real crossroads, because we weren't any good as a four-piece.

ROB: We already had a reputation around eastern Ontario by the time Davis left, and I think a lot of people saw him as a big part of what made us different. But we were pretty focused on the songwriting by that point and we didn't feel he was what made us stand out. We really felt we were going to find our way through it, but we had to play a bunch of gigs as a four-piece, which was not ideal.

GORD D: Paul joined later on, after we parted ways with our sax player. We had a saxophone player in the early days. We were very wacky and zany.

BERNIE BREEN: It was a weird time when Davis left the band. There were a couple of gigs booked and the guys were thinking of cancelling them. Gord Sinclair suggested a friend who could fill in on sax; I remember him playing with them at the Rainbow in Ottawa and, no offence to the guy, who did his best, but he was no Davis. Afterwards we were all shooting the breeze and Robbie said that they were thinking of bringing in a guitar player to replace Davis. When I heard that, my first reaction was, 'No way, man. It's gotta be sax. Are you kidding?'

A few weeks later I was at the Langlois house and Paul was preparing to go jam with the boys. There was some nervousness that day but also a buzz and excitement. I get goosebumps right now thinking about Paul going off and then coming back three or four hours later and everyone asking how it had gone and Paul answering in his way, 'Well … it was OK.' Lo and behold, I think it was a week later he debuted on acoustic and figured his way into it. And the rest, as they say, is history.

Above: The band as a four-piece, after Davis Manning and before Paul Langlois, Kingston, ON, 1986

Right: Gord Downie and Paul Langlois, Kingston, ON, 1981 (top) and 1983 (bottom)

PAUL: After high school I went to Ottawa to study at Carleton but by Christmas of my second year I couldn't take it anymore. I dropped out, moved back to Kingston and got a job driving a cab. I was very down at the time. I was out of money, so I was living with my folks and I wasn't hanging out with anyone. When I wasn't working I was playing piano and guitar and starting to write songs, but they weren't happy songs.

So there was a year and a half where Gord and I didn't see each other much at all. But one night I was waiting in my cab outside Alfie's and there was Gord coming out. He was so much happier to see me than I ever had pictured in my stupid head. It was like it had made his whole year that I was back in town. And then I started hanging out with him again. He made me feel so good and then we never stopped hanging out after that. I'll always be grateful to him for lifting me up and bringing me back to looking at life as something that I could enjoy again.

When I'd made enough money to be able to move away from home, I shared a house on Brock Street with Gord Sinclair and Gord Downie and another guy called Johnny Newman. The house belonged to Gord Downie's dad, Edgar. It was a good place to hang out and a guitar would come out once in a while, mostly just a guy strumming on the couch.

The house was right across from Victoria Park, which has a great rink, so it was a regular thing through the winter to go play some hockey. It was a very happy time, but I was drifting and didn't know what to do next. I was writing country-type songs so I was thinking of hitchhiking to Nashville to take a shot, though I'm sure I would have been eaten alive if I'd gone there.

GORD D: Paul was going to leave for Nashville and I was worried that I'd never see him. We were getting guest sax players to cover for Davis, but then I went to the guys and said, 'How about having two guitar players? How about my buddy Paul?'

PAUL: Gord used to get me in all the shows and I would just marvel at how much better they were than everyone else, but they weren't having a great time as a four-piece. They didn't feel like they were powerful enough, so they wanted to add a guitar. Still, it was really a shock when Gord called me. As soon as he asked, I wanted to do it, because I knew they were going to be big.

ROB: Gord suggested Paul and we all thought it was a fantastic idea, there wasn't a moment's hesitation. Paul was Gord's oldest friend and a chum of all of ours. It's hard to find somebody that you get along with as well as that. And so we got Paul in the band knowing he'd be great. He learned the songs really quickly and he was immediately an incredible, indispensable member of The Hip.

I didn't like being the only guitar player in the band, particularly without another instrument. When we had a sax player it wasn't so bad, but without Davis I just felt pretty naked when I went to take a solo. It was like the bottom dropped out. So having someone else who was good made a big difference.

JOHNNY: I think it was important for Gord to have Paul in the band. Gord Sinclair and Robbie were best mates growing up, so it was good for Gord to have his best mate in the band too.

In a way, The Hip was really Gord and Robbie's band, because they were together in The Filters and that glued them together. Then they each brought their best friend in and I was somewhere in the middle. So there was no power dynamic between different friend groups. The whole thing kind of gelled.

BERNIE BREEN: When Paul joincd Thc Hip, they really found their legs and discovered what rhythm guitar could do for them. I realised just how wrong I'd been that night in Ottawa. Paul anchored the band – they don't call him Rock for nothing.

ROB: Paul was a solid centre of the band. Put any five people together and you'll get a divergence of opinions. How are we going to make our way forward with five differing views? Paul generally held the centre down. Both extremes would get mad at him because he'd sit on the fence, but it was actually a pretty strategic position to take.

PAUL: Those four guys had everything going for them. Johnny decided very early on he was going to be a great drummer. Robbie, same thing on guitar. Gord Sinclair was a songwriter and Robbie put him on bass when they were teenagers. Gord Downie announced to me in grade 11 that he wanted to be a singer and was determined to make at least some sort of living doing it. They were all so driven and I became driven the day I joined, and I didn't look back.

Joining The Hip was surreal. I remember the feeling of being backstage at my first gig pretending not to be nervous. I had rehearsed with the band a couple of times but not as much as I would have liked. Going in, I thought, 'Well, Robbie's a great guitar player. I can play rhythm.' It didn't even cross my mind that I'd start singing back-ups, but there was a mic in front of me and I knew all the songs.

BERNIE BREEN: Paul was just the coolest motherfucker there was. First of all, he could smoke a butt from start to finish without ashing it. He was playing and strumming and faking his way through a lot of it. And secretly minding his Ps and Qs. He was mindful of where he was and wanting to fit in, but he was just so smart, so musical.

Paul, 1989 (top left)

Lee's Palace, Toronto, 21 October 1986 (top right)

Johnny Fay and Paul Langlois passport booth photos (above)

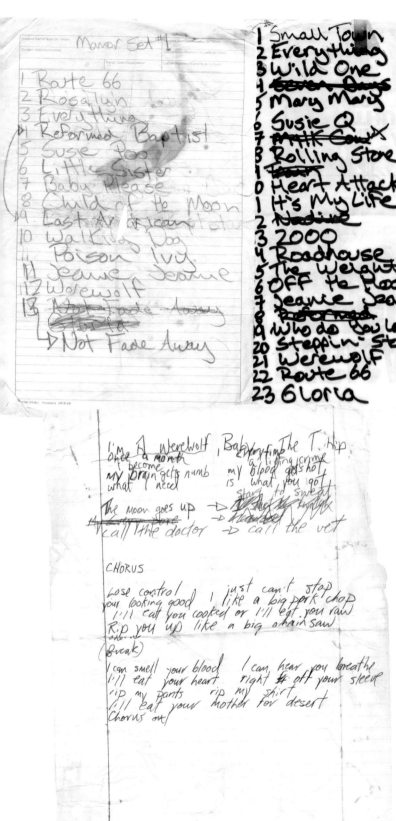
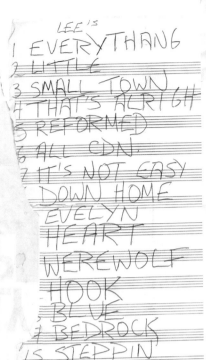

Set lists with early Hip songs 'I'm a Werewolf, Baby', 'Small Town Bringdown', 'All-Canadian Surf Club', 'Last American Exit' and 'Evelyn', as well as covers of songs by The Rolling Stones, The Band, David Bowie and The Doors

Lyrics to 'I'm a Werewolf, Baby'

PAUL: 'I'm a Werewolf, Baby' had been written and played before I joined. For some reason, instead of me learning and playing the guitar on it, someone suggested I play the shaker. Then, over time, me dancing and doing back-ups with the shaker brought the werewolf out in Gord and he thought it'd be fun to tackle me. It was staged, but it was very realistic. He would genuinely charge and tackle me, while making sure I didn't get hurt. Eventually, I got sick of it but we had fun with it for a good year and a half.

BERNIE BREEN: It was awesome. They brought the house down. Everyone loved them. You don't have to look much further than 'I'm a Werewolf, Baby', when Gord would attack Paul every single night and literally take him down to the ground and they would roll around on the stage. The band would power through and never stop. That was the beginning of it all.

ROB: By then, our fans were a much wider group of people. We weren't seeing so much of our high school friends, but we were our high school friends. The five of us were all KC guys and you'd see other KC guys at the gigs and know they were pulling for us.

I think everyone champions their own, so it makes sense that a Kingston band would have Kingston folk behind them.

PAUL: We were lucky because we had that connection to Queen's University from Gord, Gord and Robbie, so there was a Queen's crowd and they would have a Battle of the Bands. We were kind of a fun band – we were doing mostly covers, but beginning to write songs. The university kids helped a lot and then we picked up the local fans too.

JOHNNY: We never did one of those Battle of the Bands competitions. But if there was a band coming to Kingston, we'd offer to open for them or do a co-bill and then we'd blow them off the stage. So we were secretly competitive.

GORD S: There were a few other bands playing in town, so you had to get up pretty late in the middle of the night to tear their posters down and get yours up.

PAUL: All the guys were trying to come up with posters that were different and hip, so to speak. Even before I was in the band, I used to help Gord put them up. He'd post them all over town.

GORD D: I made a poster by collaging a racy shot of a girl dancing on Joe Namath's table the night before the 1969 Super Bowl. I remember being marched into the Queen's campus office, because the poster was considered sexist.

JOHNNY: Gord always wanted the shows to be special. One time, we were playing a gig at Queen's and he didn't want it to look like the band from the night before, so he put a backdrop up. But when he was trying to cut a hole in this thing to hang it up, he ended up slicing off the tip of his thumb with a craft knife.

ROB: You learn to get along with people. There was always a willingness of The Hip to play anywhere and everywhere – we'd play a sweet 16 party and then a week later a biker picnic. There weren't many bands that could do that.

I think a lot of it probably stems from our time at KCVI. Those very first few shows we played, certainly as The Rodents, we were surrounded by people cheering us on. We were as excited to be playing to them as they were to have some of their own playing for them, and they were very supportive. Then some of that high school set carried over to The Filters. By the time The Hip came along, we would do two, sometimes three shows in a day. We'd play a downtown place in the afternoon, Queen's in the evening and then whip over and play a late set at the Lakeview Manor or a private after-hours party.

PAUL: We didn't have a manager, so everything had to be taken care of by the band. A big thing was to try and fill your local clubs. We figured that if we couldn't get popular in Kingston, it wasn't going to happen anywhere.

The Lakeview Manor was our main place. It was a stripper bar in the afternoon and then had bands at night. We'd sound check after the last stripper was done, and then we would hang out upstairs.

All the strippers would stay over – there was a row of 15 small rooms for them, and then one or two set aside for the bands.

To get into the main room and up to the stage, we had to go through a little hallway that would sometimes be full of people still coming in and then we would have to walk through a bunch of tables and the crowd. My first time playing the Manor was a pretty intimidating experience. There were some tough characters, a lot of biker types. But we played there a bunch and I became very comfortable there, after a while.

JOHNNY: It was hard for a Kingston band to get a gig in a Kingston bar. There's a mentality in small towns that anything that's any good must have come from somewhere else. Robbie and Gord handled the bookings, because they had the connections from their Filters days. We'd get paid 50 bucks, which went into beer and gas.

ROB: Kingston gave us lots of opportunities. If we'd been in a smaller town, a Brockville or a Belleville, it would have been harder to build up an audience. And if we'd been in a big city like Toronto it would have been much more difficult to get into the venues.

We had the Manor, which was good for three well-paid gigs a month in front of a dedicated rock audience. We had Queen's, we had St Lawrence College, we had a few gigs at the Royal Military College. But then there were all these other places around town. It seemed at the time everyone wanted to try their hand as a live music venue, so there were a bunch of different pubs where we would play at least three or four nights.

It was nuts. Everyone thought they could run a show and make money and we didn't care where we played, as long as they gave us our money. We came up at a pretty good time. We were pretty lucky.

JOHNNY: Gord was the guy who was always dreaming of bigger and better places. Every time we got to where we were supposed to be, he'd set his sights on the next big thing – whether that was doing three nights at the Manor or getting out of Kingston and playing in Ottawa. Because I hadn't really been in a band before, I wasn't thinking in those terms. He invested heavily and he dreamed big. It took a long time for us to get there but we did it.

SET - Larry's
1 CAN EVERYTHANG
2 SMALL TOWN
3 HEART ATTACK
4 ROADRUNNER
5 ~~XXXXXXXXXXX~~ EVELYN
6 IT'S NOT EASY
7 BABY BLUE
8 REFORMED
9 U.S. CHICK
10 BEDROCK WITHOUT DOUBT
11 ~~XXXXXXXXXXXXX~~
12 I'M OK YOU PRAY
13 WEREWOLF
14 HELL
15 ALL CDN SURF

THE TRAGICALLY HIP

GORD S: One of our very first triumphs as a group was when we got signed by Jake Gold and Allan Gregg. We didn't even know what a manager was until X-Ray Macrae, our buddy who was running the Horseshoe at the time, told us we needed one.

Jake set up a gig specifically so that he and Allan could come and see us. We played in front of a crappy Stones cover band at Larry's Hideaway in Toronto. They saw us, loved us, all great – the first step on our way to world domination.

JAKE GOLD: One Friday afternoon in August 1986, Allan gave me a call saying he'd heard an interesting tape that I should listen to. We were driving to a baseball game that Sunday and he played me the tape in the car. I agreed that it was interesting and so we decided to set up a gig so that we could see them.

I called the guy who ran Larry's and he fitted them in as an opener for this Rolling Stones cover band at eight o'clock on a Saturday night. From the tape you could tell that this was a rock and roll band, but I didn't pick up their Stonesy influence. So I probably couldn't have chosen a better crowd for them to perform in front of.

The gig was explosive. I can still picture them walking on stage. They hit the chord, Gord grabbed the mic and did that jackknife thing that he does, started singing, and every hair on my body and neck stood up. I didn't really know what a star was until I saw Gord. Up until that point, I had never seen anybody that dynamic with that ability to communicate with an audience. They played

Above left: Set list from Larry's Hideaway, Toronto, August 1986

Above right: First promo photo of The Hip under Jake Gold's management

Opposite: Memo by Allan Gregg outlining his vision of The Hip's image and strategy, 22 October 1986

mostly original material, with a few covers. At Larry's Hideaway people sat at tables. And here was a place that had never seen these guys before and it was early on a Saturday night, but when the band finished their 40-minute set the whole place stood up and cheered. This was lightning in a bottle. I looked at Allan and said, 'We're signing these guys tonight.'

ALLAN GREGG: I was mesmerised. I watched Gord Downie and said to Jake, 'This guy is going to be a superstar.' He was the most alluring human being I'd ever seen onstage.

ALLAN GREGG: When we signed The Tragically Hip, my outlook changed and I became very invested on a number of levels. First, emotionally. I really liked the guys; they just were the kind of people you'd want to be your buddies. But also, commercially, we really knew, right from the start, that they could be something special.

JAKE GOLD: My gig is to spot charisma, and there was so much charisma coming off the stage. It wasn't just Gord; the way they played as a unit was so dynamic. That's what made them who they were. They had this super-powerful rhythm section – the four of them were a machine that allowed Gord to do whatever he wanted.

After the show we went over to the Pilot Tavern and made a verbal deal with the band to take them on as managers. The relationship started that night.

JAKE GOLD: The first thing we did was write the famous 'memo' to them. The guys still joke about it, especially the 'no hats' line [page 4, right]. But I think it was important to identify what they were and I don't think anybody had ever done that before. That was Allan coming from his research side and being a guy that consults big companies on brands. So we gave them that. I don't know how seriously they took it. They were kids – they just wanted to be in a band, play music and have fun. But we were starting to show them that this was a business and that if they wanted to be successful they had to start treating it like a business.

PAUL: **Jake Gold and Allan Gregg were both slightly older than us. They were partners in their own management company and they wanted to manage us. They were trying to conceive who we were, what our band identity was, but they actually ended up figuring out who we weren't. So they sent us this fax listing things that we should never do: 'You should never wear a hat', 'No primary colours'. We had good fun with them about it for a few years, but their hearts were in the right place.**

JOHNNY: Jake and Allan were kind of an odd couple. Jake wore these ill-fitting grey leather pants and Allan had long hair and a leather jacket.

Allan put together a little memo introducing us to people who might be interested. It talked about us being boys next door from good, wholesome, middle-class families. We maybe found it a little bit embarrassing, but this was our first time with managers so we went with it. And Jake and Allan made things happen for us pretty fast. There was always something moving forward with those guys.

Also, with Jake on our team, no one was going to screw with us again. When the Manor got pissed off that we'd done an afternoon show somewhere else before playing there that night, Jake told them that we'd play where we wanted and that, by the way, our price was double now.

JAKE GOLD: I wasn't intentionally being intimidating. I just didn't take any bullshit. For people who didn't come from the background that I came from, maybe that would seem intimidating.

When we didn't want to do something, we'd just say we weren't going to do it. Then people would have to bend. That was the ultimate leverage.

MEMORANDUM:

TO: JOHN PARIKHAL
                JAKE GOLD ✓

FROM: ALLAN R. GREGG

DATE: OCTOBER 22, 1986

RE: TOWARDS A MORE FOCUSSED IMAGE FOR
                THE TRAGICALLY HIP

THE MOTIVATION/THEIR POSTURE

The Tragically Hip are the boys next door... no leathers.. no spikey hair... no anarchy.

They come from good families and good wholesome middle-class upbringings... and they find nothing embarrassing about that fact.

They enjoy life and are not afraid to show either their intelligence or their sense of humour.

High school friends, just like all the rest, with one major difference. While others were hanging around the malls or playing basketball in the gym, they were in their parents basements playing records. But, they weren't listening to Genesis or Def Leppard or even the Who or Bruce Springsteen. They were listening to Pretty Young things and Jimmy Reed. And even when they were listening to the Rolling Stones, it wasn't "Beggar's Banquet" but "12 x 5" that was on the turntable.

-2-

John Parikhal
Jake Gold   October 22, 1986

And what they heard, over-time, began to change them.

..."It's my life and I'll do what I want"
..."Don't play with me cause you're playin with fire"
..."Bright lights, big city"

The music was dangerous; screaming out a sense of urgency and emotion that made small town Ontario seem inappropriate and foreign. The danger and the urgency made them want to eschew the mall and basketball courts of their contempories even more.

But small town Ontario wasn't foreign or inappropriate. It was home. The Tragically Hip weren't a bunch of gnarled Chicago bluesmen or bourbon swilling rebels from the sixties.

They were the boys next door.

So The Tragically Hip never even entertained the prospect of emulating their basement heroes. No attempt to revive the 60's; the creation a "roots rock" band was never contemplated.

It is the emotion and urgency of the music they listened to, rather than the music itself that motivates the band. And in 1986 this is what they have set out to bring to its audience.. a rawness, an energy and unbridled commitment to straight ahead, honest rock and roll like it's going to be heard tomorrow... not like it was yesterday.

-3-

John Parikhal
Jake Gold   October 22, 198-

THE MUSIC
The Tragically Hip are loud... but their sound is clean. The Vocals are always right up front. Plenty of guitar hooks provide a second melody to many of their songs. The rhythm section is simple but solid and driving. All the players attack their instruments, frustrated that emotion must be transmitted through an inanimate object.

They take their craft seriously. No gag songs or cornball jokes. No phoney contrived smoke bombs or leaps into the air to introduce a song.

But, the seriousness is paralleled by an intense energy. The energy starts half way through the first song and never lets up. The singer and guitar player provide the visual focus for the band, with Rob moving across the stage to interact with the other players and Gord up front relating directly to the audience. Everyone sweats.

The intensity and energy shows throughout the pacing of their set. They start on time; have only the briefest of pauses between songs; and they finish late. They're there to make their audience have a good time and are missionary in their commitment to emotional release through music. Like all missionaries, from time-to-time, they are not afraid to admonish those who fail to share their zeal. Rebels with a cause.

-4-

John Parikhal
Jake Gold   October 22, 1986

THE LOOK
The Tragically Hip exudes a combination of empathy and deference which is transmitted through their appearance, as well as their music. Musically, they play harder and with more commitment than their audience could ever imagine themselves copying. But, they play music their audience can relate to and understand. Similarly, their dress is something their audience could imagine themselves wearing...but not something they would wear to the venue where the band is playing. If a band member is wearing jeans, it's jeans with paisley and suede patches. If one's wearing a vest, it has a fob chain and watch. Shirts are normal in their cut but, done up to the collar. Boots are polished and pointed. No t-shirts, runners or hats.

Yet, the look is casual. Missionary musician's going to work. No ties or dress pants. Some may wear jackets but only for the first half of the first set... until they really get down to work.

The visual continuity is in style, not in the clothes. Colours are dark but not morose. Lots of black, some navy blue, deep grey and even white. No primary colours. In short, accessibly hip.

-5-

John Parikal
Jake Gold   October 22, 1986

THE PLAN
This is a working band. In fact, the key to establishing a more focussed image is the demonstration of commitment to their music through work.

The first six months of 1987 should be dedicated to constant playing. Virtually all engagements will be outside of the Toronto area. The focus will be on clubs and college dates where the atmosphere is party-like. No more opening dates. The purpose is to hone the act and create fan loyalty among 18-30 year olds, male and female, who like to be part of the music, not simply observers.

At the same time, the band should continue to write. By the end of this period, the group should have 20 original songs which are "stage ready." In this period, the mix should be one-third orginal material to two-thirds covers -- at least half of which should be material that the audience has at least heard, if not intimately familiar with (a review of the existing song list should be completed before this period kicks in). Also, by the end of this period, the band should be able to rank the audience appeal of each of its own songs and be prepared to drop half of the weaker tunes.

The next step is to demo the ten remaining songs. Once completed, three showcase events will be arranged in the same week in successively larger venues in Toronto throughout the week-- The Horseshoe, The Diamond and the Copa; the last of which would be an opening set for a major headliner.

-6-

John Parikhal
Jake Gold   October 22, 1

Depending on the response, it is into the studio or back on the road. If we are unable to secure a major deal at this juncture, the goal at least should be to put the band on an existing tour through label or corporate sponsor co-operation.

ARG:cs

It's quite fantastic, really, the intensity Allan brought and the way he could articulate his ideas in writing. It's suitable for framing, actually, in how ridiculous it is. We played along with that manifesto for about half a day and then just did our own thing. (GS)

JAKE GOLD: It was really obvious that the band all had great relationships with their parents and that the parents cared about their careers. Being in a rock and roll band probably wasn't the direction they thought that their kids were going to take, most of them having gone to Queen's.

The guys came from solid backgrounds, which informed their work ethic. Duncan Sinclair was the Dean of Medicine at Queen's, Johnny's dad was a heart surgeon and Robbie's dad was a judge. As much as they liked to party and be on the road and play music, they were intellectuals.

At one point, Duncan Sinclair called Allan up to take his temperature on whether the band really had a chance. I think he saw Allan as this established corporate guy, who was just shy of a PhD in political science, so if Allan thought that they had a shot, then he felt comfortable letting us guide his son's career.

GORD D: Allan loaned us money to make our first EP, which was great for us. He took an interest in the band and enabled us to get out of our hometown and play a little bit. He just wanted to get into the music biz and he let Jake handle the day-to-day stuff. He had some coin, we used it, then paid him back.

JOHNNY: Among their group of friends, who were doctors and lawyers and whatever, my parents weren't shouting from the rooftop that their kid wanted to be a musician. But if someone asked them what they were going to do when I fell flat on my face, my mom would reply, 'He's gonna do what he wants to do, whereas your son's doing what you want him to do.' Or she'd say, 'He's gonna buy your house, knock it down, and build a tennis court.' That shut them up!

ROB: Jake and Allan were our team for a while there. Allan was supposed to be the ideas guy and Jake was the day-to-day guy. It turns out that Jake was a great day-to-day guy and he was also the ideas guy, because most of Allan's ideas got rejected to the point that eventually Allan just left the fold.

JAKE GOLD: In the early days, we talked to Gord Sinclair and Gord Downie more than anybody. They were the guys who were leading the charge. The two Gords, as Allan and I always called them. I think Sinclair saw himself as the business guy and Downie, obviously, was the creative guy. They made a good team for us to talk to. But I never felt that there was any sort of 'my way or the highway' dynamic from any one of the band members.

To all National Staff,

The following are The Tragically Hip's tour dates for January, February and March to date.

January	22 & 23	Café Jacob, Quebec City, Quebec
	24,25 & 26	Cosmo Club, Moncton, New Brunswick
	27-31	Crazy Horse, Dartmouth, Nova Scotia
February	2-6	Rosy's Cantina, Halifax, Nova Scotia
	11	Bannisters, Hamilton, Ontario
	12 & 13	University of Western, London, Ontario
	18	Club Richards, Mississauga, Ontario
	19 & 20	Dutchmill, Trenton, Ontario
	26	Lakeview Manor, Kingston, Ontario
	27	Bishops College H.S., Lennoxville, Quebec
	29	Mc Master University, Hamilton, Ontario
March	3	Jock Hardy Arena (Queens University) Kingston, Ontario
	4 & 5	Horseshoe Tavern, Toronto, Ontario

******More To Come

Yours truly,

Jake Gold

Jacob J. Gold

GORD S: We'd begun our conquest of the world in 50 to 100 kilometre expeditions outside Kingston. Before that, we'd been shoving all our amps and as many drums as we could get into the trunk of Robbie's dad's car and then the Judge got tired of lending his vehicle. I had a good chat with my dear mother, who I knew was a soft touch and loved all the boys and what we were doing, and she ponied up to buy us this crazy, crappy old Dodge van. It had two front seats, a bench seat and enough space in the back for all our gear. And it had a spotlight on the roof that you could move around from the inside. Johnny always referred to it as the 'leg light'.

PAUL: Gord Sinclair's parents probably paid around 1,500 bucks for it. We called it the 'Lisa Marie'.

One time we played a couple of shows with the van, stayed over, and then we went up to Renfrew to do three or four nights at the Shady Lady Disco Lounge, where the van broke down. So we had to bring it into a mechanic to get it fixed and that basically cost us the whole tour. It had a good life, took us to a lot of places. And then, after a couple of years, it couldn't do it anymore.

After that we got another van called the 'R9', only because there was an 'R' sticker and a '9' sticker on the back window. The R9 lasted a long, long time.

I saw a lot more of the country when we were driving ourselves in the van, as opposed to being in the tour bus with the curtains closed.

GORD S: This was the era that set the template for what we did our entire career. It was all about getting the next gig. Then that morphed into a chance to make another record, and the chance to do another tour. But at this stage it was really, 'We got another gig! Yes!' We were having a blast.

ROB: Trucking around in the van was a good time, our little gang out doing our thing. It's a good time for any band. Everyone's on the same page, pushing in the same direction. We were all on our little galley ship and everyone had an oar. We were out collecting ideas and experiences which became songs.

There was no real sense of sacrifice at that point. That came later. And that's fine too. Sacrifice is a good thing. But at that point it was a non-stop party bus. We weren't out of control. Everyone was very focused on what we were doing. But part of that was having a better time than anyone else on this planet. That's what we were focused on doing.

JAKE GOLD: With The Hip, there wasn't the typical band stuff to deal with, like mental health and drugs. Yes, they smoked weed, they smoked hash, but there weren't any hard drugs like you heard about from other bands. These guys were just having fun.

This page and opposite:
January 1987

Students left wanting more Hip

By GRANT DALY

Last Thursday evening saw another return engagement of the Tragically Hip to Alfie's. That they were playing on the eve of one of the biggest weekends of the year did not seem to phase the Hip in the least. They seemed to enjoy the fact that they had been picked to begin the weekend's festivities and the crowd appeared to share the same feeling as the dance floor was almost continuously full.

The Tragically Hip is one of Kingston's most popular bands and is comprised entirely of ex-Queen's students, a fact which explains their immense popularity whenever they play at a campus pub. Led by vocalist Gord Downie, the band plays a mixture of both popular cover songs and a good selection of their own material. As in most cases, the crowd responded more positively to the cover songs but also gave the original songs the respect they deserved.

The Hip opened the show with their ever-popular cover of "Route Sixty-Six" establishing a good rapport with the audience from the opening note. This positive link between band and audience was not lost for the duration of the evening and it seemed at times that the band was playing one continuous set.

Although the Tragically Hip has performed at Alfie's numerous times, the band always seems to retain a certain magic and mixes enough variety into their shows to keep people coming back for more. For instance, during the first set they combined their musical talent with a little dramatic display. As they were playing their rendition of "I Am a Werewolf," the crowd got a little surprise as Downie and a fellow band member began a mock battle on stage, the outcome of which is still undecided.

The band members were sporting a look that was different than in previous appearances here at Queen's. The longer hair style and laid back wardrobe may have been an attempt to cash in on the popularity of the revitalized "Dead" look that is sweeping campuses nationwide.

While the Tragically Hip always seems to be striving for diversity in their live performances, this quest for something unique is tempered with the familiar, a prime example being the inevitable performance of the hit "Gloria" which once again was greeted by a stampede for the dance floor.

The band played until well past last call as they were repeatedly encouraged for encores. It was obvious from the reception that Tragically Hip fans are alive and well here at Queen's and that they will anxiously await the return of the Hip. For those who enjoy good music and a great time, the wait will hopefully not be too long.

The Tragically Hip work up a sweat at Alfie's.   *Polley*

Opposite: Fanshawe College student union pub night, London, ON, 1 October 1987 (top)

PAUL: The eastern Ontario circuit was basically Kingston, where we had three or four different places, a couple of gigs in Gananoque, a couple in Brockville, one in Cornwall, where we would do four or five nights at the Northway. Then we'd swing up to Ottawa and on to Renfrew. Going the other way, it was Harrowsmith, Belleville, Trenton. And those were kind of the limits of our circuit. Then we got a gig in London and we'd go back and forth between London and Kingston.

A lot of places had band rooms where you'd just sleep. It was squalor. Those were crazy days. We were hardly making any money. We made some, but nothing that we were bringing home.

GORD D: We played around eastern Ontario a lot, which can be pretty desolate at times as live music goes, playing in front of the salad bar, and stuff like that. And then gradually moved towards Toronto and then played around Toronto on the Golden Horseshoe, which now refers to all the cities that go around the western tip of Lake Ontario as far as Niagara Falls.

ROB: We'd show up at some places and there'd be tables of people up front eating chicken wings. Some people wanted to dance, but other people were just having a night out at a roadside restaurant.

GORD D: Sometimes in the college gigs, you're up there and you wonder if you're basically a backdrop for some huge beer-up. And that can be more frustrating than playing to no one.

JOHNNY: We were a slow-moving freight train – just don't get in our way because we're going to drive over you. It took us forever to get out of the 613 area code and on to Toronto. It was a long, long haul.

ROB: The logical extension for us was to go to London, because London and Kingston are similar cities in a way. They both have the snooty university, the Canadian Ivy League, as it were, and they both have a darker underbelly, both of which were very good to us. Then from London, it was Cambridge, Stratford, Sarnia – there were lots of places to play out that way. Then it was the Golden Horseshoe. We didn't have a lot of conscious thought about how we were going to conquer the next province or the country, but, as much as there was any plan, it was to saturate the B and C markets until we really had a following in those places.

Then when we made forays into Toronto to play the Horseshoe, everyone flooded in from Kingston, Ottawa, Belleville and London to see us. It became a destination venue and then the Toronto people started to wonder who this band was that none of them had heard of that had sold out the Horseshoe four, five, six times. That then drew interest from record companies, and that turned the tide for us.

PAUL: In those early days we were more focused on Kingston and London than Toronto. We would try to hit Toronto and then leave, rather than becoming part of that scene, and it worked for us. It meant that there was a bit of mystery surrounding us there and people were intrigued enough to come and see us.

ROB: We were booked at a place called Chevy's and the marquee outside said 'Thursday Night: Shepherd's Pie and The Tragically Hip'. I remember calling them up and saying, 'We are not opening for shepherd's pie.' We had never cancelled a gig before, but we had to draw the line somewhere.

JAKE GOLD: We got them a 15-passenger Econoline van and I started booking them gigs myself, everywhere from Windsor to Montreal. They were working every day except Sundays, travelling back and forth along the 401, and every offshoot. The goal was to do three nights in each city, so people who came the first night would tell their friends about it, who would then come the second night. By the third it was always packed – lines around the block.

18 June, 1987

Manifest:
The Tragically Hip

item: make/model	serial number	owner
Epiphone Broadway Semi-Acoustic Guitar	# 58850	P. Langlois
Nashville M Series Acoustic Guitar	# 7610119	P. Langlois
Fender Precision Bass Guitar	# 301593	G. Sinclair
Univox Professional Bass Guitar	# 034900	G. Sinclair
Fender Stratocaster Electric Guitar	# 580617	R. Baker
Squire Telecaster Electric Guitar	# 3678765	R. Baker
Mesa Boogie Amplifier	# 15936	R. Baker
Roland Cube-60 Amplifier	# 153976	R. Baker
Traynor YBA-1A Mark II Amplifier	# 2090456	R. Baker
HH Electronic Bass Baby Amplifier & Pedal	# 3168	G. Sinclair
Traynor Super Twin 15 YT-15 Speaker Cabinet	# 7330	R. Baker
Traynor Super Twin 15 YT-15 Speaker Cabinet	# 3460	G. Sinclair
Slingerland Snare Drum	# 112640	J. Fay
Paiste 2002 Cymbal	# 141122	J. Fay
Paiste China Type Cymbal	# 592678	J. Fay
Sonor Bass Drum Pedal	# 3849	J. Fay
Gretsch 20-inch Bass Drum	N/A	J. Fay
Gretsch 12-inch Rack Tom	N/A	J. Fay
Gretsch 14-inch Floor Tom	N/A	J. Fay
Zildjian 20-inch Ride Cymbal	N/A	J. Fay
Two (2) Zildjian Hi-Hat Cymbals	N/A	J. Fay
Two (2) Cymbal Stands	N/A	J. Fay
One (1) Hi-Hat Stand	N/A	J. Fay

... 2

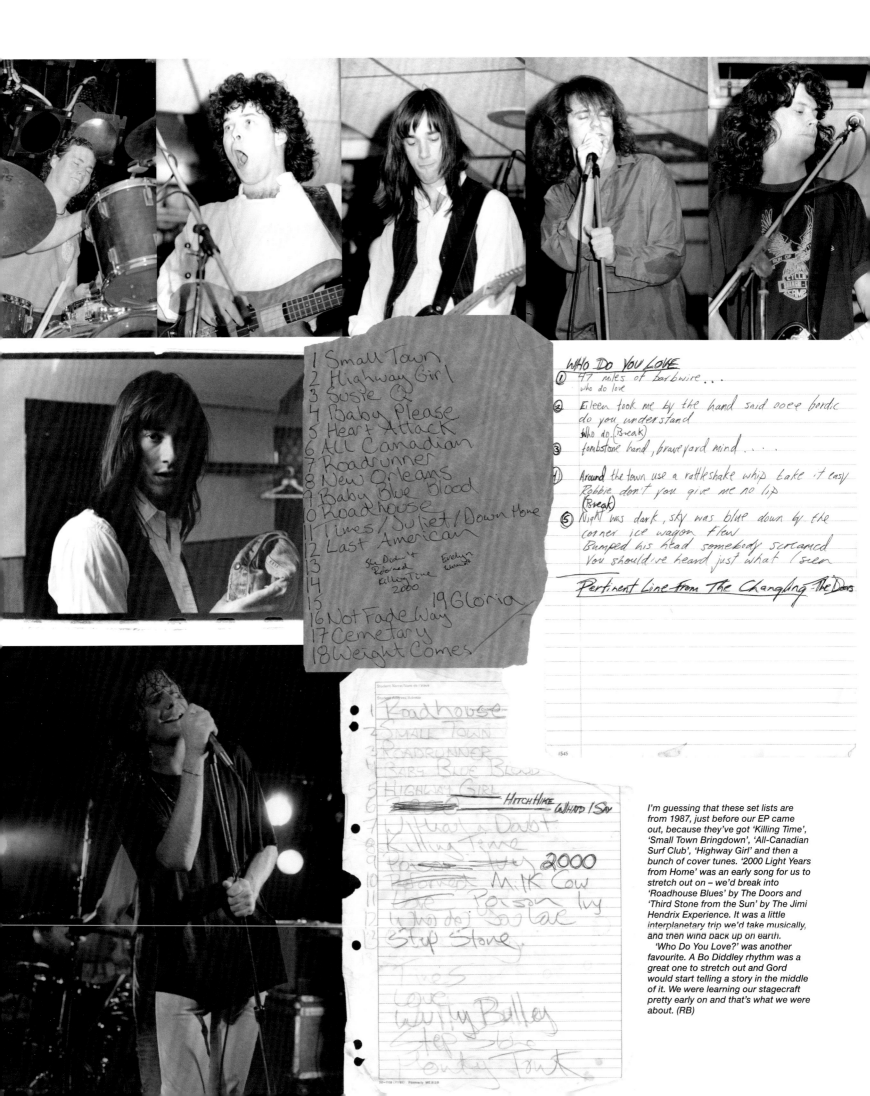

1 Small Town
2 Highway Girl
3 Susie Q
4 Baby Please
5 Heart Attack
6 All Canadian
7 Roadrunner
8 New Orleans
9 Baby Blue Blood
0 Roadhouse
11 Times/Juliet/Down Home
12 Last American
13   She Didn't   Evelyn
14   Returned   wants
15   Killing Time
      2000   19 Gloria
16 Not Fade Way
17 Cemetary
18 Weight Comes

WHO DO YOU LOVE
① 47 miles of barbwire...
   who do love
② Eileen took me by the hand said ooee bordic
   do you understand
   who do (Break)
③ tombstone hand, graveyard mind.....
④ Around the town use a rattleshake whip take it easy
   Robbie don't you give me no lip
   (Break)
⑤ Night was dark, sky was blue down by the
   corner ice wagon flew
   Bumped his head somebody screamed
   You should've heard just what I seen

Pertinent Line from The Changling - The Doors

1 Roadhouse
2 Small Town
3 Roadrunner
4 Baby Blue Blood
5 Highway Girl
6 ~~Hitch Hike~~ Whatd I Say
7 Without a Doubt
8 Killing Time
9 ~~Poison Ivy~~ 2000
10 ~~Roadrunner~~ Milk Cow
11 ~~Love~~ Poison Ivy
12 Who do you love
13 Stop Stone
   Tues
   Love
   Wully Bulley
   Stop Stone
   Funky Town

I'm guessing that these set lists are from 1987, just before our EP came out, because they've got 'Killing Time', 'Small Town Bringdown', 'All-Canadian Surf Club', 'Highway Girl' and then a bunch of cover tunes. '2000 Light Years from Home' was an early song for us to stretch out on – we'd break into 'Roadhouse Blues' by The Doors and 'Third Stone from the Sun' by The Jimi Hendrix Experience. It was a little interplanetary trip we'd take musically, and then wind back up on earth.
   'Who Do You Love?' was another favourite. A Bo Diddley rhythm was a great one to stretch out and Gord would start telling a story in the middle of it. We were learning our stagecraft pretty early on and that's what we were about. (RB)

Walk Away (A D Minor Thang)

1 I need your confidence
I need to know you're mine
When it gets right down to the killing time

I know your heart is bad
But it's all I've ever had
We can live our lives on a righteous crime

Chorus
How can you walk away
How do you walk away
Walk away from a woman
that gone and done
you wrong?

2 The woman of my dreams
Took me 'part at the seams
But I can mend wounds with alcohol

Got kicked when I was down
A sailor took my girl to town
Then she licked my wounds with the sea dog's salt

Drank half a bottle of Jack
Swore I'd never take her back
By the bottle's end I was on the phone

Give our love one more try
Make it best three out of five
And winner can take the trophy home

[I know your heart is bad
But it's all I've ever had]

Don't call it compromise
I know a one night stand
Won't stand one night for another man

INTRO ? UNISON
½ VERSE
½ VERSE
1 VERSE — FORTE
BRIDGE — Bb/C/F/A/Bb/C/Asus4/Csus2/
CHORUS (x2)
   INST. OVER ½ VERSE — SOLO + ROCKIN RHYTHM (Dm F C)
   "   " ½ " — PEDAL LICKS + INTRO ARPEGGIO
½ VERSE — UNISON
½ VERSE —
CHORUS (x2)
   INST (SLIDE, SAX ?)
VERSE — FORTE
BRIDGE
CHORUS :// OUT

The Killing Time

1 I need your confidence
Need to know you're mine
When it gets right down
To the killing time
I know your heart is bad
But it's all I've ever had
We can live our lives
On this righteous crime

2 I got kicked when I was down
And a sailor took my girl to town
Then she licked my wounds
With the sea dog's salt
I drank a half a bottle of Jack
Swore I'd never take you back
By the bottle's end
I was on that phone

bridge
What you call compromise
I don't understand
What you call compromise
I don't understand

chorus
How do you walk away?
How do you walk away?
How do you walk away from a woman
that gone and done you wrong

— Repeat #1
— Chorus → guitar break
— Chorus
— Repeat first 4 lines of #1

Evelyn

chorus
Evelyn - Evelyn
Where were you last night?
Evelyn - Evelyn
Where were you last night?

Waited on your front porch 'till the
break of day
But when dawn broke I could no longer
wait for ...

chorus

Must have phone a million times no
answer came
What kind of fool am I to play
this game with ...

chorus

This has gone on before
I can't take it no more
I'll even up the score and
Get away from . . .

chorus

If you must have your way you won't
have me
I won't be fucked around I must get
free from...
chorus

CEMETARY, SIDEROAD

I had near - but I used to be older
I'm not - like I used to be
Had years - but I guess it's all over
You talk - but you're not like me

Bridge: you talk & you talk like some weird saint
What do you think that we could taint
when you're nothing I am & I'm something you aint

Told me 'till the night makes you colder
me - How life's made you bad,
And kick me - when I choke & I smoulder
where am - not what you had

Bridge

Chorus - I'm looking for a Cemetary Sideroad
I'm screaming like a lighthouse lamp
I'm chasing after what I think that I'm cold
Like a French Foreign Legion tramp

Breakdown:
You swim - in an ocean that's storming
Double Verse: You eat - when the wolves all do
Repeating: You ache - like a mother in mourning
Verse 2: when you're - left alone with you

Bridge

Double Chorus

All Cdn. Surf Club

Well there's a rockin' little spot next to the Regent Theatre
And if want to make the scene, I'll make ya sooner or later
When ya hang out with the crowd, you know the ins & the outs the
All Cdn. Surf Club, Denim jackets & long hair

We're getting hip now to the sound that rocks the waves as they roll the
Man, I really dig ya baby, ya make me wild with your blond hair
When you dance up next to me, I wanna grow old & die here
Cleaning sand out of my back seat, while I'm thinkin 'bout you

Walkin cross the sand
With another friend
My love depends
Oh when summer ends

When you cruise down to the beach, there's lots of things that you need here
I got my guitar, camel, lights, a chick, & 24 cold beers
See me waxing up my board I look so cool in my surf gear
All Cdn. Surf Club, denim jackets & long hair

HIGHWAY GIRL

① I'm going down to see my highway girl
She just got back from around the world
Gonna get me a gun, gonna stand on guard
Gonna set up shop in her front yard

Don't you think baby you push it a bit too fast
She said slowing down won't make it last

I've got bourbon playing on my mind
It's sweet yet so unkind

bad memories aren't gonna set you free
Go out and see the world & bring it back to me

True love is a girl with long blond hair

It's so hard to be sincere
when you're always telling people what they want to hear

She said I never met a man I didn't like
But I've only met two in my life.

I'm Man standing out in the rain

I'm not tired
just a little worn

= August is the sleeper month

+ you play with the wolves
you've got to eat a few lambs

the original horse's ass
Cemetary Sideroad

Do you think you push it a bit too fast

and slowing down won't make it last

by running my back 10 times it's normal speed

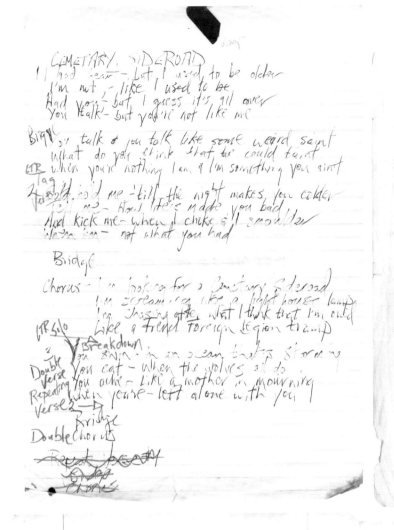

This page: Lyrics for 'Cemetery Sideroad' (top left), 'All-Canadian Surf Club' (top right) and 'Highway Girl' (bottom)

Opposite: Lyrics and notes for 'Walk Away' (top), 'Killing Time' (bottom left) and 'Evelyn' (bottom right)

Small Town Home Town

verse 1 {
Been to Reno
Drives an El Camino
Can you dig that style?
}

{
Mic Canteen you
Always make the scene
You're a crazy child
}

chorus {
It's a sad thing
Bourbons all round
To stop that feelin'
When you're livin' in a small town
You're mod and mean (long and lean)
Things don't get you down
A top ten King pin
In the borders of you're home town
}

verse 2 {
Can't get hip
You work the jobs I've quit
Can you dig my style?
}

{
Won't admit
You just don't give a shit
You're a crazy child
}

bridge {
Can't live to die, too easy
Why stick around?
I want my life to please me
Not another small town home town bring down
}

verse 3 {
This is it
You might as well get pissed   Make your trip toe
You're a crazy child   There ain't that much to miss
        Can you dig my style?
}

Small Town Bring Down

0:05
Been to Reno drives an El Camino
Can you dig that style
Mic canteen you always make the scene
You're a crazy child

0:40
It's a sad thing bourbons all round
To stop that feelin whenyou're livin in a small
                                                        town
You're long n lean things don't get you down
You're a top ten Kingpin in the borders of your
                                                        home town

1:03
Can't get hip you work the jobs I've quit
Can you dig that style
Won't admit you just don't give a shit
You're a crazy child Cause your mind's
1:20 CHORUS   gone wild
1:31 Can't live to die, too easy
Why stick around
I want my life to please me
Not another small town hometown bring down

2:05 This is it you might as well get pissed
DON'T YOU DIG THAT STYLE

Make your trip there ain't that much to miss
Can you dig that style
2:16 CHORUS   WHEN YOUR MIND IS GONE WILD

2:34 REPEAT

JAKE GOLD: I used to play hockey on Sunday nights with a bunch of other musicians and radio guys at Forest Hill Arena in Toronto. One of the guys that played with us was Ken Greer, who was in Red Rider, which then became Tom Cochrane's band. Kenny had always wanted to produce records so I suggested putting him together with The Hip.

Allan knew a guy who owned a studio called Sounds InterChange, and he gave us some time, really inexpensively. Kenny worked with the guys in rehearsal and we went in there, originally to make some demos. But then we realised we needed a piece of product to use as a calling card so we could get the band out of Ontario and western Quebec, and right across the country. So after they'd done five songs we put them back into the studio and grabbed a couple of songs live off the floor. And that became the first EP.

GORD S: 'Small Town Bringdown' wasn't my first song, but it was certainly among the first. The title was not without irony.

We were enjoying a level of success within the confines of our hometown. There were a couple of other local bands, like The Raging Groovies, which was another Queen's band, and Finny McConnell had carried on in another iteration of The Filters. The local scene was not explicitly competitive, but it was competitive. We resolved that no one was going to beat us in our own shop. And that inspired me to write a song about what it's like being the biggest band in your hometown and aspiring to break out of the confines of where you live, but not quite achieving it.

In no small way, the irony never really stopped because we went on to become quite popular in Canada, but never matched that level of success in the rest of the world.

JAKE GOLD: Gord Sinclair wrote 'Small Town Bringdown' and 'Last American Exit', two of the singles from the EP. He had the pop sensibility and understood how to write songs with a linear structure. He wrote everything on them. In the early years, everyone got credited individually for what they did.

BRUCE DICKINSON: I thought 'Small Town Bringdown' was a great song. I identified with it. That's the way I felt about the town I grew up in. There were lots of things about my hometown that I couldn't wait to get away from.

ROB: I remember the day Gord Sinclair presented the song to the band. It was very much a finished piece – lyrics, music, concept. Everyone obviously came up with their own parts, but it was 100 percent written by then. We rehearsed it and I remember thinking it was pretty good. It was different.

RB: It was chosen to be the first single by Allan and Jake. Allan financed the video and brought in a friend of his to shoot it.

ROB: We worked it up with Kenny Greer from Red Rider. He had some good suggestions on honing in on parts and simplifying lines to make it a little more concise.

PAUL: 'Small Town Bringdown' captures the angst and frustration of being in a small town in your early twenties. You always see the same people, you feel kind of stuck, and you just want to get out and do bigger things.

We did the video at the Lakeview Manor, our go-to bar. It seemed like a natural fit. Budget is always a concern for young bands, so to do it all in Kingston was the simplest way to get it down quickly.

It was our first video, ever, and it's just us playing at the Manor with a bunch of our friends on the dance floor, cut with shots of things going on in the town. In the video, we're introduced – 'Ladies and gentlemen, The Tragically Hip ...' – which never happened in real life. At the end, I give Gord a slap in the face out in front of the Downie house, which was fun. My first acting scene. I didn't hit him hard, just a little whip. We learned quickly that a lot of making videos is sitting around and waiting.

GAVIN BROWN: The first time I encountered The Hip was watching Toronto Rocks or MuchMusic in the late Eighties and seeing the video for 'Small Town Bringdown'. It didn't seem like an introductory song or a demo of something that they were just trying out. No, these guys were committed to this sound. This was who they were.

ROB: It's hard to even imagine now, but Canada used to have a music TV station called MuchMusic. They played music videos, live concerts, did interviews with musicians, reviewed albums, and they even sent teams on the road to see Canadian bands in other locations. On a Friday night everyone I knew had MuchMusic on. If you went to a party, MuchMusic was cranked up on the TV; it was like the jukebox and people were excited about it.

The 'Small Town Bringdown' promo gave us an opportunity to play to people across the country who paid attention to music videos. It was an opportunity that we capitalised on.

JAKE GOLD: It was all part of the plan that people needed to see this band live – and what better way to sell that than to put them in a video playing live and show how exciting it was.

We were going to put that record out in Kingston alone, because we wanted to make the people of Kingston feel a part of the success of the band. So why not shoot it in the biggest venue that the band was playing in Kingston, where we knew we were going to have the most enthusiastic crowd? It was a big deal – a video crew coming into town. We got initial support from MuchMusic, enough that people started to see the band as legit, because having a video and a record in stores right away legitimised you.

GORD S: We were young guys at the dawn of the video age and we were tuning in. But when you're lip syncing to your track repeatedly, after a while it's hard to take this dubious art form seriously. The way we looked at it, video was just another avenue to promote what we did best, which was gigging. We knew that our best foot forward was to get in front of people and actually play our instruments and perform. Playing a song live was our best opportunity to sell a record, and selling the record was our key to making another one.

'Small Town Bringdown' promotional CD

Opposite: Gord Sinclair's handwritten lyrics for 'Small Town Bringdown'

This photo is for our very first, what we call 'baby' record. And we look very angry. This is on a roof in Toronto, down in the industrial east end. (PL)

The Tragically Hip (EP)
RECORDED: SPRING 1987
SOUNDS INTERCHANGE, TORONTO, ON
PHASE ONE, TORONTO, ON
PRODUCER: KEN GREER
ENGINEERS: SCOTT BOYLING, RANDY STAUB
MIXING: DON WERSHBA
RELEASED: DECEMBER 1987 (KINGSTON AREA)
JANUARY 1988 (NATIONALLY)

Small Town Bringdown
Last American Exit
Killing Time
Evelyn
Cemetery Sideroad
I'm a Werewolf, Baby
Highway Girl
All-Canadian Surf Club (CD only)

JAKE GOLD: We did a distribution deal with BMG for the EP and told the guys that it was going to come out before the end of the year in 1987. But BMG said we couldn't do that because all the big acts put out records in the fourth quarter. When we explained this to the band, they said, 'But we told all our friends that it was gonna come out for Christmas.' So we went back to BMG and suggested putting it out just in Kingston in December 1987 and then releasing it to the rest of the country in the new year. They said they couldn't do that because of retail systems and this and that, but we said that there were only two record stores in Kingston and we could just put some records in our trunk, drive them down to Kingston and put them in the stores ourselves. We fought them and we won.

When the record came out nationally, we put out a press release saying that while the rest of the country was listening to this, this and this, in Kingston the number two record, directly behind U2, was by a band called The Tragically Hip. All of a sudden, everyone was wondering who this new band was.

So that became our whole M.O. When the record company said no, we said, 'Well, why not?' And every time they gave us a reason why not, we would give them a reason why.

Prior to putting the record out we wanted them to do a gig once a month at the Hotel Isabella in Toronto. Our plan was to bring some people out from the industry that Allan and I knew. By maybe the third time we had them there, the place was lined up around the block. The stage was so small that Robbie was set up on the floor because there wasn't enough room for all of them on the stage.

We didn't think the EP was going to be a big radio record, but we felt there were about eight radio stations that would play it out of the 30 stations across the country. Our attitude was that if the record company could get eight – and we got all eight – we'd have a feeling of success around the project. But if they went to all 30 and they only got eight, we'd be a failure. We took the same approach with print media. We didn't send it to dailies, only to weeklies. And before you knew it, the phone started ringing from the ones we didn't send it to, asking how come they didn't get a copy.

THE TRAGICALLY HIP play straight ahead, unadulterated honest music - raw dirt mixed with sweat. Identifying them as one of Canada's hot new bands to watch, the North American music magazine _Rock Express_ described their sound as... "a cross between the Saints (DOWNIE's growl sounds damned close to Chris Bailey's), Georgia Satellites (in velocity and energy), The Doors (untamed '60s animal rock) and R.E.M. (jangley guitars and rootsy atmosphere)".

While the band themselves eschew such comparisons, this is not bad company!

Consisting of GORD DOWNIE (vocals), GORD SINCLAIR (bass and vocals), ROB BAKER (guitar), PAUL LANGLOIS (guitar and vocals) and JOHNNY FAY (drums), THE HIP have been together since high school. While their contemporaries were hanging around the malls in Kingston, Ontario, they were in the basement listening to and playing along with the likes of Jimmy Reed, The Pretty Things and early Animals.

This exposure to '50s and '60s music is still apparent every time they play. But, unlike the spate of 'roots bands' on the scene today, theirs is not an attempt to resurrect an era of time gone by. Their sound is anything but dated. Where you can see THE TRAGICALLY HIP's early influences is in their obvious commitment to their music and the energy levels with which they express that commitment.

For the last year, the band has been paying dues and collecting the benefits of playing the club circuit all over Ontario. With the advent of '88, all who have seen them agree that their apprenticeship is over.

January of this year marks the release of their first eponymous seven-song mini-LP, produced by Ken Greer of Red Rider fame for Rock Records and distributed in Canada by BMG Music. The video for SMALL TOWN BRINGDOWN provides evidence of the excitement generated through their live performances. This is a band which believes that when they hit the stage they are there for the audience and not the other way around. Their U.S. debut in New York's CBGB's and the rave reviews garnered from the critics there, also suggests that this fact is not lost on American audiences either.

THE TRAGICALLY HIP will be touring Canada from mid-January to April in support of their record release. If you're not ready for sweat on the ceiling and fanatical dancing throughout any particular venue at any given time, stay away from this band. Conversely, if you can feel it, do it!

For furth[er]
Feb. '88

CBS

CBS Records Canada Ltd.
CBS Disques Canada Ltée
1121 Leslie Street
Don Mills, Ontario M3C 2J9
(416) 447-3311, Telex: 06-966792

November 6, 1987

9236

Dear Jake:

Thanks for your tape on The Tragically Hip.

I thought the sound was exciting and fresh but the songs were a little weak.

I didn't think that an act like this would be right for CBS, especially with lyrics like "I don't give a shit."

Thanks again,

David Bendeth
Staff Producer

encl. sample cassette

Jacob Gold
372 Richmond Street West
Suite 110
Toronto, ontario
M5V 1X6

The Tragically Hip
The Tragically Hip
BMG Music

By TED BETTS

The Queen's Journal, Tuesday, January 26, 1988

The tragic story of the highly-touted Tragically Hip's debut album starts with the first track.

Normally, a good album revolves around three pivots: music, vocals, and lyrics. The music is there. But the latter two drag them down like a ton of cement. One out of three just does not cut it.

Musically they hold their own. Gordon Sinclair's solid bass line anchors the band. The guitar also plays a vital role and Bobby Baker does the instrument a service, giving the Hip a fresh sound. The talent is best expressed live where their music is emphasized and allowed to live.

Gordon Downie's voice is very hard to swallow. It only becomes a little more bearable after a few plays. Jagged and quavering, he bites chunks out of the songs. Define his drawling as raw and appropriate for only one or two cuts. Most of the time he clashes with the music which, to give him a little credit, might be less his fault than Ken Greer and Don Wershba's, who produced and mixed the record.

The bitterest taste of the record, though, can be found in the lyrics. The band is tragically lacking in this department.

Take, for instance, the song "I'm A Werewolf, Baby" and its final verse: "I can smell your blood, I can hear you breathe/ I'm gonna eat your heart, right off your sleeve/ Eat you cooked, eat you raw/ I'm gonna rip you up like a big chain saw." These are not the lyrics of a great band.

Contributions to the album were distributed among the band but most lyrics were by Downie. The strongest two cuts, "Small Town Bringdown", and "Last American Exit," were written by Sinclair. Even here, there is desperation. The ideas and words come across awkwardly and repetitively.

The small town influence comes acrss clearly in songs like the aforementioned two and is notable in a few others like "Highway Girl." The image appears to be that of a seemingly insignificant band trying to fend off the big world while in the same instance cursing their present one.

RPM - February 20, 1988

Vol. IV No. 3 March 3 - April 6 Wednesday

ALBUMS

ZK1-0590

THE TRAGICALLY HIP — Rock
Self-titled
Rock/BMG - KZLI-0590-N

A disappointing album from a group of talented young musicians, who to listen to live, don't sound like this. New Regime's management pushing hard with a different marketing approach, inevitably though, it must be in the grooves first. Unfortunately Red Rider guitarist Ken Greer couldn't pull off the vocals, yet remixing efforts will help the single choices. Next time.

The Tragically Hip
RCA   Myles Chilton

This Kingston band's first release, a seven-song self-titled mini LP, picks up the trend towards country and folk oriented rock and drops it into the three chord stick- it-your -socially-conscious-ear without so much of a gregariously left-wing stance for extra publicity. This debut is a well-timed effort that may yank them from obscure bars and clubs but may only make them an obscure opening band for REM and the like. Perhaps that's a bit unfair, but after listening to this uneven offering, it seems that their limited songwriting range won't pull them out of the garage.

They can sound like a talented and sincere bunch; songs like the country-tinged "Last American Exit," and the brooding, passionate and ANIMALS like "Killing Time," are as good as anything by Blue Rodeo or The Northern Pikes (bands who could be their distant cousins). But silly songs like "I'm a Werewolf, Baby," which sounds like THE SCREAMING BLUE MESSIAHS playing a RAY STEVENS song with WEIRD AL YANKOVIC doing backup vocals, and "Cemetery Sideroad," which is plain dull, pull them way down.

potential

But not irredeemably down, they exhibit potential, and their live shows are reported to be tops. The solid, snarling, and twanging vocals of Gordon Downie, which range from ALICE COOPER to ERIC BURDEN to JIM MORRISON, carry all the songs. There is real energy in his voice, but it unfortunately lacks enough range or distinction to make anything truly stand out.

Date	Venue	
1,2,3,	The Grand Central, Ottawa	225
15	Call The Office, London	75
16	Queen's University, Kingston	100
22,23	Cafe Jacob, Quebec City	50
24-26	Cosmo Club, Moncton	
27-31	Crazy Horse, Halifax	} 200
2-6	Rosy's Cantina, Halifax	150
12, 13	University of Western Ontario, London	200
15-17	Downstairs John, McMaster university	180
18	Richards, Mississauga	75
19,20	Dutchmill, Trenton	160
24	Club High Life, Bramalea	80
25	Hideaway, St. Catherines	75
26	Lakeview Manor, Kingston	150
27	Bishop College, Lennoxville	160
29	The Diamond, Toronto	125
March 1	Rock Express Awards, The Diamond, Toronto	
2	The Grand Central, Ottawa	300
3	Call The Office, London	85
4,5	The Horseshoe Tavern, Toronto	135
9	Elusions, Oshawa	100
11,12	Crocks & Rolls, Thunder Bay	80
14	Garden City Inn, Winnipeg	
14	Red River College, Winnipeg	
16	Cornerboys, Winnipeg	
17	University of Winnipeg	
18	University of Winnipeg, nooner	} 250
18	University of Winnipeg,	
19	Portage Village Inn, Winnipeg	
21	Louis Pub, University of Saskatchewan, Saskat	
22	The Venue, Regina	
23-26	Mayfield, Edmonton	

JAKE GOLD: Part of our ethos was that you build the fan base and nobody can take that away from you. Media wasn't in control of your destiny. You were in control of your own destiny because you had fans.

RB: Through the years we'd get bad reviews, and we'd rejoice in them. We would have so much fun reading the bad reviews and plotting revenge. We never thought we would take revenge, but it was fun to plot.

JOHNNY: Our first time in New York, Allan Gregg very nicely paid for us to stay at the iconic Gramercy Park Hotel. We played CBGBs – we were pretty nervous and the gig wasn't particularly great.

We had stuff stolen a couple of times in New York. I don't think you're a band until you get ripped off in New York.

JAKE GOLD: Allan was a wealthy man. That gave us so much autonomy, which is why we were always able to say to the record company, 'Well, if you don't want to do it, we'll do it ourselves.' His financial backing meant that we were able to turn down a lot of shitty offers and also make our own rules. Allan probably put a couple of hundred thousand dollars into the band for trips to New York, demos, videos. Licensing the EP to BMG meant we were paying for all of that as well.

GORD D: We went down to New York City in January and got our butts kicked badly. And that was probably the best thing for us because the record was just coming out and we thought we must be really something. And then we went down to New York City. We were playing CBGBs and although it was a horrible night for sound and just a technical nightmare all the way around, it was really good for us. After that we sort of attacked everything really great guns.

PAUL: Starting to tour the whole country instead of just shuttling up and down the 401 between London and Cornwall felt like a big step forward. But it dawned on us that we had to keep writing songs if we were going to get anywhere, and we needed to be the tightest band alive.

JOHNNY: When we got into Manitoba for the first time, we were kissing our biceps. We had a week booked at the Diamond in Winnipeg, with accommodation included. The owner went to see a sold-out John Cougar Mellencamp show at the hockey arena and then he came back, drunk, and saw that there were maybe 50 people for our gig. He watched our first set, decided that we were shit and fired us.

JAKE GOLD: When the band went on stage the place was empty, because everybody was at the arena watching John Mellencamp. There were only so many people to see rock and roll in Winnipeg.

JOHNNY: We really didn't know what to do, so we had a couple of days off and then Jake got us a gig at a place called Corner Boys and that really saved us. What was cool was that people were phoning in on the radio to say they'd seen us at the Diamond; some said we were great, others disagreed. But it kept interest alive and then when we played Corner Boys the place was packed. So getting fired was one of the best things that ever happened to us in Winnipeg.

JAKE GOLD: John Kendle, who was a writer for the *Winnipeg Free Press*, got wind of the story and wrote this whole piece about how this band had got fired and they shouldn't have been fired, because they were amazing. And all of Winnipeg came to the support of this band that were basically left high and dry with no place to stay, and no place to play.

By Saturday night, there were line-ups around the block. We managed to make back about half the money we would have made had we done those other shows, but we now were established in Winnipeg. We blew up Winnipeg because of that.

The Last American Exit

A w
You know the reasons I can't conceal
G
You know I'm leavin' you obviously know how I feel
It's not as easy as calling out your name when I'm down
F#   A

weird
wierd
It's not a matter for wrong or right
It ain't much better than drinkin' and lookin' to fight
You know I'm tired of crawling 'hind my name among
                                              the crowd

bridge
G
{ *Know our neighbours and knew they'll take us*
A
{ *I know my city it's just like theirs are*
{ *I hope I'll make it, I know I'm gonna make it somehow*
G   A A

chorus {
I'm on the last American exit to the heart land
                              to my home land
"   "   "   *to my last chance*
They keep calling out my name - I shout it down
G   F#   A

They made you wonder and knew for sure
You've made them hunger at night and then run for the
                                              door
You know you'll probably cry like Caesar's son when you're
                                              found

It's not you're place it's another town
Face it baby I'm up and then baby I'm down
You'll watch the border after out yootane and watch
                                          you drown

I know your saviour he knows you shakers
You know my city I'll see you later
I'd like to stay but I know it doesn't
                              matter somehow.

PRODUCTION PERSONNEL

TRAGICALLY HIP MUSIC VIDEO

POSITION	CREW	PHONE NUMBER
DIRECTOR	Don C. Archbold	450 - 8146
D.O.P.	Richard McNeal Mayfield	484 - 0821
ASSISTANT DIRECTOR	Martin Wood	436 - 8000
CAMERA ASSISTANT	Steve Miko	484 - 0821
GAFFER	Rob Bittner	962 - 8158
BEST BOY	Martin Wilde	475 - 5997
KEY GRIP	John Adshead	425 - 9753
SOUND PLAYBACK	Jeremy Sager	425 - 8794
EDITOR	Wendy Vincent	597 - 1137 (416)
SET PA	Bruce Bossier	455 - 3656
	Carolyn Bristow	487 - 0371
	Guy Knight	465 - 0041
	Tracy Mcdonald	469 - 6961
	Drew Martin	429 - 0277
Flaffer	Wendy O Tobias Jr.	

BAND:

ROAD MANAGER	Trevor Johnson	MAYFIELD INN ROOM 232
ASSISTANT ROAD MNG.	Boyd Baley	484 - 0821
LEAD VOCALS	Gordon Downie	
LEAD GUITAR	Robert Baker	
DRUMMER	John Fay	
BASE	Gordon Sinclair	
RHYTHYM GUITAR	Paul Langlois	

Location: Dancing Shoes, Mayfield Inn
16615 109 ave   Phone: 484-0821

SHOOTING SCHEDULE | | DAY 1 THURS. MARCH 24

Sc.No.	Set/Description	D/N	Cast
Shot 1	Singer Closeups Lead CU entire song Backup on Harmony only	Day	Band
Shot 2	Singles of each member performing	Day	Band
Shot 3	Full master shot of band performing	Day	Band
Shot 4	Dolly L-R then R-L Band in front of crowd	Night	Band/ Crowd
Shot 5	Curved Dolly Track in audience. Full,Med,Tight	Night	Band/ Crowd
Shot 6	Singles of 7 Females in audience	Night	Audience
Shot 7	Full shot of people dancing	Night	Audience
Shot 8	Med. full shot of people dancing	Night	Audience

JOHNNY: On that first tour, we shot the video for 'Last American Exit' in Dancing Shoes in Edmonton. It was another one of those cavernous places that were hard to fill, so we told people that we were shooting a video and we needed extras.

Alberta was a hard place to play, back in the day. You had to be really good for them to like you, but once they liked you they loved you.

GORD S: Our first time in Edmonton was coterminous with us shooting our second video, 'Last American Exit'. We were booked in a club in the West Edmonton Mall called Dancing Shoes, but when we got there we realised immediately that this was not a rock club. It was a chicken wing, salad buffet place, more like a restaurant masquerading as a rock club. But in our minds, it was a shit gig because we were making this video. We never really had an affinity for videos as an art form and this confirmed it.

It was a real eye opener. We learned really quickly how to temper our expectations, because otherwise you can let a series of disappointments ruin your resolve to be world musical conquerors. We were facing down obstacle after obstacle and certainly our first experience in Edmonton was like that. That was just the nature of being on the road. We learned a lot that first cross-country run that made us a better band and a tighter band as a performance unit.

JAKE GOLD: That first Canadian tour, Alberta was a wasteland. There was even talk about skipping Alberta the next time we were going to go across the country. The mistake we made the first time was to play clubs, but the next time it became obvious that we needed to play schools like the University of Alberta and University of Calgary. That's where their like-minded fans were.

```
                    LAST AMERICAN EXIT
                       LYRIC SHEET


1     MUSIC INTRO (INSTRUMENTAL)


2     YOU KNOW THE REASONS I CAN'T CONCEAL


3     YOU KNOW I'M LEAVING YOU, OBVIOUSLY YOU KNOW HOW I FEEL


4     IT'S NOT AS EASY AS CALLIN' OUT YOUR NAME WHEN I'M DOWN


5     IT'S NOT A MATTER FOR WRONG OR RIGHT


6     IT AIN'T MUCH BETTER THAN DRINKING AND LOOKING FOR A
      FIGHT


7     YOU KNOW I'M TIRED OF CRAWLING 'HIND MY NAME AMONG
      THE CROWD


8     I'M ON THE LAST AMERICAN EXIT TO MY LAST CHANCE
      I'M ON THE LAST AMERICAN EXIT TO MY HOMELAND


9     I'M ON THE LAST AMERICAN EXIT TO MY LAST CHANCE
      THEY KEEP CALLING OUT MY NAME- I SHOUT IT DOWN


10    INSTUMENTAL BRIDGE
```

DATE		CITY	VENUE
June	10	London, Ontario	Call The Office
	11	Ottawa, Ontario	Congress Centre(Award Ceremony)
	12	Montreal, Quebec	Café Campus
	14	London, Ontario	C.O.C.A. Conference (Awards Ceremony)
16	16	Montreal, Quebec	Foufounes Electrique
	17	Montreal, Quebec	Le Spectrum
	19	Moncton, N.B.	The Cosmopolitan Club
	20	Moncton, N.B.	The Cosmopolitan Club
21	21	Moncton, N.B.	The Cosmopolitan Club
	22	St. John, N.B.	The Aquarius Club
	23	Halifax, N.S.	Pub Flamingo
	24	Halifax, N.S.	Pub Flamingo
	25	Halifax, N.S.	Pub Flamingo
	26	Dartmouth, N.S.	Crazy Horse Cabaret
July	1	Ottawa, Ontario	Parliament Hill
	14	Toronto, Ontario	The Diamond Club
	15	Toronto, Ontario	The Horseshoe Tavern
	16	Toronto, Ontario	The Horseshoe Tavern
*******		More July Dates To Follow	

Opposite: Gord Sinclair's handwritten lyrics for 'Last American Exit' (top)

The director, Don Archbold, and two crew members during the filming of the 'Last American Exit' video, Edmonton, AB March 1988 (middle)

THE TRAGICALLY HIP

CANADIAN SUMMER TOUR

1988

DATE		CITY	VENUE
July	25 & 26	Saskatoon	Louis Pub
	27 & 28	Regina	The Venue
	29 & 30	Calgary	The Westward Club
	31	Edmonton	Barry T's
Aug.	2		T.B.A.
	4	Victoria	Harpo's
	5 & 6	Vancouver	The Town Pump
	8 & 9		T.B.A.
	10	Red Deer	Red Deer Community College
	11	Saskatoon	Nervous Harolds
	12 & 13	Winnipeg	B-Ways

PAUL: To tour Canada in a van you've got to want to do it, because all the drives are long and you generally have to do them at night. In those early days we were driving ourselves, then unloading, sound checking, grabbing something to eat quickly somewhere (unless the club fed us), then loading up after the show and driving to whatever the next city was. Managing to stay happy and motivated was pretty difficult. The show was the good part, then most of the rest of the time was the grind part.

JOHNNY: It was long, long hours between cities. We had a cassette deck in the van and everyone brought their tapes. When he started touring with us, Mark Vreeken, our sound engineer, would put a Steve Vai tape in, which Gord wasn't crazy about. Gord brought *Nebraska* by Bruce Springsteen. It was a bonding experience – driving across the country in a van together, making each other laugh, making ends meet.

GORD S: The biggest part of being in a group is the dynamic that you have off the stage when travelling the country, especially a country like Canada. We had a van full of great personalities.

On stage Johnny was the backbone of the performance, but he was the backbone of the whole enterprise as well. Life on the road is not easy, so a good, self-effacing sense of humour is a really important element of any touring band. Johnny is a naturally comedic guy – he sees the humour in just about everything – and he could deflate any pressure situation and turn a bad gig into a world-conquering gig. He just had that capacity to make us all laugh and not take ourselves too seriously.

Johnny was also instrumental in maintaining that 'us versus them' idea. He's a scrappy guy and he would defend the honour of the band to the last word.

Paul was the main driver and I was kind of the back-up. Maybe due to his brief stint with Amey's Taxi in Kingston, he was a good driver and he would pull the long shift. Paul was very much the quiet guy. He'd sit there smoking with the window down, passing the time on the road. But for all Paul's quietness, his songwriting was pretty deep.

GORD D: We didn't have a lot of guile. Our needs were few. With rock bands, it's really like a horse: you only feed them so much so they know that you know that they're hungry. And that's all we really needed. We were really like any rock band playing across the country – everything was brand new, everything was possible. The slightest whiff of approval or interest distilled itself into confidence. But we also had a very self-deprecating sense of humour, collectively.

GORD S: I grew up with Robbie and he remains my closest friend. That gave the two of us an advantage over the other guys. We all became really tight as brothers, but Robbie and I know each other so intimately that I don't think there's ever been – apart from maybe one tussle as middle schoolers – a sharp word between us. That helped make the band trips go pretty quickly.

And the whole time Gord Downie was writing it all down. He'd get the Moleskine out and it was amazing how often little snippets of our conversations would appear as lyrics in songs. Gord was a great listener.

He absorbed and took the meaning out of what was being said or what he was reading and intellectualised it, put it out there in his own art, with the words that he was writing.

We just had a great dynamic. We were a great band on and off the stage and really, legitimately enjoyed each other's company, which was the reason we kept doing it.

It wasn't always perfect. We scrapped a lot and disagreed a lot – but if you were down, there was always someone to pick you up.

GORD S: **The history of the road in Canada is really important from a heritage and a cultural point of view. It has a real allure, as a young musician coming up, because all the artists that you admire and aspire to be like have travelled the same road. It should almost be a requirement for a Canadian to travel east coast/west coast in the country at least once in your life. The scale of it is humbling and it puts you in perspective. Your little band in your little van in the midst of everything.**

JAKE GOLD: Our licence with BMG for the EP was only for a year, after which we decided to walk away and start looking for a new deal. Prior to us putting out the EP, Capitol had shown some interest in the band. They always said to us that if we ever left, we should come and see them.

So we went and had a meeting with them and they said they wanted the band to demo for them. Allan and I didn't really want to demo, we wanted a record deal. But they weren't ready to commit. So we agreed to pay for half the cost of the demos, but we would have the rights to shop those demos. The importance of that decision became clearer as time went on.

ROB: Allan Gregg had financed the EP, the baby record, and that got released on BMG. We had a sit down with this guy from BMG who wanted to do a country rock makeover on us. We could write nine of the 11 songs on the record, but then they'd bring in professional songwriters to write two hits, and they were going to dress us up in fringe jackets.

We turned him down flat. His view was that it was better to have a record that had ten tracks of shit and one hit than one that had 11 really strong songs, none of which was a hit. But my view, which I told him, was that the record with the hit's going to sell for four months and then people are going to feel ripped off, whereas the one with 11 great tracks is still going to be selling 20 years later. He couldn't see that.

Capitol Records came and asked us to start demoing for them. They would put us in a studio and ask us to give them five tracks. So we'd record five songs and they'd tell us which two they liked and send us away to write and record another five songs and then they'd pick another two. This dragged on for a while. Meanwhile, we were playing gigs all the time and writing and doing four-track demos of our own and then we'd get into a proper studio and work the tracks up.

At a certain point, we had all of the songs for *Up to Here*, apart from '38 Years Old', written and recorded in some version. We felt like we'd got a good record, but Capitol still wanted more songs before they'd sign us.

JAKE GOLD: We recorded 'Blow at High Dough' and 'New Orleans Is Sinking' for them, and they still didn't want to put a contract on the table for us.

We decided to play CMJ, a music conference festival in New York, in late October 1988. We did a budget to put a track on the CMJ CD sampler, put a video on the video sampler and play the gig at the Big Kahuna on lower Broadway on a Saturday night and brought it to Capitol. It was going to cost about $5,000, which we asked them to split with us but they didn't want to do that.

BRUCE DICKINSON: I was listening to a sampler CD while making my breakfast and one of the tracks on it was by The Tragically Hip. I was literally cooking bacon and eggs, and through the sizzle Gord's voice cut through and I was intrigued. There was something attitude-wise, almost a caustic character, in his voice that I picked up, knowing nothing about the man. As soon as I finished eating, I grabbed the phone and called Jake Gold.

GORD D: We played in New York City in October 1988 for the CMJ Music Marathon. It's a conference there. And we were fortunate enough to get our song 'Small Town Bringdown' on a compact disc that goes out to all these programmers and college music people. And Bruce Dickinson [from MCA] happened to hear it off that CD.

PAUL: Jake invited Bruce Dickinson to a Toronto Music Awards show at Massey Hall where we were due to play two songs.

BRUCE DICKINSON: Jake picked me up from the airport and in the car he had their demo tape playing, which had about six more songs on it, including 'When the Weight Comes Down' and 'New Orleans Is Sinking'. I was just dead-on concentrating on the music while Jake was talking to me – he's the greatest salesman in the world. Jake told me later that he was worried because I wasn't really responding to him. But in my mind I was ripping apart the songs, the key they were in, the whole nine yards. What I liked about the tape was each song was distinctly The Tragically Hip but each song had its own character. I really like that in an artist, period. So I was close to being sold right then and there.

At Massey Hall the band came out and Gord somehow knocked over the mic stand. The microphone came out of the stand and fell and broke into its component parts. I'll always remember the look on Gord Sinclair's face – he was looking at the other band guys like, 'Oh, crap.' But they didn't miss a beat, which really impressed me – they all just improvised while Gord Downie did this whole story with the cable as a snake. I remember him looking out into the audience and he had a completely fearless expression in his eyes as he told the whole story – and, at that point, I'm sold.

JAKE GOLD: Part of what we were selling was this enigmatic front guy, who was spontaneous, and you never knew what was going to happen next. That's what made the shows amazing and Bruce understood that right away. He saw the electricity. It was undeniable. It was the same as the first time I saw Gord. He saw what I saw.

GORD D: We didn't know too much about it. We knew that we had to get up there for two songs and really make it happen, according to our manager. And I guess we kind of made it happen, or we were trying too hard and got nervous and got drunk or something because everything fell apart. But it seemed to be just what the show needed.

JOHNNY: We were really nervous. This was Massey Hall, a place that Rush had played; it was like our Grand Ole Opry. When the cable fell out of Gord's microphone, it could have been disastrous. But instead he saved things by making it a part of the performance.

PAUL: Bruce liked us, which we were pretty excited about. I think he was impressed with Gord's spur-of-the-moment, spontaneous mindset – when his mic came loose from the cable he managed to turn it into a story about a sperm and an egg, grabbing whatever came across his mind at the time.

Toronto Music Awards, Massey Hall, Toronto, 11 November 1988

ROB: Bruce came to see us the next night at the Horseshoe. I didn't know there was an A&R guy coming up from MCA, none of it. I didn't know who Bruce Dickinson was. I thought he was the singer in Iron Maiden. We met Bruce after the show at the Horseshoe, had a little sit down after they cleared it out. We were chatting and he said, 'I'd like to sign you to a seven-record deal.' And we said, 'Yeah, we're good with that.'

I think it was important for us on some level to sign with a non-Canadian label. We were decidedly not like other bands. We were too classic rock for the roots thing that was happening and too roots for the classic rock thing. We always seemed to slip somewhere down the middle, and never really fit into what was hot at that moment. Maybe the Canadian labels were looking for something that was going to really strike the Zeitgeist, but that was never really what we wanted to do. We just wanted to forge our own way and figure out what we were. The fact that he was from a US label seemed to carry a little extra weight for us, and I think it carried extra weight for other Canadians, which is sad and absurd, but true.

ROCK RECORDS PRESENTS:
THE
Tragically
HIP
with THE BEL-VISTAS
tickets $5·00 at the door
DECEMBER 28, 1988
tickets $5·00 at the door
at the
Horseshoe
368 Queen St West 598-4753

JAKE GOLD: At the Horseshoe, I had a Capitol guy standing to my left and to my right was Bruce Dickinson. You could feel the tension in the room, but the band played amazingly. We had a decent crowd there given that it was a last-minute thing. It wasn't like today where you could go on the internet and tell everybody you're playing. You had to get on the phone and tell your friends one by one. At one point, Bruce said to me he couldn't believe that this band hadn't been signed yet. They ended up putting a deal forward and Capitol couldn't get any of their American affiliates to agree a hundred percent to put the next record out, so we ended up signing with MCA.

ROB: We felt like we were getting demoed to death. No one would stick their neck out until Bruce saw the band and said, 'Yeah, I want that.'

JOHNNY: Gord hated all the waiting around to get signed. He knew that we were ready. Then when Bruce Dickinson parachuted in, said he didn't need to hear any more, signed us, and got his guy Don Smith to make our first record, that was a real shot in the arm. They gave us some real money. I think the first budget was $150,000, which now would be unheard of. It all went to Don and the studio, but we didn't care. We just wanted to make a really great sounding record. And we did.

On stage at the Horseshoe Tavern, Toronto, 12 November 1988, and (opposite top right) with Bruce Dickinson after the show

ENTERTAINMENT

The upcoming summer album of Kingston's Tragically Hip band will be marketed around the world

Tragically Hip signs MCA world-wide record deal

ROB: Bruce told us that we weren't the kind of band that was going to have a big hit and go racing up the charts. We just needed to do exactly what we were already doing: writing, recording, touring, writing, recording, touring. And after we'd done about four or five albums, we'd achieve critical mass. He said we'd keep growing our audience each time out, and eventually we'd become a big band. We just had to stick to our guns.

JOHNNY: If we'd had a hit song early on, I don't think we would have survived. All the experience of seeing good things happening for other bands helped us grow an armour. That stuff didn't happen for us because it wasn't supposed to. It was supposed to take longer for The Hip to make it – and when we did, we did it on our own terms.

ROB: In Bruce's mind, it was all very clear right out of the gate. He said he wanted to take us some place like Memphis to do the first record and get someone like Don Smith to produce it. We didn't know who Don Smith was, but when Bruce told us that he'd just finished doing the Keith Richards solo album we didn't need to know any more, because that was pretty much number one on our playlist at the time. Then we found out that he had also just finished doing The Traveling Wilburys and Roy Orbison's final album, and so we loved this guy. And then we met him, and we loved him even more.

It meant something to us that Bruce clearly understood the band. And then for him to suggest Don Smith, his instincts were absolutely spot on.

GORD D: When you're 16 you just want to get into a band and play; you don't even know why. The volume is turned up in your head when you're not doing anything, and the longer you don't do anything, the louder it gets. And then, in my case, once you make a record, then that volume is turned way down for a few months and you can relax and revel in a job well done. And then you go out and play live and that nightly injection of the same thing is trying to keep the volume down. Then, ultimately, you know it's time to make a record because the noise starts getting extremely loud.

BRUCE DICKINSON: Both individually and as a group, the guys immediately struck me as very intelligent. They read books. It's indicative of why they were right for me and I was right for them that they reminded me of guys that were my friends in high school.

MEMORANDUM:

TO: ALL M.C.A. STAFF

FROM: JAKE GOLD, ALLAN R. GREGG

DATE: DECEMBER 22, 1988

_____

Come out and see the hottest new act on your roster! We are delighted to announce that as of today, "The Tragically Hip" has signed a long term contract with M.C.A. America.
You are all invited to come out and see the band at "The Horseshoe" Wednesday December 28, 1988 at 10:00pm.

SIDE A

Blow At High Dough
(Baker, Downie, Fay, Langlois, Sinclair)

I'll Believe In You (or I'll be leaving you tonight)
(Baker, Downie, Fay, Langlois, Sinclair)

New Orleans Is Sinking
(Baker, Downie, Fay, Langlois, Sinclair)

38 Years Old
(Baker, Downie, Fay, Langlois, Sinclair)

She Didn't Know
(Baker, Downie, Fay, Langlois, Sinclair)

SIDE B

Boots Or Hearts
(Baker, Downie, Fay, Langlois, Sinclair)

Every Time You Go
(Baker, Downie, Fay, Langlois, Sinclair)

When The Weight Comes Down
(Baker, Downie, Fay, langlois, Sinclair)

Trickle Down
(Baker, Downie, Fay, Langlois, Sinclair)

Another Midnight
(Baker, Downie, Fay, Langlois, Sinclair)

Opiated
(Baker, Downie, Fay, Langlois, Sinclair)

THE TRAGICALLY HIP
ALBUM CREDITS

The Tragically Hip are: Bobby Baker - Guitar
Gordon Downie - Vocals
Johnny Fay - Drums
Paul Langlois - Guitar & Vocals
Gord Sinclair - Bass & Vocals

Produced by: Don Smith for Bullpen Productions
Recorded by: Don Smith and Bruce Barris at Ardent Studios, Memphis
Mixed by: Don Smith with Bruce Barris
Mixed at: The Village Recorder & Rumbo Studios
Assistant Engineers: Jeff DeMorris, Andy Udoff & Paul Eberson
Mastering by: Stephen Marcussen at Percission Laquer

Exclusive Management: The Management Trust Inc.
Allan R. Gregg and Jake Gold
Assistant to the Managers: Leigh Higgins
Crew Dudes: Mike Stock - Sound
Mark Vreeken - Stage
Dave (Boog) Powell - Road Manager

Agency: Variety Artists International
Trip Brown

The Agency (in Canada)
Peter Wheatley

Thanks to: Al, Bruce, Luke, the Jeffs and all at M.C.A. anywhere
Dave Margulies, Ken Greer, Don Wershba, Chris Wardman,
Ken Whitehead, Jody Stevens, Paul Eberson, John Fry and
everyone at Ardent, Terry Smith, Debbie Gold, Shelly Yakus,
Dave Smith, Ceaser Diaz, Memphis Drum Shop & The Drum Doctor

Special Thanks to: Don, Bruce; our friends of home and highway,
and our family.

For more information: The Tragically Hip
c/o 372 Richmond St. West
Suite #110
Toronto, Ontario
M5V 1X6

Song Credits - LABEL : Baker, Downie, Fay, Langlois, Sinclair

- ALBUM SLEEVE : All songs written by The Tragically Hip

Publishing : Roll Music/Little Smoke Music (C.A.P.A.C./A.S.C.A.P.)

THE TRAGICALLY HIP ARE:

Bobby Baker: Guitar
Gordon Downie: Vocals
Johnny Fay: Drums
Paul Langlois: Guitar and Vocals
Gord Sinclair: Bass and Vocals

All Songs Written by The Tragically Hip

Recorded by Don Smith and Bruce Barris at Ardent Studios, Memphis, TN
Mixed by Don Smith with Bruce Barris at The Village Recorder, Los
Angeles, CA and Rumbo Studios, Canoga Park, CA
Assistant Engineers: Jeff DeMorris, Andy Udoff and Paul Eberson

Mastered by Stephen Marcussen at Precision Lacquer, Hollywood, Ca

Exclusive Management: The Management Trust Inc.
Allan R. Gregg and Jake Gold
Assistant to the Managers: Leigh Higgins

Crew Dudes: Mike Stock - Sound
Mark Vreeken - Stage
Dave (Boog) Powell - Road Manager

Agency: Variety Artists International
Trip Brown

The Agency (In Canada)
Peter Wheatley

Thanks To: Al, Bruce, Luke, the Jeffs and all at MCA anywhere,
Dave Marguiles, Ken Greer, Don Wershba, Chris Wardman, Ken Whitehead,
Jody Stevens, Paul Eberson, John Fry and everyone at Ardent, Terry
Smith, Debbie Gold, Shelly Yakus, Dave Smith, Ceaser Diaz, Memphis
Drum Shop and The Drum Doctor.

Special Thanks To: Don, Bruce, our friends of home and highway, and
our family.

For More Information: The Tragically Hip
c/o 372 Richmond St. West
Suite #110
Toronto, Ontario
M5V 1X6
CANADA

Jacob J. Gold & Associates Inc.

The Tragically Hip
Album Budget

4 weeks @1100 a day X 28 days	$30,800
mixing (studio to be named later)	$30,000
tape	$ 6,000
rehearsal (rental of space)	$ 500
rentals	$13,000
hotels	$ 5,250
per diem ($20. per day @7 people X 35 days	$ 4,900
travel	$ 3,000
union	$ 5,400
miscellaneous	$ 5,000
Don Smith	$40,000
Total	$147,350

143,850
3,860

143,850
000
3,691.50   146,850
400
1,691.50   147,250
147,250

150,250

147,425

372 Richmond St. W., Suite 110, Toronto, Ont. M5V 1X6 Tel. (416) 977-8022 Fax: (416) 971-7759

Recording Up to Here *with producer Don Smith (seated right) and engineer Bruce Barris (seated centre), Ardent Studios, Memphis, 1989*

BRUCE DICKINSON: Memphis in 1988 had a really good vibe about it. Everywhere you went there were reminders of the musical heritage of the city. A lot of blues records came from Memphis. Elvis Presley. Sun Records. Ardent itself was where so much of that Stax/Volt stuff was done. It was impossible to escape it.

GORD D: Jerry Lee Lewis is from Sun Records and there's the old Stax recording studios where some of the best ever rhythm and blues was recorded. It's a music town, there's no doubt about it. And you get a sense of all that.

JOHNNY: There was tons of history at Ardent. REM had just been in there and recorded *Green*, which we all loved. Big Star and The Replacements had also recorded there.

GORD S: When we were working in Ardent Studios, Jody Stephens, the drummer for Big Star, was our studio ambassador, asking us if we needed anything. It was just unbelievable.

PAUL: The studio was great. We'd been in a couple of more commercial places in Toronto, but this was our first time in a rock and roll studio. There'd been a lot of famous records made there, like ZZ Top's *Degüello*. We were like kids in a candy store.

ROB: Bruce Dickinson hooking us up with Don Smith put us firmly on the track that we always dreamed of being on. And then we really felt we were something when we were walking into Ardent. There's a scene in the movie *Gimme Shelter* where The Stones get out of the limos and Keith swooshes his scarf around his neck with his big funky hat on and they all walk into Muscle Shoals. It was a little bit like that, although a lot less glamorous.

BRUCE DICKINSON: There was something about Don's work that really spoke to me. He captured artists' sounds, and that's not an easy thing to do. A guy who can really produce knows how to get the best performances out of an artist, and I knew Don could do that with The Tragically Hip. There was nothing fake or phony about him and the same goes for The Hip. One reason not to pick a really big-name producer is you want to ease a young band into it. I thought that Don could bring them out of the shell of Kingston – there was a whole world out there for them and Don could be the conduit for that.

I also felt that I could trust him to work with the band, and so I didn't need to be there. Because The Tragically Hip were a young band at the time, I didn't want them thinking Mr Record Company was always looking over their shoulders. I could talk to Don every morning before the band got into the studio, or late at night after the session, and the band never had to feel that the guy with the bag of money could pull the plug at any moment. I had that rapport with Don. He was the right producer for The Tragically Hip at that time.

GORD D: Don had worked at Ardent before. He liked it and thought Memphis in the offseason would be a cool place to go. We wanted to get out of the general vicinity – all the recording up to that point we had done in Toronto, where you go in the studio and then at about six o'clock you go home and everyone goes their separate ways. I think a lot of the stuff that goes on in recording happens in the off hours when you're sitting around mulling over what you've done and what you hope to do and you pull out an acoustic guitar and write a part. Being in Memphis allowed us all to be in one hotel suite. We'd come home every day and pop in one of the tapes and say, 'Well, let's change that. And let's do that.' It's way more productive when you can hang out 24 hours a day.

JF: Don was about making it alive – like we were playing the Horseshoe and he was going to capture it. I remember it being really intense and fun.

PAUL: Don Smith was our first experience of working with an LA producer whom we'd heard of. He'd recorded Keith Richards, Tom Petty. Enough said. He loved our band and he genuinely liked what everyone did, so he didn't try to change anyone. He just wanted us all to be happy with it. He knew that we were a live band and good friends, and that we just really wanted to be tight.

GORD D: Don's philosophy was very much the same as ours. We showed up and shook hands and went out on the town for a couple of days before we got down to it. I guess that, being an engineer, he's used to getting the sounds and being really happy with that aspect. And then letting the band do what they want to do. So that's what we would do. He would be very meticulous about getting the right guitar sound and tuning the drums and stuff like that. But it was never pushy. It was very casual. He was truly great to work with – very laid back, no sense of ego.

BRUCE DICKINSON: One of the main reasons why I thought Don was perfect for the young version of The Tragically Hip was that his position could be a bit like an older brother. There was nothing about Don that was overbearing. He was an extreme stickler for detail, which I loved. He could be a stern taskmaster, without being obnoxious about it. He could get what he needed to get.

ROB: I was expecting Don to tell us where to put our amps and to be twiddling and dialling stuff in. But he didn't do any of that. He just said, 'Just do what you do live. I love your band. I want it to sound like you guys are playing on stage.' That instilled us with so much confidence. We didn't need a course correction, we just needed some fuel, a little help. He was fantastic for the band.

I'd always been fascinated by the process of recording, I still am. So while I didn't know all the intricacies of compressors and tape speeds and all that shit, I was aware that most people made records by recording the bass and drums and then building everything up on top of that. But Don just put up a bunch of mics, told us to play the tunes and recorded us like we were a live band. That comes with its own pitfalls, because if there's no audience it's hard to get the energy that you get from a live show. So that was a learning curve. But it was the right approach for us.

THE HIP - MEMPHIS, TENNESSE/1989

THE TRAGICALLY HIP

C/O The Management Trust Inc.
    372 Richmond Street West, #110
    Toronto, Ontario M5V 1X6

PHOTO: KIM ELLIOTT PAULSON/1989

*The Tragically Hip,
Memphis, 1989*

*Opposite: Outside Elvis's
Lisa Marie airplane,
with Bruce Dickinson,
Don Smith and Bruce
Barris, Graceland,
Memphis, 1989.
Photo by Rob Baker*

PAUL: Going into the studio, I was always worried that the producer would question what I was doing. But Don never did that to me, and nor did Ken Greer on our first record. With Don, we were playing everything live and my sound and approach weren't questioned. The more that happened over the years, the better I felt, and by the time we were a few records in I was confident. I credit Don with a lot of that.

Don gave us the confidence for the rest of our careers to say how we wanted our records to be. We'd certainly listen to producers – there's give and take sometimes – but it was Don that really made us confident in the studio. We were already confident on the stage.

JAKE GOLD: The band understood that this was their career and that in order to be successful you had to work your ass off. They bought into the work ethic. It didn't prohibit them from having some crazy times as well. There was one night at Ardent that I remember fondly, where we were listening to Traveling Wilburys and ZZ Top tapes from the vaults, drinking Jack Daniel's out of the bottle, smoking weed. There was a time for fun and there was a time for work, and they took both seriously.

BRUCE DICKINSON: The Hip turned Ardent into a bad boy, rock and roll man cave. I don't know that they ever emptied an ashtray or took an empty beer bottle away. I guess they had to sample whatever brands of beer were available at that time.

PAUL: It spurred on our love of recording in different, special places – removing ourselves from our world and entering a new one for the five weeks or so that it takes to make an album. For that time, the record was all we thought about, all we talked about, all we did. We'd record and then we'd go back to the hotel late at night and keep talking about the songs, trying to improve them and adding new ones. We always found that isolating ourselves like that really worked well for us.

PAUL: We were recording six days a week and then Sunday was the day to get out if anyone felt like it. We did three or four trips down to Beale Street and went to clubs where we saw real blues. We toured Graceland – and Elvis's plane, the Lisa Marie. That was super fun.

ROB: The second album I ever bought with my own money was Elvis's *Aloha from Hawaii* when I was about 11 years old. For some people Graceland is a holy shrine. It would have been our inclination to joke around and make a goof of it, but we quickly realised you had to show some respect. It's meaningful to people; you're in someone else's church.

GORD S: As a young Canadian's first experience in the States, that trip to Memphis was really something. Rick Clark, a local journalist, befriended us and showed us around. He took us to the Lorraine Motel, where Dr King was shot and killed. Now it's a museum but back then the parking lot was overgrown with weeds and all the windows were smashed out. There were a couple of wreaths on the balcony, but it was neglected and abandoned. It wasn't celebrated in any way by the African American community or the community at large. Whereas, in a different part of town, there was a big statue of one of the guys who started the KKK and it was pristine, not a flower out of place. We were always curious guys so we were soaking up all that stuff.

We went to the Stax building, where so many fantastic tunes were recorded and where Booker T. & the M.G.'s were the house band. When I first started buying vintage instruments, the first set of gear I got was exactly what 'Duck' Dunn played – the Portaflex and the Fender P.

I think the honorary citizenship and key to the city were somewhere between an actual honour and a city promotion. Memphis was proud to be recognised as a music Mecca, so I suspect that many musicians who arrived there to record albums received the honour. It was certainly meaningful to us. (RB)

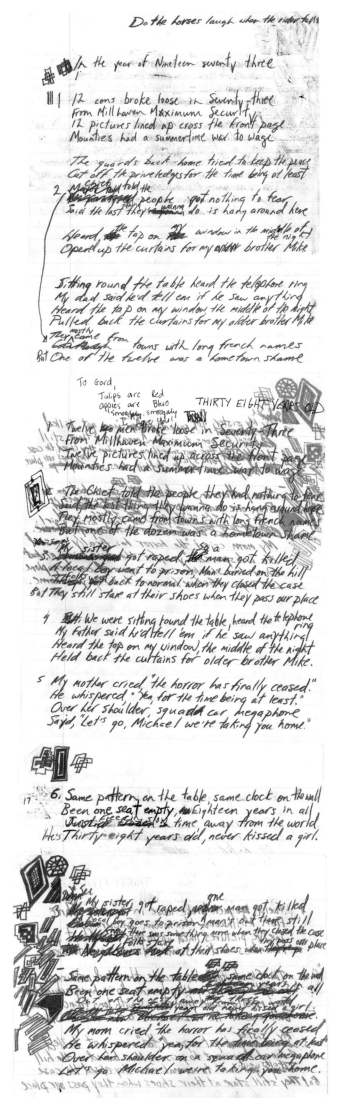

PAUL: The Hip had started as a covers band, playing the music that they liked, which was English R&B stuff like the Yardbirds and early Stones. Then when we started writing, our own songs were in that style too, but maybe a little grittier. If you listen to our first couple of albums, they are very bluesy and bare-bonesy. I don't think anyone was doing it on purpose; it just happened naturally because those were the songs we were picking up.

PAUL: Gord Sinclair came up with the riff for '38 Years Old', so he played guitar on the song and I switched to bass. Johnny made it very easy for me, because he was throwing in little rhythms where it sounded like I was doing it.

Gord Downie had been messing around with lyrics that told a story based on the big bust out down the road at Millhaven in the early Seventies. They had the pictures of the escapees right across the top of the newspaper. He and I were around eight years old at the time and Gord knew it was an event that had affected all of us.

GORD D: Close to Amherstview, where I grew up, is a place called Millhaven Penitentiary, a maximum-security institution. I remember one summer there was this huge jailbreak, which threw the outlying area into a real panic. I remember being that age and thinking, 'Wow, this is scary,' but at the same time it made that summer really memorable. I thought it would be good to pretend and take the story of the actual jailbreak on a personal level.

GORD S: We were super conscious of the Millhaven breakout. I would have been ten when that happened and that's when it became real. There was a real bad man named Donald Oag, who was among the guys who got out, and he had it in for Robbie's dad. My mom and dad sat us down and explained what was going on, and why Robbie had to leave the neighbourhood for a couple of days, why there were unmarked police cars parked in front of his house and OPP cruisers going by all the time.

I remember the night we wrote '38 Years Old' like it was yesterday. We would congregate in the common room of our three-bedroom hotel suite, which was a big deal for us back then as we were used to the cheapest motels and band houses. We were always rehearsing and trying to write. And I mistuned an acoustic guitar – I wasn't much of a guitar player back then! – and dropped the top B string down a full tone, and started playing D shapes and C shapes, and came up with the musical idea for that song.

We started writing the song and Gord stayed up all night to finish it, because we were really on to something. Really quickly we came up with a great chorus. It was like the kind of song Robbie Robertson would write, with a beginning, a middle and an end. And it was quite dramatic.

It was songwriting at its finest – to have the historical aspect of the prison break immortalised in the song and then Gord put the fictionalised family spin on top of that: his brother, Mike, was the central character of the piece, and his sisters were in it too.

JOHNNY: Unfortunately, it was tough to get Gord to play that one down the road. The lyric about 'my brother, Mike' made people think the song was about him, as his brother's name actually is Mike. He regretted using that name, but I told him that it was OK because it drew people into the story.

JOHNNY: Gord wrote the lyrics for 'New Orleans Is Sinking' before The Hip ever got together. Then Robbie came in with this amazing guitar riff, and there it was.

When Hurricane Katrina happened 20 years later, some people were saying we shouldn't play the song, but when you go to New Orleans they have a drink called the Hurricane. They know it's going to happen, they just don't know when.

GORD D: I went to New Orleans with a few Vancouver boys from Queen's for spring break. We went down there for Mardi Gras and that song was inspired by the reckless times.

NEW ORLEANS IS SINKING (AND DON'T WANT TO SWIM)

Bourbon blues on the street, loose and complete
Under skies all smoky blue-green
I can't forsake a Dixie-dead-shake
We danced the sidewalk clean
Ain't got no picture postcards ain't got no souvenirs
My baby, she don't know me when I think about those years

Uncle Tom, what's wrong, what's going on
You gotta do what you feel is real
Hey North, you're South, shut your big mouth
And Don't tie yourself up for a deal
My memory is muddy, what's this river that I'm in
New Orleans is sinking man, & I don't wanna swim

We drove down the road just like the Jodes
Chasing time with bottles of beer
And rock 'n' roll to a fading, radio station
its the last voice we'll ever hear
My memory is muddy, what's this river that I'm in
New Orleans is sinking man, and I don't wanna swim.

Blow blow, blow at high dough

He said said so you're the guy in the band
who wants to take our girl by the hand
I said I don't want nothing of yours from you
That you ain't already let slip through

The man lays down in his overcoat
He's a snow angel or a suicide note
And he jumps in the river, sinks like a stone
His enemies cry cause he died alone

If you ain't scared bout what won't last
Then you're in the past

I called in well to work today
my boss don't see it that way
Says "you feel so good why don't you quit?"
I said like all your swine, I need the shit.

Sitting smoking this cigarette
like it was a season
I watch a girl take off her clothes
for absolutely no reason
Upstairs the she's crying
She can't just strip for no reason

ANOTHER MIDNIGHT

Blow blow blow at high dough
There's always somebody who claims to know
Your fast enough is still too slow
Shut your mouth I'll learn as I go
My only advice as I watched you go
Was blow blow blow at high dough
Please spare me everything you know
Making plans for money / ain't earned
Using words I know / ain't learned

I think of my eye-glazed higher learning
Smoking the middle with both ends burning
I think of my red right tire turning
Smoking the middle with both ends burning

Wester than yesterday
hazy or the horizon

Old man puts the rope around his neck
Weight and gravity will connect
The dinner party scratches its head
Was it something that wasn't said?
wrote the time courses to cry & reflect
Close to the top, far from the end
Saying when makes too much sense

I want to devour you and all your time

Living high of the hog
Kicking time on the dog

Genuine - get it out, get it all out

You Blow, blow, blow at high dough

Re thinking bout living 40 years just to know
That you blow blow blow at high dough

I was kicking around something that kicked my
If we mate for life who mates for dead.
She's got who cares, blank stare, then recommends
We combine the two, & live each day like the end
everyday

She broke up the party screaming, get it all out

He said I don't like silence either but there's no need to sh
shoulda checked that amount at the do
Cause everyone's afraid of what using it fo

You could've heard a pin drop or a wino shout

GORD D: The songs are fairly self-explanatory if you're semi-schizophrenic. 'Don't blow at high dough' was something my grandmother used to say when you were moving too fast for your own good or learning to run before you could crawl. So that was where the saying came from. And the song sort of falls in line with that sentiment.

JAKE GOLD: None of us liked the 'Blow at High Dough' video. Looking back, I can't believe that we made it. MTV didn't play it. They weren't interested in us. I don't think the band saw videos as a legitimate creative outlet. They just saw them as something you had to do. To be honest, making videos was one of the things that none of us was very good at. We didn't make any good videos until *Fully Completely*.

ROB: The day before we made the 'Blow at High Dough' video, I went to get a haircut. The guy who usually cut my hair wasn't there and had someone filling in for him who gave me bangs, straight across, halfway up my forehead. I got out to the car, looked at myself in the mirror and started banging my head on the steering wheel. I swear if you do a freeze-frame of the video, you can see the steering wheel imprint on my forehead.

For the video we thought it would be great to do something black and white. We made it look like we were performing on *The Ed Sullivan Show* and then had a bluescreen in the background running black and white clips of all kinds of crazy shit. I loved it and I still think it's a fun video.

There was nothing revolutionary about it, but we were a young band and I felt like we were steering our own ship. There were big budget and big location videos being made at the time – guitar players standing on mountaintops with their hair blowing in the wind, playing a solo to the canyon. We hated that shit. We wanted to do ours like *The T.A.M.I. Show*, just getting up there and playing live.

JOHNNY: There was a song called 'Wait So Long' that Don Smith and the record company all thought was going to be the hit, but Gord didn't think it was finished yet. Also, it had a similar rhythm and tempo to another song that was on the radio at the time and Gord didn't want us to be compared to this other band. So we left it off *Up to Here*. I remember thinking that the song was great, but looking back it wouldn't have fit with the rest of the record.

PAUL: We would always let the record company pick the singles. We were inside the songs, so we didn't know what was going to fly on the radio. It turns out that 'Blow at High Dough' and 'New Orleans Is Sinking' were good choices. The videos made a big difference for both those songs too. The fact we were getting shown on MuchMusic really helped us. Because of that exposure, we started to get known.

We thought we were not really made for video. We just weren't made for these times, to quote Brian Wilson. It seemed like a whole other game that was played by different rules. When your record starts to break even, they need another video, which is going to cost you another $150,000 that you now need to recoup. We were always suspicious that it was just another way of keeping a band perpetually in the hole. So if we could make a video on the cheap, that appealed to us. And if we could control the messaging, which meant picking our directors or doing it ourselves, that was in our interests too. The videos we farmed out to other people, more often than not were not successful in terms of what we would call a success.

We were touring anyway, but we soon realised what a big difference it made to have a couple of songs on the radio. They were exciting times.

Promo photos, July 1989 (this page and opposite, top left)

Opposite: Backstage Platinum Award presentation for Up to Here, *Masonic Hall, Toronto, 30 March 1990 Back (l to r): Jake Gold, Rob Baker, Bruce Dickinson, Gord Downie, Johnny Fay, Allan Gregg Front (l to r): Dave Powell, Paul Langlois, Gord Sinclair (top right)*

On the roof of the MCA building, Toronto, 1990 (bottom right)

BRUCE DICKINSON: When we put out the first Tragically Hip album, *Up to Here*, we made a point, even with the album cover, that they'd just be a rock and roll band. There would be nothing phony about them. At the time, I thought what the music world needed was more bands doing what they do honestly, not dressing up in Spandex or wearing blond wigs. Guys that just pile out of a car or a van, walk to the stage and do it. There's no angle. It's just The Tragically Hip.

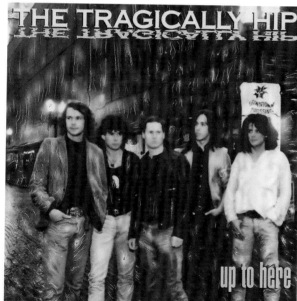

JAKE GOLD: We always knew that 'New Orleans Is Sinking' was going to be the song that would reach the most people, but we put 'Blow at High Dough' out first and had a degree of success with it. The album came out in September 1989 and coming into Christmas it had sold about 30,000 in Canada and we were building an audience in the US. Then when 'New Orleans Is Sinking' came out, the whole thing blew up. All of a sudden, in Canada *Up to Here* went gold, then platinum, then double platinum within four or five months. The next thing you know, we were selling out big venues and being offered big money to play bigger venues.

   We got some great reaction from college radio in the US. They supported us, because they saw it as a feather in their cap that we got signed out of their conference. But we still weren't getting *Rolling Stone*, *Spin*, MTV. I don't think they saw us as cool enough compared with bands like Nirvana and Pearl Jam, which were coming through, and we weren't on a cool label like Sub Pop or Geffen.

Up to Here
RECORDED: JANUARY–FEBRUARY 1989
ARDENT STUDIOS, MEMPHIS, TN
PRODUCER: DON SMITH
ENGINEER: BRUCE BARRIS
MIXING: DON SMITH
RELEASED: 5 SEPTEMBER 1989

Blow at High Dough
I'll Believe in You (Or I'll Be Leaving You Tonight)
New Orleans Is Sinking
38 Years Old
She Didn't Know
Boots or Hearts
Everytime You Go
When the Weight Comes Down
Trickle Down
Another Midnight
Opiated

Hip Dates in 1989

April 6th ,Kingston
June 7,Buffolo
     8,Rochester
     9,Washington,Mass.
    10,Rutland,Maine
    11,Portland,Maine   } 250
    13,Boston,
    14,N.Y.,N.Y.
    15,Philly
    17,Dover,Delaware
    18,Washington D.C.
    19,Pittsburgh   } 250
    20,Baltimore
    21,Viginia Beach
    23,Chicago
    24,Minniapolis
    26,Bloomington,Ind.   } 250
    27,Millwakee,Wis.
    28,Dayton,Ohio
    29,Cleveland,Ohio
    30,Detroit,Mich.
July 1,London,afternoon.Barrie,evening   500
     7,Madison,Wis.
     8,East Lansing,Mich.
     9,Kalamazoo,Mich.
    11,St.Louis,Missouri   } 250
    12,Lawrence,Kansas
    13,Wichita,Kansas
    14,Dallas,Tex.
    15,Austin,Tex.
    16,Houston,Tex.   } 250
    18,Tucson,Ariz.
    19,Phoenix,Ariz.
    20,L.A.,Ca.
    22,Long Beach,Ca.
    23,Solana Beach,Ca.   } 250
    25,San Jose,Ca.
    26,San Fran.
    27,Berkely,
Aug.22,Toronto   500 400
    29,Kinston,Ont.
Sept.1,Toronto,Ont.   500 400
     7,Erindale,U of T
     8,McMaster,Hamilton
     9,Laurentien U,Sudbury
   11-13,Saskatoon
    14,U of M,Winnipeg   } 1500
    15,Red River,Winn.
    16,U of M,Tashe Hall,Winn.
    25,Stages,Kichener
    26,Roxx,Barrie
    27,Dr.Rockets,London   } 1200
    28,Dallas,Hamilton
    29,Barrymores,Ottawa
Oct. 3, Diamond,Toronto
     6,7,Spectrum,Winn.
    10,11,Venue,Regina

Oct.-continued
    12,Old Scotch,Calgary
    13,U of Calgary
    14,U of A,Edmonton   } 2500
    16-17,Whistler,B.C.
    19,Victoria,The Forge
    20-21,86th St.,Vancouver
    26,Tramps,N.Y.,CMJ
Nov.7,Casby Awards,Toronto
    8,HMV store,Montreal
    10-12,Misty Moon,Halifax
    13,Chesnut Caberet,Fredrickton
    14,Moncton,N.B.
    16,Capri,Sydney,N.S.
    17,Mt. Alison,Sackville,N.B.
    18,Acadia,Wolfville,N.S.
    24-25,Club Soda,Montreal
    28,Channel,Boston
    29,Tramps,N.Y.
    30,Live Tonight,Hoboken,N.J. } 250
Dec.1,2,23 East Caberet,Ardmore
    4,Richmond,Virginia.
    5,Wash D.C.,Bayou
    6,Pittsburgh,Graffitti
    8,Millwakee,Odd Rock   } 150
    9,Avalon,Chicago
    15,Spectrum,Toronto
    26,Stages,Kingston   } 1000
    28,Barrymores,Ottawa
    29,30,Horseshoe,Toronto
    31,Club Soda,Montreal   850

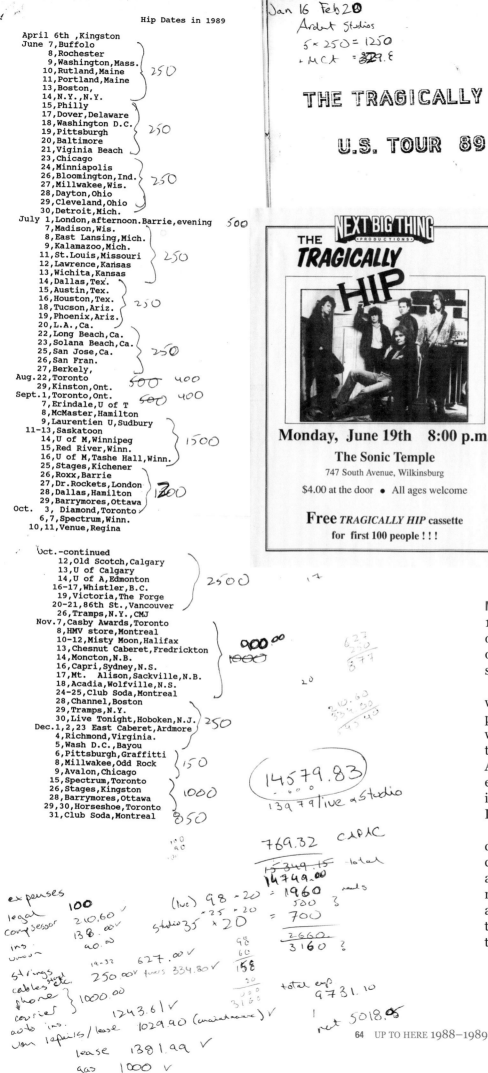

THE TRAGICALLY HIP

U.S. TOUR 89

NEXT BIG THING PRODUCTIONS

THE TRAGICALLY HIP

Monday, June 19th   8:00 p.m.

The Sonic Temple

747 South Avenue, Wilkinsburg

$4.00 at the door   •   All ages welcome

Free *TRAGICALLY HIP* cassette
for first 100 people ! ! !

JF: When we got our itinerary for our first west coast tour, we couldn't believe the places we were going to be playing – Club Lingerie in LA, the DNA Lounge in San Francisco, Under the Rail in Seattle. It was like a dream.

ROB: The Hip family was starting to get bigger, with people like Don Smith and our road manager Dave Powell. And then we were joined by Mark Vreeken – that guy's a lifer.

MARK VREEKEN: I started working with The Hip in June 1989 on their first US tour right before *Up to Here* came out. My first gig with them was doing lights at a one-off outdoor show in Ottawa. I was 17 and working for a small regional sound and lighting company.

About a year later they were rehearsing at the shop where I worked before their tour for *Up to Here*. I was packing a truck for another show at the time and they were having some trouble with their monitors. I helped them out, had a short chat and went off to my gig. About a week later, I got a call to say their monitor engineer/stage tech had left and to ask if I would be interested in flying down to Boston and doing the tour. I was super keen. And very green.

I thought they were all very nice guys, and very committed to what they were doing. They never really complained about anything, even when conditions were a bit rough. I felt pretty lucky to be there. I was in over my head at the time. I had been mixing bands in bars and some small arenas for about two years, but zero touring. They gave me a lot of opportunities. I just tried to keep up!

(handwritten notes, top right)
Jan 16 Feb 20
Ardnt Studios
5 × 250 = 1250
+ MCt = 329.8

(handwritten notes, lower left)
14579.83
13979 live & studio

769.32 CAPAC
15349.15 total
14749.00

expenses
legal   100
compressor   210.60
             138.00
ins   40.00
strings   627.00
cables etc   250.00 tunes 334.80 158
phone   } 1000.00
courier   1243.61
auto ins.   1029.90 (mountaince)
van repairs/lease
lease   1381.99
gas   1000

(live) 98 × 20 = 1960   needs   500
studio 35 × 20 = 700
2660
3160 ?

total exp 9731.10
net 5018.05

Chicago Fri June 23
1 She Didn't Know
2 3 Pistols
3 All Cdn Surf
4 Opiated
5 Baby Please Don't Go
6 Trickle Down
7 Boots -PAUL
(Acoustic 8 Last U.S.A -ROB
9 7 Days
10 Wait So Long
11 38 Years Odd -PAUL
12 Blow -ROB
13 I'll Believe
14 Small Town
15 Killing Time
16 New Orleans
17 Weight

THE TRAGICALLY HIP

Top: Rick's American Cafe, East Lansing, MI, 8 July 1989

Above right: California, July 1989

Right: Logo created as part of the Up to Here art

GORD S: Pretty soon into our first tour of the United States in 1989 we realised just how much work we had to do down there. Canada, despite how difficult it is to tour with the distances and the grind of the travel, in a lot of ways is easier. In Winnipeg, Manitoba on a Tuesday night in the middle of winter, people appreciate someone that's coming to play. In the States, it's a little more like, 'Show me what you got, because there's someone else better than you guys playing across town.' But it was great for us, because it gave us a real us against them mentality and reinforced how tight we were as a group. We literally thought it was just a matter of time before we would break in the States.

On that first tour we were in Madison, Wisconsin playing our acoustic guitars in this dingy basement bar in our cowboy boots and dungarees, and the opening band was ... Nirvana. They had twice as many people in the audience to see them as we did, and we were like, 'Holy fuck. Things have changed overnight.' It turned out that they were going to change a whole lot more for those guys. It was a different urban dynamic. In a lot of ways, it was the rebirth of a different wave of post-punk and it was very American. Again, that was a great learning experience for the group and reinforced our approach, which was always to focus on the next gig, the next record, one thing at a time. We were happy for our successes, always aspirational, but also quite humble with our status, and grateful for it too.

November 2, 1989

THE TRAGICALLY HIP

TOUR ITINERARY – SEPTEMBER/OCTOBER 1989

Sept.	25	Kitchener – Stages
	26	Barrie – The Roxx
	27	London – Dr. Rockets
	28	Hamilton – Dallas
	29	Ottawa – Barrymores
Oct.	3	Toronto – The Diamond
	6&7	Winnipeg – Spectrum
	10&11	Regina – The Venue
	12	Calgary – The Old Scotch
	13	Calgary – McKewan Hall, University of Calgary
	14	Edmonton – Dinwoodie Hall, University of Alberta
	16&17	Whistler – Buffalo Bills
	18	OFF
	19	Victoria – The Forge
	20&21	Vancouver – 86th Street Music Hall
	31	Calgary – KIK-FM Halloween Party
Nov.	2	Eastern Sound – "Command Performance"

*** The shows occurring from Sept. 25 to Oct. 3 will have
The Phantoms as supporting act.

THE TRAGICALLY HIP

TOUR ITINERARY – NOVEMBER 1989

Nov.	7	Toronto, Ontario	C.A.S.B.Y. Awards
	8	Montreal, Quebec	HMV store opening
	10-12	Halifax, Nova Scotia	Misty Moon
	13	Frederickton, New Brunswick	Chesnut Cabaret
	14	Moncton, New Brunswick	Ziggy's
	16	Sydney, Nova Scotia	Capri Lounge
	17	Sackville, New Brunswick	Mt. Alison University
	18	Wolfville, Nova Scotia	Acadia University
	24	Montreal, Quebec	Club Soda

... more U.S. dates to follow.

Nov.	28	Boston, Massachusetts	The Channel
	29	New York City, New York	Tramps
	30	Hoboken, New Jersey	Live Tonight
Dec. 1 & 2		Ardmore (Philly), Pennsylvania	23 East Cabaret
	4	Richmond, Virginia	Twisters
	5	Washington, D.C.	The Bayou
	6	Pittsburgh, Pennsylvania	Graffitti
	8	Milwaukee, Wisconsin	Odd Rock Cafe
	9	Chicago, Illinois	The Avalon

We played a lot of shows with The Phantoms and for a while we had an apartment in Toronto with Joe Toole, the band's guitarist, who was a great guy. (RB)

GORD S: One of the best learning experiences we ever had was on that first tour of the States. It was the first tour that we did in a tour bus and, as far as we were concerned, it was just a matter of time before we were going to have our own DC-10 with 'The Hip' written across the side of it. We got to Bloomington, Indiana, which is where John Mellencamp is from, and we thought that this had got to be a great rock town to produce someone like him. But when we got into the bar that we were playing, there were four people there. One table of American guys from Chicago. It was deflating, but we'd played shit gigs before and we knew that we were going to have to play them again. So we got up on stage and played. We didn't fold like a tent. We actually really dug in and played a great show.

ROB: We gave those four guys everything we had and at the end of the set one of them got up and smashed his chair on the floor, demanding an encore. So we came out and gave them a full encore. And the four people that were at that show, we must've seen them at 40 shows after that through the years.

GORD S: We learned a really important lesson that anybody can play a sold-out show in downtown Toronto on a Friday night but part of coming up is learning how to play the half-empty rooms, or the completely empty rooms. That's what makes you what you are.

We would always find a way to turn it around on stage. Johnny was remarkable for deflating really crappy situations and turning them into a laugh, and it just reaffirmed how close we were as buds and as bandmates.

It made us a better band because we went from playing 500- or 1,000-seaters in Canada to literally starting over again when we got to the west coast of the States. We realised right away that it was going be ten times as hard as Canada was.

We had learned to play a hockey rink like we were in a small club and we learned to play a small club like a hockey rink – and that's because we were jumping back and forth across the border all the time. We also learned most importantly to never take it for granted. A good show was based on how the band was playing, not on how many tickets you sold.

MONDAY SEPT 25TH

HITS RADIO AM 109 presents

THE TRAGICALLY HIP

with special guests the phantoms

Stage's

312 KING STREET W. 744-2000

advance tickets only $6.00
available at Stages, Records on wheels(Cambridge),
R.P.M. in Waterloo, U. of W. Record store & Sams(Kitchener)
proper dress is required

DATE Nov. 18 19 89
NAME The Tragically Hip.
ADDRESS
POSTAL CODE

QUANTITY	DESCRIPTION	AMOUNT
	payment for one performance	
	TOTAL	250.—

96751

The TRAGICALLY hip

*Top: On stage,
1989/early 1990*

*Above left: Leslie
Galbraith's apartment,
Kingston, 1989*

*Above right: Lakeview
Manor, Kingston, 1989*

*Left: Promo photo,
February 1989*

Co-Publishing Agreement (Executed Contract)

CO-PUBLISHING AGREEMENT

Executed Contract

THIS AGREEMENT made and effective as of the 1st day of July, 1989.

BETWEEN:

(Handwritten form — "NOTIFICATION OF NEW WORKS", Composers Authors and Publishers Association of Canada Limited. Titles of work listed include:)

Title of Work	Duration of Music
Weight Comes Down	3:50
I'll Believe in You	3:50
Just Another Midnight	4:10
Trickle Down	3:30
Roots and Hearts	3:20
38 Years Old	4:30
New Orleans is Sinking	3:30
Opiated	
Blow at High Dough	4:20
Everytime You Go	3:20
She Didn't Know	

Authors of the words / composers of the music listed as: Robert Baker, Paul Langlois, Gordon Sinclair, Gordon Downie, John Fay (handwritten throughout). Publisher: Roll / Little Smoke Music (UMP).

ROB: I think from the very beginning, everyone had aspirations to be a songwriter, but in those first couple of years Gord Sinclair was head and shoulders above everyone else. That created healthy competition; it made everyone want to step up and contribute to the songs.

GORD D: A song that we write is not really a song that *we* write until every guy has put a stamp on it. It's not really a song until Johnny plays the drums or Robbie plays his part, or whatever. Everyone seems to bring stuff, or something comes out of a jam. But we feel that it's too ridiculous to try and split hairs all the time, because we just won't last – we'll break up or something or get too egotistical about it. And I can't be driving a Rolls and poor Paul is going around with a ten speed. So it's a band credit.

It was the first and maybe the last time the five of us sat in a space with an agenda and it was very official and political. We decided we were going to share writing credits across the board. We were trying to hypothesise about the future and problems that we could foresee happening. And if we didn't do this, then we were going to split hairs over who wrote the songs, and who did this and who did that. And we thought the only way we could really make it was if the five of us were together, and relatively happy with the scene. That was the first and biggest issue to cement and it was hard. But we all agreed. And the decision we made has completely trickled down into every facet of the band, from flipping coins for interviews to who gets to ride shotgun. And it works.

PAUL: Early on, we had a meeting in my parents' basement, where we decided that all the songs should be credited to The Tragically Hip. We shouldn't say who wrote what and we should have equal credit, and therefore equal money. We all felt it was the best bet for us to stay together, because otherwise there was a danger of negative feelings of resentment and over-competitiveness creeping in. Once we all knew everything was going to be credited to the band, we kept wanting to put the ideas in and nobody lost any sleep over one of their songs not making it. We were always playing together, feeding off each other, so it really made sense to do everything as a group.

JOHNNY: Gord said it was really important that we stick together and don't screw around with money over music publishing. Because for Gord, money wasn't really very important. I never heard him talk about how much we were getting for a gig in 32 years.

Later I was talking to Dan Aykroyd and he asked me how we dealt with royalties in The Hip. When I told him that we split them equally, he was amazed that we would do things that way. But that decision is really what kept the band together. When you get money out of the way, then you just start doing the art.

PAUL: The equal-credit decision was made a couple of years before it started to become obvious that Gord was leaving us behind when it came to lyric writing. We were still throwing songs at him, but then he'd read the lyrics that someone was suggesting and be like, 'I don't get that. What does this mean?' He expressed it in a nice way, that he couldn't get his head into singing other people's lyrics. We were feeling almost overwhelmed with our roles anyway, especially in the studio, so we accepted it fairly quickly. Even though we still felt very engaged in the songwriting process, we could see that he was just better than us at writing lyrics and his unique style was giving us some identity.

GORD S: That was a difficult band meeting and I'm sure it was really difficult for Gord to bring up. At that point it was undeniable that Gord was a really good lyricist; he had a really great turn of phrase and he was the one that was up there singing the lyrics. As a performer, Gord never ever lacked for authenticity and if it meant that it was a more authentic and commanding performance for him to sing his own words, I totally got that.

Gord didn't demand, he asked, which is a tribute to him. So it wasn't contentious. He just felt that it was important, that he had things to express. I learned from him about the necessity of making the lyrics authentic and really looking deep inside.

JAKE GOLD: When Gord said that he only wanted to sing his own lyrics, he made it clear that this wasn't a cash grab. He didn't want to get half the money as the lyricist. Everyone knew that Gord was writing the lyrics, but from a financial standpoint it was a five-way split – still is to this day. I think the other guys really didn't care; they were fine creating the music with him.

Most bands over the years have broken up over publishing rights, so I think this was one of the things that kept them together.

GORD S: When Gord took over writing the lyrics it became apparent really quickly that it freed the rest of us up, from a musical perspective, to throw more ideas into the mix. Our output really increased because Gord was a prolific songwriter and a great diarist. So, while we were riding along in the van, he always had a Moleskine on the go, jotting down little turns of phrase or great words that he would stumble on while he was reading on the road.

He was prolific and we were prolific as a group. That led to a situation where we would always have more songs than we needed to choose from when we were getting ready to go in the studio.

Naturally your ego gets bruised and you slightly resent the situation. Both Paul and I got our wings clipped a little bit in terms of our ability to evolve as songwriters. But the most important thing was the band, and the band lived and died on the material.

ROB: The decision that Gord would only sing his own lyrics, while I understand it from his point of view, I do think it set parameters on the songwriting. We always came to the songwriting very open-hearted – a song can write itself in any number of ways. And when you think you've exhausted all the ways, you find a new one. But now we were limited a little bit as to where the ideas could come from and that was a tough pill to swallow for Gord Sinclair and Paul. In the early days, Sinclair was the only one writing full songs so it must have been a gut punch for him. But he did what was best for the band and sucked it up like a good soldier. He lost the battle but won the war, because the band stayed together and it benefited everyone.

It was part of a campaign of whispering in Gord's ear: 'You're the star. They're just a backup band. We can change these people out and get a really good guitar player. Johnny's a good drummer, but we could get the top LA session drummer' – that kind of shit. Gord was very resistant to it, but he did have artistic ambitions to be a poet, to be a great lyricist, and some of the people who were in the inner circle knew that and abused that. Gord was well on his way to becoming a great lyricist before this whisper campaign. *Road Apples* is full of great songs that are his lyrics. And everyone knew he was really into it. I think if it had developed in a more natural way, Gord would've ended up writing 90 or even 100 percent of the lyrics anyways.

JOHNNY: Gord was very consistent about the way he wanted things to go for him. His instrument was his voice and he just felt that the only authentic way for him to use that instrument was to sing his own lyrics.

> **GORD S: Robbie and I are the eldest, Gord and Paul are in the middle, and Johnny's considerably younger, so we were like brothers. Brothers are always resenting what the other guy has and I think Gord really wanted to mark out his piece of turf. It seems crazy to be saying that he was insecure about his position in the band, because I would stand and watch him night after night thinking, 'Damn. I wish I could do that.' But, in retrospect, perhaps he'd see us sitting around in hotel rooms playing guitar and wish that he could do what we were doing.**

Campbell St. STATION   "The FOX" 99.9 FM   505 Campbell St.
Sarnia, Ont.
336-9960

presents

"THE TRAGICALLY HIP"

Tuesday, Feb. 13/90 doors open at 7:00 p.m.
Must be 19 years and over to enter
$6.00 Advance $8.00 at the Door

Gen. Adm.   № 596

KEY WEST CLUB
WINDSOR, ONT.
PRESENTS

TRAGICALLY HIP

THURS. FEB 22   107
For Information... Call (519) 254 - 5131

ADMISSION
$8.00   advance
$10.00 at door
DOORS OPEN
AT
7:00 P.M.

107

SAT FEB 17 1990

DALLAS

GENERAL ADMISSION
ADVANCE $7.00
AT DOOR $8.00

SEC   ROW   SEAT

SAT FEB 17 1990

DOORS OPEN 7 PM

Stage

CONCERT
PRESENTATION

Monday February 19th

the
TRAGICALLY
HIP $7.00

Doors open at 7pm

312 KING ST. WEST
further info call
744-2000
must be 19 or over

SEATING NOT GUARANTEED

T H E
TRAGICALLY
HIP

Monday, March 5

Doors open 8pm. Show 10pm

$10 advance or door

The VENUE

1326 Hamilton

203

THE SUTHERLAND BAR
PRESENTS

"The Tragically Hip"
With Special Guests

March 7, 1990

Tickets $10.00 per person

121

Doors Open
8:00 p.m.
I.D. Required

$8.00

NO REFUNDS OR EXCHANGES

BUFFALO BILL'S
PRESENT

THE TRAGICALLY HIP

DOORS 9:00P
MONDAY MARCH 1   (220)

SUBJECT TO CONDITIONS ON REV

$8.00

CARDHOLDER $6

NO MINORS

GEN. ADM. 0007

SEC   ROW

$8.00

CARDHOLDER $6

NO MINORS

GEN. ADM. 0007

GEN. ADM. 002

NO MINORS

CARDHOLDERS

ADULT $8

NO REFUNDS OR EXCHANGES

BUFFALO BIL

PRESENT

THE TRAGICAL

WED MARCH 1

SUBJECT TO CONDITIONS ON

$8.00

CARDHOLDERS

NO MINOR

GEN. ADM. 00

THE REGENT PRESENTS
MCA RECORDING ARTISTS

THE TRAGICALLY HIP

WEDNESDAY APRIL 25, 1990

ADMISSION
$12.50 Tax Incl.   NO REFUNDS

/60

25

Tragically Hip: Technical Rider

.H. Specs:

king console must have a minimum of 32 inputs, with fully sweepable
q. on all channels (e.g.: Soundcraft 800B/6000, Yamaha PM 1800/3000,
C Scorpion are all acceptable consoles.)

31 band equalizers (Klark Teknik or equiv.)

compressors in line on system (dbx, UREI, BSS or equiv.)

insertable compressors (BSS 402, Drawmer, Valley People, or equiv.)

noise gates (Drawmer, Valley People, BSS or equiv.)

digital reverb units (Yamaha REV 5, Lexicon PCM 70, or equiv.)

digital delay units (Yamaha D1500, Lexicon, or equiv.)

. Specs:

stem must be in stereo

stem must also be able to provide 10 watts per person minimum (i.e.:
) seats=5000 watts)

eferred systems include Adamson, Turbosound TMS 3/ S-4, or equiv.)

rophone Specs:

vocal mics (EV 757, Shure Beta 58, or equiv.)

Shure SM 57

condensor mics

nnheiser MD 421, Or EV 408

EV RE20, or AKG D112

irect boxes

The Tragically Hip Tour 90

Feb.	13	Sarnia	Campbell St. Station
	14	Brantford	Club 234
	17	Hamilton	Dallas
	19	Kitchener	Stages
	22	Windsor	Key West
	24	Chicago	Cabaret Metro
	25	Milwaukee	Shank Hall
March	1	Thunder Bay	Lakehead University
	2&3	Winnipeg	Rendevous
	5	Regina	The Venue
	6	Moose Jaw	Watts On Main
	7	Saskatoon	Sutherland Hotel
	8	Calgary	Silver Dollar
	9	Edmonton	Dinwoodie Lounge
	10	Calgary	S.A.I.T.
	12-14	Whistler	Buffalo Bills
	15	Penticton	Tiffany's
	16	Kelowna	Sizzles
	17	T.B.A.	
	18	T.B.A.	
	19	Seattle	Backstage
	20	T.B.A.	
	21	Nanaimo	Rascals
	22	Victoria	The Forge
	23-24	Vancouver	86th St. Music Hall
	29	Cambridge	The Highlands
	30	Toronto	Concert Hall
	31	Burlington	Clancy's
April	12	Montreal	Le Spectrum

... Ottawa and Eastern Canada to follow.

THE TRAGICALLY HIP
Monitor Stand

Ch	Description	Mic	Stand	1	2	3	4	5	6	7	8	CH		Ch
1	KICK	D.I.												1
2	KICK			x	x			x	x	x		1		2
3	SNARE TOP							x	x	x		2		3
4	SNARE BOTTEM													4
5	HATS						x					3		5
6	RACK TOM						x					4		6
7	FLOOR TOM						x					5		7
8	O.H. RIDE													8
9	O.H. CRASH													9
10	BASS	D.I.		x	x		x	x	x	x		6		10
11	BASS													11
12	GUITAR S.R.				x			x	x	x		7		12
13	GUITAR S.L.				x			x	x	x		8		13
14	ACOUSTIC S.R.	D.I.		x	x			x	x	x		10		14
15	VOCAL S.R.					x	x	x				11		15
16	VOCAL C.S.	Round Base	x	x	x	x	x	x				12		16
17	VOCAL S.L.				x	x	x			x	x				17
18														18
19														19
20														20
21														21
22														22
23														23
24														24
25														25
26														26
27														27
28														28
29														29
30														30
31														31
				1	2	3	4	5	6	7	8			32

Turn over for stage plan

CLUB PLOT - THE TRAGICALLY HIP
DOWN STAGE

UP STAGE

CONCERT PLOT - THE TRAGICALLY HIP
DOWN STAGE

Pacific Coliseum V.I.P. BOX

GEN. ADM. 00600
NO MINORS
STRATHCONA HOTEL
ADULT $7.00
NO REFUNDS OR EXCHANGES
THE FORGE
PRESENTS
THE TRAGICALLY HIP
DOORS 7:30PM
THUR MARCH 22/90
SUBJECT TO CONDITIONS ON REVERSE
ADULT $7.00
STRATHCONA HOTEL
NO MINORS
GEN. ADM. 00600

THE TRAGICALLY HIP &
GUESTS PRES. BY MOLSON
& 107 KIK FM - NO MINORS
LIVE AT SILVER DOLLAR
LIGHT MEAL 6:30PM-7:30PM
THUR. MAR.8/90 8:00 PM
GENERAL ADM   ADULT
GA GEN. ADM   17.75
S/C INCLUDED
SEC   ROW   SEAT
GEN. ADM. 00159

NO REFUNDS OR EXCHANGES
BUFFALO BILL'S
PRESENT
THE TRAGICALLY HI
DOORS 9:00PM
TUESDAY MARCH 13/9
$8.00
CARDHOLDERS $6
NO MINORS
GEN. ADM. 00159
SEC   ROW   SEAT
$8.00
CARDHOLDERS $6
NO MINORS
GEN. ADM. 00159

HIGHLANDS
(519)622-0002
Ticket No   834
THE TRAGICALLY HIP
DOORS 7:30PM
THUR MARCH 29/90
SUBJECT TO CONDITIONS ON REVERSE
ADULT $7.00
STRATHCONA HOTEL
NO MINORS
GEN. ADM. 00600
SEC   ROW   SEAT
DOOR $8.00
STRATHCONA HOTEL
NO MINORS
GEN. ADM. 00600

TRAGICALLY HIP
CLANCY'S LIVE
4460 FAIRVIEW ST
(APPLEVIEW SQ.)
BURLINGTON, ONTARIO
DOORS OPEN 7 PM
SAT MAR 31 1990
$3.00
GENERAL ADMISSION

MONQUI PRESENTS
THE TRAGICALLY HIP
FLIES ON FIRE
PORTLAND MAY 14 KEY LARGO
SEATTLE MAY 15 & THE DHARMA BUMS MOORE THEATRE

No 000257
GOOD ONLY
FRI. APRIL 27
9:30 p.m.
Admission $12.50
CLUB CAPRI
Sydney, Nova Scotia
And CLUB CAPRI
Presents
TRAGICALLY HIP
in Concert
APRIL 27 1990
CLUB CAPRI
CANADA ROCKS
No 000257
TRAGICALLY HIP
FRI. APRIL 27

The Tragically Hip: Stage Rider

Backline Specs:

-2 100 watt guitar heads (Mesa Boogie, Seymour Duncan, Marshall, or Randall)

-2-4 x 12 speaker cabinets compatable with supplied amplifiers

-1 400 watt bass head with a compatible cabinet consisting of 2-10" speakers,
 and 1-15" speaker

Drum Specs:

-1-22" bass drum

-1-12" tom

-1-13" tom

-1-14 Or 16" floor tom

-drums must be Ayotte, Yamaha, or Pearl

-all necessary hardware for drums, plus three cymbal stands of heavy construction

*Live and promo photos,
New York, 1990 (this
page and opposite, top)*

*Live, circa 1990
(opposite, bottom)*

RB: We had four or five days to rehearse and acclimatise to the humidity before going into the studio. It could be 115 degrees in Phoenix, but that's not nearly as hot as 80 degrees in New Orleans.

Above: Outside Kingsway Studios, New Orleans, 1990

From l to r: Paul Langlois, Gord Downie, Rob Baker, Gord Sinclair, Don Smith, Bruce Barris, Johnny Fay

ROB: We had a lot of confidence coming off *Up to Here*; it had done much better than we ever expected. On the first record, you're kind of thrown into it and it's a whole new experience. The second time around we were more relaxed and more confident. We were working with Don again and we knew he got the band and we were able to stretch out, relax a bit and just enjoy ourselves. We were confident in the material we had.

We felt like we were a legit band. We had an album and a half or two albums out now and we felt like this next album was going to be better than the last one. Everyone knew about the sophomore curse, but we thought, 'No, we're good. We're armed to the teeth with songs.'

JOHNNY: We always were able to come up with ideas on the road, little snippets here and there. I remember how important it was to be writing for the second record while we were touring *Up to Here*. We would go back and forth with Don on the phone and he said he was going to buy some tape because he could tell we were going to be recording soon.

BRUCE DICKINSON: We wanted to continue with Don Smith producing the band because it had gone so well the first time. Often first albums are a bit of a sacrificial lamb, but that was not entirely the case with *Up to Here*. It did get some recognition and some listeners, based on its sheer quality. You're knocking on the door with the first album and it takes a lot of blows before someone opens that door. We almost got there – and if the record company had continued to work on 'New Orleans Is Sinking' we might have broken through a little more.

BRUCE DICKINSON: Don Smith was a no-brainer to me. The band loved him, and he loved the band. So it was only a matter of deciding where to record. We chose Memphis for *Up to Here* because it had this really good musical vibe, so we thought maybe we could go a little further south to New Orleans. We wanted a place where you couldn't ignore the music coming out of every little store and restaurant and club. They weren't playing the top 40 or the top AOR songs of the day; they were playing New Orleans music. Everyone thought that would be a great place to do an album. And that's how we ended up at Kingsway.

GORD S: The city is just so full of character everywhere you go, from the buildings, to the cab drivers, to the people on the street, to everybody you meet. It was unlike anything that we had ever seen. And full credit to Don Smith and Bruce Dickinson for taking us out of our element and down to that environment so we could soak it up and channel it into the record that we were making.

JOHNNY: Gord drove down to New Orleans with two or three of his buddies during a reading week break when he was at Queen's. It was a really memorable trip; he talked about it a lot. They camped out in the famous cemetery that was in *Easy Rider* and dropped acid. They didn't have a lot of money, but they soaked the city in. So when we were going to New Orleans to work with Don again, Gord was the most excited. He kept telling us, 'You're not gonna believe this city!'

BRUCE DICKINSON: Before I met up with the band, the first thing I did when I checked into my hotel room was hit the swimming pool. I distinctly remember sitting in that pool thinking, 'I cannot believe how humid this place is.' It was like you were getting a hurricane, but there wasn't a hurricane. And then, all of a sudden, this huge swarm of bats came swooping out of the sky, about ten feet off the ground, in formation. And it was like, 'Oh, welcome to New Orleans.' And then, of course, you realised that the reason there were so many bats was because there were so many bugs ...

Kingsway Studios, New Orleans

JOHNNY: Kingsway was a great old southern mansion. It had secret passageways and servants' quarters and grand chandeliers and the sound was bouncing – it was very alive. At the top of the stairs was the cross of Marie Laveau, the Voodoo Queen of all New Orleans. There were black candles that we were told not to light because they were voodoo candles. And there was a stuffed lynx and that thing was always staring at you. So it was a little weird, but I loved it.

ROB: You felt the history all around you. I don't believe in ghosts, but if there were ghosts that was the type of place where you were going to see them. The home was three storeys, but five storeys in the back where the slave quarters were once located … that is the history you are in. It was a strange place in a strange city where different cultures meet. In New Orleans, there is good history and bad history meeting in one spot and we just soaked it all up.

PAUL: We were staying in a bed and breakfast in the French Quarter, about a block away from the studio. There was no breakfast though, and there weren't really enough beds either – it involved a couch or two.

Approaching it from the street, you'd never know that Kingsway Studio was a mansion. It was just a wall, but behind it was a gorgeous house – vibes everywhere. We were very excited to be there, and very confident in the songs we had. And happy to be working with Don Smith again.

JAKE GOLD: They went into the studio for *Road Apples* less prepared than they were for *Up to Here*. There was a lot of jamming and Don was just running tape. We went through about 50 or 60 reels of two-inch tape, which was really expensive back then. The tape bill was something like $12,000 – you can make records for that today. But it gave them a chance to stretch, musically.

PAUL: We did a lot of takes with Don, with both *Up to Here* and *Road Apples*. He always wanted to grab the best one. The red light only comes on once in a while, and you want to nail it when it does. Apparently, it took Tom Petty and the Heartbreakers 125 takes to get 'Refugee' with him.

ROB: Don would say, "'Fight': take 58.' It would get harder and harder because there was a lot of guitar soloing. I'd play a solo 50 times and every time it was different because you didn't want to keep doing it the same way. But eventually he'd get one that felt good to him.

PAUL: One thing Don did for all of us was prove that a big shot producer doesn't have to act like a big shot producer. He was so down to earth, he just wanted to have fun, and he was funny.

At a technical level, what he did was separate my guitar from Rob's. There's a pan button – you used to be able to do it on the stereo in cars – and Don panned me on the left and Rob on the right, so we were kept totally separate. It freed me up but also made my role more important because you could hear both guitars. If you really wanted to know which of us was playing what, you just panned it one way or the other and you knew exactly.

Making both guitars highly audible was Don's way, I think, of identifying us as a band.

JOHNNY: Don Smith was like another drum teacher to me. He explained things about microphones and about consistency, especially with the bass drum. He spent time with me tuning the drums and helping with the set-up. We did interesting things with the drums on that record. There was a little bit of experimenting. Don had worked with the heaviest drummers in the world, so he knew what he was doing.

Opposite, top: producer Don Smith

Top right: Kingsway Studios, New Orleans, 1990. Back row (l to r): Gord Downie, Rob Baker, Johnny Fay, Gord Sinclair, Paul Langlois Seated (l to r): Bruce Barris, Don Smith, Mark Vreeken

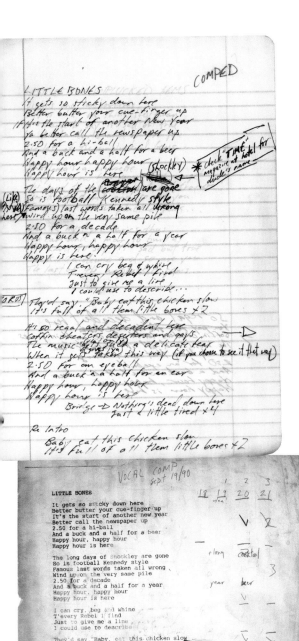

Iterations of 'Little Bones'

Opposite: Lyrics to 'The Last of the Unplucked Gems' (top)

Lyrics to 'The Luxury' and 'Twist My Arm' (middle)

Paul Langlois with cue finger buttered up, Kingsway Studios, New Orleans, 1990 (bottom)

GORD D: 'Little Bones' was intended to be about New Orleans, but it came from a lot of different things. I'd read *Last of the Crazy People* by Timothy Findley, a Canadian author. The kid in the book keeps lots of cats and one of the cats is called Little Bones. And I thought it'd be great to write a song called 'Little Bones'. This is like months before [we went to New Orleans]. I wrote it down, and then we were in a cab and a guy says something like, 'You gotta eat that chicken slow, because it's full of all those little bones.' I'm like, 'Little bones, yeah …!' So it just goes from there. And then, being in New Orleans when we put it all together, we were playing pool the first night we got there and the cue wouldn't slide through my fingers properly.

I could just dissect the song, but it wouldn't mean anything. It would just be like throwing darts at a board. But altogether it conjures up a huge whole crazy image of New Orleans for me, being from Canada. That's what the song means to me, but maybe it doesn't make sense to anyone else.

ROB: 'Little Bones' was partly inspired by our first night in New Orleans. We thought we needed to get out and see some of the city and so we decided to go to Bourbon Street. What else are you going to do when you go to New Orleans? You don't go back there, but you do it once anyways.

GEDDY LEE: **'Little Bones' is one of those songs that I adored. I don't know what Gord was talking about, but it's not required. Great art leaves you with your own interpretation. You bring yourself to a song, you bring yourself into the art.**

JOHNNY: 'Little Bones' wasn't 'New Orleans Is Sinking' Part B, but it was Gord telling his next story about New Orleans. The experience of being in the city, the guys on Decatur Street yelling stuff out and Gord writing it all down. I loved it. Paul played this riff that floated around in God knows what area code. You listen to a Hip cover band play 'Little Bones' and they never get that bit right. And then, boom, Gord Sinclair and I hit that jump-off point for the rhythm. We rehearsed for a week before we got that pop. The song had so much nuts, it was awesome.

PAUL: 'Little Bones' was a New Orleans-inspired song. It's got some great references in there. It was an obvious opener for the album.

Gord Sinclair's riff was incredible. We all knew from the start that it was going to be good. I played it upside down unintentionally and that became the intro. I'm often asked how to play the intro, and it basically involves playing Sinclair's riff in a weird way.

GORD S: You write about what you know, or what you're learning on the way. Gord was our diarist. Playing billiards or snooker, in particular, was one of our great pastimes when we were on the road. But it was so humid in New Orleans that you had to put chalk between your index finger and your thumb to get the cue to slide, otherwise you couldn't get a proper stroke on the ball. Gord being the poet that he is, wrote, 'You better butter your cue finger up,' as opposed to chalk your cue finger up.

BRUCE DICKINSON: One reason why 'Little Bones' might not have worked for radio was that it came out at the height of the parental advisory period where there was all the brouhaha about song lyrics. The chorus was, 'Happy hour. Happy hour is here.' And there was all this stuff about drunk driving and drinking and that was an excuse that radio used against The Tragically Hip. It's a great song and if it came out today there would be no problem. If it had come out 20 years ago there would have been no problem, but at that particular time some people had a problem with the lyric of that song.

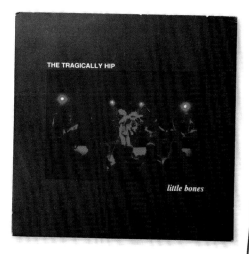

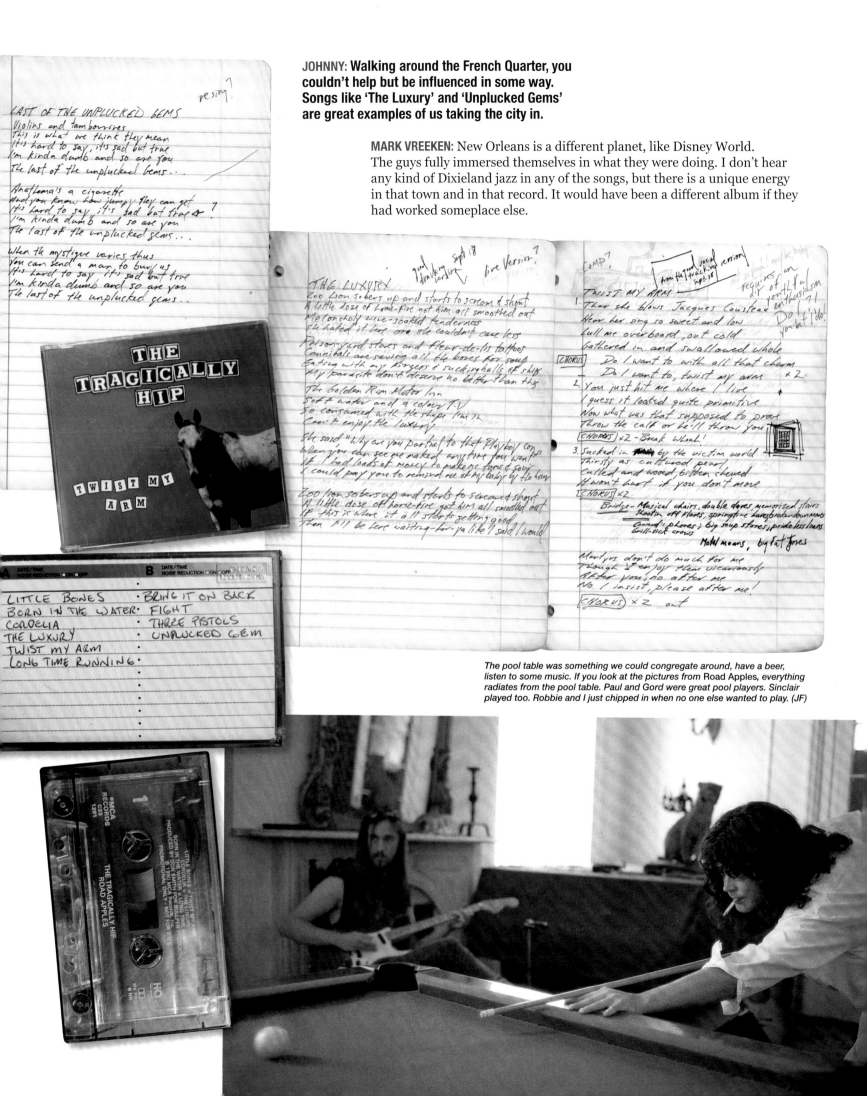

JOHNNY: **Walking around the French Quarter, you couldn't help but be influenced in some way. Songs like 'The Luxury' and 'Unplucked Gems' are great examples of us taking the city in.**

MARK VREEKEN: New Orleans is a different planet, like Disney World. The guys fully immersed themselves in what they were doing. I don't hear any kind of Dixieland jazz in any of the songs, but there is a unique energy in that town and in that record. It would have been a different album if they had worked someplace else.

The pool table was something we could congregate around, have a beer, listen to some music. If you look at the pictures from Road Apples, everything radiates from the pool table. Paul and Gord were great pool players. Sinclair played too. Robbie and I just chipped in when no one else wanted to play. (JF)

GORD S: My brother, Colin, was born with a congenital heart defect, where his heart was twisted and turned backwards in his body. He was the first kid to have what is now a common surgery called the Mustard procedure. It's open-heart surgery as an infant and very dangerous. Gord's nephew Charles had the same thing. We always had to be very conscious of Colin's level of exertion and stuff like that. We knew he wasn't going to be able to live a normal life.

He'd just gotten into KC and it was a September and I was just starting second year in university. It was his first high school dance and he was letting it go and had a massive electrical storm in his heart and died.

I was at Alfie's pub, boozing it up with some of the boys, and saw Robbie walk in. He came right over, said you gotta come with me. I was like, sit down and have a beer. No, you gotta come with me. A car was waiting out front, his girlfriend at the time was in the car and I knew something was up. We motored home super fast and my folks broke the news. Life changed immediately. There's nothing really to prepare you for not only the loss of your brother but the grief of your mom and dad. Robbie was across the street, so when my mom and dad went to bed I went right across the street to him – he was the only brother I had left at that point.

ROB: I'd never been that close to grief. As a parent you could never recover from that. Gord's dad had his work that he could pour himself into and Gord's always been a very mind over matter kind of guy and he poured himself into his school work and into the band. He just soldiered on, but we know that that stuff messes people up, festers inside you. But Gord's mom, it was so hard on her.

JOHNNY: I knew Colin Sinclair because he was a couple of grades below me. He was a beautiful, beautiful kid, always very cheerful. I was at the dance where he collapsed and passed away. I can't imagine what Dr and Mrs Sinclair and Gord went through.

I didn't know much about Colin's heart condition until afterwards. It was something he was born with and he knew about it but he didn't make a thing of it. He just lived his life with a smile. My dad was a paediatric cardiologist at Kingston General and Colin was one of his patients, but he didn't really speak about those kinds of things. We talked about it afterwards, of course.

Gord's very private and we were non-prying friends, but we knew that he was hurting. We used to rehearse at his house and there were all these great pictures of Colin, and I remember looking at them and thinking of that night. When Gord had a son, he named him after his brother, which I thought was beautiful.

GORD S: When Gord's nephew Charles died of the same thing, Gord came right over to my house. He was pretty upset. We didn't really have to talk about it because he knew that I knew what he was going through and what his family was going through. It was really something. We were always tight but that made us even tighter because we were comfortable expressing that emotion with each other. Sometimes it takes the trauma and the grief of something like that to really cement a relationship.

It wasn't long after Charles died, a couple days maybe, that I played Gord the riff for what became 'Fiddler's Green'. We were still working on our chops as songwriters individually; we hadn't got to the point where we were writing together all at the same time.

Gord was taking on the mantle as the principal lyricist of the band, which was a fantastic thing because he was so good at it. And the lyric for 'Fiddler's Green' was so profound. You think about Gord's sister, my mom, those boys and all those families that have to go through something like that and it's a beautiful song. It was life affirming in the sense that we'd grown up our whole lives being affected and inspired by the music that we were listening to, and then you cross that threshold where you're writing those songs yourself.

Sadly, we could never play the song live because our eyes would make contact from across the stage and we'd both have to turn away because the tears would well up. But, boy, it's a great piece of music. I'm still really proud of that song. We were always musically pushing things forward, always trying to become more than what we were, and that lyrical capacity to convey a narrative and an emotion and an arc all in the same encapsulating song was something that resonated with people.

If we're lucky enough to experience love in our lives, we will also experience that deep sense of loss, and it takes someone with Gord's talent as a lyricist to convey that. 'Fiddler's Green' is a nice melody, for sure, but Gord took it to another level. It inspires people and that's what we've always loved about music.

Previous pages, this page and opposite: Kingsway Studios, New Orleans, 1990

Opposite: Lyrics to 'Fiddler's Green'

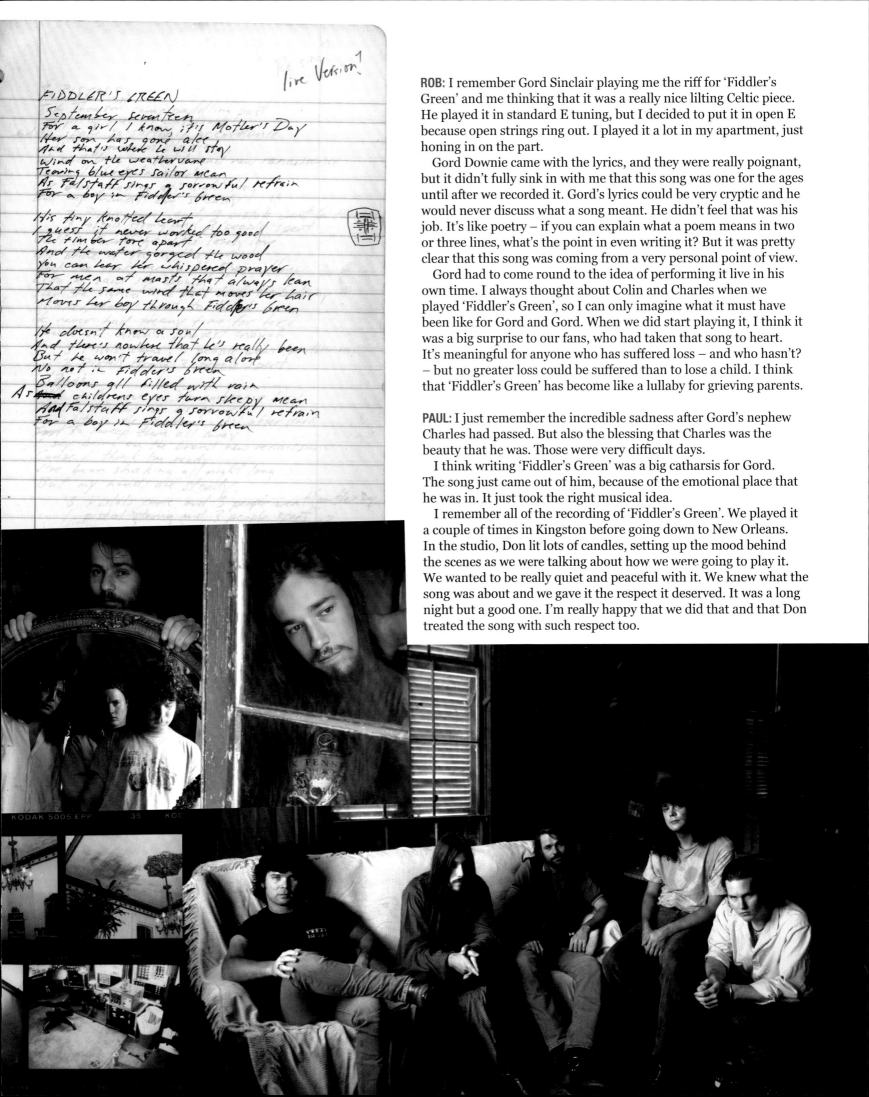

FIDDLER'S GREEN

September seventeen
For a girl I know; it's Mother's Day
Her son has gone alee
And that is where he will stay
Wind on the weathervane
Tearing blue eyes sailor mean
As Falstaff sings a sorrowful refrain
For a boy in Fiddler's Green

His tiny knotted heart
I guess it never worked too good
The timber tore apart
And the water gorged the wood
You can hear her whispered prayer
For men at masts that always lean
That the same wind that moves her hair
Moves her boy through Fiddler's Green

He doesn't know a soul
And there's nowhere that he's really been
But he won't travel long alone
No not in Fiddler's Green
Balloons all filled with rain
As childrens eyes turn sleepy mean
And Falstaff sings a sorrowful refrain
For a boy in Fiddler's Green

ROB: I remember Gord Sinclair playing me the riff for 'Fiddler's Green' and me thinking that it was a really nice lilting Celtic piece. He played it in standard E tuning, but I decided to put it in open E because open strings ring out. I played it a lot in my apartment, just honing in on the part.

Gord Downie came with the lyrics, and they were really poignant, but it didn't fully sink in with me that this song was one for the ages until after we recorded it. Gord's lyrics could be very cryptic and he would never discuss what a song meant. He didn't feel that was his job. It's like poetry – if you can explain what a poem means in two or three lines, what's the point in even writing it? But it was pretty clear that this song was coming from a very personal point of view.

Gord had to come round to the idea of performing it live in his own time. I always thought about Colin and Charles when we played 'Fiddler's Green', so I can only imagine what it must have been like for Gord and Gord. When we did start playing it, I think it was a big surprise to our fans, who had taken that song to heart. It's meaningful for anyone who has suffered loss – and who hasn't? – but no greater loss could be suffered than to lose a child. I think that 'Fiddler's Green' has become like a lullaby for grieving parents.

PAUL: I just remember the incredible sadness after Gord's nephew Charles had passed. But also the blessing that Charles was the beauty that he was. Those were very difficult days.

I think writing 'Fiddler's Green' was a big catharsis for Gord. The song just came out of him, because of the emotional place that he was in. It just took the right musical idea.

I remember all of the recording of 'Fiddler's Green'. We played it a couple of times in Kingston before going down to New Orleans. In the studio, Don lit lots of candles, setting up the mood behind the scenes as we were talking about how we were going to play it. We wanted to be really quiet and peaceful with it. We knew what the song was about and we gave it the respect it deserved. It was a long night but a good one. I'm really happy that we did that and that Don treated the song with such respect too.

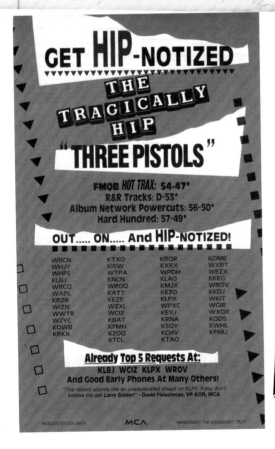

BRUCE DICKINSON: 'Three Pistols' was the first song we came up with from *Road Apples* having tested out 'Little Bones' with some radio people and gotten the negative reaction because of the drinking aspect of it. I know that Tom Thomson was a Canadian artist, but I thought the song had a universal quality to it. It didn't matter to the listener if you knew it was based on a true event in Canada, just as when you buy a paperback book it doesn't matter whether the story really took place or where it happened.

I thought it was a great song and it was a song that made you listen to the lyrics. A lot of people have said that one reason the band never broke in the States was because of all the Canadian references. I held what may have been the minority opinion that that didn't matter. All my friends knew who Leonard Cohen was. We'd all read *Beautiful Losers*, so it wasn't like a certain artistic bent or intellectual curiosity stopped at the border. The songs were great songs.

My view of 'Fifty Mission Cap' on the third album was, 'Are you gonna tell me that Americans don't know what hockey is?' What happened to Bill Barilko is actually a very compelling story. So I've never thought that the 'Canadian-ness' of the lyrics was a negative.

No one at the label ever brought up the Canadian references in the lyrics. If I remember right, some radio people used it as an excuse. I did hear an A&R guy at another company say that the Canadian aspect of some of the song lyrics was a problem. I asked him to give me an example, and he couldn't.

GEDDY LEE: I remember listening to *Road Apples* over and over again, back when I lived in the country and I would drive into the city.

The Hip's records live on because repeated listening does the music justice; you fall in love with it more and you understand the nuances. And to a Canadian audience, those nuances were born in this country.

ROB: The US is very good at tending its mythology, to the point where facts and reality are irrelevant. We always lamented the fact that Canadians were terrible with their mythology. Everyone in the US knows the story of Amelia Earhardt, but what about Bill Barilko? He disappeared in a plane too. What about Tom Thomson? How did he die? Was it a fishing accident?

Why doesn't anyone write about these people? Why do Canadian bands go to the States and write songs about going to Hollywood High? It seemed ridiculous to us not to write from personal experience. There was this vast untapped reservoir of stories. They're not our own stories, but they're all of our stories.

JAKE GOLD: I loved *Road Apples*, but the record company thought it was DOA. They didn't hear any singles. Al Teller, the president of MCA, told us that he'd pay for the record, but he wasn't going to pay for any videos or marketing. So we ended up paying for the 'Little Bones' video. Another shitty video.

ROB: A lot of the 'Little Bones' video I found embarrassing. We had a very clear concept for it, which was to film us playing at the Horseshoe then project the performance on a screen after the Horseshoe was closed and all the chairs were on the tables. The idea was to show the ghosts of all the great nights that place had seen – we'd show the records on the walls, the darkened hallways down into the basement, the cowboy and cowgirl washrooms.

But instead they injected a storyline, which looked like it was about an abortion or a miscarriage, and there was Gord in a bathtub full of milk. Where did that come from? It probably wouldn't have done as well on video stations if they'd stuck with our concept, but at least I'd be able to watch it now.

GORD D: It's easy for me to say I hate the videos because we make really shitty ones, but I don't hate them. I understand completely how they work and they're for people that really like videos, the same people that really like reading *Rolling Stone* magazine. As far as I'm concerned, it's just business and the videos sell the record. It's advertising and that's cool. I guess if we made better ones, or maybe we'd gotten more involved with them, or maybe if we were more artistic in that sense but when we finish making a record, we're pretty much spent as far as that goes. Maybe if we conjured up some video ideas when we were in the studio and the songs were freshest, they'd be OK. But we wait, and then they're just silly to us. The harder we try, the sillier they get.

Hi everyone!

Hope you had a good Christmas. Well, as you likely already know I've heard the new album and love it. As a result of loving it I couldn't help dreaming and that inevitably led to the reason for this letter. I think I have a great concept that would fit most of the tunes on the album. The pacing of the cuts and motion would be altered to fit the specific tune. It's not expensive as videos go but it is still getting into larger dollars. Anyway let me know what you think.

Hope the New Year's gig in Vancouver went well. Take care!

Sincerely,

Richard

Concept
by Richard McNeal
Unreel Film Productions Inc., Calgary, Alberta
(403) 279-2693
TRAGICALLY HIP VIDEO
Non Specific - General - New Album "Road Apples"

Location: Warehouse or Soundstage in Calgary or Vancouver

Scene: An elevated stage is dressed with a fire-proof set. The set consists of an old gas station false front with two old 8' cylindrical gas pumps. Numbers of antique signs and equipment decorate the station.

Scenario: The band plays to a live crowd with the gas station set as the background. As the band plays to the crowd Paul Langlois strikes a match on his guitar strings and lights a cigarette and drops the match to the ground. The camera follows the match to the ground where it ignites a fire trail. The fire trail rushes to each member of the band (At this point 5 stunt men would replace the band members. Having watched video recordings of the band they would imitate specific characteristics of each band member.)

Each band member (stunt man) bursts into flames and continues to play. (As well all of the guitars will be on fire to help disguise the fact that band members are not playing. The drum kit will not be on fire. It would be difficult to see Johnny Fay if the drum kit were burning. Expendable replacements would be used for all instruments.)

There would be wide shots of all five band members burning taken both facing the stage and facing the crowd. Footage of various band members burning as they play would be intercut with good clean 35mm footage of the band members not burning. Example: a shot of Bobby Baker or Gordon Sinclair burning, pans left to reveal Gordon Downie singing and not burning. Vise-versa and so on. We see the fire flicker on the faces of the crowd but turn and reveal the band not burning - it's only some of the stage lights flickering. Various shots would be taken of non-burning band members interacting with or reacting to burning band members. Some footage would be shot at normal speed and some in slow motion, and some video step printing.

JOHNNY: We were on the road trying to come up with a name for the record. I suggested 'Saskadelphia' – it was a way of saying that you could really be anywhere when you're touring. The record company hated that. There were thousands of other rejected suggestions in Gord's notebooks, like 'Looking for a Place to Happen', 'Where Is Here', 'Equus', 'Edgarland', 'Thanks, I Think' (that was one of Gord's favourites).

Finally, we came back with 'Road Apples' and they thought that was a great title. Being American, they didn't realise what it really meant.

GORD S: We thought they'd never go for it because obviously every Canadian knows road apples are frozen pieces of horse shit that you used to play road hockey with. But they loved it. We really felt that we had pulled one over, and that we were also beating the critics to the punch by calling our own record 'horse shit' before they had a chance to review it. Again, comedy wins out.

JAKE GOLD: It was up to me to sell the title to the label as signifying songs born from the road. They had no clue that it meant 'horse shit', even when we said we wanted to put a horse on the cover. At the time it was just a low-budget album cover, because MCA didn't want to support the record, but now it's looked at as iconic.

BRUCE DICKINSON: I thought 'Saskadelphia' was amusing, but I was worried that it would feed into the criticism that the band was too Canadian. I thought people would say that you couldn't expect many Americans to know where Saskatoon was or to understand the cleverness of melding Saskatoon with Philadelphia. And then they presented the name 'Road Apples' to me. I knew what road apples were. I don't know if the rest of the company did and I wasn't about to tell them.

JIM HERRINGTON: I first met the boys in a hotel room in who knows what town. I grew quite fond of them and I guess the feeling was mutual, because over the next several years I photographed them in various cities around the US and in Europe. But that *Road Apples* shoot was the first one, and we bonded during those weeks in New Orleans. I have visceral memories of being with the guys then … so many good moments – the turtle soup down the street and candlelit late nights in the opulence of Kingsway. I had a break-up with a girl that they knew and they threw out a lifeline by inviting me on tour with them to Europe. Cold, cold weather, tons of cigs, gallons of Guinness, lots of hash, laughs and fun. The lifeline worked; I abandoned the tour near the end and went off in pursuit of two different German girls I'd met. Thanks, guys, I love you and I miss you. XO, Euro-Jima.

These are all shots by Jim Herrington, who was a good friend of ours. We called him Jimbo until he came to Europe with us, and then he became Euro-Jima. He took us out to this old plantation and we took shots walking through the cane fields and up on the levees and that became the packaging for Road Apples. *If you look at us up close, you can see we're all really stoned. (RB)*

Road Apples
RECORDED: SEPTEMBER 1990
KINGSWAY STUDIOS, NEW ORLEANS, LA
PRODUCER: DON SMITH
ENGINEER: BRUCE BARRIS
MIXING: DON SMITH
RELEASED: 19 FEBRUARY 1991

Little Bones
Twist My Arm
Cordelia
The Luxury
Born in the Water
Long Time Running
Bring It All Back
Three Pistols
Fight
On the Verge
Fiddler's Green
The Last of the Unplucked Gems

Road Apples *album artwork proofs*

Opposite: Europe, 1991

MCA

To JAKE GOLD
From Randy Lennox

JAKE,
thought you'd like the 'HIP' update at HMV–MCA (U.K.)
HMV 'Worldwide' have also decided to make 'ROAD APPLES' their first worldwide 'No RISK DISK' title. This is a major undertaking / committment considering it includes Australia, Japan, U.S., etc. etc.

Regards.
Randy — MCA

cc Ross Reynolds, Stephen Tennant

AM 1380 CKLC stereo!
TOP THIRTY

PREVIEWED MARCH 18, 1991.

LITTLE BONES
WICKED GAME
SOMEDAY
ALL THIS TIME
SHOW ME THE WAY
RESCUE ME
COMING OUT OF THE DARK
IF YOU NEEDED SOMEBODY
WHERE DOES MY HEART BEAT NOW
ONE MORE TRY
SIGNS
ALL THE MAN THAT I NEED
WAITING FOR LOVE
THIS HOUSE
SADENESS
GOOD TOGETHER
SMOOTH AS SILK
I'VE BEEN THINKING ABOUT YOU
WAITING FOR THAT DAY/MOTHER'S PRIDE
GONNA MAKE YOU SWEAT
HOW LONG CAN A MAN BE STRONG
'TIL I AM MYSELF AGAIN
SAVED BY LOVE
DISAPPEAR
ROUND AND ROUND
EVERY 1'S A WINNER
YOU'RE IN LOVE
ONLY THE LONELY
HOLD YOU TIGHT
JOYRIDE

OFFICIAL ISSUE #0368		WKS
THE TRAGICALLY HIP	MCA	4
CHRIS ISAAK	WAR	6
MARIAH CAREY	SON	7
STING	A&M	6
STYX	A&M	4
MADONNA	WAR	7
GLORIA ESTEFAN	SON	8
BAD COMPANY	WAR	7
CELINE DION	SON	11
TIMMY T	WAR	5
TESLA	MCA	10
WHITNEY HOUSTON	BMG	8
ALIAS	CAP	6
TRACIE SPENCER	CAP	2
ENIGMA	A&M	2
CANDI & THE BACKBEAT	CAP	6
MC J AND COOL G	CAP	6
LONDONBEAT	BMG	2
GEORGE MICHAEL	SON	4
C+C MUSIC FACTORY	SON	9
THE JEFF HEALEY BAND	BMG	3
BLUE RODEO	WAR	7
RIK EMMETT	MCA	3
INXS	WAR	12
TEVIN CAMPBELL	WAR	2
BOOTSAUCE	POL	3
WILSON PHILLIPS	CAP	1
WORLD ON EDGE	A&M	2
TARA KEMP	WAR	1
ROXETTE	CAP	1

WHAT'S HOT!

...TES - COMPACT DISCS

...OAD APPLES - THE TRAGICALLY HIP
...HE SOUL CAGES - STING
...HAKE YOUR MONEY MAKER - THE BLACK CROWES
...O THE EXTREME - VANILLA ICE
...HE RAZORS EDGE - AC/DC

MOVIES
1. THE DOORS
2. THE SILENCE OF THE LAMBS
3. SLEEPING WITH THE ENEMY
4. GREEN CARD
5. DANCES WITH WOLVES

BRUCE DICKINSON: When *Road Apples* came out, MCA in the States did a really good job of the initial presentation. After having some resistance with the first album, we wanted to say to the industry that we mean business with this band.

We even had them play one of the big AOR conferences where radio people from all over the country came. Maybe it was idealistic of me to think that people who work for a rock radio station would at least want to stay in the room and watch the band play. But they didn't. I'd say 90 percent of them went out in the hallway with their drinks and talked among themselves. It said to me that this very sizeable percentage of radio people weren't in it for the music at all.

Radio in the States continued to shrug, whereas our friends north of the border embraced the record fully and it went to number one. Like the first album, it also sold in any place along the top of the United States that could pick up Canadian radio – cities like Rochester, Buffalo, Toledo, Detroit, on all the way across to Seattle and even down to Portland. But if you went down to Atlanta, Miami, Nashville, St Louis, Cheyenne, Salt Lake City, they just weren't interested.

PAUL: When we finished *Road Apples*, we knew we had made the right record and it sounded great. Our road manager, Dave Powell, thought 'Little Bones' was the best song he'd ever heard us do. That was a great time. We sold 100,000 copies in ten days, which meant that when we headed out on the road people knew us.

We were all feeling great and we just wanted to get to the shows and start blowing the roof off clubs across the country. It was a bit of a 'pinch me' moment, but at the same time it felt normal because we'd known each other so long. It was affirming for all of us. For me, as the new guy – I think I still hold that title – it was proof that the role I'd carved out was working. We were all pleased and proud but that just translated into being more motivated, more driven.

JAKE GOLD: *Road Apples* sold a couple of hundred thousand in the US, which was OK, and in Canada we did triple platinum, which is 300,000 records. And *Up to Here* was at 300,000 too, so we could see that we were building a constituency of serious fans who had bought both records.

Every show was sold out. Steve Tennant, the marketing guy at MCA, came up with this great line for an ad he ran for the Masonic Temple gig in Toronto: 'Even the scalpers are going to this one.'

I wanted people to feel like they were at something special. So I wouldn't let the band go to radio stations to do interviews; I'd tell the stations that they had to send their remote vans to the venue. Then when people turned up for the show, there were all these media vans lined up and it looked like there was something really big happening.

JOHNNY: We had an idea that *Road Apples* was going to do well, but we had no idea it was going to do this well. When Jake told us that it was starting to catch in Edmonton and Calgary, where we never really got a lot of play early on, we knew that it was going to be a bigger tour than we'd ever done before.

Going to Toronto and seeing a huge display for *Road Apples* in the window of Sam the Record Man on Yonge Street, that was heavy bananas for us. They only put you in the front window if they believed in you as a career band; they didn't do it as a one-off thing.

L-R BOBBY BAKER PAUL LANGLOIS GORDON DOWNIE GORD SINCLAIR JOHNNY FAY

RECIEVE THE JUNO AWARD FOR BEST ENTERTAINER OF THE YEAR
(CANADIAN GRAMMY EQUIVELENT).

Above: The band won their first two Juno awards in 1990 (Most Promising Group of the Year) and 1991 (Canadian Entertainer of the Year)

Above right: Souvenir poster in Kingston's newspaper, the Whig-Standard, to commemorate 'Hip Week', April 1991

Right: As part of the 'Hip Week' celebrations, the Whig-Standard also put the band members' parents on the front page of their 8 April 1991 edition

They're Chips Off The Old Block!
Bursting with pride
Families, fans are thrilled about Tragically Hip's success

When all these articles came out, we were on tour in the States and then we went to Europe right after that. So we only heard from our friends afterwards how ridiculous things got. I think everyone in Kingston was just proud of us for winning the Juno and they wanted to do a little something for us. It turned into a big something. And that was cool with us. Now that we were starting to do a little better, when our friends came and saw us it was a different experience for them. They felt like they were part of it. (JF)

BERNIE BREEN: The Hip have always prided themselves on not making money in Kingston, from the early days through to the final days. They always gave back or found a charity run by somebody's uncle's brother's cousin. Part of my role when I was involved with the band was finding a good reason to say why they couldn't do someone else's great cause, because if they did that cause they'd have to do them all. No one cause was greater than the others, but the band always found a couple. Camp Trillium and Almost Home were two of them. And Health Care 2000 to build the wing at the Kingston General Hospital was another.

It all started with the first two shows at Fort Henry. Mark Vreeken, the band's sound man, was charged with the first one in 1990 for KGH nurses. The next one in 1991 was the one I did for Almost Home. That was amazing, somehow figuring out how to get 5,000 people in there. It was an incredible show.

They're so humble they don't talk about it a lot, but they gave literally millions of dollars back to the community in Kingston without blinking an eye. They were never ones to look for accolades but the city has recognised them in many ways, from the street name [The Tragically Hip Way] to the Gord Downie Pier. All of that is the legacy of a philosophy that these guys had, as a group, to always want to give back and do something to help. That's just who they were.

MARK VREEKEN: It was their way to give back to their home town, a place that had given them so much and always propped them up, on and off stage. While I was working with them I don't think they ever kept any money from a Kingston show – it all went to charities. I doubt that changed after I left.

JOHNNY: Every year we liked to play one big gig at Fort Henry, which is the citadel looking over Kingston. We did a benefit in 1990 for Kingston General Hospital. The Pursuit of Happiness were kind enough to come down and play and a lot of volunteers around Kingston helped out. All the money went towards setting up a fund for nursing scholarships.

PAUL: We came up with an idea to keep our charities local and try to pour some money back. We would play benefit shows at the Manor or a United Way benefit show at the Terrapin or Alfie's. They weren't generated by us but we were always happy to play a charity gig. Then, as we got more known and more financially comfortable, we started thinking a little bigger – playing the Fort was thinking a little bigger. It felt good to give. It felt good to do a charity. And then we never took a penny out of Kingston again. Every gig we played there was for charity.

THE TRAGICALLY HIP

FORT HENRY

THE PURSUIT OF HAPPINESS

KGH NURSES

A BENEFIT CONCERT
for
Kingston General Hospital
Nursing Scholarship Fund
featuring
THE TRAGICALLY HIP
THE PURSUIT OF HAPPINESS
Fort Henry ★ August 9, 1990

CKLC AM 1380

THE TRAGICALLY HIP

IN CONCERT
WITH VERY SPECIAL GUESTS
blue rodeo

♦ Thursday, August 29 ♦ 8:00 p.m. ♦ Fort Henry
Benefit for Almost Home ♦ Ticket price $20.00
♦ Available at: GREAT CANADIAN ROCK TOURS, HOUSE OF SOUNDS, The Whig-Standard, CKLC

•SPONSORS•
HOUSE OF SOUNDS, The Whig-Standard, GREAT CANADIAN ROCK TOURS, CKLC, CKWS

TICKET
11553

THE TRAGICALLY HIP
With Very Special
Guests BLUE RODEO
A Benefit Concert For
ALMOST HOME

UNRESERVED SEATING
ADMIT 1   20.00
Thu, Aug 29, 1991   8:00 PM

The Nurses of Kingston General Hospital and 1380•CKLC present
The Tragically Hip and **The Pursuit of Happiness**
In a Benefit Concert at Fort Henry, for the Nursing Scholarship Fund, August 9, 1990
Doors open at 7:30 p.m., Rain or Shine.
General Admission Only. $15.00 Per Person
Nᴼ 4836

The Nurses of Kingston General Hospital and 1380•CKLC present
The Tragically Hip and **The Pursuit of Happiness**
In a Benefit Concert at Fort Henry, for the Nursing Scholarship Fund, August 9, 1990
Doors open at 7:30 p.m., Rain or Shine.
General Admission Only. $15.00 Per Person
Nᴼ 4836

PRESS RELEASE

August 27, 1991

KINGSTON TO HONOUR THE TRAGICALLY HIP

Mayor Helen Cooper will make a presentation to Rob Baker, Gord Downie, Johnny Fay, Paul Langlois, and Gord Sinclair, members of the rock group The Tragically Hip, on the front steps of Kingston City Hall on Thursday, August 29th, at 2:00 p.m.

"As recipients of the Juno Canadian Entertainer of the Year Award, The Tragically Hip has brought great honour and recognition to the City of Kingston" said Mayor Cooper. She added "We are very proud of the fact that the members of The Tragically Hip hail from our City and we very much look forward to this opportunity to extend our congratulations and appreciation."

Mayor Cooper invites the citizens of Kingston to gather in front of City Hall at 2:00 p.m. on August 29th, to show The Tragically Hip that Kingston is indeed proud of their accomplishments.

DAN AYKROYD: The Hip made Kingston famous. They are ambassadors for the city and gave us a sense of pride that we can say, 'I'm from Kingston.' 'Oh, Kingston. That's down the 401 between Montreal and Toronto.' 'No, Kingston is the town that built The Hip.'

The band with Dan Aykroyd, backstage at Fort Henry, Kingston, for a benefit concert for Almost Home, 29 August 1991

Dan Aykroyd was always very sweet, kind and generous to us. I think he appreciated that we were not like the other bands. At some sort of genetic level we were a blues-based band; even though we were pushing out beyond that, blues really was at the core of what we were. And that's his wheelhouse. I think he appreciated that and he and Johnny became fast friends. He just seemed like a lovely guy who was very passionate about the same kind of music that we were passionate about, and that's what it comes down to. (RB)

Hip recognized as 'true Kingstonians'

By GREG BURLIUK
Whig-Standard Staff Writer

The city of Kingston doesn't give its key to any John, Paul, George and Ringo but Mayor Helen Cooper did give one out yesterday afternoon on the steps of City Hall to John, Paul, Gord, Rob and Gord, better known as The Tragically Hip.

Along with the key and a certificate of appreciation, Johnny Fay, Paul Langlois, Gord Downie, Rob Baker and Gord Sinclair were also presented with city of Kingston T-shirts and baseball caps.

They in turn gave Mayor Cooper one of their own T-shirts, which she vowed not to surrender.

Not even to her daughter.

In her short speech, Mayor Cooper said that everyone was proud of the band, "for the honor and glory they've brought to Kingston."

Preceding her was town crier Chris Whyman, who, in his cry,

said the band members were "true Kingstonians."

Ever modest, the band was humorous in its response.

Mr. Baker said, "This really blows our mind."

The he added puckishly, "I can't think of a better way to kick off a bid for a mayoral seat."

Mayor Helen Cooper offers the Tragically Hip a certificate of appreciation and a key to the city

MICHAEL LEA/The Whig-Standard

'This is so excellent. They're putting on a really good show'
Enthusiastic crowd tunes in to a Hip night at the Fort

GORD SINCLAIR

new view Music productions

with

93 Rock
KRXQ

presents

TRAGICALLY HIP

PLUS SPECIAL GUESTS

FOOD FOR FEET
Featuring Members From Oingo Boingo

and **IAN FAITH**

TUESDAY APRIL 30

THE TRAGICALLY HIP
MUSIC/91 PRESENTS
LABATT'S CANADA LIVE
Town Pump
12:00 MIDNIGHT
FRI MARCH 1, 1991
16.00

THE TRAGICALLY HIP
MERCREDI
11 AVRIL

BAR
d'Auteuil

N° 298   20H30
s 13.

35, rue d'Auteuil, Vieux-Québec, 692-2263

KLPX & LAST LAUGH PROD.
5th & Howe

COYOTE'S - 144 W Lester

MUST BE 21/ID REQUI

THE TRAGICALLY HIP

DOORS OPEN 7PM

MONDAY MAY 6, 199

GEN   ADM   PAT P A

GA   GEN   ADM

UNBSJ SRC and **Labatt Blue**

present

The Tragically Hip

Date: March 12, 1991
Price: $13.00 per person

COCA-COLA/93xRT/JAM HELCO
THE TRAGICALLY HIP
APPEARING AT
CABARET METRO
3730 N. CLARK - CHICAGO
SAT APR 20 1991 7:30 PM

THE BACKROOM
2015 E. RIVERSIDE
Tragically Hip
May 9, 1991
Doors open 8:30 p.m.
$8.00 plus $1.00 service charge

NO ONE UNDER 18 ADMITTED

0685
GEN. ADM.

JAKE GOLD: The first time Gord did his Killer Whale Tank rant was at the Roxy show in LA that was recorded for radio and many years later put out as the *Live at the Roxy* album.

You used to service radio with CD singles of the singles and I said to the record company that we should put the live Killer Whale Tank version of 'New Orleans Is Sinking' on the B-side of one of these, because I thought some of the stations would play it. Hits FM in St Catharines played it a lot. They actually used to promote when they were going to play it and listeners would make a point of tuning in and some of them would record it off the radio. It grew into this underground phenomenon and helped build the live persona of the band.

JOHNNY: When *Live at the Roxy* was recorded, we were at the top of our game. It was mid-tour and we knew those songs inside out. Don Smith's production created this blues record but with the jazz sensibility of picking up every fibre of the room.

It was daunting playing Los Angeles, because you're not really playing to real people. But then LA is also the fourth largest Canadian city in the world, so we had lots of Canadians there.

GORD S: Gord always said that The Tragically Hip could play on the ass of an elephant if we had to. We could play anywhere because we realised it wasn't about the crowd, it was about the band projecting what we could do and it didn't matter how many people were there. If we were having a good time that translated. But it took us a lot of frustration and challenges to actually figure out that it was in us the whole time.

PAUL: When I listen to the *Live at the Roxy* album, I hear a band trying to be as tight as The Clash – hit all the spots with quick endings, play together and play to a room. We always felt like we were the best band out there, even when we were playing places that weren't full – a bowling alley somewhere, or a big empty bar in Grand Rapids on a Tuesday night. On a six-week run, it can't always be Friday night in New York City.

THE TRAGICALLY HIP

DATE:	Friday, May 3, 1991		
PLACE:	West Hollywood, CA		
FACILITY:	The Roxy		
ADDRESS:	9009 Sunset Boulevard		
TELEPHONE:	(213) 278-9457		
LOAD IN:	3:00pm		
SOUND CHECK:	5:00pm	SUPPORTING ACT:	yes
START TIME:		EMPLOYER:	Jennifer Perry
			Avalon Attractions Inc
FINISH TIME:		ADDRESS:	
SETS:		BUSINESS:	(818) 708-8855
CAPACITY:	450	HOME:	
		TECH CONTACT:	Danny O'Bryen
HOTEL:	Holiday Inn Highland		
ADDRESS:	1755 Highland Avenue, Hollywood		
CONTACT:	Viola Robinson		
TELEPHONE:	(213) 462-7181, fax 466-9072		
ROOMS:	4 doubles		
WAKE UP:			
DEPARTURE:			

Left: Call sheet for the band's show at the Roxy, West Hollywood, CA, 3 May 1991. A recording of the gig was included in the Road Apples *30th anniversary box set in 2021 and released in its own right as* Live at the Roxy *in 2022*

Above and opposite: Road Apples tour, 1991

The Tragically Hip scoort ook stoned 'n dikke voldoende

PAUL: We were pretty excited the first time we went to Europe in 1990. Our first gig was in Ghent in Belgium, and the room was full. We couldn't understand how that could be, given that no one had ever heard of us. But it was a club where people just checked you out if you were a new act over from North America. In Belgium if you're Canadian you'll get a very nice welcome, just for that liberation thing.

The same thing happened in the Netherlands. The rooms were full. It felt like we couldn't lose. They had a slightly different way of watching a show over there. During the songs, they seemed to really focus, really listen, and then they'd clap at the end of the song.

GORD S: I think the Canadian–Dutch connection was very important. To this day, on Liberation Day they honour the Canadian soldiers who lost their lives liberating the country. Kids learn about that as part of history.

In terms of entertainment, there was a genuine live music culture in the Netherlands. At the time that we started playing there, compact discs were super expensive. People would come and check out new bands instead. There were a lot of great venues and people appreciated the fact that we could play. We had a great love affair with the Dutch people throughout our career. We absolutely loved playing there.

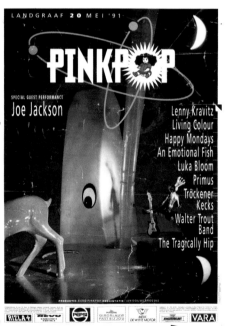

JOHNNY: Jake's strategy was for us to go over to Europe in the winter and then come back in the summer to play bigger festivals. So we were making two or three trips a year and it was getting pretty busy for us. The festivals were also a leaping-off point to get us to a different level of venue. Having played Pinkpop or Parkpop, we were able to draw enough people to be able to go into the Paradiso in Amsterdam.

From: Nigel Hassler

Date: 23rd October 1990

Re: The Hip - Money

The offers for the shows are as follows:

November 10th	–	Gent	£1,000
13th	–	Rotterdam	1,500 Dutch Gilders
14th	–	Amsterdam	1,250 Dutch Gilders
15th	–	Den Haag	1,500 Dutch Gilders
17th	–	Geneva	£1,600
18th	–	Groningen	1,500 Dutch Gilders
20th	–	Copenhagen	2,320 Danish Krona (£910)
22nd	–	Germany	T.B.A.
24th	–	Utrecht	1,500 Dutch Gilders (£210 approx)
25th	–	Cologne	£200
26th	–	Berlin	£200
27th	–	Frankfurt	£200
28th	–	Hamburg	£200
29th	–	London	£1,000 (approx) – SEE BELOW

1. Please note the German offers are only verbal and I have not
    received them on fax.

THE TRAGICALLY HIP
EUROPEAN TOUR 1991

May	16	Mean Fiddlers	London, England
	18	Apollorock	Meerhout, Belgium
	19	Effenaar	Eindhove, Holland
	20	Pinkpop Festival	Landgraaf, Holland
	22	Tivoli	Utrecht, Holland
	23	Paard	Den Haag, Holland
	24	Metropole	Hengelo, Holland
	25	De Melkweg	Amsterdam, Holland
	28	Chrougen	Lund, Sweden
	29-30	New Melody	Stockholm, Sweden
	31	Magasinet	Gothenburg, Sweden
June	1	Grosse Freiheit	Hamburg, West Germany
	3	Loft	Berline, West Germany
	4	Luxor	Cologne, West Germany
	5	B52	Munich, Germany
	6	Batschstrasse	Frankfurt, Germany
	8	King Tut's	Glasgow, Scotland
	10	Princess Charlotte	Leicester, England
	11	Solem Bar	Manchester, England
	12	Scheffield Univ.	Sheffield, England
	13	Marquee	London, England

Paradiso, Amsterdam, Netherlands, 15 November 1991

The Tragically Hip first performed in Europe in November 1990

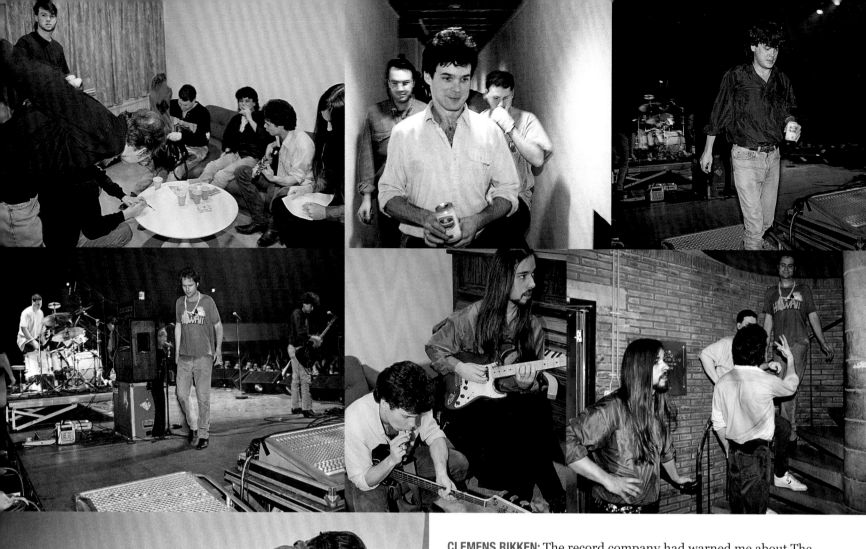

We were assigned an interview with a fairly big Dutch magazine and the journalist brought Clemens Rikken along as the photographer. He's an amazing photographer and has done a wide variety of stuff, including as a war correspondent. We all hit it off immediately with him, particularly Gord Downie. Clemens had no problem being direct and hanging around as long as he wanted, and we didn't mind having him around. Where we would normally clear the room, Clemens would still be there taking pictures of what are generally fairly intimate moments. He was always able to document. And since that time, Clemens brought his family over and vacationed in Canada. He's part of the squad. (GS)

CLEMENS RIKKEN: The record company had warned me about The Tragically Hip. They told me that the singer could be aggressive and just explode with rage. Danger! Danger!

And so I found myself standing in the catacombs of Amsterdam's Paradiso opposite that apparently very difficult to approach front man of The Tragically Hip, Gordon Downie. A somewhat shy, introspective whisperer with a stern, deep gaze searching for its own frame, he welcomed me in a single, softly murmured sentence. I saw nothing of an angry, aggressive man with a short fuse.

That welcome was the start of a very long, deep friendship. In Paradiso back then, he sometimes shuffled by with a few words, and always at the end the same mantra: 'Come on, Clemens.'

That phrase kept coming back during the years when we got to know each other better. Our lives were uncannily synchronised: children came almost simultaneously, we both heard on the same day that we were ill – with the big difference that I did recover.

I was lucky to work with the band for many years, in an always great atmosphere. Johnny, Gordon, Robbie, Gord and Paul became my new family members. And I still feel pride that in the Downie family, the youngest son is named after me – so that now I too can say, 'Come on, Clemens.'

Recently, coincidentally near the Paradiso, a Canadian pointed at my Tragically Hip hat and said, 'Hello, fellow Canadian.' I told him I wasn't Canadian, but simply from Holland. But that we were a band of brothers, even though Canada was far away. Well, go and explain that.

At the same time, I suddenly heard a voice in my head saying, 'Come on, Clemens.'

GORD S: I met Dave Powell in my first year at Queen's. I was walking by a bedroom in Jean Royce Hall and heard Jean-Luc Ponty coming out of the stereo in there. How many guys are listening to Jean-Luc Ponty? So I knocked on the door and we hit it off right away. Dave gave up everything to travel around in the van with us as our road guy.

JAKE GOLD: Dave was super, super smart. Allan and I used to refer to him as 'Big Brain'. He was like an encyclopedia about everything. We were in Australia and it was the first time he had seen the night sky in the southern hemisphere. We stood on this pier and he pointed out all the different constellations one by one. He just knew all these things.

He was super loyal and a hard worker, and he was a good go-between between me and the band. A lot of times, they would use him to do their bidding with me. If they didn't want to do something, it would be Dave that would have to tell me.

ROB: Dave Powell flew over to Europe on our first European tour two days ahead of us to get the lay of the land or, as he would have put it, for reconnaissance. He picked up a splitter van that we were going to drive around in and stopped for gas, not realising that there's Super, Euro and diesel. He thought it was all one type of gas, filled the van up with the wrong one and the engine seized, so he just left it at the side of the road. A rental van that we were completely unaware of until about a year later when he got the bill. That was one among many screw-ups.

JOHNNY: Dave was constantly wrecking cars. He was a heavy driver. On a US tour, we were driving around in two Lincolns and one of them broke down. Dave phoned the rental office in Toronto and the woman told us to bring it in. Dave explained that he couldn't do that because we were in Arizona. She replied that we weren't supposed to leave Ontario and that we needed to bring that car back right now. Dave just hung up.

JOHNNY: Dave Powell was our biggest cheerleader. When we were down because we were in Pennsylvania playing to a couple of people, he'd remind us that our first record was almost gold in Canada or tell us about the cool places we'd be going to in Europe.

He'd read the reviews and if someone panned us he'd tear the guy apart and threaten to put sugar in his gas tank. That really pumped our tyres and made us feel like the bad review didn't matter anymore.

Dave was a guy we really trusted. When we were putting *Road Apples* together, we even let him pick the versions he liked and the order he liked them in. He'd say, 'I love Robbie's guitar tone on this one' or 'I'd go with this version, because it's really aggressive.'

PAUL: Dave Powell was a riddle to himself. He had a unique persona and way of looking at life. Dave could really talk and he could really think. He'd throw these unbelievable nuggets of knowledge at you. Dave provided entertainment. You could just listen to him. We were all connected to him. He was already a buddy of Gord Sinclair's, and he became a buddy of all of ours very quickly and for a long time. No one could have made it more fun than he did.

Dave gradually developed into an excellent road manager. Jake Gold taught him how to clear a room after a show. He just went in with both feet. As we got bigger, he was handling more and more, and getting to know all the crews in the bigger arenas. He made a really good name for himself.

He was eternally single. I think he enjoyed being on the road. He liked telling stories, hanging out with us. He liked the show. He was a fan of the band. The only part he didn't enjoy was the receipts – there's quite a bit of administration to do as a road manager. He would have stuff all over his hotel room.

> **ROB: We'd be in Utrecht or Hengelo in Holland and Dave would say, 'I know the gig is right around here.' And he'd get out of the van and walk in front of us, trying to lead us, in the van, down the streets, and we'd all be killing ourselves laughing. He'd be so stressed out that it was comical, until we realised he was kind of breaking down and it was actually quite serious.**

> **MARK VREEKEN: Dave was one of a kind. He had a lot of personal history with the band so he understood what they liked and what was important to them. He'd never been a tour manager before this gig, so he was making it up as he went – learning along the way. I've never seen somebody improvise their way through problems as well as he did. Super charming, he made people that he just met feel like old friends.**

This page and opposite: Photos taken by Clemens Rikken in Amsterdam in November 1991, including (above) Dave Powell with Gord Downie, and (below) Dave working through his paperwork

JOHNNY: We had an English bus driver who always listened to his Walkman with a little pair of headphones. He pulled over somewhere in Holland to fuel up and Mark Vreeken got out in his underwear to go for a pee and get a coffee. When he came back out the bus was just pulling away. Luckily, he's Dutch, so he was able to ask for a lift and get the guy to drive alongside the bus. But it took forever to get the driver's attention because he had his headphones on and was looking straight ahead. Eventually, he noticed and Mark was able to get back on the bus. I don't think he ever got off again.

MARK VREEKEN: It was an honour to be a part of that touring family. They went out of their way to make opportunities for me to learn. I made a lot of mistakes along the way, but they kindly did not fire me!

TRAG CALLY HIP

FATIMA MANSIONS : JOHN KILZER

5 November

LAATWERK, GET, BOUDISQUE, VVV

"THE HIP" EUROPEAN TOUR NOV.4-24/91

DATE	VENUE	PLACE
NOV. 5,	KING TUT'S	GLASGOW
6,	MANCHESTER UNIV.	MANCHESTER
7,	NEWCASTLE POLYTECH	NEWCASTLE
8,	TOWN&COUNTRY	LONDON
9,	MOLES	BATH
10,	OFF	
11,	ANCIENNE BELGIQUE	BRUSSELS
12,	VOORUIT	GENT
13,	NIGHTTOWN	ROTTERDAM
14,	NOORDERLIGHT	TILBERG
15,	PARADISO	AMSTERDAM
16,	OFF	
17,	VERA	GRONINGEN
18,	OFF	
19,	MARKTHALL	HAMBURG
20,	LOFT	BERLIN
21,	LUXOR	COLOGNE
22,	OFF	
23,	NACHTWERK	MUNICH
24,	BATSCHKAP	FRANKFURT

Above left: The band's bus getting clamped, Amsterdam, Netherlands, November 1991

Above right: Poster for the show at the Paradiso, Amsterdam, 15 November 1991

Opposite centre: Gord Sinclair, Rijksmuseum, Amsterdam, November 1991

MUSIK EXPRESS **KRITIKER-TIPS**
AUGUST 1991

ZONDAG 17 NOV.
22.00 uur
ƒ10,- + maandkaart

THE TRAGICALLY HIP

+ SUPPORT: JOHN KILZER

Op het moment dat u dit leest is het concert van John Kilzer en Tragically Hip waarschijnlijk al uitverkocht. Of voltooid verleden tijd. Hoe dan ook, de kans is groot dat u naast de pot piest. Mocht u wél een kaartje hebben weten te bemachtigen dan mag u rustig doorlezen, geen probleem, maar verwacht geen nieuws. Of sappige details. Of verrassende invalshoeken. We gaan er van uit dat u, omdat u er kennelijk bij wilt zijn en dus tijdig een kaart kocht, genoeg weet.
Maar u! Jammerlijk de boot gemist! Wat gaat er aan uw arme neus voorbij?
John Kilzer! Ja, ik had er ook nog nooit van gehoord (en eerlijk gezegd zou ik er niet rouwig om geweest zijn als dat zo gebleven was) maar John Kilzer bracht onlangs een plaat uit. Busman's Holiday gedoopt. Gevuld met een soort adult orientensted rock die wat mij betreft prima deluxe geschikt is voor een twee meter sessie bij Kroeske. Op deze cd horen we een complete band, inclusief toeters en bellen. Kilzer komt echter in z'n eentje, dus is het aannemelijk dat het een intieme boel wordt.
Dan Tragically Hip. Een, Canadese band die hoe langer hoe populairder wordt. Mijn zegen hebben ze. Het mag dan 'ouderwetse' muziek

zijn en een tikkeltje belegen overkomen, maar het dampt en epibreert wel lekker. Liever belegen rock op de radio dan modern elektronisch gefröbel. Zo is dat. Rhythm & Blues, Country en Blues zijn zo wat invloeden die de canadezen in hun muziek verwerken. Ze doen dat vakkundig mét als resultaat een degelijk en stevig geluid.
Klein probleem: de trillers die, de verder uitstekende, zanger Gordon Downie op iedere tekstregel meent te moeten laten volgen. Daar wordt ik een beetje kriegel van. Beste Gordon: doe dat toch niet, laat het liever aan de vogels over. Die trillen veel beter en bovendien absoluut (oeps!) niet irritant.

Maar hé! Misschien zijn er toch nog plaatsbewijzen in omloop! Op het moment van schrijven (maandag) is er nog plek. Check it out maar wacht niet.

Arnold

John Kilzer plaat:
Busman's Holiday (1p, Geffen, '91)

Tragically Hip platen:
Tragically Hip (mlp, MCA rerelease, 1989)
Up To Here (1p, MCA, 1989)
Road Apples (1p, MCA, 1991)

...tragischerweise
Platte des Monats

THE TRAGICALLY HIP

ROAD APPLES

ON THE ROAD

.11.91 HAMBURG-MARKTHALLE
20.11.91 BERLIN-LOFT
21.11.91 KÖLN-LUXOR
.11.91 MÜNCHEN-NACHTWERK
.11.91 FRANKFURT-BATSCHKAPP

MCA

9

JOHNNY: The first or second time we went out to Europe, a big container of salad dressing spilled all over Gord's duffle bag on the flight over. When we arrived, the rest of us decided to stay up as long as we could, drink some beers and go walking around the town, but Gord had to go find a laundromat. He could never get that garlic smell off his clothes.

ROB: Gord spent a lot of time in laundromats in Europe on that tour. He'd wash his clothes, but as soon as they warmed up on his body he'd smell like Italian dressing.

ROB: Sometimes it was hard to get off your ass and out of your hotel room and check out a nice restaurant, or go to the museums. We had to make a concerted effort, and ultimately that stuff was enriching and it did inform our songs.

There were different people I did different things with. Gord Sinclair and I would often go to strange places like wax museums, Johnny and I would go antiquing and Gord Downie liked to go to the art galleries with me. Gord Sinclair also really liked certain galleries. If we were in Amsterdam, Sinclair would say, 'What time are we going to the Stedelijk?' Every time. And if we were in Washington D.C., Gord Downie would always want to go to the Hirshhorn. Different cities, different things, but you had to make the effort and get out and enjoy it. It was rewarding.

This page and opposite: Amsterdam, Netherlands, November 1991

JOHNNY: In the US, I remember a whole bunch of promises about how much people were going to love *Road Apples*. A Texas DJ named Red Beard liked the record, so we were doing OK in Texas. We were playing Chicago; San Francisco was another big area for us. So there were pockets where we were doing well.

There's a myth that it was only Canadian expats who went to see us in the States. There definitely were a lot of Canadians, but they brought their American friends.

JAKE GOLD: Canadians started doing road trips to see the band in a thousand-seater in New York or Pittsburgh or D.C., because they couldn't see them in a small venue in Canada anymore.

ROB: We did a lot of shows in the States where we were playing to 1,000 people and there are 40 Canadians right up front, and a bunch of them are wearing flags and they have a maple leaf tattooed on their face and they're more drunk – and more visible – than anyone else in the place. And the critic who goes home after the show says that the place was packed with Canadians. That happened every gig we played in the States or Europe. We could keep track of where the tickets were actually being sold, but no one wanted to know that story. That wasn't the angle. The angle was: they're not big in the US.

The Tragically Hip
North American Tour Fall 1991

September	3	McMaster University	Hamilton, Ont
	4	University of Waterloo	Waterloo, Ont
	5	University of Western Ontario	London, Ont
	7	McAlistar Auditorium	New Orleans, LA
	8	Saenger Theatre	Pensacola, FL
	10	Florida Theatre	Jacksonville, FL
	12	Carefree Theatre	West Palm Beach, FL
	13	Cameo Theatre	Miami, FL
	14	Tampa Theatre	Tampa, FL
	15	Bob Carr Perf. Arts Cntr	Orlando, FL
	16	The Moon	Talahasee, FL
	18	Centre Stage Theatre	Atlanta, GA
	19	State Ports Authority	Charleston, SC
	20	Showcase	Raleigh, NC
	21	Virginia Tech University	Blacksburg, VA
	22	George Washington Univ	Washington, DC
	24	Chrysler Hall	Norfolk, VA
	26	Club Met	Harrisburg, PA
	27	Tower Theatre	Upper Darby, PA
	28	The Beacon Theatre	New York, NY
	29	Berklee Perf. Center	Boston, MA
	30	Memorial Auditorium	Burlington, VT
October	2	Newport Music Hall	Columbus, OH
	3	Michigan Theatre	Ann Arbor, MI
	4	The Riviera Theater	Chicago, IL
	5	Club Eastbrook	Grand Rapids, MI

GORD D: I just did three interviews where the editor wanted the main thrust to be the canyon that exists between our success in Canada and our success in America. My answer to that is go check out one of our American shows. You won't see anybody too upset about us there.

GEDDY LEE: The more you saw of The Hip, the more you got into them. In America, they just needed more exposure. I remember one time Rush were in Europe and we were doing a radio interview in Germany. They asked us what other Canadian bands we liked and we said we liked The Hip. The European stations played The Hip and always seemed to dig them when we mentioned them.

You wore your love of The Hip like a badge. Everybody has a band that they feel like they've got to spread the word about. It's a delicious secret that you want to share. The Tragically Hip are a great band, and they happen to be from Canada.

GORD S: After *Road Apples*, we were touring so much and loving the writing. We hit on this formula where we would just throw songs out at rehearsals and soundchecks and Gord would grab bits of melody and then, man, the floodgates opened. That's how we became The Tragically Hip – it was all because we wanted to write songs that meant something. We weren't just jumping around as punk rockers anymore; we were trying to write stuff you could sit with and live with.

ROB: There was a feeling of confidence now that we were no longer just trying to do something. We *were* doing it. This was what we set out to do and no one could take it away from us. We'd made it, whatever that means. We were writing songs and making records and playing killer live shows all over North America and Europe, and we were all on the same page in terms of music and career.

We were firing on all cylinders, and just really, truly having the time of our lives. It was all still a grand, brand-new adventure.

THE TRAGICALLY HIP
DEC. 3-7 TOUR DATES, 91

DATE	VENUE	PLACE
Dec. 3	Aitken Centre	Fredrickton, N.B.
4+5	McInness Rm.	Dalhousie University, Halifax,
6	Day Off	Halifax
7	Moncton Coliseum	Moncton, N.B.

JAKE GOLD: There was definitely a lot of conversation with the band about what was cool and what wasn't cool. All kinds of opportunities were being presented to us that they were turning down. Maybe Allan and I could have been more forceful with them, but we also knew that if we didn't get them to buy in on things we wanted them to do, then they weren't going to be done very well.

We were offered a Rush tour in 1991, 25 dates in sold-out arenas across the US, which was something we needed at the time to get in front of a lot of people. But they didn't want to do it. This was a Gord thing. He said, 'Oh, I don't know. Rush isn't cool.' Maybe two or three years later, Gord pulled me aside and admitted he was wrong about the Rush tour. But at the time, there was a lot of piss and vinegar: 'We're a rock and roll band, we know what we're doing.'

Another time, they called us up right before they were going to do an in-store in Seattle and said they weren't going to do it. We said they had to do it because that was how you supported the label. The record company had relationships with these people. They sell your records. But the guys pulled the plug.

ROB: It never occurred to me that to have your record at the front of the store cost money. I always thought they put you there because you were in demand or because you had a good-looking cover. No, those spaces were paid for. And us making a store appearance or whatever was part of the negotiation. We probably should have played along and done some of that shit, I suppose. Should have played some programme directors' weenie roasts maybe. We could have had a career in music if we'd done that!

You do what you're comfortable doing. If you can't smile while you're doing it, you shouldn't do it.

JAKE GOLD: There was one time when the record company booked them to play on a morning television show without telling us. We had to say to the publicity guy that we didn't do television, especially morning television. I remember the producer phoned me and said that if we cancelled on her, we were never going to play *Canada AM* again. I said, 'Is that a promise?' She didn't know how to take it, because she'd never had anyone turn them down. But our ethos was, if you want to see The Tragically Hip buy a ticket.

It ended up working in their favour. They could never be accused of being a band that became famous and then stopped doing that kind of thing, because they never did that shit.

ROB: It became easier as time went on to decide what to turn down. In the beginning, you don't really know if this is going to be your only turn at bat, so you're tempted to swing at every pitch. But we stuck to our guns early on. Maybe we pumped the brakes a little more than was necessary, but we were moving forward at a speed that we were comfortable with, on our own terms, doing it our way. It didn't matter to us if we left money on the table. If we played it right, we'd be at the table for a long time. If we just grabbed as much money as we could, we were going to be out of the game quick.

We talked about running this big all-day festival at Markham Fairgrounds where we'd take as much money from as many sponsors as we possibly could, fly corporate flags everywhere, make it such an incredible sellout that it would get to a point where it became entirely meaningless. We got into negotiations about it, but they were smarter than we thought and they all wanted exclusivity, so we pulled the plug pretty quick.

You have to be vigilant about this stuff, and it never goes away. We still get offers all the time to do this, or let our music be used for that. Usually, the more uncomfortable it makes us, the more money's involved.

PAUL: If our record company suggested we should be 'a little more cowboy' or 'a little flashier', we would just say no. It became pretty obvious to everyone around us that we were going to do our own thing and see what happened.

JAKE GOLD: The band passed on the Rush tour, but they did play Rush's benefit show for United Way, which was hugely successful. That was the first time we played Maple Leaf Gardens. It was a turning point for the guys to see how a band could use its name and platform to do big things for people that needed it.

ROB: When we were asked to do the United Way benefit warming up for Rush, they told us it was going to be a 35-minute set. We were so thrilled to be playing Maple Leaf Gardens and we thought that we'd probably never play there again. So what did we do? We went up and played five songs that hadn't even been recorded yet. Some of them were only half written. 'At the Hundredth Meridian' didn't have a chorus yet and I played e-bow all the way through it, and we weren't even slightly deterred. We had some big stones on us.

The record company was telling us we were blowing this big opportunity. The five of us thought differently and it worked out just fine.

GORD D: I think I was the one who pushed for us to play only songs from our new record that wasn't even out yet. The band was game, our managers less game. Also, we were invited to play two nights and we said we'd only play one night. Really, really dumb.

The band posing with Platinum awards in front of a Tragically Hip/Sam the Record Man mural, circa 1991

THE MANAGEMENT TRUST LTD.

68 Sparkhall Ave.
Toronto, Ontario
Canada M4K 1G8
Tel: (416) 463-8444
Fax: (416) 463-4232

TO: Micheal Kopple

FROM: Jake Gold

DATE: March 17, 1992

RE: The Hip

PAGES: ~~18 (eighteen)~~ 19

FAX NO: 61-3-822-8417

If this transmission is illegible or total number of pages was not received please call (416) 463-8444.

Here are a few of the highlights that The Tragically Hip have accomplished.

1990 – Juno Award for "Most Promising Group of the Year"
1990 – Campus Entertainment Award for "Best Contemporary Recording Artist"
1990 – Triple Platinum Album for "Up to Here"
1991 – Juno Award for "Canadian Entertainer of the Year" This award is the only Juno voted by the fans. Other artists also nominated for this award were Allanah Myles, Jeff Healy, Colin James, & Blue Rodeo.
1991 – Triple Platinum Award for Road Apples, went #1 in four weeks of release.
1991 – #1 Contemporary Album Radio Artists or Band of the Year, have placed 7 of the 12 songs from Road Apples on the Canadian Album Radio Charts.
      #1 Touring Act of the Year, sold out 33 dates on Canadian Tour in 3 days.
      3 tours of Europe in last 12 months.
1992 – Have been asked to play on the prestigious Park Pop Festival in Holland June 28, 1992.
1992 – Nominated for three Junos to take place March 29.
      – Canadian Entertainer of the Year
      – Group of the Year
      – Album of the Year (Road Apples)

Here are the changes, now the tour looks like this.

Tuesday	April 21	Arrive in Melbourne (ex-United Airlines)
Wednesday	April 22	Melbourne – Press/T.V.
Thursday	April 23	Melbourne – Press/T.V.
Friday	April 24	Melbourne – Festival Hall – opening for GT&D, Ian Moss, (capacity 5,400)
Saturday	April 25	Melbourne – Corner Hotel (capacity 600)
Sunday	April 26	Travel to Sydney/Sydney – Hordern Pavilion opening for GT&D, Ian Moss, (capacity 6,054)
Monday	April 27	Sydney – Hordern Pavilion (capacity 6,054)
Tuesday	April 28	Sydney – Press/T.V.
Wednesday	April 29	Sydney – Press/T.V.
* Thursday	April 30	Sydney – Annandale Hotel (capacity 450)
* Friday	May 01	Sydney – Annandale Hotel (capacity 450)
Saturday	May 02	Sydney – Day off
Sunday	May 03	Sydney – Day off
Monday	May 04	Depart Sydney for Canada

/92 11:22   FROM MCA/GEFFEN AUSTRALIA   TO   036636988   P.02

MCA.   GEFFEN

                    Dave Powell

15th April 1992

TO: LIBBY WILSON / WENDY
    MICHAEL COPPEL
FROM: NADYA BALZAROLO
    MCA/GEFFEN

RE: THE TRAGICALLY HIP

Dear Libby

Hi there.

Details for The Hip as follows:

MCA/GEFFEN contact in Melbourne – Paul Krige.
Accommodation: The Bryson
Arrival: Wednesday, 22nd April.

In Sydney:
Paul Krige   (Tel: 900 7888)
Nadya Balzarolo   (Tel: 900 7888)

TRIPLE J – LIVE AT THE WIRELESS.

Date: Wednesday 29th, 1992
Time: Crew 12 noon
         BAND: 1.00PM
Venue: Studio 2
         ABC/Ultimo Centre
         Second Floor
         Cnr Harris Street/Ultimo Road
         ULTIMO

Contact: Paul McKercher / Stuart Matchett
         Tel: 394 1500

Performance time: 30 mins
Studio dimensions: 20m x 25m
Separate drum/vocal room.
Sound desk: SSL
Triple J can provide sound engineer if suitable.

Press day – Melbourne Wednesday 22nd April
         – Sydney   Tuesday 28th April
Schedule to be confirmed.

Best regards

Nadya

Licenced & distributed by BMG 194 Miller Street,
Phone: 02 900-7888 Fax: 02 955 2881

michael coppel presents

THE TRAGICALLY HIP

TOUR ITINERARY
AUSTRALIA
1992

4 Albany Road, Toorak, Victoria, Australia 3142
Telephone: 61-3-822 8627 Facsimile: 61-3-822 8417

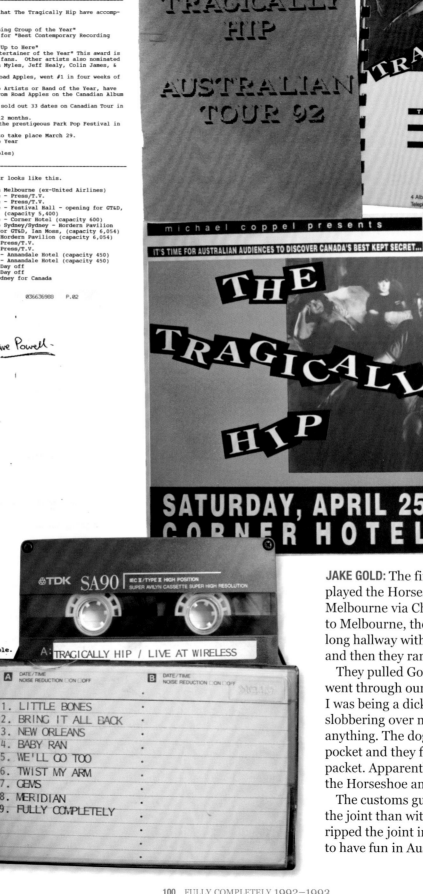

michael coppel presents

IT'S TIME FOR AUSTRALIAN AUDIENCES TO DISCOVER CANADA'S BEST KEPT SECRET...

THE TRAGICALLY HIP

SATURDAY, APRIL 25
CORNER HOTEL

• ROAD APPLES •
AVAILABLE NOW ON MCA

TDK SA90   IEC II/TYPE II HIGH POSITION
SUPER AVILYN CASSETTE SUPER HIGH RESOLUTION

A: TRAGICALLY HIP / LIVE AT WIRELESS

1. LITTLE BONES
2. BRING IT ALL BACK
3. NEW ORLEANS
4. BABY RAN
5. WE'LL GO TOO
6. TWIST MY ARM
7. GEMS
8. MERIDIAN
9. FULLY COMPLETELY

Right: Cassette tape of The Hip's Live at the Wireless session for Sydney radio station Triple J, 28 April 1992

JAKE GOLD: The first time we went to Australia, we played the Horseshoe the night before, then flew to Melbourne via Chicago, LA and Sydney. When we got to Melbourne, they lined us up on each side of this long hallway with our carry-on bags down the middle and then they ran the sniffer dogs up and down.

They pulled Gord and me aside to another area and went through our stuff on this stainless steel table. I was being a dick, complaining about the dog slobbering over my briefcase; Gord didn't say anything. The dog reacted to something in Gord's coat pocket and they found a joint in an empty cigarette packet. Apparently, someone had given it to him at the Horseshoe and then he'd forgotten about it.

The customs guy said he had less of a problem with the joint than with my attitude. I froze. Then he ripped the joint in half, threw it in the garbage, told us to have fun in Australia and let us go.

June 26, 1992
Lahr, Germany

June 27, 1992
Lahr, Germany

June 28 1992
Den Haag - Parkpop

June 29, 1992
London, England

June 30, 1992
Return to Toronto

July 01, 1992
Canada Day
Barrie, Ont.

July 01, 1992
Canada Day
Vancouver, B.C.

July 3 - Aug. 12, 1992
London, England

THE
TRAGICALLY
HIP

EURO-CAN
TOUR 92

Top: Cannabis menu,
Andersom Coffee Shop,
Utrecht, Netherlands,
1992

Centre: Germany, 1992

Centre right: Purple Haze
tour bus, band and crew,
King of Prussia, PA,
1992. Back row (l to r):
Wayne (driver), Mark
Vreeken, Gord Sinclair,
Gord Downie, Mike
Stock (front of house),
Paul Langlois
Front row (l to r): Brian
(swag man), Dave
Powell, Rob Baker,
Johnny Fay

Left: Canada Day show
at Molson Park, Barrie,
ON, 1 July 1992

JOHNNY: We played a warm-up gig at the Toucan before going out to Australia the second time, and this kid came in and helped us move stuff around. When I got back, there was a letter from him all typed out, introducing himself as David Koster, explaining how working with us was his calling, and naming some people we knew who could vouch for him. His timing was good, because we were just getting bigger and moving from the van to a bus, so we needed some extra help.

BILLY RAY (DAVE KOSTER): I finished high school and all my friends were going to university and asking what university I was going to, or what schools I'd applied to. My plan A was to get a job with The Tragically Hip. I didn't have a plan B.

I wrote a letter – Gord always joked that it was written in purple crayon, but I had typed it out – explaining that I could be their drum tech because I was a drummer and they were getting to a level where they were going to need people, and I felt that I was one of the people they needed. I was pretty confident about it and told them I'd worked for other bands, local crew work for Tom Cochrane and Bryan Adams. I wrote the same letter to Johnny Fay, Mark Vreeken and Jake Gold. Johnny called to say that they didn't really need a drum tech, they needed a guitar tech. I told him I didn't do guitars and he apologised and said that it probably wasn't going to happen.

A few weeks went by and I saw Dave Powell and Johnny trying to put a couch into an old van they had out front of Johnny's parents' place. I pulled over and offered to help and explained I was the guy who'd written the letter. I asked if I could volunteer to come up to Ottawa and just work the show. Instead, they offered to give me tickets, but I told them I didn't want tickets, I wanted to do this for a living. I think that meeting made them go back to the drawing board.

Soon after that, I had *Road Apples* cranked in my bedroom at my parents' house, and my mom called upstairs to say there was a phone call for me. It was Johnny offering me $200 a week to do drums for them across Canada. Within those five weeks I got to know the guys and really got along with them. Then they were going to Europe, but they could only take one tech. They wanted it to be me, but they said I needed to learn to do guitars. So it went from drums, to drums and guitars, to drums and guitars and monitors by the time we went to Australia.

GORD S: Billy Ray was not only a fresh face, he was a breath of fresh air for all of us. His antics were unbelievable. He's considerably younger than we are. He's like our Mal Evans. He's been through thick and thin with us. He probably knows more about the band than I do. He's part of the family.

ROB: As a band, little things make you feel more legitimate. We had a roadie now. We had someone to help us set up our shit. For me it was great because I always look for an excuse to not lift gear. And, of course, Billy was full of youthful enthusiasm. He came from a different era than us. We grew up with The Beatles, The Stones, Zeppelin and Pink Floyd, and Johnny was more The Police and Split Enz. And then along comes Billy Ray and he's Mötley Crüe and Poison. It was all very amusing to us.

BILLY RAY: I was Dave Koster for 19 years, but when I started with The Hip they had Dave Powell already and they said they couldn't have two Daves in the crew, which I thought was weird since there were two Gords in the band. They called me 'the kid': 'Tell the kid to get that guitar'. Then one night on the bus Gord Sinclair asked me to get him a beer and I jokingly said I was off duty. Mauro Sepe said, 'Oh, easy, Billy Ray, grab him a beer.' At that time, 'Achy Breaky Heart' by Billy Ray Cyrus was top of the charts and I had a mullet just like his. So everyone laughed and then it stuck. Nobody really calls me Dave at all in the music industry. The only people who still call me Dave are my family. And the bank maybe.

JAKE GOLD: Gord Sinclair's name is actually Robert Gordon Sinclair. He grew up across the street from Robert Baker and, when they started a band together, they decided they couldn't both be Robert. So Gord Sinclair changed his name from Robert to Gord.

I always found it funny that he changed his name to Gord and then they ended up getting another Gord in the band.

ROB: I remember Billy Ray on the bus, saying, 'You guys smoke pot?! Oh my God, am I gonna go to hell? I will never smoke pot.' But a month later, he was like, 'I would never buy it.' A month after that it was, 'Well, I'd never sell it.' But look at our poor Billy Ray now, 15 joints a day later …

BILLY RAY: I don't think my parents would have been happy to hear it, but after a year on the road with The Hip, I went from never having smoked a joint or done any other drugs and not being a drinker, to being a guy wearing a 'Legalise Marijuana' T-shirt and thinking that Rastafarians were the coolest people in the world. Sky High from Ziggy Marley's band said to me at the 1995 Another Roadside Attraction festival, 'My God, you smoke a lot of ganja for a white boy, man.' Which I saw as a feather in my cap.

Opposite:
Dave 'Billy Ray' Koster,
Summer Nites on the
Pier, Seattle, WA,
24 August 2002

ROB: Billy Ray is one of these guys with a certain level of confidence, sometimes completely unfounded. He decided he wanted to get a motorcycle, a Harley, but we told him he should get a Norton. So he got himself a Norton. And then he got another Norton. And he completely took it apart, down to every last screw, and put it back together and then took it apart again and put it back together again. And then he started doing that for other people, fixing their motorcycles.

He did the same thing with guitars. He didn't know how to tune a guitar, didn't know how to put strings on a guitar. Next thing you know, he's wiring guitars, taking them apart, putting them back together. He would teach himself how to do something by doing it. And he would just do it over and over and over until he mastered it. It's pretty incredible to watch someone with that kind of drive. He became an absolutely top-notch guitar tech, a guy who can't play a lick but knows how the guitar works. Same thing with the drums.

He wanted to have a life in the music business, just like we all did, so he worked out how to make himself indispensable. He's still with us.

GORD D: **Billy Ray's like my little brother. He's been with us since he was 17. My dad used to call him Radar, after the character in *M*A*S*H*, and Radar describes Billy well. He's always a step ahead of you on every level. I think he was like that from when he was a kid, just capable of everything. And he's always got my back, whatever's happening.**

PAUL: We knew, almost from the very beginning, that Billy Ray would be around a long time. He became part of the family during a tour we did of some small arenas across Canada with a bigger crew than normal. But then we went to Europe pretty soon after, and we asked Billy to come along. He immediately won us over; he was so enthusiastic and funny and good at what he was doing.

ROB: On one of our very first bus tours, we did the blood oath with trusted crew members like Billy Ray and Mark Vreeken. Everyone sliced their hand and there was blood gushing everywhere and we were all shaking hands and rubbing our cuts in each other's cuts. It was a really terrible idea.

I don't know what that was all about, except to say that we were in this for life with each other.

JOHNNY: You knew when you met Billy Ray how dedicated he was. Like a junior Dave Powell, he was ferocious in his love of the band. He's had so many cuts and bruises and broken ribs over the years – drum sets have fallen on him and he's been to the hospital and he has blood clots that he'll never get rid of.

JOHNNY: We used to give Billy Ray challenges to do for a hundred bucks. When we were mixing *Day for Night* in Morin Heights, we told him he had an hour to climb this bluff that was far away across a landscape covered in dense Quebec brush. It got to 58 minutes and there was no sign of him, but then in the distance we could see this little figure standing on top of the rocky precipice. So he got his hundred bucks, but he looked like he'd had a wrestling match with a thorn bush.

BILLY RAY: **In the first year or so the illusion of them being rock stars wore away, because I just saw that these were five regular guys that happened to have lucked out with their music. They liked having a laugh and also had moments with each other, like any group of brothers do, where you're fighting or arguing.**

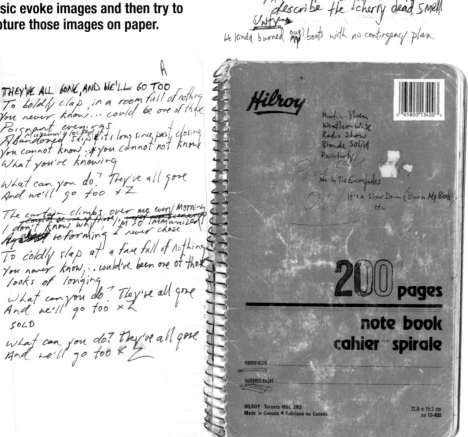

PATRICK DOWNIE: I don't know what Gord would have done if he couldn't have written, because it was a constant. Writing songs and poems was basically his elixir for life.

GORD D: In the old days, when I couldn't play an instrument at all – I couldn't bang two spoons together – I fancied myself as a bit of a poet. Because you can call yourself a poet until you realise what it takes.

Since I've become a little more musically literate, and hanging out with the guys more, I tend to write lyrics as the music suggests. I tend to wait for that, as opposed to just coming up with finished lyrical works and then seeing if I can jam it against some kind of music.

PAUL: There's a lot of cryptic stuff in Gord's lyrics and I think that's a good thing, because it keeps people listening and guessing and then everyone reaches their own conclusions. Gord loved that. He didn't want to really talk about the lyrics. You could get him going a bit, but he'd prefer that the listener decided.

ROB: Gord's writing wasn't about the grand concept; he was about the little moments that happen in conversation that you take for granted but through which you can tell a bigger story. It's like the difference between stage acting and screen acting; good screen actors can do so much more with so much less.

GORD S: Gord was an amazing diarist. I'll see a line in a song and I immediately know exactly what he's talking about.

There's a lyric in 'We'll Go, Too', which was disparaged in the English press as being asinine: 'The curtain climbs over me every morning, I don't know why I'm so immunised against reforming.' It was when we were making *Fully Completely* in a crappy flat in crappy downtown London, and every time you'd have a shower, the shower curtain, because of osmosis, would stick to your leg. I shared a bathroom with him, so I had to deal with the same shitty shower curtain all the time.

GORD D: To me the grooves are complex – they certainly evoke complex movements. The weird thing is, to me, the lyrics fit perfectly because I basically let the music do the talking and try to sit and listen to a groove established, maybe even a whole song, and let the music decide what the lyrics should be – let the music evoke images and then try to capture those images on paper.

GORD D: [Ideas for lyrics] come from all over the place. The guys in the band actually contribute a lot to the lyrics when they least expect it or know it. You spend a lot of time with people so they're wise-cracking, and things come up. Johnny'll say, 'Someone reads like a dish towel,' and I'll think, 'Jeez, that's really cool.' Maybe I'll just scribble it down and maybe it'll expand itself into some kind of larger idea. That's probably my biggest source of inspiration.

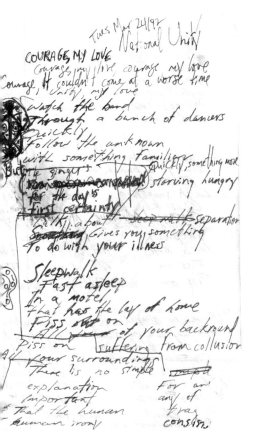

GEDDY LEE: How do you write a song about courage without it being trite? You do it with good poetry. And the band sounds so balanced and powerful; they really underscore the lyrics. Those twin guitars are fantastic and the band has such a good, grinding rock sound.

PAUL: Gord was particularly good at picking up and telling little Canadian stories that a lot of people didn't know, like 'Wheat Kings' about David Milgaard and 'Fifty Mission Cap' about Bill Barilko. They were not always good, not always rosy. He was very motivated, almost obsessed with getting to the bottom of certain stories. And if he could find a way to get them into a song, he was certainly going to try. I don't know if it helped our cause in the States, but we didn't care really.

GORD D: I go in spurts with books but for some odd reason I was drawn to Hugh MacLennan – probably more so as I'd never read anything by him – and then I just ploughed through a bunch of his books. By coupling that with the reading of the *Globe and Mail*, I found a lot of similarities and things that just hadn't changed. He's generally just a great Canadian voice. I think a lot of people in Canada are moving towards some things that identify us or that we are all interested in. Maybe there's some kind of resurgence of Canadiana.

ALLAN GREGG: Gord Downie was spectacular at telling our stories. He proved there are things to tell about Canada that are exciting and interesting and beautiful and different and compelling and that you want to know and you should know.

GORD D: I started writing pretty early on about Canada. I think I sensed even then that I didn't have a patriotic view of Canada; like almost everybody I knew, I questioned a lot of the models and the definitions and the, 'It's a great place to be' Canadian sort of things. In America there's a long history of songwriters like Randy Newman who love their country but are willing to hold it up for scrutiny – in a humorous way, which is usually the most effective – but I don't think there's really anyone doing that in popular song in Canada. If I failed in that regard, I think that it's probably because I wasn't succinct enough or wasn't direct enough, or actually didn't commit enough. I dabbled in it, but I didn't want to jump in with two feet with my version of 'love of country'. Because personally there's more to me.

GORD D: I just found a need to hear Canadian voices and that's where Hugh MacLennan comes from. It's 'For Hugh MacLennan' only because the last verse is essentially from *The Watch That Ends the Night*, entirely. I just took it and screwed around with it.

GORD D: The thing that bothers me is that the fans of our lyrics get maligned. I think ultimately what appeals to the fans of the lyrics is the sense that there's a choice in terms of their definition of their country. Because they're individuals, they like the idea of coming up with their own definition. I think they recognise that these songs that mention these Canadian places and other things about Canada are kind of blunted little barbs. They're not favourable. It's not like this country has no problems. Down in America they're shedding identities daily and weekly; up here we all grow up under this one-size-fits-all identity.

That makes it difficult to hold the country up for real review in the popular arts. When people try to do that it always sounds unpatriotic and so a lot of people don't try because it's just not worth the headache or hassle. I think the 'If you don't love it, leave it' sentiment actually is a little bit stronger up here than it is down there, if that's even possible.

JUSTIN TRUDEAU: The Hip were always grounded in stories of place in this country. You didn't have to know where Bobcaygeon was to know what the town was like. The realness of life in this beautiful land is what echoed through and made what they shared ours. I think part of the psyche of Canadians is we are constantly bombarded with American culture, in all its strength and glory, and that fills up so much of English-speaking Canada's culture. The Hip turned that on its head.

They showed that our stories were important enough to stand on their own and be these incredible works of art that The Tragically Hip shared with us. It wasn't in your face, it was so much more powerful than that, because it came up from underneath and anchored the art and the stories that The Hip delivered for us.

Lyrics for 'Courage'

Opposite: Lyrics for 'We'll Go, Too' and pages from Gord Downie's notebooks

ROB: We were set up for a couple of days in The Cowboy Junkies' rehearsal studio prepping songs for our next record, which was going to be *Fully Completely*. Gord Sinclair started playing this riff and we all picked up on it. It was a little heavier, a little more metal than anything we had done up till then. Meanwhile, Gord was standing listening to us play and he had a bunch of packs of hockey cards that he'd bought. He was opening the packs, popping the gum in his mouth and flipping through the cards. Then he came to one and stopped, turned it over and read it. And then he sang what was written on the back of the card. And that was the story of Bill Barilko.

PAUL: Bill Barilko disappeared near where my father grew up in northern Ontario, so I already knew a little bit more about his story. They thought he'd defected to Russia. There were planes all summer long after his game winner for the Maple Leafs in the finals. He went pretty soon afterwards on that fishing trip. The idea of the 50-mission cap tying the song to planes was a nice concept.

GORD D: In the Second World War, when you were a new pilot you'd be given a new cap. Of course, you'd work it in to look like a 50-mission cap so you would appear to have more experience than you really did. I just thought it was a neat idea.

Then the story itself is really haunting to me: Bill Barilko being chopped down in his prime, the end of a career. I hadn't heard it before. Once I started thinking about ripping off verbatim a hockey card, I started talking to people about him. It was interesting the different stories that came out from the old timers. I went to the reference library in Toronto and checked out the old *Toronto Star*s from 1951 and basically followed the chronology of events from the playoffs to the semi-finals, right up to the Hercules flying over Timmins looking for the wreckage, and interviews with his mother in the paper. It was creepy.

In that series all five games went into overtime and the winner was his. There are great pictures of him being held aloft at the Maple Leaf Gardens. Then, that summer, he went on a fishing trip and disappeared in a plane with a dentist and they just couldn't find the body.

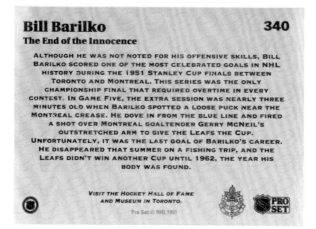

Bill Barilko 340
The End of the Innocence

ALTHOUGH HE WAS NOT NOTED FOR HIS OFFENSIVE SKILLS, BILL BARILKO SCORED ONE OF THE MOST CELEBRATED GOALS IN NHL HISTORY DURING THE 1951 STANLEY CUP FINALS BETWEEN TORONTO AND MONTREAL. THIS SERIES WAS THE ONLY CHAMPIONSHIP FINAL THAT REQUIRED OVERTIME IN EVERY CONTEST. IN GAME FIVE, THE EXTRA SESSION WAS NEARLY THREE MINUTES OLD WHEN BARILKO SPOTTED A LOOSE PUCK NEAR THE MONTREAL CREASE. HE DOVE IN FROM THE BLUE LINE AND FIRED A SHOT OVER MONTREAL GOALTENDER GERRY McNEIL'S OUTSTRETCHED ARM TO GIVE THE LEAFS THE CUP. UNFORTUNATELY, IT WAS THE LAST GOAL OF BARILKO'S CAREER. HE DISAPPEARED THAT SUMMER ON A FISHING TRIP, AND THE LEAFS DIDN'T WIN ANOTHER CUP UNTIL 1962, THE YEAR HIS BODY WAS FOUND.

VISIT THE HOCKEY HALL OF FAME AND MUSEUM IN TORONTO.

Pro Set © NHL 1951

All kinds of stories arose. It was during the McCarthy era, and so some people said he was a spy playing hockey for the Russians who defected back to the Soviet Union. Someone else told me about him hydrating gold with this dentist friend of his, which was entirely illegal.

The RCMP were right on this trail. Paul's old man had lived up in that area, in Smooth Rock Falls, and some of those people hadn't necessarily heard planes going overhead. It's a simple song, but it evokes interest.

GORD S: Our American neighbours are great at mythologising their history. They tell compelling stories with a natural fictionalised arc and they never let the facts get in the way. On the flip side, Canadians are really bad at storytelling. We stick to the facts and tell really dull, colourless, characterless stories about our history.

We were conscious of that and it's the kind of stuff that we would talk about when we were sitting in the van with each other. We'd start picking up those threads of Canadian history. Gord was amazing at that.

The Bill Barilko reference was really strong. If he had hit a World Series-winning home run for the New York Yankees and then disappeared right after that, he'd be a household name. Someone would have made a movie and he would have been played by Robert Redford and got the girl and saved the day. But we didn't know anything about Bill Barilko until we were literally rehearsing that day and Gord unwrapped that pack of hockey cards.

That reinforced what we already knew – that there are all these great stories if you actually look for them and turn them into the art form of songwriting. That was something we were just starting to get pretty good at – telling our own stories with great words, melodies, music and rhythm.

JAKE GOLD: When we delivered *Fully Completely*, Richard Palmese, the new president at MCA, said, 'You know, that song 'Fifty Mission Cap' would be a hit if it wasn't about hockey.' I told him it wasn't really about hockey, but I knew I was never going to make him understand what it was about.

Bill Barilko Pro Set hockey card, front and back, 1991

Opposite: The Hip with Bill Barilko's sister Anne Barilko-Klisanich, Hershey Centre, Mississauga, ON, 19 February 1999 (top centre)

Card from Bill's cousin Sandra Cattarello, 21 August 2016 (top right)

Lyrics for 'Fifty Mission Cap' (centre left)

Gord Downie's notes on the 1951 Stanley Cup semi-finals and finals, written in 1992 (centre)

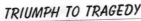

Hershey Centre - Mississauga,
Fri. February 19, 1999
Anne (Barilko) Klisanich

"Here's my fifty-mission cap"

O MISSION, CAP
Bill Barilko disappeared
That summer
He was on a fishing trip

The last goal he ever scored
Won the Leafs the Cup

They didn't win another
Until 1962
The year he was discovered

Another story from the North
I stole this from a hockey card
I keep tucked up under
My fifty-mission cap (I worked it in)
I worked it in to look like that
My fifty mission cap, my fifty mission cap
I worked it in, I worked it in
I worked it in to look like that

Bill Barilko disappeared
That summer (1951)
He was on a fishing trip (In a plane)
The last goal he ever scored (In overtime)
Won the Leafs the Cup (from 1951)
They didn't win another (from 1951)
Until 1962
The year he was discovered
works my fifty mission cap

TRIUMPH TO TRAGEDY

THE LEGEND OF BILL BARILKO
Maple Leaf Gardens • April 21, 1951
Print Size 16" x 22"

April 21st, 1951 marks the date of the scoring of one of the most famous goals in the history of the Toronto Maple Leafs and perhaps the National Hockey League. Bashing Bill Barilko from Timmins, Ontario scored at 2:53 in overtime of the seventh and deciding game of the Stanley Cup finals to give Toronto the cup.

Tragedy struck Barilko that same summer when he was returning from a fishing trip with friend, Dr. Henry Hudson, when the plane they were flying disappeared in August. The plane and its remains were not found until June, 1962 and the Toronto Maple Leafs won their first Stanley Cup in eleven years since the historic Barilko goal in 1951. You and the Toronto Maple Leafs figure it out.

"I get goose bumps every time I think of this story. What an emotional set of events this goal kicked off in the spring of 1951. To be able to capture it in art form has been an honour and a privilege. This drawing took almost 700 hours to complete and was by far the most difficult to date. His historical significance to Timmins is legendary and I'm truly proud to do something to remind people of one of the greatest scripts ever written in the history books of the Toronto Maple Leafs and the City of Timmins."
- Michael Davidson
Artist

"This beautiful print brings back very vivid memories of this wonderful moment in my life and in the rich heritage of the Maple Leafs. My father took me to this game; we sat in the south end and had a perfect view of 'the goal' that won the Stanley Cup for the Leafs. Michael Davidson's artistic rendering of the goal will be a treasured reminder to me and countless other Leaf fans of one of the most famous Maple Leaf victories. Every detail, as I recall the event, is documented in this work of art. It is a must addition for all Leaf fans."
- Harry Neale
Former NHL Coach and
Current Commentator,
Hockey Night in Canada

Michael Davidson Studios
ORIGINAL ARTWORK • LIMITED EDITION PRINTS • CUSTOM FRAMING
37 Third Avenue, Timmins, ON P4N 1B9 ♦ Phone & Fax (705) 267-2990

Bill Barilko

Game 2 - 1-1 Tie - Barilko 4 goals Series B Semi Finals
April 2 - Leafs 3 Bruins 0 - Game 3
1 win, 1 tie each
Barilko 1 assist - 2 pts, 23 minus PIM

Habs Playing Red Wings
As of Wed Apr 4 Series tied 2-2

T.O - Boston
Game 5 Sat. April 7 T.O- Bos 6-0
Sun April 9 4-1
Leafs win Semi-Final 4-1-1

Tor. to Meet Montreal - Wed Apr 11
Sat Apr 14
Tues + Thurs 17-19
Sat. Apr 21

Game 1 - Wed Apr 11 in Toronto
Leafs 3 - Habs 2 - Sid Smith in OT

Game 2 Sat Apr 14
Habs 3 - Leafs 2 - Maurice Richard OT (Harvey)

Game 3 Tues Apr 17 Kennedy OT
Leafs 2 - Habs 1

Game 4 Thurs Apr 18 - Watson OT
Leafs 3 - Habs 2

Game 5, Sat, Apr 21 - in Toronto

DOWNIE
5

South Porcupine
Aug. 21/16

Dear Mr. Downie,
I watched your last rite show & was hoping you'd include the Billy Barilko song....
T'was ecstatic to hear the opener...
You see, I am a cousin of his; my Mother was the former Mary Barilko.
I know you met Bill's sister, Anne, when you played Maple Leaf Gardens years ago.
My father coached & scouted many players into the N.H.L. including Bill Barilko.
I'd like you to have this Hockey card for your fine

When we played the rink in Mississauga in 1999, Bill Barilko's sister came to meet us before the gig. She thanked us for what we did for his memory and for his legend. To think that we had that kind of impact on someone that had lost a sibling too soon – and obviously that was something I related to – was really moving. (GS)

BILL BARILKO

Date of Birth: March 25, 1927
Death: August 26, 1951 - Age 24 years
Position: Defence - shoots right
Nicknames: "The Kid", "Bashin' Bill"

Career

Year	Team	League
1939-40	Timmins Central Public School	Junior School Champions *
1940-41	Timmins Central Public School	Intermediate Champions **
1941-42	Timmins Central Public School	Senior District Champions ***
1942-43	Timmins Central Public School	Senior District Champions
1943-44	Timmins Holman Pluggers	All Ontario Juvenile Champions
1944-45	Timmins Kiwanis Air Cadets	Porcupine Juvenile Hockey League
1945-46	Hollywood Wolves	Pacific Coast League Division Champions
1946-47	Hollywood Wolves	Pacific Coast League
1947		Pacific Coast League
1947-48	Toronto Maple Leafs - NHL	Stanley Cup Champions
1948-49	Toronto Maple Leafs - NHL	Stanley Cup Champions
1949-50	Toronto Maple Leafs - NHL	Stanley Cup Champions
1950-51	Toronto Maple Leafs - NHL	

Stanley Cup Champions
* Scored the overtime goal that won the Stanley Cup

August 26, 1951 - Disappeared after flying North to Seal River on a fishing trip with Dr. Henry Hudson. Remains were not found until 1962.

All Star Games
Three: 1947, 1948, 1949

Significant Achievements
1939 - When Bill was 11 years old, he rescued a 14 year old boy who was riding a bicycle on Gilles Lake during the winter in Timmins. The boy and the bicycle broke through the ice, and the boy was saved by Bill Barilko, who was assisted by three other youths.

1946-1951 - Bill contributed much to his community (Timmins) in terms of serving the youth as a role model during his short career.

1951-1952 - The Bill Barilko Memorial Trophy for the Best Defenseman in the Porcupine Juvenile Hockey League was established and awarded to Lloyd McKey, the first recipient, in 1952. The Porcupine Juvenile Hockey League was noted throughout the hockey world by the numerous players that were scouted to play in the OHL, and on to the NHL.

* Position played - Goal
** Position played - Goal
*** Position played - Defenseman

PAUL: We were absolutely concentrated on writing the next record. I remember all the practising and demoing in various places, wherever we could, whenever we could, for all the *Fully Completely* songs – getting 'Fifty Mission Cap' together and 'Locked in the Trunk'. By the time we went to London, England, to record the album we had all the songs written and we knew them pretty well. We always found that the best way to record is to really know your songs.

ROB: Making our first record in Memphis and then our next in New Orleans, it seemed like we were on some kind of mission to find the source, and that felt good. London seemed like an obvious choice, because the early London club scene was what really inspired the band in the first place – it was the grain in the oyster that made the pearl.

Chris Tsangarides was recommended to us by Bruce; we knew him through the band Concrete Blonde, who we all loved. I remember thinking their guitar sounds were very processed and I didn't know how that would translate for us, but we loved those records. Chris was so enthusiastic about working with us and we've always been big believers that enthusiasm conquers everything.

BRUCE DICKINSON: Allan Gregg got it immediately. He realised that the band now needed more of a father figure or an uncle, rather than a big brother.

I knew Chris and I had kept him in the back of my mind to work with some day. He was always on my list of top ten people to produce an album, even though I didn't know yet whose album that might be. What struck me was how he captured the liveness of all the metal

bands he worked with. Although The Hip certainly was not a metal band, here was another great live band that I felt he could capture in the studio. He didn't record the band live like Don Smith did. Chris was the ultimate in starting from the bottom up, with the kick drum, which was very tedious, but the end result was the end result.

ROB: We got to London and Chris didn't show up the first two or three days because he'd hurt his back, so we were just kicking around in the studio, playing through the material. We were good, hard-working Canadian kids, so we'd be there from 10 a.m. until 7 p.m., working on the material and rehearsing.

Once Chris came back, then we got on to London time: show up at 10 a.m., start doing something around 10.30, have a little break around 11.30, break for lunch at 12.30, come back at 2. Then break for afternoon tea at 4 and again at 6.30 for dinner and then you're done. We couldn't cope with how slow the process was – we were there for five weeks and in the first three weeks all we did was bass and drums.

Right: MCA press release announcing The Tragically Hip's upcoming third album, 14 April 1992

Below right: Cassette tapes of demos of Fully Completely *tracks and some unreleased songs, recorded at Street Brothers Studio, Toronto, 8 and 20 January 1992*

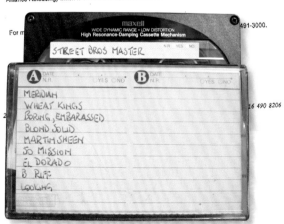

FROM MCA RECORDS CANADA (TUE) 4, 14 '92 10:57 NO. 3080693293 P. 2

For Immediate Release

THE TRAGICALLY HIP
PREPARE NEW ALBUM

Toronto, April 14, 1992:

THE TRAGICALLY HIP announced today that they will be recording their next album in England with producer CHRIS TSANGARIDES (Concrete Blonde, Ozzy Osbourne, Lords Of The New Church). Recording is scheduled to begin on July 3, 1992, with release anticipated in the fall of this year. The band's previous two albums (UP TO HERE and ROAD APPLES) have both surpassed the triple platinum mark in Canada.

In the interim, THE HIP continue their frantic pace of world-wide touring, as well as embarking on numerous new ventures in their ever-expanding musical careers. Prior to their established recording date, their schedule includes:

· Their first ever tour of Australia from april 19th to May 4th, which will see the band playing six dates in Sydney and Melbourne.

The airing of a one hour documentary slated for May 29, 1992 at 9:00 P.M. on the full CBC network. The television special centres on THE HIP's home-town annual charity concert in historic Old Fort Henry, and chronicles their thoughts and adventures on the road throughout Europe and the southern U.S.

A brief European tour from June 25th to June 29th through Germany, Holland, and the U.K. Dates include headline appearances at The Park Pop Festival in Holland, as well as the Astoria Theatre in London.

Whirlwind performances in *both* Toronto and Vancouver as part of Canada Day celebrations on July 1, 1992.

THE HIP have just inked a deal which will have them writing the full soundtrack and score for the feature film "I Love A Man In Uniform" (directed by David Wellington, produced by Miracle Pictures and distributed by Alliance Releasing) which is scheduled to premier at the Berlin Film Festival next year.

For m   491-3000.

JOHNNY: We had a good group of songs going into the studio. After making *Road Apples* in Kingsway, I found it difficult to adjust to a traditional set-up where I was playing on my own with the other guys out of the room. But Chris made it a fun experience and we were in one of the top studios in the world. He was a real breath of fresh air and that record was big for us.

The only thing that didn't work for us was that this was the first time a producer left at 5 p.m. on a Friday and didn't come back until 10 a.m. Monday. So we missed a lot of time when we should have been working.

GORD D: Chris was comfortable working at Battery Studios and, as far as we were concerned, we didn't really care where we recorded.

[Recording was the same as it had been with Don Smith] in the sense that we were all chipping in and trying out different things. Chris acted in a lot of different capacities – including nanny. They were nice sessions; there seemed to be next to no tension involved. In any sort of creative process, especially a collaboration, people normally run into snags and problems, but this seemed to be completely devoid of that, and I think it was probably because we already had the songs.

I believe that you only get so many kicks at the can as far as recording goes – it's something that's quite sacred. It's your ability to put your stamp in six weeks on something and so you've got to keep exploring different angles. There's been a lot of emphasis on trying to capture one's live sound in the studio and it's kind of a riddle as to how to do it. A lot of bands record live off the floor, which is what we did with *Up to Here* and *Road Apples*.

In this case, it was more of a basic recording method in the sense that we'd all play the songs with a thought in mind of keeping the bed tracks, being the bass and drums, and then whatever vocals or guitar that were worthy of keeping. It didn't differ too much in methodology from the last two records, but it somehow felt different.

The way I sang was also different. As opposed to singing three versions and then compiling the best parts of each, which Don was a big fan of, I would sing a song three times and we'd use the best whole take. For me, that more closely approximates the live experience.

GORD S: It was the first time we made a record where we really didn't know what it was going to sound like until the last few days of the session when Chris began to assemble all the pieces. Until then, it was kind of on the cutting room floor, so it was an interesting session.

We wrote some good songs while we were there and we had a great time. We loved Chris and loved the experience. We had some great friends there who did their best to make us feel at home, but we felt really far from home when we were making that record.

JOHNNY: I liked that Chris slowed some things down for us in the studio. He helped us understand that we didn't need to play everything at a hundred miles an hour. That was a really great learning experience.

PAUL: For the first four weeks we were just playing so we got to know all the tunes really well, and Chris and the engineer weren't in the room very often. Then all the recording was done in the last week out of five. We left and then received the mixes about a week later in Toronto and we were all very pleased with the job Chris had done – it has a certain sound, that record.

ROB: When we went to make *Fully Completely*, the songs that were already good songs live didn't elevate very much. But the songs that were a little bit half-baked that we weren't playing at the live show, those songs jumped up in a big way.

Songs like 'Eldorado' and 'Pigeon Camera' came to life with that approach, whereas with others, like 'Locked in the Trunk of a Car' and 'Fifty Mission Cap', I felt we got serviceable versions. They were never as good as when we played them live.

'Courage' is a great example of how my dyslexia made me look at the drum set in a different way. Chris suggested that the song should be a shuffle, but I didn't know how to play a shuffle. I was determined to figure out how to do it my way, so I got my foot moving fast enough to mimic what someone else would have been doing with their left hand.

We all brought our own uniqueness to the band. It never made sense when I played with other people. (JF)

Tues July 7/92 - Pre-Pro
1. Courage
2. Fully
3. Radio Show
4. So Hard Done
5. 50 Mission
6. Looking
7. U.C Detail
8. Wherewithal
9. Pumping
10. Blonde Solid
11. We'll Go Too
12. Meridian
13. Lionized
14. El dorado
15. Wheat Kings
16. Pigeon Camera

• Wed July 8,9
• Thurs

July 3 - Aug. 12, 1992
London, England

Travel:	Flight from Vancouver to London
	LV: Air Canada, FLT: 854, July 03 – 7:05pm
	AR: London, Heathrow, July 04 – 12:10pm

Hotel:	Eton Apartments
	126 Broadley St.
	London, NW8
Apt. 7, PH:	011 44 71 723 2903
Apt. 9, PH:	011 44 71 724 2279
Studio:	Battery Studios
	1 Maybury Gardens
	London NW10 2SG
	Tel: 011 44 81 459 8899
	Fax: 011 44 81 451 3900

JOHNNY: When we were in London making *Fully Completely*, I kept listening to The Skydiggers' new record on a Walkman. There was a song called 'A Penny More' that I particularly loved. I remember talking to Gord about how good their record was and how I thought it was better than what we were doing. Gord agreed with me that it was a really good record, but said that our record was going to be good too – but in a different way.

After our chat, I started to feel better about how *Fully Completely* was coming together. Gord always had a great faith that things were going the right way and he could instil that confidence in you too.

PAUL: In London, we were living in Edgware Road, which isn't a great area, in two little apartments in the same building. I was with Rob and Mark Vreeken, with two of us sharing a room; the other three guys were across the hall.

We were finishing at 10 p.m. and the studio was a long way away, in Willesden Green, so we'd take minicabs back and forth. By the time we got home all the pubs were closed, so we didn't do a lot.

GORD S: We found ourselves sitting around our crappy apartment down by Marylebone Station with no money, drinking warm, crappy beer. It was right in the middle of the Olympic Games so we thought at least we can watch that on TV. But it turns out the British are even worse at broadcasting the Olympics than the Americans. We would all be wanting to watch the 100m sprint, but there'd be a British rider who was going to do well in the dressage, so they'd show nothing but that the entire day.

ROB: The other Bruce Dickinson, of Iron Maiden, would come and hang out in the control room all the time. He was a really lovely, very disarming guy, very sweet and funny. The whole thing was a strange process for us. Chris would try to entertain us with his humour, but it was the humour that he would use with his English heavy metal bands, and we weren't always on the same page. But we found him so endearing and charming and enthusiastic. It was a weird dichotomy, working with all the English heavy metal bands and having a very blue sense of humour, and yet he was a really cultured guy and very intellectual.

I think we came up with something that sounds good. It's a very produced record, but I think it succeeds because the songs are strong.

BRUCE DICKINSON: In August '92, I went over to London to hear the mix process. The band had gone back to Canada and I was there to make sure I was happy with the mixes. Hearing those songs for the first time, I felt elated. It was the album that I knew they could make. I remember sitting with Chris at the board, thinking that this was a new level of cohesiveness and maturity. It was polished without being polished. There was a confidence from the band that came out of the speakers. They were grown up. And that was the idea.

MARK VREEKEN: Chris had a very different approach than Don. The band felt more attached and involved with the process on *Road Apple*s. Chris had streamlined his record-making techniques to a methodical art.

He was a super talented person with so much experience. It seemed like very little work was actually being done at the time. Somehow it all got done though and I think it's an amazing record.

Gord Downie's tracking diary during the recording of Fully Completely, 1992

Opposite: Lyrics for 'Wheat Kings' (top left)

Excerpts of legal correspondence regarding the band's use of Dan Gibson's loon recording on 'Wheat Kings'

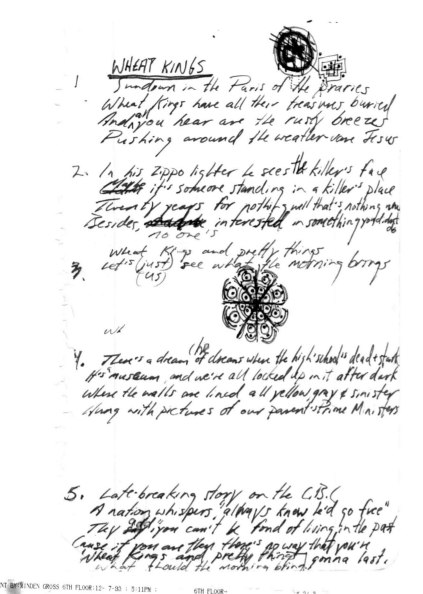

WHEAT KINGS

1. Sundown in the Paris of the Prairies
Wheat Kings have all their treasures buried
And all you hear are the rusty breezes
Pushing around the weather-vane Jesus

2. In his Zippo lighter he sees the killer's face
~~Clear~~ if it's someone standing in a killer's place
Twenty years for nothing well that's nothing new
Besides, ~~no one's~~ interested in something you did
no one's

3. Wheat Kings and pretty things
Let's (just) see what the morning brings
(us)

4. There's a dream (he dreams) of dreams where the high school's dead & stark
It's museum, and we're all locked up in it after dark
where the walls are lined all yellow, gray & sinister
hung with pictures of our parents' prime Ministers

5. Late-breaking story on the CBC
A nation whispers, "always knew he'd go free"
They say you can't be fond of living in the past
Cause if you are then there's no way that you're
'Wheat Kings and pretty things' gonna last.
What should the morning bring?

ENT BY:MINDEN GROSS 6TH FLOOR:12- 7-93 ; 5:11PM ; 6TH FLOOR→ ;# 2/ 3

RELEASE AND INDEMNIFICATION — *Fin*

DATE: December , 1993

PRODUCTION COMPANY: Dan Gibson Productions Ltd.
(hereinafter, the "Production Company")

ARTIST: Gordon Sinclair, Gordon Downie, John Fay, Paul Langlois and Robert Baker, professionally known as The Tragically Hip (hereinafter, the "Artist)

RECORD COMPANY: MCA Records, Inc. and MCA Records Canada, a division of MCA Canada Ltd. (hereinafter collectively, the "Record Company")

SUBJECT MATTER: The recording of a loon call that appears in the musical composition "Wheat Kings" (the "Musical Composition"), a track on the album entitled "Fully Completely" (the "Album"), performed by the Artist and distributed by the Record Company.

I believe a tenable argument can be made that the animal sounds which your client has copied falls within the definition of musical works (that is, harmony, melody and rhythm). The new definition of "musical work" in the *Copyright Act* does not change my view. Nevertheless, my client's recording of animal sounds clearly enjoys copyright protection pursuant to Section 5(3) of the *Copyright Act*.

Our client looks favourably on your client's suggestion to direct settlement proceeds, if any, to an environmental cause, as The Tragically Hip supports a number of environmental causes including, most recently, the Clayoquot Sound Defense Fund. My sense is that if you can provide me with evidence to support your legal position and we can work out a more reasonable number, we will be able to resolve this matter without resorting to costly legal proceedings.

PAUL: 'Wheat Kings' was about David Milgaard, who spent more than 20 years in jail for a murder he didn't commit. Following his release, we met him at Seabird Island on Another Roadside Attraction in '93. Then Gord and I went over to his apartment in Toronto three or four times, just to visit and talk. Gord was very curious about his experience, so we got to know him a little bit and had him out to shows a few times.

I was very saddened to hear that he died, but I'm happy that he was able to get some good things done and that, against all odds, he was able to recover from being locked up for so long, knowing he was innocent. The influence of his family would have been helpful, I'm sure, but we could tell when visiting him in Toronto that it was going to be a struggle.

ROB: Among people who paid attention to the news, there was a lot of debate about David Milgaard's case. My dad was a judge and so I thought that the courts didn't make mistakes like that. I never really felt that Gord was saying he was innocent in 'Wheat Kings'; I thought it was more of a 'what if' statement. Then, when it was clearly proven that David Milgaard was not guilty and we met him after his release from prison, I felt such a weird, complex range of emotions. What I remember mostly was the sense of how damaged he was by his experience and that there wasn't enough money in the world to compensate this man.

JAKE GOLD: When I came over to see them in London, the guys asked me to bring over a CD of nature sounds because they wanted to put some loon sounds on the record. I stopped at the kiosk at the airport and bought about ten different CDs. They lifted the sound of a loon, a type of water bird, from one of the CDs and put it at the beginning of 'Wheat Kings'. One day, we got a letter from Dan Gibson, who was a very famous nature sound recordist. He'd recognised the sound of his loons on our track. We had to donate $5,000 to the Friends of Algonquin Park, because otherwise he was going to try to stop us selling the record. We were all rookies about the idea of sampling, and that was a lesson learned.

JOHNNY: About five months after the record came out, some guy contacted us and said, 'I'm the creator of the loon sound,' and Chris Tsangarides said, 'You mean, God?'

ROB: Dan Gibson was very good to work with, and we were happy to donate the money to a good cause. I felt bad that we stepped on that landmine; in the age of people lifting stuff from other records, we should have known better.

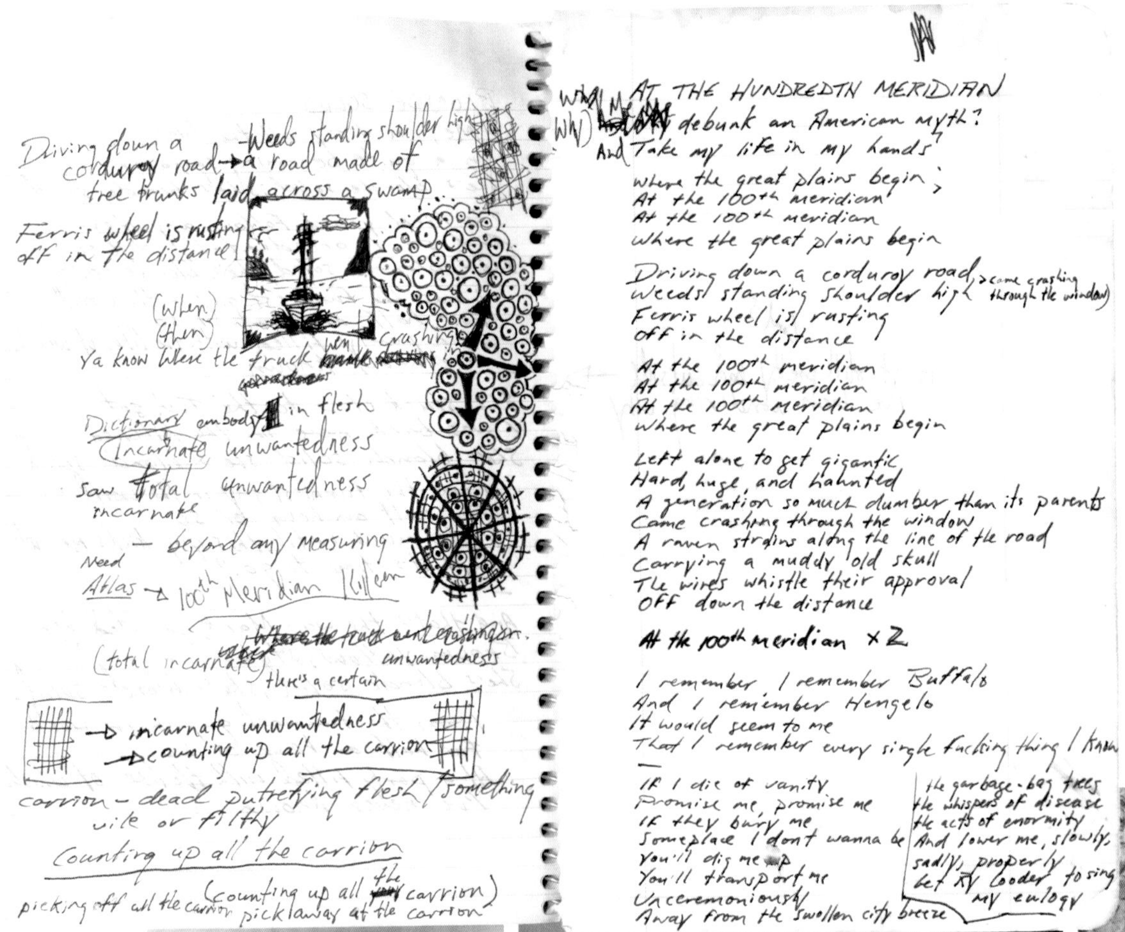

Handwritten notes (left page):

Diving down a
corduroy road → a road made of
tree trunks laid across a swamp

Weeds standing shoulder high

Ferris wheel is rusting
off in the distance

(when)
(then)
Ya know where the truck came crashing

Dictionary embody in flesh
Incarnate unwantedness
saw total unwantedness
incarnate
— beyond any measuring
Need
Atlas → 100th Meridian killem

(total incarnate) before the truck went crashing
there's a certain unwantedness

→ incarnate unwantedness
→ counting up all the carrion

carrion — dead putrefying flesh / something
vile or filthy
Counting up all the carrion

picking off all the carrion (counting up all the carrion)
pick away at the carrion

Handwritten lyrics (right page):

AT THE HUNDREDTH MERIDIAN

Why debunk an American myth?
And 'Take my life in my hands'

Where the great plains begin;
At the 100th meridian
At the 100th meridian
Where the great plains begin

Driving down a corduroy road, >came crashing
Weeds standing shoulder high < through the window
Ferris wheel is rusting
off in the distance

At the 100th meridian
At the 100th meridian
At the 100th meridian
where the great plains begin

Left alone to get gigantic
Hard, huge, and haunted
A generation so much dumber than its parents
Came crashing through the window
A raven strains along the line of the road
Carrying a muddy old skull
The wires whistle their approval
OFF down the distance

At the 100th meridian x2

I remember I remember Buffalo
And I remember Hengelo
It would seem to me
That I remember every single fucking thing I know

If I die of vanity   the garbage-bag trees
Promise me, promise me   the whispers of disease
If they bury me   the acts of enormity
Someplace I don't wanna be And lower me, slowly,
You'll dig me up   sadly, properly
You'll transport me   let my coroner to sing
Unceremoniously   my eulogy
Away from the swollen city breeze

JOHNNY: Chris and Gord had an argument about 'Hundredth Meridian'. Chris told Gord he needed to sing the chorus twice, but Gord didn't want to. He wanted the lyrics to stand as they were.

GORD D: A meridian is a line of longitude that wraps entirely around the world, a circle that never stops. I wasn't thinking this when I wrote 'At the Hundredth Meridian', but afterwards I had this idea that if you wanted to you could go to almost every town on the hundredth meridian and find out some story with an undercurrent of evil. I mean, it runs through Dodge City, Kansas and Brandon, Manitoba and then Bangkok on the other side of the world, which obviously has its darker side. That's something that I just came up with afterwards, that the hundredth meridian is a line of absolute black evil circling the globe – that idea of a black band of longitude is exciting, it's interesting.

Top: Lyrics for 'At the Hundredth Meridian'

Above and right: Filming the video for 'At the Hundredth Meridian' in Melbourne with director Pete Henderson during the band's tour of Australia and New Zealand in March 1993

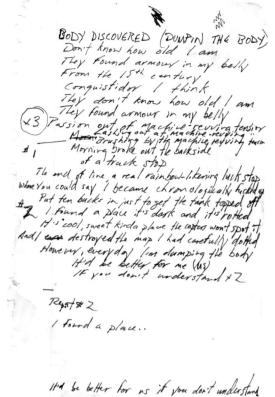

BODY DISCOVERED (DUMPIN THE BODY)
Don't know how old I am
They found armour in my belly
From the 15th century
Conquistidor I think
They don't know how old I am
They found armour in my belly
(x3) Passion out of machine-revving tension
Lashing out of machine-revving
Crushing by the machine revving tension
Morning broke out the backside
of a truck stop
The end of line, a real rainbow-likening luck stop
where you could say I became chronologically fucked up
Put ten bucks in just to get the tank topped off
I found a place it's dark and it's rotted
It's cool, sweet kinda place the copters won't spot it
And I destroyed the map I had carefully dotted
However, everyday I'm dumping the body
It'd be better for me (us)
If you don't understand x2

Repeat #2

I found a place..

It'd be better for us if you don't understand

DUMPING THE BODY
They don't know how old I am
They found armour in my belly, from the 15th century
Conquistidor I think
They don't know how old I am
They found armour in my belly
Crushing by the machine-revving tension
Lashing out of machine-revving tension
Passion out of machine-revving tension
Morning broke out the backside of a truck-stop
The end of the line, a real rainbow likening luck-stop
where you could say I became chronological fucked
Put ten bucks in just to get the tank topped off
Then I found a place, it's dark and it's rotted,
A cool sweet kind of place where the copters won't spot it
And I destroyed the map I had carefully dotted
However everyday I'm dumping the body
It'd be better for us if you don't understand
It'd be better for me if you don't understand

I found a place it's dark and it's rotted
It's a cool sweet kinda place where the copter won't spot it
And I destroyed the map we had carefully dotted
However everyday I'm dumping the body
It'd be better for us if you don't understand
It'd be better for us if you don't understand
It'd be better for me if you don't understand

JAKE GOLD: 'Locked in the Trunk of a Car' never got released as a single in America, because the band refused to edit out the 'chronologically fucked up' lyric. The Canadian company went with it, no one complained and it was a big hit, but in America they just wouldn't release it without the edit.

BRUCE DICKINSON: It's hard to pick one favourite song from *Fully Completely*, but 'Locked in the Trunk of a Car' is the song that stood out for me. As an A&R person, I always sensed a darkness in Canadian music. Maybe it comes from the long winters. You get it from Swedish people too. It's just part of the culture. 'Locked in the Trunk of a Car' appealed to me because I'm a very dark individual. I immediately thought of the Jimmy Cagney movie where the guy's locked in the trunk and he's complaining that there's no air and Jimmy Cagney says, 'Oh, you want air?' and starts shooting at the trunk.

GORD D: With 'Locked in the Trunk of a Car', I tried to use an analogy. And it happens to be a particularly grisly one – dumping a body – which, if you committed the act of murder, would be something you'd become pretty preoccupied with, and probably never forget. So it's the idea that the guilt you'd feel would be as suffocating as if you were locked in the trunk yourself. I had this idea of someone locking themselves in the trunk of a car, out in the middle of a field somewhere, and having someone take the keys and throw them off across the road into the field, and then drive away and never be seen again.

The analogy is that if you're in a love relationship and it's the absolute best thing that ever happened to you and you manage to fuck it up, as people can, you're going to feel a certain amount of regret. It sounds so maudlin, but it's just that you'll feel really horrible, like being suffocated, and you won't necessarily feel liberated from this relationship.

JAKE GOLD: Sean Valentini was a director of photography and Pete Henderson was a director who went on the road with the band for about a year and a half, following them all over Europe. They were making this mini-doc for the CBC that was going to tie in with the launch of *Fully Completely*.

Sean and Pete got to be very close with the band and so when it came time to choose a director for the 'Locked in the Trunk of a Car' video, the guys wanted Pete. It was his first real big video. And Dave Powell's first starring role. That was when we started making really good videos.

ROB: We all thought it was a great idea to start putting Dave Powell in our videos. We thought, 'Let's torture him. Let's put him in a straitjacket and hang him upside down for a few hours. What else can we do to him? Can we drag him behind a car? Can we put him in the trunk of a car for a whole day?' He was game, but it would put him in a very dark mood, which would work great for the videos.

Thanks to Pete and Sean's vision and our willingness to sacrifice Powell to whatever whims they had, we started to make cool videos. 'Locked in the Trunk of a Car' was the first one. I think it won the MuchMusic video of the year award. It had been their number one video for about two months before they realised the lyrics contained the word 'fuck'. They flipped out and called Jake. He asked them whether anyone had complained and they said no, so he said, 'So what's your problem?' And that was the end of that.

Early handwritten lyrics for 'Locked in the Trunk of a Car' which was originally titled 'Body Discovered / Dumping the Body'

Fish artwork from the 'Locked in the Trunk of a Car' video, which won the 1993 MuchMusic Best Video award

The cover art for Fully Completely was created by Dutch artist Lieve Prins in response to the idea, given to her by Rob Baker, of a 'bacchanalian sort of scene – lots of decadence, decay and rebirth'. She also drew inspiration from I Ching symbols and numbers. The final artwork was made using a Canon colour photocopier. It consists of 30 segmented photocopied images pasted together.

The band was granted licensing privileges to the artwork, but Prins retained ownership of the actual piece.

In the late Nineties, the band bought the artwork from a gallery in Los Angeles. It now hangs prominently in their Bathouse studio near Kingston.

SONG TITLES, SEQUENCE, ETC.:

COURAGE (FOR HUGH MACLENNAN)
LOOKING FOR A PLACE TO HAPPEN
AT THE HUNDREDTH MERIDIAN
PIGEON CAMERA
LIONIZED
LOCKED IN THE TRUNK OF A CAR
WE'LL GO TOO
FULLY COMPLETELY
FIFTY MISSION CAP
WHEAT KINGS
THE WHEREWITHAL
ELDORADO

SIDE ONE (cassette and LP)

COURAGE (FOR HUGH MACLENNAN)
LOOKING FOR A PLACE TO HAPPEN
AT THE HUNDREDTH MERIDIAN
PIGEON CAMERA
LIONIZED
LOCKED IN THE TRUNK OF A CAR

SIDE TWO

WE'LL GO TOO
FULLY COMPLETELY
FIFTY MISSION CAP
WHEAT KINGS
THE WHEREWITHAL
EDLORADO

RB: I had this idea of a Dutch life cycle, in a bacchanalian sort of scene – lots of decadence, decay and rebirth.

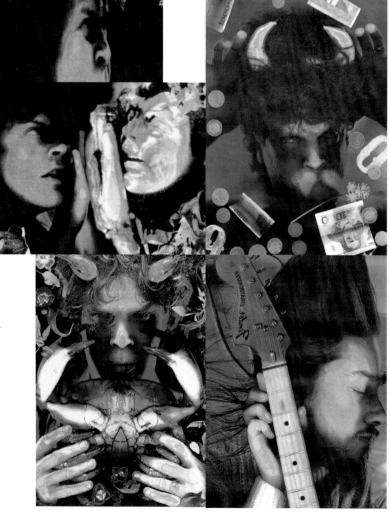

Fully Completely
RECORDED: JULY 1992
BATTERY STUDIOS, LONDON, UK
PRODUCER: CHRIS TSANGARIDES
ENGINEERS: CHRIS 'WOOD' MARSHALL
SARAH BEDINGHAM
MIXING: CHRIS TSANGARIDES
RELEASED: 6 OCTOBER 1992

Courage (For Hugh MacLennan)
Looking for a Place to Happen
At the Hundredth Meridian
Pigeon Camera
Lionized
Locked in the Trunk of a Car
We'll Go, Too
Fully Completely
Fifty Mission Cap
Wheat Kings
The Wherewithal
Eldorado

ROB: I came across the work of Dutch artist Lieve Prins, and I left the idea with her. You find people who you like and admire, and you hand the ball off to them and let them run.

We loved her interpretation of the idea of 'fully completely'. It was not at odds with anything I had suggested to her. It's the same with Gord's lyrics. They might mean one thing to him and something completely different to someone else. But isn't that kind of glorious?

GORD D: Lieve took the title of the record, and she wanted lyrics and all kinds of things from us. She mulled it over for a month or so and then came over to London, where we were recording, and we took a weekend off and set it all up in the studio. The template squares were laid out in advance on the floor in front of us. Coloured pigment powder, the shells and the coins and whatever else were also laid out in advance and then we wore heavy makeup and lay down and experimented with all kinds of different expressions. It was very immediate, and it was really cool to be part of it.

JAKE GOLD: We always wanted to create excitement around everything that we did. We decided to release *Fully Completely* at midnight on a Friday to make an event out of it. We got the radio stations to promote it and there were line-ups all around the block.

BRUCE DICKINSON: The record didn't blow up the way it was supposed to, but it was a step in the right direction. We had started with 'Courage', which was the first song on the album, and I thought it was a very good intro to the album. It did reasonably well on the AOR charts.

MCA did a very cool thing by pulling up all these people from the various sales offices across the United States to a place in Vancouver to premiere the album for the company. They went to great expense to do that and it showed some level of commitment. But I remember sitting across the table at that event from Richard Palmese, the president of the company, and he just looked at me and said, 'This better work, for your sake.'

We'd done reasonably well with 'Courage' and 'Hundredth Meridian', and I felt that 'Fifty Mission Cap' would be the one that would bring it all home. But, like the first album, where the label stopped pushing before they got to 'New Orleans Is Sinking', they stopped pushing before they got to 'Fifty Mission Cap'.

I'm still at a loss as to why they would stop, other than because they didn't hear what we heard. I think they just weren't willing or didn't have the nerve to stay with an album and keep working it. They got cold feet after two songs and pulled the plug right at that point.

Shortly after that, I was unceremoniously dumped from the label. I got to stay in touch with the band, and I'm very proud of that. They've had the career that I envisioned from day one, when we all sat down at that Horseshoe gig and I said that I saw them as a long-range career band. With all those albums, that's exactly what they became.

PRODUCED AND ENGINEERED BY CHRIS TSANGARIDES
Assisted by Chris "Wood" Marshall and Sarah Bedingham

All songs written by The Tragically Hip
The Tragically Hip are:

Bobby Baker -- Guitar
Gordon Downie -- Vocals
Johnny Fay -- Drums
Paul Langlois -- Guitar & Vocals
Gord Sinclair -- Bass & Vocals

Mixed by Chris Tsangarides
Recorded and mixed at Battery Studios, London
Engineered by Chris "Wood" Marshall
Mastered by Ian Cooper, Townhouse, London

Design & Art Production -- Lieve Prins
Adamson Acoustic Design -- Brock Adamson, Paul Bauman
Paiste -- Rich Mangicaro
Promark -- Pat Brown
Washburn U.K. -- Gavin Mortimer
Ayotte Drums -- Ray
Rock Tron
Sunshine Music -- Ron
Centre Stage -- John

Station	Comment
KLAQ	MEDIUM ROTATION...SHOWING GOOD EARLY PHONES
WRDU	NOT ON IT-NO ROOM-DOESN'T DO A LOT FOR US
WZBH	NOT ON IT-NO ROOM
WRKR	NOT ON IT-DOESN'T WORK FOR US
KRSP	NOT ON IT-NO REASON
WPYX	NOT ON IT-NO ROOM-TOO MUCH COMP.
WQWK	NOT YET-TIGHT LIST-GOOD POSSIBILITY
WNCD	NOT YET-LOOKING AT IT, SLIGHTLY
KGMG	NOT ON IT-TOO ALTERNATIVE
KUGR	LIGHT ROTATION-IT WILL MOVE UP
KATP	2ND WEEK-GREAT INTEREST
KOCD	NOT ON IT-COULD ADD NEXT WEEK
WCKW	NOT ON IT-LOOKING AT IT
KLOS	NOT ON IT-NO REASONS
WZEW	HAVEN'T HEARD-DON'T HAVE IT
WEZX	JUST ADDED IT
WMMR	NOT ON IT
KJKJ	NOT ON IT, HAVEN'T HEARD
WEQX	JUST ADDED THEM
KFMX	NOT ON IT-TRYING
KOZZ	NOT ON IT-MAYBE IN THE FUTURE
WMAD	NOT ON IT-JUST HAVEN'T GOT TO IT
KKTX	ADD LAST WEEK-GOOD PHONES
WFBQ	NOT ON IT-CONSIDERED-BUT IT DOESN'T REALLY FIT WHAT WE DO
WPXC	LIGHT ROTATION-GREAT CALLS
KZRR	NOT ON IT-NOT LOOKING AT
WNGZ	JUST ADDED THIS WEEK-LIKED THEIR LAST ALBUM
WRCQ	JUST ADDED THIS WEEK-LIKED "NEW ORLEANS SINKING' TESTED WELL
KQDI	HAVEN'T HEARD-MD LIKES IT-ON MY LIST TO LISTEN TO FOR NEXT WK
WRAI	WOULDN'T FIT WHAT I'M DOING HERE TOO "OUT THERE"
WXRC	LOOKING AT IT DOWN THE ROAD-NO STRONG FEELINGS
KCAL	CONSIDERING IT-I THINK IT'S PRETTY COOL...TOO ALTERNATIVE?
W2NF	PRETTY GOOD-UP FOR FUTURE CONSIDERATION
WIMZ	JUST OK-NO REAL PLANS FOR THE FUTURE
KTAL	LOOKING AT IT-GOOD STUFF- HARD TO SAY IN THIS MARKET IF WE START SEEING SOME SALES, WE'LL TAKE A CLOSER LOOK
WKLQ	A LITTLE "LEFT" FOR ME-BUT WE'RE KEEPING AN EYE ON IT
CFRQ	THEY'RE EXTREMELY HOT HERE
WIXV	I DON'T REALLY HEAR THAT SONG-NOT A FAVE
WAQX	NOT LOOKING AT IT-TOO EARLY
WDJR	HAVEN'T HEARD (HEARD ABOUT IT, THOUGH)
WAPL	PLAYED TWO SONGS FROM LAST LP-LIKE 'EM-REAL BACKED UP RIGHT NOW, THOUGH
WJXQ	2-3 WEEKS--IT'S A GOOD SONG
WTXQ	LIKE IT--2-3 WEEKS AWAY
KDBM	JUST ADDED TOO EARLY TO TELL
WXRK	CLASSIC STATION "OBVIOUSLY NEEDS A STORY"
KZKZ	COOL TUNE, TESTING IT RIGHT NOW 2-3 WEEKS
WRXR	HAVEN'T SPENT MUCH TIME WITH IT BUT WILL ON SUGGESTION
WKQQ	LOOKING AT IT, BUT NEED STORY
WXKE	NOT A CONSIDERATION, DOESN'T IMPRESS ME YET
KWHL	WE ARE ALREADY ON IT, GOOD REGION FOR THE BAND!
KEZE	WE LOVE IT! MORE MATURITY, JUST GETTING BETTER
WFYV	HAVEN'T HEARD, BUT WILL ON SUGGESTION
KRZQ	NOT CONSIDERING SERIOUSLY!

Station	Comment
WDIZ	HAVEN'T HEARD
WQBZ	LIKEABLE RECORD, BUT A LOW PRIORITY RIGHT NOW
WHCN	GOOD, BUT NEED A STORY AND SOME ROOM
WXLP	NOT WHAT WE ARE LOOKING FOR
KSQY	LOVE IT! ALREADY ON IT AND THERE IS A GROWING BUZZ
KNAC	CAN'T PLAY
WWTR	2-3 WEEKS AWAY, WE LIKE IT
WRXK	WE LIKE IT, BUT NEED ROOM, HAVE IT ON NEW MUSIC SHOW!
WZXL	CONSIDERING, WE ARE WEIGHING THE POSSIBILITIES
WLAV	WE LIKE THE BAND, AND WE ARE SERIOUSLY CONSIDERING
KZOQ	WE LIKE IT, VERY CLOSE
WYNF	INTERESTING, VERY CLOSE, SOMETHING'S AHEAD OF IT
KNCN	JUST ADDED, IT'S GOOD, WE'LL SEE HOW IT DOES
WIUP	HAVEN'T SPENT AS MUCH TIME WITH IT, WILL CHECK IT OUT
WEBN	HAVEN'T HEARD IT YET
WKDF	I HAVEN'T HEARD IT
WQFM	NOT A BAD RECORD, IT COULD GO SOON
KBCO	NOT SURE
KOME	LOVE IT
WTTS	LIKE THE TUNE, NO HURRY
KBAT	PROBABLY NEXT WEEK
WTPA	NICELY GROWING
WRXL	NOT YET
KLBJ	ADDED IT!
WRKI	MAYBE A LITTLE EARLY
KZRR	TOO EARLY
KFMG	ADD THIS WEEK TOO EARLY TO TELL
WWRX	NOT FOR US, SHORT LIST, ONLY 12 ARTISTS ON IT
WZYC	NEW ADD TODAY, REAL GOOD TRACK RECORD IN THE PAST WITH US
KSEZ	PROJECT FOR NEXT WEEK
WHJY	TOO EARLY. LOVE THIS BAND (IN LIGHT)
WZZQ	WAIT AND SEE ON THIS BAND IN THIS MARKET
KRQK	WAITING FOR A STORY
WROV	IN THIS WEEK IN MEDIUM...IT'S OK. TOO EARLY
KVEZ	IN LIGHT, TOO EARLY
KMBY	DON'T KNOW YET
KZAP	WAITING FOR A STORY
WIOT	LIKE IT, WAIT AND SEE
CHOM	ON DIFFERENT TRACK IN MEDIUM
KRQR	ON ONLY A WEEK IN LIGHT, TOO EARLY
CITI	ALL OVER THIS RECORD--PHONES, SALES...3 CUTS DEEP
WBGR	TOO LEFT BUT WILL LISTEN MORE
WRUF	IN NEXT 3 WEEKS
WKGR	HAVEN'T HEARD-NOT A PRIORITY-LATE RIGHT NOW
WKIT	ON IT--VERY EARLY-STAFF LIKES
KDJK	KIND-OF COOL, NEEDS BIG STORY-WATCHING CLOSELY
KKDJ	OTB DOING WELL WITH LITTLE BIT OF EARLY RESPONSE
KSJO	IT'S OKAY-SOME PEOPLE HERE LIKE IT OTHERS DON'T
WKGB	WOULD SOUND BETTER IN A BAR THAN ON THE AIR

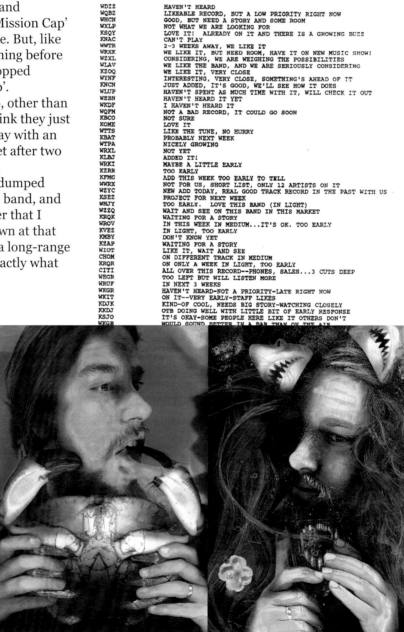

Centre: Compiled comments about Fully Completely *from US radio stations*

Critics find that it's Hip to be Canadian

The Tragically Hip

OTTAWA
NOVEMBER 16
CIVIC CENTRE

TORONTO
NOVEMBER 18
MASSEY HALL

WINNIPEG
NOVEMBER 23
ARENA

SASKATOON
NOVEMBER 25
CENTENNIAL AUDITORIUM

CALGARY
NOVEMBER 27
MAX BELL ARENA

EDMONTON
NOVEMBER 28
AGRICOM

VICTORIA
DECEMBER 1
ROYAL THEATRE

VANCOUVER
DECEMBER 2
PNE FORUM

Cdn Tour 92

smoke pot with the NHL'ers send them into slumps they can't explain to the Press like a stolen stolen stereo you can't report.

Explosions in the Narrows (75 years to the day)

showered with a generosity that left me not wet will served to make me loath him

Saskatoon - the bust - enough said
Calgary - Slugged smickin in a crowded Elevator - enough un-said
Edmonton - enough said
Victoria - I'm losing track of what I've said.

THE TRAGICALLY HIP
WITH GUESTS - PRESENTED BY
PERRYSCOPE
P.N.E. FORUM
NO CAMERAS OR RECORDERS
WED DEC 2/92 7:30PM
GA GEN ADM 24.50
8OCT 12.05 CASH 01D178
EFM1202 ADULT 24.50

The Tragically Hip

EUROPE TOUR DEC. 92

THE Tragically HIP
7 december
& Mark Curry

PROGRAMME OFFICIEL
BEST
TRANS MUSICALES
RENNES 2 - 5 DEC 92

THE TRAGICALLY HIP
Live at CBGB's (NYC 1/14/93)

1. Fully Completely
2. Looking for a place to happen
3. Courage
4. 50 mission cap
5. Pigeon Camera
6. We'll go too
7. Lionized
8. At the Hundredth Meridian
9. Locked in the Trunk of a Car
10. The Wherewithal

Right: Tivoli, Utrecht, Netherlands, 7 December 1992

Top centre: Gord Downie's notes about the 1992 Canadian tour

BILLY RAY: At the time, I didn't recognise it but me starting with The Hip coincided with their jump to the next level. I got hired because they were finally at a point where they needed crew guys. Before that, they set up their own gear, did soundcheck and, at the end of the night, had a beer before grudgingly hauling the gear back into the van and driving to the next place. When I came along, they were playing their first set of arenas, so walking into Massey Hall at soundcheck, looking around and taking in the building, was as exciting for them as it was for me.

It wasn't until we went to Europe and we were playing on festival bills with Metallica and Neil Young and Faith No More that you realised that this hometown band was one of these superstar groups that were playing to 80,000 people tonight. As a fresh-out-of-high-school kid from Kingston, I always felt they were that big and I assumed that this was what they were used to. But it turns out that a lot of those first shows I did were major milestones for the band.

I remember being in the bar of the Columbia Hotel in London, England and Lemmy from Motörhead was there and a couple of guys from The English Beat. We were just having beers and hanging out, and the news came in that the Canadian tour had sold out in six minutes flat. To see the excitement on the guys' faces that people were buying full arenas of tickets for shows that weren't going to happen for another six months was really something.

THE MANAGEMENT TRUST LTD.

66 Spadina Ave
Toronto, Ontario
Canada M5V 2H1
Tel: (416) 463-9444
Fax: (416) 463-4038

TO: Pete Hampson, Bandwidth

FROM: Jake Gold

DATE: Nov. 2, 1992

RE: The Tragically Hip, Europe & U.K. Tour

C.C.:

PAGES: 2 (two)

FAX #: 011 44 81 846 9359

If this transmission is illegible or total number of pages was not received please fax (416) 463-4038.

EUROPE DATES

Jan. 29	Gent, Belgium	
30	Tilburg, Holland	
31	Day off	
Feb. 1	Nijmegen, Holland	
2	Rotterdam, Holland	
3	Groningen, Holland	
4	Day off	
5	Amsterdam, Holland	
6	Amsterdam, Holland	
7	Bochum, Germany	
8	Hamburg, Germany	
9	Day off	
10	Berlin, Germany	
11	Frankfurt, Germany	
12	Day off	
13	Munich, Germany	
14	Stuttgart, Germany	
15	Cologne, Germany	
16	Paris, France	
17	Day off	

The Tragically Hip

EUROPE TOUR JAN/FEB.93

EUROPE

Date	City	Venue	Page
January			
Wed. & Thurs 27 & 28	Toronto/London/Brussels	Travel day	1
Friday 29	Gent, Belgium	Voorhuit	2
Saturday 30	Tilburg, Holland	Noorderligt	3
Sunday 31	Nijmegen, Holland	Day off	4
February			
Monday 1	Nijmegen, Holland	Doornroosje	5
Tuesday 2	Rotterdam, Holland	Nighttown	6
Wednesday 3	Groningen, Holland	Oosterpoort	7
Thursday 4	Amsterdam, Holland	Day off	8
Friday 5	Amsterdam, Holland	Paradiso	9
Saturday 6	Amsterdam, Holland	Paradiso	10
Sunday 7	Munich, Germany	Day off	11
Monday 8	Munich, Germany	Nachtwerk	12
Tuesday 9	Frankfurt, Germany	Batschkapp	13
Wednesday 10	Stuttgart, Germany	Day off	14
Thursday 11	Stuttgart, Germany	Longhorn	15
Friday 12	Hamburg, Germany	Day off	16
Saturday 13	Hamburg, Germany	Grosse Freiheit	17
Sunday 14	Berlin, Germany	Loft	18
Monday 15	Cologne, Germany	Live Music Hall	19
Tuesday 16	Utrecht, Germany	Tivoli	20
Wednesday 17	Glasgow, U.K.	Day off	21
Thursday 18	Glasgow, U.K.	King Tut's	22
Friday 19	Bradford, U.K.	Bradford University	23
Saturday 20	Cardiff, U.K.	Cardiff University	24
Sunday 21	Nottingham, U.K.	Day off	25
Monday 22	Nottingham, U.K.	Nottingham University	26
Tuesday 23	Dublin, Ireland	Whelans	27
Wednesday 24	Loughborough, U.K.	Day off	28
Thursday 25	Loughborough, U.K.	Loughborough Universit	29
Friday 26	Egham, U.K.	Royal Holloway College	30
Saturday 27	London, U.K.	Town & Country	31
Sunday 28	London/Toronto	Travel Day	32

The Tragically Hip

FULLY COMPLETELY

LP · MC · CD

RELEASED ON 8TH FEBRUARY

"HIP-HIP-HIP-HOORAY! THE HIP IS ONE OF THE BEST LIVE BANDS NOW WORKING ANYWHERE" THE TORONTO SUN

APPEARING LIVE

FEB 18: GLASGOW, KING TUTS · 19: BRADFORD, UNIVERSITY
20: CARDIFF, UNIVERSITY · 22: NOTTINGHAM, CITY UNIVERSITY · 23: DUBLIN, WHELANS
25: LOUGHBOROUGH, UNIVERSITY · 26: EGHAM, ROYAL HOLLOWAY COLLEGE
27: LONDON, TOWN & COUNTRY

MCA

FULLY COMPLETELY TOUR '93

Mo. 8.2. München Live aus dem Nachtwerk
Di. 9.2. Frankfurt Batschkapp
Do. 11.2. Stuttgart Longhorn
Sa. 13.2. Hamburg Große Freiheit
So. 14.2. Berlin Loft
Mo. 15.2. Köln Live Music Hall

U.K. DATES

Feb. 18	Sheffield, U.K.	
19	Newcastle, U.K.	
20	Cardiff, U.K.	
21	Day off	
22	Nottingham, U.K.	
23	Day off	
24	Liverpool, U.K.	
25	Loughborough, U.K.	
26	Munchester, U.K.	
27	London, U.K.	

These are the dates, please fax us a quote A.S.A.P. on a Super Splitter with Mervin.

Thanks

Jake Gold

The U.K. tour currently stands as follow:

FEBRUARY

18	Glasgow	King Tut's	
19	Newcastle	University	
20	Cardiff	University	
21	OFF		
22	Nottingham	Trent Poly	
23	OFF		
24	Liverpool		University
25	Loughborough	University	
26	Bradford		University
27	London	T & C	

(I may want to change the shows in Nottingham and Liverpool)

Speak to you later.

Best regards,

NIGEL HASSLER.

HARVEY GOLDSMITH ENTS.
presents
THE TRAGICALLY HIP + SPECIAL GUESTS
SATURDAY 27 FEBRUARY 1993
Doors 7:00pm
Advance £8.50

TOWN & COUNTRY

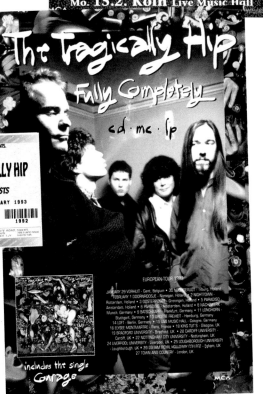

The Tragically Hip
Fully Completely
cd · mc · lp

includes the single Courage

MCA

MICHAEL COPPEL PRESENTS

The Tragically Hip

DATE	CITY	VENUE
March 10	Arrive in Melbourne	
11	Melbourne	tape Tonight Live
12	Melbourne	Central Club
13	Melbourne	Central Club
14	Travel Melbourne/Coffs Harbour	
15	Coffs Harbour	Sawtel RSL Club
16	Brisbane	Transformers
17	Travel/Media	
18	Sydney	Landsdowne Hotel
19	Sydney	Landsdowne Hotel
20	Sydney	Landsdowne Hotel
21	Travel Sydney/Auckland	
22	Auckland - Media Day	
23	Auckland	The Power Station
24	Travel Auckland/Adelaide	
25	Adelaide	Le Rox
26	Melbourne	Central Club (option)
27	Sydney	Annandale Hotel
28	Sydney	Day off
29	Depart to Canada	

'FULLY COMPLETELY' TOUR

AUSTRALIAN ITINERARY

FEBRUARY 1993

4 ALBANY ROAD, TOORAK, VICTORIA AUSTRALIA 2142

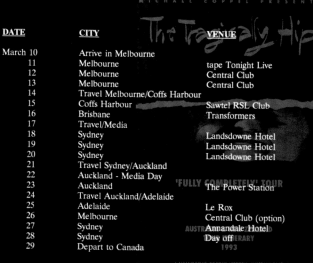

The Tragically Hip

AUSTRALIAN TOUR MARCH 93

The Tragically Hip

U.S. TOUR MAY/JUNE 93

TRICIA'S BOOK

The Tragically Hip

EUROPE TOUR JUNE/JULY 93

THE NIGHT CANADIAN MUSIC COMES HOME

ADMIT ONE ORCHESTRA B 65

SUNDAY MARCH 21ST 1993   O'KEEFE CENTRE TORONTO

10.
HALDERNER

OPEN AIR

2.7. FESTIVAL

NÄHERE INFORMATIONEN AUF DER RÜCKSEITE.

RAUM 3 GBR

89 X

2ND BIRTHDAY BASH

The Tragically Hip

JUNE 5, 1993

Budweiser Concert Series at Chene Park MUSIC THEATRE

DETROIT

© MARK L. ARMINSKI, 1993. PRINTED AT THE GHETTO PRESS, DETROIT, MI - 313-872-4026 TYPE: GREY TOMORROW

ADULT ETG6513
TM AMERICA'S TICKET

THE GRAND PRESENTS
THE TRAGICALLY HIP
CRASH VEGAS
THE GRAND
76 E 13TH STREET NYC
THU MAY 13, 1993 7:00PM

JAKE GOLD: Around the time of *Fully Completely*, people in the media started commenting on the fact we hadn't broken America yet. I didn't understand why success somewhere else was that important to them. Why were they counting our money? People didn't realise that the band had a career in America; it just wasn't as big as their career in Canada.

It was an unfair comparison anyway. Just from Boston to D.C. was 80 million people, which was three times more than the whole of Canada at the time. So it was naive to think we would ever be able to break the two countries at the same pace.

There were a bunch of bands that had some success around the world with certain songs and then you never heard anything about them again. That was never our game plan. Our game plan was to have a career.

GORD D: We're just striving to exist down there, like so many bands in the world. Breaking through is kind of a shopworn statement. There are many different degrees of breaking through. In a lot of ways I feel we've done it in pretty much the only way we've ever known, and that's through constant touring there – we've played down there a couple of dozen times. We've made a lot of friends there and there's probably anywhere from 30 to 40 cities we can go down to and play and attract a crowd. We've had a difficult time there because we've been virtually ignored by what people used to call the tastemakers, and that's *Rolling Stone* and *Spin* and maybe MTV. I don't think I would call them tastemakers anymore. So, in that sense, I think there's always hope. We've had to do it without those people and anyone will tell you it can be difficult. We don't worry about it. We're feeling very happy. We love going down there to play. I think also the attitudes are changing in Canada as well. I don't think Canadians need someone else's affirmation to tell them that it's OK to like what they like.

Below: Promo shot for Fully Completely, *May 1993*

Opposite: The Hip performing in Europe, July 1993

BOX SCORES

DATE	CITY	VENUE	ATTENDANCE/CAP	TIX	GROSS
7/16	VICTORIA	WESTERN SPEEDWAY	11,645/12,000	$35	$407,575
7/17	VANCOUVER	SEABIRD ISLAND	21,479/25,000	$35	$751,765
7/21	THUNDER BAY	BIG THUNDER	4,423/6,000	$25/30	$125,908
7/23	TORONTO	MARKHAM FAIRGROUND		$32.50	
7/24	TORONTO	MARKHAM FAIRGROUND	33,059/35,000	$45.00	$1,217,767.50
7/26	OTTAWA	LANSDOWNE PARK	11,652/15,000	$32.64	$380,321.28
7/29	WINNIPEG	STADIUM	13,875/16,000	$32.75	$454,406.25
7/31	CALGARY	RACE CITY SPEEDWAY	10,549/15,000	$35.00	$369,215.00
8/01	EDMONTON	CLARK STADIUM	11,183/15,000	$32.50	$363,447.50

GORD S: With the release of *Fully Completely*, we'd reached a point of significant mass with our audience in Canada to the point where we proposed doing our own travelling road show.

We bounced the idea off Jake, who bounced it off Live Nation, who, much to our surprise, agreed to do it. We started to assemble our dream bill, anchored by Midnight Oil, who would go on right before us. I was a particularly gigantic fan of them and still am. It was tough for us to get them – we made them an offer that they couldn't refuse. We did the whole tour with Daniel Lanois, whose band included bassist Daryl Johnson and Brian Blade, the most amazing A-list jazz drummer in the States; Karl Wallinger's group World Party did the first two shows; and we also had Hothouse Flowers, who were a great young band from Ireland.

PAUL: It was a pretty wild concept – getting together all these bands, some of them heroes of ours, and certainly all of them bands that we were fans of, and organising big shows and making it fun for them.

JAKE GOLD: *Fully Completely* came out and it was blowing up everywhere. 'Locked in the Trunk of a Car' was massive. Gord was writing more and more songs on Canadian themes, like 'Wheat Kings' and 'Fifty Mission Cap'. We needed to do something to solidify the band as the biggest band in the country, so we decided on a festival tour with really big acts opening for us. Lollapalooza had played a couple of cities in Canada, but we wanted to do it in every market. And that was the birth of Another Roadside Attraction.

The tour was going to be called Heksenketel, which is Dutch for 'witch's cauldron', but we had to run everything by Midnight Oil and they didn't like the occult connotations. So at the last minute someone suggested Another Roadside Attraction, after the Tom Robbins book, and everybody loved it.

JOHNNY: It was really cool to be organising our own festival and to be able to stay in Canada and do it. I believe that Markham Fairgrounds on the Saturday night was the biggest Hip show that we ever played – 60,000 people.

ROB: Another Roadside Attraction made us feel like we'd arrived. We got to play DJ. I used to go to high school parties with a stack of records under my arm and hijack the turntable. To be able to set up a festival and pick the bands, that was the same thing but on a very different scale. It felt awesome.

Another Roadside Attraction, Markham Fairgrounds, Markham, ON, 23–24 July 1993

Although Heksenketel was dropped as the name of the festival, it was later used as the title of a concert video recorded on the 1993 tour

Opposite: Letter and photo from a fan (bottom left)

PAUL: We were going on after Midnight Oil and didn't see that coming. It wasn't the easiest gig in the world, that's for sure. They were on fire. They hammered with all hammers. We were nervous but we were confident enough that it was going to be OK and, sure enough, it was.

GORD S: Midnight Oil clearly came fully intending to blow us off the stage every night. They're truly the proverbial hard act to follow – an intense band, very serious about what they do. We would rehearse backstage beforehand and would be really fired up. I can honestly say, Midnight Oil made us a better band. They forced us to up our game. We were good but they made us better.

ROB: Midnight Oil were a big inspiration to us. They were so tight, and they were musically, verbally and lyrically aggressive, very in your face. They weren't playing on our stage, it was their stage. They owned it and they owned that crowd. We were filled with incredible admiration for them, but it was their way. We have our own way of doing things. There are other front men, there are different approaches. I think it threw Gord for a bit of a loop to stand at the side and watch Pete Garrett come on and command the stage. But Gord didn't have to take a backseat to any of them. And we're a tight little band too. As hard as it was to follow Midnight Oil, we did!

Some of the happiest days of my life were on that tour. World Party were my favourite band in the world at that moment, and to see them on stage at Seabird Island I had tears of joy streaming down my face that we had made that happen. It was awesome.

GORD S: Roadside Attraction was yet another dream come true for us, just to get the opportunity to put that bill together. That was the most expansive one that we did and we played some crazy gigs. We built our own stage. We lost a whole pile of money, but it was worth every nickel to lose.

GORD D: That was a hard tour, in a sense. There were a lot of challenges the band faced. Going on after Midnight Oil is not the easiest thing to do – in fact, it's probably one of the harder things we ever did. But we came out of it and got to know them as people.

It was actually the picture of a utopian society. I was very impressed. I mean, it's too easy to drift into encampments, where bands' attitudes towards each other are based on the naivety that rock and roll is based on – which is that we're ultimately bent on competing with each other.

This tour had none of that. I'm a music fan – I love meeting other musicians, I love talking to other musicians – and what greater opportunity to take advantage of whatever standing we might have to try to attract people? To say 'We don't know you, but we love you, and will you come play with us?' Sometimes they actually do.

PAUL: It was so enjoyable that we did two other Roadside Attractions, in '95 and '97, with a whole bunch of other bands. We got to spend all day watching these bands that we really love and then go on at the end and play our show. It was a really positive experience for all of us, meeting all these people.

ROB: Gord would sometimes try out a new set of lyrics on stage in the middle of another song. Like the 'laminar flow' rant, which he did at Roadside Attraction – that was a song we actually worked up for *Day for Night*, but didn't end up recording.

It made every night fresh. We'd turn on a dime. You'd be playing a three-and-a-half-minute song and then Gord would start to head off in a different direction, so you'd have to cock your ear to work out where he was going with it. Was it just exposition? If it was you'd hang back and get into a little groove. But then you might hear some tension creeping in, and then it was time to get going. You just had to try to ride the dynamics.

I suppose you could go out and make every night identical and perfect, like it was a Broadway show, but that was never what we were about. We weren't Broadway. We were a rock and roll band.

GORD D: There's a section between songs where I was talking about something called laminar flow. The crowd was seeming to have a difficult time, moving around, so I was trying to do my bit at crowd control. Laminar flow is the whale's ability to move its skin and underlying layers of blubber in an undulating fashion so as to help it travel quicker through a large body of water without friction, or drag. All this comes from *A Whale for the Killing* by Farley Mowat. I realised that my memory is better than I thought it was, as I pretty much spouted it off verbatim. I want to thank Farley Mowat for that – I figure I should probably give credit where credit is due.

JOHNNY: We never knew where Gord was going to go with his stories. He kept us on our toes. I couldn't always hear where he was and sometimes I'd cut him off and then Robbie would start a solo. But we just let it happen. We were able to get out of the rhubarb if a song wasn't going that well. We could keep it positive, not throw anything anyway.

BILLY RAY: Gord had this ability to get into the flow of the rhythm that the band was jamming on and then just open his brain to whatever was running through it – it could have been the movie that was on the bus that afternoon, a book he had been reading that morning, a news story that he saw just before going on stage. His ability to spill that stuff out in a poetic rap was a gift.

ROB HIRST: Night after night on that tour I'd stand by the side of the stage and just wait for Gord Downie to erupt. And it was never the same. It was always incredibly spontaneous. Maybe something that you'd said to him and then he'd riff on that, and it was tangential and inspired and we were in stitches half the time. He'd put together a whole lot of non-sequiturs and then the band would count off the next song and off they'd go again.

The contradictions in The Hip were something we had never seen before. We knew they were a pretty straight-ahead five-piece guitar band with strong songs that spoke about Canada. Home songs with everyone singing along. But then you throw in this wild card of Gord Downie, who's barely sticking to the script, and I think that was the majesty of The Tragically Hip.

PAUL: The crowds were great, but there were a few worrisome moments where the testosterone level got too high. The bigger shows are scarier because you can't necessarily see everything that's going on. You hope that security can handle it but the person with the most power is the one with the microphone.

BILLY RAY: Gord hated it when a fight broke out in the audience; he'd stop the show and tell them to quit punching each other. Midnight Oil's set at Another Roadside Attraction in 1993 was a turning point. Peter Garrett just wasn't having it. He pointed guys out to security and got them thrown out.

JAKE GOLD: Gord followed Pete's example of calling out rowdy behaviour in the audience and getting crowds to quiet down.

Above: Gord Downie's handwritten 'Laminar Flow' rant, with an extract from A Whale for the Killing *by Farley Mowat*

Another Roadside Attraction, Markham Fairgrounds, Markham, ON, 23–24 July 1993

PETER GARRETT: Another Roadside Attraction was an incredible tour, and it was one of course that The Hip had founded. It was at a time when they were a big, exciting and growing band that people were attracted to in Canada. We had a growing audience as well.

There was a wild spirit abroad in the land and in these situations there's always a small minority of people who, for whatever reason, just want to throw their weight around. Maybe they're not in full control of themselves or they're indifferent to others. And we've always felt that that was the wrong thing to have happen, that everybody deserved to be able to be at a show irrespective of their sex, height, age, weight, whatever.

The only way that you can really deal with that behaviour is to directly confront it and call it out. And if that means stopping a show, well then stop it. Rock shows can be wild and that's fine. I love a wild rock show, I still do, but there's a difference between being wild and hurting people and you've got to draw the line very clearly. You need everybody in that place to be respected for who they are and treated in the same way.

GORD S: The moshing at those shows, in particular, was an aberration of that time. Peter's a very socially conscious guy, just like Gord, and they're standing there seeing young women up at the front to check out the band, ultimately getting pulverised in this sea of testosterone. Peter had no problem stopping the band and pointing out the most egregious offenders. Then they would launch into something like 'Dream World' and immediately fire right back up again.

Not long after that we moved to assigned seating. You could stand in your seat, but the idea of rush seating or general admission kind of went with those times. It kind of ruined itself, unfortunately.

PAUL: Sloan's lyric 'It's not the band I hate, it's their fans' – we think that's about us. There was a reputation that our core following was made up of hosers – those kind of hammerheads who drink beer with their hats on backwards – but I don't think that was the case at all.

BILLY RAY: My good vantage point of early Hip shows has left me with a phobia of crowds and being on the other side of the barricade. I've seen enough nonsensical violence: one guy elbowing another guy in the face and then that turning into five guys pounding the crap out of each other. I've seen what the crowd mentality does to a pipsqueak little wimp who decides he can punch another guy in the back of the head and no one will see him do it. It was very rough in around 1992/93. A show would start, and the audience would be a normal-looking crowd of women and men, evenly interspersed. But by the end of the first song, there were no more women at the front. They'd all either been brought over the barricade and sent back around, or they'd made their own way back through the crowd. So then it was just guys up front, elbowing, moshing, slam-dancing. In club shows in the States I spent half my night keeping guys off the stage – tackling them, pushing them back into the barricade.

ROB: We had a reputation that club owners loved of setting new bar records every place we played. Our audience came and drank themselves into a high-energy fighting stupor. It was strange to stand up there and watch it all go down. We thought it was a good sign at first, but we grew tired of it pretty fast. You don't need to see too many people get punched in the face – and in the early days there was a lot of that.

ROB: Gord really hated seeing the bullies up front rule the roost, so we set about creating a safe space for anyone who wanted to be close to the stage. For years the first few rows of a big venue would be reserved for people who were connected to the organisation that ran the building or owned the hockey team that played there. You had all these people up front that were like Captain Pikes staring at the stage – one beep for yes and two for no. They weren't necessarily huge fans of the band and it was pretty disheartening.

Then we decided to create what we called the 'henhouse'. Whoever brought the most food for the food bank would get their tickets upgraded to be able to sit up front. So the first few rows were all crazy uber fans who had earned their place through their generosity and community spirit.

GORD D: When we're on stage, we're like a school of fish that moves as a unit. The fish can tell when there's a predator coming by sensing changes in water pressure and so when the predator darts at them, the school moves but always stays intact. At our best, we're like that. We can sense the changes in each other's mood and character and behaviour and stay together.

BILLY RAY: As fans aged with the band, things got a little mellower. It helped that the music got a little mellower too – songs like 'Bobcaygeon' and 'Ahead by a Century'. There were more women coming to the show, most times with their boyfriends. Then it was nice to see, in the later years, groups of women coming together, which never would have happened in the early Nineties.

Gord thanked the women in the final concert of the final tour. The presence of women, the energy from women, the influence of having women in the room, made a huge difference.

ROB: Midnight Oil are incredible people and they put their money where their mouth is, and good on them. We were firmly in their camp with the concept of social justice, but to see the fervour and the passion and the way they used their music to do it wasn't our way. Pete Garrett is a big, brash, very self-confident Australian dude, and he comes on hard and fast and takes no prisoners. He would exhort you to his point of view, whereas we wanted to lure you and seduce you around to our point of view. Doing it in a more abstract way appealed to our little backwater Canadian senses more. Our approach was always to try to support the things we wanted and keep ourselves out of it as much as possible. When it was necessary to put our faces forward to get the message across, we would do it, but we tried to be more subtle about it, rather than 'my way or the highway'.

JAKE GOLD: Midnight Oil were environmental activists – Peter Garrett was one of the original members of Greenpeace. At the time the tour was starting, there was clear-cutting of a forest in Clayoquot Sound in BC and protesters were being arrested, so The Oils decided to go up there and play on a flatbed to show their solidarity. Gord thought that, as one of the hosts of the tour, he should be there to support them, and I think they really appreciated that.

With his commitment to the environment and to indigenous peoples, Pete was a beacon for Gord. He saw that if you're going to be the singer in a rock and roll band, you can do good and have integrity.

PETER GARRETT: I have no way of measuring my impact on Gord Downie, but if there was such a thing then I would feel that that was a great privilege. When you think about it, we're quite similar. We're in similar kinds of bands from similar kinds of countries and with, in some ways, similar preoccupations. So, if we

were long-distance soul brothers that hardly knew one another and yet affected one another, great. And I can say one thing for sure: I don't have that many soul brothers in the world and Gord Downie would surely have been one of them.

ROB HIRST: We all flew up in our light aircraft to Tofino, which was a beautiful place, but of course surrounding that was a clear-felling of Douglas firs. We were very happy to lend our name and do a dawn concert there in the woods. There were a lot of folks trying to stop the logging, the clear-felling, and there were an equal number of people from logging companies who were quite angry that this Australian rock band had turned up in their midst. Pete spoke really well to folks, said why we were there, how we were travelling the world not only doing gigs but also supporting environmental causes, including this one. We got in the van, tried to leave and that's when the logging folks and their families blocked and shook the car. We had young kids in the car so we were quite anxious.

We understood where they were coming from, really. These were people whose lives depended on logging. We understand forestry industries and we have them in Australia, but there are ways of doing it, and clear-felling large swathes of land for commercial profit is the wrong way to do it. Clear-felling destroys the environment and everything that grows in it and all the animals and birds that live in it. So we knew we were on safe ground, but we also understood there were passions on each side.

JOHNNY FAY: Going up to Clayoquot Sound and seeing Midnight Oil play there ignited something in Gord. He saw the immediacy and how a voice can be heard. This wasn't their country, but they were focused on things that were wrong across the whole planet.

I actually remember very little about the show itself. It was really brief, very early in the morning. We were travelling between gigs so it was something we had to fit in. But the most important thing was actually just to show up, give our support, and be part of that push along with Native First Nations people and Greenpeace to try to talk some sense about the way logging was done in Canada.

PETER GARRETT: We had decided to go and join the protests at Clayoquot Sound, and we flew up in a light aircraft along the coast. It was incredibly beautiful, which made the clear-felling feel even more obnoxious. The logging operations at Clayoquot were typical of early brutal clear-cuts that were happening in forests right across the world. We'd experienced some of it in our own country, and it's always an ugly, distressing sight to see the heart of a landscape and a living environment torn apart for a few bucks. I was also aware of the fact that people earned their living from it, so there had to be a

MIDNIGHT OIL

FACSIMILE

TO:	The Management Trust Limited
ATTN:	Jake Gold
FAX NO:	416 463 4038
FROM:	Gary Morris
DATE:	12th May 1993

In the event of difficulties receiving this transmission please telephone (203) 454 1006.

Dear Jake,

The Oils have asked me to convey two requests to The Hip.

Firstly, the possibility of Greenpeace having stalls at all of the shows. I would need an answer on this as soon as possible, along with venue contact numbers and addresses.

Secondly, Greenpeace are desiring to do a commando raid, raising plenty of media attention, to CLAYQUOTE SOUND BC, where there is quite significant logging of a highly destructive nature. *Clayoquot*

We would like to know if The Hip would like to join Midnight Oil in attending this commando raid, highlighting ecological carnage. A good time for this would be just after Vancouver.

We would like to hear from you as soon as possible on the above two matters.

Kind regards

Gary Morris *Rosemary*

Gary Morris

37 Cedar Hills Road, WESTON, CONNECTICUT, USA 06883
PH: (203) 454 1006   FAX: (203) 454 9651

FACTS ABOUT *LAND* AND CLAYOQUOT SOUND

April 13, 1993 - The provincial government of British Columbia announces that logging will be permitted in 74 per cent of the virgin rain forests in the watersheds of Upper Clayoquot River, the Upper Sydney River, Bulson Creek and Bedwell Sound - an area of western Vancouver Island known as Clayoquot Sound. Thousands of ancient cedar trees will die by a brutal land-clearing process known as clearcut logging. Clearcutting is an ecologically-disastrous practice which destroys the integrity of forest ecosystems and can lead to rapid erosion of soils, creating landslides, river siltation and extensive damage to coastal ecosystems and fish habitats.

July, 1993 - Five musical acts - Toronto's **Crash Vegas**, Ireland's **Hothouse Flowers**, Hamilton's **Daniel Lanois**, Australia's **Midnight Oil** and Kingston, Ontario's **The Tragically Hip** - join together for the **Another Roadside Attraction** tour, which performs 10 shows in nine Canadian cities over the next month. More than 130,000 people gather to watch these performers, who, though disparate in style, are united by their honesty, passion and integrity.

August 9, 1993 - The Day of 300 Arrests. A massive single-day protest of clearcut logging in Clayoquot Sound is mobilized by Friends of Clayoquot Sound. Nearly 1000 protesters gather to blockade logging roads, and 304 of them are arrested by officers of the Royal Canadian Mounted Police.

October 27, 1993 - Cargo Records releases *Land*, a single performed by the bands of Another Roadside Attraction. The recording was produced by Lanois during a 12-hour session at Calgary studio The Beach during the night and morning of July 30 and 31, near the end of the tour's cross-Canada jaunt.

All proceeds from the sale of *Land* will be donated to the Clayoquot Sound Defense Fund, a legal reserve set up to aid in the defense of protesters arrested at Clayoquot Sound since mid-April.

solution that provided for people and communities that were connected in whatever way, whether they were opposing what was going on or whether they felt that it should still happen. So all of those emotions and thoughts and interactions were roiling around in a kind of mad atmosphere and then you go and play a song to people and hopefully inspire them to keep doing what they're doing, because they're the ones who are doing the hard work. The musicians are just playmakers on a stage. We're not serious people, really.

Everyone tends to elevate the musician and the star, particularly in our modern culture, which is so narcissistic – a form of idolatry, if you like. All of that stuff doesn't mean anything to us; it certainly doesn't mean anything to me. What means much more is the authenticity, the integrity of what you're doing. You're going to play with people who are objecting to something that they think is fundamentally wrong, and you're trying to give them energy and inspiration and hope. When bands do that, when The Hip did it, when we did it, then they're being bands. Otherwise, whatever they're doing is just for their own fun, to play music and to enjoy it with people in a show.

GORD S: To see the guys from The Oils literally fly up to Clayoquot to lend their voice had a big effect on us. Prior to that, we were a little more meek. We wouldn't take the politics and the activism up on stage for whatever reason. Probably a lack of courage, but certainly Pete Garrett and Rob Hirst didn't lack in the courage department. It shamed us a little bit, because it had never even crossed our minds that we should go up and support the protesters that were there to protect this rainforest.

GORD S: When we got to Calgary, motivated by Midnight Oil, we decided to record a song together, produced by Daniel Lanois, which we released as a single with the proceeds going to the Clayoquot Sound Defense Fund.

ROB HIRST: The basic song was written by Jim [Moginie, Midnight Oil guitarist] and I added a section. We did an all-night session, and the idea was that the lead singers of the touring bands would take a line each. Pete took a line, Liam Ó Maonlaí from Hothouse Flowers took a line, Michelle McAdorey from Crash Vegas took a line, Gord took a line. Liam's line was flown in late. I think he was the only one that wasn't there for the session. The first line was taken, of course, by Dan Lanois himself, who then took the song away and produced it up on his mobile a little while later. With his band playing on it and all of us making contributions, it happened really quickly and organically.

PAUL: Everyone on the '93 Roadside tour recorded the 'Land' song together to bring attention to the harm being done by clear-felling in Clayoquot Sound. Rob played on it and Gord sang on it.

ROB HIRST: There are a lot of comparisons between The Oils and The Hip and I think that's why we immediately bonded on that Roadside Attraction tour. People will stay loyal to a band that continues to write music that relates to them, that talks about issues in their own country, a band that doesn't take shortcuts to get to any particular point, is clearly there for the long term and is in it for the right reasons. A band that lends its name to causes outside just playing on stage. A band that's real, that resonates. We saw that The Hip had a similar aim to ours, which was not a get-rich-quick programme by any means but was a desire to stay true to their country and to in some way interpret it in a musical and lyrical sense and put on strong shows and celebrate it.

PETER GARRETT: Anyone can put out a tweet or say something on stage, but it's what you do with the things that you're expressing that counts. We have a saying in Australia: 'Are you fair dinkum or not?' Which means, are you genuine or are you just being some kind of show pony? When we got to know The Hip a little, saw what they were doing and worked with them, particularly on the 'Land' single, we knew that they were genuine. And that's all that really matters. We didn't know one another that well, but the interactions that we had were real.

Opposite: Gord Downie's notebook and journal with handwritten entries from his trip to Clayoquot Sound on 14 July 1993 for a protest against clear-cut logging, at which Midnight Oil performed

Below: Cassette tape of three edits of the 'Land' single mixed at Manta Eastern Sound, Toronto, 1993

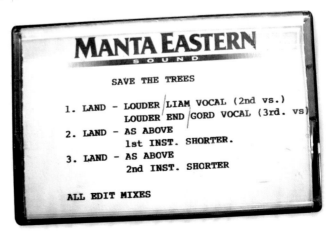

THE TRAGICALLY HIP

"Day For Night is for the fearsome and the catchy, the vice-ridden
and the retired, for the Brooders and the Bloomers..."

Gord Downie

Sometime in the early summer of '93, while planning a European tour, an idea popped into my head. We had an open period of four days between the Halfweg Festival(in Amsterdam) and the Glastonbury Festival in England. Instead of traveling to northern England before Glastonbury(as was proposed) why not remain in Amsterdam, find a small studio and work on some song ideas? The prospect of hanging out in one of our favorite cities was considerably more appealing than a few quick gigs across the channel and, fortunately, reason prevailed.

So, we found ourselves at the Sleep In---part nightclub, part youth hostel with a small studio in the basement perfect for making demos. I don't know whether this session was the very first for what would become Day For Night but, it was one of the earliest and was certainly productive. Three or four days is not a great amount of time to produce fantastic, spot-on recordings but, it's just the right amount to get the ideas down on tape and that was the main reason for these sessions. Of course, some ideas were more complete than others(Nautical Disaster was taking shape while Scared was still a happy melody on Paul's guitar) and some ideas never surfaced beyond the Sleep-In sessions. However, any idea, riff, tune or whatever, if on tape, is fair game for future poaching and a great deal of tape was run in those few days. Mark Vreeken, our live front of house engineer, was at the helm and would remain there for every session save those co-produced by the band and Mark Howard. Dave Koster(aka Billy Ray) acted as the ever-present studio assistant/whipping boy. That allowed me to roam the streets of Amsterdam in search of musical supplies or whatever else we may have needed. I did spend some time in studio each day but, not being well-versed in the art of recording it was best for me to stay out of everyone's way.

After our few days in Amsterdam we spent another twelve touring northern Europe, playing festivals for the most part. Schuttorf, Roskilde, Torhout and Werchter; these are the festivals that make Europe a fantastic place for a good band to tour. Not a great deal of bullshit, just a group of smart people doing a good job. European promoters, and certainly the fans, are broad-minded enough that a bill featuring Sugar, Faith No More and Metallica is the perfect gig for The Tragically Hip. One result of our European experiences was the confidence to put on our own festival style tour in Canada. We called it "Another Roadside Attraction", the name being stolen from a Tom Robbins novel. The Hip headlined a bill that included Midnight Oil, Crash Vegas, Hothouse Flowers, Daniel Lanois and on the west coast, World Party and Pere Ubu. The twelve dates on that tour were twelve of the best concerts anywhere, anytime. Some of the fun can be seen in a feature length video directed by Gord Downie's brother, Mike. Called "Heksenketel"(a Dutch word for witch's cauldron), it runs about 70 minutes. The title comes from the original name of Another Roadside Attraction. Aside from the filming and live show, the band was also jamming backstage almost daily and new songs were taking shape as the tour progressed.

Thugs existed as a near complete song but, would change radically with the passing months. Fire in The Hole, however, was being born out of the various dressing room jams. Everyone referred to the riff as "pointy teeth". Nautical Disaster was being jammed both backstage and onstage; it evolved in the middle section of New Orleans is Sinking from night to night. Once this tour ended we spent the last weeks of September in the U.S.. By October 2nd, the touring for Fully Completely was finished.

" A good song will continue to grow live. From there,
new songs can easily emerge."

Gord Sinclair

"The road...it's officially unfair."

Gord Downie

No longer worrying about visas, laundry or where the hell we were, we returned to the scene of many favorite crimes, the Woolen Mill. An old burlap mill in the north end of Kingston, the mill was a perfect rehearsal space but, also much more. For one, it was my home for two of the three years the band used it for rehearsals. And it was also, essentially, an impregnable fortress perfect for keeping away prying eyes and those with ears too big for their own good. With no one to hassle us(sometimes a problem in a small town), the work progressed. The months between the end of the road and Christmas were busy ones. Grace, Emergency, Inch an Hour, Impossibilium and various versions of Thugs, were either written in their entirety or re-written entirely. Various other ideas were being thrown around, including early versions of Daredevil and Greasy Jungle. We took a break for the holidays.

During the week between Christmas Day and New Year's Day, the band was back at the mill, this time working with Mark Howard. We had known Mark for a while; from back in the days when Road Apples was recorded and on Another Roadside Attraction, where he was Dan Lanois' front of house engineer. It was this week that gave the band the confidence in Howard that would result in his co-producing the album. This was the week when Thugs finally found its sound. This was also the session that captured Titanic as it appears on the album. A number of passes would be made at Titanic later in New Orleans but, none would match the atmosphere the winter lent the song. January would give rise

to Yawning or Snarling and The Inevitability of Death and February provided a chance to play some of the new songs live. Sure, some of the new material had been played live before: Thugs on Another Roadside Attraction, Nautical Disaster at the Kumbaya Festival(to benefit people living with Aids) in Toronto but, it was the College Earth Summit at Yale that saw the first performance of many of the songs. It was a small gig at Toad's Place but, the new songs were received well and it was only a month before the band would be in the studio. That month passed(and none too soon, winter was kicking the shit out of eastern Ontario) and it was time to head down to the Crescent City.

Kingsway studio, New Orleans La., is the kind of place The Hip can work. The house is a studio or the studio is a house, either way a large mansion on the edge of the French Quarter that is both familiar and practical. The Tragically Hip is not a band well suited to isolation chambers and by-the-numbers recording. Though that can be educational and productive, their best work has always come from a more fluid approach and environment. The bulk of Day for Night was recorded at the base of a large stairway, with the band within five feet of each other most of the time. Set up an amp, mike it and throw a blanket or a pillow over it, turn it up and play. Over time, patterns developed. Much of the day would be dedicated to listening and listening again to what had been recorded with the night reserved for new ideas, new tracks or new songs. Along the way, a shadow record emerged; spacey jams, old ideas reworked , generally a chance to blow off some musical steam. This music is not on the record but, it is as much a part of the recording process as anything else and much musical cannibalism will be its legacy. So Hard Done By is a perfect example. Played in concert a very few times over the years, it finally found an arrangement everyone liked. Many songs have been picked at over the years and as long as there are tapes to listen to, that will continue. When it came time to leave New Orleans, most of the recording had been done but the album was not complete. The band headed for home.

" For us, the songs are continually evolving. Months of
adding and subtracting will determine if a song is good
enough to stand on its' own."

Gord Sinclair

Three weeks after returning to Kingston, the band packed up again and headed for Morin Heights, a small town one hour north of Montreal in rural Quebec. There, with the two Marks and Billy Ray, the band began to mix everything and of course, tinker further. For two or three weeks they fiddled and mixed and generally put all the tracks together. With Morin Heights being only four hours away, the band also had the luxury of getting home once in a while and everyone took turns spending time up at the studio. It was a good choice of location for the mixing because, while relatively close to home, it was in the hills and isolated enough to allow everyone to concentrate on the songs. However, the mixing did not end in those hills and our adventures would continue into the summer.

By now, it was June. As well as the recordings to work on, we had to get ready for some live gigs. Our first big show in some time was a Canada Day concert on, of course, July 1st. It was an all day, open air show with some of our favorite Canadian bands on the bill. Change of Heart, The Odds and Spirit of the West were among the nine other acts that day. 35,000 people showed up, it didn't rain and no one was killed; so, we all had a good time. The rest of the summer yawned in front of us and we hit the road.

Whatever life a song might have in the studio, or on record, can be measured by the final product only. But on the stage, any song can have one hundred lives. Some songs really come alive only when an audience breathes life into them and thus, the purpose of the road is revealed. No matter how shitty a gig, how horrid the travel, how unpalatable the food, the songs continue to save our skins night after night. And when the gig is great, and the club within walking distance from whatever conventioneer-filled hotel we can't wait to leave, then the songs become an unstoppable juggernaut of compressed ear drums, rattling teeth and frayed nerves. Some nights we teeter between the two extremes, but the road is unending .

And so, when "Day for Night" is released in America in the new year, we will find ourselves in the midst of a Canadian tour and in the grips of whatever weather the Great Lakes might throw at us. For the same reasons we might tour Texas in July, we will tour Canada in the dead of winter; the songs demand to live, no matter how extreme life may be. Since the release of the record in Canada and Europe this past fall, we have seen both extremes again and again. We bounced around America for 19 more shows after the 20 we had played in the summer, prior to the album's release. We then trundled off to Europe for 14 shows in 6 countries. Along the way we made friends with all in the Blues Traveler organization. Another rare bonus from the road; like minded souls who have many tales of their own.

In the end, the days and nights blur together into a seamless river of misadventure and near-insanity anchored only by the music that comes from soundchecks, concerts and the uncounted beers drained in Brussels or Oklahoma City. The songs don't know where they are, and some nights neither do we. But above all the noise we might make about ourselves, or how hard the road might be, the music has always been louder.

David Powell, Road Manager, Dec.19/1994

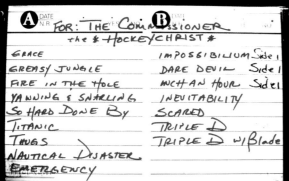
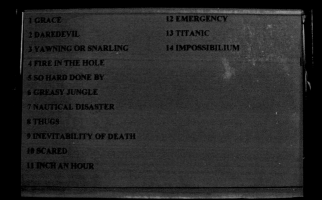

Cassette tapes of rough mixes for Day for Night, *January–May 1994*

Opposite: The Hip at Dave Powell's parents' home in Thunder Bay, ON, 1 March 1990

Nautical Disaster

I had this dream where I relished the Fray
And the screaming would fill my head all day
It was as though I'd been spit here, settled in, into the pocket of a lighthouse on some rocky socket, off the coast of France, dear.
One afternoon, four-thousand men died in the water, here and five hundred more were thrashing madly as parasites might in your blood.
Now I was in a lifeboat, designed for ten, ten only, anything that systematic, would get you hated -- it's not a deal, nor a test, nor a love of something fated - death -.
The selection was quick, the crew was picked in order and those left in the water got kicked off our pantleg and we headed for home.
Then the dream ends when the phone rings - "you doing alright?" he said, "it's out there, most days and nights, but only a fool would complain"
anyway Susan if you, like our conversation is as faint a sound in my memory as those fingernails (fing. or nails) scratching on my hull.

SCARED (The Fear Monger) The Laughing Man

I could make you scared, if you want me to
You're not prepared, but if you went
He said, "I can make you scared it's kinda what I do," If you're prepared, here's what I propose to do.
Once in Russia more than a million works of art Were out to the woods
(To save from) Down the road where, Nazis marched From
Still like on the wrong light wouldn't look any good
And through the museum the Nazis marched
There was an emptiness
to make sure the nazi music march
Through the Hermitage where the nazi's
Nazi boots
The sound of nazi boots on the march
Ran through the museum empty
Staring at the empty space where
In the museum standing empty and dark
The spirits waited for the
The spirits waited for
So that when the nazis found the (whole place) dark
They'd think that God had left the museum for good (planet)
with what good this could possibly do
It makes you scared and lucky too
I gotta say

GORD D: We use every opportunity we can get to write and to record in whatever fashion we can. Oftentimes on tours, we use our soundchecks as a brief moment to work on new material. Ultimately, writing songs requires solitude and an open-ended time schedule. With time constraints, you can't really do anything. On bigger shows, we are afforded the luxury of bringing along a crappy drum set and teeny amps and we throw them in a corner of whatever dressing room and we go in there before the show or any chance we get. I think for anyone in a band that is touring, any chance you get to create a little bit of solitude for yourself and maybe even conjure up an idea, those are moments to cherish.

GORD S: We had really hit our stride as a creative unit. We were touring the world, writing songs when we were in Australia, writing songs during soundchecks in Europe, writing, writing, writing, and coming up with what we thought was really interesting, unique stuff, like 'Grace, Too' and 'Nautical Disaster' – songs that, quite honestly, I couldn't imagine any other group ever recording. I could hear the influence of all of us in every song that we were doing. It was a really organic, cooperative approach to writing. That's what we wanted to do – extensively jam as we were writing, with Gord riffing on top of the jam, and then coddle a song together based on that.

PAUL: Travel, and especially work travel, which is what we were doing, opens up your mind and adds to your experience, maybe gets you thinking in different ways. 'Scared' is a historical sort of song and I think Gord was starting to flow into that, being in Europe. 'Nautical Disaster' is another one. If we had only ever played in Canada, maybe those songs wouldn't have come about. It's a matter of having an open mind and letting the songs come in.

GORD S: 'When the Nazis find the whole place dark, they'll think God's left the museum for good.' We probably got talking about the Nazis when we were driving around Europe in the splitter van – how, like any marauding horde, they would be coming from the outskirts of town, and that history teaches us to hide our treasures before the invaders loot them or smash them up. That wasn't lost on us. No one knows better than the Europeans how society can get turned upside down overnight.

GORD S: Art is our link between our past and our present, our now and our then. It sounds pretentious that we were thinking of ourselves in that way, but we were music fans. I have songs that still resonate with me emotionally. It's not nostalgia, but they take me back to a certain place in time while I also don't forget that I'm in this current place in time as well. That's the business we're in as creative people; we're capturing those moments of inspiration and trying to get them down as quickly as we can before they get ruined or watered down.

GORD D: I remember I saw a TV programme on the sinking of the *Bismarck*. All these German navy men went into the water when the boat was sunk, and there were hundreds of them in there. The ship that had torpedoed them was picking them up, until they got a message on the shortwave that there were U-boats in the area and they had to pull out. The idea of the boat pulling off as men were clawing away at the hull was a good starting point. But I think of that song in different ways every time I listen to it.

GORD S: Europe played a big part in 'Nautical Disaster' for Gord. I know that was quite a profound takeaway from our time spent in Europe, particularly around November, a sombre month at best. I mean, who writes songs like that? It's like prose. Nothing rhymes. It's a musical arrangement that hinges on the poetry. The melody doesn't necessarily change so much as the chords changing underneath the material. That's a reflection of our writing style. We were creating on the fly, trying to turn individual ideas into songs.

The way Gord wrote lyrics was that all of a sudden the lyric evolves and so does the song, until it becomes a complete thing, a complete thought, a complete story. That was one of our strengths. The song could stand on its own.

'Nautical Disaster' was always an evolution when we were playing it live. We used to play it as a jam in the middle of 'New Orleans Is Sinking', which was a great launching pad for 'Grace, Too' as well.

Opposite and this page:
Torhout-Werchter,
Belgium, 3–4 July 1993

Opposite: Lyrics for
'Nautical Disaster'
(top right)

Lyrics for 'Scared'
(bottom centre)

PAUL: *Day for Night* took a leap off of the song 'Grace, Too'. Everything that the album became started with that song. It wasn't a conscious decision to go in a more experimental direction. We were all just jamming at our rehearsal spot in the Woolen Mill in Kingston and this song started coming out.

GRACE, TOO – Universal conscription for Global
Peacekeeping Force
He said I'm fabulously rich
C'mon just lets go
She kinda bit her lip
Geez, I don't know
But, I can guarantee
There'll be no knock on the door
I'm total pro, that's what I'm here for
I come from downtown
Born ready for you
Armed with will and determination
and grace, too

The secret rules of engagement
Are hard to endorse
when the appearance of conflict
Meets the appearance of force
But I can guarantee
There'll be no knock on the door
I'm total pro here
That's what I'm here for
I come from downtown
Born ready for you
Armed with skill and its frustration
and grace too

**MCA RECORDS ARTISTS THE TRAGICALLY HIP
TO BEGIN RECORDING NEW ALBUM IN NEW ORLEANS;
BAND TO CO-PRODUCE WITH MARK HOWARD**

UNIVERSAL CITY, CA -- April 18, 1994 -- MCA Records announces that The Tragically Hip have entered Kingsway Studios in New Orleans, LA, to begin recording their as-yet-untitled fourth album. The band anticipates a completion date in late spring or early summer, with a scheduled release date later this fall. For the first time in their career, The Tragically Hip will co-produce, sharing production duties with Mark Howard, whose credits include work with Daniel Lanois, Bob Dylan, Iggy Pop, the Neville Brothers and Robbie Robertson.

The Tragically Hip are -- in terms of popular acclaim, gross tour revenue and total record sales -- one of the most successful musical groups in all of Canada. The band is one of only five acts to have released three consecutive quintuple-platinum albums in Canada (the others are Guns N' Roses, John Cougar, Bon Jovi and Madonna). Each of The Tragically Hip's three albums -- Up to Here, Road Apples and Fully Completely -- has passed the five-times-platinum mark in Canada, and the band's self-titled indie debut EP has sold nearly double platinum.

Last year, The Tragically Hip were voted Entertainer of the Year at 1993's Juno Awards (Canada's equivalent of the Grammys). This award carries particular significance because it is the only Juno Award determined by public ballot. This year, the band is nominated for three Juno Awards: Entertainer of the Year, Best Selling Album (Foreign or Domestic) (for Fully Completely) and Single of the Year (for "Courage"). Also, the Canadian Organization of Campus Activities (C.O.C.A.) has announced that The Tragically Hip has been selected to receive the C.O.C.A. Hall of Fame Award for 1993/1994.

The Tragically Hip are: Gord Downie (vocals), Bobby Baker (lead guitar), Paul Langlois (rhythm guitar and backing vocals), Gord Sinclair (bass and backing vocals) and Johnny Fay (drums).

"All Man's Miseries."

Contact:
Paula Batson/(818)777-8961
Caroline Prutzman/(212)841-8050

ROB: Mark Howard came to the process with a very different attitude to producing. He was all about the performance. So he wanted to be recording in the room with the band while we were playing. And when he did a mix, that was also a performance. We'd all have our hands on the faders and he'd tell each of us when to bump it up and when to fade it back down. That was fun. I don't think it was a great working method, but it never really mattered. It was about the process, and that was exciting.

MARK HOWARD: I'm a guerrilla recorder. I just get in the room with the band and we start recording. I record before they even know I'm recording – you get your best stuff that way.

ROB: We were big fans of the Daniel Lanois records. We loved their sonic atmosphere, and Mark was a huge part of creating that. He could just throw the Eventide, which was still a new thing back then, on the rhythm guitar for a little bit and then suddenly it was on something else and so the sound bounced around the room. That changed the way we played and jammed together and took us to different places.

Because Kingsway was a residential studio, we could only play electrically until about ten at night and then we would turn to what we called 'the Flintstone set-up'. Johnny had a bunch of djembes and congas and hand drums and we'd pull out the acoustic guitars. So that took us in a whole different direction.

JOHNNY: We liked the idea of making a record in a house, just setting up our instruments in a room and letting a great guy capture it. That's what Mark was really good at. If you listen to *Road Apples*, which was made by Don Smith with the same console in the same house (although in a different room), and then you listen to *Day for Night*, they sound completely different. We'd always gone somewhere new for each record, but this showed that we could go back to New Orleans and make something completely different.

With *Road Apples*, we stayed round the corner, but this time we all slept in the house. We'd stay up late and record songs that were more acoustic.

BILLY RAY: In those first days in the studio in New Orleans, there were sketches of songs. The band really fed off each other – they were open to each other's ideas. And they worked hard. There was no messing about. It was get in there, work, work, work, dinner, work some more.

They would know if a song wasn't going anywhere – they would move on to another song, try something else, have dinner, come back to a whole different group of songs, then try that other one again the next day fresh. Keeping it fresh, keeping it moving was how they created such magic.

The band loved it in New Orleans. They were really excited like kids about going to Coop's for crawfish boils and showing me the French market where I was going to pick up beer and sandwiches for them. It felt really exotic, seeing alligator heads in the shops. I remember thinking, 'How can there be any alligators still on the planet when there's this many heads for sale here?'

They all had their own little routines in the morning. Most of them would head down to a coffee shop called Kaldi's whose motto was 'Life's too short for bad coffee', which Gord was famous for quoting multiple times in concerts and interviews. Robbie would go to a place called the Richelieu for eggs benedict.

When they needed to let out their frustration and pent-up energy from being in the studio, they'd take a break and play pool or go for a swim, and then get back at it. It was like a boys' camp, and part of my job was to try to create the right kind of vibe.

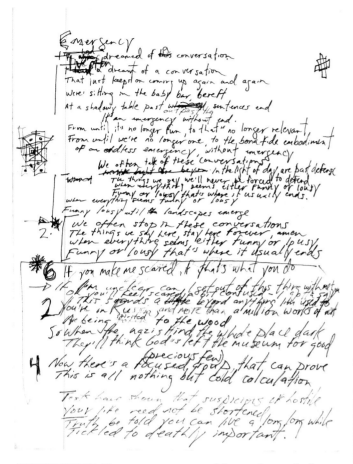

*Lyrics for 'Grace, Too'
(opposite) and
'Emergency' (left)*

*Gord Downie's notes on
Day for Night sessions
(below and opposite
bottom)*

PAUL: Mark Howard liked weird and wacky songs and he would do performance mixes. No one does a one-take mix and records it. They basically work to get closer and closer, and closer and closer. Well, Mark would start from scratch and we caught on. We still wanted to make sure we had good songs, but we were going to mess with things a bit. The only conscious decision we made was to keep growing, keep getting better – going to places we hadn't gone much was always inspiring.

There were mixes that Mark did that didn't work out, that were too out there. We had a very relaxed relationship, all of us, so we'd agree that we couldn't go down a certain route with a song. He was a little out there, but he was on the same page too. We wanted the album to have appealing songs, so, while there was some experimentation, we also dialled it back at times.

*At the start of
'Emergency' you can
hear this torrential
downpour, which we
picked up by sticking a
microphone out in the
breezeway just in front
of the house. There
were raindrops the size
of quarters bouncing
off the patio. Mark was
very good at picking up
things like that on the
fly. And then Gord
Sinclair's really cool
droning bass starts
swirling and the song
kicks in. (JF)*

MARK HOWARD: I've never seen anything quite at their level of drinking beer and smoking pot. They were smoking a quarter pound of pot a week and they got through cases and cases of beer stacked to the ceiling. It put them in a mindset where they were comfortable.

But they were stoned and they were also eating a lot of heavy food like pizza and pasta and I wasn't getting any takes out of them. So I decided to have a barbecue. We had a guy come in and cook all these special steaks and then bang, bang, bang, we got three takes in a row. I think getting a big boost of protein like that gave them a lot more energy.

ROB: While *Fully Completely* was wildly successful, the experience of making *Road Apples* had been much more enjoyable. Everyone was connected and in on it and we were relaxed and happy and so much of it came out of jamming. So with *Day for Night*, we wanted to get back to that.

It truly was a case of the five of us sitting in a circle and someone throwing out an idea and seeing where it went. We'd jam for 40 minutes, listen to the playback and pick out the 20 seconds from, say, 6.20 to 6.40 that we felt was the essence of what we were trying to get to. Then we'd hone in on that and build the song. It was not the most direct songwriting method, but it was incredibly band-focused.

MARK HOWARD: I worked with Brian Eno and he's the ambient god, so I picked up a lot from him about how to treat sounds. I discovered that the bigger the amp, the smaller the sound. Huge Marshall stacks were sounding like mosquitoes. On 'So Hard Done By' I put Robbie's guitar through this thing called a cigarette box because it was the size of a Marlboro pack. His solo on that song sounds like the Angry Birds kind of thing.

So I was very much into developing sounds for them and helping Gord with phrasing and stuff like that. I don't like to use headphones. If you're singing with the speakers on really loud, like it's a concert, you get better performances out of people. That's what I was doing with Gord and he was digging it. Once you put headphones on and you go in a little booth at the back of the studio, there's no vibe.

MARK HOWARD: I brought in Daryl Johnson, the bass player who worked with Daniel Lanois. He played some congas and a couple other things. And then I also invited this kid, Brian Blade, who was only 18 or something but was a mind-blowing drummer. We did a whole other record, like a ghost record, that's never been heard by anybody. If you think that the record that came out is dark and weird, you should hear those tracks! Like Santana but crazier.

ROB: Mark had been around when we made *Road Apples*, as he was the house engineer at Kingsway. We had a great engineer in Bruce Barris, and Mark was mostly just up to hijinks. Don Smith and Bruce Barris were so technically on it and they would be listening to a playback and they'd hear a little crackling. For the next two hours we'd be derailed while they tried to find the mic or line that was causing this crackle, and they never could. Then we'd go back to recording a little while later and there'd be a crackling again. And, of course, it would be Mark crinkling a piece of paper in front of one of the microphones just to drive them nuts. Which was kind of evil and wasting money and time, but he could also be great fun and he was a brilliant engineer in his own right.

MARK HOWARD: Don Smith and his engineer came from LA and we didn't like anybody that came through the door from LA, because they thought they knew everything. I was a little bit of a wiseass in those days and I liked messing with their brain.

JOHNNY: *Day for Night* was a really hard record to make. I love Mark Howard and he was a super talented engineer, but he'd never really produced a record before. I don't know that he was that great at managing a group. It was a weird dynamic. Whereas Don Smith had been helping to direct us in making *Road Apples*, *Day for Night* was a bit of a free-for-all.

Mark did something that we'd never had before. When he wasn't getting the results he wanted, he brought other guys in. So he brought in Bill Dillon to play some atmospheric guitar, which I don't think Robbie was crazy about. And then he brought in Brian Blade, who's one of the greatest jazz drummers of our generation, and Daryl Johnson, a bass player who was also doing vocals.

We'd started to make a little money and things were beginning to get a bit more comfortable, but now we were beginning to wonder about job security and the future of the band. We trusted in each other enough to know that we had each other's back, but this broke the trust a little bit.

Maybe it was a deliberate move by Mark to stir the pot. We certainly ended up with a pretty aggressive record, sonically. There's a real darkness to it, from the album cover to the song titles – like 'Nautical Disaster' and 'Inevitability of Death'. So it's a dark record and it was a dark period for us.

But we got through it. I remember saying to myself, 'If we can live through this, we can live through anything.'

ROB: I really like *Day for Night*. It's a dark, murky ride, but it stands up well. In a weird way, I think the moments that upset the record are the concessions we made to being more of a rocking live band. A straight, balls-out three-chord rocker like 'An Inch an Hour', which is a song I really like, stands out as not being part of the set.

BILLY RAY: Mark Howard was cool. He was this strange little guy that just had so much skill and talent. For him, it didn't matter about the studio being technically perfect. He was more about catching vibes – he'd get right in there with the band dancing away and swinging his arms and hooting and hollering to get them to put more energy into the songs.

But he also liked to screw with you. You'd make him a tea and he'd say that it was garbage and tell you to pour it out and make another one. But he wouldn't tell you what was garbage about it. You'd just have to make it differently and hope that you'd got it right this time. He'd do that for five cups in a row before he'd drink it.

GORD D: [Dark] was an adjective that was thrown around when [*Day for Night*] first came out, but I don't really see it. Some of the songs I would call downright uplifting. Even 'Inevitability of Death' is kind of a funny song more than anything. I thought it would be funny to have radio DJs cueing it up and announcing it as people were driving off to work.

Backstabber
Inevitability Of Death — Terry's Gift
Puffy lips and glistening skin
And everything comes meshing in
We don't go to hell just our memories do
I bet a sense of connectedness
exclusive, tight but nothing dangerous
We don't go to hell but memories of us do
And But If you go to hell, I'll still remember you
Lyou too
I thought you beat the death of inevitability to death just a little bit
I thought he beat the inevitability of death to death

Terry's gift is forever green
It got (us) me up and back on the scene
If we won't go hell just our memories of us do
We don't go to hell,
Fantastic gap, common space
open concept in your smiling face
But I thought you beat the death of inevitability to death
& I just thought you beat the inevitability of death to death

Day for Night
RECORDED: APRIL–MAY 1994
KINGSWAY STUDIOS, NEW ORLEANS, LA
THE DAVE CAVE, KINGSTON, ON
PRODUCERS: MARK HOWARD
MARK VREEKEN, THE TRAGICALLY HIP
ENGINEERS: MARK HOWARD
MARK VREEKEN
RELEASED: 24 SEPTEMBER 1994

Grace, Too
Daredevil
Greasy Jungle
Yawning or Snarling
Fire in the Hole
So Hard Done By
Nautical Disaster
Thugs
Inevitability of Death
Scared
An Inch an Hour
Emergency
Titanic Terrarium
Impossibilium

Day for Night *sold
300,000 copies in four
days and was the band's
first release to debut at
number one on the
Canadian album charts.
It has since been certified
six times platinum*

*Above and opposite:
Promotional shots for
Day for Night, 1994*

JAKE GOLD: I was sitting in a meeting at Universal/MCA in the States and I looked around the room and realised that I had been with this company longer than anyone else in there. They were all new people who knew nothing about the band. It became apparent that we needed to get out of this place and I knew that Atlantic Records had always wanted us to come over to them. So I asked for a release from the States on the basis that we would stay with the company in Canada.

They wanted to hold us to the contract, but I had to warn them that the *Day for Night* masters, which were on their way down from Canada, could easily not arrive and then they wouldn't get a Hip record that fourth quarter. Eventually, they agreed to release us and we signed with Atlantic.

GORD S: MCA, and certainly Jake and Allan, to no small extent, were still really fixated on radio singles. In their minds, the be all and end all was to get a big song, make a big video, put those two together and that equalled stardom. But we were growing less interested in trying to chase the radio tail the whole time.

So we presented Jake and Allan with a whole pile of great songs, about 14 or 15 of them, which we thought were exciting and were fun for us to play. Allan wrote us back in his business-ese way to say that what we had would make, at best, a good EP, essentially implying that there was nothing there of any commercial value.

We listened to what he had to say and took it to heart to various degrees, depending on which member of the group that you speak to. I still have a lot of admiration for Allan and I consider him a friend, and I certainly would never have wanted to let him down, but I wasn't going to get off the track that we were on.

'Scared' came up as one of those songs that we put together just from jamming. There's a specific line in there that I know Gord wrote with Allan in mind: 'There's a focus group that can prove this is all nothing but cold calculation.' In our minds, we were testing everything already because things were coming out from stuff we were playing live on stage. This was art, in our minds. This was the band that we wanted to become, not something that we were testing like a product in a grocery store.

We stuck to our guns and recorded *Day for Night* and Allan resigned as one of our managers, not on bad terms, but he did say that people would and did pay considerable sums of money for his advice and that snot little kids from Kingston, whom he'd effectively discovered, were the only people ever to not listen to his advice.

He clearly was upset with us but we were all quite comfortable in the direction that we took the band at that point.

JAKE GOLD: Allan told the band that *Day for Night* was unlistenable. He was always more forthright with them than I was. He'd tell them, 'If you don't do this, then this is going to happen to you.' Gord hated that kind of thing.

For a long time, I was making most of my money from them so I was happy to go with the flow, whereas for Allan the money didn't really matter. So we continued to be partners, but Allan basically stepped away from the band at this point.

JOHNNY: Allan said we should do a couple more songs because there was no radio hit on the album, which was a little deflating to hear from your manager. But we thought we'd done something good. It felt like it was time to stop building the ship and get out on tour. If we needed to, we could sort something out later.

JAKE GOLD: With the first three records, we were on a real upward trajectory. The idea was that each one was going to be better than the last. And then, with *Day for Night*, the band took a bit of a turn. It was definitely more of a sound record than a song record. But the audience still grew and *Day for Night* actually sold more in Canada, out of the box, than *Fully Completely*.

In the States, I saw *Day for Night* as a set-up record. It was clear that it didn't have a big radio hit, so instead I was going to use it as a way to tour our good markets. Next thing you know, we get *Saturday Night Live*, we get a big tour with Page and Plant, who were signed to Atlantic, and then we get four shows with The Stones in Europe.

JAMIE GOLDBERG

THE TRAGICALLY HIP
IN CONCERT
with
special guests
Odds
FRIDAY, FEBRUARY 10 • 7:30PM
MAPLE LEAF GARDENS
TICKETS ON SALE DECEMBER 10 • 10AM
(416) 870-8000

The Tragically Hip
ALL ACCESS 1995 ARTIST

Maple Leaf Gardens,
Toronto,
10 February 1995

Opposite: Catering rider
for Canadian tour,
February 1995 (left)

Tour T-shirt design and
artwork by Rob Baker
(right)

JAKE GOLD: I remember Ray Daniels, Rush's manager, once called me up and said, 'Don't play an arena in this country until you can play an arena in every city.' It was really good advice. You didn't want to appear as though you were only big in Ontario and Manitoba.

That's why *Day for Night* was our first ever arena tour. It was only then that we knew we could sell out arenas in every market.

The other big first with that tour was that it happened in winter. We figured that, because no one else was touring at that time of year, we could probably get better deals on things like buses, trucking and sound and lights. Also, we would be the big event wherever we went. We always toured in the winter after that.

GORD S: I remember that winter tour in particular. With *Day for Night* we really felt that the band had come into its own, that this was the record we needed to make. We would open every show that tour with 'Grace, Too'.

There's nothing like a winter tour for camaraderie. It's tough enough in the summer, but to do it in the winter with those long nights was something else.

I remember our line of tour buses pulling over in the Prairies because the Northern Lights were so profoundly beautiful one particular night. A bunch of people were

having a smoke and watching that happen. It speaks to the nature of the country. Where else can you possibly do it? It was just such a great tour in those terms.

ROB: Headlining Maple Leaf Gardens for the first time, you can't imagine the thrill. When we played 'Fifty Mission Cap' and the spotlight went up to Bill Barilko's banner in the rafters, the roar was so huge that I knew for a moment what it must have been like for The Beatles. It was so loud that I couldn't hear anything on stage. I looked at the other guys and they were laughing their heads off. No one could hear a thing. We got a few seconds, but The Beatles had about four years of it.

ROB: If you drive across the country in a van, and then you drive in a nicer van, and then you go on a tour bus, it all just feels like a natural progression and you grow into it. So, when we were doing those arena tours, I just felt like that was where we were at. We'd worked hard to get there and it felt good. When my socks stank I handed them to someone, and when I was hungry someone brought me a menu. Life was pretty fucking great.

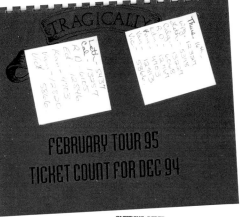

CATERING RIDER

All requirements set forth in this Catering Rider are material terms and conditions of the Production Rider, which is part of the Rider and the Agreement of which the Rider is an integral part.

• Wherever possible, Purchaser/Caterer(s) MUST use recyclable products - recycling bins should be placed in all catering areas.

• Plastic utensils and paper plates are not acceptable for any meal service. China plates/coffee cups, and metal utensils must be utilized.

• The catering requirements outlined hereunder are for Artist's and Support Act's touring personnel only. Purchaser must pre-advise Production Manager on the additional number of local persons requiring meals, which shall be subject to Artist's approval.

• There should never be a situation where clean drinking water/ice, napkins/paper towels, large plastic Solo drinking cups, plates/mugs/utensils, coffee, or any other condiments and/or necessities become in short supply.

ALL FOOD MUST BE FRESH AND HEALTHY.

a) Breakfast for (20)
• Eggs (cooked to order, any style)
• Bacon and sausages
• Hash Brown potatoes
• (1) brick medium cheddar cheese
• Assorted breads: white, whole wheat, bagels, muffins
• (1) medium-sized tub Becel margarine
• (1) regular brick of fresh butter
• Three boxes of assorted cereals
• Fresh fruit: apples, bananas, grapes, oranges, etc.
• Cream cheese, peanut butter, raspberry jam
• (4) litres of orange juice
• (2) litres of apple juice
• (6) litres of 2% milk
• (2) gallons of spring water
• Coffee (regular and decaf.), plentiful Half-and-Half, hot water and assorted teas
• (2) Four slice toasters
• Cups, bowls, plates, silverware and napkins
• Lemon, honey, sugar, cream, catsup, mayo, mustard, salt, pepper, tabasco, HP sauce

b) Lunch for twenty (20)
• Hot lunch choices: local specialty, hamburgers, spaghetti, hot turkey or roast beef sandwiches, shepherds pie, etc.
• Deli tray with turkey, roast beef, ham, assorted cheeses, tuna & egg salads
• Lettuce, onions, tomatoes, pickles
• Fresh fruit: apples, bananas, oranges, grapes, etc.
• Two kinds of assorted salads
• Potato chips, cookies
• Assorted breads: whole wheat, etc.
• (2) cases of assorted soda (some diet)
• (4) litres of 2% milk
• (6) gallons of spring water
• Plentiful coffee and tea with all necessary condiments

c) Dinner for forty (40)
Choose two types of entrees from the list below. There should be provisions for a few vegetarian meals.....Prod. Mgr. will advise. *** Local specialties are encouraged.
Entree Selections:
   i)   Fresh fish
   ii)   Roast turkey
   iii) Roast beef
   iv)   Chicken
   v)   Steak
   vi)   Prime rib
   vii) Ribs
• (1) fresh pasta dish (please be creative!)
• (2) types of salad
• (2) types of fresh vegetables
• Potato or macaroni salad
• Rolls and butter
• Fruit
• Dessert (ice cream/fruit sherbet, pies, cakes, cookies)

d) The Tragically Hip Dressing Room (120 minutes prior to show, except ***)
• Coffee, tea, condiments   *** At 4:00 PM
• (12) Classic Coke   *** At 4:00 PM
• (12) 1.5 litre bottles Evian water (or similar still water) ***At 4:00 PM
• (12) diet iced tea (on ice please) *** At 4:00 PM
• (1) litre orange juice
• (1) litre grapefruit juice
• (48) bottles of beer, exact type to be advised
• (1) veggie tray for 10 with assorted raw vegetables
• (1) assorted fruit tray for 10
• (60) plastic solo cups (large)
• (2) litres 1% or 2% milk (no homo please)
• Liquor and wine requirements will be advised
• sufficient clean ice
Prod. Mgr. will notify Purchaser well in advance of any alternate dressing room requirements.

e) Crew Room   (120 minutes before show)
• (6) gallons spring water
• (2) six-packs assorted soft drinks
• (12) assorted individual fruit juices
• (24) bottles beer
• (2) bottles non-alcoholic beer (no Sharp's)
• (1) pot of hot fresh coffee w/condiments (continuously replenished)
• sufficient ice (continuously replenished)

f) Production Office   (7:00 AM)
• (1) six-pack Diet Dr. Pepper
• (1) large container fresh apple or orange juice
• (1) pot of hot fresh coffee w/condiments (continuously replenished)
• sufficient ice (continuously replenished)

g) The Tragically Hip buses
Each bus (presently two) will receive, (30) minutes before scheduled end of Performance:
• (6) 1.5 litre bottles of Evian water or similar flat, bottled water
• (12) Coca-Cola Classic (cans)
• (24) bottles of beer (brand to be advised)
• sufficient clean ice
• Food (pizzas, Chinese, etc.) will be decided by Prod. Mgr. afternoon of show.

GORD S: The first time we played Maple Leaf Gardens, when we were invited to support Rush in 1991, all our moms and dads came because we figured it was never going to get bigger than this. Playing the Gardens, which was *the* gig, sharing the stage with Rush. This was the apex.

Then, fast forward and we're headlining there. It was such a magnificent venue to play because it was an unusual shape. It was broad and the seats went out – crappy loading for the crew, but it sounded so good.

Playing 'Fifty Mission Cap' in Maple Leaf Gardens was pretty profound in terms of what ended up happening with them retiring Bill Barilko's sweater and hanging it up in the rafters.

SATURDAY NIGHT LIVE:
MUSIC GUEST SCHEDULE

WEDNESDAY
Arrive in New York. We provide transportation from the airport to the hotel. The
Paramount Hotel is located at:

235 West 46th Street
(between Broadway and 8th Ave.)
(212) 764-5500
(212) 354-5237 - Fax

THURSDAY
11:00 am   Depart from hotel for trip to NBC.
11:30 - 1:30   Audio Balance.
2:30 - 3:30   Camera blocking.
3:45 - 4:15   Photo session for opening montage and bumpers.
4:30 - 5:15   Possible promo session - Confirm week of show.

NOTE: This is NOT a full dress situation. In order for the
Lighting Director to achieve the proper balance, band members
should not wear white.

FRIDAY
Off, unless in sketch. If so, rehearsal times will be determined Thursday afternoon.

SATURDAY
5:00 p.m.   Depart hotel for NBC.
5:30 - 6:30   Audio balance.
6:30 - 7:30   Meal
8:00 - 10:00   Dress Rehearsal (performed in real time with a live audience).
11:30 - 1:00   Live show.
1:00   Party (location TBA)

NOTE: ALL TIMES SUBJECT TO VARY

PHONE NUMBERS
John Zonars (office)   664-3777
Studio 8H   664-2300
Dressing Room   664-4430
SNL Fax   664-2485
Nice Guys Limousine   757-7788

ROB: Dan Aykroyd was asked if he would do a guest feature on *Saturday Night Live* and he ended up being in every skit and co-writing most of them. They were very eager to have him, because I think the show had been struggling a bit, and part of the deal was that he got to pick the band. To our surprise, he chose us. We had just released *Day for Night* and we went on and played two songs.

The invitation to do it was very heady stuff. It felt like a big boost to our credibility to play live on a national US TV show.

In all the years of the band, we never properly rehearsed. We'd get together with the intention of rehearsing, but then we'd end up jamming and writing songs. But for *Saturday Night Live* we actually had to rehearse to get the songs down to four minutes because they were both five-minute songs.

DAN AYKROYD: People say, 'Oh, they didn't make it in the States.' Well, they did. The Hip had a massive impact in Europe, and they had very successful tours in the States.

I was happy to help give them a little nudge when I did *Saturday Night Live* and had them on for the show. The audience reaction was outstanding, and they did get some bounce from that. Maybe the audiences in the United States didn't have the sensibility or the broad understanding and intelligence to get The Hip.

GORD S: *Saturday Night Live* was a pretty nerve-racking event. Even the soundcheck and the run-through in the afternoon were hideously oppressive. So, geniuses that we were, we thought we should maybe smoke a bit of a reefer before we went on. It had never hurt us in the past, after all. Those of us that indulged clambered into the bathroom in our dressing room in Rockefeller Centre and stood underneath the exhaust fan, blowing the smoke up there so that our moms and dads didn't catch us.

PAUL: When we got up on stage, a little stoned and a little nervous, we started with 'Grace, Too'. The intro went great and then Gord was so focused on trying to wish his nephew Jay a happy birthday that he ended up singing 'I'm Tragically Hip' instead of 'I'm fabulously rich' as the opening line. Sometimes it's not the best idea if you're super nervous to smoke a joint. I remember thinking that I should have just taken the one hit, rather than three or four. But we got through it.

Day for Night certainly wasn't very commercial sounding and I'm sure the record company felt that way too. They probably weren't too happy that we chose to play 'Grace, Too' and 'Nautical Disaster' on *Saturday Night Live*, but we were confident that this was us. Nothing had changed. We were just playing a different sort of song. We were aware that for our audience and our potential new audience these songs probably took a little more patience, but we were happy with them.

BILLY RAY: When we played *Saturday Night Live*, they had Norm Macdonald, a Canadian, do the warm-up, and every time he mentioned The Tragically Hip the audience went crazy. He said, 'Is everyone here from Canada tonight? We never get that type of reaction to the musical guest during our warm-up.' It really did feel like everybody was there for The Hip that night. I was really proud of them.

nter-Office Memo

ATLANTIC
RECORDING
CORPORATION

o	All Concerned	From	Andi Mogus

ubject | The Tragically Hip Schedule for New York

ate | *March 21, 1995* | Copies to | V. Azzoli, P. Conte, J. Billig,
| | | | B. Kaus, J. Raso

Following is the schedule for The Tragically Hip, while in New York,
Wednesday, March 22nd through Saturday, March 25th:

Wednesday, March 22nd:

8:20pm	Jim Lawrence will pick up band at the hotel to bring to dinner
8:30pm	Atlantic Dinner
	Location: Film Center Cafe
	635 9th Avenue
	(bet. 44th & 45th Sts.)
	(212)262-2525

Thursday, March 23rd:

9:00am	Load in and Crew call
11:00am	SNL will send a car to pick up band at the hotel to bring to NBC studios
11:15am	Arrive NBC studios
	Location: 30 Rock (Entrance on the 49th St. side)
1:30 - 1:30pm	Audio balance
2:30 - 3:30pm	Camera blocking
3:45 - 4:15pm	Photo session for opening montage and bumpers
4:30 - 5:15pm	Possible promo session

This is not a full dress situation. In order for the Lighting Director to
achieve the proper balance, band members should not wear white.

Friday, March 24th:
All interviews are to be scheduled.

Niagara Gazette/Phone interview with Toni Roberto (716)282-2311

Island Ear/Phone interview with Barry Stelboum (212)705-0112

Faces (Nat'l Rock Monthly)/Interview with Jennifer Rose

Westwood One (Radio Syndicate)

SW Networks (Radio Syndicate)/Interview with John Hancock

University of New Hampshire

The Source (Upstate Music Weekly)/Interview with Randy Silver

Detroit Free Press & Knight Ridder Wire Service

Grand Rapids Press/Interview with John Gonzalez

Express (Detroit Monthly)

Hit Parader/Interview with Andy Secher

11:00 - 12:00pm	Atlantic Studio (Gord Sinclair only)
	Location: 1841 Broadway, 3rd Floor

Saturday, March 25th:

5:00pm	SNL will send a car to pick up the band at the hotel to bring to NBC studios
5:30 - 6:30pm	Audio balance
6:30 - 7:30pm	Dinner
8:00 - 10:00pm	Dress Rehearsal (performed in real time with a live audience)
11:30 - 1:00pm	Live show
1:00pm	Party (Location: tba)

GORD D: We did reach a wider audience with *SNL*, but it's hard to know what attracts people to your band in the long run. Ultimately with our band, it's word of mouth. It seems to be the largest cause of the Hip outbreak – if we can align ourselves with a virus. The *SNL* thing, on a personal level, was easily the most intimate gig we've ever done. It's just you and the Cyclops. You're looking at this camera, and all of a sudden less becomes more. The gesture of a finger takes the place of the gesture of a whole waving arm.

GORD S: When we got the chance to play *Saturday Night Live*, like so many other times in our career we were like, 'OK, boys. This is it. We're gonna be farting through silk.' We took it as a sign of immediate success.

ROB: It was a most memorable night, but I think on a lot of levels we really squandered the opportunity and there was some mismanagement. In eight minutes we played to more people than we'd played to in our whole career put together up to that point. And how did we follow it up? We drove for 14 hours straight to St Louis and played to 50 people in a little punk bar.

It just seemed like there wasn't a lot of follow-through. When the pendulum swings hard in your direction, you at least want to slow down the speed at which it swings back. That pendulum swung hard and fast the other way. Boom! You're right back in Shitsville.

GORD S: Again, the dose of humility that the road gives you is really important. It fuels that sense of humour and camaraderie. Performing to so many people watching on TV, then coming down and playing a shithole club would break some musicians' backs. They just wouldn't be able to handle it. But we learned how to. In fact, it made us better at what we did. Even to this day, people talk in hushed tones about our failure to succeed in the United States. I beg to differ. We were massively successful in the United States.

PAUL: Nothing had changed. We were still on the same programme in the States, which was to build up our crowd in each city without having any national exposure to help us. We'd accepted it by then.

Boston, San Francisco, Chicago, Dallas, we kept going back. There might be 40 people this time, but there'd be 140 the next time. It literally took years to build up our crowds. I think that's a subtle thing that we were all quietly proud of. We sold out the Fillmore two nights in San Francisco, and sold out the Chicago Theatre too. How did we do that? We kept going back. It's not because they were reading about us in *USA Today* or *Rolling Stone*. It's because of word of mouth. We did it ourselves. In San Francisco we must have played seven or eight small clubs every six months to a year, to work ourselves up, finally, to the Fillmore.

GORD D: These things on your rock and roll resume probably help in a lot of ways. People say, 'Well, I don't know this band but they were on *Saturday Night Live*, they opened up for Page and Plant …'

March 18	Austin, TX	Liberty Lunch
March 21	St. Louis, MO	The Other World
March 23	Oklahoma City, OK	Bricktown Brewery
March 24	Dallas, TX	Trees
March 25	Houston, TX	Fitzgerald's
March 27	Wichita, KS	Aviator Live
March 30	Minneapolis, MN	1st Avenue
April 2	Chicago, IL	Cabaret Metro
April 4	Grand Rapids, MI	The Orbit Room
April 5	Detroit, MI	Royal Oak
April 8	Cleveland, OH	Odeon

TOUR ITINERARY

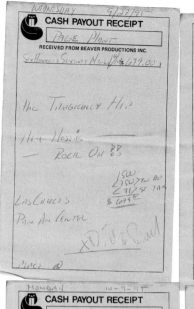

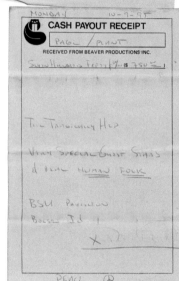

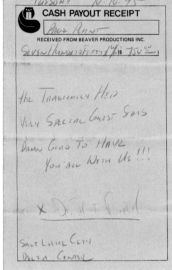

The Tragically Hip played 30 dates supporting Page and Plant in May, September and October 1995

Above: The band with Jimmy Page and Robert Plant, who is wearing a Hip T-shirt, Madison Square Garden, New York, 27 October 1995

Opposite: In June 1995 The Rolling Stones supported The Tragically Hip on four European dates on their Voodoo Lounge tour, two in Germany and two in Belgium

ROB: When we were given the opportunity to go out on tour with Jimmy Page and Robert Plant, we had a band meeting to discuss it. Four of us were very keen and one of us – Gord Downie – was very not keen. He didn't want to do it because he said they weren't his thing.

There was this Sting quote from the early days of The Police: 'We'd rather play to 40 people who paid to see us than to 4,000 people who paid to see someone else.' We thought that was true, but there were exceptions. If Bob Dylan had asked us, we would have said yes. If David Bowie had asked us, we would have said yes. So of course we should say yes to Page and Plant. The rest of us wouldn't have pushed it, but Gord actually backed down and said he'd do it. Very quickly, he was having the time of his life.

It was a low-pressure gig. We weren't expecting to turn on the audience because they weren't there for us. Gord and Paul and Sinclair had their rollerblades on, booting around playing road-hockey backstage, and we got to hang on a daily basis with Robert Plant, who was a fantastic, easy-going, funny, opinionated guy. He would get up and sound check with us and come in our dressing room. He'd got all our albums and he'd ask whether we were going to play this song from that album. It was kind of mind-blowing.

JOHNNY: The reason we got the gig was that Robert Plant was going out with Alannah Myles at the time and she gave him a bunch of Canadian things including a cassette of *Road Apples*, which he listened to and really liked. We played Madison Square Garden with them – the last time they'd been there was when they were in Led Zeppelin. Robert Plant would come in our dressing room and he was just a normal dude, one of the nicest guys in the world.

GORD D: They were very nice people. Their band is comprised mostly of members of Robert Plant's solo touring band, including Porl Thompson on guitar, who played with The Cure for many years. He was sort of an instant fan and watched every set and would walk us back to our dressing room. That made a huge impression on us because, ultimately, in this business, you start to realise that even the smallest gesture from a fellow musician can mean so much.

Robert Plant himself was very approachable, funny and self-effacing. He would drop into the dressing room and chat a little bit.

ROB: To be asked to warm up for The Rolling Stones, who were clearly the single biggest influence on the band, was such an incredible honour. And it was especially great to do it in Europe. We were sitting in our dressing room before the first show and Mick Jagger walked in. I can't tell you how surreal that was. He chatted with us for five minutes, wished us well and told us not to worry about the audience, who could be tough on The Stones' opening bands. We went out and played and it was fantastic.

LAISTER DICKSON LIMITED
2 Newburgh Street London W1V 1LH
Tel: +44-(0)171-439-7222 Fax: +44-(0)171-734-2933

* * * FAX MESSAGE * * *

TO : JAYE RIGGIO

Norman

FROM : BERNARD DOHERTY

cc Steve

DATE : 28 NOVEMBER 1995

RE : TRAGICALLY HIP PHOTO

Dear Jaye,

Fabulous news, we have found the pics of The Rolling Stones and Tragically Hip. They are B/W and sitting around a pooltable and looking very happy.
I am sending the negatives and a contact sheet over to you by courier.

Kind regards,

B.D.

Bernard Doherty

GORD D: It was very strange timing. After the Page and Plant thing, I was somewhat stunned and baffled just because of the actual experience of doing it, and then the Stones thing happens. Within a month we opened up for both these icons. I realised there must be some kind of fateful activity at work here, some kind of message from our Jedi Master telling us that we need this sort of education to see what the logical conclusion looks like, to see if, in fact, the drive is towards some kind of world domination. That's sort of what it looks like, especially in the case of The Stones. There are things that are good and things that are bad about it, but ultimately you figure out where you fit in the larger spectrum of things. And you can feel quite content with yourself.

Obviously, when I was 15 and 16 these were the people that a lot of my friends and contemporaries were into and this is what we were listening to when The Hip got started. It wasn't lost on us when we were standing backstage nervously swaying back and forth, breathing deeply, about to go on in front of 72,000 Stones fans. In fact, one way that we were able to appease the nerve gods was to realise that ten years previously we were in Robbie's basement, struggling and fumbling through 'Poison Ivy', 'Stupid

Girl' and 'Off the Hook' and you name any of the more obscure Stones numbers. It was a nice feeling, humorous, neat.

But at the same time, it's tough. You go up and play 30 or 45 minutes and you feel a bit stunted and a bit restrained – which is something I'm not personally used to dealing with.

We ran into Mick Jagger a couple of times. At the end of our four days, we posed for a picture with The Stones, which is something they like to do with all their bands. That was cool.

GORD S: The first time we supported The Stones was in Germany and it was festival seating. So there were 85,000 Germans in the Cologne soccer stadium, and I'm pretty sure that they were there to see The Stones, not us. But we'd spent our entire career hopping back and forth across the border between Canada and the States and not taking our success in Canada for granted, knowing that what mattered most was the performance and not the size of the audience. We were able to play in front of The Stones without really batting an eye. And who knows how many converts we made that night. People were applauding. It wasn't like they were trying to get us off the stage, not by any means.

ROB: The second show, in Hanover, almost got rained out. We walked on to 80,000 German fans booing us. The skies opened and the rain was splatting on us, but we just put our heads down, dug in and played harder. Five or ten minutes later, there were 80,000 people going 'Woooo!' with their fists in the air. A really great moment.

GORD D: It's a privilege that we've gained by whatever success we've managed to achieve in Canada, this ability to put these fun projects together. When I was younger I don't think I could have ever imagined being able to do that. It's funny because even to this day it takes people a long time to get used to that. They naturally assume there has to be some kind of higher power responsible, be it a beer company or somebody else.

But in this case we pick the bands, and we get a real kick out of it. It's really fun for us to do, to sit around and try and imagine what bands we think will be suitable. And it's not really an either/or proposition, it's just the five of us throwing out many, many, many bands and musicians, some that are totally out of reach, some that are flatly unavailable. It's just interesting to watch it come together.

[The Inbreds, Eric's Trip and Rheostatics] are all bands that I love and listen to quite a bit at home. In our case, it's hard to even get out and see bands that much, so in a way this tour is just a selfish way to get a very good seat for a band that you like to watch.

[The concert experience] is the theatre of the strange to begin with. It's a very manipulated kind of event, and you're reconciling a lot of different expectations – or maybe you're ignoring them – but, nonetheless, it's happening. So there's many strange and sometimes wonderful and sometimes very frightening and grotesque things that can happen. I don't particularly like watching fistfights, but I love watching people dancing off to the side. It's a living and breathing thing that's constantly ebbing and flowing – that's something that I've definitely learned – and just when you think you can figure it out, it changes.

Another Roadside Attraction, 13–23 July 1995

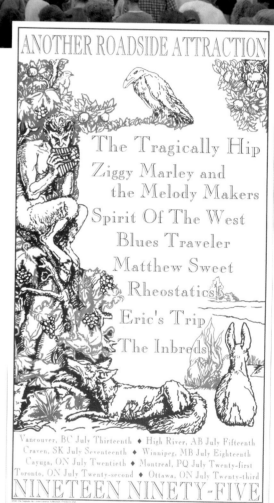

the tragically hip
trouble at the henhouse

bob ludwig's gateway mastering MCA RECORDS/CANADA 6 MAR 96
gateway mastering studios inc THE TRAGICALLY HIP EQ CD REF ALBUM
428 cumberland avenue
portland maine 04101

1. GIFT SHOP 4:57
2. SPRING TIME IN VIENNA 4:38
3. AHEAD BY A CENTURY 3:43
4. DON'T MAKE DADDY 5:08
5. FLAMENCO 4:06
6. 700 FOOT CEILING 3:40
7. BUTTS WIGGLIN' 3:47
8. APARTMENT SONG 3:57
9. COCONUT CREAM 3:21
10. LET'S STAY ENGAGED 4:53
11. SHERPA 5:13
12. PUT IT OFF 5:11

May 1996

What follows is a brief account of the making of **TROUBLE AT THE HENHOUSE**, the new album from **THE TRAGICALLY HIP**. I will begin at the end.

This record was mastered by Bob Ludwig at Gateway Studios in Portland, Maine. I know nothing of mastering, but I know everyone who made the trip to Portland raved about Ludwig. They were impressed with the man and very happy with his work. In return, Ludwig was impressed by the music and he is no lightweight. Having mastered a zillion records (Lou Reed, Rush among a host of others) and with no contractual obligation to be nice, his favourable opinion meant a lot to the band. That's because this record is their first fully self-produced project and represents them in their most natural setting: together in a room with **MARK VREEKEN** (the band's long-time soundman) at the controls. That room sits in an old limestone house on the outskirts of Kingston, Ontario. Though the bulk of the recording was done near Kingston, it was not the only session for this record.

Most of the songs from **TROUBLE AT THE HENHOUSE**, if not born on the road, were conceived on the road. When we tour and can find the time, the band steals away to a studio for a few days. We were lucky enough in 1995 to have several of these opportunities. I think the first one was in May, in Los Angeles. A month later, in the midst of a brief European swing, they spent a few days in Amsterdam putting some ideas down on tape. By the time August rolled around and hurricane season was in full swing (our driver assured us the bus was weather-proof), they had the chance to get back to Kingsway Studio in New Orleans, one of their favourites. The south is always loads of fun in the summer, especially a quiet, peaceful town like New Orleans. In October we hooked up with **MARK HOWARD** (he had co-produced _DAY FOR NIGHT_ eighteen months earlier), who had a new studio on the go in San Francisco. Usually, these sessions were a chance for the band (and crew) to have a little break from the road and to throw some ideas around, but sometimes they produced complete or near-complete songs. San Francisco gave rise to **"Flamenco"** and **"Put It Off"**. It's also where the band got the nifty jet engine sounds. Those are courtesy of the U.S.A.F. Blue Angels who were buzzing the city one day. (Drummer) **JOHNNY FAY** was on the studio roof testing a new microphone when the jets were kind enough to nearly tear our heads off. To get full effect, strap your stereo speakers to your head and turn the volume all the way up. Instant virtual reality.

The stage is also, and has always been, a favourite breeding ground for new material. Many fans will recognize **"Gift Shop"** and **"Springtime In Vienna"** from various shows from the summer and fall of 1995. Some might remember **"Ahead By A Century"** and **"Sherpa"** emerging from on-stage jams in the middle of concert warhorse **"New Orleans Is Sinking"**, a particularly fertile song. It's quite natural for the band to experiment with new material this way, as they are forever working on stuff backstage and during soundchecks. I don't think the songwriting ever really stops.

That this new records is the first self-produced effort from **THE HIP** should come as no surprise to anyone familiar with the band. It's the end of one learning curve and the beginning of another. No one was too worried that there might be some ugly ego clashes over the theories and realities of self-production. I mean after all, we've spent a lot of time together over the years. Half of any given year we're chained together in a tour bus which is like a submarine with wheels, and we surface only when we have to. Besides, producing the record themselves freed the band from the constraints of someone else's timetable. When they needed to get out of doors they could, and since **TROUBLE AT THE HENHOUSE** was recorded mostly in the dead of winter, that freedom was important. In Canada, you must enjoy winter or winter will enjoy you.

The title of the album and the artwork have their own story too. _Trouble At The Henhouse_ is actually the title the photo adorning the cover. Though everyone was thinking about, nobody had any really brilliant ideas for a concept. One day, fate smiled upon us and (guitarist) **BOBBY BAKER** stumbled on a photograph in an old magazine he'd been leafing through. Everyone thought the photo was really cool and liked the title as well. The only problem was the magazine was at least ten years old and we didn't know if we would ever find the photographer (Avery Crounse) and get his permission to use the photo. Bobby discovered that Crounse hailed from Mississippi, and promptly called directory assistance for that state. Well, a few days later he got through and presto!, instant title and cover.

With the artwork picked and the recording essentially finished, all that remained was the mixing and the mastering. The mastering you know about, for the mixing the band called on their friend **STEVEN DRAKE** (guitarist for Vancouver bands Odds). Steven is a great musician and has a great set of ears, so he and Mark Vreeken got together and began to tame the unruly beast. Working at a pace roughly equivalent to a song a day, they pushed ahead until everyone was happy with the mixes and the date for the mastering approached. Then it was off to Portland with the tapes. That is where this story began and so, that's where it will end. Put it on, turn it up and enjoy **TROUBLE AT THE HENHOUSE**.

Dave Powell, Tour Manager, March 1996

Opposite: Real estate listing for the Bathouse, Bath, ON, March 1994

Cassette tapes of tracks recorded for Trouble at the Henhouse, _1995_

March 5, 1996

To U.S. Customs,

This letter is to advise you that John Phillip Fay, drummer of The Tragically Hip, will be entering into the United States on March 6, 1996 with 21 Ampex half inch tapes and twenty Dats, to Gateway Mastering Studios, located at 82 Cumberland in Portland, Maine 04101, Phone # 207 828 9400.

The purpose of bringing these tapes into the U.S. is for final mastering of The Tragically Hip's upcoming album titled "Trouble At The Henhouse" which will be internationally released by Atlantic Records in the U.S. and MCA Records for Canada and Europe on May 14, 1996.

These tapes are owned solely by The Tragically Hip, therefore no copyright laws are being violated. The value of the tapes are a total of $700.00 Canadian Dollars.

Upon completion of mastering the tapes will be returning back to Canada on March 7, 1996.

GORD D: By the time we started to prepare to make _Trouble at the Henhouse_, it seemed like the end of a long apprenticeship, like we'd been studying for some kind of degree. The long learning curve seemed to be coming to an end and we were back to where we started, totally naive and ready to try anything.

We used to make our own posters and put them up. We used to do everything ourselves until, over time, you start getting people to help you do what you do. Those people teach you things – our managers, Jake and Allan, we've learned a lot from them, and from the record company. We've had relationships, for better or for worse, that we've learned a lot from.

Now, I feel like we're back in Robbie's parents' basement, doing it all ourselves, and we made this record ourselves. So I guess at the end of 10 or 11 years I feel independent and proud, kind of the way I felt when I was 22. Proud to be in a band, proud to do it, proud to make some money doing it.

NEW STUFF #1

AMPEX
1/95

1. 'Feverish Dream' Jam — 1/10
2. Very keef Jam
3. O'Brian's Song
4. Antares
5. Rotterdam — 1/11
6. Antares
8. Ahead by a Century

9. Paul w/delay Opvs
10. Greasy — 1/12
11. Ahead by a Century
12. Daredevil
13. Antares (no vox)
14. Cowboy Coffee
15. Like a Metaphor

Comp B 01 Dec AMPEX

1. Don't Wake Daddy 01 Dec — Run I 1979
2. Mighty Mike Run I 1:27:03
3. Apartment Song Run I 1:36:43
4. Flamenco Run I 1:42:30
5. Put it off
6. Butts Wigglin
7. Coconut.
8. Tear is Fear
10. Mankynken

ROB: We'd been looking for our own place for a long time, somewhere to store our gear, rehearse and write songs. We must have gone through 20, 25 places, but there was always an issue – the neighbours were too close or the rooms weren't big enough or it was too divided up. The Bathouse had no neighbours, an unobstructed view of the lake, big, open rooms and it could sleep a lot of people. It was just what we were looking for.

Before we bought it, the Bathouse had only had two owners in its 150 years. It was a really old, old house with rocking chairs and lace doilies on the table. It was built as a stagecoach stop between Kingston, which was not yet the capital of Canada, and York, which was a tiny shitty outpost only to become a larger shitty outpost. We were told that there had been a lynching across the street. Lots of history …

PAUL: Recording *Road Apples* at Kingsway in New Orleans was a big inspiration for the Bathouse. Kingsway was an old mansion that Daniel Lanois had converted into a residential studio – and eventually the Bathouse became a real studio with five bedrooms. We started renting it out. It was perfect if you wanted to isolate yourself, and a lot of bands did, us included. Buying and then gradually converting the Bathouse was one of the best things we ever did. And it still runs smoothly to this day. A lot of good music comes out of there.

GORD D: We had concerns, obviously, about how we would respond without a referee, nurse, psychiatrist, doctor, ship captain – whatever you want to call a producer. We were afraid maybe about ego concerns and certain problems. And, in fact, it was the opposite. We really enjoyed the individual responsibility. I think something that most musicians can relate to is, after a certain amount of time, you really enjoy responsibility. We really responded and we worked really hard.

HIP COMP D

AMPEX
22/12

1. DON'T WAKE DADDY
2. BUTTS WIGGLIN
3. SPRINGTIME
4. APARTMENT
5. GIFT SHOP
6. FLAMENCO · 23:16

7. COCONUT CREAM
8. FREAKED
9. LET'S STAY ENGAGED
10. BROOD AND BLOOM
11. AHEAD BY A CENTURY
12. PUT IT OFF
13. SHIRPA
14. FEAR
15. COOKIE
16. 700 FT CEILING
17. BYE BYE COLES
18. IF ART IS DEAD

19. COCONUT (COMP C)
20. SHIRPA (ROB ACOUSTIC)

GORD D: We started it about the end of October. We had already been writing on the road and taking little stops when there was a window of opportunity to go into a studio and try and figure out where we were at – in San Francisco, New Orleans, various places, wherever friends would let us in. That was always really refreshing as far as being on the road – having something to look forward to and listen to while you're on the bus, and something to think about, mould and shape and get into some state of order.

Then, we got a studio and started setting up and acquiring gear as we needed it and could afford it, and enjoyed building the studio. And, at the same time, building this record and really enjoying it. We had a parallel, Zen experience going on.

It was recorded all through the horrific winter. We had a rink, a pond about 1,000 feet back from the house, and the pond was sheltered by trees. It was beautiful, pure Canadiana. There was much hand wringing and discussion late into the night about how to preserve the pond, how to keep the ice in pristine condition. How can we get 1,000 feet of hose back there to flood it? How can we scrape it? Looking at the weather patterns and analysing when the thaw was going to come in to help restore the ice to its natural state. We got into a certain molecular level when it came to taking care of the ice. And that helped as far as taking our minds off the experience of making a record.

ROB: Once we got the Bathouse, the decision to self-produce *Trouble at the Henhouse* was just a natural next step. Of course, if you're not watching where you're going you'll step in a pile of shit, which is kind of what we did.

We were lucky because we had Mark Vreeken, who was a world-class, top-of-the-line engineer, so we didn't have to worry about that end of it. But it did unleash a bit of a beast. When you get into self-production, someone has to make the calls. The reason bands have producers is so that no one in the band has to take that role, because whoever does take it ends up getting resented and other people feel sidelined. You need that outside voice – someone whose ego is not involved in the creative process in the same way that yours is – to say what's working and what's not cutting it.

JOHNNY: *Trouble at the Henhouse* was the record that, pound for pound, I had the most fun making. It was just us and Mark Vreeken and we were in our own house, not in New Orleans or in England. It was a place where we could camp out and make music and come up with ideas for tours – the ultimate clubhouse.

The Bathouse was similar to Kingsway in terms of being able to record in different rooms. We kept shifting things around to see what would work. It was exciting to be building a studio and making a record at the same time. We went in with no songs really. We just thought we'd start recording. We'd start at noon and then go right through until midnight, and we could make as much noise as we liked because there were no neighbours.

We were able to take record company money and use it to buy something that was going to last for a long time, whereas if you were given a budget you usually flitted it away on other people's studios and rentals and catering. You never knew where the money went. Also, we could be more in control of the amount of time we spent on a record instead of just being told we had three weeks.

GORD S: We were selling enough records by that point that they let us produce our own record. My personality is such that I was way into that. I understand to a limited extent the technical side of producing a record, and certainly I felt we could translate the success that we were having as a cooperative songwriting unit into being able to discuss and pick versions of songs together. I thought that would be our future – we'd just make our own records in our own studio and become the autonomous working collective that we'd all dreamed of.

I love being in the studio. The hours slip away from me when I'm in there, especially when you can hear things moving forward. But self-producing didn't necessarily work out for everybody. Robbie got a little distant over the course of that session. He wasn't happy with how it was going.

We always had a pattern of laying down drums and bass first. That's how we learned to do it. You build your rhythm foundation, pick the best version, then build a song based on that. So Robbie would always have to wait, just like Gord would do final vocals towards the end of a session. It's hard to get great guitar solos or vocal performances right off the floor, especially when everything's bleeding. So you'd go back in and rerecord them. Maybe Robbie didn't like having me sitting there listening to him playing guitar solos and saying, 'Well that one's great, but that one isn't so great.' I kind of slid my ass into the more vocal producer side of things, perhaps too much.

Top: Trouble at the Henhouse *promotional photograph, 1996*

Opposite: DAT recording of 15 tracks recorded at the Bathouse in early 1996

1. COCONUT • C6
2. LET'S STAY ENGAGED • C26
3. DON'T WAKE DADDY • C17
4. BUTT'S WIGGLIN • 17
5. SHERPA • D3
6. FLAMENCO • D4

7. GIFT SHOP • D1
8. FREAKED • C20
9. AHEAD BY A CENTURY • B18
10. SPRINGTIME • C18
11. FEAR • C23
12. BROOD AND BLOOM • C7
13. PUT IT OFF • SAN FRAN
14. APARTMENT • C15
15. COOKIE • C27

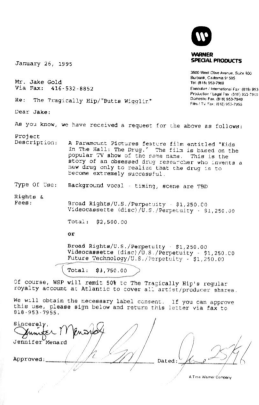

ROB: I recall the making of that record as a low time in my life. To this day, there are certain songs I can't listen to. They just irritate me, because I was there when they were being recorded and it was unpleasant. I hate 'Coconut Cream' for that reason. Gord loved the song and pushed hard for it. He wanted me to try playing it with a coat hanger, but that's not my vibe. I'm not Sonic Youth. Gord would often try to pull us in more of an indie direction, but that was a yoga pose we were never going to get into.

'Butts Wigglin'' is another song that might have been better left off the record. I'm a big believer in cutting until it hurts. That was a song we were asked to contribute to the Kids in the Hall movie *Brain Candy*. Our buddy Craig Northey was musical director on the film. We just called it 'Butts Wigglin'' because it made us laugh. The title has nothing to do with the song.

GORD S: For 'Butt's Wigglin'' I got a little Wurlitzer keyboard for that goofy bluesy keyboard riff. I got out of my bass-playing, background-singing corner and was playing piano. That was an adjustment for some people. The Tragically Hip was expanding and going beyond just the five-piece rock and roll band.

GORD D: We were passing the *Brain Candy* script around the bus laughing uproariously. We had just gone to New Orleans to do our house cleaning on the song ideas we had, trying to put songs in some kind of order. There was a line from the script, 'In my opinion, the drug is ready', that I had in mind when I wrote the lyrics for 'Butts Wigglin'', and those guys had a piece of music, but they didn't know the music they were working on at the time was for the movie. Writing with a task in hand, with something tacked to the board in front of you, creates a whole different approach. It freed me from the responsibility of anything. I felt like I could say anything or sing in any way I felt like. It allowed me to adopt a persona.

I think the ending is really cool. It was recorded in New Orleans from that session. We brought it back to Bath and tried a bunch of different things but the version on our record is slightly faster, which we like. It's a little punchier than the one that's on the *Brain Candy* soundtrack.

This Fear is Fear
Cause it's so new
Cause it's so near

I think the Fear is here
Cause it's so ~~sure~~ true
And yet so unclear

This punk is Fear
Fear of Fraudulence
But it's still ~~Fear~~ (here)

O this odious Fear
I'm out of place
I don't belong here

With the bureau chiefs
The shrugging spies
~~with the mother of all decisions~~
              The whole shadowy tradition

That poise is poise
Cause there's no trace
There's no noise
T~~he~~ The vulgar choice
Hard to make
Hard to voice

        Does it diminish your super-capacity to love +4

                    ⊗

what is on your mind
We wanna know
but we want you to take your time
C'mon make up your mind
    Will you lay low   ~~Are we Friends?~~
    Or will you combined (Or are we ~~just~~ combined?)
        With the bureau chiefs
        The shrugging spies
        The whole shadowy tradition
                        profession

GORD D: Paul's singing is amazing on '700 Ft. Ceiling', and it totally elevated that song. We had the idea and were doing it live in a much heavier landscape, originally. Then we pared it down and tried all kinds of different instrumentation and, ultimately, settled on an acoustic thing, and built that song up from the ground with just two acoustic guitars, then a vocal, then some djembe that Johnny played, and big bass.

JOHNNY: When Paul came into the band, we didn't realise he had such an amazing voice. His singing is very honest and very original – he seems to meander as if he's looking for his note and some guys would get on him for being out of tune, but he wouldn't take it to heart. He'd just carry on singing his own way. There's kind of a Neil Young quality to it. Paul's singing seemed to fit with his playing and it's another reason why he was such a force in The Hip.

GORD D: I really like Paul singing, always have. We've been friends for a long time. And we would sing together in high school. I think because we have such a friendship, such a bond with each other, that singing together is entirely natural. It's just a dialogue.

PAUL: There was a connection between Gord and me when we first started singing together, and that was long before I joined the band and long before I played guitar. We happened to sing together a couple of times and then, when I got in the band, I really thought of back-ups as my main job. Especially when we were a covers band playing Sixties songs.

Gord had a baritone voice. I have a baritone speaking voice but a high singing voice, which happened to sit nicely on top of Gord's. Sinclair's did too. Sinclair and I were very Canadian in our approach to sharing out back-ups equally, polite to a fault: 'No, you sing that one. You'll be great.' 'No, you sing it. I did the last one.'

JOHNNY: We were so lucky with how those three voices of Gord, Gord and Paul came together. They just went for it and if it worked, then great. If it didn't work, it didn't go on the record.

There was always a very honest, respectful approach. Paul and Sinclair didn't want their singing to overshadow Gord's lyrics, so they'd always talk to him first about what they were thinking of doing.

There was an upstairs room at the studio that I briefly set up as a painting studio. I'm a high functioning introvert, in that I work pretty well in group or social settings, but it drains my battery quickly and I need significant alone time to recharge. Painting does that for me. In a way I'm barely even there when the painting happens. Whatever was rattling around in my mind might work its way out, just as in dreams. Obviously '700 Ft. Ceiling' was happening that day. (RB)

TYPEWRITING?

Past strips of Serengeti
And the malls of Sleepy Hollow
Past Interstate Brickface (the Howling waters of the precipice)   *Try. rhymescheme AAB/CCB/DDB
Past the policy weary commune
Past sled-dogs after dinner
Past the bounty-hunter who shot Bigfoot
Past shelves of pussy magic
Past the asteroid that wrecked the planet
Past exhibits under repair
Past pageantry for the pot-head
                                    (Past the unbearable likeness to the Beats)
                                    (mass acceptance of the Beats)

Past the red-tape required by heaven
Past the policy weary commune
Past the roast of earthquake savvy
Past cupped hands whisperin you're damned

P

Past the most-suitable winner

Past the bounty-hunter who shot Bigfoot
Past
P
Past the asteroid that wrecked the Planet
Past leanings toward a full stop
We live to survive our paradoxes
In the summer that hissed like Tom Verlaine
Past the red-tape required by heaven
Past the policy-weary commune
Past cupped hands whisperin "you're damned"
Past strips of Serengeti
Past ol Interstate Brickface
Past the blueprints for Calt-forn-ia
Past shelves of pussy magic
Past the gates of Sleepy Hollow
Past pageantry for the pot-head

Past elephants polishing their tusks
Past waves of immigration ((At a thousand points of entry)
At the doors of the stranded palace
Past the error of catalogues and lists

GORD D: ['Springtime in Vienna' is] a song about Hitler and blues singers. Nazi Germany is I guess ingrained in all of our minds and, of course, there's the movie *The Producers* with the song 'Springtime for Hitler', so it's a quintessential paradoxical title. The song is, if nothing else, a celebration of the idea of living to survive your paradoxes by one minute, which is sort of the goal. To have one minute of clarity and then lights out.

Go Out, Get Drunk

New York PRESS

VOL. 9, NO. 40

NEW YORK'S FREE WEEKLY

TO: ALL CONCERNED
FR: DONNA JARVIS & JIM LAWRENCE
RE: THE TRAGICALLY HIP

OCTOBER 2 & 1996

TROUBLE AT THE HENHOUSE CONTAINS the funniest Kurt Cobain joke that I've heard all year (he's reincarnated as a sleigh dog—get it?), and no one's earned the right to milk that cow better than the Tragically Hip. Fabulously rich from success in their native Canada, the Hip are the only alternative group to use their wealth as a springboard for ideas, and have built a fluid and dark career on finding the happiness behind obsession. American success remains stalled ever since they cursed their career with the first few lousy albums, but they're now entering their fifth year as one of the most alluring live acts around. And since this is Ontario South, they can play the comparatively cavernous Irving Plaza, Weds., Oct. 2. 17 *Irving Place* (15th St.), 777-6800.

GORD D: Sled dogs fit as an image and when I was totally convinced that it was an image that would come forward and then drift, ebb and flow with the song like the rest of the images, then I made one of those sled dogs Kurt Cobain, who maybe can't get to sleep. I liked that, because in the song 'Pennyroyal Tea' he says, 'Give me a Leonard Cohen afterworld so I can sigh eternally.' Well, unfortunately, you can't pick how you will be reincarnated, if in fact you are reincarnated. The image has a sort of comedic value and is maybe slightly touching that, ultimately, you're still doing the same thing in the afterlife.

I liked the image, but I was worried that people's ears would be turned on an axis; they'd immediately turn to that line and stay there for the whole song.

GORD D: I like to illuminate the obvious, simulate the obvious, eliminate the obvious, it doesn't really matter. It's interesting, the idea that there's an infinite world, an infinite galaxy within the very surroundings you're in, your very house, and it's the thing that people that are single for a while really want. They want to explore that galaxy for a while. It's like when you're in there making a record in the studio versus going out and playing it live. And when you're doing each one you want to be in the other place. So when you're in a relationship, maybe the outside world seems a little more enticing and interesting and you want to explore the infiniteness of that galaxy. But ultimately, it's all right in front of you; there's as much there as you need and as much there as you need to explore.

I wanted in 'Apartment Song' to imbue certain inanimate objects in your house with a kind of beauty – the beauty that things have, in and of themselves, when you really look at them.

What our apartment does when we're not around
Does not concern us

CONCERN US (THE APARTMENT SONG)
This com's comin

Above left: Some of the lyrics from a 1995 jam called 'Past' ended up in 'Gift Shop', 'Don't Wake Daddy', 'Springtime in Vienna' and 'Vapour Trails'. A reworked version became 'Typewriting' on Gord Downie's solo album Coke Machine Glow

Left: Fragments of lyrics from 'Apartment Song'

Opposite: Some of the lyrics in this unreleased song resurfaced in '700 Ft. Ceiling' and 'Stay' (top)

Painting by Rob Baker titled '700 Ft. Ceiling' (bottom)

GORD D: We started 'Flamenco' in a session in Amsterdam and it was just a lump for a long time. I find it like a jazz recording – not musically, but the actual sound of it is like an old jazz recording; you can really hear the air in the room. It was recorded in San Francisco with Mark Vreeken and Mark Howard. Mark Howard obviously knows how to mic things because he got a cool sound. That wasn't one that we really had to arrange; we just started playing it and it was done and we knew it was done.

A good friend of the band, Marjorie Gregg [Allan Gregg's wife], inspired a lot of it. She died and it affected us. But there are certain lines, like the prostitute one, that don't fit that image of her. So it's not perfectly about her, it's just inspired by her, and also by a walk that Robbie and Gord and I took through the Vondelpark in Amsterdam. It was a really sunny day and all of Holland seemed to be out enjoying the end of the winter, as people do – creaking around with their bones and their white skin and really just enjoying being outside.

There was a bandshell and a bunch of flamenco dancers. I caught a few glimpses of the movements that they were making and they struck me as entirely poetic. I just tried to describe what I saw, kind of like when a light flashes in your eyes and you get a negative image of the last thing you saw. The hands sweeping the air – I just tried to capture that. When you see people dance that dance, they're imbued with the courageous aspect of the human spirit. And Marjorie was an incredibly courageous person.

Above: Gord Sinclair jogging in Amsterdam, early 1990s

Below: Songs recorded at the Bathouse in January 1996, including unreleased tracks 'Brood and Bloom', 'Fear', 'Freaked' and 'Cookie Factory'

Opposite: Treatment and schedule for the 'Gift Shop' music video

Sheet music book for 'Gift Shop'

GORD S: I remember walking and jogging in the Vondelpark countless times. Amsterdam's a magical city, and the Vondelpark is a magical park. It's got a great number of different trails all the way through it and there's a ring-road all the way around it. If you want to ride a horse, you can ride your horse on it. If you want to jog a lap, you can jog a lap. And, like life, you can venture off along these arterial trails and see any manner of thing. There's bandshells, there's swans, there's water features. There's farm animals wandering around. There's cafés everywhere.

The Dutch are really quite special in terms of their embrace of liberty. You should be free to do whatever the hell that you want to do, whenever you want to do it, within the bounds of respect for the person that you're with. Beyond that anything goes. The fantastic thing about the Netherlands was that soft drugs were everywhere so we weren't afraid of getting in trouble. There's just something about that place. It's grey and it's dour and they take art really seriously there. And we were taking ourselves really seriously.

So we'd be walking and puffing and talking about life and whatnot, and Gord was always chronicling stuff, always writing it down.

We wrote a bunch of songs while we were in Amsterdam. Smoking hash and smoking butts. It was just fantastic.

ROB: I loved Amsterdam. We all did. You would see so many great things just by walking around. I remember one drizzly night there was a band of buskers set up in the divider between the two lanes in the middle of the road. It was like the Quintet of the Hot Club of Paris with Django Reinhardt: stand-up bass, three guitars and a violin, playing gypsy jazz.

After that, I started travelling around the city trying to find them. We would see them sometimes in the Vondelpark, where there were always lots of great things – people dancing, people playing music, dogs shitting everywhere (we always figured 'vondel' meant 'dog shit'). I don't know what it is about Holland; it's a very progressive country, but no one picks up dog shit.

1 700 FT CEILING
2 GIFT SHOP
3 BUTTS WIGGLIN
4 SPRINGTIME
5 DONT WAKE DADDY
6 FLAMENCO

7 COCONUT
8 LET'S STAY ENGAGED
9 BROOD AND BLOOM
10 AHEAD BY A CENTURY
11 SHERPA
12 FEAR
13 FREAKED
14 APARTMENT SONG
15 COOKIE FACTORY
16 PUT IT OFF

BATH COMP F   AMPEX 12/1

PAUL: 'Flamenco' and 'Gift Shop' are similar, in that everyone is kind of stumbling as they individually discover really nice parts to play. I was loving my part in both those songs and I think everyone else was loving their own part too. Those two seemed to be band songs and they made a big difference to the album.

GORD S: We were taking every opportunity that we had to get together and get the spontaneity of creation that Gord was a big fan of. 'Gift Shop' was a riff that we'd been developing on stage and it began to evolve into a song in the studio sessions.

ROB: 'Gift Shop' was a fun one for me. I know that you don't invent anything on the guitar, but I found a tuning that allowed me to play six D notes simultaneously. That first big chord I hit in the song is just a wall of D. There's no harmony to it, it's just a big sound. It allowed me to slide around the neck and use droning D notes and open strings, which was something I'd been doing on other songs like 'Ahead by a Century' and even 'Grace, Too'.

The keyboard at the front end of the song was played by Pete Tuepah, my guitar tech at the time. He was a lovely guy and a really great musician. He went for it and got it in one take, maybe two.

The video was a lot of fun to make too, although the whole thing went completely sideways. We had a big budget and we flew out to Arizona and hiked into the Grand Canyon. The idea was that we'd have this guaranteed clear sky to use as a natural blue screen. But of course when we got there it was raining even though it never rains there. The next day we shot part of the video and it rained again. All the colours changed. We didn't have the natural blue screen and so we had to turn it into a black and white video. We were rewriting the script as we went and the whole thing was chaos, but we rolled with the punches.

The video for gift shop will be shot in black and white and will be comprised of several elements. Due to the length of the song and the way it is segmented musically, each element will be highlighted during a certain part of the song. The opening of the video will be shot in Arizona and will emphasize a contrasty black and white look with skies. We will use heat turbulence to shoot through and create a visual warbling that matches well with the Leslie organ effect and the mood of the top of the song. I will also use an intervalometer which is a fast motion effect, together with slow motion to create a feeling of floating through time and space.

The next element is actually a thread that will run through the video. A glass globe or fish bowl will be filled with water, turned upside down and placed on a base so that our own empty snow-dome will be created. We will take this dome around with us while we shoot the video and place it in the centre of the frame. The image of the world seen through a water filled dome is inverted and distorted. We will shoot buildings, tourist attractions, tourists with flash cameras, eyeballs looking back at us, people, the desert, Niagara Falls, etc. to create our own ever changing snow dome.

The third element is the band shot against the sky to use as blue screen. We will composite them on top of background plates of NYC, mesas, Niagara Falls, Mounties on horse, etc. Towards the end of the song I will introduce a sparkling snow effect by shooting an element of swirling sparkle dust in water for the background and foreground and then in the middle I will place the band who will be photographed with reflections with broken mirror bits that are glued to rotating cylinders. This will create the effect that the band are within the snow environment and will be a beautiful way to end the video. By this point the snow dome composting will be at its maximum.

Other elements will be shot as we go in a travelogue style. We will also be collecting various kitschy snow dome, postcards, statuettes etc. that can that can be photographed in studio and composted to our scenes.

GIFT SHOP
The Tragically Hip

Timings	Lyric
	0
0:33	The beautiful lull
	The dangerous tug
0:43	We get to feel small
	From high up above
	And after a glimpse
	Over the top
1:03	The rest of the world
	Becomes a Gift Shop
1:23	The pendulum swings
	For the horse like a man
	Out over the rim
	Is ice cream to him
1:42	The beautiful lull
	The dangerous tug
	We get to feel small
	But not out of place at all -
2:08	We're forced to bed
	But we're free to dream
	All us human extras
	All us herded beings
2:26	And after a glimpse
	Over the top
	The rest of the world
	Becomes a Gift Shop
2:45	*Guitar Solo*
3:01	I don't know what to believe
	Sometimes I even forget
	And if it's a lie
	Terrorists made me say it
3:20	The beautiful lull
	The dangerous tug
	We get to feel small
	From high up above
3:39	From high up above
	From high up above
	From high up above
3:56	*Guitar Solo to end*
4:49	*Last Hit*

the tragically hip gift shop

**THE TRAGICALLY HIP
"GIFT SHOP"**

SCHEDULE:

Arizona Shoot Date

Schedule:

Band to see and approve location pictures from Arizona.

Eric Yealland, Sean Valentini and Merrie Wasson, Ray Dumas, depart Toronto to Phoenix

Tech scout and lock in locations

Final prep day

The Tragically Hip departs Toronto for Phoenix

Crew and The Tragically Hip travel to location

SHOOT in location outside Phoenix

Travel to Phoenix

The Tragically Hip travels to Tucson

Eric Yealland, Sean Valentini and Ray Dumas travel to NYC

Merrie Wasson wraps out Production in Phoenix

Merrie Wasson travels to Toronto

SHOOT NYC

Eric Yealland, Sean Valentini and Ray Dumas travel Toronto

SHOOT TORONTO STUDIO DAY

SHOOT NIAGARA FALLS

If you want this, you need to tell me to have prints made - then I'll make the collage.

PAUL: 'Ahead by a Century' came towards the end of that *Henhouse* session. It was kind of quirky, different from where our sensibilities necessarily were at the time. It was pretty acoustic, with obviously Robbie playing that main riff. The track started with Robbie and Johnny and then the rest of us added our stuff.

ROB: 'Ahead by a Century' started out as a straight-ahead country-folky kind of song that didn't have a lot to distinguish it – other than great lyrics. One night after everyone else had left the studio, Johnny and I stuck around to see if we could get something to happen. We didn't feel that involved in the song the way it was.

I had an open-string guitar part that introduced the riff that you hear out of the gate and that recurs throughout the song. Johnny worked up a drum machine pattern and then kicked into real drums at a certain point. We demoed it that night and played it for everyone the next day. The song lifted right away. Sometimes it's a struggle to contribute to a song that you feel left out of and find a way to make it better, make it a band song. That one worked, others didn't.

JOHNNY: 'Ahead by a Century', I think, was when people started to really relate to us lyrically. The title itself was really cool. I wondered if that was another trinket that Gord's mom had given him – like 'blow at high dough'. People also connected with the line 'No dress rehearsal, this is our life' – the idea that you've got to make the most of life.

GORD S: My favourite thing about being in The Tragically Hip, above and beyond the friendship obviously, was that as a songwriter you were working with four other creative people all the time. And one of the other guys could take one of my ideas, which I might have considered mundane, and turn it overnight into something really special. And that's what Robbie and Johnny did with 'Ahead by a Century'.

We came in the next day and it had this different vibe, and then Gord and I started working on it and came up with the melody quickly. Maybe hearing it that way for the first time pushed him melodically, and then all of a sudden we were working on a song and, as the lyric evolved, we realised we were working on a good song. That's the most rewarding thing. That's why you do it.

BILLY RAY: We had just finished a string of club shows, and we went right from the clubs into an arena tour. On the first night of that tour, Gord walked into my soundcheck time and said, 'How's it going?' And I was like, 'It's good, man, but it's weird.' And he said, 'What's weird?' And I said, 'This is a big show tonight. Normally with high school plays and that type of thing you do months of rehearsals and pre-production before you mount the show. But this is no dress rehearsal, this is our life.' Within a couple of months 'Ahead by a Century' was well into its working and 'No dress rehearsal, this is our life' became one of the biggest lines ever in Canadian rock and roll, and I'm pretty sure it came out of my mouth.

It feels like people are going to call me a liar, but that's the way Gord worked. You'd say something and out came the notebook and next thing you knew he'd written a song based off of one line you'd said. So you had to be careful what you said or you could become a song!

Stills, artwork and treatment (opposite) for the 'Ahead by a Century' video, 1996

THE TRAGICALLY HIP
Director - Eric Yealland
Overview/Treatment

Introduction

My object in this video is to illustrate some of the images in the lyrics in a non-literal and impressionistic way. The video will be shot in colour 35mm.

The video will be structured by using two vignettes. The first one following the adventures of a young man and the second of and older man (30's) and his wife. The intention is to set up the viewer to think that the two characters are the same person at different points in his life. In reality the boy is the son of the man and woman of the second vignette.

The second vignette, we are led to believe, is about an man who has gotten involved with the local criminal element in order to help his family's income. Something has gone wrong and now there are three men in a dark car driving towards the house. The woman is aware that they are on their way, while the man remains more or less ignorant of the unfolding situation. Tension is created as the woman checks her watch and observes her husband as he gets ready for his day.
This is a setup for the viewer because these images are just metaphors for his regret and in the end of the video he is able to let-go and find comfort in the arms of his wife.

First Vignette

We begin by establishing a house with a tree in the yard surrounded by a forest. We see Gord sitting holding an acoustic guitar. The camera is focused just in front of him so that the scene seem nice and soft. In the background is the tree in the yard. As the verse begins both Gord and the camera begin to slowly crane up in the air until the top of the tree is predominant in the frame. We cut to a shot of the tree and the house that is pulling back, entering a forest. A few feet into the forest the camera begins to drop down and it reveals two 12 year-olds who are lying together amongst the leaves and needles of the forest floor. We establish that nearby is an active hornets nest. As the kids stare into each others eyes the boy says something and the girl begins to laugh at that moment the boys rolls over onto a hornet. Cut to a shot looking up from underneath a piece of plexi-glass where we have affixed a dead hornet. We see the kid roll over onto the camera and the hornet. We cut back to the kids as he screams. The two kids have the same facial expression except hers is of laughter and his is of anguish. When the line 'I had a feverish dream' is delivered we cut to a shot of the boy with a terrified look on his face. He is close to the camera and looking directly into the lens. He spins around and begins to run quickly away from the camera. At the same time the camera begins to rotate around the axis of the center of the lens. The effect becomes one of the world turning upside down and will be very dream-like. This shot is influenced by a dream-sequence in Fellini's 8 1/2.

Second Vignette

We then shift to a vignette that introduces two more characters, a husband and a wife in their home. We establish that he is involved with some shady characters in town because of his overwhelming desire to provide for his family. To create tension I have added a layer that has the woman somehow involved in the timing of the arrival of the dark men. We see her twisting the wedding ring on her finger nervously. He, however, is unaware of the building situation. We see him putting on an old dress shirt, slowly doing up the buttons as he looks over the cameras shoulder at a mirror behind us. We see him washing up and getting ready.

The Dark Men

We then introduce our final characters who are three dark men driving a dark car. All tree of the men are sitting in the front seat. They are chatting and two of them are laughing as the driver keeps stoically silent. We cut to them pulling up at the couples house. They get out and hike-up their pants at the foot of the path. They begin to walk towards the house. It is never resolved why the man are going to the house. Are they going there to kill him? Take him away? Inform him that his father has died? I want to ask more questions then create typical music video narrative.

Resolution

The man in the house sees them coming and pushes his wife aside as he splits out the back door. We see the man running towards the camera with the house in the background and the kid from the first vignette running toward the house. It is revealed here that both events have been happening simultaneously and asks another question about the relationship between the three characters. The man runs and runs and as the light begins to drop his wife materializes out of nowhere and he runs straight into his wife and falls into her arms crying.

Society of Composers, Authors and Music Publishers of Canada (SOCAN) award for 'Ahead by a Century', presented to Gord Downie on 10 November 1997

Boots made for Gord Downie for The Hip's final tour in 2016, with lyrics from 'Ahead by a Century' etched into the soles

GORD S: 'Ahead by a Century' was the final song that The Tragically Hip ever played as a band, with everyone at their campfires and town arenas all singing it out. It felt like the band jammed it out that last night for an extra ten minutes, but it was probably only a couple.

ROB: I like that the song has a life beyond us, that people sing it on TikTok and YouTube. A big car company from the States wanted to use it for a campaign, but we turned down the money because we didn't think 'Ahead by a Century' went with pickup trucks. When Canadian Tire approached us, we said we'd let them use it if they went to an inner-city school and got a kids' choir to sing it. They liked the idea and it was nice.

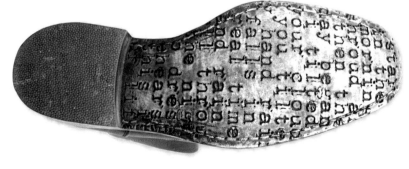

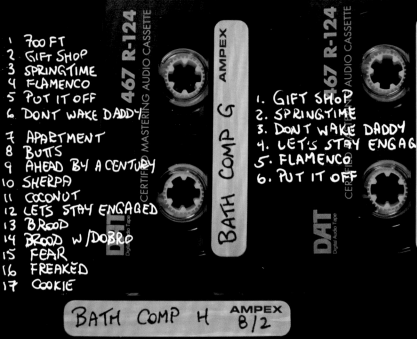

467 R-124 CERTIFIED MASTERING AUDIO CASSETTE · AMPEX · DAT

1. 700 FT
2. GIFT SHOP
3. SPRINGTIME
4. FLAMENCO
5. PUT IT OFF
6. DON'T WAKE DADDY
7. APARTMENT
8. BUTTS
9. AHEAD BY A CENTURY
10. SHERPA
11. COCONUT
12. LETS STAY ENGAGED
13. BROOD
14. BROOD W/ DOBRO
15. FEAR
16. FREAKED
17. COOKIE

BATH COMP G · AMPEX

467 R-124 CERTIFIED AUDIO CASSETTE · AMPEX · DAT

1. GIFT SHOP
2. SPRINGTIME
3. DON'T WAKE DADDY
4. LET'S STAY ENGAGED
5. FLAMENCO
6. PUT IT OFF

HENHOUSE COMP I

Previously - Un-Released

(FUJI CASSETTE)
→ Get Back Again
→ Wait So Long
→ Work That Hard
→ Blonde Solid.
(lyrics!) → If You Lived Here
(You'd Be Home By Now)
– Calico
– Just As Well.

FUJI TAPE
· Princess Tex
· Montreal

(Floater)
Gen Free Japan →
Hiccough Son
Sucker List

Henhouse
· Fear Is Fear
· IF Your Freaked, I'm Fucked,
· Cookie Factory

→ Day For Night
* "Of Course There's No Law Against Practising Demagoguery." (Heavy When You Rain)

* When the Cynic Meets The Road
(Win Win?)

· Cowboy Coffee (Driftin Away On the Purple Pain)
· Stumpy's Overthrow
· Laminar Flow

FULLY ·
· Martin Sleen (Quil Smokin'
* Painterly * I Got Today's USA, TODAY (Detail)
(Courtesy of The Hotel)
· Weather-Wise (Universal Her)
· Radio Show
· Me In The Everglades
→ It's A Slow Down (Burn My Boots)
(The Wind Always Acts Like it knows something

BATH COMP H · AMPEX B/2

1. GIFT SHOP
2. SPRINGTIME
3. FLAMENCO
4. DON'T WAKE
5. APARTMENT
6. 700 FOOT
7. BUTTS WIGGLIN
8. LETS STAY
9. ABAC
10. SHERPA
11. COCONUT
12. COOKIE
13. PUT IT OFF

FREAKED

Sugar's not the teeth, Sugar's not the calories.
It's the dents in the, the path worn in the carpet

27:21
I've seen more blurry lights than starry nights
I've seen more T.V. shows than sheer delights

'cause you gotta get to know your cage
Stress points corrosive age
The keeper's hours, throughout the day
His habits, weaknesses and ways

If you're Freaked I'm Fucked
I love you that much
(GM) If you're Freaked I'm Fucked (so)

And ya Sugar's not the teeth, sugar's not the calories.
It's the dents in the wall, the path worn in the carpet
Tell us everything you think we should know
We'd rather know something about everything
From the top floor to the shop floor
We're warm to a fancy thought.

If you're Freaked I'm Fucked
I love you (that) so much
(Gee) If you're Freaked I'm Fucked
I know it doesn't sound like much.
Guess

I Enjoy the desertos
I enjoy the desert and it enjoys me

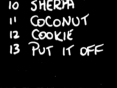

jim herrington

Here's the booty.... I've circled in yellow grease pencil (really more of a crayon) the ones I liked, although by the time you read this I probably don't like 'em anymore. Keep an open mind when looking at this stuff - some of it can look drastically better (or worse) when printed differently than the way the contact sheets are printed. I bet you think I'm bonkers by some of the frames I've selected - I like the quirkier stuff. Call me...

Above left: DAT cassettes of tracks recorded during the Trouble at the Henhouse sessions, Bathouse, Bath, ON, early 1996

Above and opposite: Handwritten lyrics for 'Freaked', 'Brood & Bloom' and 'Cookie Factory', which are all unreleased tracks from the Henhouse sessions

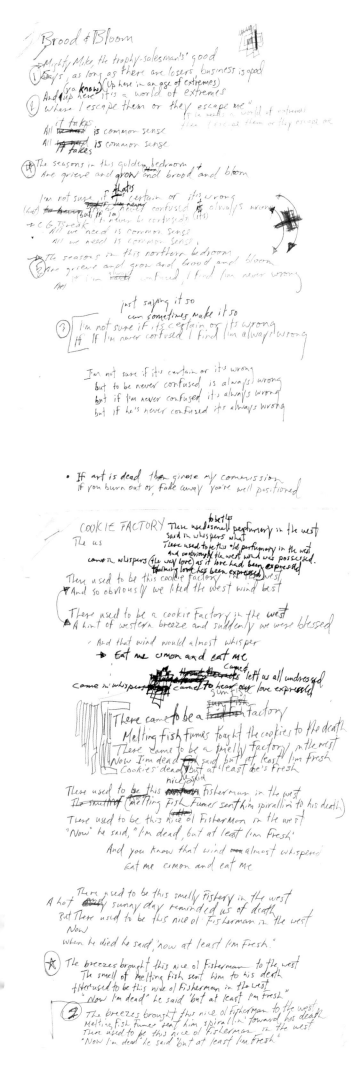

Brood & Bloom

Mighty Mike, the trophy-salesman's' good
says, as long as there are losers business is good
(ya know) (Up here in an age of extremes)
And up here it's a world of extremes
Where I escape them or they escape me

it takes
All ~~what~~ is common sense
All ~~it takes~~ is common sense

The seasons in this golden bedroom
Are grieve and grow and brood and bloom

I'm not sure if it's certain or it's wrong
but if I'm never confused it's always wrong
C.G. Break (I'll never be confused) (its)
All we need is common sense
All we need is common sense.

The seasons in this northern bedroom
are grieve and grow and brood and bloom
if I'm confused, I find I'm never wrong

just saying it so
can sometimes make it so
I'm not sure if it's certain or it's wrong
If I'm never confused I find I'm always wrong

I'm not sure if it's certain or it's wrong
but to be never confused is always wrong
but if I'm never confused it's always wrong
but if he's never confused it's always wrong

• If art is dead then ignore my commission
If you burn out or fade away you're well positioned

COOKIE FACTORY There was/is small perfumery in the west
The us   said in whispers what
There used to be this old perfumery in the west
and obviously the west wind was possessed.
came in whispers (the way love) as if love had been expressed.
hearing love has been expressed
There used to be this cookie factory in the west
And so obviously we liked the west wind best

There used to be a cookie factory in the west
A hint of western breeze and suddenly we were blessed
And that wind would almost whisper
→ Eat me c'mon and eat me
came
The toast the crackers left us all undressed
came in whispers came to hear our love expressed

There came to be a Fish factory
Melting fish fumes fought the cookies to the death
There came to be a smelly factory in the west
Now I'm dead he said but at least I'm fresh
Cookies' dead but at least she's fresh
nice ol' said

There used to be this Fisherman in the west
The smith (melting fish fumes sent him spirallin' to his death)
There used to be this nice ol' Fisherman in the west
"Now" he said, "I'm dead, but at least I'm fresh"

And you know that wind would almost whispered
Eat me c'mon and eat me

There used to be this smelly Fishery in the west
A hot sunny day reminded us of death
But There used to be this nice ol' Fisherman in the west
Now
when he died he said, 'now at least I'm fresh.'

The breezes brought this nice ol' Fisherman to the west
The smell of melting fish sent him to his death
There used to be this nice ol' Fisherman in the west
"Now I'm dead" he said 'but at least I'm fresh."

The breezes brought this nice ol' Fisherman to the west
Melting fish fumes sent him spirallin' toward his death
There used to be this nice ol' Fisherman in the west
'Now I'm dead' he said 'but at least I'm fresh'

GORD S: We always followed the formula that you've got to have three singles on your record, three 'stress tracks' in record company parlance. We knew 'Gift Shop' was a wicked tune. That's going to go somewhere. No problem. 'Ahead by a Century': great. I always thought that '700 Ft. Ceiling' could've easily been a single. So, we've got three great songs. Let's just have fun. Let's make a real proper record, based on the music that we listened to growing up. We were always LP guys: The Beatles' records would have a bunch of great hits on them. The Stones were the best example, where an album like *Beggars Banquet* had fantastic hit songs on it, like 'Sympathy for the Devil', but also less immediate songs like 'Prodigal Son' and 'No Expectations'. Those were the songs that I wanted to write. So on *Henhouse* that's 'Apartment Song' and 'Sherpa' and 'Coconut Cream' (although I love the energy of that song). Maybe with a producer that was looking to sell a whole pile of records, those wouldn't have made it on the record.

Self-production's not easy. There's a lot of diplomacy involved in production and everyone's got to buy in to the idea of one person having the final say. This is the captain of the ship and this is where we're going to go with it. When you don't have that then it can be pretty entropic.

GORD S: *Trouble at the Henhouse* was probably our last record where we religiously employed that wood-shedding approach to songwriting, where we were literally in a circle taking turns to throw out ideas. We would continue to do that, but less successfully. To try to extend that approach into the recording studio and have five producers on the project was another thing entirely.

PAUL: There were downsides of self-producing. You'd have one or two guys who liked a song or wanted the chorus in a particular place and one or two who didn't and then there'd be someone in the middle as the tie-breaker. We'd work all this stuff out in general, but it was so overwhelming. So, after that, we decided we'd always have a producer and the best one we could find. I'm glad we did the one album together, and everyone got along, but it was easier when there was a producer in control – even of little things like when we broke for dinner. We never got pushed around but we certainly appreciated a bit of guidance.

We had a couple of battle royales over arrangements on that record, which is when a producer would usually have stepped in and settled things. For example, Gord and I locked horns over the arrangement of '700 Ft. Ceiling' and we eventually came up with a compromise. I think it affected '700 Ft. Ceiling' as a song, because it sounds like a compromise. That was the peril of the collective approach, but we would never have known if we hadn't tried.

ROB: On all the records leading up to *Trouble at the Henhouse*, we had been five minds acting as one with a sympathetic producer helping us realise our vision. Stripped of the producer, we were five minds not always acting as one and getting into the weeds in certain situations.

It's a decent record and we did a pretty good job, but, in retrospect, self-producing was not the right thing for our band to do. But if we hadn't done it then, we would have done it on the next record or the one after that and we would have run into the same issues and, who knows, maybe it would have been worse.

the tragically hip to release newest album
trouble at the henhouse Saturday May 11th

TORONTO -- May 2, 1996 -- On Saturday, May 11, 1996, **the tragically hip**'s sixth studio album entitled **trouble at the henhouse** will be available in record stores across Canada. For the many fans who just can't wait, some retailers will be opening their doors at one minute past midnight (12.01 a.m.) on May 11th. The album's first single "**Ahead By A Century**" reached the #1 chart position in less than 2 weeks.

In keeping with **the tragically hip**'s ongoing concerns for the environment, the band have developed the album's packaging to be as environmentally friendly as possible. The CD for **trouble at the henhouse** does not utilize the traditional jewel box, ensuring that virtually no plastic is used for the packaging other than the shrink wrap. Due to these CD's being slimmer in design, more will fit into each shipping box resulting in another benefit of less cardboard being used. In addition, the CD package has been printed using vegetable dye inks, on 100% recycled board and coated with water based varnish. While the cassette format dictates more conventional packaging, the environment has also been taken into consideration by the band. The cassette graphics have been printed using vegetable dye inks on chlorine-free paper.

In support of the Canadian music retail community, **trouble at the henhouse** will be the first album ever to include a packaging sticker stating 'Not Available From Record Clubs'.

On Tuesday, May 7 at 6:00 p.m. eastern daylight time, the Rock Radio Network will be debuting **trouble at the henhouse** in a two hour special broadcast through 23 radio affiliates across Canada featuring an exclusive interview with **Gord Downie**.

the tragically hip is one of the most successful acts in Canada, having racked up total catalogue sales in excess of the 3,000,000 unit mark in Canada. Sales on the individual full albums range from six times platinum to eight times platinum. The release of **trouble at the henhouse** marks the first time that the band will have a simultaneous release in the U.S. (on Atlantic Records) as well as numerous international markets (such as the U.K. Europe, Australia and southeast Asia) through MCA Music Entertainment International

Trouble at the Henhouse
RECORDED: OCTOBER
1995–FEBRUARY 1996
THE BATHOUSE, BATH, ON
KINGSWAY, NEW ORLEANS, LA
SOME LOFT, SAN FRANCISCO, CA
PRODUCERS:
THE TRAGICALLY HIP
MARK VREEKEN
ENGINEERS: MARK VREEKEN
MARK HOWARD
MIXING: STEVEN DRAKE
MARK VREEKEN
RELEASED: 11 MAY 1996

Gift Shop
Springtime in Vienna
Ahead by a Century
Don't Wake Daddy
Flamenco
700 Ft. Ceiling
Butts Wigglin'
Apartment Song
Coconut Cream
Let's Stay Engaged
Sherpa
Put It Off

GORD D: We were without ideas as far as what we would put on the cover, what we would even call the record and Robbie was dabbling around with a few things.

ROB: I had all my old photography magazines that I had taken out to the Bathouse and they were just on shelves and coffee tables around the place. Between takes I was leafing through one of them and I found this shot by a guy named Avery Crounse and I said, 'Here's the album cover.'

GORD D: We all thought it was perfect and talked Robbie into dialling 411. It's not his forte to cold call. There was detective work. He left a message saying we were interested in this photograph. We waited a week and figured that maybe the guy didn't live there anymore, that he was not even alive. Then he phoned back and he was totally enthusiastic about it. He was no longer a photographer, but he was a filmmaker and putting his son through Princeton Law. He was totally into it and we told him we'd exploit the shit out of it and he didn't care.

That photograph is called 'Trouble at the Henhouse', so the photograph gave us the title of the record. The inside photo of lightning hitting the horizon line is called 'Traveller's Omen'.

JAKE GOLD: Steven Drake mixes the record. The record company in the States hears 'Ahead by a Century' and goes, 'Holy shit. We've got a real song here.' We hire a video director to make a great video. The record's due to come out.

Tower Records had just opened their store at Yonge and Queen in Toronto. It was their only Canadian location and they wanted to make a big splash when *Trouble at the Henhouse* came out by having the band play on the roof. In return, they'd offered price and positioning in America for at least two months.

Price and positioning meant that Tower had to buy a certain number of copies of the record, and they had to put it in all the right places with posters so there was no way that anyone who went in the store could miss it, as opposed to being buried in a rack under 'T'. In America, it was probably worth about $50,000 a month.

I called up the president of Atlantic and told him about this opportunity and he agreed to match whatever deal I could get. So if I got two months, they'd pay for another two months.

So we were set up now. All we had to do was play on the roof of Tower Records. I sat down with the guys and one of them said, 'Well, didn't The Beatles and U2 do that?' And I said, 'Yeah, and that's pretty good company.' And then Gord Downie said, 'But I shop at Sam's.' Which was a Canadian record store chain.

I had to go back to Atlantic and tell them we weren't going to do it. Had the band chosen to play on the roof, we would have had major retail marketing support in America, which would have then shown radio that the record company was really behind the record and therefore they would have played the record more and there would have been way more visibility on the band. And then all of the other stuff that comes with that. What happened instead was the record company lost interest, because they didn't see us doing anything to help our own cause.

ROB: When The Beatles played on a roof, that was really great. And then U2 did it and that was great too. But did we want to be doing U2 doing The Beatles?

It just didn't feel right for us. Those record store promotion things always left us cold. We did a few of them: 'Shoppers, Celine Dion's record is at the front, and, in aisle five, The Tragically Hip will now be performing.' We felt like the soup of the day or something.

GORD S: We had a big problem with multinational companies coming into Canada. We were Sam the Record Man guys. In fact, I bought my records from House of Sounds, Johnny Sugarman's store. I resisted the corporatisation of art.

It was another circumstance where I think Gord was probably the most resistant to doing this gig and he stood his ground on his principle. You could see it as a really good example commercially of us taking out a gun and shooting off the other foot. Because if we'd really wanted to be selling tons of records, we'd have done this gig and then maybe the record company would've participated a little bit more and things might be very different now.

But we didn't and they aren't. We stuck to our own trajectory and, ironically, here we are several decades later and there aren't any multinational record stores left. HMV's no more. Tower's no more. Even Sam the Record Man is no more.

Spy Gadgets

ReBoot:
An alpha-numeric
success story

THE LAST
TEMPTATION
The Tragically Hip Interview

Ice-T   Sloan   Pluto
Cub   Doughboys

The Tragically Hip
Trouble At The Henhouse
U.S. Radio Tracking

East

Date May 29th, 1996
BDS Report period: May 20-26th/96   AlbNet report period: as of May 29th

Station	City	Format	Song	TWP	LWP	2WP	Rank	BDS	AlbNet Comments
1 MUCH	New York	Adult	Album	9	0	0			• new
1 WAVF	Charleston SC	Alt	ABAC	24	A	0			• new
1 WBER	Rochester NY	Alt	ABAC	9	8	5			•
1 WBJB	NYC	Adult	Album	5	A	0			•
WBOS	Boston MA	Adult							
1 WBRU	Providence RI	Alt	ABAC	1	0	0		•	
0 WBRU	Providence RI	Alt	Gift	1	0	0		•	
1 WCIZ	Watertown NY	Rock	ABAC	21	21	14			•
WDET	Detroit MI	Adult							
1 WEBK	Killington VT	Adult	Album	16	20	21			•
0 WEDG	Buffalo NY	Alt	Gift	0	2	1			• rankdown from #14, AlbNet reports 21p20p21p
1 WEDG	Buffalo NY	Alt	ABAC	20	20	21	17		• rank up from #30, AlbNet reports 14p6p3p
1 WEQX	ManchstrVT/AlbnyNY	Alt	ABAC	19	15	4	19		•
WFUV	New York	Adult							
1 WHEB	Portsmouth NH	Rock	ABAC	14	14	14			•
1 WIBF	Philadelphia PA	Alt	ABAC	17	5	0	28		• rank debut, AlbNet reports 6p6p0p
1 WIII	Ithaca NY	Adult	Album	16	16	14			•
1 WIZN	Burlington VT	Rock	ABAC	21	18	20			•
1 WKIT	Bangor ME	Rock	ABAC	16	16	0			•
1 WKLL	Utica/Rome NY	Alt	ABAC	5	6	6			•
1 WKRL	Syracuse NY	Alt	ABAC	3	6	0			• AlbNet reports 5p6p6p
1 WKVT	Brattleboro VT	Adult	Album	7	7	7			•
1 WKZE	Sharon CT	Adult	Album	12	12	6			no spins reported
WMAX	Rochester NY	Adult							
WMVY	Cape Cod MA	Adult							
1 WNCS	Montpelier VT	Adult	ABAC	9	8	9	23		• rank debut, AlbNet reports 8p.8p.9p
WNCW	Spindale NC	Adult							
WNEW	New York	Adult							
1 WOCA	Philadelphia/Various	Adult	Album	2	A	0			•
1 WPXC	Hyannis MA/Cape Cod	Rock	ABAC	6	3	4			•
1 WQXA	York PA	Alt	ABAC	0	3	1			•
WRNX	Springfield MA	Adult							no spins reported
WROX	Norfolk VA	Alt							
WRSI	Greenfield MA	Adult							
1 WTTS	Bloomington IN	Adult	ABAC	1	2	0			•
WVAY	Wilmington VT	Adult							
1 WVBR	Ithaca NY	Adult	Album	10	10	10			•
1 WVGO	Richmond VA	Alt	ABAC	0	1	0			•
WXDX	Pittsburgh PA								
WXLE	Clifton Park/Albany NY	Adult							
WXPN	Philadephia PA	Adult							
WXRC	Charlotte NC	Adult							AlbNet reports 6p,2p,0p
1 WXRV	Boston MA	Adult	ABAC	9	1	0		•	
1 WYEP	Pittsburgh PA	Adult	Album	3	0	0			•

Totals	Stations Spinning		TWP	LWP	2WP
	27		276	214	157

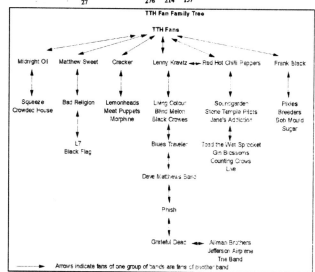

TTH Fan Family Tree

Arrows indicate fans of one group of bands are fans of another band

So what does this stuff mean?

First, we don't have one conclusive data source at this point. That having been said, a number of interesting patterns emerge here.

Generally, these runs show that TTH fans can come from all different angles... The trick is to select a short list of bands fans of whom are most likely to like the new TTH record. Given what we have here (mostly qualitative-type data based on Internet fans), we need to use judgement in the final selection, using the interesting but limited information we have here.

JAKE GOLD: Two months later on the cover of *Network*, their in-store magazine, Sam the Record Man had a drawing of Gord as Christ on the cross at the Canadian/US border, with the headline 'Why can't this band crack the United States?' It was the height of irony. Of course, they had no way of knowing what cross Gord actually got on to help them, out of his sense of loyalty to them.

US radio tracking data ('ABAC' refers to 'Ahead by a Century'), May 1996

JAM Presents
the tragically hip
with special guest
clarissa

THURSDAY JUNE 27 RIVIERA CHICAGO ALL AGES

The Hip '96

LOCAL CREW
PRESS/PHOTO/TV
LOCAL CREW
PRESS/PHOTO/TV
ALL ACCESS

The Hip '96
PRESS/PHOTO
V.I.P.
PRESS/PHOTO
V.I.P.

The Hip '96
GUEST
GUEST

The Hip '96
AFTER SHOW ONLY
AFTER SHOW ONLY

CAT'S CRADLE

300 E.

SCUD MOUNTAIN BOYS

The Hip, their crew and members of the band Clarissa and their crew, Cat's Cradle, Carrboro, NC, 29 August 1996

Back row (l to r): Dan Cassar (lights), Johnny Fay, Paul Langlois, Clarissa's sound man, Mark Vreeken, Michael Rank (Clarissa's vocalist and guitarist), Gord Downie, Gord Sinclair, Dave Gregg (merch), Pete Tuepah (guitar tech), Andy McMillan (Clarissa's bassist), Randy Kemp (monitors)
Front row (l to r): Rob Baker, Dave Powell, Sara Romweber (Clarissa's drummer), Billy Ray Koster

GORD S: Around the time of *Day for Night* and *Trouble at the Henhouse*, Gord moved to Toronto and never came back. Johnny moved full-time to Toronto a couple of years after Gord.

It changed the logistics right away. We couldn't just phone each other up and go out for a beer, let alone sit around and write songs – that ability to be spontaneous is a great thing from an art perspective.

The studio out in Bath, which we started around '94, '95, was going to be the epicentre of all things Hip creatively. Fairly quickly, we realised that for the guys in Toronto it was a pain in the ass. The others, living in Kingston, could go home at night but Gord and Johnny were having to stay out there.

If we'd all stayed in Kingston, who knows what would have happened? We might have broken up. Robbie and I grew up together and we couldn't wait to scrape the dust of Kingston's one-horse town off our boots and go see the world. But we still live a couple hundred metres from each other because Kingston is a great place, not only to be from, but to continue to live. One of the great things is that everybody knows us from beyond being in The Tragically Hip. We're just guys from Kingston, and that's a great leveller. It's not that big a deal and I think that's a really good thing for your ego.

ROB: Five late twenty-somethings living in a van together on the road gave way to five thirty-somethings with different needs and aspirations and demands on them. It was only natural that Gord would set up camp in Toronto. We spent a lot of time on the road and our partners needed to be where their support systems were. Gord's partner's support system was in Toronto.

PAUL: Friendships within the band were fairly uncomplicated for the first ten years, but then, as we went along, Gord Sinclair got married, Robbie got married, I got married the next year, Gord Downie got married the year after that. Then everyone started having kids and we were all trying to stay on the same page as to when to tour and when not to tour and, when we were recording, how to get enough time at home with the family. Fortunately, Johnny remained on the same page, even though he was fairly single, and I think that was almost the key. We all knew we'd miss things like friends' weddings because we were on the road. But we agreed, I would say, 95 percent of the time, on when we should take time off because it was really scarce.

JOHNNY: When the guys started having kids, things couldn't help but change. It was time to think about putting groceries on the table, instead of getting marijuana over the border.

Our touring cycle got a little bit easier. We were playing bigger venues, so we'd do a three-week tour then take a couple of weeks off and boot it back home. There was no time wasted just sitting around. The insane days of being in the van were long gone.

And sometimes the guys would take their families with them. When we went on the road for Roadside Attraction in '95, during Ziggy Marley's set there were kids dancing on the stage behind the band. It was awesome.

BILLY RAY: It was good for the band, morale-wise, to be able to go out on tour for three weeks, and then just at the point that people were getting sick of each other, of living on a bus, of eating truck stop food, they'd get to go home and see their wives and kids and recharge their batteries. Then they'd come back out, ready to be rock stars and kick ass again.

GORD S: Being on the road, we missed a lot of important things and we relied on each other emotionally to get through these times. We were down in Texas when my eldest son, Colin, had whooping cough really badly. I could hear in my wife's voice how scared she was. Yet, it's not a group of strangers you're with; there's a real love between us and having that emotional support was the only thing that enabled you to endure it, stop you from quitting and flying home.

PAUL: When we were opening for Page and Plant in '95, I had a pager as there were no cell phones. Halfway between Salt Lake City and Ames, Iowa, my daughter Emma was born six weeks early and the pager didn't go off. I missed Emma's birth, but we cancelled a week of shows, so I was able to get back home.

Kids change everything. It's really tough to leave them. It gets tougher the more aware they become – at six, seven and eight, they're like, 'You're going again?' It makes long days longer to be away and we were away a lot. But it makes you try harder, makes you a better person. Children bring so much joy and worry into your lives. They just make everything matter more.

BILLY RAY: I used to room with Gord Sinclair back when it was Paul and Gord Downie together, and Robbie and Johnny together. I'd be lying on my bed in a hotel in somewhere like Wichita Falls listening to Sinclair teaching his kids over the phone, having them read to him, spelling words, doing math problems. I remember really admiring his determination not to be an absent parent. All those guys really put in the effort to be in contact even if they couldn't be physically present.

These pages and overleaf: Trouble at the Henhouse tour, Canada, late 1996

THE TRAGICALLY HIP TOUR 96

REHEARSAL SCHEDULE

NOV. 5 / 96

PRODUCTION DAY 1

GOALS:

1) Load in and set up completely SOUND , LIGHTS, STAGE, BACKLINE, LASER...
2) SET Up Production Office
3) TUNE P.A. SYSTEM   2 Hours   Laser & Lights Dinner or Off
4) FOCUS LITES   2 Hours   Sound Dinner Or Off
5) LASER   2 Hours
6) Lites & Laser Overnight Programming

8:00 AM	Load in Lites & Sound Rigging -- & Stage	
11:00 AM	Load In Sound & Backbone	
12:30 PM	Split Lunch Begins	
2:00 PM	Lighting Rig in the Air	
3:00 PM	Sound Rig In the Air	
	Set Up Stage	
	Set Up Back Line	
4:30 PM	Laser In Place	
	Tune the P.A. (2 Hours)	
6:30 PM	Focus Lights (2 Hours)	House lights May Be Dimmed Now ??
8:30 PM	Laser Focus (2 hours)	
10:30 PM	Overnight Programming Begins	

GST #R897157590
THE TRAGICALLY HIP
WITH RHEOSTATICS
COPPS COLISEUM
$26.03+1.82 GST+.50 CIF
WED DEC 11 1996. 7:30PM
1026180CT11988CA 660TB200
15   1$ 31.60A

The Tragically Hip
November 1996

Sunday	Monday	Tuesday	Wednesday	Thursday	Friday	Saturday
					1	2
3	4	5	6	7	8 VANCOUVER Pacific Coliseum	9 VANCOUVER Pacific Coliseum
		REHEARSAL - VANCOUVER				
10 VANCOUVER Pacific Coliseum	11 Off / Travel to Edmonton	12 EDMONTON Northlands Coliseum	13 EDMONTON Northlands Coliseum	14 Off in Calgary	15 CALGARY Saddledome	16 CALGARY Saddledome
17 Off in Saskatoon	18 SASKATOON Saskatchew-an Place	19 WINNIPEG Arena	20 WINNIPEG Arena	21 THUINDER BAY Fort William Garden	22 Off in Detroit	23 DETROIT Cobo Arena
24 Off in Buffalo	25 Off in Buffalo	26 BUFFALO Marine Midland Arena	27 Off in Ottawa	28 OTTAWA Corel Center	29 OTTAWA Corel Center	30 QUEBEC CITY Le Colisee

@ 481.00 per page

The Tragically Hip
December 1996

Sunday	Monday	Tuesday	Wednesday	Thursday	Friday	Saturday
1 Off in St. John's 4:30 Btc	2 Off in St. John's From HA!	3 St. JOHN'S NF Memorial Stadium	4 St. JOHN'S NF Memorial Stadium	5 Off / Travel to Halifax 2:00pm	6 HALIFAX Metro Center	7 SAINT JOHN NB Harbour Station
8 Off / Travel to Montreal	9 MONTREAL Molson Place	10 Off in Toronto	11 HAMILTON Copp's Coliseum	12 TORONTO Maple Leaf Gardens	13 TORONTO Maple Leaf Gardens	14 Toronto... End of tour party
15	16	17	18	19	20	21
22	23	24	25	26	27	28
29	30	31				

IFTC Inc.   Revised 10/7/96, 2:36:13 PM

August 6, 1996

The premise behind the "Trouble at the Henhouse" art design is about this juggernaut like device which has, after traveling a seemingly endless distance by some arcane method, come to rest in the arena. It's visual weight is immense, and is composed of battered metal plate riveted together and flanked by two corrugated iron "henhouses". Behind, in the wake of the juggernaut is an immense vista of steel prairies stretching on as far as the eye can see. The prairie sky is turbulent and stormy.

The following designs then branch from this point. The "options" consist of three different treatments to the metal juggernaut. One, the oncoming tornado, two, the mystical nexus, and three, the surrealist map. The one common element to all three options is that they all are treated as revealed puzzles during the breaks between the songs finally culminating in the overall effect at the end of the performance.

Although visually heavy, the set is intended to go through a metamorphosis for every song during the performance. Composed of neutral colours, mainly grays and black with highlights of rusty brown the stage and backdrop will become distinctly different "environments" giving each song it's own signature. This will be achieved through the lighting of the set which will overpower the boilerplate look giving each song it's own distinct mood.

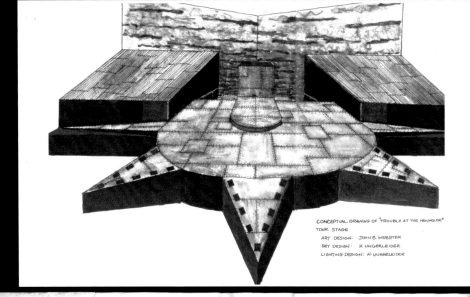

CONCEPTUAL DRAWING OF "TROUBLE AT THE HENHOUSE"
TOUR STAGE
ART DESIGN: JOHN B. WEBSTER
SET DESIGN: H. UNGERLEIDER
LIGHTING DESIGN: H. UNGERLEIDER

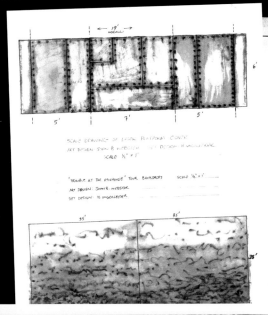

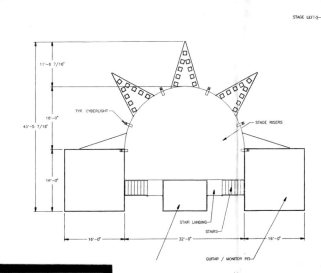

"HENHOUSE" TENT ROOF DETAIL   SCALE ¼" = 1'
ART DESIGN: JOHN B. WEBSTER   SET DESIGN: H. UNGERLEIDER

the tragically hip

on compact disc and cassette

and on the road this fall

November 8 & 9	Vancouver	Pacific Coliseum	November 26	Buffalo	TBA
November 10	Seattle	TBA	November 28 & 29	Ottawa	Corel Centre
November 12 & 13	Edmonton	Edmonton Coliseum	November 30	Quebec City	Colisee de Quebec
November 15	Calgary	Saddledome	December 3 & 4	St. John's	Memorial Stadium
November 18	Saskatoon	Saskatchewan Place	December 6	Halifax	Halifax Metro Centre
November 19 & 20	Winnipeg	Winnipeg Arena	December 7	Saint John	Harbour Station
November 22	Chicago	TBA	December 7	Montreal	Molson Centre
November 23	Detroit	TBA	December 12 & 13	Toronto	Maple Leaf Gardens

The handwritten song introduction notes read approximately:

(BANTER, ETC.)
① ▸ Grace Too ▸ ("Rheos, richer for having seen them")
  ▸ Fucked up, I just fucked up, loss of judgement — Failure to have judgement etc.
② ▸ Fully, Completely ▸
③ ▸ Springtime ▸ Fantastic to be here ▸ (we call this Springtime in Vienna.")
  Renaissance, undercover, Cold war, nothing you can't handle, no more rubbernecking (Original Mix?)
④ ▸ (Thanks a lot... the hull of Detroit")
  ▸ TWIST MY ARM ▸ (Into temptation)
  ▸ ("Yea thanks, Yea it's nice to be in a legendary room, band, crew, Rheos happy to be here.")
⑤ ▸ GIFT SHOP ▸ (I implore ... I ignore you too.)   (Mix?) B/G Singing?
  ▸ Intro: We'd like to do a song if we could
  sorta explores the realm of catharsis and my area is
  capable of more PWR and adolescence in crowd is all about trust.
⑥ AHEAD BY A CENTURY ▸   (Mix) (Wave Drum?)
  Intro: This about a man down on his luck takes to the street shotin a banana at people Skyin to convince them that it was making a sound)
⑦ THE LUXURY ("the wind always acts like it knows so much...")
  ("courage, it couldn't come at a worse time"..)   Middle
⑧ COURAGE ▸ The snow is merry is M// the snow is so merciless on poor old M//a
  (Outro) the snow is so merciless on poor old M// in spite of everything that happened inspite of it.
  Don't you worry ... Mamma's gonna make her look good etc. x5
⑨ NEW ORLEANS — Over Intro) "From the Himalayas of your mind to New Orleans"
  (Middle) China Girl — See your heart beating / I see the stars crashin' down
  China (China bir') etc." too tired to be poor
  "Don't Worry Baby" at baby just shut your mouth Everything will turn out alright!
⑩ DON'T WAKE DADDY
  (Thanks a lot)
⑪ Intro ▸ OK this holiday season you might be, by an encyclopedia salesman SCARED unsolicited, you say no thanks, it's the CD ROM age, my friend
⑫ BLOW AT HIGH DOUGH   FUCKED UP LYRICS
  Something or Richard Nix
  ▸ They're turning this song into a movie starring Peter O'Toole as the curmudgeonly light house keeper and Jodie Foster as Susan (called the Nurse Patient)
⑬ ▸ NAUTICAL DISASTER
  Outro (it's all I way do.   (c'mon c'mon c'mon I want into your temple)
  (it's a bad time to be poor)
⑭ WHEREWITHAL ▸ ("I retire to Florida, a private citizen")   OVER ▸
  Thank you Rheos, Thank you everyone thanks a lot.

▸ ENCORE
  — Sometimes you can feel a sense of confinement so crushing so
  that it actually starts to feel good at which time a member
  of your family probably rescues you.
⑮ LOCKED IN THE TRUNK OF A CAR ▸▸▸ (B/G's?)
  " the first thing I do is go to Montana to be a bronco buster"
⑯ ▸ LITTLE BONES
  (Bow down to my will / gather round the window sill")

THE TRAGICALLY HIP LIVE BETWEEN US

THE TRAGICALLY HIP
LIVE BETWEEN US
IN STORE
SATURDAY, MAY 24TH

Live Between Us
RECORDED:
23 NOVEMBER 1996
COBO HALL, DETROIT, MI
PRODUCERS:
THE TRAGICALLY HIP
MARK VREEKEN
ENGINEER: MARK VREEKEN
LIVE SOUND: MARK VREEKEN
MIXING: DON SMITH
RELEASED: 24 MAY 1997
Grace, Too
Fully Completely
Springtime in Vienna
Twist My Arm
Gift Shop
Ahead by a Century
The Luxury
Courage
New Orleans Is Sinking
Don't Wake Daddy
Scared
Blow at High Dough
Nautical Disaster
The Wherewithal

Above: Gord Downie's notes on song introductions for the 1996 Detroit show that was featured on Live Between Us, The Hip's *first full-length live album*

Opposite: Promo photos for Live Between Us, *Brussels, Belgium, 1997*

ROB: We recorded every show on the Henhouse tour, but it was only after we got back and took a little time off that we decided to put out a live record. It was something we had talked about a little bit. We were upset at the number of bootlegs out there – not that we really cared about people making bootlegs, but the quality of those things was lousy.

There were about four shows on the tour that stood out and one of them was Detroit. That was the one that we kept coming back to as the most solid from start to finish. The idea was definitely that it was going to be a warts-and-all thing, and if it didn't stand up then we wouldn't release it. We weren't going to do overdubs or make fixes. If we were looking for the best possible version of 'Gift Shop', the best version of 'Ahead by a Century', we could have pieced it together that way. But we thought that that was opening a big kettle of fish. So we didn't take a lot of care about the songs we actually put on the record. It was just that those were the songs we happened to play that night.

We also decided that the record would just include the body of the set. From the Detroit show, there were particularly good versions of 'Little Bones' and 'Flamenco' that we played as part of the encore, but we left them out because we figured that it's one thing to sit through a two-hour concert but it's another thing to sit through a two-hour record.

54

the tragically hip

November 8, 9 & 10 • Vancouver • PNE
November 12 & 13 • Edmonton • Coliseum
November 16 & 17 • Calgary • Saddledome
November 20 & 21 • Saskatoon • Saskatchewan Place
November 24 & 25 • Winnipeg • Winnipeg Arena
November 28 & 29 • Ottawa • Corel Centre

SOLD OUT

GORD D: The goalie's a fairly solitary figure within the team and very little understood, even by coaches. There's no shortage of tips and pointers for the long-haired superstars up front, but for the goalies it's just, 'You go out there, kid, and do whatever it is that you do.' It can be a pretty gut-wrenching experience.

ROB: We all came up playing hockey when we were kids. Some of us more seriously than others. Gord was a bit more serious than the rest of us and Paul was a pretty good player too. I was a terrible player, but I was big.

PATRICK SAMBROOK: The first time I met Gord, I got invited out to play hockey at a Friday afternoon league with people of all different levels, and Gord was the goalie. One thing about Gord was he did not like to be scored on. It didn't matter what your level or who you were, that's who he was when he was the goalie.

When I started working with him professionally it got worse. Before, it was more gamesy and fun, but in the moment he was incredibly intense, and then afterwards he would relax a bit. It was an incredible part of him and I think you can see it in his music and his performance.

Being goaltender really messed up Gord's hips. That was a constant physical thing that people weren't necessarily aware of. He did a lot of therapy just to get himself to a place where he was able to perform those last tours. If he had lived longer, he would have needed a hip replacement.

BILLY RAY: Gord was a very good skater. He had great form. When Gord played hockey, he always looked like a pro; it was almost like a dance, his slap shots.

MARK NORMAN: One of my titles was 'social director'. So in the summertime it was my job to set up where we were going to play golf or where we were going to go drinking. But in the wintertime, when we were out in western Canada, on several occasions I would find a hockey rink that we could go to late at night, and arrange for some sticks and gloves and that kind of stuff.

The band would get off stage, hang out for a bit and get cooled down, and then we'd go over to the other rink and play shinny until two or three in the morning. Then we'd sit around in that dressing room and drink beer.

Billy Ray was the sniper and I was always worried Gord was going to hit him in the head, because Billy Ray never let up and he could skate circles around all of us.

Above and opposite centre: Gord Downie's goalie skates and goalie helmet

Opposite: Gord Sinclair (top left), Gord Downie and Dave Bidini of Rheostatics (top right), Paul Langlois (bottom left), Rob Baker and Dave Powell (bottom right), Trouble at the Henhouse tour, Canada, late 1996

MARK NORMAN: One night in Calgary we went to the Max Bell Arena, where Wayne Gretzky's brother Glen was the general manager. So he came out and played with us and it was awesome. He had the little Jofa helmet, just like Wayne, and he knew exactly where to be, just like Wayne. We were all pretty thrilled to be playing with a Gretzky.

RICKY WELLINGTON: I started doing Hip shows in Toronto and it ballooned from there. In around '94, I got called and asked if I wanted to go on tour with them and it was a no-brainer. We never did a tour without hockey gear for several years. It was on my priority list.

We would get one of the bus drivers to drive them to a rink where a local promoter had set something up for us; or sometimes they would play the night before at the arena where the show was happening. Sometimes you would have as many as 15 people playing, including members of the opening bands. Heck, we even played with guys like Lanny McDonald.

TRISTIN CHIPMAN: Once in a while, they would get out and skate if there were NHL guys around who they could go and mess around with. Usually on Canadian tours there would be a lot more dudes around that wanted to do things like that, more people interested in the legend of 'Gord the Goalie'.

BILLY RAY: There was a great night where Lanny McDonald was coaching my team, which is a moment I won't forget. Joel Otto was there that night. I knocked out Sean Kelly, the soundman for By Divine Right, the opening act.

The band and crew sporting events used to be so much fun in the early days, until they got way too competitive and a little too violent. Touch football turned into tackle football. It ended pretty quick once that happened. People started getting injured.

BILLY RAY: If you were a hockey fan and you wanted to get an autograph from an NHL player, your best bet would be to hang out backstage at a Tragically Hip show, because if we were in Philadelphia then there'd be ten Philadelphia Flyers in the dressing room. If it was Winnipeg, you'd have ten of the Winnipeg Jets. We were private-jetted from The Who tour to Edmonton and back again to play Mark Messier's 50th birthday party.

PATRICK SAMBROOK: I remember playing Chicago when Joel Quenneville was coach of the Blackhawks. He came the first night and the whole team came the second night. It was a great moment and classic Gord, because he pretty much played a private concert to the team captain, Jonathan Toews – although nobody else in the room would have known that.

Hockey was a major part of Gord's life; it was all-consuming, whether it was the hockey pools or playing.

GORD D: My parents met [Boston Bruins coach] Harry Sinden back when I was a baby in Amherstview, Ontario. I think my mom knew his wife, Eleanor, from her school days. They asked Harry and Eleanor if they'd be godparents to me and my younger brother, Pat. As a spiritual guide, I'd say Harry's done very well. It's been an amazing thing for us, the Boston Bruins and Harry. I talk to my little brother every day and we always talk about the Bruins.

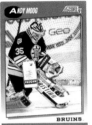

BILLY RAY: We had boxes and boxes of hockey jerseys with the band members' names on their backs. Different teams would send them over and everyone became kind of blasé about it. But Gord still seemed to be genuinely excited to have another hockey jersey with his name on the back.

TRISTIN CHIPMAN: Hockey mattered. There was hockey life around them all the time. The Boston Bruins, of course. If there was anything Bruins related, that was the conversation all day long for Gord.

PATRICK DOWNIE: Our relationship with Harry Sinden and the Bruins gave Gord and me an excuse to connect daily. I worked for the Bruins in the 1990s and 2000s playing music at the Boston Garden. I played many Hip tunes at their games, some of which they still play today. What more could you ask for from a godfather? We are eternally grateful to Harry.

MARK NORMAN: There were always a lot of hockey players dropping by, like Brendan Shanahan, Kirk Muller, Doug Gilmour. The Hip did a lot of stuff with the NHL and with the Olympic hockey team, so the guys in the band got to know these really great players and they'd come and hang.

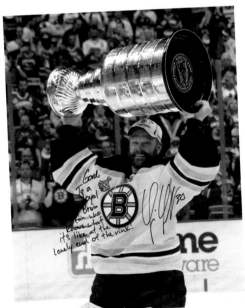

PATRICK SAMBROOK: A lot of hockey players listened to The Hip. The connection was authentic. Gord's lyrics for 'Fifty Mission Cap' were posted up in the Toronto Maple Leafs dressing room. It was inspirational for those players to have the words there. When the Canadian Olympic team won the gold medals, they listened to The Hip.

The number one broadcast in the history of Canada is the Canadian Olympic game, the second biggest is The Tragically Hip's final concert. Those two things sit there together.

JOHNNY: I was having dinner with Ray Daniels one night and he said, 'You know, the three most Canadian things are hockey, beer and The Tragically Hip. And I manage Rush so that's hard for me to say.'

RANDY LENNOX: Hockey is a sporting metaphor for The Tragically Hip. Both come from Canada and have some success in America, but have over-the-top success back home. The Tragically Hip is as indelible a source of pride to Canadians as hockey is.

1987 2nd Annual Real Cool
Hockey Pool

Round 1
1 Johnny — GRETZKY (EDM)
2 Gord S — MULLEN (CAL)
3 Paul — KURRI (EDM)
4 Rob — GILMOUR (ST.L)
5 Gord D — BOURQUE (BOS) (D)
Round 2
5 Gord D HUNTER (PIM) CAL
4 Rob — KERR (PHIL)
3 Paul COFFEY (EDM) (D)
2 Gord MESSIER (EDM)
1 Johnny KORDIC (MTL) PIM
Round 3
1 Johnny NILAN (MTL)
2 Gord S MacINNES (Cal) (D) PIM
3 Paul McClelland (Edm) Pim
4 Rob ZEZEL Phil
5 Gord D HOWE Phil (D)
Round 4
5 Gord D. YZERMEN (Det) PIM
4 Rob TOCCHET (Phil) PIM
3 Paul GARTNER (Wash)
2 Gord S. Hextall/Fresch Phil Goaltenders
1 Johnny WILSON (Chic) (D)

Round 5
1 Johnny HUDDY (Edm) Def
2 Gord S MURPHY Wash (D)
3 Paul Moog/Fuhr Edm Goaltenders
4 Rob LOWE Edm D
5 Gord NEELY (Bos)
Round 6
5 Gord FRANCIS (Hart)
4 Rob CROSSMAN Phil D
3 Paul NASLUND (Mont)
2 Gord S HAWERCHUK (Winn)
1 Johnny Hayward/Roy Mont Goaltenders
Round 7
1 Johnny LEMIEUX (Mont)/Pim
2 Gord S. OTTO Cal/Pim
3 Paul TIKKANEN Edm
4 Rob SMITH Mont
5 Gord Ranford/Keans Bruins
Round 8
5 Gord REINHART (Cal)
4 Rob St Louis goaltender blaskr Hawks
3 Paul PROPP Phil
2 Gord S SIMMER Bos
1 Johnny POULIN Phil

Round 9
1 Johnny ANDERSON Edm
2 Gord S FERDERKO StL
3 Paul ROBINSON Mtl (D)
4 Rob GOULET Que.
5 Gord KLIMA Det.
Round 10
5 Gord LAWLESS Hart.
4 Rob HUNTER St.L
3 Paul WALTER Mtl
2 Gord S DINEEN Hart.
1 Johnny CARBONEAU Mtl.

Opposite: GD's Boston Bruins memorabilia

This page, clockwise from top left: The Hip in Calgary Flames jerseys, 1996; Team Canada 2002 Olympics jersey; Montreal Canadiens jersey (PL's team); Toronto Maple Leafs jersey (RB's team); signed hockey cards, Bobby Hull from the Chicago Blackhawks (GS's team); more signed hockey cards; The Hip in Buffalo Sabres jerseys with Brad May, November 1996
Centre: The Hip's 1987 Real Cool Hockey Pool

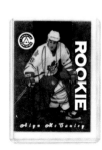

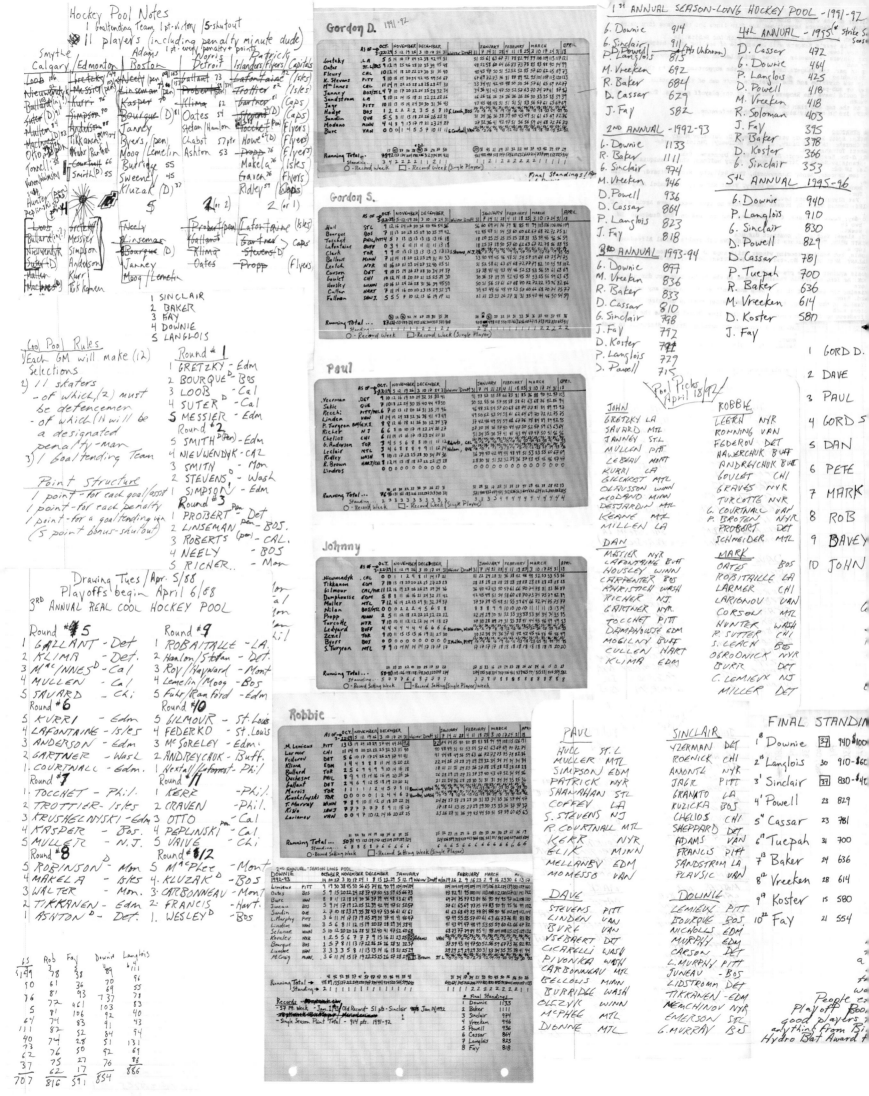

Hockey Pool Notes
1 goaltending Team 1 pt-victory / 5-shutout
11 players (including penalty minute dude) 1 pt. every penalty + points

Smythe	Adams	Norris	Patrick
Calgary / Edmonton	Boston	Detroit	Islanders/Flyers/Capitals
Loob 86	Gretzky 149	Neely (pen) 1934	Gallant 73	Lafontaine (Isles)
Nieuwendyk	Messier	Linseman (pen)	Probert (pen)	Trottier 82 (Isles)
Bullard	Kurri 96	Kasper (pen)	Klima 12	Gartner (D) (Caps)
Suter (D)	Simpson 90	Bourque (D) 81	Oates 54	Stevens (D) (Caps)
Mullen (D) 93	Anderson 88	Janney	Stefan/Hamlon	Tocchet (pen) (Flyers)
MacInnes (D)	Tikkanen 74	Byers (pen)	Chabot 57 pt	Howe (D) (Flyers)
Otto 58	Weir/Barford	Moog/Lemelin	Ashton 53	Propp 76 (Flyers)
Tonnelli	Courtnall 66	Burridge 55		Makela 76 (Isles)
Hunter/Peplinski	Smith (D) 55	Sweeney 45		Graven 76 (Flyers)
		Kluzak (D) 37		Ridley 57 (Caps)

4   5   2 (or 2)   2 (or 1)

Cool Pool Rules
1) Each GM will make (12) Selections
2) 11 skaters
 - of which, (2) must be defencemen
 - of which (1) will be a designated penalty-man
3) 1 goaltending Team

Point Structure
1 point - for each goal/assist
1 point - for each penalty
1 point - for a goaltending win
(5 point bonus-shutout)

Round #1
1 GRETZKY - Edm
2 BOURQUE (D) - Bos
3 LOOB (D) - Cal
4 SUTER (D) - Cal
5 MESSIER - Edm

Round #2
5 SMITH (D)(pen) - Edm
4 NIEUWENDYK - Cal
3 SMITH - Mon
2 STEVENS (D) - Wash
1 SIMPSON - Edm

Round #3
1 PROBERT (pen) - Det
2 LINSEMAN (pen) - Bos.
3 ROBERTS (pen) - Cal.
4 NEELY - Bos
5 RICHER - Mon

Drawing Tues / Apr. 5/88
Playoffs begin April 6/88
3RD ANNUAL REAL COOL HOCKEY POOL

Round #5
1 GALLANT - Det.
2 KLIMA - Det.
3 MacINNES (D) - Cal
4 MULLEN - Cal.
5 SAVARD - Chi.

Round #6
5 KURRI - Edm.
4 LAFONTAINE - Isles
3 ANDERSON - Edm.
2 GARTNER - Wash.
1 COURTNALL - Edm.

Round #7
1 TOCCHET - Phil.
2 TROTTIER - Isles
3 KRUSHELNYSKI - Edm.
4 KASPER - Bos.
5 MULLER - N.J.

Round #8
5 ROBINSON (D) - Mon
4 MAKELA - Isles
3 WALTER - Mon.
2 TIKKANEN - Edm.
1 ASHTON (D) - Det.

Round #9
1 ROBITAILLE - LA.
2 Hanlon/Stefan - Det.
3 Roy/Hayward - Mont
4 Lemelin/Moog - Bos.
5 Fuhr/Ranford - Edm.

Round #10
5 GILMOUR - St. Louis
4 FEDERKO - St. Louis
3 McSORELEY - Edm.
2 ANDREYCHUK - Buff.
1 Nextall/Foresst - Phil.

Round #11
1 KERR - Phil.
2 CRAVEN - Phil.
3 OTTO - Cal.
4 PEPLINSKI - Cal.
5 VAIVE - Chi.

Round #12
5 MacPHEE - Mont
4 KLUZAK (D) - Bos.
3 CARBONNEAU - Mont.
2 FRANCIS - Hart.
1 WESLEY (D) - Bos.

1ST ANNUAL SEASON-LONG HOCKEY POOL - 1991-92
G. Downie	914
G. Sinclair	911 (4th Unknown)
P. Langlois	815
M. Vreeken	692
R. Baker	684
D. Cassar	629
J. Fay	582

2ND ANNUAL - 1992-93
G. Downie	1133
R. Baker	1111
G. Sinclair	974
M. Vreeken	946
D. Powell	936
D. Cassar	864
P. Langlois	823
J. Fay	818

3RD ANNUAL 1993-94
G. Downie	897
M. Vreeken	836
R. Baker	833
D. Cassar	810
G. Sinclair	798
J. Fay	792
D. Koster	771
P. Langlois	755
D. Powell	715

4TH ANNUAL - 1995 (* strike season)
D. Cassar	472
G. Downie	464
P. Langlois	425
D. Powell	418
M. Vreeken	418
R. Soloman	403
J. Fay	395
R. Baker	378
D. Koster	366
G. Sinclair	353

5TH ANNUAL 1995-96
G. Downie	940
P. Langlois	910
G. Sinclair	830
D. Powell	829
D. Cassar	781
P. Tuepah	700
R. Baker	636
M. Vreeken	614
D. Koster	580
J. Fay	

Pool Picks April 18/92

JOHN
GRETZKY LA
SAVARD MTL
JANNEY STL
MULLEN PITT
LEBEAU MONT
KURRI LA
GILCHRIST MTL
OLAUSSON WINN
MODANO MINN
DESJARDIN MTL
KEANE MTL
MILLEN LA

ROBBIE
LEETCH NYR
RONNING VAN
FEDEROV DET
HAWERCHUK BUFF
ANDREYCHUK BUFF
GOULET CHI
GRAVES NYR
TURCOTTE NYR
G. COURTNALL VAN
P. BROTEN NYR
PROBERT DET
SCHNEIDER MTL

DAN
MESSIER NYR
LAFONTAINE BUFF
HOUSLEY WINN
CARPENTER BOS
KHRISTICH WASH
RICHER N.J.
GARTNER NYR.
TOCCHET PITT
DAMPHOUSSE EDM
MOGILNY BUFF
CULLEN HART
KLIMA EDM

MARK
OATES BOS
ROBITAILLE LA
LARMER CHI
LARIONOV VAN
CORSON MTL
HUNTER WASH
R. SUTTER CHI
S. LEACH BOS
OGRODNICK NYR
BURR DET
C. LEMIEUX NJ
MILLER DET

PAUL
HULL ST. L
MULLER MTL
SIMPSON EDM
PATRICK NYR
SHANAHAN STL
COFFEY LA
S. STEVENS NJ
R. COURTNALL MTL
KERR NYR
GILK MINN
MELLANBY EDM
MOMESSO VAN

DAVE
STEVENS PITT
LINDEN VAN
BURE VAN
VERBEEK DET
CICARELLI WASH
PIVONKA WASH
CARBONNEAU MTL
BELLOWS MINN
BURRIDGE WASH
OLCZYK WINN
McPHEE MTL
DIONNE MTL

SINCLAIR
YZERMAN DET
ROENICK CHI
AMONTE NYR
JAGR PITT
GRANATO LA
RUZICKA BOS
CHELIOS CHI
SHEPPARD DET
ADAMS VAN
FRANCIS PITT
SANDSTROM LA
PLAVSIC VAN

DOWNIE
LEMIEUX PITT
BOURQUE BOS
NICHOLLS EDM
MURPHY EDM
CARSON DET
L. MURPHY PITT
JUNEAU BOS
LIDSTROM DET
TIKKANEN EDM
NEMCHINOV NYR
EMERSON STL
G. MURRAY BOS

FINAL STANDINGS
1	Downie	940	$100
2	Langlois	910	$60
3	Sinclair	830	$40
4	Powell	829	
5	Cassar	781	
6	Tuepah	700	
7	Baker	636	
8	Vreeken	614	
9	Koster	580	
10	Fay	554	

1 GORD D.
2 DAVE
3 PAUL
4 GORD S.
5 DAN
6 PETE
7 MARK
8 ROB
9 BAVEY
10 JOHN

2ND ANNUAL "SEASON LONG POOL"
Records:
- 57 Pt. Week - Jan 14/92 Old Record 51 pts - Sinclair Jan 14/1992
- Single Season Point Total - 914 pts. 1991-92

Final Standings
1 Downie 1133
2 Baker 1111
3 Sinclair 974
4 Vreeken 946
5 Powell 936
6 Cassar 864
7 Langlois 823
8 Fay 818

---

1. SINCLAIR
2. BAKER
3. FAY
4. DOWNIE
5. LANGLOIS

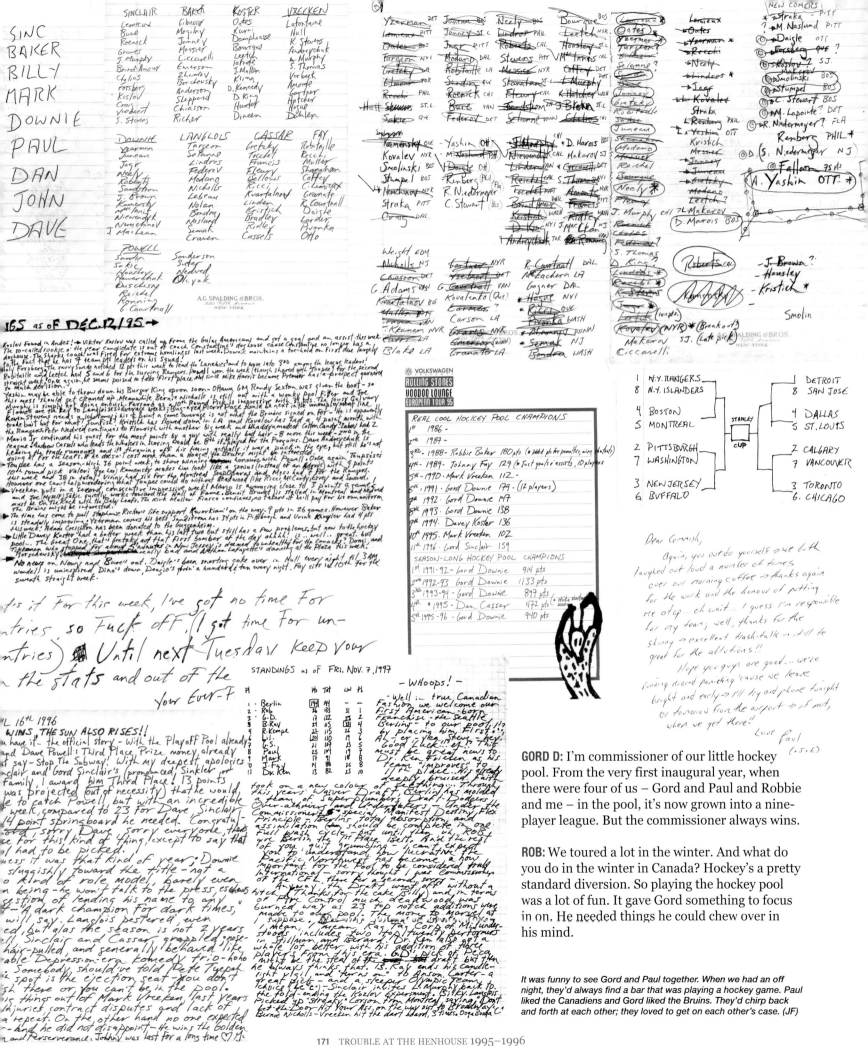

GORD D: I'm commissioner of our little hockey pool. From the very first inaugural year, when there were four of us – Gord and Paul and Robbie and me – in the pool, it's now grown into a nine-player league. But the commissioner always wins.

ROB: We toured a lot in the winter. And what do you do in the winter in Canada? Hockey's a pretty standard diversion. So playing the hockey pool was a lot of fun. It gave Gord something to focus on. He needed things he could chew over in his mind.

It was funny to see Gord and Paul together. When we had an off night, they'd always find a bar that was playing a hockey game. Paul liked the Canadiens and Gord liked the Bruins. They'd chirp back and forth at each other; they loved to get on each other's case. (JF)

GD: Ultimately, you're just trying to have the music move you to the point where you become a fan of yourself.

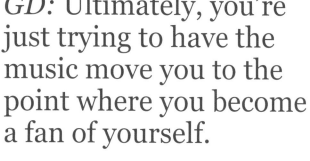

GORD D: What I've learned is that a demagogue's got to keep moving. If I can get on stage and establish a line of movement, I can follow it all through for hours. I just start by starting. And then it feels more like a dance from one thing into another into another that begets a frenetic movement into a karate kick into a twist, a turn, a drop, a dip, and then a wiggle, a jump, a hop.

PAUL: Gord would quickly get inside a song, which might almost have been out of shyness; he was very good at immediately being Gord on stage. He was a master of the mic trick. Some of the crazy things he did, he seemed totally in his own world.

He was really a dancer at heart and I think that helped him, wanting to move in certain ways. He had so many great little bits, all of which he discovered on stage. He wasn't a guy to be rehearsing things at home in front of the mirror.

He had a knack for ranting and making up stories on the spot. The more experienced he got, the better he became at it. He always wanted to be doing something. Sometimes he was just standing if his head was really inside the song. Other times, it involved some sort of dance, as if he were a mime artist.

BRUCE DICKINSON: Gord Downie was an optimum front person. That person can sing the phone book and you'll pay attention. And Gord Downie had that quality. You could throw any random sheet of words in front of him and he would sell it to an audience.

BILLY RAY: Gord used to always say, 'For a show to be great, something's gotta happen.' When the lights went down and the crowd roared, he was on 12 out of 10. And any little thing that went wrong would send him flailing. Gord's best shows were his worst shows. If something went wrong for him he would decide to destroy the next five mic stands he was given or kick over the monitor wedges just out of frustration. It became completely entertaining and defined his stage persona as 'anything can happen, and will'.

JOHNNY: Gord loved the idea of being the front man of a band, not just an individual. He and I went to see INXS in Ottawa and it was really important for him to observe Michael Hutchence, who was an incredible performer but also very much part of the band.

STEVE BERLIN: Seeing The Hip live for the first time, one of the most powerful things was watching Gord. I remember thinking, 'Does he do that every night?' It was hard to fathom that happening every show. This can't be coming off the top of his head. And then to watch him do it completely differently, with completely different characters and stories, show after show after show. My goodness. That is a remarkable dude up there. That is some serious shit happening.

It's about as close to rock and roll shamanism as you can get. Mick Jagger is often thought of in that way, but he's not doing what Gord was doing. He's not coming up with seven-minute raps, like a screenplay, off the top of his head. I mean, who does that?

ALLAN GREGG: Gord was so unusual, because he was so natural. When you look at great front men like Mick Jagger or Michael Hutchence, you know that they practise what they're doing. But when you look at Gord, you can tell he'd never practised any of this shit. He couldn't help himself. He'd be singing away and all of a sudden he'd hit himself on the side of the head and then he'd do a little leap up in the air. It wasn't how he was supposed to look or what others had taught him to do. This was just a totally unique, charismatic individual.

BILLY RAY: Gord was a nervous guy. He'd say at the start of every tour that he was just going to go up there, stand still and deliver the songs, and that would be enough. But the second that the crowd roared and the guitar solo came, he realised, 'Oh, I'm not playing the guitar solo, I've got to do something else because all the eyes are on me.' He didn't plan to pick bugs out of Paul's hair and eat them, stalk the stage like a tiger in a cage, or jump around like a monkey. It was just whatever happened to come into his mind at that point to keep from just standing there waiting to sing the next line.

He used to love to bend a mic stand in half like he was riding a motorcycle, sit on it and then stand up and show the audience it was at 90 degrees. Then he'd grab it and straighten it up again. It was really impressive. Gord was a tough guy. I saw him take that mic in the back of the head. He was starting to get one of those lumps like Fred Flintstone, and he looked over at me like, 'Oh, that hurt,' and then just kept going on with the show. He would fall on one of the wedges. For anyone else, that would be the end of the concert, maybe the tour. But he'd just jump back up and carry on.

ROB: Every single tour we did, Gord would say that he didn't want to go out there and dance like a monkey anymore, that he was just going to stand there and sing. But then when all eyes were on him the nerves would take over and he'd start dancing. We were glad he got performance anxiety, because it was the best thing for us.

JOHNNY: Gord was able to divorce himself from the day-to-day when he got up on stage. We always had people thinking he must be drunk, or on acid or coked out of his head. And we'd tell them that he was just on life. He was doing his thing, entertaining people.

Pinkpop Festival, Landgraaf, Netherlands, 6 June 1995

Opposite: Pacific Coliseum, Vancouver, 25 February 1995 (top)

Trouble at the Henhouse tour, Canada, late 1996 (bottom)

Tragically Hip keep fans guessing

— Bruno Schlumberger, Citizen

PLUGGED IN: Hip singer Gordon Downie leads the faithful through some new material at a sold-out Barrymore's Wednesday

BILLY RAY: If there was a video or audio of the show, we would watch or listen to it on the bus afterwards, open a beer and make fun of each other's clams. One night, we were watching a show on the bus and Gord had been particularly manic and animated that night, running across the stage and jumping over monitors and climbing things.

We were laughing and saying what a great show it had been, but then I looked at Gord and he was totally serious, staring at the TV. He said, 'I'm a clown. I don't want my children growing up thinking daddy was a clown. I want to be a musician. Tomorrow, plug in Paul's acoustic for me at soundcheck.'

Gord was not a great guitar player. He was learning to play in front of the audience. And for a long time, the only place the sound of his playing went was to his in-ears. But for him it was a grounding spot. He could stand and strum along during Robbie's guitar solo and it was his way of saying that he wasn't a clown or a dancing bear, he was Gord Downie the musician.

The problem was, the audience wanted Gord Downie the crazy circus clown. They wanted to be able to say to each other, 'Holy crap, look what he's doing now!'

GORD D: I did a lot of guitar playing on this record, just basic stuff. It's interesting how you sing when you're splitting your attention between playing and singing. Obviously, you don't focus quite as much on the actual notes as they're coming out of your mouth because you can't. You have to have some kind of blind faith that what you're singing is something approximating your real voice. Oftentimes, I think it's a secret voice or something. I found that I plugged into the music at a different level by playing and singing at the same time, and was a little more reverent about singing, and was forced to sing a little quieter. When you sing quieter, you can actually hit higher notes. So I found that my range increased for this record and I discovered a lot more melodic possibilities. In the evolution of my singing voice, I feel like I'm getting closer.

PAUL: We were all aware that a big part of our entertainment value was Gord as a front man, without a guitar. But, by the time of the Henhouse tour, we were also aware that he was enjoying himself more if he got to do at least a few songs on guitar.

I didn't mind the concept of him playing on stage, but for a couple of the songs, like 'Ahead by a Century' and 'Gift Shop', I was worried that we would miss the good stuff he was doing back there when he was dancing around and playing with the mic stand. I thought that there would be too much of Gord on guitar and not enough of Gord the showman, but he managed to balance it out. And then on some of the later tours he didn't play at all.

Trouble at the Henhouse tour, Canada, late 1996

ROB: Gord playing guitar on stage ... are you kidding me? I hated it. It detracted from him being a focal point, a front man. And, honestly, he was one of the best front men anywhere ever. When you strap an acoustic guitar on, it pins you down. That's not to say that you can't still be a great front man and play guitar. But Gord wasn't a good enough guitar player to be able to do that. He had to look down at his fingers to make the chord changes and in the early days there was a real disconnect between what his two hands were doing.

It wasn't up to me to tell anyone what to do on stage. If Gord wanted to play guitar, that was his call. We survived it. I think Gord came to the decision in his own time that it wasn't in his best interests to keep on playing and he let it go by the wayside at a certain point.

JOHNNY: Gord was a leftie but he played guitar right-handed. Because of that, he had a very percussive style of playing. He just picked the notes where he wanted them. And that's also how he wrote.

GORD S: Gord was really conscious as a performer of not repeating himself and not getting into schtick. But after a decade and a half of being the front guy, it's hard to be 'on' all the time. I think playing the guitar gave him a sense of relief from that. It took the pressure off.

Also, for Gord it was never enough just being the lyrics guy. When we were writing songs, it was rare for us to start with the words. We always started with a musical idea that would inspire a melody, and then the lyric would evolve from there. I think Gord wanted to get good at playing principally because he wanted to be able to bring a song to the group and say, 'This is how it goes and here's what I've done.' He'd see us going into hotel rooms carrying our guitars and then playing them and maybe he wanted to feel a little more integrated with the musical side of the band.

ROB: Dave Powell was our International Man of Mystery and there were lots of things going on in his life that we knew nothing about. One of the things we did know was that Gord was frustrating him, in particular his guitar-playing. But it wasn't just that that made him leave. I think he just felt like he'd taken the job as far as he could with us.

GORD S: For Dave, it was anathema to step out of your box in The Tragically Hip. So I think he was put off by Gord slapping on the guitar and me playing the shitty little riff and throwing in the piano on 'Butts Wigglin''. And Gord was put off by the fact that Dave was put off by it, and their relationship became a little more fractious at that point, unfortunately.

JOHNNY: I think Dave wanted us to always be the little band in the van going around and doing gigs. He wasn't crazy about other people coming in, other than Billy Ray and Mark Vreeken. He liked it as that little unit.

GORD S: When Dave left it was really hard. It's hard to know who outgrew who in that situation. It was at a time when we all had partners and families going. Dave was living in our rehearsal space. He did not have a partner and family. But maybe at that point he was looking for something else to do as well. Road managing a group is a huge job; there are a lot of moving parts and you have to be super-organised. Dave wasn't the most organised guy in the world.

BILLY RAY: In Europe back then, you were supposed to have your gear processed at every border and get a stamp in a booklet called a carnet, which is like a passport for goods. Nearing the end of one European run, Dave realised that he hadn't had the carnet stamped once. This would be a big problem when we went back into Canada. So, the night before we flew home, Dave took a glue stick and went through the whole carnet sticking every page to the next page so it became a solid chunk of paper that could not be separated. Then he wet it a little around the edges, and his plan, which worked, was to tell the customs officer that there had been a rainstorm and his briefcase had flooded, and that it was all stamped, but, oh no, now it's all stuck together.

The guy looked at this brick of paperwork, knowing how fully illegal it was, and said, 'Well, I guess you did your best,' stamped it back into Canada, and that was that.

PAUL: There were multiple reasons why Dave left. For one, it semi-bothered him that we were all becoming family guys and it bothered him when Gord played acoustic guitar instead of being the front man. But the biggest reason was within himself. He'd been our tour manager for a long time. He had a big brain, not that tour managing is easy or doesn't require a lot of brain power, but he needed to get back to himself. There are frustrating times on the road and I think he just got fed up with it.

Team Crew, 5 vs 5 soccer, US tour, circa September 1993

Back row (l to r): Dan Cassar, Monitor guy, Mark Vreeken
Front row (l to r): Dave Powell, Billy Ray Koster

Opposite: Dave Powell during the 1991 tour of eastern Canada (bottom)

Dave Powell died on 27 November 2018

3 pages total

TO: JEFF, MCA CONCERTS 206-803-0707

FROM: DAVE POWELL, THE TRAGICALLY HIP
416-532-7080(416-927-9214 AFTER 3:00PM PST)

RE: BACKSTAGE HOSPITALITY, SECURITY ETC.

HOWDY JEFF, PLEASE SUPPLY MY GUYS WITH THE FOLLOWING CRAP EACH EVENING:

48 MILLER LITE(NOT GENUINE DRAFT! AND NO BUD LITE!)
4 GALLONS OF BOTTLED WATER
2 LARGE BOTTLES OF GATORADE
12 ASSORTED SOFT DRINKS
2 LARGE BAG REGULAR POTATO CHIPS
2 LOAVES BROWN BREAD
1 SMALL JAR PEANUT BUTTER
1 SMALL JAR STRAWBERRY JAM
5 PACKS SUGARFREE GUM(VERY IMPORTANT!HAH!)
10 CLEAN LARGE TOWELS(NO BLEACH PLEASE)
TEA AND COFFEE
$10.00 PER NIGHT PER HEAD BUYOUT
BOWL OF FRUIT

AS A ONE TIME PURCHASE, WOULD YOU PLEASE BUY A BOTTLE OF TYLENOL, A BOX OF ASSORTED BANDAGES AND A WHOLE BUNCH OF TUMS AND PEPTO-BISMAL(TABLETS IF POSS.) NOW, ON TO OTHER MATTERS...

MY MAIN CONCERNS IN MY ABSENCE NATURALLY REVOLVE AROUND THE BANDS SECURITY. IT IS VERY

IMPORTANT THAT THEY HAVE UNFETTERED ACCESS TO THEIR DRESSING ROOM. THEIR FANS ARE GENERALLY WELL BEHAVED IF SPOKEN TO IN A DECISIVE MANNER BUT ARE ALSO NOTORIOUS DRUNKS. KEEP ALL DRUNKS AWAY FROM THE BAND ESPECIALLY IF THEY'RE CANADIAN. AS A GENERAL RULE, CANADIANS HAVE NO SPECIAL STATUS WITH THE BAND WHEN WE'RE IN A FOREIGN COUNTRY, SO DON'T LISTEN TO ANY SOB STORIES ABOUT HOW FAR THEY DROVE ETC. ETC. ANY TRUE FRIENDS OF THE BAND KNOW TO WAIT PATIENTLY UNTIL SUCH TIME THAT THE BAND CAN DEAL WITH THEM. THIS WILL BE AT LEAST 20-30 MINS. AFTER THE FINAL ENCORE. NO EXCEPTIONS UNLESS A SPECIFIC BAND MEMBER APPROVES. THEY MAY NEED CABS TO GET AWAY FROM THE GIG FAST, DEPENDING ON HOW THINGS GO. RE THE GIG ITSELF: DUE TO MY ABSENCE ABSOLUTELY NO ONE, AND I DO MEAN NO ONE , IS TO INTRODUCE THE BAND. NO RADIO BULLSHIT WHATSOEVER, NO SIGNAGE ON STAGE NO JOCKS HANGING AROUND JUST IN CASE THE BAND CHANGES THEIR MINDS. THEY WON'T. OUR SOUND MAN WILL PLAY A DISC OR TAPE AND THEY JUST WALK ON. NONE OF US ARE TOO HAPPY ABOUT MY SITUATION, SO IF THEY SEEM A BIT WEIRD DON'T TAKE IT PERSONALLY. IF THERE IS A BACKSTAGE PHONE THAT IS NEAR THE DRESSING ROOM PLEASE GET ME THE NUMBER IF YOU COULD. WHEN IN DOUBT ERR ON THE SIDE OF CAUTION, THIS IS THE FIRST REGULAR TOUR GIG I HAVE MISSED IN OVER FIVE YEARS SO IT'S IMPORTANT TO KEEP THINGS LOW KEY AND ORGANIZED. ONE FINAL NOTE, PLEASE CHECK WITH THE BAND REGARDING THEIR GUEST

LIST. IT PROBABLY WON'T BE MORE THAN A COUPLE OF DOZEN AT MOST. PLEASE ADD TO IT BOTH NIGHTS IN SEATTLE : LISA ROSENBERG +1
DAMON STEWART +1

NO STAGE DIVING! KEEP THOSE BASTARDS OFF THE STAGE. BE PREPARED FOR CRAZINESS, THERE IS NO SUCH THING AS TOO MUCH SECURITY!!!ABOVE ALL KEEP THE BAND SAFE...BEST OF LUCK, CALL ME ABOUT THAT BACKSTAGE NUMBER...ADIOS DP.

URGENT!!

... I am hoping this is fairly complete! Thanks Dave

TEAM HOTEL

Telefax / fax letter

Datum 22-6

An JERRY FOX - GUEST
COPTHORNE HOTEL
Fx# 9836667

Von DAVID POWELL
THE TRAGICALLY HIP
QUALITY INN PLAZA
Ph. 33880

Hello, Jerry
will be sure to see you today!
Here's the list...

HANNOVER : BIRGIT WEIKHOF - 5 TIX + PASSES
LYNN TAMBURRA - 1 TIX + PASS

Bitte sofort an den Gast weiterreichen. Die Nachricht ist sehr wichtig!

• Diese Faxmitteilung umfaßt incl. Titelblatt ____ Seite/n   • This fax letter contains 2 page/s including front page.

Gord,

The wheels have fallen off for me.

Dave

Jan 2 1997

BILLY RAY: At a certain point, I think Dave realised that he was in over his head, that this was no longer fun and the band needed a real tour manager. It wasn't five guys and him in a van travelling across the country playing club shows and leaving when they felt like it and finding a sports bar to watch the Bruins play. It had become a job that needed someone to be really on top of their game. All of a sudden, you've got to deal with a guest list of 300 people at the Air Canada Centre. Dave didn't want to be looking for earplugs for the toddlers and making sure that the wives weren't being hassled by a security guard because they left the backstage compound without their pass. He didn't want to be on the hook for every little thing.

When he quit, he quit in a real blaze of glory. Anyone who left broke Gord's heart. You weren't allowed to leave on good terms, really. Because when you left The Tragically Hip you were saying to Gord Downie that you no longer believed in him and his hopes and dreams.

Everything changed after Dave. There's The Hip with Dave Powell, and there's The Hip without Dave Powell. He used to say, 'Pee if you got to!' That was his little five-minutes-to-showtime signal. I remember saying, 'Pee if you got to!' on the tour after Dave had left, and Gord quickly said, 'That era's over. We know when to go pee.' I thought, 'Point taken.' Dave broke Gord's heart.

ROB: Dave was a fascinating, complex and difficult man, but above all he was a brother, a good friend to all of us. He was a guy's guy, our personal butler, and we were kind of lost without him and didn't know how we were going to replace him. So we decided we needed to do something totally different. From that point on we used only female road managers. They brought a different energy and were much better organised than any of the guys we ever worked with. So, enter Tristin Chipman.

Tristin had been hired by the promoter to set up the backstage area on one of our early arena tours. She knew we had young children, so she'd organise an ice sculpture in the family room that had little dinosaurs frozen into it surrounded by pop and fruit. The kids would be busy chipping away at that for hours. We thought, 'Who's responsible for this? We need people like that.' So that's how Tristin became our road manager.

My Dear Friends,

I write to let you know that I can no longer be your tour manager. I don't have any more tours in me. It's not a job one can fake and if I were to carry on I would be faking it. You deserve better than that. I write to you as a band because it causes me the least distress. I don't think I could face writing five of these. I like to think of you as a band anyway. And as my friends. So please understand that writing you is easier on my nervous system right now. Besides, I couldn't very well drop in and say "how's it going? I quit...". And frankly, this is really not very easy. But, its time for me to make a move in my life. Time to turn a corner. This is not going to happen for me on our bus.

You have always been generous to me and I thank you for that and the chance to see the world and the laughs along the way. I've always been proud to say I was your tour manager. I don't know what I might do now but, fear of failure has always been good motivation for me. I will land upright. So tell anyone who might ask that I'm on a permanent vacation; I hate to think of it as quitting but, there she be.

I know the timing of this isn't perfect but, how could it be anyway? I think it only fair that you have as much time to find a replacement as I can give you, and I need to get on with gettin' on. I'm not really interested in discussing this(nothing personal but, I don't want anyone trying to dissuade me), so if you don't hear from me for a couple of months, don't worry. I'll resurface eventually. The great unknown has never been too unkind to me but, it takes a while to get used to the terrain. No matter, I've learned all sorts of strange stuff during my time as your tour manager. It will come in handy. Peace and good luck.

Your Friend,

Dave

Dave

04/14/1997 9:07   4169617898   JE   PAGE 01

April 14

Dear Gord,

Sorry to disturb you at home, but I thought a fax was less troublesome than a phone call. After our last conversation I owe you an apology as I had misstated some things. In my defence I didn't know what I was really talking about until last night. Last night I found out a lot of things. Your involvement in my breakdown was, at best, peripheral. Even as a catalyst, barely worthy of mention. My breakdown was predetermined long ago and would have happened if I were the CEO of IBM or a janitor at the ITC. Hardly the result of anything the band did or did not do. My life was no longer mine to control, the compass that had guided me for 34 years ceased to function and now I must replace it entirely. I think I knew intuitively that modest changes in my life would be insufficient. Thus, I had no choice but to go for for the big play, total deconstruction, nothing else would do. I suspect you may feel some of these same things. Superficial changes will only delay what you will find out: the skin you used to be comfortable living in just doesn't and won't fit anymore. Gotta have new skin. I don't know what any of this might mean to you, but it's the only advice I can give you. If it doesn't make sense now it might later, but if you don't do what you really have to do you won't do what you need to do. And don't do it for anybody else but yourself and I mean nobody else. Sorry for the pain and trouble I've caused and I mean that. It can get ugly along the way that's for sure and there seem to be false endings to the journey once you start out. I think I got lucky and found my way. I hope you find yours. For me, the wheels really did fall off but I have a new set. I'll let you know how they work out. Good luck on tour and in the hockey pool.

Love
Dave

P.S. Sorry about typing this out but, I wanted it to be legible.

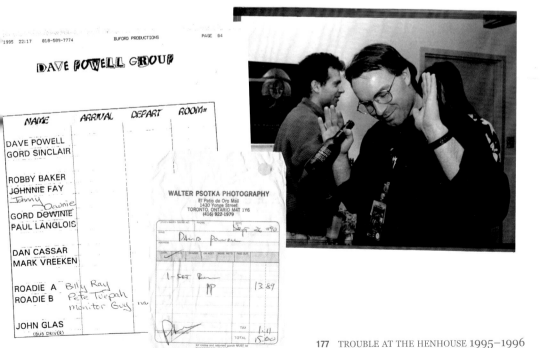

'1995 22:17   818-589-7774   BUFORD PRODUCTIONS   PAGE 04

DAVE POWELL GROUP

NAME	ARRIVAL	DEPART	ROOM#
DAVE POWELL			
GORD SINCLAIR			
ROBBY BAKER			
JOHNNIE FAY *Johnny*			
GORD DOWNIE *Downie*			
PAUL LANGLOIS			
DAN CASSAR			
MARK VREEKEN			
ROADIE A *Billy Ray*			
ROADIE B *Pete Toepah monitor Guy*	*na*		
JOHN GLAS (BUS DRIVER)			

WALTER PSOTKA PHOTOGRAPHY
El Patio de Oro Mall
1430 Yonge Street
TORONTO, ONTARIO M4T 1Y6
(416) 922-1979

Sept 26 '90

DAVID POWELL

1-SAT Room   13.89
MP

TAX   1.11
TOTAL 15.00

14958   Thank You

BUFORD PRODUCTIONS ...and Travel

Design 1   Detail of P.A. tower artwork

Roof facing trim

Front wash truss trim

Lighting truss and riser trim

Design 1 Border details

*Another Roadside
Attraction,
17 July–2 August 1997*

Design 1   Initial Daylight stage

Design 1   Evolved Daylight stage

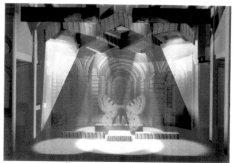

Design 1   Night stage

Design 1   Detail of Backdrop artwork

ROB: I loved the Roadside Attractions – a village that springs up where there was nothing and 40,000 people come and then the next day you would have no idea that anything had happened there. That was the original concept, but then the promoters got involved and wanted to do it in football stadiums because they already had washrooms and concession stands and there was parking so they could make money on that. Things got co-opted and it undermined everything we were trying to do.

The whole thing was supposed to be about bringing in international acts from places like South Africa and Ireland and Australia, but certain provinces set tax penalties for having non-Canadian acts on the bill. We thought we were doing people a service, so why should we pay the provincial government for that?

Suddenly there were festivals everywhere, all happening in places that had washrooms and concession stands and parking, and it felt like we were fighting an uphill battle to do things the way we wanted to do them. So we decided to stop. I enjoyed all three Roadside Attractions, but the pressure from promoters and agents, governments and tax collectors, took a lot of the fun out of it.

You Are Invited To The
End-Of-Tour Wrap Party
For

ANOTHER ROADSIDE ATTRACTION

When: Saturday, August 2nd
Where: Molson Park, Barrie
Festivities Begin At 11pm
Please, Come As You Are!

VIP
GUEST
LOCAL CREW
PRESS PHOTO

ANOTHER ROADSIDE ATTRACTION 97

March 15, 1997

The following two design proposals are inherently diverse in their concepts but I believe both to be exciting and interesting ideas. For the sake of titling these concepts I have simply named them Design 1 and 2. I hope you find both worthy of the project.

Design 1

I personally call this one the butterfly idea. The concept was to use two dissimilar visual elements and combine them to achieve something greater than it's sum. In this design I have thrown together some very interesting 17th Century Dutch perspective drawings with metamorphosing butterflies. At the beginning of the day the stage will be set with what appears to be some colorful caterpillars crawling on it. As the day progresses these caterpillars will transform into some very colorful butterflies. Then as night falls the audience's attention is drawn into the interior of the stage where the lunar moth presides over a now vibrantly colorful set which reverses the appearance of the stage from it's daytime look. This brings the design full circle in a very elegant fashion.

Design 2

My thanks go to Robbie Baker for starting me on the road to this idea. As he was the one to mention " Why not try a literal translation of "Another Roadside Attraction" ?" Well after some good research I found the turn of the century miracle cure handbills and posters. Using these elements as the basis of this concept I then veered from the straight and narrow and went in a Barnum and Bailey direction. As a result this very playful and vibrant stage has come about complete with it's own flag waving enthusiasm. As night falls the scrims drop the drum rolls out and the excitement escalates. Although there is very little in the way of transformation to this design I believe it's inherent vibrancy can carry it through the event.

One more thing I'd like to mention, Dan Cassar gave me the lighting truss layout over the phone and I may have not got it completely right, but I hope I have as I think it's a very intriguing design. Thanks, Dan.

Once again I'd like to thank you all for including me in the festivities this summer!

Yours,

John B.

SPRING TIME
PLANET
GRACE
TWIST
HEAD   SASKATOON
700 FT
MEMBERSHIP
BLOW
=lAMENCO
DADDY
Fully
FIRE
NAUTICAL
WHEAT
GIFT SHOP

1 Spring
2 Planet
3 Grace   #7 Winnepeg
4 Twist
5 ABAC #20
6 Greasy
7 700 Ft
8 Membership
9 New 0
10 Scared #14
11 Daddy
12 Fully
13 Nautical
14 Fire
15 Wheat
16 Gift

1 Spring
2 Planet   Darrien
3 Grace   Lake
4 Everytime
5 ABAC
6 700 Ft
7 Member
8 NEW 0
1 Flamenco   MERIDIAN
2 10D
1 Vapour
2 Coconut
3 Wheat
4 Nautical
Fire
5 Gift

GORD S: We got ourselves to the point with Roadside Attractions where we could put our own bill together, carte blanche, and Los Lobos were always at the top of the list. As young men, if we'd gotten the call from Los Lobos to go and tour Jupiter with them, we would have gone.

To our great fortune they came on the '97 Roadside Attraction with us, and we discovered that not only were they a fantastic band but they were fantastic people. We got to know Steve Berlin very well in particular. We were familiar with records Steve produced and, although we didn't discuss it when we were doing the tour, it was certainly in the back of my mind that he would be a great guy to produce our band.

ROB: We loved Los Lobos. We had 'Don't Worry Baby' from their first record as a staple in our set for a long time. So when we got them for the Roadside Attraction, that was awesome. At one of the venues on the tour the catering was not up to par, so Louie Pérez came through and said they were taking up a collection to improve the food situation. Everybody kicked in 20 bucks and off they went. They came back and pulled these hibachis out from under their bus and set up a massive Tex Mex kind of barbecue and fed everyone backstage. They're a great band – just a bunch of guys on one page doing their thing.

STEVE BERLIN: I had made records in Canada and I was always conscious of The Hip, but hadn't committed my attention to their stuff until we joined them on the Roadside Attraction tour. Once we started talking, I was front and centre every show and it was revelatory. The audience bond was one of the more remarkable things. I've never met anybody, in any age or demographic, that didn't like The Hip.

I've been in lots of places where fans are in love with the band that they're seeing. But on the Roadside Attraction tour it was more than that; it was national pride. It's possibly a uniquely Canadian thing: 'These are our dudes and they're bad-ass.'

ANOTHER ROADSIDE ATTRACTION
THE TRAGICALLY HIP
SHERYL CROW
ASHLEY MacISAAC
WILCO ★ LOS LOBOS
CHANGE OF HEART · THE MUTTON BIRDS · RON SEXSMITH · VAN ALLEN BELT
www.roadside.ca

JulY
17 - Vancouver, BC Thunderbird Stad.
19 - Camrose, AB Camrose Exhib. Grnds.
21 - Saskatoon, SK Saskatchewan Place
23 - Winnipeg, MB Assiniboia Downs
26 - Highgate, VT Franklin County Field
28 - Ottawa, ON Rideau Carleton Rcwy.
30 - Buffalo, NY Erie Cnty. Fairgrounds
AuGusT
2 - Barrie, ON Molson Park

COPYRIGHT 1997 HATCH SHOW PRINT ☆ HAND MADE QUALITY POSTERS SINCE 1879

10. Dressing Room Compound

A dressing room compound will be designed and contain the following:
a) [1] new 20 x 40 tent with floor and a combination of window walls and solid walls. The tent is to have a carpeted floor, decorative lighting and should house the following:

i)	pool table
ii)	fountain
iii)	foos ball table
iv)	lamps / comfortable chairs
v)	video games
vi)	basket ball hoop
vii)	ping pong table
viii)	internet station
ix)	computer games/nintendo, etc.

b) Please use your imagination for this area and present your ideas to the Site Coordinator prior to committing to any particular enhancement.

11. Dressing Rooms

a) We will require the following dressing rooms in Atco-style trailers:

i)	The Tragically Hip	1	10' x 40' with 2 rooms & 2 doors
ii)	Sheryl Crow	1	10' x 40' with 2 rooms & 2 doors
iii)	Ashley MacIsaac / Wilco	1	10' x 40' with 2 rooms & 2 doors
iv)	Los Lobos / Change of Heart	1	10' x 40' with 2 rooms & 2 doors
v)	Ron Sexsmith / Van Allen Belt	1	10' x 40' with 2 rooms & 2 doors
vi)	Mutton Birds / Tour Crew		1 10' x 40' with 2 rooms & 2 doors

b) If possible there should be a washroom with a shower in each trailer. If not we will need access to showers or a shower trailer. Each trailer requires stairs with hand rails, locking doors with keys, air conditioning, working lights and window coverings.

c) We will require the following furniture:

i)	The Tragically Hip	1 couch, 1 love seat, 1 arm chair, 2 end tables, 3 lamps, 1 throw rug, folding tables and chairs.
ii)	Sheryl Crow	1 couch, 1 love seat, 1 arm chair, 2 end tables, 3 lamps, 1 throw rug, folding tables and chairs.
iii)	Ashley MacIsaac	1 love seat, 1 arm chair, 1 end table, 2 lamps (one is a floor lamp), folding tables and chairs.
iv)	Wilco	1 love seat, 1 arm chair, 1 end table, 2 lamps (one is a floor lamp), folding tables and chairs.
v)	Los Lobos	1 love seat, 1 arm chair, 1 end table, 2 lamps (one is a floor lamp), folding tables and chairs.
vi)	Change of Heart	1 love seat, 1 arm chair, 1 end table, 2 lamps (one is a floor lamp), folding tables and chairs.
vii)	Ron Sexsmith	1 love seat, 1 end table, 2 lamps (one is a floor lamp), folding tables and chairs.
viii)	Van Allen Belt	1 love seat, 1 end table, 2 lamps (one is a floorlamp), folding tables and chairs.
ix)	Mutton Birds	1 love seat, 1 end table, 2 lamps (one is a floor lamp), folding tables and chairs.
x)	Tour Crew	1 couch, 1 end table, 2 lamps (one is a floor lamp), folding tables and chairs.

Backstage Layout

FIRST AID

WHEEL CHAIRS

VIP AREA

ARTISTS COMPOUND

CATERING

PRODUCTION

Backstage BBQ with members of Los Lobos (bottom), Another Roadside Attraction, 17 July–2 August 1997

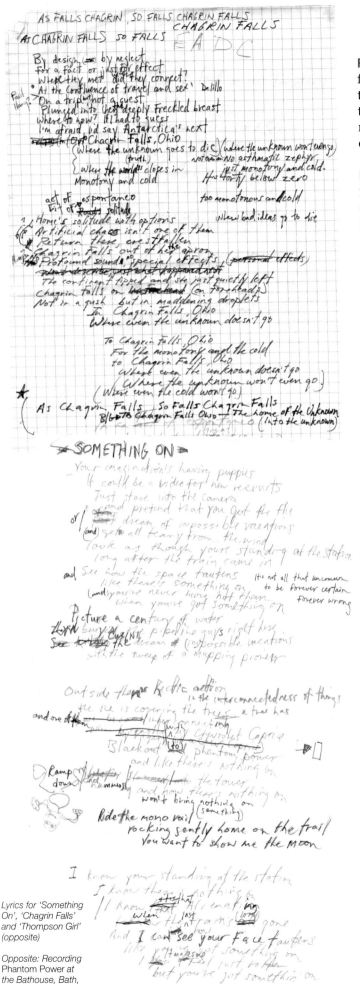

Lyrics for 'Something On', 'Chagrin Falls' and 'Thompson Girl' (opposite)

Opposite: Recording Phantom Power at the Bathouse, Bath, ON, 1998

PAUL: It's an achievement to even make a second good record, let alone five as we had by this point. It takes your whole life to write the first and then, all of a sudden, you've got to fit the next one around a relentless touring schedule. So coming to *Phantom Power*, our sixth album, you might think we'd be running out of energy and inspiration – but it was quite the opposite.

ROB: I don't recall if we had discussed Steve Berlin producing our next record while we were on the road. Maybe towards the end of the tour some kind of noise was made about that. Whenever that decision was made, I think it was a really good call by us. He was a member of a long surviving band, so he understood the dynamics. Every band has poles that attract and repel and Steve was able to observe that interaction within our band and knew how to negotiate it.

STEVE BERLIN: One of the things that struck me on the road was how similar they were to my band. The guys went to the same high school, grew up together, went through all their first everythings together.
  I understood that dynamic well. In Los Lobos I was more or less the outsider coming into a band of guys who had been together forever. There is a certain vibe of guys who are friends with or without the band. They are guys who have protected each other from early on, held their head while they puked and that kind of stuff. It's a different level of brotherhood.

GORD S: We were a number of records in and we wanted to figure out how to keep doing the same thing but with a different flavour. We thought Steve would bring that sensibility to how we wrote songs and make us better. We asked him, and to our joy and shock he said yes.
  Steve's the consummate musician – he's got a great ear for an arrangement, a melody, a song. He knows how to be a songwriter and how to get it properly down on tape. We knew he would bring something special because you can hear what he does in Los Lobos – he brings a musical element to them that floats around the edges, but he also floats around the middle of it. So we thought he would be fantastic to produce our band.

STEVE BERLIN: I tried to approach it as if it was a new band. I didn't want the weight of their history or anybody's expectations. I felt that if I literally de-educated myself about what I was about to do, I wouldn't be worried about anything but making a great record. So my approach from early on was to focus on the songs. If they wanted me to reference stuff from their past records I was happy to do that, but I wanted to treat them like this was their first record.

GORD S: After our experience self-producing *Trouble at the Henhouse*, we went right back to our usual way of doing things. It was great to have someone helping us develop songs from the ground up. As we were demoing them, we were sending them straight to Steve. It was very much what we used to do with Bruce Dickinson when he was our A&R guy.

STEVE BERLIN: They sent me tons of stuff and the batting average was high, to say the least. But it was a lot of disconnected ideas and great jams. Not a lot of fully coalesced songs.

Take	Title		Time
1	SOMETHING ON	Ⓜ	
2	" VOC↑		
3	CHAGRIN FALLS	Ⓜ	

JOHNNY: In a lot of ways, Steve was the best producer we ever had. He was a great structural guy and would talk about the shape of a song. He recognised what we had and he knew what we needed to get. So he'd say, 'This song's done. That one's really close. We need to do more on these ones.' Being a musician, he knew that you can't beat the demo, so don't try.

'Bobcaygeon' is an example of that. I heard the original take that we did, and what Gord Sinclair and I play on the final recording is no different. There was more guitar on it, and then Steve played at the end. We played it twice and that song was done.

PAUL: Working with Steve Berlin on *Phantom Power* was a really positive experience. He was so thoughtful and musical and he had a very open mind, so he was almost like another sounding board for Gord.

STEVE BERLIN: I've been lucky to work with a lot of great singer-songwriters, but Gord was on a different level.

The sound of every syllable and how the syllables left his mouth, not just the words, was so important to him. We would talk about 'a' and 'the' way more than people could possibly imagine. It was inspiring, the intensity of his commitment to making every single thing great.

Chagrin Falls From her apron
then borne on a light spring zephyr

No one calls cause we answer
our phone.
Prefer to leave a message

Chagrin falls from her
apron swept up in an
asthmatic zephyr
barely held aloft

THOMPSON GIRL

Thompson girl's stranded at the Unique Motel
Thompson girl - winter fighters shot on the car as well
Christmas (There's trouble) at 55°
this latitude weakens my knees
Thompson girl

Thompson girl walkin from Churchill
Thompson girl with Polar Bears and mostly up hill
When she saw that Nickel stack
She whistled hard and (I) whistled back
Thompson Girl

Thompson girl we're down to the dead house plants
Thompson girl jettisoned everything we have
She says springtime's coming wait'll you see
it pokin through with them shoots of beauty
(Thompson girl)
It's the end of Rent-a-Movie weather
Time to end this seige together
Thompson girl

pokin through with those shoots of beauty
smokin grunt work, dream state, Villeneuve on (active) duty
and I'm off duty

grunt work between dream state and duty
will be pokin through with those shoots of beauty.
the token moments

STEVE BERLIN: By the time I worked with The Hip, they were friends with a lot of pro hockey players. I think that, as much as they were fantastic musicians, they came at their job more like athletes than musicians. They had this musical aggression almost; it was like they were trying to score a goal or knock somebody's block off, without it escalating into anything toxic.

Sometimes I would say to bands, 'OK, just imagine this is the last time you're gonna play this. Play it as hard as you possibly can.' I never had to say that to The Hip.

ESCAPE IS AT HAND (For the travellin' Man)

Our 1st time in New York, You're second time in New York
we were 3RD (5th) and 4th on the bill
we talked a little about your band
we talked a little bout your future plans
It's not like we were best friends
(or enemies or anything)
but that number scheme comes back to me
at times like these little
in time with these little heartbeats in a time beyond my heartbeat
– at times beyond my heartbeat –
we hung around for the final band
called Escape is at Hand for the Travellin' Man
you yelled in my ear this "Desire turns Concrete"
"Music Speaks to me"
they opened with Lonely from Rock n' Roll
then a cover of You Checked Out An Hour Ago
Closing with All Desires turn Concrete
It's not like we were best friends nor enemies nor anything
(they) melody colour scheme (came back to me) in between
Melody had ceased to be all down the street that melody comes back to me
froze melodies at times beyond my heartbeat
the time beyond my heartbeat I'm in a time beyond my heartbeat
I guess I'm slow I guess I'm too slow
but you said any time of the days fine
you said any time of the night is also fine

I walked through your revolving door
elevator take me to your floor I called up to 7th floor
the music's soft the lights are low The elevator gave a low moan
the pigeons sagged the wire with their weight
listening to the singing chambermaid
singing you Checked Out An Hour Ago.

(Melody could cease to be
in time beyond my heart beat)

(that melody's an enemy no enemies
the enemy's not anything
thought it would be)
Son with Fury
it's a 66
it's in a hurry
Son with Fury
the Ol' Saskatchewan
(rollin') Flowin' early

BOOKCITY # 3
348 danforth avenue toronto 469-9997

Escape is at hand
for the travellin man
He'll turn his concerns
from the road.
He'll make a transition
make peace with ambition
take a break from ambition
Load

~ 45/.9211 ~

Lyrics for 'Escape Is at Hand for the Travellin' Man' (above) and 'Fireworks' (opposite)

GORD S: 'Escape Is at Hand for the Travellin' Man' is another song that evolved out of a jam in the middle of 'New Orleans Is Sinking'. 'New Orleans' was a big hit for us, so we played it every night and, to keep it interesting, we would break it down in the middle and goof around with something.

As so often happens, we would cut an idea out of that jam and try to develop it into a song. We had a verse and a bit of a chorus, not your traditional hooky chorus, but it had a place to go. And then it had a bridge, another place to go. But Steve wanted to figure out how to make it a complete song instead of just an idea.

We'd recorded a version of the song onto two-inch tape (this was pre-Pro Tools), and then Steve wanted to add a second bridge to make it a little bit longer and complete the thought after a bit of a breakdown. But we were having problems recapturing the vibe of how we had originally recorded it.

So we wound up cutting the two-inch tape, duplicating a section and then cutting it back in – literally old-school movie splicing. This was being done by Ken Friesen, who was helping us engineer, while the rest of us were out for dinner. Steve couldn't sit down at the table, he was so nervous that we were going to fuck up the one and only version of the song that we had in the attempt to make it better. But it turned out that refraining the bridge did make it a much better song. All Steve's idea.

PAUL: When we were doing 'Escape Is at Hand', Steve helped us identify the chorus – before that, we hadn't really thought of it as having one. So Steve had good thoughts about songs and music, he was experienced and we got along very well with him. We all trusted him, right across the board.

For a long time we referred to the song as 'Stereolab' because Gord Sinclair and I particularly were fans of the band Stereolab and they influenced it. Then, when we recorded it, 'Escape Is at Hand' came out as the title.

There's a particular lyric that I love: 'It was our third time in New York, it was your fourth time in New York.' That totally brought me back to the 1988 CMJ Music Marathon, which was actually our first time in New York. Gord was talking to Jim Ellison, who was the singer of Material Issue, a band from Chicago that we kind of knew. It was their first time in New York as well. We were fifth and sixth on the bill.

GORD S: It was back in the day when CMJ, the College Media Journal, was a really big deal. We were all trying to get on to college radio stations; kids didn't listen to Spotify then. CMJ would have this great conference each year where bands would play all over New York City.

PAUL: Later that night, Jim showed up at our hotel. Gord and I were rooming together and Jim needed a place to crash so he slept on the little armchair in our room. The song just speaks to me of bands on the road going to the big city to take their shot and getting a full dose of it.

Some years later, Jim died by suicide. When Gord found out, he remembered that night and wrote the song. The lyric 'It's not like we were best friends' isn't negative. It's not saying that they didn't like each other, it's just that they never became best friends. It's a mutually respectful thought.

GORD S: Material Issue was a great band, but they could only take it so far. Gord perfectly captured in the lyric of 'Escape Is at Hand' how we felt when we heard that Jim Ellison had taken his own life. Gord was always very reluctant to talk about what the song meant. There is no one way of interpreting it.

GORD D: I write songs as though I were talking to a friend. When you're talking to your friends, you understand each other without having to make sense. The guys in the band never seem to question my lyrics. They understand them perfectly.

GORD S: For me, 'Escape Is at Hand' captured not only what it is that we and countless other bands did for a living, but the toll it can take when your aspirations confront your realities and your frustrations.

In America there's a higher premium on commercial success than maybe there is elsewhere. We were always really fortunate: signed out of the States, we made the record company money because of our album sales back home. But we never made them so much money that they wanted to meddle with what we were doing, and that allowed us to evolve artistically.

Our American buds didn't necessarily have that opportunity. We have lots of great friends from American groups that had gigantic hits. But then that wound up fucking up their careers because the record company wanted another hit and another hit. And when they couldn't deliver, all of a sudden they were on the radar of the CEO and they got dropped. It's a cruel industry.

STEVE BERLIN: The way that Gord sings that song, it's so matter of fact. It wipes me out every time.

In the life of the travelling musician there are moments when it's the best job in the world. For two hours a night, you have this ecstatic, beautiful energy with people screaming, but then you come down and you're stuck in a hotel room in Des Moines, Iowa feeling lonely and depressed and missing your family. Gord's lyrics capture that milieu, the whole bright/dark, happy/sad thing. And Gord is talking to Jim, saying he didn't pick up that he was depressed and in crisis, that if he'd known he could have done something before it was too late. It's an overwhelmingly powerful song; every time I hear it, I start crying.

PETER GARRETT: As a touring musician, you're in a little bubble of your own. And so occasionally when you prick that little bubble that you're travelling in and fly into someone else's bubble with whom you can break bread and share common ground, then that's a nourishment for you.

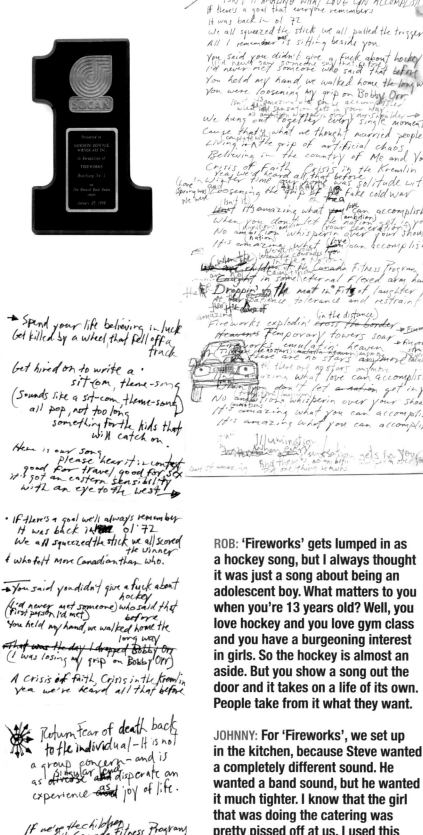

ROB: 'Fireworks' gets lumped in as a hockey song, but I always thought it was just a song about being an adolescent boy. What matters to you when you're 13 years old? Well, you love hockey and you love gym class and you have a burgeoning interest in girls. So the hockey is almost an aside. But you show a song out the door and it takes on a life of its own. People take from it what they want.

JOHNNY: For 'Fireworks', we set up in the kitchen, because Steve wanted a completely different sound. He wanted a band sound, but he wanted it much tighter. I know that the girl that was doing the catering was pretty pissed off at us. I used this miniature drum set that I'd played on 'Ahead by a Century' and 'Poets'.

Above centre: SOCAN award presented to Gord Downie for 'Fireworks', 25 January 1999

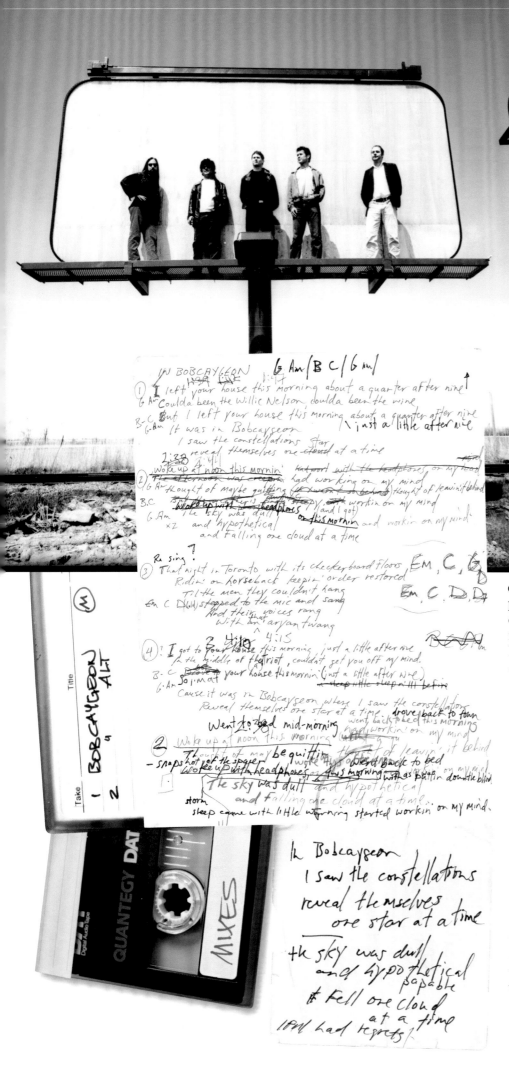

ROB: I did a demo at home on a dobro, where I took inspiration from the open G guitar part from a Led Zeppelin song called 'That's the Way'. I put my own spin on it, but it was definitely the inspiration for that guitar riff. I worked 'Bobcaygeon' up and brought it to the guys and everyone thought it sounded pretty good.

The form was there, so we kept that and everyone just arranged their parts. I remember thinking that what I'd done was like zappy folk, but when we played it together it sounded like The Band, which was way better. That was one of the great things about working with this group of guys. You could have an idea that you blueprinted out, and then you handed it over and it became something different. You had to be on board for that ride, because it could go places you didn't expect.

BILLY RAY: Gord was in this corner of the players room downstairs at the Bathouse. We'd set up a plexiglass barrier, a big comfy chair, some pillows and a microphone – it was kind of Gord's nook. The band were jamming, as they do, because that's how they write. Gord fell sound asleep in the chair with his headphones on and then the band finished up and went home, and I went to bed – I lived there at the time.

When he woke up and realised that everyone had gone home and just left him, he was pretty pissed off, so he wrote a line, 'I woke up with headphones on this morning, about a quarter after nine. I thought of maybe quittin', thought of leavin' it all behind.' That was later changed to 'I left your house this morning, about a quarter after nine. Could have been the Willie Nelson, could have been the wine' and became the opening lines of 'Bobcaygeon'.

STEVE BERLIN: Gord is one of the best at capturing and conveying a feeling in oblique lyrics, not telling you what it is that he's singing about, but you still get all of it when you let it hit you. Like the scenes in 'Bobcaygeon' and 'Thompson Girl' – how do people live in these places? He would capture the feeling of these places and people. It's a rare gift.

I couldn't tell you what 'Bobcaygeon' is about, but you get the sense that something large is happening. It's like an opera or something. You feel like you've been somewhere when he sings that song.

GORD D: I think maybe it's OK if people don't understand what a song's about. Even if you get a sense of the mood or the landscape or the character of the song, and it's taken you off somewhere else so you're not even listening to the lyrics by the end, then it's succeeded.

The handwritten lyrics (top left):

BOBCAYGEON: Thanks. HONOUR YOUR TEACHER.
I left your house this morning 'bout a quarter after 9
Coulda been the Willie Nelson, coulda been the wine
When I left your house this morning
It was a quarter after Nine
It was in Bobcaygeon. When I saw the Constellations
reveal themselves one star at a time.

Drove back to town this morning
with working on my mind
I thought of maybe quitting. Thought of leaving it behind
I went back to bed this morning and as I'm
pulling down the blinds
The sky was dull — hypothetical — and falling one
cloud at a time
BRIDGE — That night in Toronto with its checkerboard floors
Riding on horseback and keeping order restored
til the men they couldn't hang stepped to the mic & sang
and their voices rang with that Aryan twang.

BREAK —
I got to your house this morning 'bout a quarter after 9
In the middle of that Riot — couldn't get you off my mind
I got to your house this morning it was a little after Nine
It was in Bobcaygeon when I saw your
constellations reveal themselves — one star
at a time.

ROB: Gord's lyrics are brilliant. And it was Steve's idea to have Bob Egan. He was playing with Wilco on one of the Roadsides and he loved it so much up here that he picked up stakes from where he was living in the Chicago area and moved to Canada. We got him to play on that song and a couple of others, like 'The Rules'. I'm a huge fan of pedal steel. And Steve played keyboard on it. He added a whole new level to the band.

STEVE BERLIN: I thought it would be a cool idea to play it like an R&B song, and specifically I was thinking about a Shuggie Otis record called *Inspiration Information*. All the guitars on that record have very specific parts that shift subtly from section to section. It sounds simple on the surface, but it's kind of complex rhythmically.

So my suggestion was to give it a little wilty R&B swing and groove. Johnny could really swing. I think that's one of the things that made The Hip's rhythm section so powerful; like John Bonham, he has this built-in swing to his playing, which makes everything sound heavier.

But I think the secret sauce was when we had Bob Egan come and play pedal steel. What's so great about that song is the feeling of longing, like you're missing somebody or something, and I'm pretty sure it's the pedal steel in the background that makes you feel that beautiful sadness.

'Bobcaygeon' is the most played Hip song on Spotify, which boggles my mind, certainly when you look at their entire catalogue. It just affects people. When I saw them on that last run I was crying the whole show, but especially during that one.

PAUL: Early on, we just thought that 'Bobcaygeon' was a nice riff Robbie brought in. I remember when we were first playing it thinking it was a cool tune. Once we had made the video, we knew it was going to be a single and we hoped that maybe it would do OK. It was only later that it became a touchstone song for us because of the way our fans connected with it. We ended a lot of our shows with 'Bobcaygeon'.

GORD S: It became a really popular song for the band. Pick any of our gigs and you can look out and see great big burly guys with their arms around each other and tears rolling down their face. That's the song that triggers those emotions for people. It evokes this kind of ethereal, very pastoral view of Canada. Cottage country Canada. It really has a resonance, and I think it continues to this day: just this right place, right time kind of song.

JOHNNY: I really had no idea how big 'Bobcaygeon' would become. It was maybe the biggest track that we had. It really sounds like a Canadian song. Like Gordon Lightfoot, Blue Rodeo, Anne Murray. It's just a great Canadian sound.

JAKE GOLD: I think 'Bobcaygeon' represents the feeling of most Canadians. The very Canadian thing of being up at the lake. You're up at the lake, you're seeing the stars, you don't see the city. And everybody across the country has a lake they go to at some point: it's a very Canadian experience.

GORD S: Bobcaygeon went on to be the most stolen road sign in Ontario. It used to be a couple of times a year the MTO guys would be like, 'The kids have stolen the sign again … fuckin' Hip.'

'Bobcaygeon' was released in February 1999 as a single from The Hip's sixth album, Phantom Power, produced by Steve Berlin

The song is named after Bobcaygeon, ON, a town in the Kawartha Lakes region about 160 kilometres northeast of Toronto. The song's narrator works in the city as a police officer, a job he finds stressful and sometimes ponders quitting, but unwinds from the stress and restores his spirit by spending his weekends with a loved one in the rural idyll of Bobcaygeon

The song resulted in the town of Bobcaygeon coming to occupy what has been described as a 'mythical' place in Canada's collective imagination, as the archetype of a cottage country paradise

'Bobcaygeon' won the Juno Award for Single of the Year in 2000

Top left and opposite: Lyrics for 'Bobcaygeon'

DAN AYKROYD: 'Bobcaygeon' is such a hit because we've all, figuratively, woken up that morning, like Gord, and started thinking about work. There is power and connection in that imagery because we've all lived it.

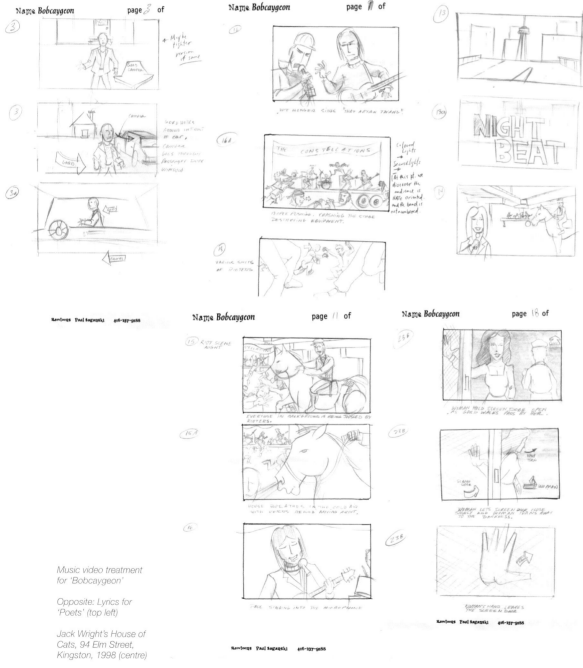

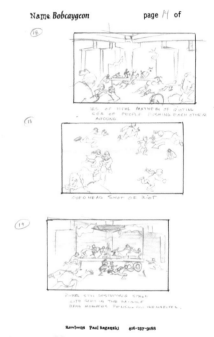

Music video treatment for 'Bobcaygeon'

Opposite: Lyrics for 'Poets' (top left)

Jack Wright's House of Cats, 94 Elm Street, Kingston, 1998 (centre)

GORD S: Gord was great at writing prose lyrics, but he was also great at telling a story. Robbie Robertson from The Band would always write a song with a beginning, a middle and an end, like a little short story. Springsteen writes that way too. 'Bobcaygeon' is one of those songs, and so it lent itself to the video treatment really well – the idea of a cop by day, lover by night, trying to reconcile his past, present and future.

Hugh Dillon is a trained actor and very old friend. He was at our high school at the same time as us and is yet another great artist and musician to come out of Kingston. He was perfect as the character to have in there, playing Gord, the singer of the band, in terms of the narrative of the video.

Handwritten lyric sheet (left column):

POETS — Speaker's Corner —

the Coast
Spring starts with a heart beat pounding
the birds can be heard
above the
Lava's flows the Super Farmer direction
he's been getting relief from the heat
in the Frozen Food section.

don't tell me what the poets are doin
don't me that they're talkin' tough
don't tell me that they're anti-social
not anti-social enuff.
somehow

when Porn speaks to its splintered legions
to the Pink amid the withered corn stalks
in their winter regions
(while) aiming at the archetypal Father
you say with such broad and tentative swipes
maybe you shouldn't bother — yea
why do you even bother —

Don't tell me what the poets are doin
(that he's everywhere and on his way)
Those from the himalayas of the mind
Play from the epitome as well as
at with the creation's place
to the epitome of vague
SOLO
Those high grasses of the mind
Don't me what the poets are doin
Don't show me how a writer gets laid / that
Don't tell me how (your) universe was altered
When you find out how they got paid.

If there's not anything (more) that you need now
your leaves raked by bare-breasted women ? against
your beach bleached ? (made out of real) the high grasses
so now women reach you by swimming.
reach your towel w

In the high grasses wrapped in a towel after swimming
If there's nothing more that you need now
your beach bleached by bare-breasted women
For the women who try and make it by swimming.

PAUL: I liked 'Poets' as soon as we first started playing it. I thought it was Stonesy and a solid contender to make the record and then it became more than that. It got catchier and then we did the video, and it was a single by the time the album came out. People liked it.

JOHNNY: The original version of 'Poets' was with a drum machine and it sounded almost Lynchian in a *Twin Peaks* kind of way. It was very strange. Steve Berlin was very responsible for the drum track on that song. He worked closely with me and he made the group play over and over. It was like working with Don Smith, in that sense.

Steve didn't like the industrial thing we were trying to do. He thought we were experimenting too much and that it needed to sound more like a song. The great thing about Steve was that he knew how to get a vibe and 'Poets' ended up sounding kind of like a party.

The song was called 'Super Farmer' at one point. I think that was a Dutch term. Gord loved Holland, so he was always scribbling down things from being over there.

STEVE BERLIN: 'Poets' was two different ideas. The verse was one thing and the chorus was a completely different thing. Listening to it now, you wonder how those things could ever have been separate. But at one point, it was this from cassette A and that from cassette B.

GORD S: 'Poets' was a really big single for us, but Gord hated the song. I think the vocal performance that's on that track is the one and only time he actually sang that song. He may have done it twice.

PAUL: The video for 'Poets' was shot in a semi-famous house in Kingston, Jack Wright's House of Cats, where he had literally hundreds of cats. The director, Mike Downie, Gord's elder brother, told us to wear the kind of thing that we might have worn to a high school dance – something that is maybe slightly not right, because you're a high school kid and you don't exactly know how to dress. I was the only one that took that instruction to heart, so I had these crazy leggings that were actually my wife Joanne's. No one else played along, so all day I could see the crew looking at me, thinking, 'What is that guy wearing?' That's one strong memory of the day – being quite privately embarrassed.

I do remember the smell too. It was not a clean environment. But it was a fun day and a fun song to play, and it was nice to do a video that was three blocks away from where you live. I would say there was less waiting around on that video than on most of the others. There was a sense that we wanted to get this done so that we could get out of the stinking cat house.

JOHNNY: Sinclair and I were allergic to cat dander, so Billy Ray got us whacked up on Sudafed before we went in. It was horrible in there – it was humid and smelled of cat piss. All the things you want on a hot summer day. Gord kept telling us to show more enthusiasm, but we were pretty drowsy. He was really pissed off at us. It was a crazy concept for a video; I didn't really get it.

GORD S: The 'Poets' video was our first experience of working with Mike Downie cinematically and it was also Gord's first foray as a director, as Gord and Mike were co-directing. That was a new step for the group. Gord was always out front of the band, literally and figuratively, but now he was stepping out and taking more of the creative load on his shoulders. By that time video had become a necessary evil, but we thought it would be good if we could keep this aspect of the operation in-house and on-budget.

AMPEX

June Session Comp

1. Vegas strip
2. Membership
3 Save the Planet.
4. Chagrin Falls.
5 Vapor
6 Bob Cajun
7. Nothin but heartache.
8. Bobby Orr.
9. Saskatoon Boat Race from the Delta
10. Have You Been Injured? | Hotel
11. Have You Been Injured? (Up tempo) (Gtoe)
Aug. 8-9, 1997 A9LC9?
12. Insomniacs (Chorus Idea D-E)
13. Empire Waist - 6, CD
14 Elvish H; comed - AD Moody Bch
15 Surf Foot sea n'seashell - Maine
16 Stereolab (New Chords)
17 Bumblebee → (5th Fret so called C#F)
18 Rain w bugzapper? →

19 - People are Bunks. (in D)?
20 - Much 2 -

AMPEX

Pre ProComp 1

1 BOBBY ORR   4-5:10
2 BIGGER LIGHT   4-19:00
3 BIGGER LIGHT   4-31:00
4. BOB CAJUN   4-47:20
5. VAPOUR TRAIL   4-55:10
6. VAPOUR TRAIL   4-105:19
7 DESERT SONG-NO VOCAL 4-18:20
8 DESERT SONG   4-124:40
9 CHAGRIN FALLS 3-59:13
10 SAVE THE PLANET 3-117:17
11 SONGWRITERS CABAL 3-132:24
12 MYSTERY 4-1:30:00
13 MYSTERY 5-5:00
14 DR. HOOEY 3-49:30
16 STEREOLAB 7-30:50
17 SONGWRITERS CABAL 7-22:50
18 DR. HOOEY 7-16:04
19 DESERT SONG 5-51:40
20 BOBBY ORR 5-111:35
21 VAPOUR TRAIL 6-5:52
22 INSOMNIACS wT6-40:36
23 SAVE THE PLANET 6-105:25
24 BOB CAJUN 6-128:50

AD124 APOGEE

The Tragically Hip Test Sequence   01/03/08

ARTIST: THE TRAGICALLY HIP
PROJECT: ALBUM '98 TEST

WS CLIENT

TITLE: Test Sequence	DATE: Jan 3/98
PRODUCER: Steve Berlin	
ENGINEER: Jim Rondinelli	

WS THE WAREHOUSE STUDIO

CLIENT:

A to D CONVERTER: Apogee AD 500 No Softlimit
RECORDER: Pana 3800   SAMPLE RATE: 44.1 K

CLIENT FILE #

REF: -12 dbFS = 0 VU   TONE: 1 khz ☐

980301

T/C: NONE   T/C REF: None

ID:	TITLES:	MIX #
1	Poets	Master 6 Pass 1/6
2	Bobby Orr	Master 1 Pass 1/1
3	Chagrin Falls	Master 2 Pass 1/2
4	Membership	Recall 1 Pass 3/1
5	Thompson Girl	Master 2 Pass 1/3
6	Save The Planet	Master 10
7	Bob Caygeon	Master 3 Pass 3
8	Something On	Print 8 Pass 1/8
9	Vapor Trails	Finally Done Pass 3/5
10	The Rules	Master 3 Pass 1/3
11	Bumblebee	Final Master Pass 1/1
12	Escape	Master 6 Pass 1/6 Eq'ed
13	Tremelo	Edited Master Eq'ed
14	Mystery	Choice Mix 2.46/3/1.2(8)

ROB: Weird things happened in the mix. It felt over-compressed, which is great on certain songs, but it's like too many steak meals in a row. So we had to get it mixed a couple of times.

STEVE BERLIN: At the end of *Phantom Power*, there was an issue with the mixing. I had hired a guy named Jim Rondinelli, who I thought did an amazing job. But some of the mixes were bold by what had gone before, so there was a little uneasiness. Gord Sinclair was worried that it was too crazy and people wouldn't get it. I got the sense that Gord Downie liked what we had done and understood that the bold step was probably the right move. But in that moment he realised he had to acquiesce to the band. So they had Don Smith and Mark Vreeken mix the entire record without me in the room.

Listening to it again recently, I couldn't understand what the hell we were fighting about. But in that moment, it was a big deal. Clearly, it didn't sound like what The Hip had sounded like before, but I didn't see the point of hiring me if they wanted to sound like the Don Smith version. I knew that they were The Hip and I knew that they meant a lot to people, but I didn't have the other records in my head as a continuum the way the guys in the band did.

Afterwards, we had this meeting in Vancouver, where we sort of horse-traded mixes. It was mildly contentious by Canadian standards; by American standards, it was like an afternoon tea. There was an interesting dynamic at play and I learned a lot about give and take.

Obviously, we did it in a way that I was invited back for the next record, but I think they were a little more wary of me after that.

PAUL: Steve cared so much about the mixes. Of course, any producer should care, but you could see in his face the way he was hunkering down on his thoughts about particular songs.

JAKE GOLD: *Trouble at the Henhouse* took a long time to make. *Phantom Power* didn't take as long. But, all of a sudden, what was going to be an inexpensive record turned out to be an expensive record because we spent as much on the mixes for *Phantom Power* as we did on the recording.

Top and centre: DAT cassettes of songs and song ideas recorded for Phantom Power, 1997. Some tracks were later retitled. For example, 'Bobby Orr' became 'Fireworks' and 'Stereolab' became 'Escape Is at Hand for the Travellin' Man'. Some of the outtakes included here, such as 'Vegas Strip', 'Insomniacs', 'Bumblebee' and 'Songwriters Cabal', were released in 2023 as part of the box set commemorating the 25th anniversary of the album

Bottom and opposite: DAT cassettes of test sequences for Phantom Power with the different mixes of the tracks clearly labelled, January and February 1998

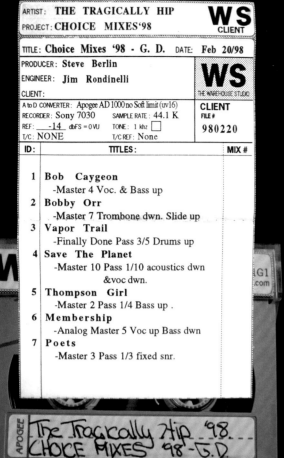

ARTIST: **THE TRAGICALLY HIP**
PROJECT: **CHOICE MIXES '98**

WS CLIENT

TITLE: **Choice Mixes '98 - G. D.**   DATE: **Feb 20/98**
PRODUCER: Steve Berlin
ENGINEER: Jim Rondinelli
CLIENT:

WS
THE WAREHOUSE STUDIO

A to D CONVERTER: Apogee AD 1000 no Soft limit (uv16)
RECORDER: Sony 7030   SAMPLE RATE: 44.1 K
REF: -14 dbFS = 0 VU   TONE: 1 khz ☐
T/C: NONE   T/C REF: None

CLIENT FILE #
980220

ID:	TITLES:	MIX #
1	**Bob Caygeon** -Master 4 Voc. & Bass up	
2	**Bobby Orr** -Master 7 Trombone dwn. Slide up	
3	**Vapor Trail** -Finally Done Pass 3/5 Drums up	
4	**Save The Planet** -Master 10 Pass 1/10 acoustics dwn &voc dwn.	
5	**Thompson Girl** -Master 2 Pass 1/4 Bass up .	
6	**Membership** -Analog Master 5 Voc up Bass dwn	
7	**Poets** -Master 3 Pass 1/3 fixed snr.	

The Tragically Hip '98. CHOICE MIXES '98 - G.D.

ARTIST: **THE TRAGICALLY HIP**
PROJECT: **CHOICE MIXES '98**

WS CLIENT

TITLE: **Choice Mixes '98 G. D.**   DATE: **Feb 20/98**
PRODUCER: Steve Berlin
ENGINEER: Jim Rondinelli
CLIENT:

WS
THE WAREHOUSE STUDIO

A to D CONVERTER: Apogee AD 1000 no Soft limit (uv16)
RECORDER: Sony 7030   SAMPLE RATE: 44.1 K
REF: -14 dbFS = 0 VU   TONE: 1 khz ☐
T/C: NONE   T/C REF: None

CLIENT FILE #
980225

ID:	TITLES:	MIX #
1	**Bob Caygeon** -Master 4 Voc. & Bass up	
2	**Bobby Orr** -Master 7 Trombone dwn. Slide up	
3	**Vapor Trail** -Finally Done Pass 3/5 Drums up	
4	**Save The Planet** -Master 10 Pass 1/10 acoustics dwn &voc dwn.	
5	**Thompson Girl** -Master 2 Pass 1/4 Bass up .	
6	**Membership** -Analog Master 5 Voc up Bass dwn	
7	**Poets** -Master 3 Pass 1/3 fixed snr.	
8	**Chagrin Falls** -Master 2 Pass 1/2.. Robbies gtr up	
9	**Membership Recall** -Recall 1 Pass 3/1	
10	**Something On** -Print 1 Pass 1/1	
11	**Escape** -Master 3 Pass 1/3	

The Tragically Hip '98 CHOICE MIXES '98 G.D.

AD94

APOGEE

QUANTEGY **DAT** Master Digital Audio Tape **R-124**

PREMASTERING COMP. 4/98

1:1 Safety Copy   **JAKE G.**

1 POETS
2 SOMETHING ON
3 SAVE THE PLANET
4 BOB CAYGEON
5 THOMPSON GIRL
6 MEMBERSHIP

7 FIREWORKS
8 VAPOR TRAIL
9 RULES
10 CHAGRIN FALLS
11 ESCAPE
12 TREMOLO

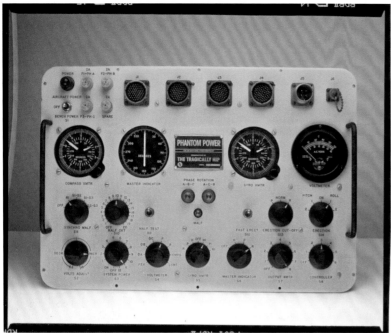

The Tragically Hip
November 1997, Rough Board Mixes

The Tragically Hip
November 1997, Rough Board Mixes

Side A	Side B
1. Save The Planet	1. Thompson
2. Membership	2. Bumblebee
3. Bob Caygeon	3. Escape
4. Bobby Orr	4. Tremolo
5. Poets	5. Vapor
6. Rules	6. Vegas
7. Chagrin	

© Little Smoke Music 1997

JOHNNY: I was in New York City with this girl I was going out with and we were walking on Houston. I looked across the street and saw this big yellow thing in the window of a prop store. We went across the street and took a closer look. It was a device for testing the hardware in planes for malfunctions and checking the circuitry.

The guy sold it to me for a hundred bucks and I took it back to Bath. We just had it at the house and we kept on looking at it until eventually I think Gord and Robbie said, 'Well, that looks like a cover to me.'

Phantom Power

RECORDED: 1997–1998
THE BATHOUSE, BATH, ON
PRODUCERS: STEVE BERLIN
MARK VREEKEN
THE TRAGICALLY HIP
ENGINEER: MARK VREEKEN
MIXING: JIM RONDINELLI
DON SMITH, MARK VREEKEN
RELEASED: 14 JULY 1998

Poets
Something On
Save the Planet
Bobcaygeon
Thompson Girl
Membership
Fireworks
Vapour Trails
The Rules
Chagrin Falls
Escape Is at Hand for the
Travellin' Man
Emperor Penguin

Phantom Power, *The Tragically Hip's sixth studio album, won the 1999 Juno Awards for Best Rock Album and Best Album Design*

GS: We caught a great wave. The record reenergised not only the group, but our fanbase. For many people *Phantom Power* was their entrée to The Tragically Hip. It was almost like the start of another chapter in the band's evolution.

ROB: Songs like 'Bobcaygeon', 'Ahead by a Century' and 'Flamenco' presented a rounder, softer side to the band. I don't think it was a conscious effort to diversify our audience, so much as a wish to present who we were more clearly. Those songs brought something else to the party that was very much of us. And I think it brought other people to the party as well, or made them feel comfortable at the party.

JOHNNY: The sound comes from touring, from understanding the country, from spending our time out there. Towards the end, we really wanted to do some gigs way, way up north. We always wanted to keep on going to new places. If Gord had had more time, he would have woven every single nook and cranny, every cool little Canadian town, into a song, for sure. To him, those little places were what made Canada unique. Mistaken Point, Newfoundland. Moonbeam, Ontario. He might have passed through them just once, but they stayed with him.

GORD D: [We use place names], but never to be patriotic or nationalist. Not once.

GORD S: *Phantom Power* was a really important record for us at a really important time in our career. We had been making records kind of the same way five times: let's plug in and bash out these tunes and see what comes out the other side. We had to start thinking outside of our little box. Steve was instrumental in making, from beginning to end, a really strong record for the band with different flavours and sounds and songs.

STEVE BERLIN: A lot of what I was doing was throwing them for a loop, getting them to concentrate on not doing it the same way they'd always done it, and that took a minute. Eventually we became a well-functioning unit.

ROB: I would say that, in terms of our entire discography, *Phantom Power* is good but overrated. That album won a lot of awards: Album of the Year, a Juno for art design, some single awards. And, like all awards, they always get it wrong. We didn't even get nominated for *Up to Here*, *Road Apples*, *Fully Completely* or *Day for Night*. I think the record industry in Canada must have known something was up. *Day for Night* sold 300,000 copies in under a week. The Canadian record industry must have been saying, 'Huh? What? Who are they?' So, two albums later, they start piling the awards on.

It's the critical mass thing that Bruce Dickinson had talked about when he signed us. He said it would happen around our fifth record. In our case, it happened with our sixth. *Phantom Power* has some really great songs on it, songs I'm very proud of. But I feel it planes a little bit – there's a couple too many mid-tempo numbers, not enough variety for my personal taste.

THE TRAGICALLY HIP

1/29	Saint John, NB	2/7	Ottawa, ON	3/2	Regina, SK
1/30	Charlottetown, PEI	2/15	Sudbury, ON	3/4	Calgary, AB
1/31	Moncton, NB	2/17/18	Hamilton, ON	3/6	Red Deer, AB
2/1/2	Halifax, NS	2/22/23	Toronto, ON	3/8	Prince George, BC
2/3	Sydney, NS	2/26	Winnipeg, MB	3/9	Kamloops, BC
2/5	Montreal, PQ	2/27	Saskatoon, SK	3/11/12	Vancouver, BC
2/6	Quebec City, PQ	2/28	Edmonton, AB		

The Tragically Hip Winter Tour 1999
Preliminary Set Design

John B. Webster

The Phantom Power Tour
"escape is at hand for the travellin' man"
US West Setlists and Pictures- March 29th to April 9th

The Phantom Power Tour
"escape is at hand for the travellin' man"
Atlantic City to Dewey Beach September 1-11

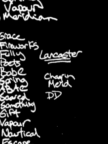

The Phantom Power Tour
"escape is at hand for the travellin' man"
Minneapolis to Cleveland Sept 22-26

JOHNNY: It wasn't really until *Phantom Power* that we spent a ton of time in the States. We kept going back. I think we did three tours for that record.

Wayne Forte, our agent at the time, was smart about it. He told us not to go to Europe on this tour, but just concentrate on the States because he thought it would pay off. And it did. He was a great agent.

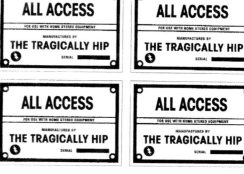

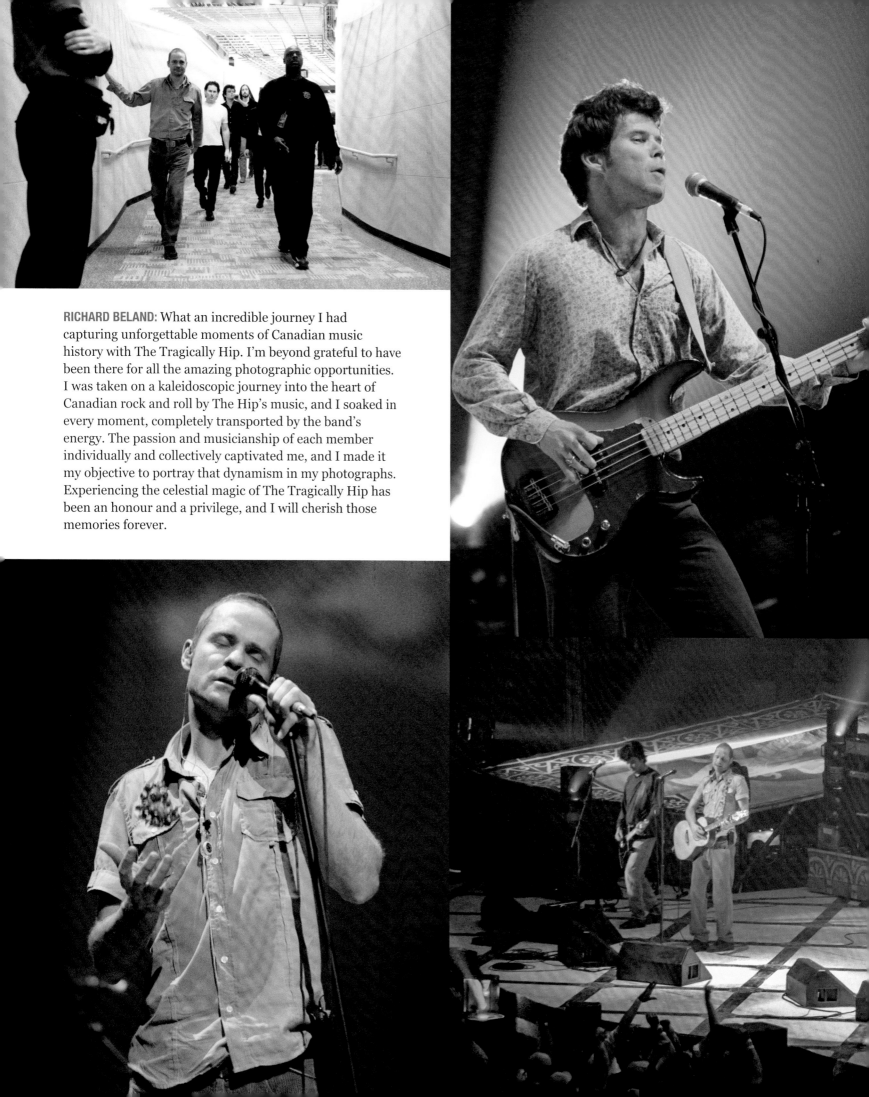

RICHARD BELAND: What an incredible journey I had capturing unforgettable moments of Canadian music history with The Tragically Hip. I'm beyond grateful to have been there for all the amazing photographic opportunities. I was taken on a kaleidoscopic journey into the heart of Canadian rock and roll by The Hip's music, and I soaked in every moment, completely transported by the band's energy. The passion and musicianship of each member individually and collectively captivated me, and I made it my objective to portray that dynamism in my photographs. Experiencing the celestial magic of The Tragically Hip has been an honour and a privilege, and I will cherish those memories forever.

Phantom Power tour,
Canada, February 1999

JOHNNY: We were actually the closest band in origin to the festival. Rome is just over the border from us, in New York State, which has always been mega for us. There's this great camaraderie between Canadians and Americans that live close to the border like that.

On the Friday night some stuff went down and they were expecting it to escalate. So we figured we would get in there and play our set, stick around for a little bit, and then get out. We were happy to leave when we did. You could definitely feel that it was going to go off. Like the first Woodstock, it wasn't really well organised.

GORD S: The MTV cameras were rolling all the time, so you were super conscious of that. It was pretty nerve-racking. There were 100,000 people in the crowd. We played and we kind of nailed it. It was wicked, and you could see lots of Canadian flags out in the audience.

GORD S: Woodstock '99 really sticks out in my mind because obviously it was a super big deal. The Woodstock concept had become such a huge cultural icon. Anybody who's anybody was invited to play at it, and so when we found ourselves invited we were stoked.

ROB: I grew up with the *Woodstock* album and I've seen the movie a ridiculous number of times. Michael Lang, who put the original festival together, was a hero of mine growing up. It's a weird thing to have a rock promoter as one of your heroes, but he truly was.

JAKE GOLD: Woodstock was the television side of the American market for us. It was live on MTV with pay-per-view or whatever. We wanted to be a part of something like that.

JAKE GOLD: They've had all these documentaries about the aggro that went on at Woodstock '99 but we aren't mentioned because ours was a happy set. It was people celebrating. We were on early in the day, so people hadn't gotten drunk enough yet and we weren't there to rile up the crowd.

JOHNNY: We thought it could be cool to play in front of a whole bunch of people. But it was a pretty bizarre line-up – people I'd never heard of before, like Kid Rock and Limp Bizkit.

GORD S: We opened the main stage on Saturday. It was certainly weird when we arrived. It was not peace, love and music. It was anonymous trailers and not a lot of interaction with other artists.

ROB: The Hip were a very confident band at that time, so going on to a crowd that size didn't faze us whatsoever. But it was nuts – like being on the deck of an aircraft carrier with this roar all around you.

JOHNNY: It was strange because behind the stage there were three other stages with band set-ups on them ready to be wheeled out. You're seeing everybody's gear back there with the pyrotechnics and all of that stuff. And then we were just a little band from Kingston.

ROB: After we did our set there was a press conference straight afterwards and one of the journalists said, 'We've just had Michael Lang in here and he said that of all the bands on the bill you're the only one he could imagine playing at the original Woodstock.' It may have been meant as a gigantic insult, but I took it as a great compliment. That just meant to me that we were a very basic, straight-ahead band: what you see is what you get. It wasn't lights and a big show, it was five people on a stage doing the best they can with what they've got in their hands.

GORD S: Later in the day, I had my kid out in the crowd and it was getting too much. We had to get out of there. We pulled the bus out of there as the crowd was booming towards the stage for Metallica. As we were driving out, you could feel the vibe change. You could literally feel the air going out of the balloon. It was going to be the continuation of that iconic Woodstock vibe, but, in retrospect, what happened became the opposite.

JAKE GOLD: During Limp Bizkit's set on the Saturday night, I was out in the audience for a minute and saw the sound towers starting to get torn apart. When we were backstage, I could hear people freaking out on the radios. They thought the towers were going to come down. So they had to end Limp Bizkit's set for the safety of the crowd and the crew.

Woodstock '99,
Griffiss Air Force Base,
Rome, NY,
22–25 July 1999

STEVE BERLIN: Los Lobos's manager at the time, John Scher, was putting on Woodstock '99. So we were doing it, it wasn't an option. As soon as we drove in, I sensed this unpleasant vibe – people were fighting. The water was $12 for a little bottle. I looked left and right and thought, 'What the fuck is going on here?'

During Rage Against the Machine people started burning stuff; this black cloud of smoke came over the stage and it smelled like burning shit. Zack de la Rocha doing Rage stuff, dressed all in white, looked like he was holding back this malevolent horror movie cloud of awfulness.

I watched him for a while and I realised we had to get the fuck out of there, right then and there. It felt like something really bad was about to happen and I didn't want to be anywhere close to it. We just drove out, in the middle of the night, to where our next gig was. I didn't see any of the real shit that went down later, but, man, it was palpable, like a mustard gas attack.

ROB: What really got me was a few months later *Rolling Stone* did an exposé on what went wrong and they basically said that the trouble kicked off when The Tragically Hip took the stage. Their theory was that we'd brought a frat boy audience and that they started it all. Looking out at the crowd, that wasn't what I was seeing.

I thought, 'Oh, now you decide to mention us. Not your fucking darlings Limp Bizkit or Rage Against the Machine. It's our fault. Fuck you very much.'

Dear Jake,

As you probably already know, at the end of the Woodstock weekend, several fans staged a massive riot on the festival grounds. The riots eventually became centralized in the festival village where the Aware tent was located. As the events escalated, Aware employees, in order to protect themselves from harm, left the tent where they were selling CD's. As a result, the rioters looted the CD store and a large amount of product was lost to theft.

Aware is covered by insurance and we have already begun the process of filing a claim. Nevertheless, it could take some time for us to collect on our losses. In the meantime, we ask that you please be patient with our payment. We fully intend to pay each label; however, we need to collect on our damages before we begin sending out checks. If you have any questions please call me.

Regards,

Will Healy

1536 W. Adams • Unit 1 North Rear • Chicago, IL 60607
phone: 312.226.6335 • fax: 312.226.6299
www.awarerecords.com ~ will@awaremusic.com

THE TRAGICALLY HIP PERSONEL LIST FOR WOODSTOCK-99

35 909 22

NAMES	TITLE
Baker, Rob	band
Downie, Gord	band
Fay, Johnny	band
Langlois, Paul	band
Sinclair, Gord	band
Lorimer, Bea	tour manager
Vreeken, Mark	production manager
Lamarche, Matt	moniter tech
Scrutten, Gary	guitar tech.
Koster, Dave	stage/ guitar tech
Cormier, Mike	drum tech
Forte, Wayne	agent
Stertz, Shelley	management
Gold, Jake	manager
Sinclair, Chris	family
Sinclair, Colin	child
Davidson, Merideth	family
Pearson, Shannon	family
Baker, Borris	child
Galibraith Leslie	family
Newfeld, Rick	bus driver
Glass, John	bus driver
Younge, Evan	truck driver
Wellington, Rick	security director
Forte, Alexandre	family
Davie, Karin	family
Cleghorn, Cathy	merchandise
Gregg, Dave	merchandise
Hamilton, Deb	family
Langlois, Joanne	family
Walton, Ross	website/fanclub
Rioux, Lissette	Sire Records
Blumenthal, Lori	Sire Records

already has receive
sent to NY

already has receiv

JOHNNY: We had this opportunity to play a big show at the Air Canada Centre to bring in the new millennium. We weren't too worried about whether the bug would shut down the power grid, because I could imagine Gord singing to 18,000 people with a candle and a megaphone. I think he would have enjoyed that actually.

ROB: John B. Webster was doing stage design for us at the time, and he had this idea that we would have a gigantic snake filled with confetti that would be wrapped around the inside of the arena. As the night went on, the snake would shed its skin to represent casting off the old year, and then there'd be a massive balloon and confetti drop at midnight, with the snake spewing confetti all over the crowd.

   With an hour to go until doors opening, John was sitting on the floor crying because they couldn't get the snake up into the ceiling. Eventually, they got it up there but they clearly didn't do it right.

JAKE GOLD: Partway through the show, I could see that Gord was struggling with his voice. I heard over the intercoms that they couldn't get the door of the loading dock closed and there was this massive cold draught blowing onto the stage. Gord couldn't get warm and he needed to be warm to be able to sing. Eventually, someone took an axe to the door and got it to close, but by then it was a long way through the show and Gord was really, really pissed off.

ROB: When midnight struck, there was just a little cough of confetti and no balloon drop.

JOHNNY: Gord invested a lot in those shows, not only as the singer but as the designer of the event, and so when things like that didn't work it set him off a little bit.

ROB: Finally, they managed to get the balloons to drop, and Gord lost his mind. There were balloons all over the stage and he was determined to pop every one of them. He was stomping on them and hitting them with his mic stand and then throwing his full body weight on some of them. There were a lot of balloons, so this went on for a long time.

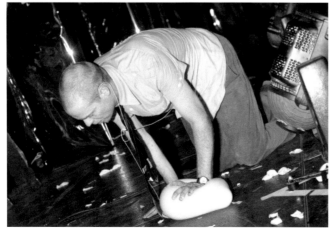

GORD D: The entire thing was a fit of rage. There was nothing artistic about it at all. It got ridiculous to the point where I think the crew were all in tears from witnessing the worst blowout they'd ever seen. I don't do that anymore.

Left and above: DAT recording of new songs played at the New Year's Eve 1999 and New Year's Day 2000 shows at the Air Canada Centre. All six tracks became part of Music @ Work ('Drakes' was retitled as 'Stay')

THE TRAGICALLY HIP

MUSIC@WORK
March 2000

1	My Music @ Work	3:07
2	Tiger the Lion	5:31
3	Lake Fever	4:34
4	Putting Down	3:14
5	Stay	3:22
6	The Bastard	4:54
7	The Completist	3:08
8	Freak Turbulence	2:53
9	Sharks	4:15
10	Toronto 4	2:57
11	Wild Mountain Honey	3:57
12	Train Overnight	3:18
13	The Bear	3:56
14	As I wind Down The Pines	2:34

MGMT
TRUST

CONFIDENTIAL

JOHNNY: We had Steve Berlin back to do *Music @ Work*, but it was a different record from *Phantom Power*, a different mindset, a different atmosphere. It had nothing to do with him, but it just didn't click this time. We never used a producer more than twice. The second record was always different. I don't know why.

ROB: The first time around, with *Phantom Power*, we really put our trust in Steve and we did a great record with him. The next one was not a great record. But it wasn't his fault. We began to second-guess him and the whisper campaigns started up – the stupid shit that bands do.

STEVE BERLIN: *Music @ Work* was a harder record to make, beyond a shadow of a doubt. On *Phantom Power*, songs like 'Fireworks', 'Poets' and 'Bobcaygeon' were effortless. We didn't have to talk or think about them, they just showed up. I don't remember that ever happening on *Music @ Work*. There was a lot more talking and thinking, and a little less free-wheeling and willingness to experiment. My bag of tricks is only so big, so some of the stuff that was new on *Phantom Power* was old hat by *Music @ Work*.

I got the feeling as it went along that they were kind of half-assing some of the stuff I was asking them to do. During *Phantom Power* Gord Downie and I would have these exchanges in what I considered to be a gentleman's discourse, where he'd push back. But somewhere in the middle of *Music @ Work* he was pushing back on everything. It was like he was testing me.

There was one day I remember thinking, 'What's the point? I'm not really affecting this in a positive way. I should just go.' Then I got up the next day, told myself that that was a quitter mentality and decided to stick around. And eventually the contention with Gord stopped. I guess he figured out that he couldn't make me quit, so he might as well deal with me!

GORD S: Post-*Phantom Power*, our young children were now functioning little people and we were all at a stage of our lives where home responsibilities were becoming way more important. It was getting harder and harder to bring the five of us together to write songs.

So, going into the studio, we weren't ready to make *Music @ Work*. We had a lot of great ideas but the majority of the songs were unfinished, and there was no clear single. Steve got thrust into the middle of it, and it was a really untenable situation.

Top: Gord Downie, Gord Sinclair, Johnny Fay, Steve Berlin and Paul Langlois in the control room at the Bathouse, 2000

Music @ Work *promo photos, Bathouse, Bath, ON, 2000*

GORD S: By that point we'd had the Bathouse for quite a while, and it was actually a going concern. We were starting to rent it out, we had a house engineer, and people were coming in and making records. It's a great studio, based on the residential model that we lifted from Daniel Lanois. You wake up and get the sleep out of your eyes, brush your teeth and go down in your pyjamas and start making a record with the rest of the guys that are all staying there. When you're young and dumb ... fantastic!

But, by the end of the Nineties, Gord was in Toronto, so he had to live out of the studio, while the rest of us could go home to our wives and families. And it wasn't fair, and he was right that it wasn't fair. We had a couple occasions where, out of respect for him, we'd all stay there with him, but this issue meant that making records in our own studio was becoming impractical.

ROB: When we recorded at the Bathouse, I had to watch how much I drank and smoked because I'd have a 25-minute drive home on a shitty road at night. And when you drive to the studio, it takes an hour or two to get settled back into where you were.

Going away someplace where you live and record creates a natural focus. It's a sacrifice, but everyone's making the same sacrifice so you feel like a team.

BILLY RAY: One of the reasons the band bought the Bathouse was to be able to make records without having to rent a studio, which cost so much money. But by the time *Music @ Work* rolled around, the convenience of being only 20 minutes away from home, not having to spend the night away, being able to go out and get milk and a loaf of bread, meant that home life was beginning to intertwine with work life in a big way. Instead of there being a group of guys on a mission to make a record, now families came into play and trying to get everyone on the same page became more and more difficult. Being in your own studio, the clock wasn't ticking like it would be if you were renting a studio for 12 days, and that wasn't great for productivity.

It got to a point where they had to start going to other studios again. If the lid's not on the pressure cooker, then the meal's not getting cooked. You're just blowing steam into the air all day long, every day.

JOHNNY: The first couple of records we did in Bath were good, but it started to become just too convenient. Sessions didn't start until twelve o'clock and then that turned into one, then two, then three. When we finally got started, we only had an hour before dinner and we really didn't get as much work done as we had hoped. Going away is always the best. You're in the studio at eleven and tracking by twelve and then you're on your way.

STEVE BERLIN: When you make a record, you're capturing a moment – the people, the smells, the sounds. You're literally capturing what happened in this room, in this five-week period. And sometimes that room is leaky; there's things happening around you, behind you. You don't really know what's going on when the guys leave the studio. They were the same people in the same room but they were just in a slightly different head space. There was a little bit more family time that we had to bake into the cake. Certainly, the pressures outside of them had grown since we made *Phantom Power*.

GORD S: We were starting new song ideas in the studio while we were supposedly making a record. Gord was writing lyrics on the fly and not liking what he was doing and going back and redoing them.

JOHNNY: Gord was starting to really labour with his lyrics. Previously, we'd be ready with the music and Gord would be ready with the lyrics, and he'd just commit to them. Sometimes he'd come in the room with lyrics he'd just finished writing, throw them down proudly and say, 'Hot off the press. Wanna read 'em?' But now he was probably feeling a lot of pressure, because he'd gone from being the quirky front guy who danced around a lot to someone that people were interested in for what he had to say. He had a briefcase full of pages and pages of stuff. He was overthinking and overwriting.

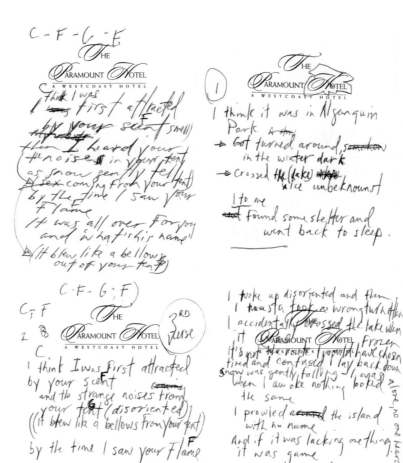

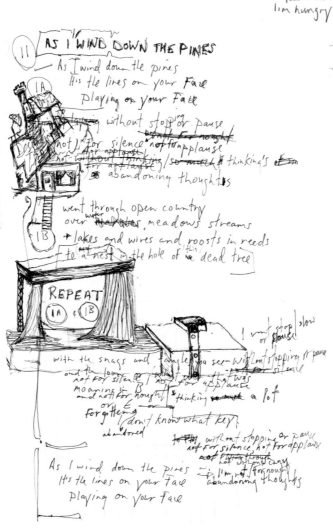

Gord Downie's handwritten notes and lyrics for songs on Music @ Work, including 'The Bear', 'As I Wind Down the Pines', 'Tiger the Lion', 'Lake Fever' and 'My Music at Work'

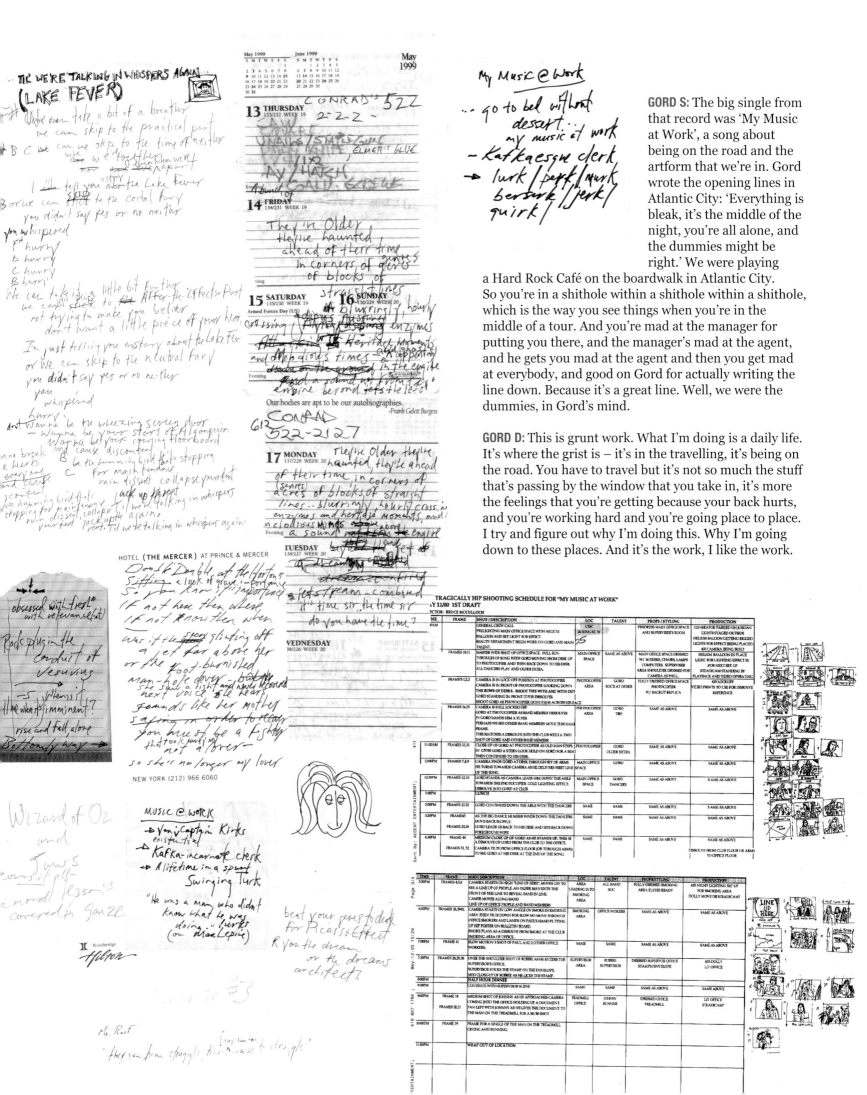

GORD S: The big single from that record was 'My Music at Work', a song about being on the road and the artform that we're in. Gord wrote the opening lines in Atlantic City: 'Everything is bleak, it's the middle of the night, you're all alone, and the dummies might be right.' We were playing a Hard Rock Café on the boardwalk in Atlantic City. So you're in a shithole within a shithole within a shithole, which is the way you see things when you're in the middle of a tour. And you're mad at the manager for putting you there, and the manager's mad at the agent, and he gets you mad at the agent and then you get mad at everybody, and good on Gord for actually writing the line down. Because it's a great line. Well, we were the dummies, in Gord's mind.

GORD D: This is grunt work. What I'm doing is a daily life. It's where the grist is – it's in the travelling, it's being on the road. You have to travel but it's not so much the stuff that's passing by the window that you take in, it's more the feelings that you're getting because your back hurts, and you're working hard and you're going place to place. I try and figure out why I'm doing this. Why I'm going down to these places. And it's the work, I like the work.

PAUL: There were two main differences between the recording of *Phantom Power* and *Music @ Work*. One was that Steve wasn't there all the time for *Music @ Work*, so a lot of the time we'd be talking with him on the phone or exchanging emails.

The other difference was Pro Tools, the recording program, which changed everything. It was our first experience with Pro Tools. You could write as you were recording, so the decision scope increased massively. You could play a solo and then play another one and mix them together. And you could record forever. You really need to make quick decisions in songwriting and recording. You can't put them off. With Pro Tools, you can put them off and mess around in a way, so that probably threw all of us a little bit. I think the introduction of Pro Tools changed us and not for the better, at that time.

ROB: I still think that two-inch tape is a way better medium than digital, but this is the world we live in.

There are advantages to Pro Tools. If you want to know what the guitar would sound like flipped backwards, you can do that in 30 seconds, whereas if you did that with two-inch tape it would take hours. The disadvantage is that with Pro Tools you don't have to make all your decisions on the fly, so problems can pile up at the end. When you're recording a song on two-inch tape, you have to know in advance how long each section is, you have to dial in your guitar tones and your drum tones – there's work to be done up front, but then the actual recording takes four minutes. With Pro Tools, it's very different. We had one song – 'Tiger the Lion' – that had something like 78 tracks. Up until then, the most we'd ever used was 16. And it was because no one made any decisions. When we got to mixing, no one really knew what the songs sounded like, because you can't get a proper sense of playback with so many things undecided.

PAUL: *Music @ Work* **has a few songs that we might look at as filler. Maybe some of the songs weren't as finished as we thought, and yet we were recording them anyway. That probably didn't affect our relationships in a good way. I'm sure we were all struggling individually with a bit of self-doubt.**

JOHNNY: We had lived in the last golden age of making records on two-inch tape. You took a blank piece of tape, sat in a room and made music, and then you mixed it. And there it was. With Pro Tools, it was on a hard drive. People started asking why their guitar track was colour-coded brown and the snare drum was pink. It was confusing – it's like you're making music with your eyes and not with your ears. The Pro Tools experience is lousy. It does sound incredible, but it's not like running tape at all.

ROB: Coming off of *Phantom Power*, which was a much more focused record, *Music @ Work* spread out in different directions. It's got a lot of really good moments, and I don't think there are too many real stinker tracks, but it's not a very cohesive record. The big problem was editing. Steve said working with us was like trying to get something passed by the UN Security Council. And he wasn't wrong. We were five guys, each with a veto. Steve wanted us to cut back to 11 tracks and he had a definite opinion about which songs should be left off, but we just couldn't agree on it between the five of us. We should have stepped aside and left it to him; it would have been a much more powerful album if we had.

JOHNNY: In my mind, I don't think the songs were there on *Music @ Work*. We maybe weren't ready to make a record then. We should have taken some time off. The title song became a staple of the live shows, but I can't remember playing a lot of the other tracks from that record. It wasn't hugely well received.

GORD S: Gord was really frustrated when *Music @ Work* was finished. There were a bunch of songs on there that he was really unhappy with, lyrically. 'Sharks' was one, which I thought was such a great song idea but it was incomplete. 'Wild Mountain Honey' was another one he was really unhappy with, and so was Steve. It's a feeling that we'd never really had before. In the past, we'd walk out of the studio thinking that we'd just made the best record not only that we'd ever made but that anyone had ever made, period. This time, it was like, 'Is this done?' Well, no, it wasn't done. It was a bummer.

THE FINANCIAL POST
THURSDAY, MAY 11TH, 2000

Tragically Hip fans rail at online piracy of unreleased CD

Cyber fans of Gord Downie, above, and the rest of The Tragically Hip, have been singing an angry tune.

Music @ Work
RECORDED: 1999–2000
THE BATHOUSE, BATH, ON
PRODUCERS: STEVE BERLIN
MARK VREEKEN
THE TRAGICALLY HIP
ENGINEER: MARK VREEKEN
MIXING: STEVEN DRAKE
RELEASED: 6 JUNE 2000
My Music at Work
Tiger the Lion
Lake Fever
Putting Down
Stay
The Bastard
The Completists
Freak Turbulence
Sharks
Toronto #4
Wild Mountain Honey
Train Overnight
The Bear
As I Wind Down the Pines

PAUL: *Music @ Work* got leaked and we flipped out. We never found out how it happened. You hate to have your record leaked, if it's not on purpose. You have a release date two months away and then, all of a sudden, people can hear your record. It was off-putting for all of us.

JOHNNY: This guy at the gym told me he'd heard our record on Napster. I could understand the attraction. If I could get music early from a band that I liked, I'd think that was cool. But it really took the wind out of our sails and was another thing that didn't help *Music @ Work* at all.

PAUL: Napster and free file sharing was worrying. We were all wondering how it would work, where the money would come from. If it's all accessible and free, we're getting the rug pulled out from under us, was the way it was looking. Turned out to be true.

We still made money selling tickets but it ended up taking a major chunk out of musicians' income. It's become a tougher business for everybody.

JAKE GOLD: Word got out that *Music @ Work* had leaked. But when I spoke to the guy who was running all our web stuff, he told me that the fans were starting to shut down the people who were doing the leaking. He could see, in real time on message boards and on Napster, fans turning against these people who they saw as ripping off the band.

So we managed to spin what could have been a 'Holy fuck, what are we gonna do?' type of situation into a positive story about the fans supporting the band and getting the leak shut down.

But it made us realise that we were now in this digital age, where there were platforms available for people to share music, and we were either going to have embrace it or get killed by it.

GORD D: [*Music @ Work* leaking] tells me that the day you finish mastering your record you should think about putting it out, rather than having all this time leading up to a splashy release.

Most musicians make their money from playing live anyway. Oftentimes, if they're with a big record company, they get their money up front so they're not necessarily clear whether people are actually stealing from them or the record company. People back in the Eighties used to come up to me and say, 'I taped your record. Does that bother you?' And it didn't bother me at all.

PAUL: By the time *Music @ Work* came out, we had been at an arena level for quite a while in Canada. But we noticed that the top bowl wasn't full, the single tickets that used to be a no-brainer were not selling. All our fans were getting older with us. And they also had young kids, less time. They're not going to buy a single ticket in the nose bleeds.

So we had a rethink and moved back to doing multiple nights at theatres. We hopped back and forth for many years. It's fun to play Maple Leaf Gardens and the Air Canada Centre, but it's also fun to play Massey Hall and the Roy Thomson.

JAKE GOLD: I could see that Gord Downie hated being up on stage in these cavernous places and I thought we needed to do something to reinvigorate the audience. In 2002 we created the Theatrical Extravaganza. We had these great circus-style posters with two purple hippos dancing [page 218]. When you walked into the buildings there were stilt-walkers and clowns, because we wanted people to feel like they were at something special. And the shows themselves were incendiary. We got amazing reviews right across the country.

ROB: I was fine with the decision to play more theatres and do multi-nights. Staying in a city for three nights can be more fun than being on the bus every night and gives you more chance to play. We had lots of material, which meant that we could do three nights in a city and do three different shows. So it was all good. But I think there was some concern on the band's part that if we bumped down to the theatres, there would be a perception that we couldn't sell the arenas and then bumping back up might prove more challenging.

GORD S: There were thoughts that this might be the beginning of the end, or the end of the beginning. We'd spent our entire career just working project by project, but now we were facing a new parcel of challenges. We had lives outside the band that we were responsible for, and the band was creatively not as satisfying as it had been. So we started to question each other and management and what we were doing, looking for a way out of the trajectory that we were on. That led to a bunch of interesting times.

*HSBC Arena, Buffalo,
NY, 20 December 2000*

VIVA LE HIP!

MADE AT WORK

An Evening With The Tragically Hip
North American Tour

2000

ALL ACCESS

AN EVENING WITH

THE TRAGICALLY HIP

WINTER TOUR

NOVEMBER 2000

15 VANCOUVER, BC
16 VANCOUVER, BC
18 KELOWNA, BC
19 PRINCE GEORGE, BC

AN EVENING with
THE TRAGICALLY HIP
tTH

WINTER TOUR 2000

Dec 3, Toronto   Dec 5, Sudbury
Dec 6, Ottawa   Dec 21, Hamilton   Dec 23, Toronto

AN EVENING WITH
The Tragically HIP
WINTER TOUR 2000
CANADA   CANADA

Dec 7, Montreal, PQ
Dec 9, Saint John, NB   Dec 14, Corner Brook, NF
Dec 10, Moncton, NB   Dec 15, St. John's, NF
Dec 12, Halifax, NS   Dec 16, St. John's, NF

AN EVENING WITH
THE TRAGICALLY HIP

Dec 1, CHICAGO, IL
Dec 2, DETROIT, MI
Dec 20, BUFFALO, NY

NORTH AMERICAN TOUR
2000

Limited Edition 40 of 1000

THE TRAGICALLY HIP

LIVE IN CONCERT

... GUEST ...   · LOCAL CREW ·   ... GUEST ...

PRESS·PHOTO

An Evening With
THE TRAGICALLY HIP
LIVE
WINTER TOUR 2000

Nov 21 Edmonton, AB   Nov 25 Lethbridge, AB
Nov 23 Calgary, AB   Nov 27 Saskatoon, SK
Nov 24 Red Deer, AB   Nov 28 Brandon, MB

THE TRAGICALLY HIP
LIVE IN CONCERT
·LOCAL CREW·   ···GUEST···   ·ALL ACCESS·

THE TRAGICALLY HIP
LIVE IN CONCERT
·LOCAL CREW·   ···GUEST···   PRESS·PHOTO·TV

THE TRAGICALLY HIP · U.S. OCTOBER/NOVEMBER 2000
DATES STILL TENTATIVE AND FOR INTERNAL USE ONLY

The Tragically Hip
World Tour 00

All Access
Guest
Local Crew

The Tragically Hip
World Tour 00

All Access
Guest
Local Crew
Press / Photo

:AN EVENING WITH:
THE TRAGICALLY HIP
:LIVE IN CONCERT:

North American Tour
Itinerary

Erie
Albany
Atlanta
Denver

CHANGES MADE ARE IN BOLD TEXT

DATE	DAY	VENUE		CITY,STATE	Status	Announce	On S		MV
OCT 2	MON	AUDITORIUM THEATRE	20,000	ROCHESTER, NY	Confirmed	21-Aug-00	11-Aug-00	✓	✓
OCT 3	TUE	LANDMARK THEATRE	20,000	SYRACUSE, NY	Confirmed	22-Aug-00	11-Aug-00	✓	✓
OCT 4	WED	PALACE THEATRE	10,000	ALBANY, NY	Confirmed	22-Aug-00	11-Aug-00	✓	✓
OCT 5	THU	OFF							
OCT 6	FRI	TOWN HALL		NEW YORK, NY	Confirmed	14-Aug-00	11-Aug-00	✓	✓
OCT 7	SAT	TOWN HALL		NEW YORK, NY - OPTION	Confirmed				
OCT 8	SUN	WARNER THEATRE	25,000	ERIE, PA	Confirmed	14-Aug-00	21-Aug-00	✓	✓
OCT 9	MON	OFF							
OCT 10	TUE	OFF							
OCT 11	WED	NORVA THEATRE	6,000	NORFOLK, VA	Confirmed	12-Aug-00	12-Aug-00	✓	✓
OCT 12	THU	ROXY THEATRE	6,500	ATLANTA, GA	Confirmed	16-Aug-00	18-Aug-00	✓	✓
OCT 13	FRI	HOUSE OF BLUES	6,250	NEW ORLEANS, LA	Confirmed	19-Aug-00	19-Aug-00	✓	✓
OCT 14	SAT	WALLER CREEK AMPHITHEATER	10,000	AUSTIN, TX	Confirmed	24-Aug-00	26-Aug-00	✓	✓
OCT 15	SUN	OFF							
OCT 16	MON	OFF							
OCT 17	TUE	OFF							
OCT 18	WED	WEB THEATRE	5,250	PHOENIX, AZ	Confirmed	5-Sep-00	16-Sep-00	✓	✓
OCT 19	THU	RIALTO THEATRE	10,250	TUCSON, AZ	Confirmed	5-Sep-00	9-Sep-00	✓	✓
OCT 20	FRI	HOUSE OF BLUES	17,500	LOS ANGELES, CA	Confirmed	17-Aug-00	17-Aug-00	✓	✓
OCT 21	SAT	HOUSE OF BLUES		LOS ANGELES, CA - OPTION	Confirmed				
OCT 22	SUN	OFF							
OCT 23	MON	OFF							
OCT 24	TUE	FILLMORE	17,000	SAN FRANCISCO, CA	Confirmed	13-Sep-00	17-Sep-00	✓	✓
OCT 25	WED	FILLMORE		SAN FRANCISCO, CA - OPTION	Confirmed				
OCT 26	THU	OFF							
OCT 27	FRI	AGGIE THEATER	5,500	FT. COLLINS, CO	Confirmed	11-Sep-00	16-Sep-00	✓	✓
OCT 28	SAT	PARAMOUNT THEATRE	9,000	DENVER, CO	Confirmed	11-Sep-00	16-Sep-00	✓	✓
OCT 29	SUN	OFF							
OCT 30	MON	TBA - OFF		TBA					
OCT 31	TUE	TBA - OFF		TBA					
NOV 1	WED	MOORE THEATRE	18,000	SEATTLE, WA	Confirmed	15-Sep-00	22-Sep-00	✓	✓
NOV 2	THU	MOORE THEATRE		SEATTLE, WA - OPTION	Confirmed				
NOV 3	FRI	MOORE THEATRE		SEATTLE, WA - OPTION	Confirmed				
NOV 4	SAT	ALADDIN THEATER		PORTLAND, OR	Confirmed	8-Sep-00	8-Sep-00	✓	✓
END									

The Tragically Hip World Tour 00 — Massey

1 Tiger
2 Something
3 Music
4 Gift
5 Down
6 Spring
7 To #4
8 Fireworks
9 Freak
10 Nautical
11 Daddy
12 Completists   Money / ABAC
13 Bob C   Blow
14 Fully
15 Fever   Flamenco
16 Meridian   Poets

Montreal

1 Tiger
2 Something On
3 Grace + Down
4 Music
5 Escape
6 Stars
7 Poets
8 Poets   To #4
9 Courage
10 Vapour
11 Completists   Train
12 Completists
13 ABAC   Gift
14 Fireworks
15 Fever   Bastard
16 Meridian   Bob C / Toronto

1 Tiger   Bones
2 Something
3 Gift + Music
4 Down   Sharks / Money
5 Fully / Spring
6 Money / Tom   ABAC
7 Poets / Fireworks   Blow
8 To #4 / Stay / Freak
9 Nautical   Flamenco
10 Daddy
11 Completists / Stay Gone? / Poets
12
13 Bob C
14 Fireworks / Spring / To #4 / Fully
15 Fever
16 Meridian

GORD S: When we were finishing off *Music @ Work*, Steve was contributing an awful lot of keyboard to turn a six into a nine. Then, when it came time to tour, we didn't have the instrumentation to effectively present the material. So the logical step was to add a keyboard player. Chris Brown and Kate Fenner came as a unit. It started off with them playing on three or four songs, but by the end of the tour, because they were also our support act, they were on stage longer than we were.

BILLY RAY: Gord Downie was very much against the idea of side musicians. He thought that if Chris and Kate were going to be on stage with them then they had to be in the band. As far as he was concerned, The Tragically Hip now had seven members and he didn't want anyone on the crew treating Chris and Kate any differently from anyone else in the band.

GORD D: By bringing in Chris and Kate we're adding two new, very original sounds. It multiplies the variables of what we can do.

I think it was a good decision on our part. It's coloured things quite significantly, had a real ripple effect, and over time those two have managed to eke out an existence up there. I'm really proud of what they've done, because it's not easy. Their whole attitude and approach have been really contagious.

In terms of singing, it's suggested this whole new universe to me and allowed me to really stretch out to the point where I don't even remember what song I'm in. I feel pretty supported. On this tour, I've had certain people comment to me, 'You know, I expected to come and see a guitar band, and it was like a singer's band.'

JOHNNY: Chris and Kate are two of the nicest people you'd ever want to meet. They were in The Bourbon Tabernacle Choir, which had a great following, and then they came and did some solo stuff with us. And then all of a sudden they were in with us playing. When we did a performance on MuchMusic, we stepped out through this window to the people that were out on the street and Chris and Kate came out the window with us. It was confusing to some people – and it was definitely confusing to me.

GORD S: Having Chris and Kate on stage forced a reinterpretation of certain songs. All of a sudden, we were playing 'New Orleans Is Sinking' with a keyboard solo in it. And Kate needed more to do than play the tambourine, so she started singing a verse here and there and doing some back-ups. Then that snowball started steaming down the hill until, before we knew it, Kate had taken over from Paul and me as back-up singer.

GORD S: It was different from what we were used to doing and also different from what the audience was used to hearing. In small doses it could have been a really good thing, but changing everything to accommodate this big band wasn't easy. It was a fraught time and a difficult tour.

BILLY RAY: I hate to throw those guys under the bus but it was not beneficial to have them in the band. Kate's a beautiful singer, but sometimes it was distracting the amount she was singing. Some songs became almost a duet between her and Gord, except it wasn't a duet because they were just singing in unison. And Kate had a habit of tossing her tambourine to the side when she wasn't playing it and letting it hit the stage and then roll. It would drive Johnny crazy because he would hear this off-beat sound and he'd be looking for where the sound was coming from. And, sure enough, it was Kate's tambourine rolling around.

Chris played a lot of busy Clavinet stuff and there became this volume war on stage where Paul would turn his amp up to try to hear himself over the sound of the Clavinet going full-blast behind him, which led to a cascade of other things happening.

BILLY RAY: I also think putting Kate and Chris between Paul and Gord was detrimental to the band. Paul and Gord had been great friends for so long, and worked off of each other so much during the live show, that to separate them like that on stage made for some rough times between the two of them.

PAUL: I was protective of my role and of the five of us playing together. I fought against bringing other people in. I would have been against adding anybody. I just thought, the five of us is a lot already. We don't need anybody else. I think Gord wanted to switch it up a bit and that having a keyboard player and a female back-up singer would be fun. It was a tough position, mentally, for Chris and Kate to be in. Playing with them wasn't so bad. Once it was happening, I was quite accepting of it. And, of course, they brought their talents.

JOHNNY: I think maybe Gord wanted to go in a different musical direction. He had music in his head that he couldn't always get out. I remember when we came back from Europe and we were at Pearson Airport, about to go our separate ways, I said to Gord that it had been a great tour and he replied, 'It would have been so much better with Chris and Kate.' I couldn't answer that; I just stood there shaking my head. Then when we met up again a couple of weeks later, Gord and I had words over it. He knew the way the rest of us felt about it, but he still kept pushing. It felt like a real breach in the friendship.

TRISTIN CHIPMAN: Gord wanted Chris and Kate fully integrated, and part of that was his feeling of alienation from the rest of the guys. Then that created two different camps. Chris walked the line, but Kate was a draw for Gord – she had a different type of energy and he spent a lot of his time with her. In fact, that's how Gord started getting his own dressing room; he loved Kate's because it was girly – mint-green velvet and candles – and he wanted to be in there, not with the other guys. It became a source of division.

BILLY RAY: For my entire career, I treated The Hip as one unit consisting of five very individual guys. Part of this was making sure that they always had one dressing room. When Chris and Kate were in the band we had an extra room where Gord would end up hanging out a lot with them. I felt like that was bad for the dynamic of the band. But there was never a time that they walked on stage without everyone meeting up first – shaking hands, hugging, kissing, whatever it would be. They knew that you couldn't hide it from the fans if you went out there and you weren't getting along.

PAUL: During the Music @ Work tour we had not been as tight and together as before. We agreed that things were weird. Gord was desperate to work it out so he had the idea of getting a therapist to ask us some questions. There were about 15 written on a sheet of paper – things like 'What are you least happy with?' and 'What are you most happy with?' I remember a couple of my answers pissed Gord off.

I don't think the questionnaire really worked. Then we all had a conversation in the driveway along the lines of, what's next after this? Gord suggested we should have a retreat and talk this out. Robbie said we should bring our guitars and play, because that's what we did. Which I thought was fairly perceptive. Yes, we were friends, but the five of us sitting in a room just talking about our friendship wouldn't work. People would blow up. So we had the idea of re-focusing and re-kindling our friendship through writing songs together. And that really did work. We avoided the group therapy thing like the plague. The music calmed us down, we got a good one going and then it was like, 'OK. This is great. What was the problem again?'

Opposite: Music @ Work tour with Kate Fenner (top and fourth photo from top) and Chris Brown (centre)

Copps Coliseum, Hamilton, ON, 21 December 2000 (second photo from top); Molson Centre, Montreal, 7 December 2000 (other four photos)

This page: Copps Coliseum, Hamilton, ON, 21 December 2000 (top); Air Canada Centre, Toronto, 3 December 2000 (above); Cobo Hall, Detroit, 2 December 2000 (left)

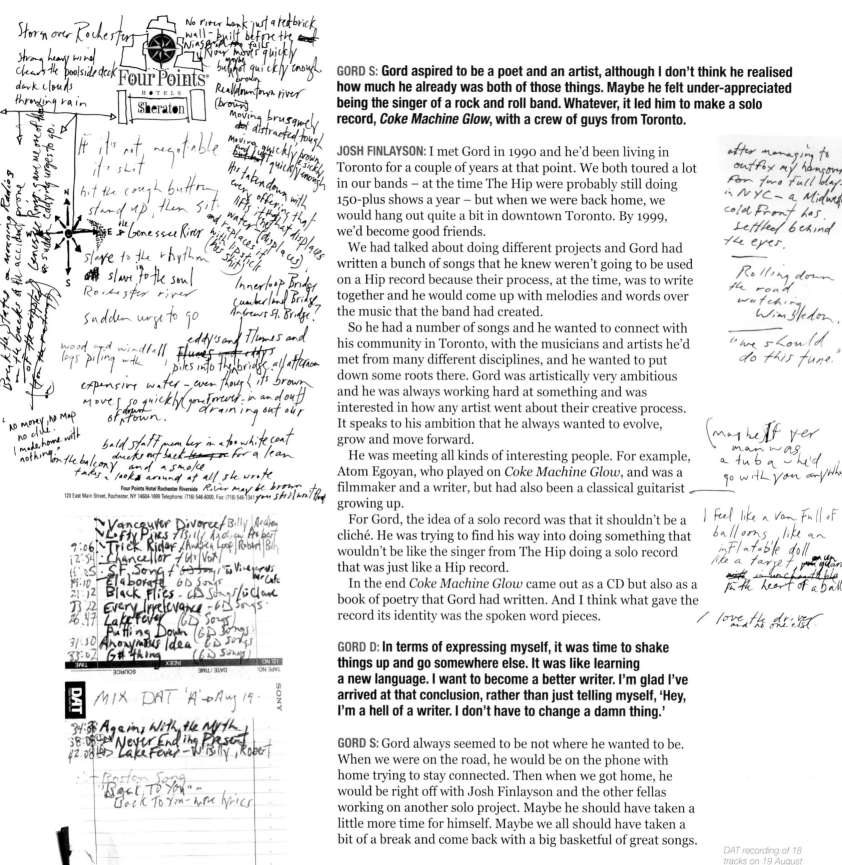

GORD S: Gord aspired to be a poet and an artist, although I don't think he realised how much he already was both of those things. Maybe he felt under-appreciated being the singer of a rock and roll band. Whatever, it led him to make a solo record, *Coke Machine Glow*, with a crew of guys from Toronto.

JOSH FINLAYSON: I met Gord in 1990 and he'd been living in Toronto for a couple of years at that point. We both toured a lot in our bands – at the time The Hip were probably still doing 150-plus shows a year – but when we were back home, we would hang out quite a bit in downtown Toronto. By 1999, we'd become good friends.

We had talked about doing different projects and Gord had written a bunch of songs that he knew weren't going to be used on a Hip record because their process, at the time, was to write together and he would come up with melodies and words over the music that the band had created.

So he had a number of songs and he wanted to connect with his community in Toronto, with the musicians and artists he'd met from many different disciplines, and he wanted to put down some roots there. Gord was artistically very ambitious and he was always working hard at something and was interested in how any artist went about their creative process. It speaks to his ambition that he always wanted to evolve, grow and move forward.

He was meeting all kinds of interesting people. For example, Atom Egoyan, who played on *Coke Machine Glow*, and was a filmmaker and a writer, but had also been a classical guitarist growing up.

For Gord, the idea of a solo record was that it shouldn't be a cliché. He was trying to find his way into doing something that wouldn't be like the singer from The Hip doing a solo record that was just like a Hip record.

In the end *Coke Machine Glow* came out as a CD but also as a book of poetry that Gord had written. And I think what gave the record its identity was the spoken word pieces.

GORD D: In terms of expressing myself, it was time to shake things up and go somewhere else. It was like learning a new language. I want to become a better writer. I'm glad I've arrived at that conclusion, rather than just telling myself, 'Hey, I'm a hell of a writer. I don't have to change a damn thing.'

GORD S: Gord always seemed to be not where he wanted to be. When we were on the road, he would be on the phone with home trying to stay connected. Then when we got home, he would be right off with Josh Finlayson and the other fellas working on another solo project. Maybe he should have taken a little more time for himself. Maybe we all should have taken a bit of a break and come back with a big basketful of great songs.

DAT recording of 18 tracks on 19 August 1999. Includes songs from Music @ Work *and* Coke Machine Glow

Gord Downie's first solo album, Coke Machine Glow, *was recorded 2–12 May 2000 and released 3 July 2001*

His second solo album, Battle of the Nudes, *was released on 3 June 2003*

GORD S: I knew Gord's solo record was going to be completely different from The Tragically Hip, because I knew what Gord was writing, knew how he played the guitar, knew what his sensibilities were. But you never want to hear that a guy in your band is doing his own thing. It suggests that he's unhappy with the situation he's in. It was a worrisome time.

I read his poetry book first, which I really quite enjoyed. It gave me a lot more insight into Gord as a writer, because I understood right away how he was restricted by the songwriting form. There were tons of lines that I recognised from songwriting sessions and it was interesting, from a creative perspective, how he reworked those ideas into the poems. Then I listened to the record and I felt reassured right away that he wasn't mowing The Hip's grass at all; he was totally making his own music in a completely different setting.

ROB: I felt threatened, angry and probably a little betrayed when I heard that Gord was doing a solo record. Threatened more than anything. I thought that if his record took off that would be the end of the band. We were in a five-way marriage with no sex, just a lot of love and a lot of frustration. And when you find out your partner is stepping out, you feel like you're being left behind.

I think Gord probably felt constrained by us; he wanted to be in a situation where he could make his own decisions and the buck stopped with him. Also, there were lots of people trying to get in his ear about this or that. Some people in management and the record company had a strong impulse to carve him away from the band. And when he moved to Toronto, he was surrounded by musical wannabes who saw in him the great front man that they lacked. The fart whisperers, we used to call them, because they would tell him every one of his farts was sacred.

When I heard *Coke Machine Glow* I thought it was good, but I was also a little relieved that it was more of an arty record. I thought, 'Well, that's not his meal ticket. He's stuck with us if he wants to pay the bills.'

TRISTIN CHIPMAN: When Gord had his solo record coming out, he started playing guitar more. There was a shift in the way that he wanted to be on stage, and I think he was bringing some of the quieter part of himself into his performance. That stirred up some feelings in Paul and Robbie about how this new creative presentation wasn't collaborative. At that time, Paul and Gord weren't as close friends as they had been. They were conflicted in a lot of ways, and Paul would instead go golfing with Gord Sinclair.

BILLY RAY: Gord got really irked when the band would have a soundcheck scheduled and some of the guys would not be there because they were still golfing – these became known as 'golf-checks'. It made him feel that he was pulling more weight or working harder or having bigger dreams, that maybe some of the others were happy with where they were at.

JOHNNY: What I really respect about Gord is that he may have wanted to do his own things but he still loved The Hip and he didn't want to trash the band. Some singers will say, 'Oh, I'll just go do it on my own. I don't need these guys.' But Gord was never about that.

His writing on that record was like it had been in the early days of The Hip. He was in the infancy of his solo career and he didn't have to deal with the pressure that was on The Hip to deliver something new and different.

BILLY RAY: Some of the other guys would say no to things that an agent might bring to them, but Gord never wanted to say no to anything. He wanted to just play shows and work and work and work. I think he thought that if they weren't going to work as hard as he did, then he needed to do some of his own work. I certainly wouldn't say that the other four guys in the band didn't work hard enough, or that they were golfing all the time; that's not the case. But it's hard to keep up with someone who doesn't stop and who is constantly looking for the next outlet to throw their art towards.

PAUL: I was probably slightly tweaked that Gord was going to make his own record while still being in The Hip. But then I went up to Toronto and sang on two tracks and I heard the rest of the record and realised it didn't sound anything like us. We understood pretty quickly that we weren't going to have to compete with Gord's solo career. In fact, Gord doing that first solo record opened the gates up for all of us to be creative outside The Hip.

Something I struggled with in my own solo work is it's hard not to sound like The Hip when you're in The Hip. You almost have to force yourself to sound different. I would say Gord probably had the same problem. It's a mental struggle. But that's making music for you. Or making any art.

JOSH FINLAYSON: Gord was sensitive about *Coke Machine Glow* coming out and how that would impact the relationships in the band. He was an incredibly loyal person. If his solo record had been like a Tragically Hip junior record, it would have been a very different statement. But the record was not that, it was a total left turn. It was meant to be an artistic statement, ultimately, and I think people that were Tragically Hip fans may or may not have liked it, and people that weren't fans may have gone, 'Wow, this is different. I didn't expect this from Gord Downie.'

Gord was very aware that he didn't want it to compete with The Hip. And, even when we toured the first two records, *Coke Machine Glow* and *Battle of the Nudes*, almost all the touring was in the States and he was very consciously wanting not to ruffle any feathers.

JOHNNY: One of the last times I saw Gord, I walked past this picture he had on his piano and saw him out of the corner of my eye. He had the biggest smile on his face. I stepped back to see where I was in the picture. But it wasn't a picture of The Hip; it was a picture of Gord with the guys he loved playing with on his other projects, like Kevin Hearn and Josh Finlayson. They made up for the stuff that probably drove him crazy about The Hip.

Seeing that picture made me think about how he got to do it a couple of times: with his best mates and with The Hip, who were also his friends. Gord really loved making music. It was what kept him going right to the end.

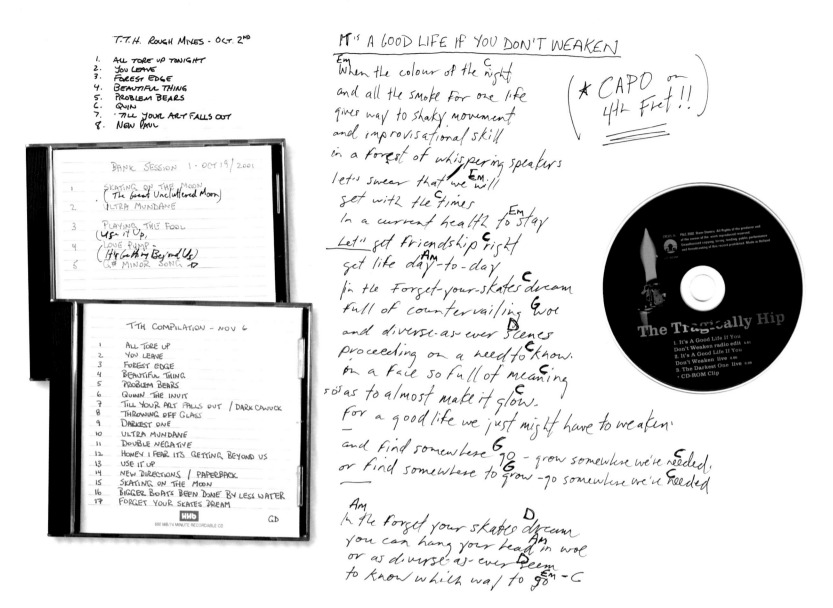

IT'S A GOOD LIFE IF YOU DON'T WEAKEN

(* CAPO on 4th Fret !!)

When the colour of the night
and all the smoke for one life
gives way to shaky movement
and improvisational skill
in a forest of whispering speakers
let's swear that we will
get with the times
In a current health to stay
Let's get friendship right
get life day-to-day
in the forget-your-skates dream
full of countervailing woe
and diverse-as-ever scenes
proceeding on a need to know.
on a face so full of meaning
so as to almost make it glow.
For a good life we just might have to weaken!
and find somewhere to go - grow somewhere we're needed.
or find somewhere to grow - go somewhere we're needed

In the forget your skates dream
you can hang your head in woe
or as diverse-as-ever seem
to know which way to go

The Tragically Hip

GORD S: We followed up *Music @ Work* with *In Violet Light*, which was another occasion where we were due to make a record but, again, we didn't have the material together. Life started getting in the way as it should. Our families became way more important than our careers.

BILLY RAY: *In Violet Light*, which nobody talks about, is an incredible record. The problem The Hip ran into was people wanted more *Road Apples* and more *Fully Completely* – more hard-punching rock and roll and dirty little grooves. But The Hip weren't a band with a formula. They weren't just going to go in and make the same songs with different words. It didn't work that way.

ROB: We wrote and rehearsed for what became *In Violet Light* in Johnny's place on Princess Street, which was an old bank that got decommissioned because it had been robbed too many times. It was a very strange session. Gord showed up with a massive stack of lyrics. We'd never had this experience before. Normally, we would jam an idea and while we were jamming Gord would hum along a melody and maybe the music might suggest a phrase or an emotion that he'd work on, and we'd build the songs that way. But this time we'd play a piece of music and then Gord would grab a lyric off the top of his pile and try to sing it to what we were playing. Occasionally, it would work but mostly it didn't, so he'd go to the next piece of paper. This went on for months.

We got some really good songs out of it, but it was a long, frustrating process. At a certain point, he'd gone through the stack and didn't have anything left, but the musical ideas were still coming in. I had a riff and everyone played behind it and then Gord just started singing the way he used to. That's where 'It's a Good Life If You Don't Weaken' came from. I liked those songs that came about at the last minute better.

JOHNNY: 'It's a Good Life' is a great, great track. We all got behind Robbie's riff and the lyric has a little thread that came from something Bea Lorimer, our road manager at the time, said to Gord after a gig.

CDs of rough mixes and tracks for In Violet Light, *recorded October and November 2001*

Lyrics for 'It's a Good Life If You Don't Weaken'

posed
cording
dget

WORLDS END

163 N. Martel Avenue, Suite 270
Los Angeles, CA 90036
Ph: 213-965 1540 Fax: 213-965 1547

The Tragically Hip	Budget Record & Mix at Compass Point,		ID: 3180
: Hugh Padgham	for: **Nassau, Bahamas**		Start Date: 11/19/01
	Approved:		Prepared: 11/5/01
: Terry Manning	Project Coordinator: Cindi Peters		Version: 1

Category	Units	%	Budget
TRACKING/MIX STUDIO "A" : (12-hr lockout / studio time on hold)	48 days	1,200.00	57,600.00
PRO-TOOLS RENTAL	1 flat	6,000.00	6,000.00
MEDIA: Harddrives, Tapes, etc.	1 flat	4,000.00	4,000.00
CARTAGE:	1 est	2,000.00	2,000.00
		Total Studio:	**69,600.00**
BAND AIRFARE: 5 rdtrips w/taxes x 2 trips - YTZ/NAS/YTZ - Air Can Coach**	10 rdtrips	420.00	4,200.00
BAND ACCOMM: Tiptop Apts - 5 Apts @ $75/ea (No Tax)	57 nights	375.00	21,375.00
BAND PER DIEM: 5 members @ $40/day	58 days	210.00	12,180.00
GUITAR TECH AIRFARE: 1 rdtrip w/taxes x 2 trips - VTZ/NAS/VTZ - Coach	2 rdtrips	420.00	840.00
GUITAR TECH ACCOMM: Orange Hill Inn - 1 Rm @ @ $75 + 18% Tax	57 nights	90.00	5,130.00
GUITAR TECH PER DIEM:	58 days	40.00	2,320.00
		Total Talent:	**46,045.00**
PRODUCER AIRFARE: 1 rdtrip w/ taxes x 2 trips - LHR/NAS/LHR - BA Bus. Class	2 rdtrips	5,010.00	10,020.00
PRODUCER ACCOMMODATIONS: Island Outpost Hotel - 1 Rm $195+ 18% Tax	57 nights	232.00	13,224.00
PRODUCER PER DIEM:	58 days	40.00	2,320.00
		Total Producer / Engineer Expenses:	**25,564.00**
MISCELLANEOUS: Phone, Faxes, Couriers, Etc.	1 flat	500.00	500.00
		Total Misc:	**500.00**
PRODUCER ADVANCE:	1 flat	75,000.00	75,000.00
ENGINEER & PRO-TOOLS OPERATOR FEE:	48 days	800.00	38,400.00
		Total Fees:	**113,400.00**

PLEASE DISCUSS ALL ROYALTY ISSUES DIRECTLY WITH SANDY ROBERTON
NOTE: There will be a holiday break commencing around 12/17/01 and resuming
approximately 1/7/02, working through 2/3/02.
**There are no flights on Sundays!!!!

Currency: USD

Budget Total   255,109.00

TTH

COMPASS POINT   rough mixes
Nov-Dec '01

1. Use It Up
2. Ultra Mundane
3. All Tore Up
4. Forest Edge
5. Beautiful Thing
6. The Darkest One
7. Til Your Art Falls Out/Dark Canuck
8. Problem Bears
9. Throwing Out Glass
10. Bigger Boats
11. You Leave
12. Forget Your Skates Dream
13. Oh Honey

COMPASS POINT

The Tragically Hip
(M---i Red Fire)

1. ↑ All Tore Up - and Tonight?
2. ↑ The Darkest One - Vox ??
3. The Ultra Mundane (Another Ocean)
4. ↑ A Forget Yer Skates Dream
5. ↑ Throwing Off Glass
6. ↑ Use It Up
7. ↑* Beautiful Thing - cover some ground
8. ↑* Forest Edge
9. Bigger Boats Been Done less Water
10. ↑ You Leave
11. The Problem Bears
12. Oh Honey
13. Til Your Falls Out/ The Dark Canuck
- Silver Jet
- Are You ... Into the Nite
Raw unmastered mixes

Above: CDs of rough and raw, unmastered mixes for In Violet Light, *recorded in Compass Point, Bahamas, late 2001*

Top right: Compass Point, Bahamas, 2001

JOHNNY: All the stars seemed to align when we made *In Violet Light*. We had the opportunity to work with Hugh Padgham, who was the guy who produced *Ghost in the Machine* and *Synchronicity* for The Police. He also worked with XTC and produced 'In the Air Tonight' for Phil Collins. Originally, he wanted to do the album in London, but we ended up in the Bahamas because [Island Records founder] Chris Blackwell had given him access to Compass Point, which was a very well-known studio there. When the car came at four in the morning to take me to the airport, there was a meteor shower and I took that as a really good sign.

PAUL: We all believed that we needed to go away and do a record, isolate ourselves like we used to for all those other records – *Up to Here*, *Road Apples*, *Fully Completely* and *Day for Night* – where we were living together, whether it was in a motel or in the studio.

ROB: We had a narrow window to jam the recording into, because Gord had his solo record coming out and some tour dates lined up. So we were in a scramble to find a producer and a bunch of names came up. When Hugh Padgham was mentioned, we thought that might be an interesting choice. So we got in touch, Hugh was available, and off we went to the Bahamas.

Compass Point was a great studio. It looked right out over the Caribbean and we each had our own apartment next to the studio. It was where Talking Heads did a bunch of their albums and AC/DC did *Back in Black* there. Terry Manning and his wife, Sherrie, who ran the studio, were fantastic people. I was in the studio 12 hours a day and then completely alone the other 12 and that

suited me perfectly. I woke up every morning, had fresh fruit and juice, did yoga for an hour, sat by the pool and read for another hour, then went into the studio and recorded all day. Came back at night and did it again. Had some fresh fruit and juice, did yoga for an hour and went to bed. It was kind of good. But it wasn't a great record. There are some good moments on it.

BILLY RAY: Making *In Violet Light* was one of Gord's 'every song is a novel' moments. He had a stack of rewrites three inches thick. I can still picture him sitting on the outside porch of Compass Point with the ocean crashing in, with this huge pile of papers that could have been three albums' worth of stuff but was just the one song.

JOHNNY: One Sunday, which was always a day off, I met Hugh on the beach. We walked together for a while and he said, 'Your singer said he was going to change some of the lyrics and he's gone and changed them all. What's that all about?' He wasn't used to that. When Sting said to him that he was going to change some lyrics it would just be an 'and' and a 'the', not the whole lot.

British producers have a very strict way of going about things. You do the tracking and then you finish the mix and when it's done it's done. You can't jump in and change things once the record's been stitched up. Hugh didn't understand that Gord couldn't sing it if he wasn't feeling it. I don't think that those two gelled.

From that point, Hugh became uninvested in the project and just really wanted to finish the record and move on. But I loved working with him. He was a drum producer and he had a very precise miking technique. This was a guy who had worked with Stewart Copeland on two of his biggest records and so I asked him a lot about that.

ROB: Hugh was a funny guy to work with. He hated guitar solos. He said to me, 'I hate it when you play a guitar solo. It sounds so country and western.' You just take the shit in your stride, smile, swallow, carry on.

PAUL: It was a good experience and a nice studio, nice people. I look at that record pretty fondly.

PAUL: 'The Dark Canuck' is a particularly out-there bunch of lyrics. Some people like it a lot, but we didn't play it too much. It did seem sometimes feel that Gord was trying to jam these pre-set words into a space that didn't quite fit. I remember Hugh Padgham commenting the odd time, 'What is he on about?' A classic Brit thing. It was a tough song to sing to.

I had a little incident with Hugh when I was trying to sing back-ups on 'The Dark Canuck', and it was insane. After I did the first take on that track, Hugh said to me, 'What was that?' I said that I was just trying to get comfortable. He came back with something offensive and I stormed out. But we made up later.

The Dark Canuck — 1

This one is for you
and it goes on and on and on
when nothing seems to do
for when the doubtless and the wrong
ask, 'can I help you?'
in that way that says; ' I can't'
or claim we're all the same
just inconsistent
or pretend all understanding
turned out to be pretense
then pretend the pretense of understanding.
'how long does it take' - depends

you can cast your doubts
turn em inside-out
hang em upside-down
til their art falls out - BV(the short answer's; 48 hours)
let your heart all out - BV(the short answer's; 48 hours)
til your art falls out - BV(the short answer's; 48 hours)
let your heart all out - Summon up your power

if you need a good connection for drugs
or a strong tolerance for alcohol
too little religious education
some pain threshold
if from the outside
there's no demand for what you do
and inside there's an army waiting
for their marching orders from you
come sit on my swing-seat
come sit on my porch
after 10 at night, smoke your cigarettes if you like -of course

you can cast your doubts
turn em inside-out
hang em upside-down
til their art falls out - (the short answer's 48 hours)
let your heart all out - (the short answer's 48 hours)
til the art falls out - (the short answer's 48 hours)
let your heart all out - Summon up your power

and it goes on and on and on

In Violet Light promo photo, April 2000

Lyrics for 'The Dark Canuck' and 'Use It Up' (this page), and 'Leave' under its working title 'Bird' (opposite)

USE IT UP – (6D Gtr)

Use it up - Use it all up - Don't save a thing for later. yea

#1 If there's music out there laying in wait.
to pounce and drain every ounce if you wait or hesitate.

#2 and music that'll help you be tough
and come together on more than Springsteen. though most days
it's been enough yea

Then there's music that can take you away - away, away, away
Break -

So use it up, use it all up - don't save a thing for later
use it up, use it all up - don't save a thing for later

#3 If there's music out there staying awake.
to cry and drain every eye until hatred's eliminated
and music that can help you feel great
and write som come together in the fictive dream with a
kinda Randy Newman take - yea

E.A Then there's music that can take you away, away, away, away

Bridge - Where we can jump to our feet agape - cause nothing is cruel
and even if it is or was - indefatigueably cruel.
we don't care because... yer a fool - and I'm a fool
yer a fool and I'm a fool.

For music that can take you away.
music that can take you away.
music that can take you away.
music that can take you away.
so use it up
use it all up
don't save a thing for later

PAUL: 'Use It Up' – those words came pretty easily to Gord. Some songs you don't have to beat up or tear apart or rethink or mess with. But some songs you do, because you haven't got to where you wanted to get, so you keep trying. Gord did that a lot. It was an obsession, but in a good way.

With 'Use It Up' I remember thinking at the time there was something there, that it was a cool concept. He used that phrase sometimes to describe what he felt we should do, which was basically use everything we had. Don't save it. Let's record it now and put it out. It was kind of his mantra, really.

JOHNNY: When we went to the Bahamas, Hugh just tracked different versions of the songs we'd already demoed with Mark Vreeken and I think the demos for that record are way better.

Gord recorded a vocal for 'Leave' on the morning of 9/11, just after he'd watched what everyone else watched. He sang about the twin towers and terrorism, and then he never sang those lyrics again. I think they were too personal. But they're there on the demo.

GORD S: One of the biggest fights Gord and I ever had was during *In Violet Light* about 'Leave'. It was written from the perspective of a bird, and the lyrical denouement of the song was 'Where there's love there's hope,' but at the last minute Gord wanted to change 'love' to 'worms'. I get the analogy that if you're a bird it's worms that are your sustenance, but the original lyric resonates more universally. Hugh tasked me with getting it changed back.

We duked it out down in the Bahamas over that one and eventually we used the take where Gord sang about love not worms. But he was very angry and he didn't talk to me for about six months after that.

Bird - (Leave)

'Do you mean the attack is routine?'
A bird asked of a bird.
'In this context - a concave nest,
how do we learn to learn to hurt?'

'Do you mean there's no variation?'
watching a dog charge a flock
of birds exploding (in) congregation
"Why plan; when we stop?" (Lowell)

'I dunno...but, why suppose it's not the way it should be?'
When you can fly beyond the Great Waiting List
As the crow implies; 'we won't be missed'
we can leave..
leave
leave

It's a routine flight for this bird tonight
She heard there's more worms than earth in the Afterlife
the blind feed the blind, whistling things like;
'on the money' and 'bulls-eye'
she picks up the little leaves
where human wrecks are taking (to) seed
and re-painting their deities
and plastering away at their villainies
where there's worms..there's hope

'Do you hope those earthbound poets
(could) learn to sing as good as us?'
so we can sit back and enjoy our illusions
and our quietus?'

I dunno...but why suppose it's not the way it should be?
when you can squawk and wait for word from above
and 'change yourself into something you love' (O'Meara)
when you leave
leave
leave

PAUL: A couple of days after coming back from the Bahamas with the material we realised we needed two more songs, so we went into Bath and recorded 'Are You Ready' and 'Silver Jet'. I'm not sure that Gord was a big fan of 'Silver Jet', but we all thought it was a good one and just sealed the deal, ensuring that *In Violet Light* could be up there with the rest of what we like.

GORD S: We did two or three extra tracks with Mark Vreeken and we got a couple of good ones, but Gord was still changing lyrics. He wasn't sure of what he had and where it was going and things were falling into a bit of a 'last thought, best thought' situation.

ROB: 'Silver Jet' and 'Are You Ready' rounded things out, but it still wasn't a super great, focused record.

SILVER JET

There's a still in the night - a tuneless moonlight
Just the I-need-you-and-here's whys of snorin' bords n'Cheryls
there's a heron outside - inviolate light
with an urge to go, & shadow, a heightened air of peril
My heart jumps to and your heart jumps too.
I think to myself - I don't really know my heart
and as you whisper, 'me too.'
Silver Jet - roars over head - rocks the nocturne - all everglade
and grey steer
Silver Jet - so far off already - with an I need to and
here's why - all the way) to Cape Spear.

It's quiet again when a car like Big Ben (with) it's radio
dopplerin; 'and for all you Gregory Peck fans!'
Let us now praise famous men - for puttin' pressure
on the wonderous to Fight and.
Your heart jumps to and my heart jumps too.
I'm thinking to myself - Packing is the secret heart
as if the Wolves of Northumberland, themselves
were coming to the rescue (were rumoured to be en route)
Silver Jet way overhead.
in the archipelagoes with satellites and green stars
Silver Jet - so far off already,
with you I need to and here's why - flying to the next part.
My heart jumps to and your heart jumps too.
I think to myself - always packing is the secret heart
and as you whisper 'me too.' —
Silver Jet - roars overhead (Silver Jet) flying to the next part.
(silver Jet) - so far off already (silver Jet) - a satellite, a green star
(silver Jet) - way overhead (silver Jet) - everglade and gray steer
(silver Jet) - so far off already (silver Jet) - Cape Spear

One of 51 pages of Gord Downie's handwritten lyrics for 'Silver Jet' and one of 10 pages for 'Are You Ready'

ARE YOU READY   Gb.A.
① Hear the ol whistle blowin - they're pulling the plug
we got to get goin' - they got our hole dug.
Are you ready? - are you ready, are you ready to love.

② the Devils in the Blues - smoked to the stub.
Never accept - then accept with a shrug.
Are you ready? - are you ready are you ready to love-
to love - to love - to love - to love

③ So They got safety fifth - and they take the world straight
whatever it is - they'll just have to wait.
to get pretend back - who wants to be tough.
to be permanent - permanent enough.
Are you ready? - Are you ready are you ready to love
to love / to love / to love / to love

In Violet Light
RECORDED: NOVEMBER–DECEMBER 2001
COMPASS POINT, BAHAMAS
PRODUCER: HUGH PADGHAM
ENGINEER: TERRY MANNING
MIXING: HUGH PADGHAM
TERRY MANNING
RELEASED: 11 JUNE 2002

Are You Ready
Use It Up
The Darkest One
It's a Good Life If You Don't Weaken
Silver Jet
Throwing off Glass
All Tore Up
Leave
A Beautiful Thing
The Dire Wolf
The Dark Canuck

*Above: Original painting
by Rob Baker which was
the basis for the cover of
In Violet Light*

*Promo photos for
In Violet Light*

The Tragically Hip

In Violet Light

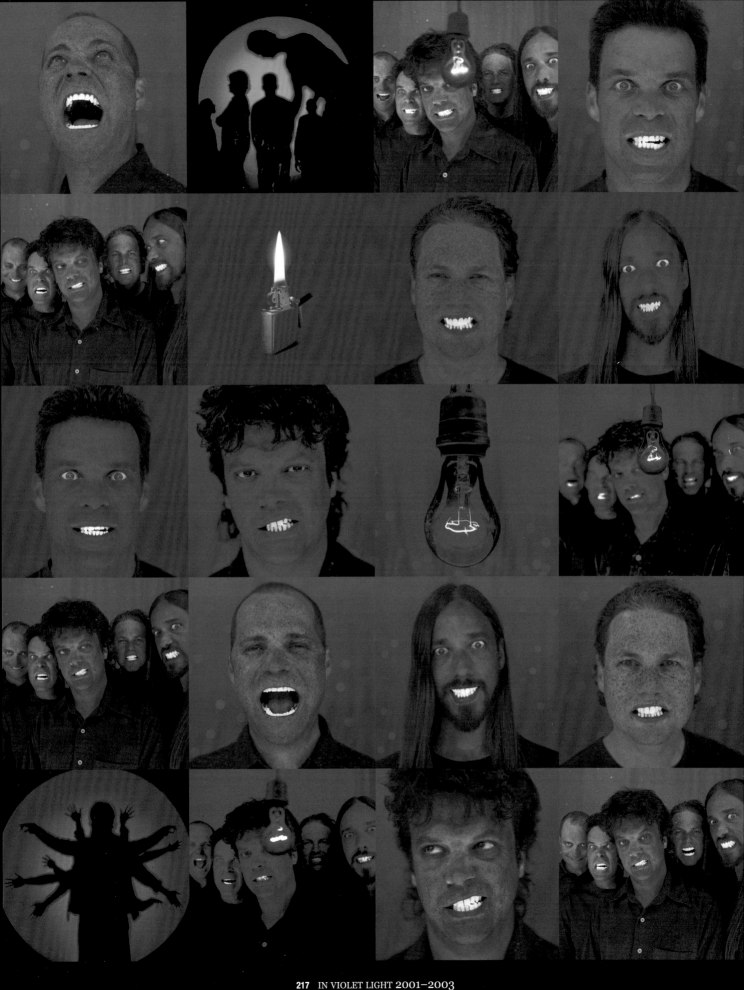

MEN WITH BROOMS

MEDIA ALERT!!! MEDIA ALERT!!! MEDIA ALERT!!! MEDIA ALERT!!!

THE TRAGICALLY HIP ON THE SET OF MEN WITH BROOMS

(Toronto – May 2, 2001) Canadian recording stars The Tragically Hip will be joining the hot cast of the Canadian comedy, *MEN WITH BROOMS* today, Wednesday, May 2nd. Band members Robby Baker, Gord Sinclair, Johnny Fay and Paul Langlois are all avid curler and have had their own Kingston, Ont. based curling team,_____, for years. Lead singer Gord Downie will join his fellow band-mates on set when they make their cameo appearance as a curling club competing for the prestigious Golden Broom. The Tragically Hip's latest CD, MUSIC @ WORK, is distributed by Universal Music.

Written by Paul Gross and John Krizanc and produced by Robert Lantos (*Sunshine, The Sweet Hereafter*), *MEN WITH BROOMS* is a romantic comedy in which four friends reunite after ten years for their former curling coach's funeral. The foursome try to sweep the past behind them to win the coveted Golden Broom championship and bring honour and pride to their small home town.

Starring **Paul Gross** (*Sunshine, Kissed*), **Molly Parker** (*Sunshine, Kissed*), **James Allodi** (*Top of The Food Chain*, TV's "The Associates"), **Kari Matchett** (TV's "Nero Wolf," "Power Play"), **Michelle Nolden** (*Century Hotel*, TV's "Foreign Objects"), **Peter Outerbridge** (*Chasing Cain, Kissed*), **Jed Rees** (*Lake Placid*, TV's "The Chris Isaak Show"), **Polly Shannon** (upcoming *Harvard Man*, "The Sheldon Kennedy Story") and the legendary Leslie Nielsen (*The Naked Gun's* series, *Airplane*), *MEN WITH BROOMS* is a Alliance Atlantis and Serendipity Point Films presentation, in association with Whizbang Films. Alliance Atlantis owns worldwide rights with Serendipity Point Films handling U.S. sales.

***

For more information please contact: Stephanie Keating – unit publicist (416) 516-4170.

MWB PRODUCTIONS INC.
940 Lansdowne Ave., Bldg. 13A, Toronto, ON M6H 3Z4
Tel: (416) 516-4170   Fax: (416) 516-9550

GORD S: *Men with Brooms* was a fun experience. The only problem was that there were five of us and a curling team has four members. Paul, who was a natural athlete and by far the best curler among us, got lost on the way to the shoot, so he missed out on being in the movie entirely.

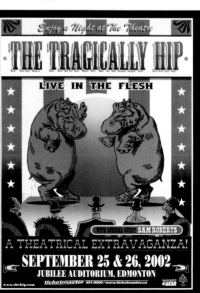

Right: Queen's Golden
Jubilee Gala, Roy
Thomson Hall, Toronto,
10 October 2002

Below: In Violet Light
summer tour, 2002

Bottom: Band and crew
photo, theatre tour,
fall 2002

THE GOLDEN
JUBILEE
GALA

GORD S: We were invited to perform for Queen
Elizabeth and Prince Philip on their Golden Jubilee visit.
My mom and dad were there, for sure. My mom was an
unrepentant monarchist. The picture of me shaking the
Queen's hand was on her piano for the rest of her days.
But for me, truthfully, the most amazing thing about
it was that we were on a bill with Oscar Peterson.
Now there's royalty.

We played 'It's a Good Life' and 'Poets'. Afterwards, in
the receiving line, Prince Philip said to me, 'I'm bloody
deaf after you lot.'

HAMMER IN THE NEW YEAR

THE HAMMER

THE TRAGICALLY HIP
Copps Coliseum
Hamilton, ON
DEC 30 & 31
2002

THE TRAGICALLY HIP

WITH SPECIAL GUESTS SARAH HARMER & SAM ROBERTS

TICKETS AVAILABLE AT ALL TICKETMASTER OUTLETS. COPPS COLISEUM BOX OFFICE
(905) 527-7666 IN HAMILTON OR (416) 870-8000 IN TORONTO
ticketmaster.ca   THE HAMILTON SPECTATOR   www.thehip.com

World Tour

The Tragically Hip
LOCAL CREW

2002

This band began, more or less with one decision - that has spawned many decisions — That songwriting royalties would be split - 5 ways. After that everything—every profit, tangible or intangible ~~cost to all~~ every opportunity, ~~an~~ every hardship, every compliment— would split 5 ways. At th time, there was no way of knowing what that would mean - but the decision ~~it was~~ agreed, ~~provided~~ the best chance of attaining our goal- to create a band. ~~Our goal was~~ to create a band ~~that has~~ been interpreted many ways over th years ~~hasn't changed~~ within and from without — It is elusive and could remain elusive because ~~the goal~~ is happiness and happiness can't be defined by a group, but by individuals who discover, share and timelessly promote happiness within the group. We have in recent years stopped searching - stopped creating our band.

We ~~are~~ slow, top-heavy, dysfunctional - a burden to ourselves. We are starting to become our own worst enemy and maybe even the very picture of ~~the organization~~ we swore we'd never become. We're distrustful of one another and that distrust is coming perilously close to damaging the one pure thing we ~~r~~ made together — a ~~strong~~ strong beating communally creative heart.

We have compartmentalized our roles to the point where our decision-making resembles the worst aspects of a Union mentality. We are spending an unhealthy and increasing amount of time concentrating on the outer speculative vagueness of our business ~~~~ rather than on the inner world of our expertise. We resent each others opinions to the point where in order to avoid resentment - we have stopped listening to one another; ~~a dangerous predicament.~~ if we are

To continue - this must change — much must change. ~~~~ The band needs to re-evaluate, re-energize and most importantly re-create itself. There is undeniably a lot of work to do - in a lot of areas. One of those areas is Management. The band feels it is time to part ways with the Management Trust. We have enjoyed many great times and experiences together but for the reasons stated ~~~~ the band feels - a change and new start will be good - in fact essential for ~~~~ all parties to move toward ~~~~ and perhaps attain, if ~~only~~ briefly, ~~~~ something approximating a definition of happiness.

We hope you understand the effect of the weight of this decision. We love you and respect you. We will miss you and honour the memories of all the many things we built together. We will speak ~~only~~ of you only, ~~~~ in a warm kindly manner - of the things we did, not the things we didn't. ~~in the end~~ is all that matters. ~~we hope that we can still be friends~~

— We intend to take the high road and honour the provisions of our amended contract including its sunset provisions for the payment of your commission

— the band would appreciate if Management Trust would continue to manage the day-to-day affairs of the band during the transition ~~period~~ to new management.

— and that the press/media are kept out of what we feel is our/your personal business — entirely.

— G would like to continue working with you in a full capacity on his/my solo career.

GS: None of us wanted to break the band up, but something had to change. So Jake took the fall, sadly.

ROB: It doesn't matter if you're Scotty Bowman and you have a Stanley Cup ring for every finger and toe, at a certain point you lose the dressing room and there has to be a change. And that's where we'd got to with Jake.

He was doing other things at that point. He wasn't just the manager of a rock band, he was playing at being a music manager on TV. *America's Got Talent*, *The Voice*, I hate that shit. It's always been lurking around in the music industry, like a fucking big turd in the punchbowl, and suddenly our manager's doing it. So that was a problem. It wasn't the only one. Jake can be very pointy. We used to say, 'He's an asshole, but he's our asshole.' Normally, he might have three or four guys in the band really pissed at him at any given time, but he'd always have at least one ally. But this was a moment where we were all on the same page and we decided that it was time to act.

JOHNNY: One night while we were in the Bahamas, Paul and I were sitting drinking Heineken at Jake's little cottage on the north coast. Jake was concerned we didn't have the right amount of material. On previous records, we'd had three or four songs on the radio. Now we were getting one. Jake quipped, 'Feels like the end to me.' And I remember thinking, 'Well, if you think it's the end, it's the end for you. Because it ain't the end for me.'

GORD S: Our tendency as human beings is to allocate blame. So when the business side of things isn't going the way you want it to, you blame the manager. Jake and Allan were aspiring to establish their record company at the time and we maybe felt that Jake was taking his eye off the prize pig. Namely us.

JOHNNY: Jake had moved to New York and we wanted him to have a presence in the States so that we could at least push the yardsticks a little further. We needed an office down there, but Jake had no interest in working with anyone else. He was used to doing things his way.

We held a meeting and talked to Jake about our future. He could see that the writing was on the wall, but he wasn't too happy about it.

To be honest, with our indecision and the time it takes us to come up with things, we burn people out. Jake had got divorced because he put The Hip first and his marriage second. He was Hip-centric. But now he was wanting to do other things. So I think the change was good for all of us.

A week later, Gord turned around and hired Jake as his manager. At the time, it felt like he was throwing the four of us under the bus, making us look like the villains. We were too impassioned and stupid to see the bigger picture, which was that Gord needed someone to manage his solo project. (GS)

JAKE GOLD: I had been negotiating a new deal with the Canadian label, so when the band called a meeting at a hotel in Toronto I thought that's what we were going to be talking about.

When I arrived, there was kind of a sombre tone in the room. Gord sat down next to me at this round table and pulled out a letter, which he started reading. It talked about the band becoming 'slow, top-heavy, dysfunctional, a burden to ourselves' and needing to 'evaluate, reenergise and recreate'. Basically, Gord was saying that they had become so dysfunctional that somebody had to go, but it wasn't going to be any of them. So it had to be me.

It came as a surprise, but I wasn't really pissed off. I was sad, but at the same time it was almost like a weight had been lifted off my shoulders. Because they were right that things were dysfunctional.

PAUL: It was heavy bananas at the time, particularly for Jake. He took it well, although he was upset, of course. He was very loyal and did a lot of great things for us. It was a tricky meeting for us all. We maintained being friendly whenever we saw him. We just didn't see him as much.

ROB: After a lot of wrangling over who should manage us and no consensus, Johnny suggested we meet with Sam Feldman. We met in a hotel room and talked about our situation for over two hours. At the end of it Sam agreed to take us on. We said, 'We'll contact our lawyer and have him write up something and ...' Sam interjected and said, 'We just did that. Now we shake hands. If at any point things aren't working out we'll go out for a meal, talk honestly, and if we can't resolve our problems we'll shake hands and walk away.' We shook hands. Sam was now our manager.

A few years later when it was time to move on, we went out for a meal, spoke honestly, shook hands and moved on. A truly rare and honourable man.

JOHNNY: I wanted to stay with a Canadian manager. Sam managed Joni Mitchell and Norah Jones, so he was pretty plugged in. We were going to move agencies and he was also an agent group, which was exciting to us. He said we weren't going to do anything crazy big right off the bat, but then we played SARSFest at the Skydome, which was huge.

We weren't with Sam for very long. He didn't like that Gord was still with Jake for his solo stuff and I think Jake was double-booking Gord a little bit. I don't blame Sam. We were at the lower end of the totem pole for him and he didn't need the aggravation.

CDs and cassette tapes of songs and song ideas recorded February–March and October–December 2003 for The Tragically Hip's ninth studio album, In Between Evolution

Opposite: Recording In Between Evolution, Studio X, Seattle, 2003

1 ballroom hanging 04:05
2 dance steps 03:42
3 life is forgetting 02:54
4 painting is my guess 03:10
5 as make shift as we are 04:15
6 fighter fighter 03:48
7 custom hitches 03:52
8 are we family 04:48
9 josephine 03:38
10 vaccination scar 04:08
11 beautiful you/nowhere else 02:44
12 gus 05:19
13 cooking in wartime 04:00
14 copenhagen 02:21
15 new orleans is beat 03:25
16 bracelet falls away 02:50

JOHNNY: Sam Feldman brought us out to Whistler to do some writing sessions. We met Adam Kasper while we were out there and Sam thought he'd be a great guy to produce the next record, *In Between Evolution*.

ROB: We knew of Adam Kasper through his work with Nirvana and Pearl Jam. He was different from how we thought he would be. We were expecting him to be like a Marine, but he seemed more like he might be in the CIA. He had this no-nonsense vibe to him.

Seattle in December and January was dark. There were maybe three days that it didn't rain in the whole two months we were there. You walked with your hat pulled down and your shoulders hunched up, looking at the ground. And even if there had been any sun, the studio was a windowless room inside a room inside a room. We got some good work done, but I think it's an inconsistent record. It had a more aggressive sound than a lot of our other albums. I don't know if that's where we were at or where Adam was at, or a combination of the two.

GS: There's a reason that grunge came out of Seattle: it's called January.

JOHNNY: Adam was a good guy to be with. He kept things interesting, although it was a little confusing at times. We'd go into a studio, then he'd send us away for a couple of days and when we came back he'd be at a different studio. We were living in these crazy little two-storey bunkers with a coffee maker and a bed upstairs. There was no cell phone service and it rained all the time. I love Seattle, but it rains a lot.

We would just go to the studio and then go home. That record seemed to take a while to make. There was a lot of back and forth.

PAUL: As great as things were in the studio for *In Between Evolution*, our living situation in Seattle wasn't ideal. We were in this massive apartment building and none of us ever knew what apartments the other guys were in. We had Sundays off, but we never got together once.

Every night we'd get in the elevator, go to our different floors and then we wouldn't see each other until we were in the studio at noon the next day. Sundays, I'd just go out and get something to eat and watch football, and I was recording every night on my laptop. I'm assuming that the other guys were doing the same thing. So there was a certain kind of on-your-own vibe about making that album, for sure.

GORD S: *In Between Evolution* was another one like *In Violet Light* where we came out of the studio not knowing if we had a record. We actually reconvened with Adam at another studio to record a couple more tracks. There were some great songs on that album, but there were a couple of stinkers too.

PAUL: Studio X was great, the city was cool and Adam Kasper was a great producer and a great guy. We were feeling good and we were getting along well. We were recording six days a week, noon 'til midnight. I remember that we were playing particularly well, like we knew these songs better for some reason.

I like how that record was mixed. I like that I can hear the good playing and the band sounds tight. There were very few overdubs, fewer than on a lot of records.

I like the collection of songs. I wouldn't say it's our strongest batch, but it's a good batch. Gord didn't really like 'Vaccination Scar'. I think that he had a problem with some part of the lyrics, but I really thought that one jumped out of the speakers. 'Heaven Is a Better Place Today' is a nice, quick rocker. That's a Johnny idea, a good one.

We actually went to a different studio outside Seattle for a switch up. We didn't even stay over there, just went for the day and recorded 'Are We Family' and maybe one other song.

ROB: We all really liked 'Vaccination Scar', but Gord hated it. He couldn't get his head around the lyrics.

Adam used to invite Eddie Vedder over to the studio and he and Gord would play basketball and hang out. One day Eddie told Gord that Adam had been playing him some of the songs we were working on and that he loved 'Vaccination Scar' and thought it was one of the best Hip songs he'd ever heard. Gord was like, 'Really? You liked that one?' It ended up on the record. So thank you, Eddie!

BILLY RAY: Every Tuesday, Gord would play basketball with Eddie Vedder and his gang. One night, Eddie came to the studio with Mexican wrestling masks. He was wearing one when he got there and he gave another one to Gord. I wish I'd taken a picture of Eddie Vedder and Gord Downie sitting on the couch at Studio X, listening to the record while wearing Mexican wrestling masks. They had them on for the whole night.

Eddie stopped Pearl Jam's show on the final night of the final Hip tour to send love up to Canada. That was a pretty special moment. The guys from Pearl Jam definitely had a real appreciation for The Hip.

Lyrics for 'Vaccination Scar', 'It Can't Be Nashville Every Night', 'As Makeshift as We Are', 'If New Orleans Is Beat', 'One Night in Copenhagen', 'You're Everywhere' (working title 'Ballroom') and 'Goodnight Josephine'

'It Can't Be Nashville Every Night' is a great Hip song. It encapsulated what we did our entire career. Every gig was a big gig, even when it was a shit gig. We always had that work ethic. We opened that tour a bunch with 'Vaccination Scar', but we should have used 'Nashville'. It's a wicked tune and I used to love playing it. (GS)

ROB: *In Between Evolution* was the culmination of Gord writing and rewriting lyrics in the studio. If you looked through his stack, you might find 100 sheets of the same lyric. Sometimes it felt like days went by where nothing happened, because we were waiting for him to sing. It started to get to Adam and he looked like he was coming unglued in front of us.

It was frustrating for all of us. At the time, I thought there was maybe an element of power play in it – an 'I'll sing when I'm ready' kind of thing. But now I wonder if there were physical, emotional, mental things going on. Some early sign of things to come. I don't know. I just know that it was a behaviour that seemed to be taking root and was odd.

Part of it may have been that Gord was becoming interested in other forms of writing than just song lyrics and he was trying to push lyric writing maybe further than it would go. Songs can exist for a lot of different reasons, but when you try to be deliberately artistic you can get in the weeds pretty fast. Successful rock songs go for your heart, your crotch, your gut. They don't try to seduce your auditory nerves or tickle your hypothalamus.

GORD S: When we were making *In Between Evolution*, Gord set this rule for himself where he was going to introduce a word in every song that had never been used in any other song lyric. Maybe William S. Burroughs would think that was a great idea, but it goes way over the head of the average music listener. I just thought that instead of following this arbitrary rule, why not find the right word? It was art and craft crashing into each other.

JOHNNY: I think Gord was feeling the weight of people hanging on every word and trying to decipher things – like they did with Jim Morrison. He always said, 'Everybody needs an editor.' But maybe he was editing himself too much. He'd write a really great lyric and then he'd change it all and it would disintegrate.

GORD S: I think Gord always thought we had it pretty easy, that we would just bash out our tunes, get a great take and then celebrate together by drinking 100 beers, while he was chained to his desk trying to find a word that rhymes with orange.

In Between Evolution
RECORDED:
DECEMBER 2003–JANUARY 2004
STUDIO X, SEATTLE, WA
BEAR CREEK STUDIOS, WOODINVILLE, WA
PRODUCER: ADAM KASPER
ENGINEER: SAM HOFSTEDT
MIXING: ADAM KASPER
RELEASED: 29 JUNE 2004

Heaven Is a Better Place Today
Summer's Killing Us
Gus: The Polar Bear from Central Park
Vaccination Scar
It Can't Be Nashville Every Night
If New Orleans Is Beat
You're Everywhere
As Makeshift as We Are
Mean Streak
The Heart of the Melt
One Night in Copenhagen
Are We Family
Goodnight Josephine

JOHNNY: *In Between Evolution* was part of a kind of mid-career slump. I'd say we might not have been ready to go into the studio. There wasn't any pressure from the record company, but we knew they needed a record from us and we had to go in and do it. If there was any pressure, we put it on ourselves. That group of three records starting with *Music @ Work*, we were just squirrelling around with no direction.

GEDDY LEE: The middle years are the toughest because each musician has their own ideas and has maybe a bit too much confidence in their own ideas. So personalities can butt heads, and that's when you can disagree on a more serious level.

The Hip skirted that dangerous period. I think pressure brings something else out in you and either you can rise to it or be crushed by it. A good, healthy, creative mind can benefit from that even at the worst times.

The In Between Evolution *cover art was by Cameron Tomsett, who also produced the band portrait (centre right) that was used to promote the album*

ROB: We'd always been adamant that we weren't going to stop and look over our shoulder and see where we'd been. We wanted to keep pushing forward always. But *Hipeponymous* was one where we agreed to do a 'best of'. Instead of doing a greatest hits record, we thought we'd put it out to the fans and let them pick the songs they wanted. And that turned out well.

GORD D: I wanted to make sure the package was as forward-looking as it could possibly be, but, as a good friend of mine says, every now and then you have to stop the tractor and look back at the field you just ploughed.

Hipeponymous / Yer Favourites
RELEASED: 1 & 8
NOVEMBER 2005

Hipeponymous is a limited edition box set, containing a two-CD compilation titled Yer Favourites, *a full-length concert DVD recorded on 26 November 2004 at the Air Canada Centre titled* That Night in Toronto, *and a DVD of bonus features. These include all of the band's music videos, a backstage documentary titled* Macroscopic, *and a short film titled* The Right Whale, *which features 11 visual vignettes set to new original scores written by the band. The box set is packaged in a 48-page hardbound book depicting various Hip memorabilia*

Yer Favourites contains tracks selected by Hip fans on its website and remastered. It also includes two new songs, 'No Threat' and 'The New Maybe'. It was released both as part of the Hipeponymous box set and as a standalone two-disc set

the tragically hip

YER FAVOURITES

the tragically hip

YER FAVOURITES

CDR74Gold   650 MB/74 minute CD-R 1x-8x

	MUSIC FOR DVD	4/19/05
1	FISH	
2	MARVIN/HIDE AND SEEK - SUBWAY	
3	ECHOSPACE/SKY BUILDING·COOKING	
4	PAUL 2 EYES/STRANGER OF THE KING	
5	OPEN G · THE RIGHT WHALE · SNOW	
6	PAUL 4	
7	BHOOP	
8	PAUL 1 · DR.VING@NIGHT·EDIBLE PAPER	
9	SONG 3 (MEN w/BROOMS) DRIVING #2/MIND FAME	
10	SCREEN 1	
	SPEAKER SONG/NoYORK DENISE	

The Right Whale

late perception equals late response equals abrupt response.
If you change your mind - no problem.
If you live too long - no problem.
If you're sure they've stopped wondering about you by now-
   no problem. - go to sleep...dream.
   sound-dive to your Forever place
no one on earth is doing this now.
yea, Sleep..dream- leave the black counter-top
   the blood-stars and the ~~long~~ great blonde moon.
there'll be some more blowing and drifting while
you sleep.
   Sleep, dream and awake
     to a virtual fraud of a morning-
a world with a care
a world dark but for some laggard stars.
and the post-ponement of the great blonde rose
over there.
the water emptied of spectacular accidents
a world without a care.
Awake..
   taken.
   sentenced to Paradise
   nobody's casualty-
    nobody. these,

Above: Sessions at the Bathouse that provided two new songs for the Hipeponymous/ Yer Favourites package, 2005

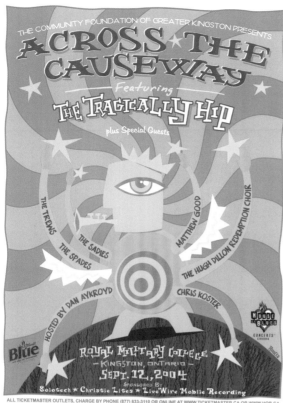

JOHNNY: By now we had a lot of material to choose from and Gord insisted on changing the set list every night. But he always wanted to focus on the new stuff. He'd have us play the whole of the new record before we played one song from *Road Apples* or *Up to Here*. I was always of the thought that you can't trick people to come and see you on the strength of those records and then play a bunch of B-sides. I didn't like playing the same set every night, but there were certain songs that we had to play every night. You've got to keep it interesting for you, but you've also got to keep it interesting for the people who are coming to see you.

PATRICK SAMBROOK: When Bernie Breen and I started managing the band, part of our job was to bring them back to arenas. I think they always thought that's where they should be, and it didn't take long to get them there.

Gord loved playing arenas and being back in the bigger spotlight, but he didn't want to have to do the bigger gestures. We found a way to make an arena performance intimate by using screens, so people could see his subtleties. It meant that he could keep his performance a little bit tighter and he didn't have to be the dancing monkey, as he often described himself.

Canada tour, 2004

ROB: After we fired Jake, we were with Sam Feldman for a few years and he was really important in keeping our heads above water. When we came out of that arrangement we hired Bernie Breen and Patrick Sambrook, largely because Gord wanted Patrick and we wanted Bernie and so we compromised and got both.

PATRICK SAMBROOK: Bernie Breen and I shared an office, but we had our own clients. We got this call asking us what we thought about managing The Hip together. This was my favourite band in the world, so to have the opportunity to be their manager was nuts. We went down to the Bathouse during the early days of making *World Container*. We sat down in the kitchen and Robbie said to us, 'OK, what's your plan?'

TRISTIN CHIPMAN: Patrick and Bernie offered a very personalised and warm relationship. They were people that the guys would hang out with around campfires at parties. I think that appealed to the band, even if it didn't bring a promise of huge stardom.

BERNIE BREEN: Our official pitch meeting was awkward because we were friends with the guys. We were very confident, as we'd been around the block and had made our way with other artists. I think, in hindsight, that we were a good, logical choice.

PATRICK SAMBROOK: It was not lost on Bernie or myself that this was a very successful band. People have always asked me what it was like to be given the keys to the Cadillac. However, when we came on board the band was in a natural dip. They had been on such a historically high level, but that was impossible to maintain.

BERNIE BREEN: They were getting ready for the next phase. They'd had this huge success in the early Nineties when they'd become Canada's band, but what were their goals now? We talked about everything, including the rest of the world and certainly the next record, which Bob Rock had committed to making. That was very exciting for us, as Bob Rock is a legend.

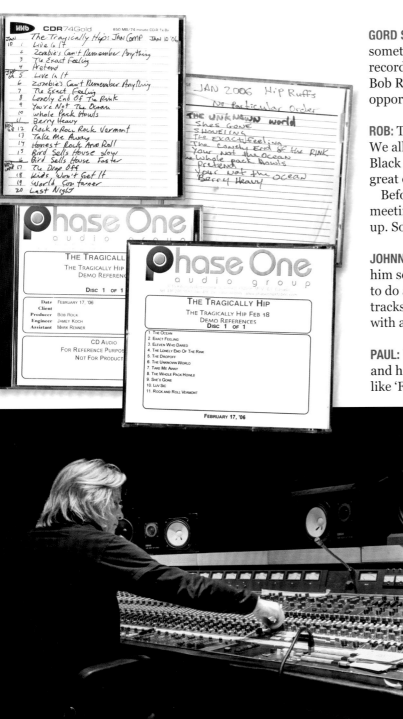

GORD S: We were at another juncture where we needed to bring in something new. We'd had a fun time making the previous two records, but they didn't really have many stand-out singles on them. Bob Rock was a certified hit-maker, so we jumped at the opportunity to work with him.

ROB: The thought of working with Bob Rock had come up before. We all loved the Mötley Crüe album *Dr. Feelgood* and Metallica's Black Album. He made great sounding records and knew how to get great drum sounds.

Before Patrick and Bernie took over, Sam Feldman had set up a meeting between Bob and Gord and Gord came back very charged up. So we started working with Bob and things moved fast.

JOHNNY: Gord had gone over to Bob's place in Hawaii and shown him some demos. Then we flew out to Vancouver and met with Bob to do a week's session to see if it was going to work. We got some tracks then and there. It was really exciting to be working in Canada with a big Canadian producer.

PAUL: We started strong with Bob and he had it sounding good. Songs like 'Family Band', 'World Container' and 'Yer Not the Ocean' definitely had a bit of muscle. Bob was quite reserved in the studio but confident, and everyone took notice of what he had to say.

BOB ROCK: As soon as I met Gord we made a connection, so I was very into doing the record.

JOHNNY: Bob was definitely a triple threat. He was an engineer. He was a producer. And he was a musician. He got bands, because he'd been in one himself. I remember seeing him in The Payolas when I was younger. So he was the guy.

BOB ROCK: Like every great band, The Hip had its own sound. If you took any one of those players out of the picture, it wouldn't be the same. Gord was very important in that, being the voice. The thing that always stood out to me, besides their groove and feel, was Gord's lyrics. I think he's comparable to the greats. He wrote about and found the beauty in Canada; he's about as Canadian as it gets.

GORD D: Bob was the right man at the right time. He was a very focusing influence on the group. In rehearsals, he went around to each of the guys suggesting ways to make the songs more interesting. I think he was really jazzed that whatever he asked for, the band could deliver. These guys in The Hip are very agile, which maybe I'd forgotten.

He was interested in showing people what our influences were. As a band, you engage in this dogged pursuit of your own sound and, in the process, you tuck all those influences under the hem of the garment. But it's fun to go back to the music you loved in your youth and recognise your place in the grand scheme of rock.

BOB ROCK: I don't know what they were expecting with me. I'm not what you would call a record company kind of producer. Coming from being an artist myself, I respect a band's sound and I just try to bring that out.

Opposite: Amsterdam, Netherlands, July 2006

This page: Bob Rock, Phase One, Toronto, 2 March 2006

CDs of tracks for World Container recorded at Phase One, Toronto, January and February 2006

JOHNNY: Bob Rock doesn't do anything miniature. When you get in the studio with him, you put the drums up, you get the guitars going, and then you listen to it and it sounds ginormous.

Bob had an incredible work ethic, like nobody I've ever known. His dad had passed away and he phoned me up and said he was going to go to the funeral service and then he'd meet me at the studio afterwards to work on drum sounds. I told him he didn't need to do that, but he insisted. So he sat there and mixed for a couple of hours, just silently doing his thing. He had limited time to work on projects, so he didn't fluff around.

I loved sitting with Bob and picking his brain. You could ask him anything about sonics and he'd explain it all to you. Like the way he tuned the guitars a little bit flat, because he was already thinking ahead to the mix when he was going to put them through a processor. I don't know that the other guys liked that, but he had everything sculpted the way he wanted it to sound on the record.

ROB: We were pretty impressed by Bob's bag of tricks out of the gate – miking techniques for the drums and little arrangement ideas – and we liked the fact that he didn't auto-tune everything or cut to the grid so that every beat was perfectly in place. He said that songs were supposed to speed up and slow down, and we absolutely agreed. So we were thinking that this was the guy for us.

GORD S: Bob was very much in charge. It was his record and he was going to make it his way. It dawned on me fairly quickly that he was a 'build the tracks up' kind of guy. So he'd work with each of us individually to draw the parts out. Get a good drum take, build onto that, and so on.

The sounds that Bob was getting were fantastic. He's a great engineer, both in terms of old-school set-up and working with Pro Tools. But it also became fairly obvious that Bob employed a kind of divide and conquer approach to extract performances from the band. And the principal performance that he was hoping to extract was from Gord. It was all about trying to get Gord to make the best record that Gord could make.

ROB: Bob had a way of sussing out who the key man was and carving them off. He was very much like that with Gord. We've never had a producer come in who so blatantly whispered shit to one guy that was hurtful to band relationships. As an example, there was a thing with our tuning. We tuned to 440 Hz, which was standard pitch the world over. Some singers as they age tune down a semitone to make it easier for them to hit the high notes. So Bob was saying to Gord that any band that respected their singer would tune down to 430. But no one asked us to tune down in the first place.

BILLY RAY: I had to explain to Bob Rock that The Hip was five guys and Gord was not the leader of the band, but Bob was saying that the other guys weren't the ones who wrote the hit songs and that they should be recognising Gord's artistry. It was like he was saying they should just be happy to be along for the ride.

BOB ROCK: Working with me was different from the way they'd worked before. Not to say that what I did was better, I'm just saying it was different and some people don't like change. Maybe before, some members of the band got more attention.

ROB: Bob wouldn't let me tune my own guitar. He had to do it himself, because that way he knew it was in tune. I thought, 'Are you for real?'

He didn't like Paul's voice or Gord Sinclair's voice. He didn't like Gord's approach to bass playing, which was very melodic. Gord's a superb bass player with a unique style that kind of evolved from Andy Fraser from Free with a bit of Paul McCartncy thrown in. But Bob wanted him to play quarter notes and eighth notes to leave more room for guitar overdubs. He had a profound lack of understanding about what we did as a band. He wanted us to be a different band than we were.

GORD S: I've played with the guys my whole life, so I know I can find holes to put melodies in. Bob was a guitar player, so his perspective was that all the melodic elements should come from the guitar. He thought that the bass should just be 'chunk, chunk, chunk, chunk' – nothing but note foundations. They weren't the most creatively satisfying sessions that I've been involved with.

JOHNNY: We're not great communicators, we sweep things under the rug. So I didn't always know how the other guys were feeling. Everyone took away something different from every session.

Really good producers get the lay of the land pretty quick. Bob maybe felt that we were fine as a band and that he didn't need to change too much playing-wise, but he saw that Gord needed help and direction and so he focused on him. That was my take on it anyway.

GD: I tried to be more succinct on this record. That's the logical conclusion of the road I've been on for a long time – of trying to be a better writer and a better singer.

GORD D: Most producers treat the singer the way hockey coaches treat the goalie: 'You guys, go there and stretch. You guys, go to the pylons. And you, fatty, you stop the puck.' I'm a goalie too, so I accept it, but I always felt a bit lonely in the studio. I don't think anybody feels lonely around Bob.

BERNIE BREEN: Bob really gravitated to Gord, and Gord to him. Gord gave himself to whoever he was working with, at whatever level and for whatever it may have been. If it was the guy flipping the burger, Gord would work with that guy to make that burger the best fuckin' burger the guy could make.

JOHNNY: Bob was someone that Gord really trusted. When Gord was wanting to change a lyric, Bob would let him go down that path but then show him that what he'd already done was really great and suggest combining the two. So he let Gord have the freedom, but he also directed him in a certain way. I don't think anyone else had really invested the time in Gord that Bob did. That was really good for Gord, because it made him realise that he still had it.

Phase One, Toronto,
2 March 2006

ROB: The title track started with a long poem that Gord had written. I was lucky that I had a little piece of guitar music that he was able to recite his poem over. That evolved into a song and Bob brought in a really great piano player he knew. He was just warming up and he started going through Bowie tunes like 'Aladdin Sane', so we hit it off with this guy. Having a stranger play with us, we were always on our best behaviour.

JOHNNY: 'In View' is a great song to play and it did well for us too. The video was really cool, but I didn't know until recently that while Gord was shooting it he was running hard and he tripped and fell and hit his head pretty hard. I think he was concussed after that.

PATRICK SAMBROOK: The impact of 'In View' was considerable. The keyboards and vocals were not something you would have heard on other Tragically Hip songs. That turned off some fans, but it also turned on others and it attracted a lot more women to the band. The song crossed over to other formats that weren't just rock, which was also good.

GORD D: I've stumbled on the idea of writing about love lately. I'd been kind of avoiding it all those years, probably because I didn't trust myself to not lapse into sappy sentimentality. In my line of work, sentimentality is really, really dangerous. So I was coming at a lot of songs from the head, not the heart. But since I've started writing about love, I've realised it's the taking a crack at it that's the important thing, not necessarily the understanding of it.

GORD S: The culmination of Bob's divide and conquer approach was Gord going out to his place in Maui for months to work on the vocals. I was in the middle of a divorce at the time, so I couldn't go, but Paul was there.

PAUL: Recording *World Container* was a very positive experience, which was what I was expecting. The mixing phase in Maui, which is where Bob lives and has a studio, I didn't enjoy as much. I was out there basically on my own for four or five weeks, waiting for Gord to finish the vocals so that I could do the back-ups. It was crazy-making to sit on the driveway in the car because there was no room in the studio, waiting for 12 hours a day, and not get called until the last week.

There was a perception that Bob was almost trying to put a wedge in between Gord and the rest of the band. Maybe Gord felt a bit isolated and leaned on Bob because of that. Bob said to me that he thought we should treat our singer better. But when you create a situation where the singer has to go to Maui and the rest of the band (except me) doesn't, well, of course that's going to make Gord feel isolated.

JOHNNY: I think Gord needed Paul out there, but Paul didn't like just hanging around. If he was working, he was working. If he wasn't working, he wanted to be with his family or playing golf. So Paul was parked there and it wasn't pleasant for him, but somehow he managed to keep the peace and keep things rolling.

Lyrics for 'World Container' and 'In View'

Opposite: Draft album artwork for World Container *(top)*

PATRICK SAMBROOK: As with some of their previous records, there was a goal with *World Container*, which was to make The Tragically Hip a global phenomenon. I don't think that was lost on Bob Rock. Bob made some changes that some of the other guys in the band did not connect with, and took things to a place they weren't comfortable with. Gord sang differently on that record and changed lyrics for Bob, so he was very invested in doing what it would take to expose the band's music to a larger audience.

GORD S: Bob really helped Gord regain his songwriting confidence and got him back into the discipline of crafting lyrics that fit within the structure of meter and melody. But having this exterior force dividing the unit was a problem, and it got worse on the next record.

World Container
RECORDED: SEPTEMBER 2005
FEBRUARY–APRIL 2006
THE BATHOUSE, BATH, ON
PHASE ONE, TORONTO, ON
THE WAREHOUSE, VANCOUVER,
BC, ARMOURY, VANCOUVER, BC
PLANTATION RECORDING,
MAUI, HI
PRODUCER: BOB ROCK
ENGINEERS: JAMEY KOCH
ERIC HELMKAMP, BOB ROCK
MIXING: JENS
RELEASED: 17 OCTOBER 2006

Yer Not the Ocean
The Lonely End of the Rink
In View
Fly
Luv (Sic)
The Kids Don't Get It
Pretend
Last Night I Dreamed You
Didn't Love Me
The Drop-Off
Family Band
World Container

PATRICK SAMBROOK: We did things for *World Container* that we didn't ever do again, which included getting Gord to go across the country co-hosting morning radio shows. He would never have done that before and he never did it again, but he did it then – and, of course, he was great at it.

It was hard to look at the record commercially because the music industry was changing. It was about the impact it had on the fans. It got more American radio play than we had received in the past. It was a step back into the spotlight for the band in Canada. Multiple number one singles.

PAUL: *World Container* took some flak for being over-produced. I think Bob gets that sometimes. But I didn't agree. The title track was one of my favourites. I think it's kind of cool. Overall, in my opinion, the album stands up pretty well.

ROB: It was probably our best record since *Phantom Power*. Maybe it lacked for really great songs, but it was focused and it sounded good.

World Container debuted at number two on the Canadian Albums Chart, selling 27,000 copies in its first week, and was certified Platinum in Canada within a month of its release

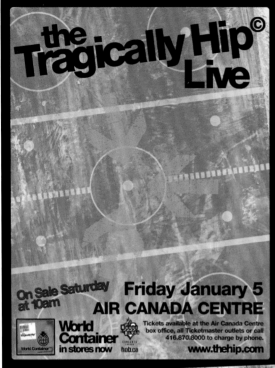

PATRICK SAMBROOK: Every night on the World Container tour was different. I remember our agent coming down to one of the shows. Afterwards, he looked at Bernie and me and said, 'Wow. What's happening? They didn't play a single hit.' They wanted to challenge the audience and play them songs that they'd never heard before.

Luckily the fans were still into it, but not to the same extent. The Hip's biggest records had their own life, but their less commercial records were equally good and needed to be heard. Gord would almost over-perform the new or more obscure songs to try and win people over.

GORD S: I thought *World Container* was a really strong record and it was a great record to tour. Songs like 'The Drop-Off' and 'Yer Not the Ocean' lent themselves well to The Hip's live show, whereas a bunch of the songs on the previous two or three records were tough to play live.

World Container tour,
summer 2006

Sudbury Community
Arena, Greater Sudbury,
ON, 27 January 2007

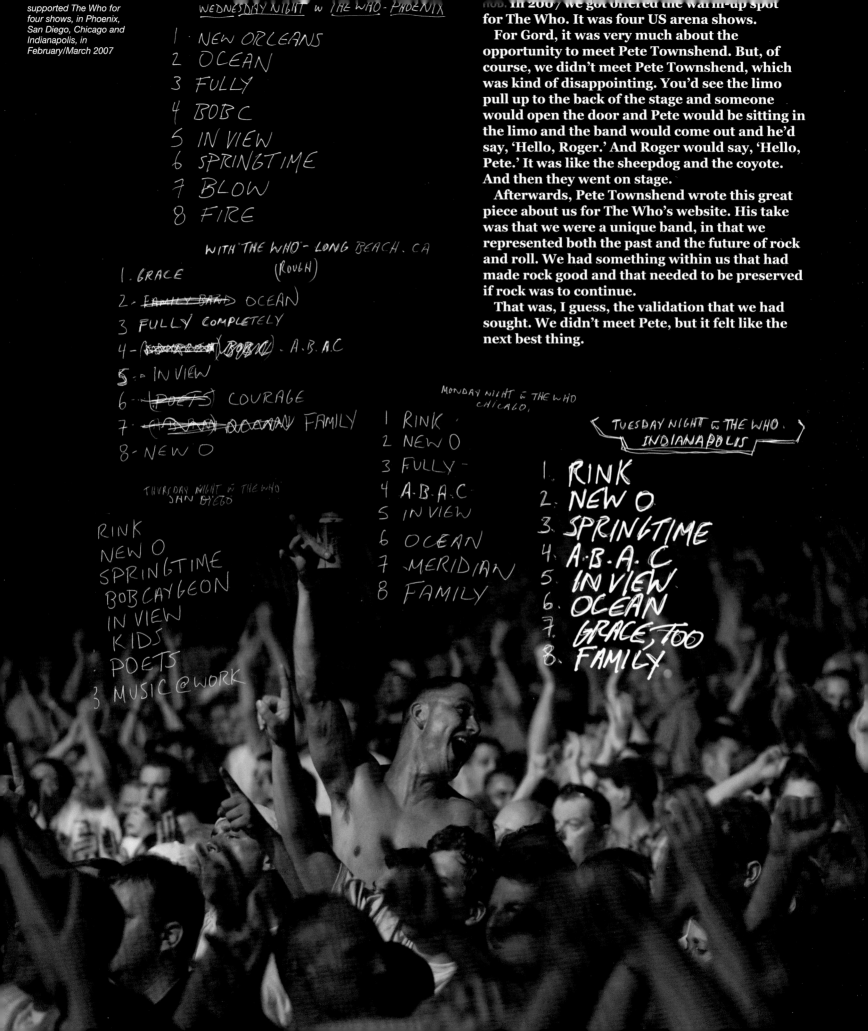

supported The Who for four shows, in Phoenix, San Diego, Chicago and Indianapolis, in February/March 2007

WEDNESDAY NIGHT w THE WHO - PHOENIX

1. NEW ORLEANS
2. OCEAN
3. FULLY
4. BOB C
5. IN VIEW
6. SPRINGTIME
7. BLOW
8. FIRE

WITH THE WHO - LONG BEACH, CA
(ROUGH)
1. GRACE
2. ~~FAMILY BAND~~ OCEAN
3. FULLY COMPLETELY
4. ~~(xxxxxxx)~~ ~~(BOBX)~~ . A.B.A.C
5. IN VIEW
6. ~~(POETS)~~ COURAGE
7. ~~(xxxx) xxxxx~~ FAMILY
8. NEW O

THURSDAY NIGHT w THE WHO
SAN DIEGO

RINK
NEW O
SPRINGTIME
BOBCAYGEON
IN VIEW
KIDS
POETS
3 MUSIC @ WORK

MONDAY NIGHT w THE WHO
CHICAGO,

1 RINK
2 NEW O
3 FULLY
4 A.B.A.C
5 IN VIEW
6 OCEAN
7 MERIDIAN
8 FAMILY

TUESDAY NIGHT w THE WHO.
INDIANAPOLIS

1. RINK
2. NEW O
3. SPRINGTIME
4. A.B.A.C
5. IN VIEW
6. OCEAN
7. GRACE, TOO
8. FAMILY

In 2007 we got offered the warm-up spot for The Who. It was four US arena shows.

For Gord, it was very much about the opportunity to meet Pete Townshend. But, of course, we didn't meet Pete Townshend, which was kind of disappointing. You'd see the limo pull up to the back of the stage and someone would open the door and Pete would be sitting in the limo and the band would come out and he'd say, 'Hello, Roger.' And Roger would say, 'Hello, Pete.' It was like the sheepdog and the coyote. And then they went on stage.

Afterwards, Pete Townshend wrote this great piece about us for The Who's website. His take was that we were a unique band, in that we represented both the past and the future of rock and roll. We had something within us that had made rock good and that needed to be preserved if rock was to continue.

That was, I guess, the validation that we had sought. We didn't meet Pete, but it felt like the next best thing.

BILLY RAY: The handkerchief gag started from Gord just having a handkerchief that he would use to wipe the sweat off his brow and then it evolved. We got these white handkerchiefs and he started using them in his hand as a puppet, as something to express his creativity, turning them into a bird or laying them over his face so that the crowd couldn't see him.

Then it became something more than that. Gord would throw a handkerchief into the audience and then spin around and I'd throw another one to him in a ball and he would catch it. This would look like magic to the audience. They'd see him throw a handkerchief, do a spin, and then he'd have another one in his hand. Where did that come from? It got to a point where every night I'd have maybe 50 handkerchiefs laid out in a row in the guitar area. When we ran low, I used to have to go to a Sears or a Hudson's Bay Company and buy every white handkerchief that they had. It got a little expensive at times. I had a special way of rolling them and tying them so they'd fly better. He and I really got a rhythm going, where I was tuning guitars but watching him and the

second that he threw a hanky I'd throw him another one. Some nights we got it where he was just batting the ones I was throwing him straight into the audience and then catching maybe every third one. Or he'd go way out into the audience and say, 'Billy, hit me!' and I would step out from the side of the stage and throw this ball of white handkerchief ten rows out, and he'd catch it and the place would go wild. We developed a great understanding, like a quarterback and a wide receiver.

Paul Langlois's worst nightmare was that one of these hankies would land on him, because to get them to Gord I had to throw them past Paul. Out of the thousands of hankies that got thrown, there's only one time I can really remember that happening. I threw one, but the light above where I was standing had a strong fan on the back of it, which blew the hanky right down onto Paul's shoulder. Paul was playing and he glared at me with this look that said, 'See? I fuckin' told you so.' Gord went over and carefully took it off Paul's shoulder because he was well aware that Paul didn't love this gag. In fact, no one else really liked it in the band. At all.

Ottawa Blues Festival, LeBreton Flats Park, Ottawa, 3 July 2008

Opposite: The Fillmore, Detroit, 30 May 2009 (bottom left); Hamilton Place, Hamilton, ON, 30 September and 2 & 3 October 2009 (other photos)

Gord Downie's handwritten recording session notes, including a sketch of a van/bus.

Handwritten notes:
```
START APR. 17/08 - Bathouse
1  Wolfgang
2  Skeleton Park - 3rd Verse
3  65 After Wichita
4  Queen Of The Furrows
5  The Rock    - Standard - Chorus
6  Speed River → 6D" Open D
7  It Kills Me Too
8  Cuzza U
9  You Can't See Me (Just Mics)
10 R Grey Skies Beckon
11 → New New Orleans World ?
12 All Morning Moon    — OPEN A
13    Morning Moon - tag
14 o At The End Of The Day - DEMO
15 o This Ocean Is Dead
16 A  Who Are You.
17    Moon Over Glenora — E . A . C# . A . C# . E
18    Moonslow Yer Lashes - OPEN A
19    Moonslow Yer Lashes - tag
20 → Don't You Wanna See How It Ends
21 o This Is Where I Sleep
22    Let Them Fall
23 → Broadcast — Standard — DEMO
24    Country Day
25    This Will Be The Last Time
26    Frozen In My Tracks
27    The Black Canoe — DEMO
28    tag of Centre — Standard
```

Side annotations:
```
Skeleton
Morning
Queen
After Wichita
Country Day
Frozen
Who Are You

Depression Suite
The Rock
New Orleans World
See How It Ends

tuning!
- LLO - Open A
- Low river Standard
- 6D" Open D

Moonslow · The Rock
```

CDR 74 Gold   650 MB/74 minute CD-R 1x-8x
The Tragically Hip Writing   Dec 20th
1 Wolfgang
2 Skeleton Park
3 Queen of The Furrows
4 After Wichita
5 The Rock

CDR 74 Gold   650 MB/74 minute CD-R 1x-8x
The Hip Writing   Dec 20/21
1 Wolfgang
2 Skeleton Park
3 After Wichita
4 Queen Of The Furrows
5 The Rock
6 Speed River
7 It Kills Me Too
8 Because of You
9 You Can't See Me
10 Grey Skies Beckon
11 New Orleans World
12 Morning Moon T1
13 Morning Moon T2

CDR 74 Gold   650 MB/74 minute CD-R 1x-8x
The Hip Writing   Jan 23 2008
1 AT THE END OF THE DAY / I DON'T WANNA WAIT
2 THIS OCEAN IS DEAD
3 WHO ARE YOU?
4 MOON OVER GLENORA
5 MOON SLOW YOUR ASHES
6 MOON SLOW YOUR ASHES TAG

ROB: *World Container* had been a pretty happy record up until the mix, but then it went south. At the end of the whole experience, at least three of us were eager to see Bob Rock's tail lights fade. But he had insinuated himself into Gord's life not just as a music producer, but as a life coach, personal guru and best buddy. So when it came to the next record, Gord basically said that if we didn't use Bob he wasn't going to do it. It was that cut and dried.

BERNIE BREEN: After *World Container*, Gord wanted to work with Bob again. I think that the other guys played ball because that's how you get along in a band for as long as they have. You recognise when somebody feels passionate about something, and that's how Gord felt about Bob producing.

BOB ROCK: When I was asked to do another record with The Hip, I was very happy. I enjoyed working with them and I was excited.

But coming into *We Are the Same*, it felt different from the first album. *World Container* was like a first date, when everything's exciting. *We Are the Same* felt more like a strained marriage. There was an edge to the atmosphere. I'd like to believe it wasn't just because of my involvement. Gord and I had become friends and maybe that changed the dynamic … I don't know. Bands are weird.

JOHNNY: Gord did the majority of the demos for *World Container*. They were his songs, lyrics and music. But for *We Are the Same*, there was more of a group songwriting effort. We were writing in a circle, like we used to in the early days, but there was a lot more orchestration and time spent sculpting the parts.

Gord was getting his confidence back. He wasn't trying to jam in a bunch of words; he was letting the songs come naturally, the way he used to.

GORD D: Control is a commodity that people cling to and hide behind. But there's no place for control in a studio or on a stage. It's about faith and trust. Those are the paramount goals that you have to aim for. And that's what I've got with Bob Rock. It's a thrilling freefall.

GORD S: Gord and Bob maintained a very close relationship after we finished *World Container*. I think that their ambition for *We Are the Same* was to make the great Canadian record, without telling the rest of us what they had in mind. I felt super dislocated from the project. By this point, we weren't writing together in a room any longer. We were each giving Gord our own musical ideas on a Dictaphone and he was cherry-picking from that.

The great thing about being in The Hip was that you didn't have to finish an idea. You could come in with something and then the creativity would start flowing from all directions and it would all come together. And Gord was totally in the middle of it. While we were riffing, he'd be writing and singing and it was great. But making records with Bob didn't give us many of those moments, because we weren't pulling on the oars together. In some cases, we didn't even know where the boat was.

THE DEPRESSION SUITE

THE ROCK ⑤

Under. the pillow.
I bury my head and try n shut Chicago out.
As it turns out, there's a whole other world of sounds
of perfect fifths; low skids and Arctic howls.
(All saying) "Are you goin through, somethin?"
"Are you goin' through somethin?"

Under the pillow, / a little room to breathe,
the early morning light's a pale cranberry
I hear "the Aaaaah-'aah, that Nowwow-wow
of a siren Far away and closing steadily.
way far off
(I'm saying) - Are you going through somethin?
And- Are you going through somethin'?
Are you going through somethin'?
E D A cuz I - I - I - I - I am too.

Under. / the pillow
I can hear you whispering- 'Are you going through somethin
(well honey) 'Are you going through somethin?
Are you going through somethin?
Then I - I - I - I - I : I am too
Then I - I - I - I - I - I . I am too

fea- / . I . I . I . I am too

tambourine?
organ
⑥ OPEN D   Away from this
            Away this minute +
            Away for one moment
    OPEN A   Away from this feeling
             From Away -ny oy

SPEEDRIVER
You're Drinally
stunning / I'm almost shivering   ↑TAG
You'd second   A
    anyone. don't hate who you have to be
Speed River take me away   Away from this worn
Speed River take me away   Away From the feel
Speed River take me away   From falling this
                              Away -ny o
Hard stuff.   Away -o y ny
    bring a dose of the Hard Stuff.   From this n
OK! Enough!   -Ooooooo-
    OK is enough of the 'hard stuff   Away from this
Speed River take me away   Away from the feel
Speed River take me away   From feeling the
Speed River take me away   Away from worn
                               Away from
A   D   E   A   D   E   Feeling this
Away From this. Away From this. Ooo-
Awake   At the
OK! Enough.
    This feels like I been here before
    you said, "Don't be tough. let's go back.
whispered, said, "Lets go forward.
Speed River took you away
Speed River took you away
Speed River took her away
Away from this. Away this minute
BREAK - BREAKDOWN-
This house
    sounds just like a bomb hit it
it's an old sound
that says "if you asked me to I'd deliver (all of) it.
Speed River take me away x3

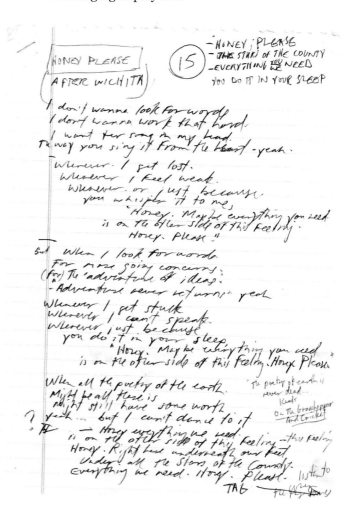

HONEY PLEASE
(AFTER WICHITA)   ⑮   - HONEY; PLEASE
                           - THE STAR OF THE COUNTY
                           - EVERYTHING YOU WE NEED
                             YOU DO IT IN YOUR SLEEP

I don't wanna look for words
I don't wanna work that hard.
I want her song in my head.
The way you sing it From the heart -yeah.
Whenever. / I get lost.
Whenever / feel weak.
Whenever. or just because.
    you whisper it to me,
    "Honey. Maybe everything you need
    is on the other side of this feeling.
    Honey. Please "
But When / look for words
For more going concerns:
(for) The 'adventure of ideas:
-Adventure never returns yeah
Whenever / get stuck
Wherever / can't speak.
Wherever just because
    you do it in your sleep.
    "Honey. Maybe everything you need
    is on the other side of this feeling. Honey Please
When all the poetry of the earth   The poetry of earth is
Might be all there is   never dead.
Might still have some worth   Keats
yeah... but I can't dance to it   On The Grasshopper
                                    And Cricket
- Honey everything we need
is on the other side of this feeling -this feeling
Honey. Right here underneath our feet
Under. all the Stars, of the County.
everything we need. Honey. Please.
TAG

JOHNNY: There are some great tracks on that record, like 'The Depression Suite'. We'd never done anything like that before.

BOB ROCK: 'The Depression Suite' started off as three fragments that we could have developed into individual songs, but we had a lot of solid songs, so I wanted to see if we could tie them together to make a long song, almost like a movie. It was maybe a silly idea, but what I admire about The Tragically Hip is that they went for it and they achieved it.

ROB: We took three half-formed turds, none of which had a chorus or were going anywhere, and melded them into something far more interesting. I don't know whose idea it was to start doing them as a suite – the 'Hopeless Opus', we called it – but that was one of the more successful moments on the record, and it was fun and challenging to play live.

ROB: If there's one track from that record I could send to the Mariana Trench, it would be 'Speed River'. What a plebeian song that is. We had done that song much more successfully several times already in our career. For a band that tried not to repeat itself, boy, we were treading some shallow water there.

ROB: We had a song called 'After Wichita', which everyone liked. We worked it up as a demo, recorded it a number of times in Bath and it went off to Maui to be mixed. When we got the mixes back, 'After Wichita' was now called 'Honey, Please', the lyrics were completely different and the vocals were in a different spot. If I'd known Gord was going to sing in that spot I wouldn't have played there, because now guitar and vocals were banging into each other. There was no discussion. It just came back as a different song.

ROB: I started to find Gord more difficult to work with around the time of *Trouble at the Henhouse*. But you learn to compartmentalise and squash your emotions down at an early age. Talk about hockey instead. It's part of the dysfunction of my gender. By the time of the second Bob Rock record, it had got to the point where Gord would walk into the room and I would instantly stand up, like Pavlov's dog, and pour myself a drink. It was my way of coping. I might already have a Solo cup full of vodka and Red Bull sitting beside me, but I'd go and make another one.

For a couple of years things were pretty tough, but we worked through it and got to a very good place. It didn't happen until too late.

PATRICK SAMBROOK: I never saw an open chat within the band and the opportunities for that to happen dwindled because Gord listened to the other members less as time went on. It became tricky, as it is for any family that's not communicating. I'm not sure they ever really fixed it to the level that they would have liked. There was a difficult grey area between Gord as the front man and as one of five members of a democratic band.

CDR74Gold   650 MB/74 minute CD-R 1x-8x

The Tragically Hip Writing
Feb 19 2008
1 Don't You Want To See How It Ends
2 This Is Where I Sleep
3 Let Them Fall
4 Broadcast T8
5 Broadcast T9

CDR74Gold   650 MB/74 minute CD-R 1x-8x

The Tragically Hip   March Writing
                      28th/08
1 Country Day
2 This Will Be The Last Time
3 Frozen In ~~the~~ My Tracks
4 The Black Canoe
5 Target Centre

CDR74Gold   650 MB/74 minute CD-R 1x-8x

THE TRAGICALLY HIP PRE PRO   APRIL 08
           DISC 1 OF 2
1   AFTER WICHITA
2   MORNING MOON
3   IT KILLS ME 2
4   WHO ARE YOU
5   QUEEN OF THE FURROWS
6   SPEED RIVER
7   SKELETON PARK
8   IF I'M ANY GOOD AT ALL (IT'S BECAUSE OF YOU)
9   MEAN IT (YOU CAN'T SEE ME)
10 GREY SKIES BECKON
11 THE DEPRESSION SUITE
(THE ROCK, NEW ORLEANS WORLD, DON'T YOU WANNA
                        SEE HOW IT ENDS)

Recording We Are the Same, *Bathouse, Bath, ON, 24 April 2008*

Opposite: Lyrics for 'The Depression Suite', 'Speed River' and 'Honey, Please'

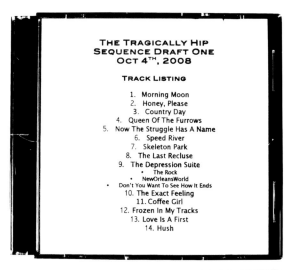

THE TRAGICALLY HIP
SEQUENCE DRAFT ONE
OCT 4TH, 2008

TRACK LISTING

1. Morning Moon
2. Honey, Please
3. Country Day
4. Queen Of The Furrows
5. Now The Struggle Has A Name
6. Speed River
7. Skeleton Park
8. The Last Recluse
9. The Depression Suite
   • The Rock
   • NewOrleansWorld
   • Don't You Want To See How It Ends
10. The Exact Feeling
11. Coffee Girl
12. Frozen In My Tracks
13. Love Is A First
14. Hush

ROB: Bob had Paul and me come to Maui for the mixing of the record. Sinclair, who was the musical core of the band in a lot of ways, didn't go to Maui either time. He wasn't asked to be there for overdubs, back-ups, thoughts, nothing. We were holed up in our little condo units and every morning we drove to Bob's studio and got told to stay close and they'd call if they needed us. Day in, day out, never a phone call. I played for an hour one day. Waste of our time and money.

GORD D: I think anybody in a long-term relationship will tell you it has its challenges. We're five guys trying to make things every couple of years, and sometimes you gotta break some eggs to make the cake.

PAUL: I accepted going to Maui for *World Container*, but when they suggested it again for *We Are the Same* I was very against the idea. It was probably the biggest fight that Gord and I had, certainly our biggest fight in the band. I think he was surprised that I didn't want to go, but my point was that I didn't think anyone should go. I didn't see why we couldn't just do the vocals in Bath.

Gord and I made up pretty quickly. He was a formidable foe whenever we were on opposite sides of an issue but he was always quick to apologise. He was very self-aware; it would drive him nuts if he thought he'd offended anybody.

We got to the end of the schedule and Gord's vocals weren't done yet. You can't really sing back-ups if the lead isn't done. So I went back to Canada and Gord stayed in Maui to try to wrestle these songs into place. The plan was to do the back-ups later in Toronto – Sinclair and I had some ideas.

GORD S: When Paul and I showed up at the studio in Toronto, we found out that the back-ups had already been done by Gord, Bob and Eric Helmkamp, the guy that was engineering the record. It was like, 'OK, fuck you too.' Paul and I walked out on that session. It was the first time I'd ever been fired from a job in my entire life, and it was in my own band.

PAUL: Gord was just living and breathing the album. Part of me understands why he'd sing a few back-ups. That's his total right. But I was disappointed Bob and Eric sung on them. It should have been Gord Sinclair and me singing them. Sinclair and I only ended up doing back-ups on 'The Depression Suite'.

To me, back-ups add such personality. They can really make a song. And so to have them sung by people who weren't members of The Hip felt like it was going behind our backs. I took it personally. I got over it, but at the time I wasn't too happy.

With time, I grew to accept and like how those songs were sung. I would sing back-up on them live just like Gord did. I can't say I imitated the other two guys, really, but I got the concept. It was quite a vocal extravaganza.

BOB ROCK: We did all the tracks and some vocals in Maui, so Gord came early. I work quickly with vocals, so we did a lot of back-ups without the band, which was a huge mistake. I never know how to finish a record until you have vocals, because it's only then that you understand what the song is. I'm used to doing things in the moment, but when you're in the moment sometimes you get things wrong.

When they heard it, they were put off because they weren't involved. It was a bit uncomfortable. I never want to interfere or change a band; I just want to help them make the best album that they can make. I wanted to make a better record than *World Container*, and in my mind I did.

BERNIE BREEN: Once Gord gave his trust to somebody it was unwavering, but the other guys were more sceptical of Bob's motives. I don't think that Bob's approach was self-serving; he was doing what he thought was best for the band. It might not have sat well all the time, but he did the best he could.

BILLY RAY: I remember meeting up with Paul and Gord Sinclair and handing them the CD of the rough mixes of *We Are the Same* and Sinclair just took it and pitched it into the seat of his convertible MG. I was like, 'Really?' And he was like, 'Pfft, I don't care to listen to it.'

PATRICK SAMBROOK: *We Are the Same* came together as this acoustic-guitar-driven, around-the-campfire record. Some members took to it better than others, which may be why it sounds like it does.

ROB: *We Are the Same* is my least favourite Hip album. A lot of that is probably subjective because I had a bad time making it. It had some good moments, but it would have been stronger minus two or three tracks. We had a meeting – not a happy meeting – where we settled on which tracks to cut, but when the record came out it had all the tracks still on it, because Bob and Gord were holding the reins.

JOHNNY: It's interesting that Robbie doesn't like *We Are the Same*, because I think that some of my favourite solos of his are on that record. Songs like 'Morning Moon'. Maybe he didn't want to be there, but he certainly played well.

PAUL: I think there's some cool songs on *We Are the Same*. I don't hate it. I think Bob did good work on it. It's certainly not *World Container*, but it was a step somewhere.

JOHNNY: I think Gord felt that Bob wasn't respected for what he did for us. Things didn't end in a great way. I certainly thanked Bob, and Gord kept his friendship with him intact. In fact, one of the last things Gord did was make a record with Bob.

I talked to Bob years later and he has no bad blood about it. He's still proud of the records he made with us, and so am I. Those two albums put us back on the radio when we needed to get back on the radio. Bob got us back to being a rock band instead of experimenting. It was exciting to be in the band again. We couldn't make another record that didn't have any real direction.

BILLY RAY: I know a few of the guys think the records they did with Bob are the worst they've ever made. I disagree. I think *World Container* and *We Are the Same* are two masterpiece records. But I think all Hip records are masterpieces, so I'm kinda biased.

We Are the Same
RECORDED: DECEMBER 2007–OCTOBER 2008
THE BATHOUSE, BATH, ON
THE WAREHOUSE, VANCOUVER, BC
PLANTATION RECORDING, MAUI, HI
THE ORANGE LOUNGE, TORONTO, ON
PRODUCER: BOB ROCK
ENGINEERS: ERIC HELMKAMP, AARON HOLMBERG
MICHAEL GILLIES, ROGER MONK
MIXING: JENS
RELEASED: 7 APRIL 2009

Morning Moon
Honey, Please
The Last Recluse
Coffee Girl
Now the Struggle Has a Name
The Depression Suite
The Exact Feeling
Queen of the Furrows
Speed River
Frozen in My Tracks
Love Is a First
Country Day

HHb CDR80   700 MB/79 minute 59 second CD-R 1x-12x
The Tragically Hip
1 Morning Moon
2 The Depression Suite (DAY1)
3 Honey Please
4 Last Recluse
5 Coffee Girl
6 Now The Struggle Has A Name
7 The Exact Feeling
8 Queen Of The Furrows
9 Speed River (DAY1)
10 Frozen In My Tracks
11 Luv Is A First
12 Country Day
                          56 min
Rehearsal from
THE LOFT
03/25/09

On 6 April 2009, to coincide with the release of We Are the Same, *The Hip performed at the Bathouse in a concert that was screened live in Cineplex theatres across Canada*

BILLY RAY: For the We Are the Same tour Gord wrote out the set lists for every show by hand. It was the only tour he did that for. He demanded that I get those set lists at the end of each night and keep them together. And so, for an entire world tour I collected every one of his handwritten set lists and kept them in a drawer in my workbox.

On the final night of the tour, as I went to tape his set list down to the floor, I realised he'd written at the bottom: 'Thanks, Billy, it's been real.' At the end of the night I took the whole pile of set lists to him but he told me to keep them and do something with them. A couple of years later, we were joking about how they were still sitting in my workbox and he said, 'You better do something with them soon, my stock's dropping.'

Song list and rehearsal set lists, We Are the Same tour, 2009

Billy Ray Koster, 2009

Opposite and overleaf: Massey Hall, Toronto (including Jim Bryson on keyboards, opposite top left), 11–19 May 2009

PAUL: On the We Are the Same tour we brought in Jim Bryson to cover the orchestral parts on keyboard and he also sang extra back-ups. He's a great guy. So touring with Jim was fun, but I don't necessarily think *We Are the Same* advanced us or made us popular in any different way.

BILLY RAY: When Paul and Gord were repairing their relationship, there were nice moments every night during 'Morning Moon' when they would both be playing acoustic guitar and they'd turn and catch each other's eye and then play off of each other.

Other times, I witnessed Gord and Paul miss that bit a few times, or one of them would not recognise it or time it right, and it hurt in the heart that these two guys who loved each other had missed a moment to reconnect.

JOHNNY: I didn't know anything about the material on Gord's next solo album, but I knew that he was very excited about it. I had people whispering in my ear all the time that it was called *The Grand Bounce* because Gord was getting ready to bounce out of the band. Would he have left The Hip if the record had been a huge success? Who knows ... but I don't think so.

GORD D: I read in a book by Evan S. Connell about the Battle of the Little Bighorn that when a soldier decided to desert in the middle of the night it was said he was 'taking the grand bounce'. It was only after the record had gone to print that I realised people might think I was deserting from The Hip, but that's not what I meant by it. I think we're deserting all the time – deserting our best thoughts, values and ideas to embrace something else.

Canada is kind of where desertion was born. It's the Great White Plan B, the place where Americans come if it doesn't work out for them down south.

PATRICK SAMBROOK: Gord's solo career was filled with guilt. He was incredibly loyal to The Tragically Hip and recognised that he owed his position in life to the band, but he also wanted to explore other things and play with other people. By the time of *The Grand Bounce*, he was beginning to feel OK about having a solo career while still being in The Hip. He needed to express himself elsewhere to keep the band going.

RB: Gavin Brown was a good choice to make our next record. He fit right in on a personal level. He worked really hard. And he seemed to get us.

PAUL: *The Grand Bounce* was out and Gord was touring it. When you're doing your own thing like that, you're not really communicating that much together. Then we got together and started writing in Bath, which takes time. I don't know how Gavin Brown's name came up. Maybe because he had produced some of Sarah Harmer's records. Eventually, we landed on him being a good choice for *Now for Plan A*. He was enthusiastic and he came to Bath and it was a pretty natural fit.

GORD D: **This record matches up with what I needed emotionally, which was to sing with a blown-out voice, giving everything I've got. I asked the guys to give me five musical ideas from their cupboards and let me react viscerally, spontaneously to the ones that attracted me.**

GAVIN BROWN: It was a unique juncture in The Hip's career because they had taken some time apart, which for any band that has been together for 20-plus years is probably a good idea. They were best buds but I think they might have lost sight of that and they were hurting.

I was asked to get the guys reacquainted and see how it would go. Each of the members of the band had made some demos and Gord had selected five of them and these were going to be the jumping-off point for us. When they were sent to me, I was a little taken aback at how raw and unfinished they were. Sometimes bands have these very developed ideas because they want to show off and put their best foot forward, but this was quite the opposite. When I got to Kingston, I realised that these demos were actually a gift that each guy had given to the whole band – a gift of openness to see where the music could go.

PAUL: Most of the ideas in our career were small musical ideas. One guy would start playing a riff, then another guy would join in. Then Gord would start rapping or singing something over the top of that. The ideas would chase each other.

The best feeling was when everyone liked your idea and it turned out nice. We were lucky that we had a lot of songs like that.

GAVIN BROWN: We were in their studio for months, recording piece by piece, drums and bass, and then overdubbing guitars, but we weren't getting to where I felt we needed to be.

In one rehearsal Sinclair started playing 'Grace, Too' and I suddenly realised, 'Oh, this is where I am. This is The Hip.' These songs are part of our DNA. They ran through a bunch of them and I just sat in the room, transported to another world.

As they played their songs during that rehearsal and at the concert in Bobcaygeon, I witnessed the band gelling into the unified organism that we know as The Hip. I was no longer trying to battle the process, no longer trying to find the way through. I realised that we had to scrap what we'd done and start again in a different studio with the band playing together.

Now for Plan A songs recorded at the Bathouse, Bath, ON, January and June 2011

GORD S: I thought it was a really good idea of Bernie's and Patty's to play Bobcaygeon. You're asking people to travel a long way to see us play, so it behooves the mountain to go to Muhammad every once in a while. It went back to the Roadside Attraction days, where we'd pony up for the staging and the sound reinforcement and the security. So we weren't making a huge profit, but we sold enough tickets to have a fantastic show in a place that we wouldn't normally play.

BERNIE BREEN: Bobcaygeon was a significant event. It just seemed an obvious thing to do. There was no intention other than to do what the band had done their entire careers, which was to go and play live to people who wanted to see them. We found a field and worked with a promoter. The show sold out in a minute. It was the event of all events there and one they still talk about. Everyone in the community embraced it. We knew we had to film it – it would have been crazy not to. So it all came together very quickly and it was magical.

PAUL: I was excited about playing Bobcaygeon. Big outdoor festivals like that are always fun. We hadn't played there before so we were all curious too. And we got a little movie out of it. The only downside was that it wasn't the nicest day.

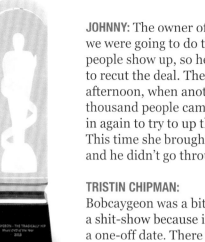

JOHNNY: The owner of the property where we were going to do the gig saw all the people show up, so he called in Tristin to recut the deal. Then, later on in the afternoon, when another couple of thousand people came in, he called her in again to try to up the fee a bit more. This time she brought the police with her and he didn't go through with it.

TRISTIN CHIPMAN: Bobcaygeon was a bit of a shit-show because it was a one-off date. There was a lot of forcing magic out of something that was big for many people, which meant a lot of pressure. There's always pressure around a big conceptual show like that. It's never going to be perfect, and it's never as romantic as it ends up looking like it was.

Nobody was eating that day because we were all so anxious. And there was nothing nice about it – it was just a field with tents, port-a-potties and plywood. In the end the energy was good, but we were glad to be getting back on the bus.

*Big Music Fest
Bobcaygeon, ON,
25 June 2011*

*The 2012 movie
The Tragically Hip in
Bobcaygeon, directed
by Andy Keen, won a
Juno award for Music
DVD of the Year in 2013*

BERNIE BREEN: Gord was becoming immersed in what was going on in the lives of Indigenous people up north, so he brought the idea of playing at the Great Moon Gathering to us and we brought it to the rest of the guys. We had to figure out what it would look like, and we wanted to livestream it, which at the time was something completely new.

PAUL: The events took place in a nice community school, where a local band opened for us. There was a good vibe in there. We all stayed in the same house and we loved being a part of the community for a little while. We met so many great people, so friendly and welcoming. We took part in these sessions of communal talking and playing music.

We were honoured to participate and we really were properly treated and welcomed, and so that was a bonding experience.

GORD D: Joseph Boyden was the keynote speaker at the Great Moon Gathering in Fort Albany and he asked us to go up there with him. He thought playing a rock show and having some fun would build that bridge of communication.

ROB: Going to play places like that is a lot of logistics for something that ends up costing you money. But you don't have to make money every place you play. You make good money in some cities and other places maybe it's going to cost you, but you should still go. As a Canadian band, you should be embarrassed if you don't go.

JOHNNY: We flew from Toronto to Sault Ste Marie and then the rest of the way north on another little plane. We could see the guys that were packing the plane doing the math on the weight of all our gear, which didn't seem good at the time.

When we got up to Fort Albany, there was zero cell service. And, lo and behold, we started talking to each other. Everyone had a great time and it was an incredible vibe. Playing a gymnasium, it was almost like we were back at KCVI. We stayed in one big building that we had to ourselves and we were able to hang out and bury the hatchet a little bit.

The people were so kind and generous. That's true Canada up there. It was very different from Bobcaygeon, where everybody was trying to work out how they could get more money out of us.

ROB: Anytime we performed in a new, special place, we'd all go through a fascinating learning experience and that couldn't help but pull us together. And Fort Albany was a very special place. We met a lot of lovely people there. I was given a beautiful red fox fur hat that had been made for me by the elders in the community and I wore it with such pride. When we landed back in Toronto, I was still wearing it and people looked at me like they were going to stab me or throw red paint on me. I was like, 'Oh, fuck, I forgot.' But on the coldest days of the year, I still pull that hat out.

PAUL: It was quite eye opening. First of all, it was insanely cold. Also, I was struck by how expensive everything was. You went into the grocery store and a head of lettuce would be 18 bucks. I couldn't understand how they could deal with that, especially when you know that the income level is lower. It was a difficult life up there. Cold. Expensive. Not many services or places to go. A pretty harsh environment, certainly in the winter.

ROB: You certainly come face to face with your ignorance of this country when you go north and meet these incredible people that have a very different way of life. You realise that you can't judge them by your metrics. People who live in the Arctic Circle have tiny homes and so you think that they must be so poor, but it's just that it's a lot easier to heat a one-room place.

We don't understand the way a lot of people in our own country live.

Great Moon Gathering,
Fort Albany, ON,
15–17 February 2012

GORD S: What struck me the most when we went up to Fort Albany was that we were with our Northern Cree brothers. First Nation Canadians, but Canadians nonetheless – more Canadian than we were, in fact. They were just lovely to us and we had a whip snapper of a party afterwards.

I went out on a snowmobile onto James Bay with Gavin Brown until we lost sight of land. The expanse of space was incredibly life-affirming.

One of the few regrets I have from being in The Hip is that we didn't get north more often. We never played Yellowknife or Whitehorse or Iqaluit. We should have pursued that more.

GORD D: We think we have so much stuff to teach the people of the north, but we could take a lot of lessons from the way they run their communities. The way they take care of each other and the way they stretch a buck.

BERNIE BREEN: Sharing that experience was really something, and I think they were all grateful for it. It reminded them that they were brothers.

GORD S: Gord's involvement with First Nations communities had a spiritual underpinning. He really embraced the idea that we are of the land and, as such, we have a duty to protect it.

NOW FOR PLAN A

GORD D: We liked *Now for Plan A* as a title. It has many connotations. The return to the original premise, which is to survive. The title really resonates for me because when we were making this record we had a bunch of setbacks, but none as long and involved as my wife, Laura, getting diagnosed with breast cancer in August 2011.

GORD D: Tess Gallagher, Raymond Carver's wife, wrote that poetry is a place to be ample and grateful to those nearest and dearest to our hearts. I've always adhered to that idea, but it seemed like nothing I had written lately, or maybe ever, was cutting it in that regard. I just wanted to be able to show my love and gratitude and devotion, and express my fear, for my wife.

It makes you want to hurry up and change, because you know that nothing will be the same anymore. You're going to try to live a beautiful life with your family, without illusion, and that's very freeing.

PAUL: When Laura was diagnosed with breast cancer right in the middle of *Now for Plan A*, we, of course, stopped recording, knowing what she, Gord and the kids were going through. It was all-consuming and highly scary and emotional.

GORD D: The band is very much a big family. We're all integrated now, so a torpedo midships to somebody hits us all. There'll probably be more of that, where we have to put things aside and rally and help and support.

PAUL: We all just tried to be supportive friends and check in. But it was a tough time. I remember Gord running all over the place, driving the kids around, going to get the groceries. Stuff that he would normally do anyway, but just with both feet in, no question. He was busy holding the fort down, while trying not to show too much fear or emotion in the hospital visits.

Gord wrote about part of their experience in hospital on 'Now for Plan A' and 'The Lookahead'. He says, 'Her blood is still clear and sanguineous' – I think I looked into that at the time. We didn't necessarily know what he meant. The verses are him at the hospital trying to be the supportive guy he wanted to be.

There was a sense of a greater connection within the band because of everything Gord was going through with Laura and his family, and also from our experience up at the Great Moon Gathering.

GORD S: Laura was sick and Gord was dutifully investing his time in her care and recovery and we had this album to make. I don't know why we had to make a record right then, but we moved the sessions to Toronto so that Gord could get home every night.

We were trying to write songs and make music and not 100 percent ready to get into it, but it was a fun studio to play in and Gavin Brown was an excellent producer who got a lot out of us.

GAVIN BROWN: Overdubbing a band, piece by piece, as we had been doing at the Bathouse, is no fun after a while, but working with this living unit was so much better. I needed to capture the other guys peppering in with their instruments and speaking around the vocals, and we weren't getting that with them playing by themselves.

Lyrics for 'The Lookahead', 'Now for Plan A' (under its working title 'Wisteria'), 'About This Map' and 'Goodnight Attawapiskat'

GORD S: 'Now for Plan A' is a beautiful little song and Sarah Harmer is a lovely singer. We've known her since she was in high school. Her elder sister Mary was a great bud of ours at university and Sarah used to come and visit and we'd hang out. It was nice, knowing what Gord and his family had been going through, to present that song as a duet.

'Nothing short of everything's enough' – that was definitely Gord's approach to work and that's how he expected us to approach our work with the group too. I sent him the riff for that song, and when he came back with that lyric I thought maybe it was a criticism, that he thought it was a shitty song and that I wasn't fully invested in the process. But he said it was about him not me. When you're writing remotely, you don't have the benefit of eye contact with your co-writer, where you can throw something out there and if you get the stink face back you know that it's a fart in a space suit.

PAUL: It always goes great with Sarah Harmer. She's an excellent singer and very good in the studio. We'd already done a song with her for the film *Men with Brooms*. It was a natural fit.

The lyric 'nothing short of everything's enough' resonated with me when we first started playing 'Now for Plan A'. It's about an insatiable appetite for more, which the band had, and Gord really embodied. He must have been talking to himself a little bit, maybe talking to the band as well. Nothing we did was ever going to be enough, but we had to keep trying.

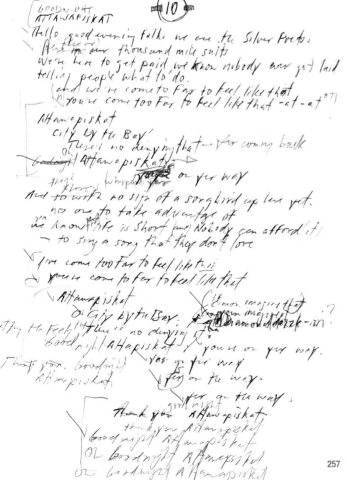

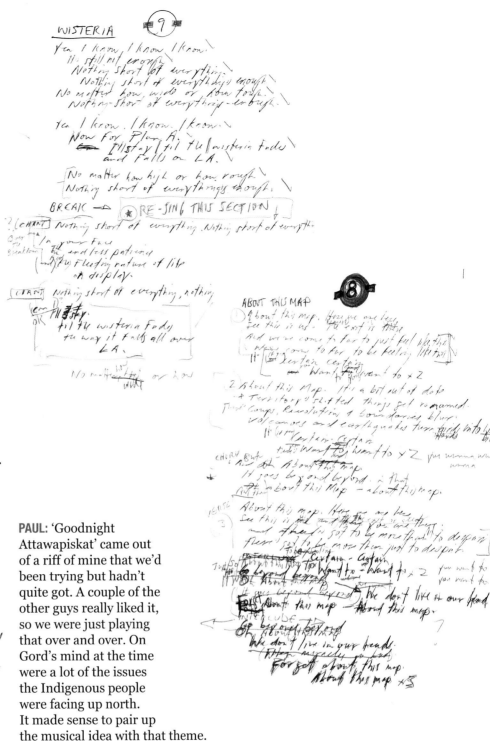

PAUL: 'Goodnight Attawapiskat' came out of a riff of mine that we'd been trying but hadn't quite got. A couple of the other guys really liked it, so we were just playing that over and over. On Gord's mind at the time were a lot of the issues the Indigenous people were facing up north. It made sense to pair up the musical idea with that theme.

JOHNNY: The Great Moon Gathering had been a great little break while we were doing *Now for Plan A* and it was good for Gord because he wrote 'Attawapiskat' on that trip.

GORD D: On the surface, 'Goodnight Attawapiskat' is about a band that shows up in Attawapiskat to play. They've got no real idea of where they are; they're just there to play their gig because it's on the way to somewhere else. Which is kind of ironic, because Attawapiskat isn't on the way to anywhere. Oftentimes, we hear it referred to as a fly-in, fly-out community.

But I wanted people to think differently about that part of the world. When Attawapiskat was flooded three times in 14 months, the government reaction was, 'Let's relocate you. Why are you even living here?' But the people there didn't want to be relocated, because they'd hunted and fished on those lands for 10,000 years.

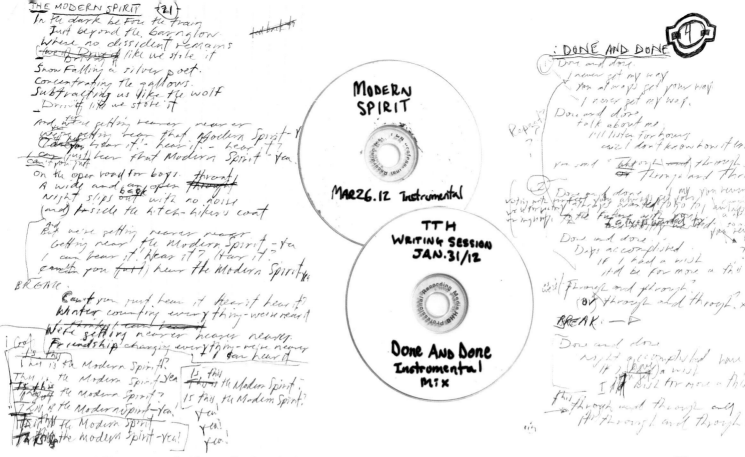

ROB: We recorded basically the whole album at the Bathouse and then went to Toronto and rerecorded everything from start to finish in ten days. For the most part, it was really successful. But at the last minute we lost a couple of really key tracks, two of the more rocking songs.

One of them was a song called 'Intensity', which Paul had brought in. It was during that whole Occupy Wall Street protest and the title was a play on the phrase 'in tent city'.

GORD D: The songs I laboured over, I don't like as much. The more you work at them, the more you start thinking, 'Why am I doing this? Why do I care about this? Do I care?' I wanted to care about everything I said on this record. I've always wanted that, but sometimes you get caught up in trying to impress, in worshipping the intellect, which will eat you up.

We had a killer version worked up, a very raw, in your face Stooges kind of thing. But then Gord changed all the lyrics and 'Intensity' became 'Along the Albany'. He was struggling to make the new lyrics fit and so the song fell by the wayside.

GAVIN BROWN: Trying to get Gord to nail down his 65th draft of a song … one day he said, 'These words are killing me.' He took it very seriously. I hope we got what he wanted.

JOHNNY: I listen to that record now and I still like it, but it was poorly mixed. I think we all got to a point where we thought, 'OK, it's finished. Let's just mix it and get on with it.'

GORD S: There are a couple of wicked songs on *Now for Plan A* – 'At Transformation' is a great opener – but it's an uneven record. Not many of the songs translated to the stage all that well, which is always my acid test.

ROB: We ended up with an underwhelming record when we were on the cusp of having a really strong rock album. It felt like we cut ourselves off at the ankles a little bit.

258 NOW FOR PLAN A 2010–2012

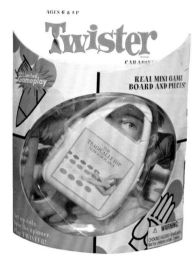

GAVIN BROWN: The album was not as well received as I would have liked, but that's a by-product of having been an awesome band for 30 years. Like The Rolling Stones, who I think are similar in that respect, some of The Hip's later records aren't given the dues that they deserve. It was their most lucrative tour up to that point and their worst selling record.

For me, a lot of the process of making a record is about singles, but it was very clear that that was not going to be the case with this record. Gord didn't care about having any singles. We got one, 'At Transformation', and that's the track that is most like their old songs in the tempo, engagement and the bass-driven riff.

PATRICK SAMBROOK: Gord's biggest desire was critical success, which a lot of people find surprising. Maybe because he had commercial success early on, he really cared about the music critics, his contemporaries and other musicians. He did a lot to try to win that acclaim, sometimes successfully, sometimes not. He would often set his sights on the highest cliff and then if we didn't get there he would be devastated.

ROB: As the visual focal point of the band, Gord was in a different position than the rest of us. He was interfacing with the audience, while the rest of us were interfacing with each other. Gord's looking outward also included being much more interested in and concerned with critical approval than we were.

GAVIN BROWN: I think Gord is naturally interested in counterpoint and the positive side of being different. He's a contrarian, and when you're the most important vocalist in the country, who do you get to be a contrarian against? Yourself. So, he became his own worst enemy at that point. Like, 'Who am I gonna push back against?' Well, there's nobody other than himself.

Now for Plan A
RECORDED: 2011–2012
THE BATHOUSE, BATH, ON
NOBLE STREET, TORONTO, ON
PRODUCER: GAVIN BROWN
ENGINEERS: LENNY DEROSE
NYLES SPENCER
AARON HOLMBERG
DAVID MOHACSI
MIXING: MICHAEL H. BRAUER
RELEASED: 2 OCTOBER 2012

At Transformation
Man Machine Poem
The Lookahead
We Want to Be It
Streets Ahead
Now for Plan A
The Modern Spirit
About This Map
Take Forever
Done and Done
Goodnight Attawapiskat

Top: Mini-game promo pack to tie in with the album's Twister-based cover, 2012

Opposite: Lyrics for 'The Modern Spirit', 'Done and Done' and 'At Transformation' (under its working title 'Glittering Chance')

THE
TRAGICALLY HIP
NOW FOR PLAN A

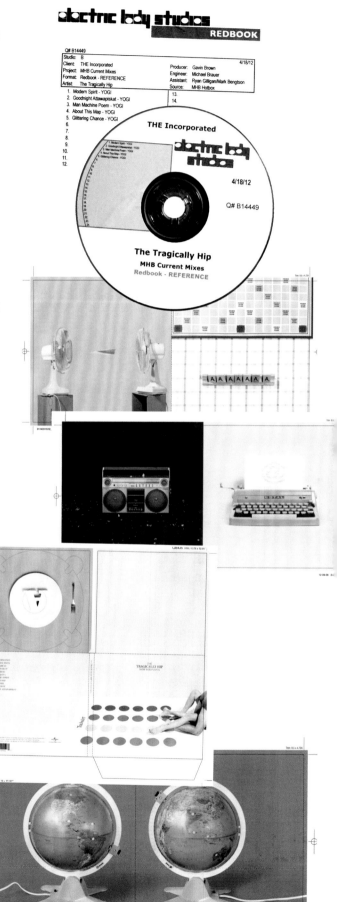

Stills from the
'At Transformation'
video, 2012

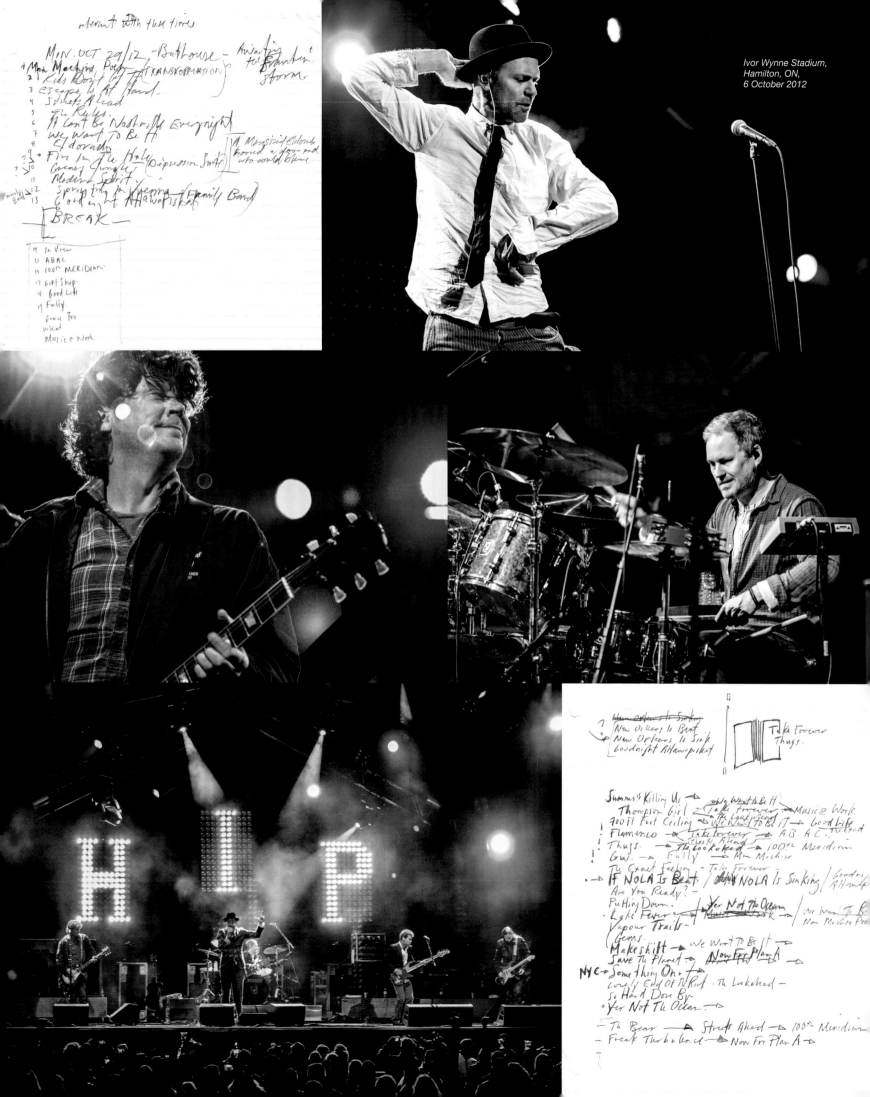

Ivor Wynne Stadium,
Hamilton, ON,
6 October 2012

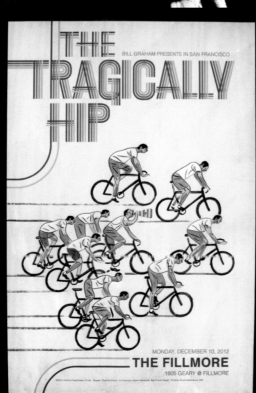

JF: We needed to get back into bigger venues. And to get back into bigger venues you've got to play the hits, and people have got to know that's what you're going to do.

This page and overleaf: Fully and Completely tour, January–October 2015

Opposite: Leather jacket that Gord Downie had custom made for the tour (top)

PAUL: Some bands had started to play entire records as shows and the idea of us doing that with *Fully Completely* appealed to me. We thought it would be one way to fill the seats up in the top bowl. And it turned out we were correct.

We wanted it to be exactly right, as it's a challenging record to play. But because it was so challenging, we didn't get sick of playing it. We also played other songs, either before or after we did the *Fully Completely* record. And the challenge of it meant that we managed, for the most part, to avoid thinking that we were selling out, or that it was a cheesy thing to do. It was actually a very successful tour and way more fun than I expected.

ROB: The idea that you're going to reissue an old record from your glory years and then go out on tour and play it in full, we just thought that stank. A lot of bands were doing it. And then the next thing I know, we were doing it too.

We sat down and talked about the idea and we all expressed our reservations. But at the end of the day, any show that we played would have had six or seven songs from *Fully Completely*, so to play the other five didn't seem like that big a stretch. If it gave the promoters something they could hang on a billboard, then, you know, that was playing the game. We went out and did the tour that we were going to do anyways, just with a few extra tunes from one of our records. And I know that that tour bumped us back up in a big way into larger venues.

GORD S: I was totally down with the idea, but Gord was very resistant. I wrongly assumed it was because he thought we should be creating new stuff, but it was actually just that he didn't think people would give a shit about a 20-year-old record of ours.

When he finally agreed to do it, the tickets went on sale and sold out immediately.

PATRICK SAMBROOK: When looking at the consumption of The Tragically Hip's music, it still leans to those earlier records. There was a discussion as to which one of the older records to highlight. *Up to Here* was another candidate, but Gord loved *Fully Completely* and ultimately that was the record he was willing to tour. It took some pushing; he wasn't into it until he wrapped his head around it being his idea. Gord was like that.

BERNIE BREEN: Our challenge was to make it fresh, exciting and engaging for Gord. Patty and I talked to him a lot about his job as an artist and performer. B.B. King said, 'The audience is my boss, and I want my boss to be happy.' Once we got Gord to put himself in the position of a Hip fan, it was off to the races. We knew it would be big and it was.

ROB: We always felt like we had a core fan base that was along for the journey wherever we went. They wanted to see how we were going to change, what the next step would be. And that's who we focused most of our attention on. Management and agents, to their credit, said, 'That's great, but it's not enough. What about the people that have drifted away over the years? What about the people you haven't reached yet? Let's do something for those people.' And they weren't wrong. It was good to take stock, and that was a pretty damn good record.

BILLY RAY: When it came to it, Gord rose to the occasion. He never went out there and showed the audience that he wasn't totally into it.

GEDDY LEE: Gord had a quirky, charismatic stage presence and he clearly was in his own world on stage. That's one of the things that people loved about the way The Hip presented themselves. On a basic level, they were a hard rockin', grinding band, yet there was poetry and charisma at the core.

PATRICK SAMBROOK: Gord wanted to surprise us all on the Fully and Completely tour by getting three Elvis-style leather suits made, the black one being a full homage to Elvis's Comeback Special. But he sweated like a lunatic and couldn't perform in them, so he asked the designer to chop them in half so he could wear them as a two-piece. This then fuelled his interest in accentuated outfits for the final tour.

BERNIE BREEN: Once we had that concept down it happened fast and the tour did very well throughout North America.

JOHNNY: We played a set, took a break and then we played *Fully Completely*. It was supposed to tie in with the 20th anniversary of the album, but by the time we came round to the idea it was actually the 22nd anniversary. That's how long it takes us to agree to things.

GORD S: The fans loved it, but more importantly it was a gas for us. We weren't putting pressure on ourselves to write new material or switch up the set every night. The weight of the world had all of a sudden been lifted off our shoulders.

It was funny, because we would sequence a record based on imagining how we would do it as a live show and now that's exactly the order we were playing the songs in. So it was already baked into the equation.

PAUL: There was this thing going on in the crowd and you could feel it. They had each made their own connections with those songs more than 20 years earlier. But now they were also developing connections with each other. They had never met, but they were on the same page. They were Hip fans. A lot of people out there would have had their songs on that album that really affected them – 'Wheat Kings', 'Courage', 'Locked in the Trunk', 'Fifty Mission Cap'. It feels very good to play to crowds that really know your songs. And that was certainly the case on the Fully and Completely tour.

JOHNNY: That tour was good for the band – to be able to play a record from beginning to end and look back to when we were that age and reflect. A lot of bands don't get that chance. Everyone was in a good mood and we were happy to be playing those venues again. Seeing how much that particular record meant to people washed the bad stuff away. After all the years of things not going great, it seemed like we had a better path in front of us.

Fully and Completely 2015 tour crew (l to r): Jeremy Van Delft, Justin Schnell, Mike Cormier, Tyler Pigeon, Billy Ray Koster, Andrew 'Juice' Werlick, Matt Kirby (behind), Lee Moro and Ricky Wellington

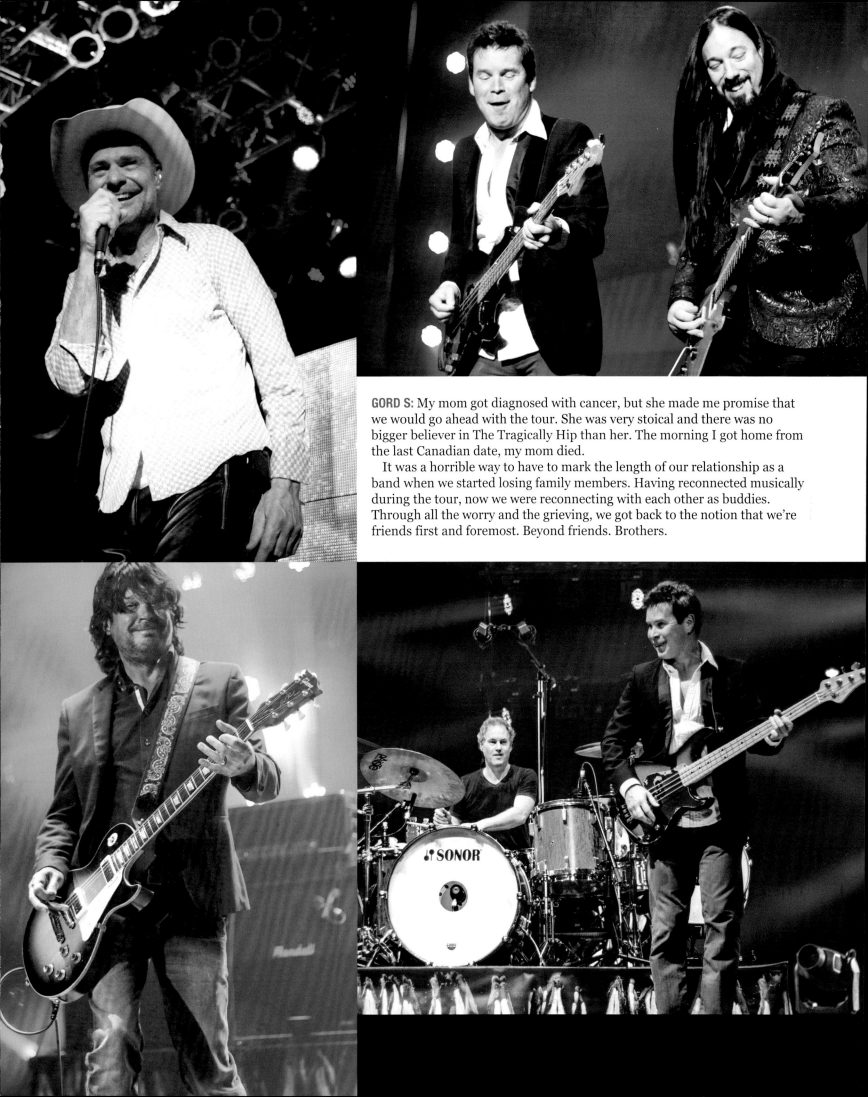

GORD S: My mom got diagnosed with cancer, but she made me promise that we would go ahead with the tour. She was very stoical and there was no bigger believer in The Tragically Hip than her. The morning I got home from the last Canadian date, my mom died.

It was a horrible way to have to mark the length of our relationship as a band when we started losing family members. Having reconnected musically during the tour, now we were reconnecting with each other as buddies. Through all the worry and the grieving, we got back to the notion that we're friends first and foremost. Beyond friends. Brothers.

JOHNNY: Everybody's got a certain record that they didn't enjoy working on. For me, it was *Man Machine Poem*. It was super confusing and it felt like hard work. Sonically, it's not up to par with our other albums. So I didn't love that record and I didn't love the people that were involved in making it.

PATRICK SAMBROOK: *Man Machine Poem* had a purpose to it. It went to a whole other place that was not commercial-leaning. But, in the end, I don't think they had the songs.

GORD S: *Man Machine Poem* was a tough record to make. Like he had on the previous record or two, Gord was getting us to send him little demos of what we'd been working on for him to see if he could put something on top. He brought in Kevin Drew from Broken Social Scene to take on the Bob Rock role of helping us see the songs through to fruition.

It took us a long time to make a record that way. Gone were the days of packing up the band and heading down to Memphis for a month. We recorded *Man Machine Poem* over three or four pretty long sessions at the Bathouse. A record is always going to be like a photograph. It captures the way you were playing the day that you recorded it. The problem with having your own studio is that you always want to go back and fix every last thing. I think that Gord and Kevin were trying to make a perfect record, so it was kind of fraught at times.

ROB: While we were making the last record, Gord came to me and we sat in my room at the Bathouse and talked to each other face to face, as real friends should do, but rarely do.

Gord had come to an acceptance that his marriage was slipping away from him and with that acceptance came a realisation about the effect he had been having on a lot of other relationships in his life. He felt like he'd been pushing away most of his friends, pushing away his bandmates, in an effort to sustain his marriage. And now he'd reached a point where his home life had come apart, there was a sudden opportunity for healing his other relationships.

GORD S: Having been through a marriage breakdown myself, I was there for Gord. Despite everything, he was happier. It was like this challenge was a reminder to propel yourself forwards instead of backwards.

We'd been together through this whole thing and we'd got past that tough time where we were working things through and now we felt like it was onwards and upwards.

And then Gord goes and gets fuckin' sick.

ROB: Those few weeks in the studio together felt like years of therapy. We were writing, making music and great things were happening. Gord and I were working hard together planning how the album artwork would roll out. There was a lot of love and trust and respect.

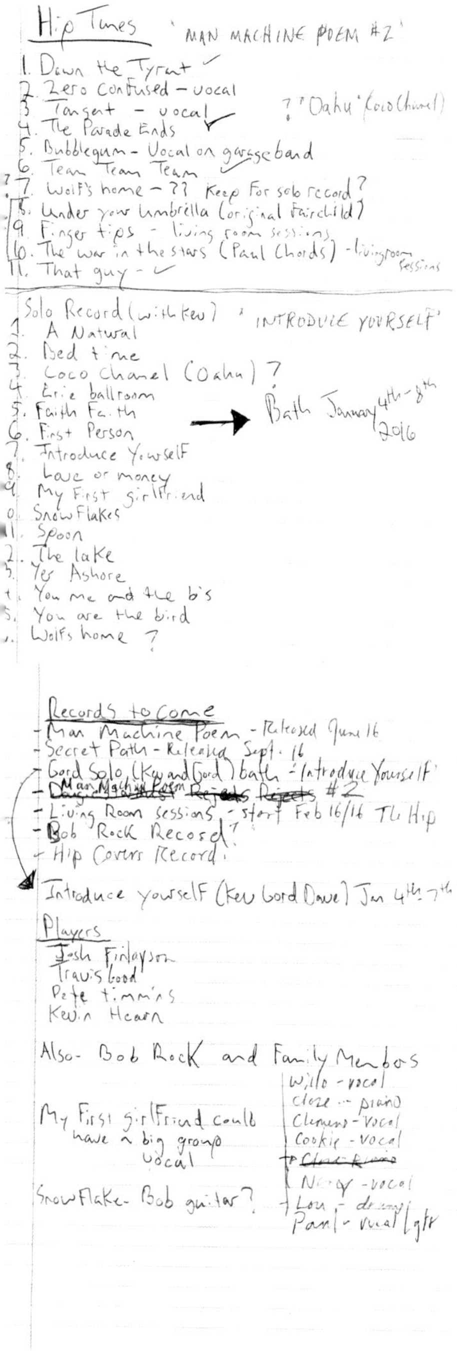

Handwritten notes (left margin):

Hip Tunes   'MAN MACHINE POEM #2'
1. Down the Tyrant
2. Zero Confused - Vocal
3. Tangent - vocal   ? 'Oahu' Coco Chanel
4. The Parade Ends
5. Bubblegum - Vocal on garage band
6. Team Team Team
7. Wolf's home - ?? Keep for solo record?
8. Under your umbrella (original fairchild)
9. Finger tips - living room sessions
10. The war in the stars (Paul Chords) - living room sessions
11. That guy

Solo Record (with Kev)   'INTRODUCE YOURSELF'
1. A Natural
2. Bed time
3. Coco Chanel (Oahu) ?
4. Erie ballroom   → Bath January 4th - 8th 2016
5. Faith Faith
6. First Person
7. Introduce Yourself
8. Love or money
9. My First girlfriend
10. Snow Flakes
11. Spoon
12. The lake
13. Yes Ashore
14. You me and the b's
15. You are the bird
16. Wolfs home ?

Records to come
- Man Machine Poem - Released June 16
- Secret Path - Releasing Sept 16
- Gord Solo (Kev and Gord) bath - Introduce Yourself
- Man Machine Poem Release Reports #2
- Living Room Sessions - start Feb 16/16 Th Hip
- Bob Rock Record?
- Hip Covers Record?

- Introduce Yourself (Kev Gord Dave) Jan 4th-7th

Players
Josh Finlayson
Travis Good
Pete Timmins
Kevin Hearn

Also- Bob Rock and Family Members
willo - vocal
close - piano
Clemens - Vocal
Cookie - Vocal
Chuck ?
Nancy - vocal
Lou - drums
Paul - vocal/gtr

My First girlfriend could have a big group vocal!

SnowFlake - Bob guitar?

Handwritten notes (centre):

Lou COMPULSISM GRADE 11
Met2 → Mixed Map
English → University level

"But rest assured it's nothing you did and nothing genetic"
- D J. Cook

Shopper:
- Dental Floss
- Dental Paste
- Dental Brushes
- Big Bottle of Water
Meeting or big field guys

Pages from Gord Downie's notebooks, containing plans for future Hip and solo projects and notes from a conversation with his neurologist, circa 2016

Opposite: Gord Downie's handwritten lyrics for 'Man' and 'Machine'

The first writing session for Man Machine Poem produced 'Tired as Fuck' and 'In Sarnia'

JOHNNY: Our parents taught us everything we know about family and gave us that shot in the arm when there was nobody coming to the shows, and now they were passing away. My dad, Gord Sinclair's mom, Gord Downie's dad, Robbie's parents, Paul's mom. That pulled us closer together. Mending our relationships was really important at that point. You know that whatever you've been through with these guys you can always rely on them, and that's true friendship.

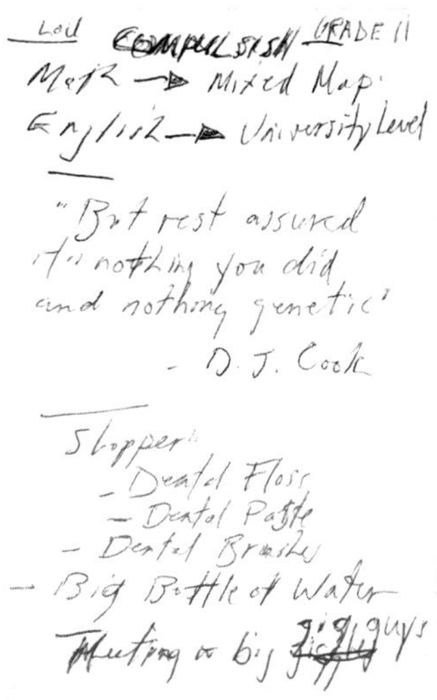

GORD S: When Gord's dad, Edgar, got sick, we saw a lot more of Gord and the energy that we had got from hanging out together on the road was made even stronger.

BERNIE BREEN: The first Downie I met was Edgar. After high school I got my real-estate license, and I walked into the offices of Pratt and Murray and the first person who stuck his hand out and introduced himself was Edgar Downie. He was a beauty, such a warm, wonderful man and so welcoming to me as a young kid. The apple doesn't fall far from the tree, because Gord certainly was a beauty of beauties too.

Given what happened straight after, I guess that losing Edgar was the beginning of the end for all of us.

ROB: We'd been at Edgar's memorial the day before and the following day I'd got tickets for Gord and me to see Daniel Romano play at the Grad Club. Gord texted to say he wasn't going to be able to make it and he'd fill me in later. What I didn't know was he'd had a big seizure while out on a walk earlier that day with his mom and sister and now he was at hospital undergoing a battery of tests.

GORD S: I'd been out with Gord at a club in Kingston when he'd had a seizure. We'd been smoking pot and it was noisy and hot and the lights were flashing. My eldest son has epilepsy, so that's what I thought was going on. When I heard he'd had another seizure the day after his dad's funeral, I thought it was a reaction to the accumulation of stress. Obviously, that was not the correct diagnosis. We were told that he had a tumour in his brain, but not to worry because it was the good kind to have. Then a couple of weeks went by and they found out with better imaging that in fact it wasn't the kind of brain tumour that you wanted to have.

BILLY RAY: The meeting where Gord received his diagnosis was at his sister Paula's house. The neurologist, D.J. Cook, delivered the horrible news that Gord had an aggressive form of brain cancer called glioblastoma. He basically said, 'We've found it early ... we should have 15 months.' Gord's other sister, Charlyn, said, 'Excuse me, Doctor, 15 months until reoccurrence?' And D.J. looked up and said, '15 months until death.' I saw Gord write in his notebook, '15 months until death.' Then he asked, 'OK, and when you say "quality of life", what do you mean by that?' D.J. answered, 'Well, you're walking and you're talking.' And Gord said, 'Walking, talking ... good.'

I sat in disbelief, watching this man I loved take this news with such strength and calmness. He asked a few more questions about what the treatment could be, would be, what his chances were. None of the news was good. D.J. told Gord to enjoy Christmas with his family, because he wouldn't have another Christmas like this. Meaning, if he made it to next year he most likely wouldn't be walking and talking.

Afterwards, we drove to the Bathouse and started working on *Introduce Yerself* almost immediately. The album consisted of songs that were like individual love letters to the people who meant the most to him. He lived his life in an artistic way in that he turned whatever was happening to him into something good.

JOHNNY: When I saw him after the operations and the chemo, it was still the same Gord. And when he hugged you, it was still the same hug. Gord was always tough. He didn't let it get him down, that's for sure.

ROB: Once Gord got the diagnosis, it all came into focus pretty quickly. I knew it was bad and then, over the course of a couple of days of doing research and talking to various people, I found out just how bad. And then you realise that life as you know it is over.

PATRICK DOWNIE: Gord idolised our father. Having just seen him die and the way he had handled it gave Gord what he needed to face his own death with the same dignity and grace.

PAUL: We all knew that this was, besides being so bad for Gord personally, really the end of the band, though he would have disagreed. I still can't believe it. But I'm less weak about it. Time has helped, but it's still just one of those things that no one saw coming, including him.

RB: Our fun period, which had started with the *Fully Completely* reissue tour, turned out to be very brief. We were all in this holding pattern, not knowing what was going to happen with this record or, more importantly, with our friend.

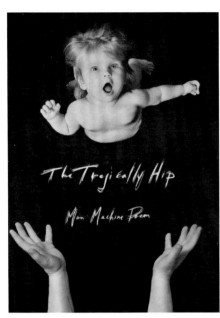

JOHNNY: In the old days, we seemed to be able to keep the lid on a record for six months while the record company was getting it pressed and preparing the promo. That was always an exciting period where you'd be able to listen to this music that you knew was going to be coming out.

When we were keeping a lid on Gord's diagnosis, it was absolutely the opposite. It was dread, because we knew that things weren't going to get better. Then when I turned the news on, the same news programme that I watch every night, and the news presenter was saying what was going to happen to my friend and my band, I think that's when it really sank in for me.

Dougie To Stardust
Transformation is birth/death/rebirth/re-death -witnessing death, a birth (humans, animals); animal euthenasia
Dougie Stardust is a record about transformation.
DOUGIE (formerly known as 'Reprise Machine') [jogging]

Man Machine Poem
RECORDED: 2015
THE BATHOUSE, BATH, ON
PRODUCERS: KEVIN DREW, DAVE HAMELIN
RELEASED: 17 JUNE 2016
Man
In a World Possessed by the Human Mind
What Blue
In Sarnia
Here, in the Dark
Great Soul
Tired as Fuck
Hot Mic
Ocean Next
Machine

ROB: When the diagnosis happened, we were about to release our record. It was off in the Czech Republic being printed.

The album was going to be called 'Dougie Stardust'. In our world, Dougies and Tammies are your typical hosers, so the idea was that Dougie Stardust was going to be like Ziggy Stardust's dumber Canadian brother. There was going to be a fun campaign including a line of beer – 'make mine a Dougie.' The beer label had a 'mullet mirror' on it so when you looked at it you could see your face wearing a mullet.

By the time we got the record back from the Czech Republic, David Bowie was dead and Gord had cancer and it was clear we were going to have to change things. We destroyed all the records – I kept one for myself – and redesigned the package.

ROB: It took Gord's diagnosis for them to realise how petty their differences were in the face of something so much more important. Through the course of Gord's illness, Paul was very much there for him.

PAUL: When Gord got sick, his younger brother, Pat, was keeping me updated. In February 2016 Pat phoned up and told me I should come up and visit for a night. So I went up and I ended up staying for months. Gord didn't want me to go. I'd just read, or talk if he wanted to talk. He was playing records and working on his shit – he still had a lot left to do. So that stage of our friendship was another gift to both of us. Thirty years of small tensions over all the decisions you have to make together as band members just peeled away.

ROB: Paul and Gord were inseparable friends, but over a period of probably the last four or five albums things got progressively rougher between them. By the time of the last couple of records, they were getting into verbal arguments, which I'd never seen from them before. Paul was always the guy who sat on the fence on every issue, but now he started to really assert his opinion on things.

PATRICK DOWNIE: We grew up with Paul. His nickname is Rock and that's not for 'rock and roll', it's because the dude's a rock. He doesn't suffer any fools, he doesn't overreact, he thinks everything out. He's a very careful observer. And he just has this really calming way about him that I know Gord relied on most of his life.

You feel this very steady force with Paul; as long as he's around, then everything's OK. So, at such a time of need, Paul's presence was everything.

GORD D: Paul's been helping me out a lot, as he has since we first met in grade 11. He's always been a great help to me. Beyond everything else, I love him so much.

PAUL: Gord and I remained best friends throughout, but we had a few tough times. The way we handled our tough times was to have a blowout. I wasn't afraid of him and he wasn't afraid of me. It didn't happen often and we were always able to resolve any problems we had. But our friendship was a hell of an arc.

PAUL: He didn't need much help really, he just needed company. I went to all the radiation treatments with him and there was more of a connection between us, like it was in high school, when we were drinking coffee at HoJo's. I feel lucky about all of it.

Right: Recording 'Happy Birthday' for a friend of the band at the end of a soundcheck, Metro Centre, Halifax, NS, 5 December 2004

PAUL: While I was helping Pat look after Gord as he was going through the radiation and chemo, Gord kept asking me whether we were going to tour *Man Machine Poem*. It wasn't like he was in total denial about his situation, but maybe he was a little bit. There was something beautiful in that, and then it became beautiful for everybody that that tour actually happened.

PATRICK SAMBROOK: Making Gord's illness public was intense. We tried to be calculated in the way we did it; nothing was left to chance.

BERNIE BREEN: Over the May holiday weekend, Patty and I had a lot of conversations with the band, and Gord's oncologist, Dr Perry, came in and talked it through with us all. We had two different versions of the press release ready to go, one announcing the end of the band and the other announcing the tour. We only decided on that Monday whether to greenlight the tour or not. It was a weird weekend.

PATRICK DOWNIE: In the build-up to the announcement no one could really tell how big the news was going to be, but when Gord and I took his youngest son to school that morning all the staff in the school were lined up outside staring at us as we were walking along the street.

Then we went to Loblaws to buy peanut butter and Patrick Sambrook came flying into the store and he was a sweaty mess. 'This is blowing up! International news! CNN!' He was freaking out and Gord said, 'What if I live for another seven years? Everyone's gonna think I'm an asshole.'

GORD S: When Gord announced that he wanted to go back out on the road, I never thought for a second that we were going to be able to pull it off. I just saw it as a chance for us to hang out and listen to music and play guitars, kind of like we used to do before we put the band together.

But then it really started happening. The surgery they'd done on Gord's left temporal lobe had caused him to lose his capacity to remember words, so Billy Ray committed all the lyrics to a computer file and we had monitors so Gord could read them Frank Sinatra-style. Interestingly, even though he couldn't remember the words, he still knew how to sing them. The meter was still there.

GORD D: The worst punishment I've had to take from this is I can't remember people's names and I can't remember lyrics. That's one savage kick in the pants.

ROB: We just thought it was a silly idea, but what do you do? This was our friend, our brother, so we got together and started to rehearse. I would have bet everything I had that we'd never play another note in public again, but Gord was very determined. He was on the exercise bike and working the songs over and over, trying to build his memory back up.

JOHNNY: I knew Gord would be able to do that final tour. His phrasing was good and he was singing in time. I didn't ever think that he would bow out of a tour and he never did.

PATRICK DOWNIE: Gord was pretty good at disguising his apprehension. It was really him who was driving this from the very beginning and he knew that everybody else's confidence was depending on what he was like when he walked into that first rehearsal.

Leading up to that we were trying to get him to practise, because he couldn't remember anything that required real memory. But he didn't want to do any of that. I don't think he wanted to know if he was really going to be that handicapped or not.

We went in there and everybody was on pins and needles. They chose to do 'Escape Is at Hand for the Travellin' Man', which is a great song, but a tricky one. And, fuck, it was like 'Happy Birthday' coming out of his mouth. It just flowed right out, and you could feel the room relax.

BERNIE BREEN: The team, loved ones, crew and everybody did whatever it took to make that tour happen. It was very special.

TRISTIN CHIPMAN: I couldn't have imagined not being part of that final tour. I couldn't have been anywhere other than with them all during that time.

ROB: You're talking about a dying man and you grant him his last wish, regardless of what it is.

Left: CDs of songs rehearsed at the Bathouse for the Man Machine Poem tour, 18 June and 11 July 2016

Opposite: Gord Downie's rehearsal notes for the tour, listing the songs The Hip practised each day, May and June 2016 (left)

Master song list, showing the tracks from which the set for each show was built (right)

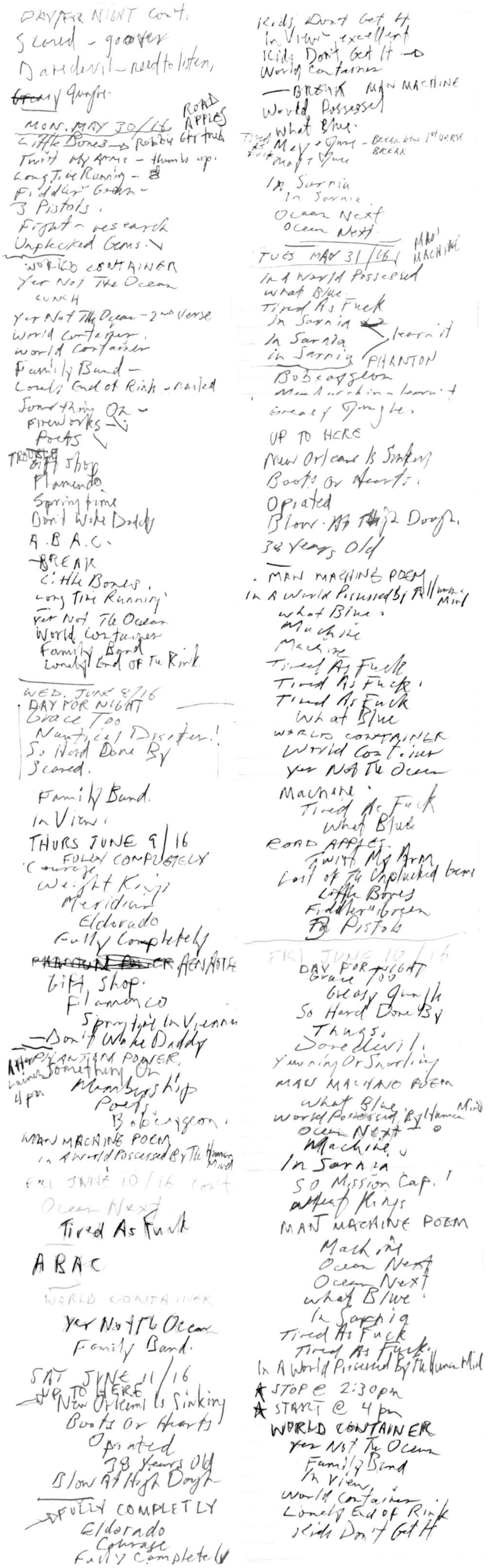

(handwritten setlist / rehearsal notes, left columns)

BILLY RAY: We rehearsed more for that final tour than any other event ever in the 30 years that I worked for the band.

We worked really hard on getting Gord back to a point where we could make people believe he wasn't just reading lyrics off of a teleprompter, but the fact is he was. He had to read every lyric of every song, because, no matter how many nights we played, those memories weren't there anymore.

On the very final night he was still reading, still just as terrified of forgetting all the lyrics or skipping a section. He worked right to the very last note. And I was really proud of him for it.

GORD D: I wanted to do the whole of the new record, but we slowly moved away from that idea. Instead we designed it so that you would get mini-sets of four songs from seven or eight records. We went on the road with about 90 songs and then Paul rearranged them so that every night would be different. He picked songs he knew were my secret favourites. He didn't tell me, but I know that's what he did.

PAUL: Gord wanted to play quirky songs that we'd only played once or twice, ever. He'd listen to Hip records and try and find songs that really intrigued him. I'd have to tell him that no one knew how to play that one, because we'd only done it once and that was 16 years ago at the album release party. Gord liked pushing the envelope and he wanted to make it as challenging as possible, for all of us. Everyone played ball.

JOHNNY: Some of those songs I don't think we'd ever played as a band and now we were doing them on tour.

GORD S: Paul had this idea that we would start the show really tight like when we were a club band, then we'd play more like a theatre band and then we'd do the last bit like we were an arena band. We broke the show up into mini-sets featuring each record so that Gord could have a break in between.

JOHNNY: I know that Gord's doctors didn't think the tour was a great idea. They thought he should be spending time with his family and getting his affairs in order. But he was doing that final tour for us too. He wanted to make sure that we were set up. So he was taking care of us and he was taking care of his family. He was really stitching things up at the end.

GORD D: When I was getting ready for the last tour, I listened to all our records for the first time in a long while and realised how wordy they were. I'd take up all the spots and leave no room for anyone else until I ran out of breath and then Robbie would close out with something really cool. I'd never noticed that before. I think I apologised. I've been doing a lot of apologising.

MASTER SONG LIST
7/20/16

UP TO HERE	ROAD APPLES	FULLY COMPLETELY
Blow	Bones	50 Mission Cap
New Orleans	3 Pistols	Fully
Boots	Twist	Courage
Opiated	Luxury	100th Meridian
(38 Years Old)	Fiddler	Eldorado
	Long Time	Wheat Kings
		Looking
		(Locked)

DAY FOR NIGHT	TROUBLE AT THE HENHOUSE	PHANTOM POWER
Grace	Gift	Poets
Daredevil	Springtime	Something On
Greasy	Ahead by a Century	Bobcaygeon
Yawning	Daddy	Membership
So Hard Done By	Flamenco	Fireworks
Thugs		Escape
(Scared)		(Rules)
		(Chagrin)

MUSIC AT WORK	IN VIOLET LIGHT	IN BETWEEN EVOLUTION
Lake Fever	Good Life	Summer is Killing Us
Puttin' Down	Dire Wolf	Gus
Music at Work	Are You Ready	Nashville
Toronto #4	Throwing Off Glass	New Orleans is Beat

WORLD CONTAINER	WE ARE THE SAME	NOW FOR PLAN A
Ocean	Morning Moon	Transformation
Lonely End of the Rink	Last Recluse	Man Machine
In View	Coffee Girl	Look Ahead
Family Band	Struggle Has a Name	We Want to Be It
Kids		Streets Ahead
World Container		

MAN MACHINE POEM		
Machine		
What Blue		
Tired as Fuck		
Possessed		
Sarnia		
Ocean's Next		

ROB: Even the night before the tour started, I didn't see it happening. Maybe we'd get one show or part of a show, but with every successive show it became more obvious that Gord was getting stronger. He was drawing more from the crowds than he was giving, so he came off stage each night exhausted but invigorated.

GORD D: That last tour, I enjoyed every second of it. Wished it would go on forever. I guess that's why at the end of it I felt so great.

Maybe people were showing up worrying that I was going to be hobbled over, but, no, it was the best singing I've ever done. I'm not saying that to brag, but just to thank whoever was giving me that stuff.

ROB: I still thought it was a terrible idea and I was way beyond reluctant. I just thought that any moment there'd be 10,000 phones taking footage of Gord having a seizure on stage. That was the worst thing I could imagine.

So I just put my head down and did my job to the best of my ability, but I couldn't be in the moment of what was happening because it was too much for me emotionally. I had a hard time looking out at the audience and seeing people singing with joy or crying in despair. I still haven't watched the movie. If I see it on TV, I just turn it off.

GORD S: I don't think Gord was ever more sure about anything in his life, and I was never more unsure. If he had said after the soundcheck for the first show that he couldn't go through with it, I would have been perfectly fine with that. Perhaps I saw a little glimpse of fear in Gord's eyes when he stepped up to the mic on that first night in Victoria, but then it vanished and off we went.

Given his prognosis, most people would curl up into a ball. But Gord just kept getting stronger. It was great to see him in his element. He loved performing and he was really, really good at it.

STEVE BERLIN: The thing that everybody saw on the last tour was that Gord was about as brave as a guy could be. Every night, he went out on a high wire over the gorge without a net. He took risks that nobody else would be willing to take.

BILLY RAY: The first time that Gord ever went on stage feeling completely comfortable was the final tour. It was very odd that it took him that long to get there. Within two minutes into any concert he was drenched as if he had been in the shower, but on the final tour he barely sweat at all. It was because he had finally come to this place of 'What am I nervous about? This is what I do, this is who I am.'

The first three dates of the Man Machine Poem tour: Memorial Centre, Victoria, 22 July 2016; Rogers Arena, Vancouver, 24 & 26 July 2016

BILLY RAY: To watch Gord go from this Grizzly Adams, shades-on, frail, soft-spoken man, to a god in leather suits and fancy feathered hats was an incredible experience.

GORD D: Every fantasy I'd ever had for a show was coming true. I played every other day, which for a singer is heaven on earth. And I got to wear seven leather suits.

PATRICK SAMBROOK: The first night of the tour as Gord headed to the stage was the first time I saw the pink suit, because that's what he wanted. Nobody saw it until he made his grand entrance like Liberace, and it was spectacular. We all loved it.

JOHNNY: If you look at the clothing that Gord wore for 90 percent of our career, it was moth-eaten Star Wars T-shirts, brown corduroy jackets, cowboy boots. Then at the end it was Ziggy Stardust. Nobody else could pull off suits like that, at that point in their career. I think he wanted to go out with a bang. 'Get a load of this!'

PATRICK DOWNIE: Gord had lifelong dreams of wearing fantastic suits and plumy hats like his heroes Dylan and Bowie, but he had never quite gone for it. I personally think he didn't need the suit. He could have been up there in rags and would still have looked good. But in that final tour the fancy costume finally matched the stage persona.

TRISTIN CHIPMAN: If Gord wrapped himself up it made his throat feel better. It became a running joke; if there was a breeze at soundcheck, you'd throw all kinds of things at him to get him warm and keep the mood up.

I sent socks to a seamstress to put a button in and he liked that, so we kept buying these crazy socks. Everyone else thought it was stupid, but we thought it was funny.

JOHNNY: Gord wanted to say goodbye and thanks to all those great people and all those great cities. We didn't get to Montreal or Halifax or Newfoundland and I think he was upset about that, but he got out to most of the places he wanted to, and he did it on his terms.

BILLY RAY: For the last two minutes at the end of each night Gord stood and absorbed the moment and smiled. He said that he tried to make eye contact with every person in the room to say goodbye.

GEDDY LEE: I went to a show in Toronto and I watched Gord bathe in the music, taking in every person in that room. There were moments where it looked like he was trying to devour the love that was being thrown at him.

PATRICK DOWNIE: In retrospect, you see how important that final tour was in terms of Gord's legacy. He really did get to see how appreciated he was, to see how cherished he was. It was so special to witness that, to see him finally get his dues.

DAN AYKROYD: It was a national goodbye, so it was bittersweet, triumphant, joyous and sad ... but it also gave us hope. Here's someone going through this very personal challenge, and he still wants to go on stage and embrace the fans.

GD: Thank you for keeping me pushing, and keeping me pushing.

DAVID BASTEDO: When I look at this image from Winnipeg [below], and I disassociate myself from the process of capturing it, and from the pain and sadness and emptiness that I feel at the absence of Gord – my friend, a supporter and an influence in my life and many others – I get to joy.

I think of everything that went into the moment of this image. The years that we all had together. As fans and as friends. The love that it represents. The creativity of the words and music that The Tragically Hip made, which brought us all together. Which changed my life.

I think of the passion and the talent and above all the strength. To fight, to challenge, to struggle and to go on. To go out dancing, on a stage.

GORD S: What became really apparent to us as we went along on the tour was the genuine affection between the audience and the band. People were very aware of what Gord was going through, but the atmosphere wasn't sorrowful. It was joyful.

In the old days, we found people singing along to our songs a little off-putting, but if you get out of your own way and look at it from a positive perspective you realise that these pieces of music and lyrics that we've put together have meant something to a lot of people out there. That's a good foundation for culture and heritage. It's the power of art to bring us together in a positive, celebratory way.

BILLY RAY: The Hip crowd was distinctive. For me, there was no better moment than when I called house lights and it would go black, and then you'd hear this jet taking off as everyone screamed their lungs out. That sound always gives me goosebumps.

On that final tour, in Vancouver the crowd was so loud that I actually had to pull my in-ear out to make sure that the sound I was hearing was the crowd and not something that had gone wrong.

PATRICK DOWNIE: The shows were incredible. You could feel the gratitude, the excitement, the sadness, the awe. The energy in those buildings was indescribable.

the tragically hip

Friday August 12th
Toronto Ontario
Air Canada Centre

Day Schedule

Lunch: 12:00 - 3:00pm
Dinner: 4:30-7:30pm

PA Tuning: 1:00pm
Line Check: 4:00pm
Tour Photo: 4:45pm
Soundcheck: 5:00pm

Doors: 6:30pm

The Tragically Hip: 8:30-10:30pm

Curfew: 11:00pm

info to know
No Load Out
TOUR PHOTO
Welcome Lee Moro to the Tour
Say Goodbye and Thank you to Mark Vreeken
No More Tickets Available for Toronto Shows.
Have a Great Day!!

PAUL: In the last ten to 15 years of the band, whenever we had a day off on the road we'd take the crew out for dinner. On the last tour the shows were every other day, which meant that every other night we could all have dinner together. I think that made us a little more social, as opposed to everyone running out and grabbing their own stuff.

TRISTIN CHIPMAN: As the tour was coming to an end, it was starting to get really heavy, but we weren't talking about it either. The whole thing felt like exaggerated pretend. Like, let's drink and dance on the bus, and try to make it feel normal. I think that got to Gord.

There was a moment when Gord and I were in the dressing room. He said something like, 'It's just the same. Everybody's just the same,' and he was down. It was a very dark sentiment. I remember kneeling in front of him and saying, 'Nothing is the same, but nobody knows what to do. Everything is different.'

Gord taught me how to be a better friend to someone who dies in the future.

RICKY WELLINGTON: Everybody in the crew had their moments because we all knew what the end was, but we also knew to put our emotions to one side. Everybody stepped up and did their job, which was to make sure that The Tragically Hip put on a fantastic tour. The crew did a phenomenal job and the end result was a phenomenal tour.

That final tour was the best and worst of both worlds. The best was that we were all together, and the worst was that we were never going to be together again.

BILLY RAY: My friendship with Gord was real, although he would sometimes jokingly call it 'paid friendship'. He knew me better than anybody else on this planet. I trusted him and I really felt like I could say anything to him. I miss him a lot.

Tour crew (l to r): Aven Hoffarth, Katy Sluzar, Jenn Pressey, Courtney Yuchtman, Tess Minor, Gillian Reiss, Dr Lindsay Voigt, Tristin Chipman (third row, left)

Billy Ray Koster and Ricky Wellington (third row, right)

Patrick Downie (left) and Gord Downie (fourth row, left)

Billy Ray Koster and Gord Downie (fourth row, right)

RB: In retrospect, it was obviously the right choice to finish in Kingston.

JOHNNY: When we were out west at the beginning of the tour, people left us alone and it was just like old times. But when we got to Ontario, things started to happen fast. We did this great show in Ottawa and we were able to have our final party there. It was just the band and crew hanging out having a great time. In many ways, that felt like the real end of the tour.

Then when we came to Kingston everything got really locked in and it wasn't fun. Kingston's always a difficult place to play, because there are all these people that we've got to take care of and so your brain is taken away from the show itself.

JOHNNY: **Our first ever gig, which Robbie set up for us, was at the Kingston Artists Association on Queen Street. Now, 32 years later, we were playing our final show in a hockey arena built, literally, a stone's throw away. From the back door of the arena to the KAA must be about 60 feet.**

GORD S: The day of the Kingston gig was super-crazy busy, which in retrospect I'm grateful for. I didn't have time to be bummed that this was going to be the last show we'd ever do. Then when we were performing, the focus was on delivering the best possible version of that song in that moment. As it always was.

PATRICK DOWNIE: We were staying out at Paul's place, away from Kingston, to get away from the hype. On the morning of the show, I had to go into town and Kingston was transforming into Disney World for The Tragically Hip. Every restaurant, every public space had banners and Hip music playing. It was like walking through a fairground.

JOHNNY: The morning of the show I got up and it was a beautiful sunny day. It was weird for me to be staying in a hotel downtown. I remember walking over to the gig much earlier than I normally would have done. I looked around the venue and then I went and sat in the back lounge of the bus.

It was like I was looking at everything through someone else's eyes. I didn't even feel like I was there. I was doing all my normal things – putting a guest list together, having something to eat, warming up. I've watched it on TV and it still feels like it's somebody else on stage.

BILLY RAY: The afternoon of the final show, I was polishing Paul's sunburst Les Paul and wondering why it was taking so long. And then I realised it was because my tears kept landing on the guitar. Everyone else had this sense of celebration, that we'd managed to get to the end of the tour. But I wasn't happy. I didn't want it to end. I didn't believe that Gord wasn't going to make it through this. I remember it being a hot, muggy, windy, strange-weather day, and the whole town was alive with this crazy Hip energy.

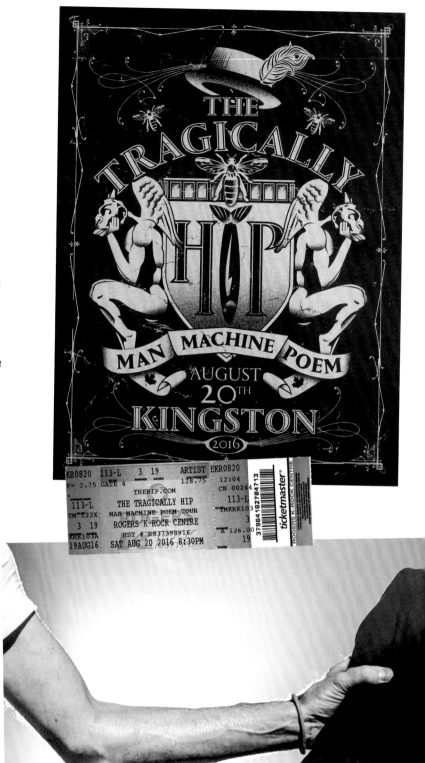

DAN AYKROYD: **When the guys came around Gord, I saw the essence of four great souls coming together to protect and nurture one of their own. Like crows, when one of their number is sick or dying, come together in a circle and recognise their fallen member.**

It was a beautiful moment. But then they started, that dragon started, and, man, we rode the dragon that night.

MARK NORMAN: Justin Trudeau came to the last show and what I loved about it was he had his can of beer and was wearing his Hip T-shirt and jeans. The prime minister of the country, just showing up. When he came in he waved to the crowd and the crowd waved to him and burst into 'Oh, Canada'. It was such a wonderful moment that showed the importance of The Hip to the nation.

JUSTIN TRUDEAU: I like to think that Gord saw in me some of the things I saw in him, which was someone who loved this country and wanted to bring Canadians into that place of a deep love for this country, which he had. Not through a sense of what this country is, so much as what this country could be. What this country is in the stories we live every day.

I think we saw that in each other, and connecting on that was the basis for a friendship that was deep and real, even though we didn't get to see each other nearly as often as we would have liked.

DAN AYKROYD: I remember that it rained late that night, washing all that music off us, so that we could get up and begin again the next day. Because the music sticks to you. I think the rain helped us to wash away the experience into a beautiful memory in history, which it became. Because there was no more after that.

BILLY RAY: After the show, everyone had gone to different places to do their own thing; Gord had gone up to Robbie's house. The city went from being so full of people to a ghost town in a matter of hours. I went back and sat on the security guard's chair outside the band bus, waiting for them to get back from Robbie's because Gord was going to get on the bus back to Toronto. When they showed up at about 2 or 3 a.m., Gord asked me what I was still doing there. So I told him I had already gotten a new gig as the security guard at the K-Rock Centre. He laughed at that and said, 'No, no, we've got more to do.'

The next morning the weather was really horrible – dark grey, windy and rainy – which I thought was fitting. I woke up in a hotel in Kingston, because I didn't want to go home that night. There was a feeling that it wasn't really over until I went home. I just remember it being among the darkest, most melancholy couple of days of my life, because I never expected to be saying goodbye so soon. Even though it had been 30 years, it seemed like we had 20 more to go. I wasn't ready for it to end.

BERNIE BREEN: The day after Kingston was a great relief. Just fundamentally, from a business perspective, we were on pins and needles from day one. The first song of the first show in Victoria was the most emotional I was on the whole tour. What happened before, during and after every show, everybody coming together afterwards and celebrating every night ... that's where national celebration came from.

It was the best tour they ever did, without question. The set lists, pacing, show, look, feel, sound, the crowd's response, the tears ... it was incredible. You couldn't dream it. Sad but triumphant.

PAUL: We'd been thinking we might extend the tour beyond Kingston, maybe play Montreal and Halifax. But the first thing Gord said after Kingston, backstage, was 'That felt like the last show.' He was half smiling. He was happy. He knew it was obvious to us. Because it was Kingston and it was being broadcast and everything had gone right, it really did feel like the last show.

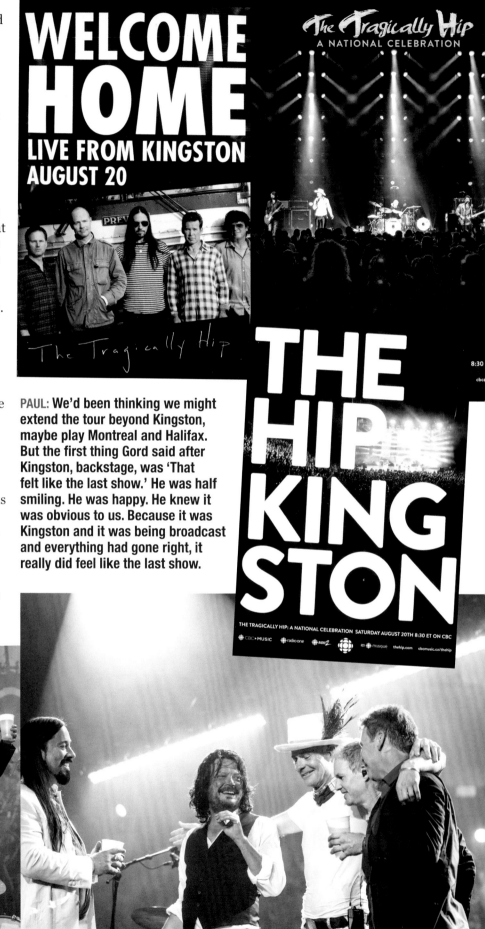

PROCLAMATION

PATRICK SAMBROOK: The impact that The Tragically Hip had on Canada was demonstrated by that tour and especially by the number of people that tuned in to the final show, which was historic. To this day we don't know the exact number, because there were so many people that watched it communally. But it showed me that The Hip connected to people in this country like no band ever has or ever will.

ALLAN GREGG: That last concert was the second most watched television event in Canadian history. Eleven million people. There are only eleven million households in Canada.

MARK NORMAN: The entire nation was so focused on that show – every town and hamlet in the country had PAs and big screens set up in the parks.

BILLY RAY: Seeing the way that all of Canada pulled together on 20 August 2016 to watch the final show, I felt vindicated in saying that The Hip were more than a rock band, that they were a part of the fabric of this nation.

You'd hear people say all the time that The Hip got them through cancer, or bereavement, or divorce. Or they chose something by the band as their wedding song, or they were listening to The Hip when their baby was born. And to this day, whenever I meet someone new and they find out that I worked for The Hip they'll tell me where they were when they watched that final show.

TOM POWER: I was at a festival in Milwaukee and we were the only Canadian band on the bill. We asked for a backstage dressing room with internet so we could watch the concert. But it was on a laptop and it wasn't loud enough, so we took the laptop and shoved it in a big frame drum to get the amplification. As people walked by, they'd ask what we were watching. We explained it to them and more and more people gathered around to learn what it meant to us as Canadians to have that concert.

ROB: A few weeks after the tour ended, I received a long letter from a guy named Dave Bielanko, who was in a band called Marah. He told me all about how he'd watched the final show by himself in a barn in Philadelphia, because it was such an intense, private moment for him. In a weird way, it was the first time that I'd engaged beyond my family and the band and crew with what had transpired. It was profoundly moving to read the perspective of someone to whom the band had meant so much. I still pull that letter out every once in a while.

JOHNNY: Playing that last show was a little like being in a spaceship with everyone observing what was going on. For the rest of our lives, we'll have all those stories about where people were in the country on that night. I love that.

GORD S: Canada is an amalgam of three territories and ten provinces that couldn't be more dissimilar from each other. The fabric that holds this country together is pretty thin. And so it's important for us to go out of our way to listen to each other's stories. It's important for a young artist in Newfoundland to be able to hear what a young artist in Victoria's up to, and all points in between. It's important for newcomers to Canada to find their place within the national milieu and tell their stories of coming to this country, and it's important for our First Nations people to tell their stories about having always been here.

We were in the listening business. Maybe the reason we lost our way in the early 2000s was that we stopped listening to each other and we lost sight of the congregation. But we found the path out of the woods, and when we got to that last run in 2016 we realised that people had been listening to us all along.

Fans gather to watch The Hip's final show on a big screen, Springer Market Place, Kingston, 20 August 2016

GD: If this is the last thing I do, then I'm happy.

GORD D: *Soon, in a few days, a couple of weeks, there's 150 years that Canada wants to celebrate, and I will personally then celebrate the birth of our country, celebrate the next 150 years. It will take 150 years or seven generations to heal the wound of the residential school.*

To become a country, and truly call ourselves Canada, it means we must become one. We must walk down a path of reconciliation from now on. Together, and forever. This is the first day of forever: the greatest day of my life, the greatest day of all of our lives.

ASSEMBLY OF FIRST NATIONS,
6 DECEMBER 2016

Secret Path

Between the early 1880's and 1996, over 150,000 Indigenous children were systematically taken from their families.

They were sent away to residential schools run by church organizations and funded by the Canadian government.

PAUL: I've never come across anyone who made as much out of the last two years of their life as Gord did.

GORD S: The moment that the tour was finished Gord pivoted right into *Secret Path*. He was mad at me for a while because he wanted me to come out and play with him, but I'm glad that I didn't. This was something that he owned and I didn't want The Hip to define it in any way.

    Secret Path spoke not only to Gord's advocacy and courage but to him as Gord Downie the person, not the singer for The Tragically Hip. It wasn't just a one-off thing, but has had a lasting effect in bridging the gap between First Nations people and us newcomers to Canada.

GORD D: My brother Mike gave me this piece from *Maclean's* magazine about a boy called Chanie Wenjack who ran away from a residential school in 1966 and died trying to get home. A friend of mine, Kevin Drew, asked me one day to make a record with him. I said that I would like to, but I didn't think I had any songs. But the weird thing is, I'd been writing about Chanie. So we made the *Secret Path* record and it's an attempt to capture the feeling of trying to get home. It's the best thing I've ever done. By 'best', I mean that it helps my heart a little. Nothing else really matters to me.

ROB: *Secret Path* is something that probably wouldn't have flown as a Hip project. We would have found it interesting and we would certainly have entertained it as an idea, but it would have been a very different thing had we done it. Really, it needed to be done the way Gord did it, which worked out beautifully.

JOHNNY: *Secret Path* was Gord's most important work, apart from being a dad. It was a story that he needed to get out. While we were doing our final tour, he was working day and night to get that record ready to release on the 50th anniversary of Chanie Wenjack's death.

PATRICK DOWNIE: There were so many people that wanted to visit Gord for a last goodbye or to keep him company, but he wanted no part of that. Gordie wanted the Irish exit, to slip away without really saying goodbye. Some people copped onto that. His best Toronto buddy and constant collaborator, Josh Finlayson, figured out that the way to stay in Gord's orbit was to find work for him to do. Gord had all this material that was flowing out of him. So instead of Josh coming over just for visits, they were writing a record.

BOB ROCK: Gord was always happiest when he was creating. The hardest thing, thinking about him, is that he was living a full life and hungry for the future. Great songwriters like Gord want to share their thoughts, to be heard, and he had a lot to say.

JUSTIN TRUDEAU: Gord was an extraordinary presence. He was speaking to you individually, and he was speaking to everyone at the same time. He filled the space with an ability to draw you in and feel what he was feeling. And what he was feeling every time he sang any song was full and complete every step of the way. That authenticity and that depth of strength and passion that just shone through every time … it was an absolute marvel to be in his presence when he was bringing us along in this beautiful rant about where and who we are. He was someone who took so much space up on stage, yet in conversation, he left so much room for you.

BILLY RAY: Gord was seen as this iconic rock star, but he never thought of himself that way. Because he wasn't. He was a regular guy with all the problems that regular guys have. He knew that he wasn't perfect; he actually said to me, 'Billy, I wasn't the easiest guy to love,' to which I replied, 'Well, I found it pretty easy.'

GORD D: I've just got to keep doing things. I want to keep going to the point where people start saying, 'Jesus, is that guy not dead yet?'

Gord Downie's Secret Path album, released on 18 October 2016, was the focal point of a multimedia project telling the story of Chanie Wenjack and the wider story of the Canadian residential school system. The project also comprised a tour, a graphic novel, an animated film and school teaching materials.

Secret Path was a shortlist nominee for the Polaris Music Prize, 2017

Opposite: Secret Path tour, Roy Thomson Hall, Toronto, 18 October 2016

Secret Path band (l to r): Kevin Drew, Charles Spearin, Dave Hamelin, Gord Downie, Josh Finlayson and Kevin Hearn at the Dream Serenade benefit concert, Massey Hall, Toronto, 22 October 2016 (centre left)

PAUL: When I got the call from Pat to tell me Gord had died I knew what he was going to say. I was on a train and I could almost feel things go extra quiet.

Obviously, it was big news and I saw a bit of that on TV. Seeing people talking about Gord was quite affecting. People felt so connected to him, and it was a sad day for the whole country. He affected a lot of people with his words and his singing and his actions, his kindness with people. It was a bigger deal than he probably thought it would be.

ROB: We had a good songwriting session with Gord a few months before he passed. He was still looking forward, which was so admirable and inspiring.

When I got the word that he'd passed away, I felt a bit of relief for him. There are things worse than death, but it's hard going on.

JOHNNY: A couple of days later, there was a ceremony at Nathan Phillips Square in Toronto. Gord's brother Mike got up and spoke and then Don Kerr sang 'Fiddler's Green'. It was a very still night and I remember looking up at a Canadian flag just as a wisp of air came out of nowhere. The flag billowed in the breeze and then was still again. I thought about what a Buddhist friend of mine said to me ... she said Gord's spirit would still be here with us for a few more days after he passed. I think she was right.

CITY OF
TORONTO

Expression of Condolence for Gordon Downie
by Toronto City Council

The Mayor and Members of Toronto City Council are deeply saddened to learn of the passing of Gordon Downie, widely known as Gord Downie, of the band "The Tragically Hip." The legendary band's frontman passed away on October 17, 2017 at the age of 53.

Gord is an iconic Canadian born singer-songwriter who gained worldwide recognition as lead singer of The Tragically Hip. Their music is associated with the great talent and true patriotism we have here in Canada, and they remain a prolific band that is commonly recognized as the most Canadian band in the world.

In his personal life, Gord Downie is known for his advocacy for environmentalism and indigenous affairs. Gord leaves behind a strong legacy and commitment to Canada's First Peoples by way of the Gord Downie and Chanie Wenjack Fund to support reconciliation between Indigenous and non-Indigenous peoples.

Gord was a long time Toronto resident, and was known for steadfast support for local Toronto music and musicians. In addition to regularly showing up to venues as a fan, he performed for Toronto audiences countless times.

Gord Downie was an inspiration to us all. His music is an essential part of the soundtrack of Canada. His diagnosis was heartbreaking but he faced illness with courage and a commitment to continue doing what he loved.

Gord Downie will be deeply missed by the entire nation.

The City Clerk is requested to convey, on behalf of the Members of Toronto City Council, our sincere sympathy to Gord Downie's family.

November 8, 2017

ALLAN GREGG: The Tragically Hip has become an integrated part of the Canadian fabric. And Gord Downie's passing was a thread that was pulled from that fabric.

Gord Downie died on 17 October 2017 in Toronto, at the age of 53

Above: Toronto, 1999

Left: Candlelit vigil, Bobcaygeon, ON, 18 October 2017

Opposite: Backstage, Fillmore, San Francisco, 7 April 1999

Overleaf, page 292: Toronto, 19 June 2012

Page 293: Air Canada Centre, Toronto, 14 February 2013 (top)

K-Rock Centre, Kingston, ON, 20 August 2016 (bottom)

A lyric from 'Escape Is at Hand for the Travellin' Man' (bottom left)

PAUL: I lost a lifelong friend. The fact that we were able to stay friends while working together for 30-some years says something. Gord was a guy that was fun to laugh with and that I had great respect for – both for his talent and for him as a person. I knew it would be difficult to get through it, but I didn't know it would be as tough as it turned out to be. I had a couple of years of not wanting to do anything. So trying to move on like I knew he would want me to do didn't happen right away.

I was depressed that Gord was gone and at the unfairness of it all. I wasn't really going through too much sadness about the band. After a year or two, people started asking me whether I missed playing, and, yes, I did miss it. But I was also grateful that I got to do it for so long. It wasn't a three-year run or anything. It was 32 years. And little by little I healed. I felt less apt to get emotional. I still feel Gord with me, helping me, like he always did. You've got to take any help you can get.

ROB: There was a lot that was lost. We lost our best friend. We lost our jobs. But I kind of felt we lost the brotherhood as well. The best part of being in a band is you go through everything together. The good moments, the bad moments, the great reviews, the bad reviews. Whereas we went through grieving Gord separately. And that was hard.

PAUL: I think we were all in that general state where we weren't looking to do much, or really talk much. We could have handled it better, in hindsight. Got together and talked about it. But we know how to be together and how not to be, so we were all on the same page. We could tell, even without talking.

ROB: I've watched people of my father's generation who identified who they were with what they did. And when you took away what they did, in their own minds there was nothing left of them. When they retired my old man, it was like he'd been unplugged from the wall and shoved into a corner.

I always swore that wouldn't happen to me, but it did. I spun out, drank a lot, ran away from home, generally fucked up, until I realised how much I was actually losing. You think you've lost everything, but then you see just how much you still have. So I was able to right the ship of state and resume my life.

Now I spend my days in creative pursuits, painting, recording. I sit on the front porch with my guitar every day and entertain the squirrels. I'm not making any money from any of it, but that's OK. I did pretty well.

JOHNNY: I don't see us touring with another singer. People say, 'Well, INXS did it. Journey did it. Queen did it.' But we're not those bands. Those bands are machines. We were just a group of friends that liked making music together.

Partly it's out of respect for Gord, but it's also just hard to wrap my head around going on the road with somebody else. Would we do new songs? Would we do old songs and some new stuff? Any time I give it some thought, ten minutes later it doesn't make any sense at all.

JOHNNY: **I don't see the other guys as much as I'd like to. Each guy's got a solo project or music they're working on with other people and I think that's how you honour the band – by having a life outside it.**

We have this brotherhood that is so important in my life. I didn't know how important it was until we started to reconnect.

ROB: I have less than zero interest in playing shows and getting someone else to sing. I would be actively opposed to the concept. Gord was a key member of the band and I would feel the same about any of us. When John Bonham passed, Led Zeppelin said they were done and they were. I always admired that.

GORD S: I'm in the 'never say never' camp. But The Tragically Hip's not The Tragically Hip without Gord. And, if I were gone, I'm sure he would say the same thing about me.

They're my best friends. Even though Gord's gone, even though the band isn't together anymore, the music still has a really strong resonance with people and hopefully that will never go away.

ROB: We get offers and we look at them and then say no, which is kind of what we did most of our career anyways. Every once in a while, a good one comes in – like the Buffy Sainte-Marie tribute with William Prince, because we love William Prince and it was for a good cause. So we'll carry on picking and choosing things on a piece-by-piece basis.

PAUL: Gord tried to convince me about a year before he died that we should get another singer, but I said we weren't going to be doing that. Then when there were just the four of us left, certain things came up. People talking about a tribute show with different singers. We managed to talk about it without talking about it, and so it went away.

I wouldn't rule out another chapter. We're trying to rerelease and remaster everything we have and do special things for the Hip fans who would be interested in that kind of thing. It's maybe crossed our minds that we could jam. We know we play together well. None of us do a lot of gigs. Gord Sinclair did a little run and he played a few Hip songs, because why wouldn't he? We all wrote them. I've thrown some in here and there. The reaction is always positive – people are happy that we're keeping the music alive.

As a four-piece, it just seems to ebb and flow. The day after Gord died, my dad was asked in an interview whether the rest of us were going to keep doing music, and he said that we would but our hearts would never be in it like they were for The Hip. He was probably right about that. I don't mean to be depressing, but it's just that The Hip was what we did.

no more doing the best
we can
get the sun will hit
his eyelids
feet will hit the sand

GORD S: Patrick and Bernie saw us through a fraught decade, including that last tour, which they handled magnificently. They were our spokesmen when we didn't really want to do a lot of press after Gord's diagnosis.

Then when we weren't recording or going on the road, they had to be a little more creative to come up with ways to generate income. They put in a lot of hard time and I think it burned them out.

ROB: After Gord died, there were a lot of contractual questions hanging in the air about where our songs were and who owned them and we weren't getting any answers. Bernie and I had a tough phone call and then two weeks later I was in a Canadian Tire parking lot when I received a very formal email that basically said Bernie and Patrick were firing us as clients. Five minutes later, I spoke to Paul and he said, 'We're gonna have to rehire Jake. It's the only thing that makes sense.' I never thought I'd ever hear those words, but he was right.

JAKE GOLD: When I heard that Bernie and Patrick had resigned, I wrote the band a letter telling them that they needed someone to steer the ship and make things happen. Before they fired me, I had started building a fan database, but nothing was happening with that. Their social media was a mess. Everything was a mess. They needed to embrace the digital age.

We had a meeting where they invited me back into the fold. I remember Paul asking me whether I was sure I wanted to do this and I replied that this was as much my legacy as it was theirs. I think that was when they realised there was nobody better to take this on than me – because no one cared more about it than I did.

JOHNNY: Jake Gold was our manager for 17 years and then he wasn't for 17 years. And now he's back. We don't know whether it will be for 17 years this time, but he's definitely who we need right now to help us.

GORD S: Jake was the one who shepherded us from crummy little bars to hockey rinks and beyond. And now he's devised a plan to repackage what we did together and, specifically, to get the unheard music from our catalogue out in front of people. The idea is not just to sell stuff, but to celebrate the legacy of the group.

ALLAN GREGG: Jake really loves The Hip. He's going to make sure this band's legacy is not forgotten, that people are going to be singing 'Ahead by a Century' a hundred years from now. He'll make that happen.

JOHNNY: A few years ago, there was a fire at a Universal warehouse and some of the master tapes in there were destroyed. Our name was on the list, but when we started asking where our tapes were and what we owned no one was giving us any answers. So we realised that we needed Jake the pit bull to go find those tapes. Our songs are all we have, and we need to take care of them for our kids.

ROB: The Universal fire and the quest to track our tapes down was the spark that pulled us back together. It turns out that they'd been shipped up to Toronto, I guess when we left MCA USA but stayed with MCA Canada. So that was a relief, but we still haven't found them all.

JAKE GOLD: None of the guys had really talked to each other since Gord passed away. They'd all gone into their own little shells where they were grieving independently and it was paralysing them.

So when I came back in, it was like a wake-up call. Now they're back communicating with each other. We have meetings every two weeks, where Gord is represented by his brother Pat. I ask a lot of hard questions on those calls and I expect answers. I tell them that if they're uncomfortable talking about something they should say they're uncomfortable and tell us why. A lot of stuff has come out.

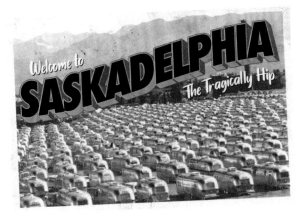

Saskadelphia
RELEASED: 21 MAY 2021
ENGINEER: BRUCE BARRIS
MIXING: MARK VREEKEN
Ouch
Not Necessary
Montreal
Crack My Spine (Like a Whip)
Just as Well
Reformed Baptist Blues

The Saskadelphia *EP consists of six previously unreleased songs that were recorded during the* Road Apples *sessions in 1990, although one of the tracks, 'Montreal', is a later live recording (from the city of its title), as the original studio version could not be located. The* Road Apples *master tapes were among those that the band tracked down in 2019–2020. The title of the EP, a portmanteau of Saskatoon and Philadelphia, is one of the rejected titles for the record that became* Road Apples

GORD S: The 50th anniversary of the Junos was coming up. This was an important Canadian institution that we had always supported and that had always supported us. They wanted us to do something, but we had zero interest because Gord wasn't there. Jake, being Jake, kept suggesting different singers until eventually he came up with Leslie Feist.

We started playing with Leslie back when she was in her early twenties and playing guitar in By Divine Right. She was wicked then and she's even better now.

JOHNNY: It felt like the right time to do something and the right person to do it with. I know that Gord would have fully approved.

GORD S: Paul came up with the idea of doing 'It's a Good Life'. Lyrically, it seemed perfect for that moment. We had to change the key for Leslie, which gave the four of us a reason to get together and relearn this song that we'd played hundreds of times over the years. It's quite a delicate song and moving it up four or five tones made it even more delicate and ethereal.

JOHNNY: We went back to Bath and we were up in the rafters at the back of the house where we had last been rehearsing five years earlier with Gord. And there was his exercise bike, right there. That was a very heavy moment.

While Robbie and I were waiting for the others to arrive, he started playing a riff that wasn't from the song we were there to rehearse. And I started playing with it. It made me realise how much I had missed that creative process.

It was nice to be in that room, making music again. And then it was a great performance. We weren't nervous and it didn't feel weird, because we've got this connection with Leslie.

GORD S: When we got to Massey Hall to shoot on the floor, we did three takes and nailed it each time. Then Gordon Lightfoot turned up to record the introduction to our little segment and we fired everything back up and did it three more times for him. Just like Gord, Leslie never sang it the same way twice, because she occupies the lyric. She's great that way.

GORD S: It all came back really quick, once Paul got the mouse nest out of his amp.

The Tragically Hip received the 2021 Humanitarian Award during the 50th annual Juno Awards

At the event on 16 May 2021 the band performed with Leslie Feist on vocals

Above: Rehearsals at the Bathouse, May 2021

PATRICK SAMBROOK: The legacy of The Tragically Hip is the songs. In the end, it all comes down to that: will people still be listening to those songs in 20, 30, 40 years? In my opinion they will. The band's legacy has continued to grow because of that.

PATRICK DOWNIE: I'm one of those weirdos that actually thinks The Hip's biggest days are ahead of them – because of their story and because of the sheer power and beauty of the music.

JAKE GOLD: I don't think anybody has unabashedly written about Canadian things the way Gord did. I also think that the band's Canadian-ness, their non-confrontational, non-boastful nature, which was such an important element of their success in Canada, probably held them back in other places.

JUSTIN TRUDEAU: The Hip gave us so much substance. So many layers to unpeel, and the wordplay … it spoke to me in a way that was really personal. For me, it was a language and story that gave a sense of legitimacy to, and pride in, Canadian culture that is hard to explain to anyone who isn't deeply grounded in it.

But they still sold a million and a half records in the United States and toured some decent-sized places there and in Europe. If you took their American and European tours on their own, without Canada, you'd say they had a pretty good career. Putting that next to how they did in Canada was always an unfair comparison, because nobody did what they did in Canada.

JOHNNY: It's hard to say why the country embraced us the way it did. We just came at it with as honest an approach as we could. We never tried to jam it down anyone's throat. You either liked us or you didn't.

Maybe Canadians like us because we didn't make it big in the States. Maybe it made our fans more protective of us, like, 'We love you better than anyone. Who cares about anyone else?' I think it would have been very different if we'd really made it in the States. When Alanis Morissette went down there and made it uber-huge, she became less popular in Canada.

BERNIE BREEN: The first thing everyone says is 'Too bad they didn't make it in America.' But The Hip are a global band, they made it everywhere. They're not an arena band everywhere, but any band who can play anywhere in the world to thousands of people every night have made it, and The Hip did it consistently for 25 years.

DAN AYKROYD: We felt, with The Hip's music, that we were living along with them. When any artist can express themselves and nail that common experience that they have with the audience, that's magic. That's what makes superstardom and that's what makes valid, enduring art. That's what The Hip bring.

As a Canadian audience, we always felt that The Hip were our own, even though they toured around the world. We will share you, but we want you back.

PAUL: Some people would tell you that The Hip are Canada's favourite band. That's not what I feel, though I'm happy we're considered in that way. You go out to a bar and people tell you here and there that our band affected them in some good ways. I'm proud of that and proud of what we got done.

We were a hard-working Canadian band, and we happened to click. We managed to write consistently good songs for long enough to make a lot of records, which meant that we started seeping from parents to kids and became almost like a cult – in a good way.

The records were mini-marathons to make and that's where the tension was, but once we'd written the songs and recorded them we'd go out on the road and have a good time. Our aim was to blow the roof off the place, every time.

ROB: We used to get asked a lot about what it was that made us a Canadian band. It's a really hard thing to put your finger on. I think it comes down to being yourself. Neil Young is the same guy backstage that he is on stage. He walks on wearing his jeans and his plaid shirt, picks up his guitar and projects his soul out to the crowd. And people appreciate him for his directness and his honesty. I think that Joni Mitchell is the same. And maybe Leonard Cohen, certainly Gordon Lightfoot.

When I get up on stage, I'm not playing a character. I'm not being a rock star. It's just a twist of fate that I'm the one on stage instead of the one in the crowd guzzling beer and throwing his fist in the air. Because if there was a band like The Hip, I'd be in the crowd cheering them on.

Above: In 2012, Kingston city council voted to rename the portion of Barrack Street that runs in front of the K-Rock Centre after The Tragically Hip

Opposite: The Tragically Hip, Port Lands, Toronto, 19 June 2012

A fragment of a handwritten note by Gord Downie

GORD S: When we started out trying to make our career as a rock and roll band, job security wasn't our first thought. We approached it song by song, gig by gig, album by album, year by year – and always with gratitude that we were able to make a living doing this.

Over time, we had to use our wits to overcome the obstacles in front of us and chart new paths. The trajectory of our career was quite amazing. At the end of that final tour, we got spit out exactly where we started. It was like going off on a mission to Mars and coming back 30 or 40 years later, sadly not with everyone that you left behind waiting for you.

PAUL: We're all still friends with each other and with Gord's brothers, sisters and kids. It's always been a family. All our kids are like cousins to each other. Fortunately, we all agreed on the things that were important. No one was saying we should move to LA and start doing loads of drugs. Though appealing, it just wasn't us.

Our biggest achievement is that we were able to do all this and be friends, enjoy it and not get weird.

GORD S: I would give back everything that we experienced if we still had the opportunity to hang out with each other, the five of us, playing music and writing songs. I loved being on stage, but sitting around with the guys listening to songs and talking about music is what I miss the most.

JOHNNY: I don't know too many people who could start a job at 17 and 40 years later still be doing this thing that they love. I feel so lucky. Going out on the road with my friends, I was like a frog jumping from one lily pad to the next. It was amazing.

PAUL: Gord made my life the day he asked me to be in the band. I couldn't fuck that up. From that moment on, I was determined to chisel out a role in this thing. Stick to my guns and be good enough for these guys to want me to stay around. My life could have gone a whole bunch of different ways. I'm sure I would have found something to do, but it wouldn't have been being a rock star in The Hip. So I'm forever grateful to Gord for that, and to all of them really. It's been the best sort of career anyone could hope for.

ROB: I got to live the dream I'd been pursuing since I was ten years old, to make a living out of writing music and playing songs and to do it with my best friends on Earth. To be able to pull that off even briefly would be a genius moment, but to do it for 30-something years? That's ridiculous. No one should be so lucky.

I want what takes a lifetime to learn and after that to sigh and turn around and start all over again with no more pause than I had back then.

EPILOGUE BY ROB BAKER

I had a front row seat and a backstage pass for 30-plus years of touring … the thrill of victory, the agony of defeat. The mud, the blood and the beer. Tons of hard work and sacrifice, gallons of tears and frustrations, even occasional flashes of anger, but more than anything it's the many laughs and ridiculous shenanigans that I remember and choose to focus on. For those on the outside, which is everyone but the five of us, a couple of very close aides and our immediate families, it was our music – the albums and the concerts – that was our content. For us, or at least for me, the albums were the frame and the shows were the canvas, but it was our lives painted on that canvas. We have been very privileged, through hard work, tenacity, reasonably good instincts and sheer dumb luck, to have been able to live our dreams and build a life out of our imaginations.

There was no shortage of darkness in our internal relationships, but that's our business, not yours. There was also more laughter than one lifetime is entitled to, and the cornerstones on which it was all built were love, respect, dedication and loyalty. Anything one builds on a foundation like that has a great chance at survival and success.

It is no secret that I had serious trepidation about going on our final tour with a bandmate and buddy who had terminal brain cancer and was having grand mal seizures.

But to go on tour was the dying wish of a creative brother, and 'no' was not an option. I didn't look at that tour as a career move or album promotion – I was there to support Gord. He needed me. He needed us, all of us, and it turns out millions across the nation too. Through it all, the one thing that made it more than worthwhile, a true joy, was the time on stage. I was not paid to play music with my pals, I was paid for all of the other stuff that we had to put up with just to get those two hours of peace, release and community.

A lot of profound love and friendship, and deep emotions, were shared on that tour, but we needed to keep both hands on the reins and our eyes on the prize. After the last chord had been played and the last bows taken, we set about emptying our wardrobe trunk just as we would at the end of any other tour. We'd just attended a massive retirement party for ourselves but we had to work at it. We cleaned out our proverbial desks and put our shit in boxes and headed home to try and make sense of it all – in silence.

I'm not a solo artist and I've never wanted to be. All I've ever wanted was to be part of a really good band.

I was.

The Tragically Hip, Toronto, 19 June 2012

Opposite: Gord Downie and Mike Downie, Secret Path tour, Roy Thomson Hall, Toronto, 21 October 2016

AFTERWORD BY MIKE DOWNIE

In October 2021, I conducted my first feature interviews with the four surviving members of The Tragically Hip for our documentary series *No Dress Rehearsal*. Those initial interviews took place in their venerable old high school, KCVI, in downtown Kingston. It had recently been closed down, sold off to Queen's University, but for four beautiful fall days we had the full run of the place.

For the first time in over a century of supercharged, teenage action, the old building was now resting, so empty and quiet. The long hallways, lined with lockers, the high-ceilinged classrooms with dusty blackboards, created a wonderfully nostalgic setting for our interviews.

In 'Wheat Kings', a song from 1992 album *Fully Completely*, Gord sings, 'There's a dream he dreams where the high school's dead and stark. It's a museum and we're all locked up in it after dark.'

All those years later, the dream was now reality, like it was somehow always meant to be.

My brother Gord had been gone four years, almost to the day, when we showed up at KCVI. Looking back now, I'd say that was just the right amount of time to have passed. The emotion, the gravitas of Gord's passing still hung in the air but there was also clarity and fresh perspective. The boys were ready to tell their once in a lifetime, meteoric story of how five high school friends became Canada's most iconic and cherished band.

The following year there were two more long days of interviews with each member. We moved slowly through the years. Going deep into each album and tour, and what was happening, personally and professionally, behind the scenes with the band. The guys were honest and revealing, with no punches pulled. These were marathon interviews, the longest I've ever done. And we were all emotionally exhausted at the end of those days. There were an additional 55 interviews with people like Jake Gold and Billy Ray Koster, fellow Canadian musicians and actors, family, friends and a bunch of Hip insiders for our series.

In a documentary like *No Dress Rehearsal* you end up using just a sliver of the hundreds of hours of interviews. It's a frustrating part of filmmaking but that's how it works. I'm so pleased that this beautiful book, *This Is Our Life*, will allow Hip fans to take in so much more of this fascinating content.

Doing these interviews was simply the highlight of my 30-year directing career. And having the opportunity to hear new stories and insights about my brother Gord was something I'll carry with me always. To Robbie, Johnny, Paul and Gord, thank you for trusting me with your story. What a gift.

GORD DOWNIE'S SET-UP

Gord's onstage microphone of choice was the Shure SM 58, mostly on account of its durability (he was very hard on microphones). Billy Ray had a drawer of 12 SM 58s with a custom-made desiccant pack that lay on top of the ball screens to absorb the sweat. Over the course of a concert, the microphone would have to be switched about once every four songs, or sooner if Gord destroyed one. As for mic stands Gord only used straight, round-based models. He would destroy at least one stand, and as many as seven or eight, every concert, by sitting on them, riding them like a horse, a motorcycle or a recliner, or whatever he felt like doing with them in the moment.

Ever present in Gord's pocket was his four-colour pen, which he used according to a strict method. For example, if the last word in a blue ink line was traced over in red, that meant he had finalised that line.

Gord's Moleskine notebooks and four-colour pen were as important to him as phones, keys and wallets are to the rest of us. He never left home without them.

The original banana shaker was given to Gord by the boys from Van Allen Belt, a Kingston band that opened for The Hip in the Nineties. He loved it for its quirky ability to be a phone or a gun or even just a banana. Anything he could dream up.

To Gord the most important item in this photograph would probably be the coffee mug, which was named Deb, after Debbie Hamilton, the Bathouse hospitality manager. Debbie gave the mug to Billy Ray as a Christmas present in 1997, and shortly thereafter Gord poured himself a coffee in it for the drive home to Toronto. For 20 years virtually every cup of coffee he consumed was from this mug.

The metallic leather suits, feathered hats
and side-zip leather boots displayed in
these photos were custom made for Gord to
wear on the 2016 Man Machine Poem tour.

Gord's seven suits were by Izzy Camilleri.
Each was named after a person of influence
in Gord's life: gold suit, 'Paul'; hot pink,
'Isabel'; acid green, 'Jenn'; silver, 'Patrick';
turquoise, 'Edgar'; mirror ball, 'Bowie'; and
purple, 'Prince'.

Gord wore the gold 'Paul' suit eight times
on the tour (Victoria, Vancouver 1,
Vancouver 2, Edmonton 1, Calgary 1,
Winnipeg, Toronto 2 and Ottawa), and the
hot pink 'Isabel' suit nine times (Victoria,
Vancouver 2, Edmonton 1, Edmonton 2,
Calgary 1, Calgary 2, Toronto 1, Hamilton
and Kingston).

The hats were by Karyn Ruiz of Lilliput
Hats in Toronto. Karyn wrote out lyrics
from two of her favourite Hip songs,
'Bobcaygeon' and 'Done and Done', and
screenprinted them on the silk lining of
the hats.

The boots, featuring lyrics from 'Ahead
by a Century' etched into the soles and a
small Hip crest on the sides, were by Jeff
Churchill of Toronto shoemaker Jitterbug
Boy. He was tasked with recreating a
cherished old pair of boots Gord owned.

ROB BAKER'S GEAR

AMPS (TOP TO BOTTOM)
1) 1957 Fender Super. A work horse in the studio, but I never took it on tour.
2) Mesa Boogie Trem-O-Verb (on its road case). Live there would have been two Trem-O-Verbs or two Mesa Boogie Lone Stars (or one of each). This was the basic rig for the last dozen or so years. I used Mesa Boogie amps live from the very beginning – first a MkIII combo, then head and cab. For Fully Completely and Day for Night I used a TriAxis preamp with a Strategy 500 power amp and rack effects with an Abacus foot switcher … all a bit too much like flying a plane for me. I settled on the Trem-O-Verb/Lone Star set-up because it was just a bit more direct. Of course, there was also a pedal board loaded with a Boss tuner, Vox Cry Baby wah and an assortment of Line 6 modellers and expression pedals. (The yellow box on the Trem-O-Verb is a line tester for checking cables and batteries – a mini version of the cockpit line tester featured on the cover of Phantom Power.)

GUITARS (LEFT TO RIGHT)
The five guitars shown made up the core of an evening set, though there would have been others on the road as well.
1) Oskar Graf, custom made to allow baritone tuning. I kept it in open C tuning (CGCGCE) and used it for 'Ahead by a Century', 'Stay' and 'Train Overnight'.
2) PRS. This was my main standard-tuned stage guitar from the late Nineties on. I rarely used it in the studio.
3) 1974 Fender Stratocaster. This was my first electric and was my main guitar through Fully Completely.

I played it on virtually every song I ever recorded up until 1994. After Fully Completely it became my open E guitar (EBEG#BE) and was used for 'Grace, Too', 'An Inch an Hour', 'My Music at Work', 'Use It Up', 'It's a Good Life If You Don't Weaken', 'Problem Bears', 'In View' and 'The Kids Don't Get It', as well as live versions of 'Fiddler's Green'. It made an appearance at every Hip show from the first one to the last.
4) 1987 Fender Custom Telecaster. I used this primarily for drop D tuning ('So Hard Done By'), open G (DGDGBD) ('Fireworks',

'Don't Wake Daddy', 'Putting Down'), DGDGAD ('Gift Shop', 'Butts Wigglin''), and DADGAD – a tuning I use extensively, but I don't know if I ever recorded a song in that tuning with The Hip.
5) Yamaha Navarro. I have two of these. The one shown has had the low string and tuner removed to make it a five-string open G (Keith Richards tuning – GDGBD). This was the live guitar for 'Bobcaygeon'. The second Navarro was used for standard tuning ('Thompson Girl').

JOHNNY FAY'S GEAR

DRUM KITS

Sonor drums have been a constant in my life. From my early days gigging at the Lakeview Manor to our final show, I have played Sonor. They are built to last and tough on the road. And that's because Germans don't build Scheiße.

For the final tour, I used a Sonor Horst Link Signature Series kit from the Eighties, consisting of a 24" bass drum with three floor toms (14" x 14", 16" x 16" and 18" x 18") tuned really tight. My B-kit on that tour was a Gretsch cocktail kit built for me by the 'Drum doctor', Ross Garfield. He specially painted it in copper mist nitron as a tribute to Elvis Presley's drummer D.J. Fontana.

Ray Ayotte, the master drum builder from Vancouver, made me a few kits. One of them, from the mid-Nineties, was an amazing, almost Lego-like set consisting of a 14" bass drum, 10" snare and a 10" tom. I took these drums everywhere on the road as my warm-up kit, and they were at every session too. These were the drums on 'Ahead by a Century' and 'Poets'.

SNARE DRUMS

I've had a few favourites over the years, but these are my absolutes.
1) Barrrett Deems custom 12-lug 14" x 6" copper-plated Slingerland snare, used for many live shows.
2) Two soprano snare drums custom built for me by Joe Montineri. They were 12" x 4", one wood and one brass, and they sounded like little Gatling guns – some of my favourite snare drum sounds on our records. I used these a lot on recordings, especially in the Don Smith era (for example: 'Twist My Arm', 'Born in the Water' and 'Cordelia').
3) An original Eighties Tama 'Terminator', 18-pound cast-bronze shell, which Bob Rock turned me on to. It was mega and used on 'In View' from World Container and on We Are the Same.

CYMBALS

My cymbals have always been Paiste, which was my first endorsement. I started with 602 blue Stewart Copeland 13" hi-hats, and later gravitated to larger 15" Crunch hats and 18", 20" and 24" Giant Beat crashes for playing live.

DRUM MACHINE

My Linn LM2 drum machine was at every session. In fact, I always had two of them in case one broke down. I used it on 'Ahead by a Century'.

STICKS

I used my Johnny Fay signature Regal Tip drumsticks, which were mega sticks made for me in Lewiston, New York.

PAUL LANGLOIS'S GEAR

AMPS (LEFT TO RIGHT)

1) 'Bernie' amp. I got this from Colin Cripps (Blue Rodeo, Crash Vegas) in the mid-Nineties. Gord S, Robbie, and Gord D all got one too around then. Bernard Raunig was an electronics repair person and tinkerer in Hamilton, who purchased a lot of surplus Bell & Howell Filmosound 385 film projectors being auctioned off by a school board in the early Nineties. He had a notion he could extract the audio amplifier sections from the projectors and repurpose them as guitar amplifiers. The cabinet is homemade from solid pine and covered in sail canvas, which was then brushed with lacquer. Colin recommended the amps to us in The Hip, and also refurbished the wiring with the help of Tim Dudley (Songbird Music, Toronto, now closed). It's a killer amp. Mine stays at the Bathouse and gets used fairly often by the many people that record there.

2) Randall amp head (top). I have a bunch of these and would change them up over the years both live and in the studio. I started early in my Hip life with a Randall combo amp and was easily able to find a sound that I felt fit the band's sound well – then never looked back.

3) Celestion speaker cabinet with two 10" speakers (bottom). I eventually switched from a Randall combo to a Randall head and this cabinet was my main amp rig for stage and studio. Of course, in the studio many different amps and speakers were tried, but this was what I always used live.

GUITARS (LEFT TO RIGHT)

1) 1979 Les Paul Custom Black Beauty. I bought this in New Orleans when we arrived to begin recording Day for Night. I actually used it on every song on the album except 'Scared'. I'd found my new main guitar! I then started buying the odd Les Paul over the next couple of years, including a '72 Custom Sunburst, which became my main guitar from Trouble at the Henhouse on. This black one remained in action, though, for various songs like 'At the Hundredth Meridian', 'We'll Go Too' (tuning F#BDF#BE) and 'My Music at Work', to name a few.

2) 1972 Fender Telecaster Custom. This was my main guitar (and my first electric guitar in The Hip) for our first three albums. Most of the songs on those records employed this Tele. After that, I switched mostly to Les Pauls, but I still used the Tele for certain songs, like 'It's a Good Life', 'Fireworks' and 'Pigeon Camera'.

3) 1992 Takamine acoustic. My wife, Joanne, surprised me with this guitar in 1992 at a Massey Hall soundcheck in Toronto. It has always been my main acoustic for songs like 'Wheat Kings', 'Fiddler's Green', 'Opiated', 'The Depression Suite', and many more.

GORD SINCLAIR'S GEAR

AMPS (TOP TO BOTTOM)

This is the rack I had on the road for the last 20 years or so of touring. I would switch around or update bits of gear over time as needed, but my approach was pretty consistent, even back in our bar gig days. I would run signal from the bass straight into a compressor, then to a DI for the sound engineer, then into the amplifier and speaker cabinet, then try to drown out the guys on stage! From my perspective, simpler is always better. I found this set-up to be clean and powerful, always reliable and sonically consistent.

1) dbx 160SL compressor.
2) Coolohm Audio preamp/DI combo. A custom piece of equipment made by my friend Phil Presnal in Toronto.
3) Gallien-Krueger 800RB 300/100 bi-amp bass amplifier. I always carried two just in case one blew, but that never happened.
4) Adamson Systems custom bass cabinet with single 10" and 15" EV speakers and a built-in crossover. I had this box, and a duplicate for arena gigs, made for me by an engineer named Paul Bauman. Adamson is a great Canadian PA company known all over the world, but to my knowledge these were the only two onstage instrument enclosures they ever made.

BASS GUITARS (LEFT TO RIGHT)

1) 1959 Fender Precision Bass. The first vintage instrument I ever bought, which I found on tour in Chicago in 1989. I used it for years on stage. I think it has always been on the road, much loved and much played.
2) 1990 G&L SB-1. An early example from Leo Fender's last guitar company. This became my main onstage instrument around 1993. The hot, humid and sweaty club shows had been taking a toll on my old P, but this bass was always up to the challenge. I have played it at every show since. Sturdy, reliable and loud.
3) 1968 Gibson EB-2. I often brought this bass on the road, especially after we did a stripped-down acoustic set in theatres for Music @ Work. It offered a nice tonal alternative to the P-bass sound for quieter songs. It also reduced the stage-left guitar ratio between Robbie and me from 8:1 to around 5:1.

CONTRIBUTORS

DAN AYKROYD *found fame as a regular performer on the sketch comedy series* Saturday Night Live *before leaving in 1979 to star in hit movies including* The Blues Brothers *(1980),* Trading Places *(1983) and* Ghostbusters *(1984). He returned to* SNL *for the 1995 episode in which he introduced fellow Kingstonians The Tragically Hip to a national US audience.*

DAVID BASTEDO *is a multi-disciplinary artist, photographer, storyteller and creative technologist based in Kingston, Ontario. For 12 years, from 2004 to 2016, he was the exclusive tour photographer for The Tragically Hip, capturing the band's essence in evocative still and motion images both on and off stage. David also documented Gord Downie's 2016 Secret Path tour.*

RICHARD BELAND *is a music photographer based in Toronto. He has shot more than 3,000 shows in his career, including 100–150 Tragically Hip concerts. For his work on Gord Downie's 2003 record* Battle of the Nudes, *Richard received a Juno Award nomination for Album Design of the Year.*

STEVE BERLIN *is a producer, arranger, session player, saxophonist and member of Los Lobos. Clients for his arranging and session work include REM, John Lee Hooker and Willie Nelson, and he has produced records by Faith No More, Rickie Lee Jones and Buckwheat Zydeco. Steve also produced two albums for The Tragically Hip:* Phantom Power *(1998) and* Music @ Work *(2000).*

BERNIE BREEN *has worked in music for more than 30 years, as a club owner, concert promoter, booking agent and artist manager. He has handled the careers of acts such as Tom Cochrane, Big Wreck and Crash Vegas. For 15 years he co-managed The Tragically Hip with Patrick Sambrook.*

GAVIN BROWN *is an accomplished songwriter and the recipient of the Juno Award for Record Producer of the Year. He has produced a wide range of artists, including Barenaked Ladies, Billy Talent, Three Days Grace, Sarah Harmer and Metric. In 2012, he produced The Tragically Hip's penultimate studio album,* Now for Plan A.

TRISTIN CHIPMAN *took over as The Tragically Hip's road manager in the early 2000s. She has also managed tours for The Indigo Girls. Tristin left the Hip family to pursue a career in clinical social work, but returned temporarily to manage the band's final tour in 2016.*

BRUCE DICKINSON'S *long and varied career in the music industry has included spells at Columbia Records (where he coordinated Bob Dylan's* Biograph *box set), Chrysalis, EMI and MCA. One of his first moves as Vice President of A&R at MCA was to sign The Tragically Hip to a worldwide deal in 1988.*

MIKE DOWNIE *is a documentary filmmaker and the elder brother of Gord Downie. He has made award-winning films on a wide range of subjects, from hockey to the world of parasites. Mike also directed the 2018 documentary* Finding the Secret Path *as part of Gord's* Secret Path *project and* No Dress Rehearsal *(2024), a four-part series about The Tragically Hip.*

PATRICK DOWNIE *is Gord Downie's younger brother. A fellow Boston Bruins obsessive, he stepped up to the role of Gord's chief carer following his diagnosis of glioblastoma in December 2015. Pat was there to support his brother through everything that he endured and achieved during the last two years of his life.*

JOSH FINLAYSON *is the lead guitarist of the Canadian band Skydiggers, which he co-founded in 1987 with singer Andy Maize. He also contributed, as a musician, co-writer and/or co-producer, to four of his friend Gord Downie's solo records:* Coke Machine Glow *(2001),* Battle of the Nudes *(2003),* The Grand Bounce *(2010) and Gord's last recorded work,* Away Is Mine *(released posthumously in 2020).*

PETER GARRETT *is an Australian musician, campaigner and politician. He served as a cabinet minister in the Rudd/Gillard Labor governments from 2007–13. Peter has been the lead vocalist of Midnight Oil since 1977. The Oils joined The Tragically Hip on the first Another Roadside Attraction tour in 1993.*

JAKE GOLD *is a music manager. He managed The Tragically Hip from 1986 to 2003, guiding the band's rise to national icon status, and has also handled The Watchmen, Sass Jordan and The Pursuit of Happiness among others. Jake is also known for his role as a judge throughout the six-season run of* Canadian Idol. *He returned to managing The Hip in 2020.*

ALLAN GREGG *has combined a career as a public opinion researcher and political strategist with that of a music manager. He and Jake Gold co-founded their company the Management Trust in 1985 and signed The Tragically Hip the following year. The company has been cited as Manager of the Year by the Canadian Music Industry Awards on three separate occasions.*

JIM HERRINGTON *is an American photographer whose portraits of people including Willie Nelson, Morgan Freeman and Dolly Parton have appeared in magazines such as* Vanity Fair, GQ *and* Esquire. *He photographed The Tragically Hip at various points in their career, including for their* Road Apples *and* Day for Night *records and on tour in Europe in 1991.*

ROB HIRST *is the co-founder and drummer of the Australian rock band Midnight Oil. During the band's fallow periods, Rob has pursued various other musical projects, including Ghostwriters, Backsliders, The Angry Tradesmen and The Break. He bonded with the members of The Tragically Hip when Midnight Oil took part in the first Another Roadside Attraction tour in 1993.*

MARK HOWARD *is a record producer, engineer and mixer. Working with producer Daniel Lanois, he engineered records by artists such as The Neville Brothers and Bob Dylan. Mark first encountered The Tragically Hip when he engineered their Don Smith-produced* Road Apples *album (1991) and three years later he produced The Hip's* Day for Night.

DAVE 'BILLY RAY' KOSTER *joined The Tragically Hip's road crew as a drum technician in 1992. His responsibilities soon expanded to cover guitars and monitors and all other items of stage equipment, from mic stands to banana shakers. Billy Ray became a valued member of the Hip family throughout the rest of the band's touring and recording career.*

GEDDY LEE *is a musician and songwriter, best known as the lead vocalist, bassist and keyboardist for the Canadian rock group Rush. Along with his Rush bandmates, he was made an Officer of the Order of Canada in 1996 and was inducted into the Rock and Roll Hall of Fame in 2013. Geddy has described The Tragically Hip as one of the greatest bands Canada has ever produced.*

RANDY LENNOX *is a music and media executive. He is currently the president of Bell Media, Canada's largest music label and media company. As president and CEO of Universal (formerly MCA) Canada, Randy oversaw the development of some of Canada's best-selling artists, including Justin Bieber, Drake, Shania Twain and The Tragically Hip.*

MARK NORMAN, *also known as The Hip's Social Director, has been a promoter and producer of major global music tours since 1981. He passionately promoted The Hip across Canada in clubs, theatres and arenas and co-produced all three Another Roadside Attraction festival tours. Mark misses The Hip and their live music dearly.*

TOM POWER *combines careers in music and broadcasting; he is the vocalist and guitarist with Canadian folk band The Dardanelles as well as the host of arts magazine show* Q *on CBC Radio One. In 2021 he interviewed The Tragically Hip shortly before their performance at the Junos with Leslie Feist.*

CLEMENS RIKKEN *is a Dutch photographer, particularly known for his photographs of musicians (including Björk, Prince and Jeff Buckley), sportspeople and politicians. He hit it off with The Tragically Hip when photographing them on their early European tours and continued to work with them regularly thereafter.*

BOB ROCK *began his music career as co-founder and guitarist of The Payolas, before focusing on producing. Perhaps best known for his work with Metallica, he has also produced and engineered records for Aerosmith, Bon Jovi, Cher, Nelly Furtado and many others. Bob produced The Tragically Hip's albums* World Container *(2006) and* We Are the Same *(2009), and collaborated with Gord Downie on the album* Lustre Parfait *(released 2023).*

PATRICK SAMBROOK *is a music manager, who handles artists such as Sarah Harmer, Ellevator, JayWood and Mappe Of. He co-managed The Tragically Hip with Bernie Breen from 2005 to 2020.*

JUSTIN TRUDEAU *currently serves as Canada's 23rd prime minister. Appointed leader of the Liberal Party in 2013, he won a majority government two years later and has since earned second and third mandates in 2019 and 2021. Justin is also one of the proudest and most prominent fans of The Tragically Hip.*

MARK VREEKEN *spent 17 years with The Tragically Hip, from 1989 to 2006, as their front of house sound engineer and production manager, receiving co-production credits for the band's albums from* Day for Night *(1994) through* In Violet Light *(2002). More recently, Mark has been working as the broadcast music mixer on NBC talk shows* Late Night with Conan O'Brien *and* The Tonight Show with Jay Leno.

RICKY WELLINGTON *became a member of the Hip family in the mid-Nineties and was the band's head of security from 2005 to 2016. He currently works as a security officer for MLSE, parent company of major Toronto sports teams including the Maple Leafs (NHL), Raptors (NBA) and Toronto FC (MLS).*

PUBLISHER'S NOTE

With immense gratitude to The Tragically Hip – Rob Baker, Gord Downie, Johnny Fay, Paul Langlois and Gord Sinclair – for creating so many unforgettable songs which continue to inspire a nation, and to The Hip's fans, without whom this book would not be possible.

For Genesis Publications it has been an honour to celebrate The Hip in their 40th year during our 50th year.

The publishers would like to thank:

The authors, Rob, Johnny, Paul and Gord, for their dedication and time spent in creating this book.

Gord Downie's brothers, Mike and Patrick, for their collaboration and enthusiasm.

Jake Gold for his vital role in making this book happen.

All friends and family of The Hip for their support.

Thanks to everyone who contributed to this book, with a special mention to:

David Bastedo, Richard Beland, Jim Herrington and Clemens Rikken.

Elspeth Domville, Guy Elsmore-Paddock, Simon Evers, Summer Figueroa, Ryan Hefford, Dave 'Billy Ray' Koster, Brad Mindich, Brandon Schmidt, Colin Sinclair, Ian Thuillier, Crystal Van Dee, Dave Wells, Eric Woodruff and James Young.

And the Genesis team, especially Sally Millard, Nicky Page, James Hodgson, Katy Baker, Megan Lily Large and Alexandra Rigby-Wild.

ACKNOWLEDGEMENTS

The Downie family would like to thank:
The band and all those who worked diligently with them over the years, especially Jake Gold, Allan Gregg, Shelley Stertz, Sarah Osgoode, Bruce Dickinson, Wayne Forte, Mark Norman, Randy Lennox, Sam Feldman, Bernie Breen, Patrick Sambrook, Riley O'Connor, Cathy Cleghorn, Courtney Yuchtman and THE one and only Jenn Pressey.

Johnny Fay would like to thank:
Lara Noack, for always being there for me, and my beautiful boys, Finn and Will, for giving my life such purpose. I'm forever grateful for all the love and support over the years from my family – my parents Loretta and John Edward Fay, who let me be who I wanted to be, and Paul, Philippa, Donna and Mark Fay for never being too far away.

Paul Langlois would like to thank:
My family and all of my friends, and especially my three favourite girls, Joanne, Emma and Sophie.

Jake Gold would like to thank:
Allan Gregg, whose guidance and friendship enabled me to be a better manager and a better person, and Shelley Stertz, whose loyalty knows no bounds and at difficult times always stood by my side.

CREDITS

TEXT
The vast majority of the text in this book comes from the interviews conducted by Mike Downie for the documentary series No Dress Rehearsal. *These have been supplemented by archive quotes from the following sources.*

Interviews
Rob Baker: *Steve Newton,* Georgia Straight, *25 June 1997;* **Gord Downie:** *Jennifer Baichwal and Nicholas de Pencier,* Long Time Running, *2017; Michael Barclay,* Eye, *24 November 2000; Laurie Brown,* On the Arts, *CBC, February 1992; CBC, 1989; Jian Ghomeshi,* Q, *CBC, October 2012; John Kendle, 26 Oct 2005; Ron Maclean,* Hockey Night in Canada, *CBC, 23 February 2002; Peter Mansbridge,* The National, *CBC News, 14 October 2016; Wendy Mesley,* The National, *CBC News, 9 October 2012; MuchMusic, 2000; Steve Newton,* Georgia Straight, *20 October 1989, 26 November 1992, 6 July 1995 & 7 November 1996; Matt Schichter,* Matt Schichter Interviews, *2011; George Stroumboulopoulos,* The Hour, *CBC, 22 October 2006 & 26 May 2010; George Stroumboulopoulos,* Tonight, *CBC, 15 October 2012; George Stroumboulopoulos,* We Are the Same *release performance at the Bathouse, 6 April 2009; Steve Warden, Rock Radio Network, 1996;* **The Tragically Hip:** *Tom Power, CBC Music in Studio at the Junos, CBC, 1 June 2021*

LIMITED EDITION COPIES

Vinyl
A-side: *'Get Back Again'*
Written by The Tragically Hip; produced by Chris Wardman; mixed by Mark Vreeken
Copyright © Arte Humane Inc., Bhaji Maker Inc., Ching Music Inc., Dirty Shorts Music Inc., Wiener Art Inc., Southern Music Pub Co. Canada Ltd

B-side: *'Get Back Again'* (Live)
Written by The Tragically Hip; recorded by Doug McClement/LiveWire Recording at the Misty Moon, Halifax, NS, 26 April 1990; mixed by Phil Hotz
Copyright © Arte Humane Inc., Bhaji Maker Inc., Ching Music Inc., Dirty Shorts Music Inc., Wiener Art Inc., Southern Music Pub Co. Canada Ltd

Postcard prints
Copyright © Clemens Rikken

8" X 10" photo print
Copyright © 2023 Ian Thuillier

Backstage pass
Copyright © 1988 Rob Baker
Drawing of a sculpture by Clodion (circa 1800)

MANAGEMENT
Jake Gold, The Management Trust
Assisted by Ryan Hefford

Social media and content
Summer Figueroa

INDEX

INDEX OF CONTRIBUTORS